Inside the Fashion Business

KITTY G. DICKERSON

Professor and Chairman
Department of Textile and Apparel Management
University of Missouri–Columbia

Prentice
Hall

Upper Saddle River, New Jersey 07458

Library of Congress Cataloging-in-Publication Data

Dickerson, Kitty G.
    Inside the fashion business / Kitty G. Dickerson.—7th ed.
        p.   cm
    Includes bibliographical references and index.
    ISBN 0-13-010855-3
    1. Fashion merchandising—United States. 2. Clothing trade—United States.   I. Title.

HD9940.U42 D525   2000
338.4'7687'0973—dc21

                                        2002072843

Editor-in-Chief: Stephen Helba
Executive Assistant: Nancy Kesterson
Executive Editor: Vernon R. Anthony
Director of Manufacturing and Production: Bruce Johnson
Associate Editor: Marion Gottlieb
Editorial Assistant: Ann Brunner
Managing Editor: Mary Carnis
Production Liaison: Adele M. Kupchik
Marketing Manager: Ryan DeGrote
Production Management: UG / GGS Information Services, Inc.
Production Editor: Nancy Whelan
Manufacturing Manager: Ilene Sanford
Manufacturing Buyer: Cathleen Petersen
Creative Director: Cheryl Asherman
Senior Design Coordinator: Miguel Ortiz
Design Coordinator: Christopher Weigand
Interior Design: Angela Foote/Julia Zonneveld Van Hook
Printer/Binder: Courier Westford
Cover Designer: Amy Rosen
Cover Illustration: Zoe Worley, SIS/Images.Com
Cover Printer: Coral Graphics

Pearson Education LTD.
Pearson Education Australia, PTY, Limited
Pearson Education Singapore, Pte. Ltd.
Pearson Education North Asia Ltd.
Pearson Education Canada Ltd.
Pearson Educación de Mexico, S.A. de C.V.
Pearson Education—Japan
Pearson Education Malaysia, Pte. Ltd.

10 9 8 7 6 5 4 3 2
ISBN 0-13-010855-3

Dedication

This edition is dedicated to the original author, Jeannette Jarnow, who was deceased in 1998. I took this photo of her on the one occasion when we met. In her eighties, Mrs. Jarnow continued to have a keen interest in the fashion industry and this book.

Kitty G. Dickerson

Source: Kitty G. Dickerson

Brief Contents

CHAPTER 1

*The Business of Making
and Selling Fashion*   1

CHAPTER 2

Principles of Fashion   34

CHAPTER 3

*Globalization of the
Fashion Industry*   68

CHAPTER 4

The Consumer   114

CHAPTER 5

The Materials of Fashion   157

CHAPTER 6

*The Women's and Children's
Apparel Industry*   210

CHAPTER 7

The Menswear Industry   282

CHAPTER 8

*Fashion Accessories, Intimate
Apparel/Undergarments,
and Cosmetics*   322

CHAPTER 9

*Fashion Producers in
Other Countries*   369

CHAPTER 10

The Retailers of Fashion   418

CHAPTER 11

*Auxiliary Fashion
Enterprises*   474

Fashion Business Glossary   **511**

Appendix A
*Select World Wide Web
Sites* 523

Appendix B
The Influential Designers 528

Appendix C
*Career Opportunities
in Fashion* 533

Index 543

Contents

Preface   **xiii**

About the Author   **xvii**

CHAPTER 1

The Business of Making and Selling Fashion   *1*

The Business of Fashion: An Overview   2
   Scope of the Fashion Industry   2
   Economic Importance   3
   The Democratization of Fashion: A Brief Historical Perspective   5

The Fashion Pipeline: Channel of Distribution   6
   A New Classification System for Various Segments of the Industry   6
   Timing of Product Development and Showings   8

Fashion and the Profit Motive   10

The Consumption of Fashion Goods   12
   The Role of the Consumer   12
   The Power of Fashion   13

Major Industry Trends   14
   Influence of the Electronic-Information Age   14
   Mergers and Acquisitions   16

Vertical Operations   17
Globalization   18
Virtual Companies and the Growing Role of the Logistics Industry   20
A Changing Consumer   21
Rapid Transfer of Fashion   21
Reducing Response Time   22
Companies Have Redefined Their Businesses   23
Improved Industry Relationships   23
Increasing Customization   23
Social Responsibility   24

Readings   **26**
   Video Conferencing: Cutting Cloth and Costs over the Telephone in a Global Way   27
   E-valuating B2B Exchanges: Trading Relationships That Pay Off   29

CHAPTER 2

Principles of Fashion   *34*

The Language of Fashion   34
   A Style: Distinctive Characteristics   35
   A Design: Variations of a Style   35
   Fashion Means Consumer Acceptance   35
   Other Key Fashion Terms   36

The Constant in Fashion Is Change   37

Why Fashions Change   37

Changes in Fashion Are Gradual   39

Fashion: A "Follow-the-Leader" Process   40

The Fashion Cycle   40

Theories of Fashion Leadership   42

How Fashions Develop   46

The Role of Designers   46

Fashions Reflect Their "Times"   47

The Prediction of Fashion   52

Recognizing and Evaluating Trends   53

Sources of Information   54

Readings   56

The American Way   57

A Century of Change: Jeans   59

Gimme a "T": Nearly a Century of T-Shirt Wearing Reveals Something Unique about the Character of Americans   61

Marketplace Aesthetic Goes, Like, Totally '80s   63

CHAPTER 3

Globalization of the Fashion Industry   68

Overview of Globalization   70

All Industry Segments Are Affected by Globalization   71

Brief Background of Globalization of the Fashion Industry   74

Who Imports and Why   75

Imports by Retailers   77

Imports by Manufacturers   80

Imports Versus Domestic Production   81

Textile and Apparel Trade Deficit   81

The Global Trade Battle   83

The World Trade Organization (WTO)   84

The Multifiber Arrangement (MFA)   84

Quotes and Bilateral Trade Agreements   87

Getting Around the Quotas   89

Country-of-Origin Rules   90

Taxes on Imports: Tariffs/Duties   92

Preferential Programs: Exemptions from Tariffs or Quotas   93

The Politics of Textile and Apparel Trade   96

Promotion of Domestic Products   97

Selling U.S. Products in Other Countries   98

Licensing Agreements   98

Direct Exporting   99

Joint Ventures   101

Direct Ownership   101

The Importance of Preparing for Globalization   103

Readings   104

Streetwear Brands Take to the Streets of Europe   105

Wal-Mart Plots Big Global Expansion   107

CHAPTER 4

The Consumer   114

Background: Never Take the Consumer for Granted   116

The Power of the Consumer   119

Organizing the Industry Around the Consumer   121

The Marketing of Fashion   124

The Marketing Approach   124

Target Customers   125

Macroeconomic Factors That Affect Consumption of Fashion   128

Analysis of Customers' Fashion Preferences and Trends   136

Quick Response as a Marketing Strategy   138

Push System   139

Pull System   140

The Marketing Concept and Manufacturing/Distribution   141

Serving Consumers in the Next Millennium   142

Federal Legislation Affecting the Fashion Business   143

Federal Laws Regulating Competition   143

Product Labeling Laws to Protect Consumers   144

Readings   145

   Latina Fashionistas   146

   Reaching the Aging Boomers   148

   Commit to SINS, Win Lifelong Customers   150

CHAPTER 5

The Materials of Fashion   157

From Fiber to Fabric   157
Fiber Producers   158

   Suppliers of Natural Fibers   159

   Manufactured Fiber Producers
   (NAICS Subsector 325)   161

   Impact of Chemical Fiber Producers   162

Textile Component Producers (NAICS 313, most relevant to the fashion industry, and 314)   167

   Economic Importance   168

   History and Growth   170

   Geographic Location   173

   Different Types of Textile Producers   174

Fashion Research and Development   175

   Specialized Fashion Staffs   176

   Early Color Decisions   176

   Textile Design   177

   Fashion Presentations   177

   Seasonal Lines and Sales Presentations   179

   Textile Trade Shows   179

The Technologies Required to Compete   180

   Quick Response (QR): Computerized
   Partnerships   180

   Computer Aided Design (CAD)   182

   Computer Aided Manufacturing (CAM)   182

   Shuttleless Weaving   183

E-Commerce for the Textiles Sector   184
ISO 9000   186
Environmental Issues   186
Imports and Exports   188

   Expansion of Business into Mexico   189

Furs and Leathers   189

   The Fur Industry   190

   The Leather Industry   193

Readings   197

   Color Forecasting: From Runway to Real World   198

   Dot-Coms Are Making the Textile
   World Go 'Round   201

   Burlington Launches Super Fabrics   203

CHAPTER 6

The Women's and Children's Apparel Industry   210

Economic Importance   210
NAICS Groupings for Apparel   211
History and Growth of the Women's Industry   212

   Ready-to-Wear in the Nineteenth Century   213

   Developments in the Twentieth Century   214

   Industry Restructuring   217

   Development of the Unions   217

The Organization of an Apparel Firm   219
An Industry Reshaped by Computer Technology   221

   Quick Response   221

From Design Concept to Consumer   224

   Line Development—Preadoption Steps   224

   Line Development—Postadoption   230

   Product Sourcing and Production   232

   The End Result: A Finished Garment for Sale   235

Distribution   237
Marketing Procedures   238

   Presentation of Lines   238

   Reliance on a Sales Force   239

   Advertising and Publicity: National and Trade   239

   Designer Trunk Shows   240

   New Technology   240

Apparel Manufacturers' Relationships with Retailers   241
Manufacturers into Retailing   242

   Manufacturer-Owner Retail Stores   242

   Manufacturers' Shops within Stores   243

Nature of the Industry   243

   Different Types of Producers   244

   Size of Apparel Companies   246

   Specialization by Products and Prices   248

Prevalence of Style Piracy   249

Proliferation of Industry Licensing Agreements   250

Financing by Factoring   252

Location of Fashion Market Centers   254

New York, the Leading Market Center   254

Secondary Fashion Centers   257

Apparel Marts: Regional Selling Centers   258

Future of New York as a Fashion Center   262

Children's Wear   262

Nature of the Industry   262

Industry Specializations   263

Marketing Activities   264

Readings   266

Apparel E-Commerce: Online and Kicking   267

VF Extends Its Mass Appeal   270

Improving Product Development with E-Commerce Tools   273

CHAPTER 7

The Menswear Industry   282

Economic Importance   283

History and Development   283

Early Beginnings in the Nineteenth Century   283

Twentieth-Century Developments   285

Nature of the Industry   287

Men's and Boys' NAICS Groupings   287

Types of Firms   288

Geographic Locations: Decentralized   288

Design and Production Procedures   289

Tailored Clothing   290

Casual Office Wear   295

Sportswear Design and Production   296

Marketing of Menswear   299

Manufacturers' Brands   300

Targeted Customer Approach   300

Designer Labels and Designer Licensing   300

Retail Channels of Distribution   302

Manufacturer-Owned Retail Stores: Dual Distribution   304

Marketing Activities by Trade Associations   306

Fashion Explosion in Men's Accessories   309

Readings   310

Help Wanted: Career Counselors Ponder What's Suitable   311

Brooks Brothers: Repositioned for Success   313

CHAPTER 8

Fashion Accessories, Intimate Apparel/Undergarments, and Cosmetics   322

The Accessories Industries   323

The Business of Accessories   323

Economic Importance   325

Marketing   325

Shoes   327

Nature of the Industry   327

Development of Athletic Shoes   328

Economic Importance   328

Marketing   329

Extensive Competition from Imports   330

Hosiery   332

Nature of the Industry   333

Economic Importance   333

Hosiery Construction   333

Marketing of Hosiery   334

Global Activities   335

Handbags and Small Leather Goods   336

Nature of the Handbag Industry   337

Economic Importance   337

Handbag Construction   337

Global Activities   338

Small Leather Goods   338

Gloves   338

Nature of the Industry   339

Economic Importance   339

Glove Construction   340

Glove Marketing   340

Millinery/Hats   340

Nature of the Industry   341

Economic Importance   341

Construction of Millinery   341

Marketing of Millinery/Hats   342

Jewelry   342
    Precious or Fine Jewelry   343
    Bridge Jewelry   344
    Costume Jewelry   345
    Economic Importance   345
Other Accessories   345
Accessories Designers   346
Intimate Apparel/Undergarments   346
    Industry Segments   348
    Economic Importance   349
    Marketing   350
    Global Activities   351
The Cosmetics Industry   352
Readings   **356**
    A Century of Accessories   357
    Consumer Infidelity   362

CHAPTER 9

Fashion Producers in
Other Countries   369

Different Types of Producers in
Other Countries   369
Paris Haute Couture   370
    Chambre Syndicale de la Couture Parisienne   370
    Designer-Name Couture Houses   373
    Semiannual Collections and Showings   373
    Status of Couture Today: Other Sources
    of Income for Couture Houses   375
    Italian Couture   377
Ready-to-Wear Fashion Centers   378
    French Ready-to-Wear Industry   378
    Italy   381
    London   383
    International Shows in Germany   385
    Japan   385
    Canada   387
Fashion Producers in Lower-Wage
Countries   389
    Lower Labor Costs   390
    Major Countries of Asia   392
    Central and Eastern Europe   398
    Latin America and the Caribbean   399

Shift of Foreign-Owned Factories
to the United States   401
Sweatshops: The "Third World"
in the United States   402
Fashion: A Global Business Today   405
Readings   **406**
    Not So Haute: French Fashion Loses Its
    Primacy as Women Leave Couture Behind   407
    The Barons of Far East Fashion   411

CHAPTER 10

The Retailers of Fashion   418

Fashion Retailing in the Past   418
Different Kinds of Retail Operations   419
    NAICS Codes for Retailing   419
Department Stores   421
    Origin of Department Stores   422
    Branches: From Suburban to National   422
    Competitive Changes by Department Stores   424
    Store Ownership Groups   425
Apparel Specialty Stores:
Large and Small   427
    Large Departmentalized Specialty Stores   427
    Small Apparel Specialty Shops   428
    Boutiques   428
Chain Store Retailing   429
    Specialized Apparel Chains   431
    Apparel Retailing by General Merchandise
    Chains   433
Discount Retailing:
Underselling Operations   434
    Full-Line Discount Stores   435
    Hypermarkets and Supercenters   436
    Warehouse Clubs   436
    Category Killers   437
    Off-Price Apparel Chains   437
    Factory Outlets   439
Franchised Retailing   440
    Designer-Name Franchised Boutiques   441
Shopping Centers and Malls   441
Nonstore Retailing   444
    Mail-Order Houses   444
    Growth of Mail-Order (Catalog) Retailing   445

Mail-Order (Catalog) Apparel Specialists   445

Catalog Operations by Department and
Specialty Stores   447

Catalog Showroom Retailing   447

Electronic Retailing   448

Online Retailing ("E-Tailing")   448

Home Television Shopping   449

CD-ROM Computer Shopping   451

Flea Market Retailers   451

Direct Selling: Door-to-Door and Party Plans   451

The Changing Dimensions of Fashion
Retailing   452

Growth of Private Labels: Retailers into
Manufacturing   452

Concentration of Retail Power   456

Partnerships in the Softgoods Industry   457

Logistics and Distribution   457

Globalization of Retailing   459

Relationship Marketing   460

Readings   462

Retailers are Flocking to the Web—
Like It or Not   463

Mackey McDonald: 2020 Vision of the Future   465

Relationships. Experiences.
Don't Hit the Market Without Them   466

CHAPTER 11

Auxiliary Fashion
Enterprises   474

Fashion Information and
Advisory Services   474

Fashion Information Services   475

Fashion Consultants   477

Merchandising, Buying, and Product
Development Organizations   477

Independently Owned or Fee Organizations   478

Store-Owned Organizations: Cooperative
Groups   479

Computer Technology and
Service Providers   481

Testing Laboratories and Services   483

Management Consultants   484

Consultants in Technical Areas   484

Import and Export Consultants   485

News Media for the Fashion
Industry   486

Fashion Magazines   486

Newspapers and General Magazines   489

Trade Publications   490

Electronic Media   491

Advertising and Publicity Agencies   494

Advertising Agencies   494

Publicity and Public Relations Firms   495

Mall/Property Management
Specialists   496

Trade Show Enterprises   496

Trade Associations   498

The Fashion Group International   500

Other Fashion Enterprises   500

Readings   501

Styleexpo.com: New Venue for Trade Shows   502

TextileWeb Introduces E-Commerce
Solution for Fabric Sourcing   504

TradeTextile: Source Link in Asia   506

All for One—and One for All: Footwear, Apparel, and
Fashion Associations Ink Three-Way Merger   507

Fashion Business Glossary   511

Appendix A
Select World Wide Web Sites   523

Appendix B
The Influential Designers   528

Appendix C
Career Opportunities in Fashion   533

Index   543

P*reface*

I*nside the Fashion Business* is a book for those who have a particular interest in what is called *the fashion industry*—that complex of enterprises concerned with the design, production, and marketing of men's, women's, and children's apparel, accessories and cosmetics.

The fashion industry of the new millennium is one that is quite different from the one that existed only a decade or two ago. This industry has become one of the most globalized of all sectors, with a vast worldwide production and distribution network that includes almost every country of the world as a participant in some way. New technologies have made for fast, easy communication with industry partners on other continents. Similarly, new computer technologies have been incorporated into virtually all aspects of the industry to increase efficiency, save time, and produce value for the consumer. Additionally, the industry and companies have restructured through mergers to enhance efficiency and market strength and sometimes have divested of certain operations to focus on core businesses.

New to This Edition

This seventh edition has been revised to reflect the phenomenal changes taking place in the industry today. The book has been completely updated to prepare individuals for careers in this transformed industry. Similarly, the book can be of value for those already in the industry by serving as a comprehensive reference.

Every segment of the industry has been required to change to meet new competitive challenges. The industry has been vastly restructured through these shifts in emphases and activities. These changes are discussed in several chapters.

A particularly important aspect of the revision is the inclusion throughout the book of information on how new computer technologies have reshaped the industry. Of particular note are tables in Chapter 6 that outline the apparel production process in sequential order and identify how computer technologies are incorporated at each stage.

Globalization is also a theme found in many chapters. In fact, this is now such an important aspect of how the fashion industry works today that the chapter entitled "Globalization of the Fashion Industry" has become Chapter 3 in this edition, rather than as Chapter 8 in the last edition, thanks to a reviewer's suggestion. Of special note is a summary table highlighting the impact of globalization on various segments of the industry.

Other examples of the new material in this edition are:

- The use and impact of the *Internet* for various aspects of business.
- *Electronic commerce* (e-commerce), as found in both business-to-consumer (B2C) applications, such as online sales, and business-to-business (B2B) applications, such as online sourcing.
- Information on *sources that facilitate B2B commerce* in the fashion industry.
- *Supply chain management*.
- The growing importance of *logistics activities* and changes in the distribution process such as *cross docking*.
- The *growing power of the consumer*, with a profile of various groups. Special attention is given to marketing to *Generations X, Y, and Z* as well as to *growing minority markets* in the United States.
- The use of *data mining* to better understand consumers and their buying patterns.
- Current aspects of retailing such as *"lean retailing," global retailing, and "e-tailing."*
- The tension between manufacturers and retailers over *chargebacks*.
- *New and updated information on trade policies* that affect the fashion industry.
- A short discussion of *high-performance textiles*.
- A new section on the *cosmetics industry*.
- The *NAICS (North American Industry Classification System)* used to classify industry segments.
- An extensive *listing of websites for job hunting*.
- *Additional designers and glossary terms* have been added to appendixes.

Organization

The book first presents an introductory overview of the fashion business and another chapter on principles of fashion. Then a chapter on globalization follows. The book is organized to follow the stages through which a product goes. Because the consumer is the focal point around which the whole industry must be organized, a chapter on the consumer comes next. The following chapters each deal with one particular segment of the fashion industry and go through the stages of production: the raw materials of fashion—the fibers, fabrics, and so on; apparel production; and finally distribution through various forms of retailing. A final chapter discusses a variety of support services available for the industry.

The chapters first include an organized fact-filled body of knowledge. Next comes a series of industry readings carefully selected to complement, supplement, and illustrate the subject matter of the chapter. The readings may describe the operations of leading companies or may reflect significant trends occurring in the industry. Then, to facilitate further research, each chapter has an updated bibliography, list of trade associations, and list of trade periodicals related to the subject. In each case, the chapter concludes with suggested review activities. Following the final chapter are a fashion business glossary and three appendixes. New to this edition, Appendix A provides an extensive list of online job-hunting sources.

Content

Chapter 1, "The Business of Making and Selling Fashion," presents an overview of the fashion industry and its scope, economic importance, and major trends affecting the industry. The trends discussed are those of a broad nature that are reshaping the industry and that apply to virtually all segments of the fashion sector.

Chapter 2, "Principles of Fashion," discusses the generally accepted definitions of fashion and the principles governing its origin and dynamics, along with the implications for the marketers of fashion. It also discusses the role of designers today.

Chapter 3, "Globalization of the Fashion Industry," considers why globalization has occurred for this sector, how it affects the industry, some of the issues involved including trade policies, and the importance of being prepared to function in a global economy.

Chapter 4, "The Consumer," is designed to help the reader understand that the consumer is the reason the fashion industry exists. As consumers change their priorities and spending habits, fashion marketers must be increasingly sensitive to consumers' needs in order to succeed.

Chapter 5, "The Materials of Fashion," examines the industries that provide the raw materials from which apparel and accessories are made: fibers, fabrics, leathers, and furs. Each is discussed in terms of its economic importance, its method of operation, and its strategies for meeting present market conditions.

Chapter 6, "Women's and Children's Apparel," discusses the design, production, and marketing of women's and children's apparel. It includes the history, development, growth, and practices of this segment on the fashion business. This chapter has been revised significantly to incorporate new technological changes used in apparel manufacturing today.

Chapter 7, "The Menswear Industry," reviews the growth of this industry, the growing influence of fashion in menswear, changes affecting the industry, and its changing methods of operation.

Chapter 8, "Fashion Accessories, Intimate Apparel/Undergarments, and Cosmetics," deals with the economic importance and operations of these specialized industries that produce for specialized segments of the fashion industry. The section on cosmetics is new to this edition.

Chapter 9, "Fashion Producers in Other Countries," discusses the fashion producers in other countries who supply fashion merchandise to the global market, with an emphasis on the U.S. market. These producers range from internationally famous designers to contractors in low-wage countries.

Chapter 10, "The Retailers of Fashion," explains the different types of retail operations, the part each plays in the business of fashion, and how retailing is changing. New forms of retailing, particularly online retailing, are discussed.

Chapter 11, "Auxiliary Fashion Enterprises," covers the service enterprises that contribute to the effective functioning of the fashion business, such as news media, fashion advisory and information services, management consultants, advertising and publicity agencies, and buying/sourcing offices, among others.

The "Fashion Business Glossary" provides help with the vocabulary fashion professionals need to master. Appendix A gives an extensive listing of websites available to assist in job hunting. Appendix B is an annotated list of influential designers. Appendix C, "Career Opportunities in Fashion," provides guidance for those seeking a niche in the fashion business. Entry-level opportunities are discussed in terms of personal qualities, skills, and preparation.

The author feels strongly that readers need statistical yardsticks against which to measure the importance of various industries, trends, and individual enterprises in the fashion business. This is included in the text, within the limits of what was available up to the time of publication.

Acknowledgments

This book, like its predecessors, reflects the assistance of many other people. I appreciate the industry professionals who shared their knowledge and insights and to the publications and organizations that granted reprint permissions for readings or other items. Special thanks go to the reviewers contracted by Prentice Hall for their helpful comments, which were used in the revision of this edition.

Special appreciation goes to Jeannette Jarnow, the original author (deceased in 1998), who developed the original edition of this book, which has become known to virtually everyone who has studied the fashion industry. Several coauthors worked on the book with her over the years. Many friends in the academic and fashion worlds gave advice and counsel, helping to shape the previous editions.

I appreciate the important role Editors Vernon Anthony and Brad Pothoff played in launching this edition. Monica Ohlinger of Ohlinger Publication Services assisted in valuable ways in preparing the manuscript for production. Nancy Whelan of UG / GGS Information Services, Inc. ably orchestrated final production as Production Editor.

Kitty G. Dickerson

*A*bout the Author

Kitty G. Dickerson is Department Chairman and Professor, Department of Textile and Apparel Management, University of Missouri–Columbia. Dr. Dickerson is a Fellow in the International Textile and Apparel Association (ITAA) and has served as president of that group. She serves on the Board of Directors of Kellwood Company, a *Fortune* 700 apparel firm, which is the fifth-largest publicly owned apparel firm in the United States and the fifteenth-largest in the world, with sales well over $2 billion. She serves as Chairman of the Board's Corporate Governance Committee and is also a member of the Executive Committee and the Audit

Source: Photo by Carole Patterson.

Committee. With previous experience in retailing, Dr. Dickerson's work focuses on the total softgoods industry. Also author of another Prentice Hall book, *Textiles and Apparel in the Global Economy*, Dr. Dickerson was an early leader in focusing on globalization in the industry. She was invited to write the apparel chapter for *U.S. Industry and Trade Outlook*, published by the U.S. Department of Commerce, and has been asked by Standard & Poor's to write various softgoods industry analyses. She was chosen as the *Bobbin* "Educator of the Year," an award presented through ITAA. Additionally, she was named to *Textile World's* "Top Ten Leaders" list and has received numerous other academic and industry awards. She has published widely in scholarly and trade journals and has been invited to address academic and industry groups in the United States and in other countries.

CHAPTER 1

The Business of Making and Selling Fashion

*F*ashion in the global market and the United States today is big business. Its component parts—the design, production, and distribution of fashion merchandise—form the basis of a highly complex, multibillion-dollar industry. It is a business that began with small entrepreneurs at the turn of the century and today is a huge, many-faceted business. It employs the greatly diversified skills and talents of millions of people, offers a multitudinous mix of products, absorbs a considerable portion of consumer spending, and plays a vital role in the country's economy. The industry employs advanced computer technologies in producing, selling, and distributing the merchandise. The industry is dynamic, volatile, and ever-changing—often it is challenging to synchronize with consumers' fickle tastes. It is, moreover, a business of curious and exciting contrasts. On one hand, there is the rarefied air of Paris couture salons presenting collections of exorbitantly priced made-to-order designer originals; at the other extreme are giant factories that mass-produce and distribute endless quantities of low-priced apparel to towns and cities across the country.

The fashion-related industries play a very important role globally. Almost every country in the world depends on the textile and apparel sectors as important contributors to their economy. Fashion products are made under an astonishing range of circumstances, from the high-fashion houses of Europe to dreary, cramped sweatshops in the poorest developing countries. Amazingly, nearly all those starkly different operations can be linked electronically to create and produce fashion products for today's consumer.

This chapter presents an introduction to the fashion industry—the scope, economic importance, and trends that affect nearly all areas of the industry. The readings that follow address some of the changes taking place in the industry and encourage us to think about what the industry may be like in the future.

Subsequent chapters discuss in detail the various segments of the industry that are involved in the design, production, and distribution of fashion merchandise: fibers and fabrics, apparel and accessories production, sources of supply in other countries, retailing, and related auxiliary services.

1

The Business of Fashion: An Overview

The impact of fashion is all-pervading, but when we speak of the *fashion business*, that term is generally understood to refer to all companies and individuals concerned with the design, production, and distribution of textile and apparel goods.[1] See Figure 1–1 and also the more detailed graphic inside the back cover. Unlike industries such as tobacco and automotive products manufacturing, the fashion industry is not a clearly defined entity. It is a complex of many different industries, not all of which appear at first glance to have anything related to fashion among their products.

Scope of the Fashion Industry

Plainly recognizable as part of the fashion business are industries devoted to the making of inner- and outerwear articles of women's apparel; those involved in the production of menswear; those that make children's apparel; and those that make accessories such as scarfs, jewelry, handbags, shoes, gloves, wallets, and hosiery. Some of these industries serve one sex or the other; some serve both sexes.

When one moves back to an earlier stage of production—to the fibers, fabrics, leathers, furs, metals, and plastics from which the finished products are made—the line between what is and what is not the fashion business becomes harder to draw. Some textile mills that produce dress and coat fabrics also produce bedsheets, carpets, or industrial fabrics. Some chemical companies that produce fibers that are eventually spun and woven to make garments are also producers of explosives, fertilizers, and photographic film. Some producers and processors in fields normally remote from fashion find themselves with one foot temporarily in the fashion business when prevailing styles demand such items as industrial zippers, decorative chains, quilted fabrics, or padding materials, for example. A season or two later, these people may be as far removed from the fashion business as ever, but for the time being, they, too, are part of it.

The fashion business also includes different types of retailers, such as stores that sell apparel and accessories, mail-order catalogs, and Internet websites from which many consumer purchases are made. It includes businesses that neither produce nor sell merchandise but render advice, assistance, or information to those that do.

In this last category are consumer publications that disseminate news of fashion, ranging from the daily newspaper to magazines devoted primarily to fashion, such as *Glamour, InStyle, Vogue, Harper's Bazaar*, and *GQ*. Also included in this category are trade periodicals, such as *Women's Wear Daily, Stores, DNR* (*Daily News Record*), and *Bobbin*, that carry news of fashion and information on production and distribution techniques to retailers, apparel manufacturers, and textile mills. It also includes publicists and advertising specialists, forecasting services, industry consultants, mall management experts, and organizations that help both apparel manufacturers and retailers produce their lines in other countries.

All these and more are part of the business—farms and mills and factories, blue-collar and white-collar workers, tycoons, and creative artists. All play their parts in the exciting, dynamic business of fashion.

---

[1]Beauty and grooming products are frequently included in the fashion industry. Space permits only a brief overview of this segment of the industry in Chapter 8.

Figure 1–1

The industry is composed of many segments that must work together to provide fashion goods to the consumer.

Source: Illustration by Dennis Murphy.

Economic Importance

Global Importance

Business sectors related to the fashion industry play important roles in the global economy. Since launching the Industrial Revolution in England centuries ago, the textile and apparel sectors have been, and continue to be, leaders in **industrialization** and trade in nearly all parts of the world. Beyond providing fashion products and textile home furnishings as basic human necessities, the manufacture of these products provides the means of earning a living for an impressive portion of the world's population. *These industries are, by far, the world's leading manufacturing employer* (Dickerson, 1999).

The textile and apparel industries have been important engines of economic development worldwide. That is, the economies of many countries began to improve because they focused on these industries. In countries such as Pakistan and Bangladesh, for example, textile and apparel products count for nearly 70 percent of the country's total exports. In other words, those industries are the economic lifeblood for many individuals and families. Similar examples of the importance of the industry can be found around the world because *no other manufacturing sector today is even close to being as globalized as textiles/apparel.*

National Importance

The business of fashion contributes significantly to the economy of the United States both through the materials and services it purchases and through the wages and taxes it pays. In assessing the importance of this contribution, it helps to consider consumer expenditures, the number of people employed, and the amount of wages and salaries paid to them.

In 2000, U.S. consumers spent over \$319 billion[2] for clothing, shoes, and accessories—an amount that constituted more than 5 percent of what they spent for all purposes from food to foreign travel. The outlay for fashion goods ran well above that for furniture, household equipment, or even personal savings for the year (U.S. Department of Commerce, 2001). Typically, the sales of men's, women's, and children's apparel and accessories account for well above half the total volume of general merchandise stores.

Still another indication of the industry's importance is the number of jobs it creates—and it creates them in every state of our country. Nearly 1.4 million people in the United States are employed in industries that produce apparel for men, women, and children or in the textile plants that produce the materials from which the garments are made (American Textile Manufacturers Institute, 2000, based on U.S. Census of Manufacturers data).

Apparel manufacturing alone employs more people than the entire printing and publishing field and more than the automobile manufacturing industry. Many additional workers are employed in producing such items as fur and leather garments, accessory items, shoes, and jewelry. In addition to the industries that *make* fashion products, we find that the sectors that *sell* fashion products also add greatly to the economy and provide employment for large numbers of workers. More than 22 million Americans, 18 percent of the nation's workforce, are employed by retailers. Among these, more than 3.8 million are employed in general merchandising and apparel specialty stores (National Retail Institute, 1999).

To see the full picture of the fashion industry's contributions, we must add the employment in finance, transportation, advertising, utilities, and other essential services that devote part of their efforts to the fashion industry. It soon becomes obvious that the industry has an astounding impact on our economy. We must keep in mind the mammoth national and global industry that makes these fashion goods

---

[2]This figure is in current dollars.

available to us. At the same time, all the segments of the industry that make these fashion products available represent career opportunities for those who wish to enter the industry.

The Democratization of Fashion:
A Brief Historical Perspective

The textile and clothing industries have played an important role in the history of the United States. Besides contributing a great deal to the economy, the development of an industry that produced affordable clothing for the population added to the spirit of equality and democracy that were important principles of American life. Mass production of clothing has provided a majority of Americans with a more than adequate supply of good-quality garments. One should keep in mind, however, that the generous supply of ready-made apparel, as we know it today, was not available during a good portion of our country's early history.

In 18th-century America, two types of textile fabrics were available: the high-quality textiles for the rich and the low-quality textiles to clothe the poor. There was very little in between. Rich Americans took advantage of the products from the English textile industry, because the U.S. industry had only begun to develop by the latter part of the century. Not only was there virtually no U.S. textile industry at that time, but the apparel industry did not develop significantly for nearly another century. Therefore, early clothing for Americans varied both in the quality of the textiles and in the construction of the clothing. Wealthy Americans had their clothing custom produced from fine fabrics. In contrast, those of less fortune wore clothing of fabrics characterized by a common quality of coarseness (Dickerson, 1991).

Kidwell and Christman (1974) noted that in colonial America, obtaining clothing was more difficult than securing food or shelter. A majority of families of ordinary means produced all their own clothing by raising flax and keeping sheep to provide fiber, which was transformed through time-consuming hand methods into fabrics and garments. Fabrics made from home-grown fibers were made into clothing for families by wives and mothers who had few tools and usually no training. Housewives made clothing to protect family members from the elements rather than to look fashionable. Consequently, in these early years, one's financial standing was readily apparent by one's clothing.

Kidwell and Christman's book, *Suiting Everyone: The Democratization of Clothing in America* (1974), focused on the development of the U.S. **apparel industry** and the role the industry has played in making "average Americans the best dressed average people in the world." The authors cited a quote by William C. Browning, a second-generation clothing manufacturer, as the essence of what they call the "democratization of clothing":

> And if it be true . . . that the condition of a people is indicated by its clothing, America's place in the scale of civilized lands is a high one. We have provided not alone abundant clothing at a moderate cost for all classes of citizens, but we have given them at the same time that style and character in dress that is essential to the self-respect of a free, democratic people. (p. 15)

In summary, the apparel industry that developed not only became a major U.S. industrial sector, providing employment and income for large numbers of workers through the years, but it also became an industry that manufactured products that enabled the population to have clothing that obliterated ethnic origins and blurred social distinctions. Although the apparel sector played a vital role in the economic development of the country, the industry made important contributions beyond that to the spirit and climate of equality on which the new independent nation was founded (Dickerson, 1991).

The vast selection of fashion goods and the competitive prices found in the U.S. market are the envy of much of the world. Even today, individuals from almost any socioeconomic group can be well dressed.

The Fashion Pipeline: Channel of Distribution

There are three main links in the production and distribution of fashion products. These are referred to as the **channel of distribution**—that is, the network of interrelated functions involved in moving products from where they begin to end with the consumer. Other terms used to describe these linkages are the *production-distribution chain* or the *fashion pipeline*. The major segments are:

- **Component suppliers.** Companies in this group provide the raw materials of fashion, such as fibers, fabrics, leathers, and furs. They may also be the suppliers of buttons, zippers, threads, and other products required to produce finished items.
- **Finished product suppliers**. Firms in this group manufacture finished apparel and accessory products.
- **Retail distributors.** This group includes all forms of retailing—stores, catalogs, television shopping, Internet shopping, and so on—that provide the link to move fashion products from the manufacturer to the consumer.

These three segments must work together closely to produce and deliver products quickly. The term **softgoods industry** refers to the total network or chain of these interconnected segments and generally includes textile home furnishings and other textile products, as well as apparel and accessories.

All three segments of the industry are interdependent. The challenging business environment in recent years has forced all segments to work together more closely to respond to consumers' needs. The component suppliers depend on the finished product suppliers for the sale of their products; the finished product suppliers depend on the retailer, who is the final link between the consumer and the vast network of the fashion-producing industry. Within that network are enterprises of many different types. Figure 1–2 provides a flowchart to illustrate the main segments and the interrelationships of each. More competition and less **concentration** occur in the downward segments of the channel of distribution. That is, there are more companies to compete.

Subsequent chapters will discuss the activities of each in detail. A detailed graphic inside the back cover of this book depicts the numerous segments of the industry involved in producing a garment. To obtain a four-color brochure featuring this graphic in greater detail, contact Textile/Clothing Technology Corporation, [TC]^2, at 211 Gregson Drive, Cary, NC 27511-7909 or FAX: 919-380-2181.

A New Classification System for Various Segments of the Industry

Often it is important to be able to look at the overall business activities of specific segments of the fashion industry. For example, we might want to compare the value of product shipments for a particular segment of the industry (e.g., sheer hosiery mills) from one

| Figure 1–2 | The Fashion Pipeline (The Softgoods Industry) |

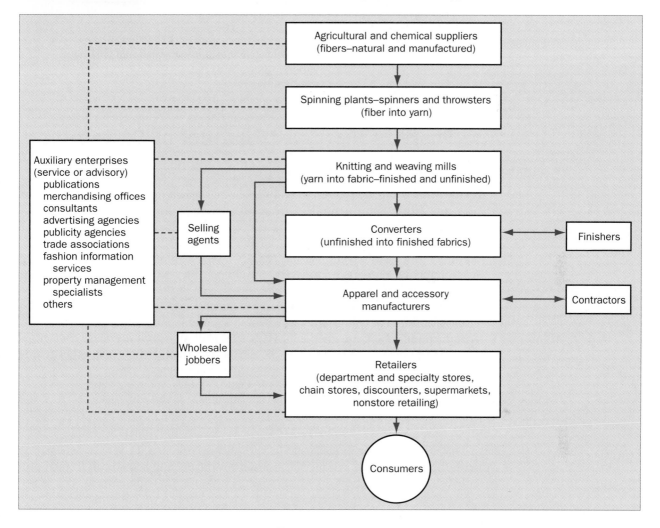

year to another and need consistent product categories to make that comparison meaningful. Or, we might want to compare the U.S. industry's output of sheer hosiery with that of Mexico or Canada. A government system exists to make that possible.

On January 1, 1997, a new classification system, the **North American Industry Classification System (NAICS)**, replaced the former system, the Standard Industrial Classification (SIC). The new NAICS system was designed to provide the United States, Mexico, and Canada with a common system to review NAFTA[3] trade. The NAICS system uses a *product* orientation whereas the SIC categories had a *process* orientation.

NAICS industries are identified by a six-digit code, with the first five digits standardized for the three North American countries. The sixth digit can be specific to a country. The digits are shown in Table 1–1.

---

[3]NAFTA is the North American Free Trade Agreement, which allows trade without restrictions between the United States, Canada, and Mexico.

Table 1–1	NAICS Industry Codes
Digit(s)	**What Digits Represent**
First 2 digits	NAICS industry sector
Third digit	Subsector (e.g., 315 is apparel manufacturing)
Fourth digit	Industry group
Fifth digit	NAICS industry
Sixth digit	National industry (if applicable)

The major NAICS categories in the fashion industry are:

- **Textile Mills** comprise the **NAICS 313** grouping, which includes fiber mills, fabric mills, and fabric finishing mills. (Group 31 is *manufacturing*, the third digit, "3," represents *textile mills*.) In later chapters, we will see that additional digits define the specific type of products within the major groups.
- **Textile Product Mills** comprise the **NAICS 314** grouping, which includes textile furnishing mills (carpets, rugs, linens, and draperies); textile bag and canvas mills; and rope, cordage, and tire fabric mills.
- **Apparel Manufacturing Mills** comprise the **NAICS 315** grouping, which includes both apparel-knitting mills and cut-and-sew apparel manufacturing.
- **Manufactured fibers** are in the **NAICS 315** grouping, *the chemical and allied products grouping*, because of their chemical origin, rather than with other textile components.
- **Retailing** of fashion products is in Groups 45 and 46 (see Chapter 10).

Timing of Product Development and Showings

Each link in the fashion industry chain periodically presents its new styles early to those in the next level of production, so that producers and sellers can in turn prepare their lines or collections in advance of the consumer buying periods. For example, the colors, weaves, and fabrics that are expected to receive consumer acceptance are researched and selected a year or more before the consumer will see them.

In the past, each branch of the industry announced its new lines according to a fairly traditional schedule based on several factors: the change of the season; the time required to produce goods after buyers placed their orders; and the time required by product developers (whose titles might have been fashion director, designer, stylist, or creative director) to assess the pulse of the market. Products often took a year or more to get from the design stage to the consumer.

Today, however, a changing market and new computer technologies have drastically changed traditional merchandising practices for apparel manufacturers and retailers. We have seen a dramatic compression of the time sequence required to develop new products and to get them to the customer. Many of the previously time-consuming activities now use computer techniques that reduce the time required for various stages. For example, using computer-aided design, the apparel manufacturer works with retailers to develop new lines that can be viewed on the computer and adapted on the screen, rather than going through the time-consuming stages of making samples to see if designs produce the desired effect (Figure 1–3).

Figure 1–3

Computer technology has reduced the time required to bring a garment from the conceptual stages to the final product. This program, by Lectra Systems, speeds the time from initial concept to the finished prototype sample.

Source: Reprinted courtesy of Lectra Systems.

Changes of this type have revolutionized the traditional timetable for getting products to market. Fashion merchandising has increasingly moved away from the traditional cycles and, instead, has evolved more and more toward a continuous flow of new products.

Using these newer approaches to producing fashion merchandise, many retailers and manufacturers have formed partnerships to make the work flow even faster. Both want to please the customer. As part of this, many companies use consumer style testing to determine through early, small orders if customers do actually like what is being produced. If they do, modern manufacturers can produce and ship quickly because they have new technologies that permit rapid response.

Fashion and the Profit Motive

Although the fashion industry is seen as a glamorous, dynamic field, companies are in business for one reason only—to make a profit. If they do not succeed in being profitable, even the most dazzling fashion lines will not continue. Creativity and dedication mean nothing if an enterprise is not economically viable.

From Neiman Marcus in New York to Wal-Mart in Peoria, garments must appeal to customers willing to buy the merchandise. Customers who vote with their dollars are necessary, so those who work in the production and retailing of fashion products find it financially worthwhile to be involved.

Although the fashion industry is among the most exciting fields in the world, it is also difficult, demanding, and unpredictable. Despite the enchanting interplay of creativity, marketing wit, business acumen, and media hype, *everything comes down to the bottom line*. The accountant's financial statement must show a profit for an enterprise to continue. The fashion business is not a charitable business or a kind business. To be *in* business, a company—no matter how large or how small—must be a *profitable* business.

Companies must be profitable because those who own the firms are expecting profits. This applies to all segments of the fashion industry. Ownership may be considered in two major groupings:

- **Privately held companies** are owned by individuals, partners, or groups. Financial information about the company does not have to be made public, and profits go to the owners. In early days of the fashion industry, a majority of companies were started and owned by individuals; thus, they were of this type. Most small firms today still fall into this category. Privately owned companies are one of the following:
  - *Sole proprietorships* are owned by one person who has control over the business and who must bear all risks.
  - *Partnerships* are owned by two or more persons who share control over the business and who also share the risks.

  Privately held companies can also be very large. Two major U.S. companies of this type in the fashion business are Levi Strauss & Co., one of the largest apparel firms in the world, and Milliken & Company, one of the largest textile firms worldwide.

- **Publicly held companies** are those owned by shareholders who have purchased stock in the company. Most of the largest textile, apparel, and retailing firms are of this type. Publicly held companies are required to regularly report their financial performance to **shareholders** (or stockholders). Depending on how well the company is performing, people may want to buy or sell stock in it. If a company is doing well, potential buyers are attracted to buy that company's stock. If the company is doing poorly, shareholders may be inclined to sell their stock and invest in another firm that provides greater rewards for their investments. Therefore, large, publicly owned companies must strive to please their owners—the shareholders—who want a return on their investment in the form of **dividends**.

Sometimes, publicly held companies in the fashion industry go through highs and lows of popularity with potential shareholders. For example, when The Gap's products are popular with consumers and selling well, investors are attracted to the

Figure 1–4

An example of Standard & Poor's *Stock Reports.* The report plots the trend in the stock performance and gives the Standard & Poor's analyst's views on whether the company appears to be a good investment prospect at the time.

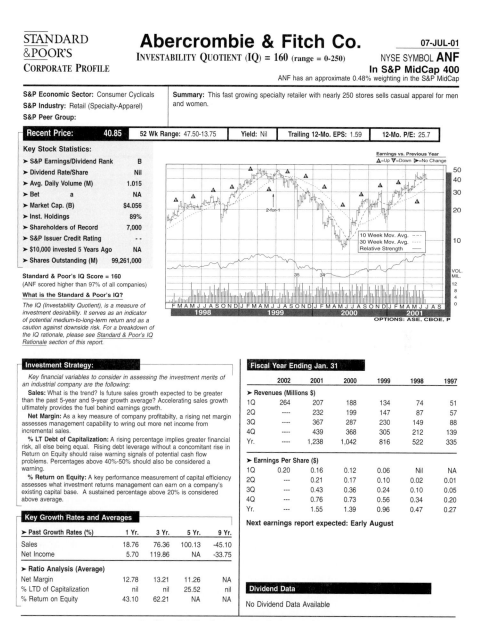

Source: Reprinted courtesy of Standard & Poor's, a division of the McGraw-Hill Companies.

company's stock. For many years, The Gap has been successful and this has been the case. But when the company miscues on its fashion offerings, the stock loses some of its appeal, and the value of the company's stock tends to decline. During a company's "low" time, potential shareholders may lose faith in the firm and are less inclined to buy the stock. Similarly, existing shareholders may sell.

Publicly owned companies publish **annual reports**, which give a review of the firm's business activities for the year and a statement of its current financial position. These provide important profiles on companies. Annual reports also provide tangible evidence that the fashion business is also big business.

Anyone wishing to follow the stock of a publicly held company may do so in various ways. The *Wall Street Journal* is a primary source used to follow the performance of company stocks. A number of other services provide updates on companies' performance and even make recommendations on whether a company's stock is a good buy at the time. Examples of these are Value Line and Standard & Poor's. These services usually use a graph to illustrate the company's stock price over a period of time. An example is shown in Figure 1–4.

The Consumption of Fashion Goods

The fashion industries, as in most other consumer goods industries in the United States today, have a production capacity beyond what the public actually needs. At the same time, most consumers have incomes in excess of what their households require for such absolute necessities as food and shelter. This combination of ample production capacity and ample discretionary spending power means that consumers have a wide choice as to how they will spend their money. A woman, for example, does not merely choose between one dress or another; she may also choose between a new dress and a new household appliance. Likewise, a man may choose between one jacket or another, or he may choose between a jacket and new golf clubs.

The Role of the Consumer

The role of the ultimate consumer in the fashion business is an important one and, in the final analysis, controlling. This fact is recognized by all successful fashion professionals. Ordinarily, the part that consumers play is a passive one. People do not actually demand new products and designs of which they have little or no knowledge; neither do they demand change. Their individual and collective power is exercised in the selections they make, on the one hand, and in their refusals to buy, on the other. It is by their acceptance or rejection that they influence the goods that will be presented for their favor and even the methods of presentation. Consumers' collective acceptance or rejection results in annual figures on the industry, as shown in Table 1–2.

The controlling role of the consumer is not unique to the fashion industry. Every business that serves the public has to guide its operations in light of consumer demand. The fashion industry, however, moves at a faster tempo. The rewards of success are great, and the cost of failure is correspondingly high. As the late Dr. Paul H. Nystrom (1929) put it:

> Consumer demand is the guide to intelligent production and merchandising. . . . A knowledge of the fundamental facts of what consumers want and why, is clearly of the first importance . . . to those who plan the poli-

		Clothing and Accessories		
Year	Total	Men's and Boys'	Women's and Children's	Shoes and Other Footwear
1970	$52,396	$15,539	$28,794	$8,063
1975	70,021	20,807	38,519	10,695
1980	102,831	30,142	56,909	15,780
1989	200,100	55,900	115,100	29,100
1995	254,400	77,900	140,300	36,200
2000	319,135	97,203[*]	175,117	46,815

Table 1–2 **Selected Components of Consumer Expenditures (in millions)**

Source: Department of Commerce, Bureau of Economic Analysis, *Survey of Current Business*, various years.
*Includes clothing issued by military.

cies, design the product, determine the price lines, prepare the advertising and sales promotion, sell the goods and make the collections, in fact all who deal with the problems of the consumer.

The role of the consumer will be examined in greater detail in Chapter 4.

The Power of Fashion

Few words in any language have as many different implications as the word *fashion*. To the layperson, it implies a mysterious force that makes a particular style of dress or behavior acceptable in one year but quite the reverse in another. Economists view fashion as an element of artificial **obsolescence** that impels people to replace articles that still retain much of their original usefulness, even though the new articles may not greatly differ from the old ones. It is the power of fashion that encourages individuals to cast aside narrow-legged jeans still in excellent condition for baggy-legged ones, and later to swing back again to tight-fitting jeans. As one writer noted:

> The economic, as distinct from social, *raison d' être* of fashion resides in the need to make people buy things they don't need. If the clothes can't be relied upon to wear out fast enough, something must be found that will wear out faster; that something is what we call fashion. But fashion is one form of the familiar capitalist technique of planned obsolescence which can be enjoyed with a clear conscience. Many of the world's people wear secondhand clothes, which are available in good condition at low prices because of the fickleness of their original buyers. (Gopnik, 1994, p. 16)

To sociologists, fashion represents an expression of social interaction and of status seeking (Barber & Lobel, 1952; Merton, 1949). Psychiatrists find indications of sex impulses in patterns of dress (Bergler, 1953). But whatever fashion may mean to others, it represents billions of dollars in sales to the group of enterprises concerned with the production and distribution of apparel and accessories. As one fashion scholar said, "Everything that matters, everything that gives their trade its nature and place in the world must be ascribed to fashion" (Robinson, 1962).

Fashion, in and of itself, does not create consumer purchasing power, but wherever there is such purchasing power, there is interest in fashion. In times past, when purchasing power was concentrated among the wealthy few, they alone pursued fashion. Today, with a widespread ability to spend, great masses of people follow fashion, and thus fashion determines both the character and the direction of consumption. Although such factors as price, durability, convenience of use, and quality of workmanship are also of concern to the consumer, they mean relatively little unless the purchased articles are also clearly identified with the prevailing fashions. Fashion is also an important factor in the replacement market for such utilitarian items as household goods; it is often more important than wear and tear in motivating the discard and replacement of furniture, kitchen utensils, and automobiles, for example. Businesses that serve the consumer succeed when they go with the fashion, but are doomed to failure whenever they go against the tide.

Major Industry Trends

In recent years, the fashion production-distribution chain has undergone dramatic **restructuring**. The industry does not resemble the one that existed 25 years ago. Just as fashion products change, *the industry itself* keeps evolving. These changes reflect the dynamic nature of the industry as it responds to economic conditions, to business trends in general, and to consumers whose purchasing patterns vary from one time to another.

We shall discuss briefly some of the changes here to highlight trends that have affected the whole fashion industry. Most of these will be covered further in detail in later chapters.

Influence of the Electronic-Information Age

Computer technologies have exploded on the scene to reshape the softgoods industry as well as every other segment of commerce. In fact, the "digital revolution" is the catalyst driving the new global economy. Just as the Industrial Revolution dramatically changed the lives of citizens in the 18th and 19th centuries, the two interrelated "revolutions" of digital information technology and globalization have transformed our world profoundly in our lifetime.

For today's fashion firms, technology enables teams from around the world to work together without ever meeting face-to-face. Through today's communication systems, a firm in New York can transfer its designs and markers (diagrams or layouts of pattern pieces to be cut from fabrics) via satellite to a firm in Hong Kong, where they are printed to be cut and produced. Or, a U.S. firm may communicate easily by electronic mail, telephone, or fax with a company in Indonesia that is contracted to manufacture its line. Through videoconferencing, retail buyers may view lines of fashions available to them from Asian producers without having to leave their offices. Companies may also conduct business among its various distant segments or with partner firms via the Internet. See Figure 1–5 for examples.

In the United States, major apparel firms such as VF Corporation and Kellwood Company have computer systems that hook to those of retailers such as J.C. Penney and Wal-Mart. This computer connection for exchange of information is known as **electronic data interchange (EDI)**. The reordering systems are so precise that when a pair of jeans is sold in a store, a replacement pair is back on the shelf in a matter of

Figure 1–5

"Cyber-Fashion" Today

Digital information technology permits the fashion industry to function in exciting, innovative ways that were beyond our imagination only a few years ago. Examples include:

- **Fashion Trip** combines an interactive CD (which must be purchased for $39.95) with Internet access. Using Fashion Trip, shoppers can walk through a three-dimensional mall and control their shopping trip with a mouse. Then they shop online in individual virtual stores in which they choose and try on apparel, using digital mannequins that reflect their body type and skin tone. If shoppers want to purchase items, they can go from the CD to the websites of companies such as Wet Seal, Bongo, Guess, Nicole Miller, Almay, and Clinique. They can buy directly from a company's website or find the closest retail outlet. Although the first CD is aimed at young women ages 15 to 28, the service is expected to expand to other groups. Fashion Trip can be accessed at the following website: www.fashiontrip.com

- **Duck Head Apparel** supplies its retail customers that have Duck Head in-store shops with software that acts as a virtual store planner. The technology assists retailers with merchandising, sales tracking, and replenishment. The software lets retailers lay out a floor plan for Duck Head shops, and when the shop is in place, it permits the retailer and Duck Head to communicate with each other electronically. The software is tied to the retailer's **point-of-sale (POS)** system, so that sales can be tracked by style, size, or individual merchandising displays. As each item is sold, the electronic data interchange connection to Duck Head's offices permits the manufacturer to automatically replenish standard items such as twill pants.

- **The Limited** uses an **intranet** computing platform to track orders for fashion items that have been placed with overseas companies making garments for this major retailer. Based on Internet technology, this internal network tracks shipments once they have been sent to the shipping dock by the manufacturer. If a shipment is running late, the intranet automatically alerts the buyer who placed the purchase order. The Limited's goal is to use its intranet to track orders through the entire manufacturing process. Authorized business partners anywhere in the world will be able to cooperate and help the company monitor orders through the manufacturing process.

- **Lands' End** has expanded its efforts to sell globally by developing a website in Japanese at www.landsend.com.jp

- **J.C. Penney** has developed high-tech conferencing technology that permits a linkage between its private-label designers in the Plano, Texas, headquarters with overseas partners that produce Penney's brands such as Hunt Club, St. John's Bay, and Arizona. Using Penney's system, which permits audio and video exchanges, designers and partners can interact about elements of a design and discuss what will work, reducing costly mistakes. The system is expected to be enhanced to allow users in several locations to work on a design simultaneously and view changes as they are being made.

- **Bloomingdale's** website has two features to enhance service to customers and also allows the company to reach and understand a broader base of customers who do not live near one of the company's 23 stores: (1) "My b. profile" allows consumers to give information on their personal preferences about product categories, styles, and designers. This is used to provide customized information on sale events, promotions, and targeted e-mail. This feature keeps track of a consumer's purchases, permitting the retailer to better tailor its future marketing and merchandising efforts. (2) A personal shopper program provides a one-on-one interaction previously possible only in the stores. It allows customers to ask Bloomingdale's personal shoppers about fashion items and availability via e-mail.

days. This keeps the retailer from maintaining large inventory investments at any given time. In *A Stitch in Time* (Abernathy, Dunlop, Hammond & Weil, 1999), researchers noted that many of these **"lean retailing"** efficiencies that first developed in the apparel industry are being propagated through a growing number of other consumer product industries.

Computer technologies have reshaped the fashion industry in nearly every aspect of the business. These advances have increased the variety and availability of products, shortened production time, improved design and manufacturing procedures, and in general eliminated many time-consuming manual operations in every facet of the industry. The Internet brings to both industry and consumers a plethora of new ways to transmit information. A number of relevant website addresses are given in Appendix A. Additionally, the new technologies permit many new ways to conduct business, as noted in Figure 1–5.

Computer technologies are dramatically transforming the way consumers shop. As growing numbers of consumers—in the United States and around the world—log on, the truly revolutionary impact of the Information Revolution is beginning to be felt. Internet traffic is doubling roughly every 100 days. Instead of a physically defined marketplace, new technologies have created a "marketspace,"[TM][4] an electronically defined arena in which business occurs and customer relationships are built.[5] The information superhighway has made possible electronic interactive retailing (Ernst & Young, 2000). Some experts estimate that ultimately between 20 and 40 percent of apparel sales will occur online (Seckler, 1999). The consumer can stay home and buy his or her new fashion products online via the Internet—even through a virtual mall and trying the items on virtual mannequins that resemble the shopper. See Figure 1–5.

Through online shopping, the consumer is increasingly empowered by being able to shop and compare products and prices from more sources in a short time frame. The use of credit cards (i.e., the **"plasticizing"** of the purchase process) has facilitated easy purchases from almost anywhere. Added to this the advent of 800 numbers, WATS lines, fax machines, computers, efficient delivery services such as United Parcel Service and Federal Express, shopping and shipping can occur with the ease of a call or a few strokes on a keypad. Moreover, these systems have almost eliminated geographical shopping boundaries.

Mergers and Acquisitions

Many companies, both manufacturers and retailers, have **merged** with others to form larger, stronger firms. Some companies have acquired others. Table 1–3 gives examples of some of the industry mergers and **acquisitions** in the late 1990s. The net result of these business moves has been the formation of many very large and very powerful firms. For example, Federated Stores purchased Macy's. Even before the acquisition, each was among the largest retailers in the industry. Together, these megamerchants have enormous control over the marketing system and manufacturers' access to consumers. To illustrate this, Wal-Mart's annual business is now *larger than the next dozen or so largest retailers on the list combined*.

On the manufacturers' side, the large companies have also grown larger. For apparel firms, Kurt Salmon has noted that the top five apparel firms now account for

---

[4]A trademarked term coined by Jeffrey Rayport and John Sviokla of Harvard Business School.
[5]The Fashion & Beauty Internet Association is a network of businesses and individuals with a World Wide Web presence that have come together to interact and forge relationships and to promote their businesses. FBIA can be found at http://www.fbia.com

Table 1–3	Examples of the Mergers and Acquisitions in the Industry

Buyer	Company Acquired
VF Corporation	The Bestform Group and others
Galey & Lord	Dominion Textile (apparel fabrics)
Tommy Hilfiger Corp.	Pepe Jeans
Dillards	Mercantile Stores
Profitts's	Saks
Dan River	Bibb Co.
Hudson Bay Co.	Kmart Canada
Claire's Stores	Lux Group (The Rags) and Bijoux One
Jones Apparel Group	Sun Apparel, Nine West
Kellwood Company	Koret of California and Fritzi of California
Fingerhut	Arizona Mail Order
The Leslie Fay Cos.	Warren Apparel Group

about 75 percent of the total sales of all publicly held apparel firms (about half the total market). Similarly, the two top footwear firms account for 55 percent of the sales of publicly held footwear companies.

A leader in this movement toward becoming a megaplayer in apparel, VF Corporation has continued to acquire apparel firms in many product categories in the United States and abroad. This strategy provides VF with product lines that have been targeted at various channels of distribution. For example VF sells its Vanity Fair lingerie in department stores, its Vassarette line to discount stores, and also produces private label undergarments for stores such as Victoria's Secret.

In general, mergers and acquisitions lead to a concentration by a small number of firms, especially in some industry segments. In many areas, these industry giants control a major portion of the market. Although the move toward forming giants may lead to greater efficiency and productivity, there is also the risk that this strategy reduces the innovation and creativity needed in the industry. In other words, the growth of these giants has the potential of adding to the "sameness" that has characterized the industry in recent years. Consumers want fresh looks and grow tired of finding essentially the same thing everywhere they shop.

Although the high-fashion segments of the industry often receive a great deal of attention, those portions generally represent a relatively small portion of the total fashion industry business. On the other hand, the giants, often formed through mergers and acquisitions, dominate the industry. Most of these giants serve the **mass market** with mass-produced products and account for the major portion of the business in the industry. Although the high-fashion part of the industry adds excitement and, often, a sense of fashion direction, the "big bucks" generally are connected to companies that serve the mass markets.

Vertical Operations

Companies in different segments of the industry have taken on activities that were previously handled by other players in the industry. For example, manufacturers have expanded into the retail business, and retailers have entered the manufacturing area. Although these **vertical operations** are not new in the fashion industries, the dramatic increase in the number of firms using this strategy *is* a significant change. In the menswear industry, manufacturer-owned retail stores have existed for decades. More recently, however, these vertical ventures have also proliferated in women's wear and accessories areas.

Examples exist at all levels in the industry, but it is most obvious and visible at the manufacturer–retailer interface. Some of the most successful companies on both sides of this divide are taking over functions that once were performed exclusively by their suppliers or customers. For example, many retailers are involved actively in designing and overseeing production of a growing share of the merchandise they sell. The Gap used to sell just Levi's jeans, but in 1984 it decided to contract all its own Gap-brand merchandise. Similarly, The Limited's companies develop their own lines and oversee contractors' production of virtually all the merchandise sold in their stores. That is, rather than buying their merchandise from manufacturers, these two major retailers have become "manufacturers" themselves. Conversely, many manufacturers have opened their own retail stores. Levi Strauss & Co. opened retail stores in the mid-1990s. Guess's retail stores generate more than 40 percent of the company's total revenue. NikeTown stores lure customers with a blend of dazzling entertainment and Nike products. Outlet malls, an outgrowth of this trend, sell directly from manufacturers.

In the manufacturing sector, some apparel firms have become vertically integrated so that they have control over the supply and quality of fabrics needed to produce their garments. Today, many yarn spinners, knitters, weavers, apparel producers, and retailers, who formerly were mutually exclusive and distinctive segments of the fashion industry, are losing their familiar identities and have taken over some of each others' roles.

Verticalization, like mergers and acquisitions, has led to a smaller number of companies—many of them giants. These vertical operations have added to the intensely competitive conditions of the fashion industry. Although verticalization may reduce the number of competing firms, those that remain are larger, more powerful industry players.

Today's competitive business conditions have also led to an ironic reversal of this trend. In recent years, Sara Lee (one of the top two U.S. apparel firms and parent company of brands such as Hanes, Playtex, Bali, and many others) announced plans to **deverticalize**. The company made a strategic decision to drop all the manufacturing aspects of its apparel business and become a marketing company for its brands, much as Nike and Coca-Cola have done. Sara Lee sold off or closed most of its factories, contracting its production with other companies in the U.S. and abroad rather than making garments in company-owned plants. Instead, the company focused on brand management and marketing.

Globalization

Advances in communication and transportation systems have changed the world from a collection of fairly independent national economies to a **global economy**. For example, when Asian economies go through troubled times, a ripple effect is felt around the world, and most other markets are affected.

A global influence is not new for the textile and apparel industries. The fashion industry has long functioned in response to international events such as the European couture showings, and for centuries, textile products played an important role in international trade. Although textile and apparel products have been part of international commerce for decades, the earlier activities were hardly a warm-up for the rapid **globalization** of the industry occurring today. Now, the fashion industry is very global in nature—requiring those of us who follow the industry to think globally. Today, the labels on our fashion products resemble a geography course. Consumers are wearing garments from countries they may be unable to find on a map. Apparel manufacturers frequently have their garments assembled in remote nations that were unlikely production sites a few years ago, such as the factory in China shown in Figure 1–6. Retailers travel worldwide to find products for their stores, often arranging for the production directly themselves, just as manufacturers do.

U.S. textile and apparel manufacturers are now setting their sights on the markets of other countries, after many years of focusing on just the domestic market. For many years, U.S. manufacturers spent a great deal of their time and resources fighting imports rather than considering potential markets for their products in other parts of the world. Today, a number of U.S. textile and apparel firms sell their products overseas, including Levi's, Russell, Lee, Sara Lee, and many others. Designers such as Calvin Klein, Donna Karan, Ralph Lauren, and Joseph Abboud have opened their own stores in other countries.

Retailers are rapidly developing a global presence, too. As the U.S. market has become overstored, expansion in other countries has become a major avenue for growth. The Gap now has more than 200 international stores. U.S. retail chains such as Talbots, Kmart, J.C. Penney, and Wal-Mart are opening stores in many other countries as part

Figure 1–6

Many garments sold in the market today are made by workers in other countries. Here, young women in China are producing blouses for a major U.S. apparel firm.

Source: Photo by Kitty G. Dickerson.

of ambitious global expansion plans. J.C. Penney has a store in Chile that is much larger and carries more high-visibility brands than its U.S. stores. L.L. Bean distributes its catalogs in more than 145 countries. Globalization of retailing is expected to continue.

Globalization is discussed in more detail in Chapters 3, 9, and 10.

Virtual Companies and the Growing Role of the Logistics Industry

As part of this globalization, many large apparel firms and the private-label divisions of major retailers have become "**virtual companies.**" In these companies, more and more functions of the business are contracted to other sources—known as **outsourcing.** For fashion goods, the sewing operations are sent to contractors, usually in other countries. As other functions are farmed out, the home company becomes a base for orchestrating the numerous outsourced operations, thus becoming more and more a "virtual" company. The fashion industry, like many sectors, now has a significant new partner—the **logistics** industry—which plays a vital role in coordinating and managing companies' far-flung global produduction and distribution activities. Logistics firms not only bring overseas merchandise to the United States, but they also send the orders to a company's distribution center, where they may continue to be involved in warehousing activities.

Although businesses have always had to move and store goods, the modern approach to logistics came from World War II, when the United States had to send soldiers and supplies to many countries. The corporate emphasis on logistics started in the 1990s, as companies hired logistics firms to help speed up transportation and reduce the costs of holding large inventories. Logistics firms include some familiar names that do far more than the public generally knows about: Emery Worldwide, United Parcel Service, CNF Transportation Inc., and Federal Express.

Today, the logistics industry performs many hidden but very important functions, and this little-noticed business has become one of the fastest growing worldwide, with about $900 billion in revenue in the year 2000. About 75 percent of all major manufacturing firms (including retailers' private-label divisions) use logistics firms. Logistics firms provide a growing range of services—the shipping and warehousing of merchandise, as well as even packaging and labeling of items if desired by the client firm. These companies know and understand customs regulations for shipping products; they also prepare the documents needed for shipping and can save the client company many headaches.

Some logistics firms have divisions that specialize in serving the fashion industry and provide special shipping containers to keep garments from being wrinkled during shipping. As another example of the tailor-made services for clients, Nike's new athletic equipment division contracts with a logistics firm to transport basketballs, soccer balls, and footballs. When the balls arrive half-inflated to take less space in shipping, the logistics firm pumps the remaining air into the balls, puts them in colorful packages, and even adds the price tags for some sports retailers (Mathews, 1998).

The logistics industry relies heavily on the electronic technologies discussed earlier. Global positioning technologies allow logistics companies to track a shipment anywhere in the world; the customer can be advised of the location of a shipment at any time. Customs documents and invoices can be sent electronically. The forklifts in some logistics companies even have tiny computers so that drivers can get instructions on their screens for when and where they should pick up and deliver their next loads.

A Changing Consumer

The industry has found it difficult in the last decade to cater to a consumer whose priorities seem to have changed. In the 1980s, consumers were eager fashion spenders. Brand names were important, and consumers were willing to pay for status products. In the 1990s, however, consumers became very value driven, demanding more for less. Roger Blackwell, a marketing consultant, noted: "We are entering the century of the consumer, and the consumer knows it" (Seckler, 1998, p. 9).

Consumers make apparel expenditures much more cautiously than in the past and are not easily manipulated by promotional efforts geared to encourage them to buy things they don't need or want. Caution is in part related to concerns over the economy. Priorities have changed; for many consumers, new clothing is no longer a high priority. Additionally, consumers are exerting a new independence. They are more likely to define their own styles and more likely to resist being dictated to by industry. Moreover, because they have so many choices, consumers have no reason to feel they have to buy a particular brand or shop at any special store.

Several studies have suggested that consumers' expectations about what they want in their apparel and their shopping experiences are rising but are not being met. David Cole, chairman and chief executive officer of Kurt Salmon Associates, a major consulting firm for the softgoods industry reported to apparel executives, "Though 70 percent of consumers enter a store knowing exactly what apparel they want to buy, 49 percent leave empty-handed, according to the seventh annual KSA nationwide consumer outlook survey" (Ostroff, 1998, p. 2).

Firms in all segments of the industry are scrambling to find ways to attract and satisfy an increasingly demanding consumer. Many are using new computer technologies to track the needs of more and more narrow segments of the consumer market in hopes of tailoring products more carefully to those individuals' needs. Companies like The Limited are creating vast consumer data banks that allow them to follow and service those individuals most likely to be loyal, profitable customers.

Rapid Transfer of Fashion

Because of satellite communication systems, consumers see new trends and want them quickly. Before these communication advances, new trends from the European fashion shows might have taken two years to reach the mass markets. Now, consumers almost anywhere in the world can see the fashion shows in Paris and Milan as they occur. Rather than waiting for two years, the fashion-forward consumer wants the new fashions immediately. This rapid transfer of demand places pressure on the whole manufacturing-distribution chain to be able to respond more quickly than ever before.

Rapid worldwide communication of fashion trends also means that consumers in many parts of the world may also be wearing fairly similar new lines. They also show amazingly similar attitudes and shopping patterns. Today's youth are the first generation to be tied together by a worldwide electronic web that quickly transmits fashion trends around the globe. For example, the MTV generation in Los Angeles, Jakarta, Mexico City, and Taipei may be listening to the same music and wearing clothes that look amazingly similar. This electronically connected generation may be the first truly global consumers (Figure 1–7). In fact, they are likely to be wearing clothes more like their peers in other countries than like those of an older generation in their own country.

Figure 1–7

Global Consumer

Source: Illustration by Dennis Murphy.

Reducing Response Time

All segments of the industry have had to rethink and reorganize the way products are made and distributed to reduce the time required to get merchandise produced and to the retail sales floor. This trend, like others we have discussed, depends heavily on new computer technologies. Computers are used in all aspects of making and distributing fashion goods, greatly compressing the time required previously to bring a garment from concept to the consumer. These response strategies go by names such as **Quick Response (QR)** and **rapid replenishment**. These quick turnaround schemes have become important because no company wants to have a large investment tied up in inventory sitting in warehouses.

Retailers want to be able to move merchandise quickly from apparel manufacturers when needed rather than keeping large inventories themselves. Similarly, apparel firms do not want large inventories of fabrics sitting idle in warehouses; therefore, the garment manufacturers expect to obtain deliveries of fabrics and other components quickly, as needed. This pattern occurs throughout the industry, forcing each segment to respond quickly to its respective customers. Because of these schemes, the time required to get fashion items produced and to the customer is much shorter than was true only a few years ago. These strategies have also reduced consumers' out-of-stock shopping frustrations. Although these changes have required major adjustments from the companies involved at each stage, these new strategies are beneficial to an industry based on responding to consumers' needs and interests in the latest trends.

Companies Have Redefined Their Businesses

In their quest for improved profits, a number of companies have taken on new identities. Some have expanded the types of products they produce or sell; others have narrowed their focus to serve a specific market more effectively; others have simply shifted in what they do.

DuPont, a major fiber producer, surprised the industry by announcing the company would become involved in some areas of apparel production (which the company later discontinued). Similarly, textile firms Guilford Mills and Burlington Industries launched apparel firms in Mexico. Jockey, once a producer of only men's undergarments, now has a thriving business in women's lines. Sara Lee, once known for cakes and other baked goods, bought one apparel company after another, including names such as Playtex and Hanes, making it one of the largest U.S. apparel firms. Hanes, once known for undergarments and hosiery, now has a very large knit activewear business. Nike, formerly known for athletic shoes, now produces a wide range of activewear and has also opened its own retail outlets. Similarly, Wilson, the maker of sports equipment, now has a line of activewear apparel.

Among retailers, J.C. Penney stores moved away from hard lines (appliances, furniture, automotive areas) to emphasize primarily soft lines (apparel, textile home furnishings) and to serve a target market with somewhat higher incomes than had been true earlier. The chain transformed itself from a stodgy store for low-priced basics into a store that attempts to attract the traditional department store customer. Similarly, after many years of struggling to find a successful identity, in the early 1990s, Sears stopped selling through its "big book" catalog and also placed greater emphasis on fashion areas. Both chains have struggled in recent years because they can provide neither the high-profile name brands found in department stores nor the price-value relationship found at discount stores. In addition, through its purchase of the Eckerd Drug Store chain, J.C. Penney hopes to be positioned to serve the aging U.S. population with growing medication needs.

Improved Industry Relationships

In the past, manufacturers and retailers had many areas of disagreement and dissension. Prices, delivery dates, quality, terms of sale, advertising costs, and many other issues led to ill will between them. When business did not go well, it was easy to blame the other player.

More recently, however, many manufacturers and retailers have realized that both have a great deal to gain by working together. They now realize that both gain by cooperating in ways that permit them to serve the consumer more effectively. Today, we see many manufacturers and retailers connected via computers to share information on consumer purchases. When products are sold in the store, the manufacturer is able to replenish the store's stock. This way, the next consumers find what they want in the store rather than being disappointed. Today, we see a growing number of these industry partnerships that are built on trust and a commitment to serve the consumer well.

Increasing Customization

As consumers have become less interested in shopping, they are expecting more from the softgoods industry. They have become more demanding of product value, quality, and service that meet their needs. Many consumers are tired of the "sameness" that is part of mass production and merchandising. They are tired of the "one-size-fits-all" approach. A number of companies are responding to consumer demands for more **customized** products.

Coca-Cola, for example, now offers a much more extensive array of products than in the past. Besides Classic Coke and regular Coke, each is available in choices that include with or without sugar and with or without caffeine. Similarly, the Lee Company offers women's jeans in an almost mind-boggling array of choices: denim, corduroy, or twills; denim in traditional, stonewashed, pepperwashed, or other spattered finishes; wrinkle-free or regular; short, regular, or long lengths; relaxed fit or close fit; narrow, medium, or full leg width; elastic waist or regular waistband; and jeans for women with full thighs or those with slim thighs.

New developments in body scanning are on the horizon, which may change the way shoppers buy their apparel—and the ultimate fit of those garments. Using scanning devices that record a shopper's unique body shape, images and data—often with 3-D graphics—can be stored on smart cards that consumers carry when shopping (see Figure 1–8). The data on the smart cards can be provided at the time of purchase to have garments made specifically for that shopper's unique body size and shape. A Kurt Salmon Associates survey found that 60 percent of all customers have difficulty finding apparel that fits well, and *only 29 percent are satisfied with the fit of the apparel purchased.*

The trend toward increased customization of products and services will continue, particularly as companies compete to win market share. Computer technology permits both retailers and manufacturers to track specific consumer groups and their needs. This increased customization will place added demands on firms, however, as they are required to produce and manage a wider array of products in smaller quantities.

Social Responsibility

As industries become increasingly global and as segments of the industries become more powerful, a heightened need for social responsibility emerges. Moreover, consumers are becoming increasingly sensitive to the need for social responsibility among all segments of business. Many consumers are now beginning to demand ethical and socially conscious conduct from the enterprises that supply their goods and services. Among the issues of growing importance are sweatshops, child labor in some countries, prison labor, unsafe working conditions, harmful environmental practices, and violation of trade policies.

Increasingly, industries, along with consumers, are faced with choices that have implications for the environment. These concerns include: manufacturing processes that pollute the air and streams, processes that use natural resources that are in short supply, and the proliferation of products and packaging that cannot be recycled.

Consumer and labor groups have begun to expose violations of environmental, labor, and human rights codes at both the national and international levels. Resulting negative publicity has focused on some of the United States' leading firms. In a number of cases, these embarrassments were unjustified when socially conscious companies had attempted to comply with the codes. In short, companies are expected increasingly to be responsible citizens, both globally and in their local communities.

This chapter has provided a brief overview of the fashion industry and has considered some of the major trends affecting most industry segments. We see that the industry itself is in transition. When we consider both the rapid turnover of fashion goods that propels the industry, along with the revolutionary transformation occur-

Figure 1–8

The Textile/ Clothing Technology Corporation [TC]^2 has developed body scanning technology to help fashion manufacturers produce garments that are customized to fit the customer.

Source: Courtesy of the Textile/Clothing Technology Corporation [TC]^2.

ring in the way the industry goes about its business, the combination is indeed challenging. However, we must also remember that most of the transformation of the industry continues to make it stronger and more efficient.

Individuals with careers in the various fashion fields must follow the major industry trends to be aware of how their own area of business is affected by the broader changes. We might say that the only thing constant about the industry *is the change*. The fashion industry provides many exciting careers for those who are informed, energetic, persistent, and resilient.

Readings

The fashion industry has been transformed greatly by new technology and competitive forces. Because of these forces, the industry functions very differently from what it did a decade or two ago.

Video Conferencing: Cutting Cloth and Costs over the Telephone in a Global Way

New technologies save time and travel costs for companies that connect with business partners in other countries.

E-valuating B2B Exchanges: Trading Relationships That Pay Off

Business-to-business (B2B) electronic commerce is changing how companies work with their business partners. The results are new partners, new relationships, and new ways of communicating within the industry.

Video Conferencing: Cutting Cloth and Costs over the Telephone in a Global Way

by Evan Rosen

The sign on the door reads creativity cannot be rushed. Inside the office, a designer and merchandiser feel pieces of black fabric, as one would stroke silk. "I can float some paisleys and flowers on this," says the designer, who sits among racks of clothing, piles of swatches, and empty bottles of spring water.

In the beehive of creativity that is the San Francisco headquarters of Koret of California, the bees of the clothing business sift through samples, study color and concept boards, and produce the styles they hope will sell. Often developing three seasons of clothing at once, merchandisers and designers examine the look and feel of tomorrow's skirts and sweaters. The apparel industry is a classic "touchy, feely" business that has used technology only to a point. Sure, PCs sit atop most desktops and CAD plays a role in developing styles, but professionals still place a premium on the senses of touch and sight.

Nevertheless, videoconferencing is making inroads in this industry because of the need to link geographically distributed work teams. Also, global competition is forcing the industry to embrace efficiency. While the American Apparel Manufacturers Association reports that output-per-worker has risen 50 percent since 1980, there is a continued demand for faster and greater output. For many companies, videoconferencing is part of the efficiency solution because it brings professionals together in a virtual workspace with higher impact than phone conversations or e-mail and more affordably than travel. Koret is one apparel manufacturer easing into videoconferencing, testing the water before taking the plunge.

Jacqueline Hamm, the product manager for Koret's Stephanie K line, is the "queen of videoconferencing," using the technology more than any other Koret merchandiser. For Hamm, the biggest pay-off is the non-verbal communication. "I know my buyer well enough that when she makes certain faces, I know she doesn't like something," Hamm explains. She uses a PictureTel 200 system running at 128 kbps to link with Koret's New York office. And while Hamm gets on a plane four times a year for sales trips, she conducts previews to those trips via videoconferencing.

The Need to See and Feel

Koret has tried using an auxiliary camera so buyers for retail chains can examine clothing samples during videoconferences. However, this approach has fallen flat. "You can't distinguish the color or the fabrications," insists Denise Johnston, Koret's senior vice president of merchandising. "Everything is going to drape differently." Walking through Koret's design rooms stuffed with racks of garments, Johnston pauses and pulls a knit top from its hanger. "Here you'd want them to see the detail of the popcorn stitch and the detail on the button. You could never see that through videoconferencing."

To circumvent color variations and lack of detail, Hamm sends fabric, button and trim samples mounted on a color and concept board to Koret's New York office before the videoconference. During the session, Hamm watches for the nonverbal cues

Source: From Apparel Industry Magazine, *December 1999, p. AS10. Copyright Bill Communications Inc. Reprinted by permission.*

27

that tell her almost everything about her customer's reaction to the clothing line. Previously, Hamm would rely on Koret's New York sales staff to interpret customer reaction. Like a game of "telephone," however, something would often get lost in the translation. Videoconferencing bridges the gap.

Future uses of videoconferencing could include linking the San Francisco headquarters with sewing plants in Asia. Currently, the factories FedEx garment samples to headquarters for approval, and merchandisers send back color copies of patterns with written comments. These packages must also clear customs. "If we could just point the camera at the garment and tell them where we liked the technique and where we didn't, the quality control people could understand how to fix problems," Hamm points out.

What about selling apparel lines through videoconferencing? Not a chance, says Hamm. "I need to build rapport and find out about other business."

Johnston agrees. "You have to be able to touch, feel and visualize," she says. "But if you could get a truer picture, [videoconferencing] would be more useful at a design level."

As competition increases in the clothing industry, this traditionally "touchy, feely" business may be forced to implement such technologies more widely. "It's turn time or die in the apparel industry. If you can shorten that time, it's golden," insists Jack Morgan, director of communications at the AAMA.

E-valuating B2B Exchanges: Trading Relationships That Pay Off

by Richard Romer

The Internet has opened new channels of distribution and provided new opportunities to **apparel** manufacturers and retailers of all sizes. B2B e-commerce, in particular, is changing the way business is conducted by facilitating the further evolution of new buyer and supplier relationships. Rather than buying, selling and sourcing through existing, often limited, channels, the Internet has helped the apparel industry evolve into a truly global buying community.

Within the realm of e-commerce, there are three primary arenas of opportunity for retailers and manufacturers—sourcing, closeouts and B2B sales—as well as three platforms facilitating these transactions: vertical, horizontal and X to X exchanges.

- *Sourcing.* Through the Internet, apparel manufacturers and retailers can now source fabric and finished goods throughout the world. This grants small- and medium-sized companies access to a global playing field—one that was previously available to only larger counterparts—for the buying and designing of apparel and finished goods.
- *Closeouts.* Online auctions and direct-sale exchanges enable the quick liquidation of excess merchandise to a seemingly endless supply of new domestic and international customers. On an online auction, a seller can entertain bids for a fixed duration from multiple buyers. On a direct-sale exchange, closeout goods are inventoried and purchased in much the same fashion as regularly sold goods. Both formats offer manufacturers and retailers better pricing than in the past, using brokers or a limited number of known distribution points.
- *Direct sales.* Several platforms enhance the process of apparel sales for online retailers. Software companies have bred online trade shows, which reduce travel to showrooms and trade shows to see next season's presentations. Many solutions are affiliated with inspection and shipping companies, warehouse facilities and financing partners, enabling the entire process, from purchase to shipping, to be accomplished through a single contact on a single network.

The aforementioned e-commerce opportunities are exercised on several 13213 platforms or Internet exchanges, including vertical, horizontal and X to X exchanges.

- *Vertical exchanges.* Vertical exchanges are narrowly defined e-marketplaces that provide, within a specific industry, everything from liquidated merchandise, overstocks or RFPs to online auctions. The benefits to buyers include access to: (1) a purchasing catalog of goods within the specific market segment; and (2) a global source of suppliers and merchandise. Examples of this type of exchange include TextilEdge.com, TexTrade.com and TradeOut.com.
- *Horizontal exchanges.* Horizontal exchanges span a number of different product categories. Rather than simply being a textile marketplace, a horizontal exchange brings together retailers, manufacturers, technology companies, equipment manufacturers

Source: From Apparel Industry Magazine, *September 2000, p. 84. Reprinted by permission. Copyright Bill Communications, Inc., September 2000.*

and financing partners, among others. Examples include fasturn.com, retailexchange.com and ftadirect.com.

- *X to X Exchanges.* The most recent trend in the market has been the formation of alliances across a number of horizontal exchanges. These X to X sites encompass a number of different industries and exchanges that typically include everything from procurement, RFPs and auctions to overstock and liquidations. These exchanges provide one-stop shopping for everything from office supplies to goods and services.
- *Financing.* For sellers, gaining the financial backing necessary to meet the growing demands of a new customer base goes hand in hand with the desire to grow sales. As businesses gain access to a larger community of new buyers and sellers, many companies are concerned about who they're conducting business with. Credit protection takes the worry out of B2B e-commerce.

With credit protection, a factor credit checks potential buyers on the site, extends lines of credit to those buyers, and guarantees payment of the resultant accounts receivable to sellers. This enables manufacturers to be secure in the creditworthiness of new customers and allows buyers to make purchases quickly and easily with preapproved lines of credit. In some cases, the manufacturer can receive advances against its receivables and improve its cash flow.

The Internet has caused a fundamental shift in the buying and selling process for the retail industry. This shift has a new beneficiary: the buyer of goods. The customer now has the opportunity, as never before, to purchase the best products from the most expansive assortment of suppliers at the most competitive prices. The more customer-driven the exchange, the more likely it will succeed.

Chapter Review

Key Words and Concepts

Define, identify, or briefly explain the following:

Acquisition	Industrialization	Privately held companies
Annual reports	Intranet	Publicly held companies
Apparel industry	Lean retailing	Quick Response (QR)
Apparel manufacturing mills	Logistics	Rapid replenishment
Channel of distribution	Manufactured fibers	Restructuring
Component suppliers	Mass market	Retail distributors
Concentration	Merger	Retailing
Customization	North American Industry	Shareholders
Deverticalize	Classification System (NAICS)	Softgoods industry
Dividends	Obsolescence	Textile mills
Electronic data interchange (EDI)	Outsourcing	Textile product mills
Finished product suppliers	Plasticizing	Vertical operations
Global economy	Point-of-sale (POS)	Virtual companies
Globalization		

Review Questions on Chapter Highlights

1. Name the different types of industries involved in the business of fashion and explain their interrelationships.
2. How is the fashion industry important globally?
3. Explain the importance of the fashion business to the economy of the United States.
4. List the three main links in the production and distribution of fashion merchandise and explain their interrelationship.
5. What is the likely fate of a company that has terrific fashion lines but is not profitable?
6. What is the difference between a publicly owned company and a privately held one? A sole proprietorship and a partnership?
7. How can one follow the success of a publicly held company that produces fashion-related products?
8. What are some examples of how the fashion industry has been affected by the electronic-information age?
9. What are logistics firms? How are they involved in the fashion industry?

10. How have a growing number of industry mergers and acquisitions affected the fashion industry?
11. Have your fashion purchases been affected by globalization? By the electronic-information age?
12. How do today's consumers differ from those of a decade ago? What are the implications of these changes for the fashion industry?
13. What does Quick Response mean to a manufacturer? A retailer? A consumer?
14. What does it mean to say a company has "redefined its business"?
15. Are there reasons why fashion manufacturers and retailers should have positive working relationships? Explain your answer.
16. Do you purchase any "customized" products? What are they and why do you buy them? Are there ways you would like to see fashion items more customized?
17. Can you think of any social issue in the news in recent times that relates to the fashion industry? Identify the issue and list how it relates to the industry.

References

Abernathy, F., Dunlop, J., Hammond, J., and Weil, D. (1999). *A stitch in time: Lean retailing and the transformation of manufacturing—lessons learned from the apparel and textile industries.* New York: Oxford University Press.

American Textile Manufacturers Institute (2000, March). *Textile HiLights.* Washington, DC: Author.

Barber, B., & Lobel, L. (1952, December). Fashion in women's clothes and the American social system. *Social Forces.*

Bergler, E. (1953). *Fashion and the unconscious.* New York: R. Brunner.

Department of Commerce, Bureau of Economic Analysis. (2001). *Survey of Current Business.*

Dickerson, K. (1991). *Textiles and apparel in the international economy.* Upper Saddle River, NJ: Merrill/Prentice Hall.

Dickerson, K. (1999). *Textiles and apparel in the global economy.* Upper Saddle River, NJ: Merrill/Prentice Hall.

Ernst & Young (2000, January). *Global online retailing.* A special study sponsored by National Retail Federation. Washington, DC: Author.

Gopnik, A. (1994, November 7). What it all means. *The New Yorker, LXX*(36), pp. 15–16.

Kidwell, C., & Christman, M. (1974). *Suiting everyone: The democratization of clothing in America.* Washington, DC: Smithsonian Institution Press.

Mathews, A. (1998, June 2). Logistics firms flourish amid trend in outsourcing. *Wall Street Journal,* p. B6.

Merton, R. (1949). *Social theory and social structure.* Glencoe, IL: Free Press.

National Retail Institute. (1995). *Retail industry indicators.* Washington, DC: Author.

Nystrom, P. (1929). *Economic principles of consumption.* New York: Ronald Press.

Ostroff, J. (1998, May 12). AAMA parley told: Satisfy consumers. *Women's Wear Daily,* pp. 2, 4.

Robinson, D. E. (1962, August). The economics of fashion design. *Quarterly Journal of Economics,* p. 75.

Seckler, V. (1998, June 24). On-line reminders: What's in store. *Women's Wear Daily,* p. 13.

Seckler, V. (1999, January 28). Study: Retailers better get online. *Women's Wear Daily,* p. 9.

United States Department of Commerce, Economic and Statistics Administration, Bureau of Economic Analysis. (1995, April). *Survey of current business,* Table 2.6, Personal consumer expenditures by type of product. Washington, DC: Author.

Selected Bibliography

Abernathy, F., Dunlop, J., Hammond, J., and Weil, D. (1999). *A stitch in time: Lean retailing and the transformation of manufacturing—lessons learned from the apparel and textile industries.* New York: Oxford University Press.

Celente, G., & Milton, T. (1991). *Trend tracking.* New York: Warner Books.

Craik, J. (1994). *The face of fashion: Cultural studies in fashion.* New York: Routledge.

Davis, F. (1994). *Fashion, culture, and identity.* Chicago: University of Chicago Press.

Dickerson, K. (1999). *Textiles and apparel in the global economy.* Upper Saddle River, NJ: Merrill/Prentice Hall.

Feather, F. (1994). *The future consumer.* Buffalo, NY: Firefly Books.

Kotler, P., & Armstrong, G. (1994). *Principles of marketing* (6th ed). Upper Saddle River, NJ: Merrill/Prentice Hall.

Kurt Salmon Associates. (1995). *Vision for the new millennium . . . evolving to consumer response.* New York: Author.

Onkvisit, S., & Shaw, J. (1993). *International marketing: Analysis and strategy* (2nd ed.). Upper Saddle River, NJ: Merrill/Prentice Hall.

Peterson, R. (Ed.). (1992). *The future of U.S. retailing: An agenda for the 21st century*. New York: Quorum Books.

Standard & Poor's. (various years). *Industry survey: Textiles, apparel, and home furnishings* and *Industry survey: Retailing*. New York: Author.

The world of fashion. (1994, November 7). *The New Yorker, LXX*, (36).

Trade Associations

American Apparel and Footwear Association, 1601 N. Kent Street, Suite 1200, Arlington, VA 22209.

American Textile Manufacturers Institute, 1801 K St., NW, Washington, DC 20006.

Canadian Apparel Federation, Suite 605, 130 Slater St., Ottawa, Ontario K1P 6E2, Canada.

Canadian Textiles Institute, 280 Albert St., Suite 502, Ottawa, Ontario K1P 5G8, Canada.

National Retail Federation, 325 Seventh St., NW, Suite 1000, Washington, DC 20004.

Retail Council of Canada, 210 Dundas St. W., 600, Toronto, Ontario M5G 2E8, Canada.

Trade Publications

Textile Industries (formerly Americas Textiles International), 2100 Powers Ferry Rd., Atlanta, GA 30339.

Bobbin, 1110 Shop Rd., Box 1986, Columbia, SC 29202.

Canadian Apparel Manufacturer, 1 Pacifique, Ste Anne de Bellevue, Quebec H9X 1CS, Canada.

DNR, 7 W. 34th St., New York, NY 10001-8191.

Stores, 325 Seventh St., NW, Suite 1000, Washington, DC 20004.

Textile World, 4170 Ashford-Dunwoody Rd., Suite 420, Atlanta, GA 30319.

Women's Wear Daily, 7 W. 34th St., New York, NY 10001-8191.

*P*rinciples of Fashion

*F*ashion, which is as old as time and as new as tomorrow, is one of the most powerful forces in our lives. It influences what we wear, the way we talk, the foods we eat, the way we live, how and where we travel, what we look at, and what we listen to. Fashion is what leads us to discard a product that is still useful but is no longer "in." It is also what makes us sometimes wear more clothes than we may actually need and sometimes less than is needed to protect us from the cold or the sun.

Fashion even influences how society sees the human body. In the 18th century, plumpness was seen as a sign of prosperity and health, and a thin person was seen as too poor to afford enough to eat. In contrast, today's obsession with thinness has spawned a $33 billion-a-year weight-loss industry and has led to an epidemic of eating disorders such as anorexia and bulimia among young women (Powers, 1996).

The intensity with which changes in fashion are followed by people everywhere on all levels of society is evidence of its social significance and its impact on human behavior. To be "out of fashion" is indeed to be out of the world.

This chapter discusses the generally accepted definitions of fashion and the principles governing its origin and dynamics. It also suggests some of the many implications of the fashion process for the producers and sellers of fashion goods. The readings that follow cover changing trends in fashion and topics related to fashion design.

The Language of Fashion

Many definitions of fashion have been given by wise and witty or learned men and women. For example, to Oscar Wilde, "[F]ashion is a form of ugliness so intolerable that we have to alter it every six months." And according to Ambrose Bierce, "[F]ashion is a despot whom the wise ridicule . . . and obey." Thoreau philosophized that "every generation laughs at the old fashions but follows religiously the new." And Shakespeare wrote that "fashion wears out more apparel than the man."

Because an understanding of fashion is obviously of primary importance for fashion practitioners, let us begin by defining the terms that are used by everybody and confused by some. Although the definitions that follow are formulated largely with respect to textiles and apparel—the subject of this book—it must be emphasized that they also apply to music, painting, architecture, home furnishings, automobiles, telephones, and any other consumer goods or services that one can think of.

A Style: Distinctive Characteristics

The terms **fashion** and **style** are confused by many people who say, "That's the style," when they really mean "That's the fashion." There is a world of difference in the meanings of these two terms. *A style is a type of product that has one or more specific features or characteristics that distinguish it and make it different from other products of the same type.* For example, a crew neck is one style of neckline and a turtleneck is another. All blazer jackets have certain features in common—features that make them different from, say, safari jackets—just as bow ties differ from four-in-hands. Baggy jeans have a common characteristic—fullness—that distinguishes them from other types of jeans. Shirtwaist dresses have a distinctive feature that makes them different from wrap, sheath, or other types of dresses.

Similarly, there are different styles of fabrics, each of which has its own distinctive features, such as denim, gabardine, chiffon, and seersucker, to name but a few. In automobiles, there are such styles as convertibles, station wagons, and vans. Art has such styles as pop art, art deco, and impressionism; houses may be colonial, ranch, Victorian, or other styles. There are styles in penmanship, interior decoration, and advertisements. In any one category of product, there is usually an endless variety of styles.

A Design: Variations of a Style

Within a specific style, there can be many variations in trimmings, texture, decoration, or other details. A cardigan sweater, for example, is a distinctive style, but within that style, individual variations could include different types of knits, embroideries, pockets, and necklines, to name but a few. *These individual interpretations or versions of the same style are called* **designs**. Compared to the number of styles in any given product, the possible variety of designs is limitless. Each design is different from the others in detail; they are all individual interpretations of their respective style.

In the fashion industry, when a style becomes popular, many different designs or versions of that style may be produced. In the trade, each producer assigns a **style number** to each design in the firm's line, which is used to identify it in production, selling, and shipping.

Fashion Means Consumer Acceptance

Among the countless definitions of *fashion*, the one from Webster's latest unabridged dictionary comes very close to what professionals mean when they use the word: *the prevailing or accepted style in dress or personal decoration established or adopted during a particular time or season.* The most widely recognized fashion authority, the late Dr. Paul H. Nystrom (1928, p. 4), defined fashion in similar words as "nothing more or less than the prevailing style at any given time." Thus, a fashion is always based on a specific style. A style, however, does not become a fashion until it gains consumer acceptance, and it remains a fashion only as long as it is accepted.

For example, bow ties, tapered jeans, crinoline skirts, and chemise dresses are and will always be styles, but they can only be called fashions if and when they become prevailing styles. It is clearly possible, moreover, for a particular style to come in and go out of fashion repeatedly. Some examples of such "ins and outs" of fashion are peasant blouses, sheath dresses, padded shoulders, and circular skirts, to name a few.

The element of social acceptance is the very essence of fashion. Acceptance, however, does not mean that a style is necessarily worn by everyone or even by a majority of the public. Acceptance can be and usually is limited to a particular group of people or to a particular location. For example, what New York men and women wear is often unacceptable in other parts of the United States that have markedly different climates or mores. Furthermore, what is popular among a particular age or occupational group may not be accepted by those of different ages or occupations.

Other Key Fashion Terms

There are, of course, many more key words commonly used in the fashion business, and it is necessary to understand their precise meanings to understand fashion itself and follow a discussion of fashion principles.

Classics and Fads

A classic is a style that continues to be accepted, to a greater or lesser degree, over an extended period of time. In the fashion world, this means that its acceptance endures for several seasons, or even longer. Typical of **classics** are blazer jackets, crewneck shetland sweaters, and men's oxford cloth button-down collared shirts. From time to time, some classics can achieve a peak in popularity and become a mass fashion. That happened to the examples just cited, which in 1983 constituted the "preppy look."

In contrast to classics, there are styles that sweep suddenly into popularity, are adopted with great fervor, and then just as quickly disappear. Their acceptance is generally for a brief period of time and among a limited following. *These short-lived fashions are called fads*, and they seldom have any lasting impact on future fashions. An example is the Nehru collar, which was adopted by men almost overnight several years ago and died as abruptly as it was born. Often there is a capricious aspect in a fad, as in the case of "pet rocks" and "mood rings," which were briefly and suddenly seen everywhere and then just as suddenly were gone. Fads go up like rockets and sink without a trace once their brief popularity is over.

Prior to her death, Princess Diana had become a fashion icon who chose more classic styles as she matured. However, her playful nature also enabled her to enjoy occasional fads, or sometimes even to launch a fad through her own appearance.

Limited and Mass Fashions

The term **high fashion** is commonly used to describe a *very new style, whose acceptance is limited to those who want to be first to adopt the very newest fashions and can afford their often astronomical prices.* Some of these styles are limited in appeal primarily because of the high prices they command. Their intricate design and costly workmanship keep some of them out of reach of all but people in top income brackets.[1] Other styles may be limited because they are too sophisticated or extreme to be

---

[1] Despite its glamour, high fashion is only a marginal moneymaker. Design houses such as Dior, Yves St. Laurent, Givenchy, and many prestigious U.S. designers rely on fragrances and accessories bearing their names to provide their profits. More recently, many of these designers have created "secondary lines" within the reach of the upper middle class as a way to support their enterprises. Examples include Ungaro's Emanuel line, Anne Klein II, and Donna Karan's DKNY (Riemer, Zinn, & Dapner, 1991).

attuned to the needs of the average man or woman. In either event, high-fashion styles are generally introduced, produced, and sold in relatively small quantities until their newness wears off. If the style has the potential for appealing to a broader audience, it is generally copied and sold at lower prices. The originator and the early purchasers, meanwhile, have gone on to something new.

Karl Lagerfeld, head of three fashion houses—Chanel, Lagerfeld, and Chloé—and perhaps the most powerful designer in the world today, noted the role of high-fashion houses. He reflected that the broader public would be unlikely to buy his clothes: "I don't buy. You don't buy. I propose" (Lane, 1994, p. 86). That is, the high-fashion houses set the pace for trends through their creative offerings.

In contrast with high fashion, which accounts for a relatively small portion of the fashion industry's business, there are **mass fashions** or *volume fashions*. These are *styles* that are accepted and worn by a large number of people. Mass fashions are produced and sold in large quantities at moderate prices and constitute the bread and butter of the fashion industry.

Fashion Trends

Fashions are not static; there is always movement, and that movement has a direction, discernible to careful observers. *The directions in which fashions are moving are called fashion trends*. For example, skirt lengths have moved up from the calf to the knee to well above the knee—perhaps almost imperceptibly from one season to the next, but generally in an upward direction. Short jackets, as another example, sometimes gain at the expense of hip-length styles. Men's lapels or ties may become wider or narrower; women's shoes may become clunkier or more elegantly slim; the athletic workout look may be getting more or less popular than other leisure-time clothes; fabrics may go from wrinkled to creaseless; and so on. The changes from season to season may be slight, but they generally have a direction. The ability to recognize that direction or trend is vital to fashion practitioners. Because these people must work far ahead of consumers' buying periods, much of their success depends on their ability to read the signs and promptly recognize the incoming and outgoing trends in fashion. The term *fashion-forward* may be used to describe styles that are gaining in acceptance. *Avant-garde* fashions are those that are unorthodox, experimental, perhaps unusual, or shocking. Although avant-garde fashions may be noticed, they may not gain broad acceptance.

The Constant in Fashion Is Change

If there is one absolute constant pertaining to fashion, it is the fact that it is always changing—sometimes rapidly, sometimes slowly, but it is never static or dormant. This element of change is recognized in the definitions of fashion itself cited earlier, by the use of such words as *prevailing* or *a given period of time*. To ignore the element of change is like looking at a still photograph in place of a motion picture. The still photo tells you what is happening here and now; the motion picture shows you what came before and what may lie ahead.

Why Fashions Change

To understand the constant changes in fashion, it is imperative to understand that fashions are always in harmony with their era. As a famous designer expressed it, "Fashion is a social phenomenon which reflects the same continuing change that rides through any given age." Changes in fashion, he emphasized, "correspond with the subtle and often hidden network of forces that operate on society. . . . In this sense, fashion is a symbol" (Beaton, 1954, pp. 335, 379–381).

Differing views exist on how fashion changes are started. Sproles (1981; Sproles & Burns, 1994) categorized these views into two groups, as follows:

- *The industry as initiators of change.* Because the fashion industry thrives on change, this idea suggests that different segments of the industry "force" change on the consumer by dictating new trends. Traditionally, the European fashion houses exerted a powerful influence; the trade media such as *Women's Wear Daily* shaped the industry's choices and, therefore, consumers' choices; and retailers dictated what would be worn by what they carried. Although all these forces are important, Sproles noted, "changing fashion is a far more complex phenomenon than those with the industry-centered views might wish to believe" (1981, p. 118). In recent years, many consumers have become increasingly resistant to having new fashions forced on them. Often, consumers now exert a spirit of independence in their dress by wearing what they feel is right for them, regardless of what the industry promotes.
- *Consumers as the initiators of change.* Others who study fashion change believe consumers are responsible for what becomes fashionable. Given an array of products from which to choose, certain trends develop because a group of consumers establishes that these fashions are "right." Four major theories suggest how consumers determine the course of new trends: (1) some trends may begin with the upper socioeconomic consumers; (2) others may occur simultaneously within all socioeconomic groups; (3) sometimes fashions rise from subculture groups, such as urban African Americans, youth, blue-collar workers, and ethnic minorities such as Native Americans; and (4) nearly any creative or innovative individual can launch fashion trends if they are consistent with the social climate and lifestyles of the times (Sproles, 1981).

Some of these theories are discussed further later in this chapter. Some of the factors that cause consumers to initiate change are discussed next.

Psychological Reasons

Men and women are complex creatures whose actions are seldom governed by reason alone. Change comes about for psychological reasons. People grow bored with what they have; the eye wearies of the same colors, lines, and textures after a time; what is new and different appears refreshing; and what has been on the scene for a while appears dull and unattractive. Thorstein Veblen, writing at the beginning of the century, made this clear in his *Theory of the Leisure Class*. As he pointed out: "A fancy bonnet of this year's model unquestionably appeals to our sensibilities today more forcibly than an equally fancy bonnet of the model of last year; although when viewed in the perspective of a quarter of a century, it would, I apprehend, be a matter of the utmost difficulty to award the palm for intrinsic beauty to one rather than to the other" (Veblen, 1963, p. 97).

Changes for such psychological reasons occur also in the fashions for products other than clothing. Auto manufacturers introduce new colors because potential buyers tire of the same colors. Further, for example, nothing could be more utilitarian than a broom, a refrigerator, a telephone, a teakettle, or a hand tool. Yet people about to buy such things will be attracted to, for instance, a broom with a coppertone handle to go with a similarly colored refrigerator that has recently been purchased to replace a quite adequate white model that they discarded. This element of change for the sake of change—artificial obsolescence, in fact—touches nearly all products today. Along with boredom, human curiosity or an innate desire for new sensations leads to change for its own sake.

Rational Reasons

Changes in fashion are also caused by rational reasons, such as environmental factors that create new needs. A classic example of a social change that brought about a drastic change in fashions occurred in the early decades of the 20th century, when women sought, gained, and enjoyed new political and economic freedom. Their altered activities and concepts of themselves encouraged them to discard the constricting garments that had been in fashion for centuries and to adopt shorter skirts, relaxed waistlines, bobbed hair, and other fashions more appropriate to their more active lives. Generations later, as women moved into top executive positions in the business world, the tailored suit, femininely soft blouse, and attaché bags became the "dressing for success" fashion among career women.

Similarly, in the decade following World War II, when the great trek to the suburbs began, those who joined the exodus from the city found themselves needing cars and car coats, garden furniture, and casual clothes for backyard barbecues. The physical fitness movement in the 1970s and 1980s brought about a need for exercise clothing, and as the interest in jogging, hiking, tennis, and aerobic dancing mushroomed, so also did the need for new and different fashions appropriate to each of these active sports. "Casual Fridays" and a shift toward working at home have changed the way many people dress for work in the 1990s and 2000s. Even environmental concerns influence fashion by avoiding the use of certain dyes and finishes harmful to nature.

Changes in Fashions Are Gradual

Although fashions change constantly and new ones appear almost every season, a full-scale changeover is never completed at any one time. In studying the pattern of change in fashions, scholars have observed that changes in fashion are **evolutionary** in nature, rather than revolutionary.

It is only in retrospect that fashion changes seem marked or sudden. Actually, they come about as a result of a series of gradual shifts from one season to the next. For example, when women's skirts began inching up from midcalf length in the 1960s, this gradual shortening was not particularly noticeable at first. It was only when skirts moved thigh high, in the form of minis and microminis, that people took notice of the approaching extreme. Similarly, when men began to abandon ultranarrow ties and suit lapels in favor of more and more width, the changes were not noticed at first. Then, when wide ties and lapels began to lose their appeal and progressively narrower styles made their appearance, people again mistook their belated recognition of these gradual shifts for a sudden change in fashion.

Even today, when the rate of fashion change has accelerated sharply, the pace of change is really slower than it appears to the unskilled observer who has failed to notice the early evolutionary movements in a new direction.

The evolutionary nature of fashion change is a fundamental principle that is recognized by fashion practitioners; it provides them with a solid, factual foundation for forecasting and identifying incoming fashions. When planning and developing new style ideas, they always keep the current fashions and evolving directions in mind. Thus, the acceptance of a particular coat or dress fashion during a current season becomes a straw in the wind for experts in search of clues to the next season's trends. The degree of its acceptance provides needed clues as to what will or will not be welcomed by the consumer in the next season. Knowing that people do not respond well to sudden changes, the fashion experts build gradually, not abruptly, toward new ideas.

An exception to this principle occurred just after World War II. During that cataclysm, fabrics were in decidedly short supply; fashion was at an enforced standstill; women's clothes were built along straight, skimpy lines. By 1947, however, fashion was on the move and making up for lost time. Dior introduced his famous "new look," with long, full skirts and pinched waists. The radical change was accepted overnight. This unique event in fashion history was possible because the years of wartime shortages had precluded the gradual changes that would otherwise have taken place.

Even the slowest, most gradual of evolutionary changes in fashion, however, do change direction eventually. Once an extreme has been reached, shifts begin to occur in a new and different direction—often as a complete reversal, such as the returning swing of a pendulum. "All fashions end in excess" is a saying attributed to Paul Poiret, an outstanding couturier of the 1920s, and his remark carries as much weight today as it did then.

Examples are readily found in both history and recent times. Eighteenth-century hoopskirts and the crinolines of the 19th century ballooned to diameters of 8 feet. Later, both exploded into a fragmentation of trains, loops, and bustles that nevertheless provided a far slimmer silhouette. Similarly, when the miniskirts of the 1960s moved up to the microminis of the 1970s, hems began inching downward. Whether it be skirt lengths, silhouettes, suit lapels, or general fashion looks, all fashions tend to move steadily toward an extreme, at which point a new direction develops.

Fashion: A "Follow-the-Leader" Process

In the constant change and movement of fashion, there is a definite orderliness about the pattern of acceptance. Styles become fashions through a "follow-the-leader" process. Understanding this acceptance pattern is a key to understanding fashion movements; it explains how a look or idea begins with a few and spreads to many.

The Fashion Cycle

Every fashion has a life span, known as a **fashion cycle**. This consists of three major stages: a beginning, or rise; a peak or very popular stage; and a declining stage. The acceptance patterns of individual styles and of overall fashion looks both fall into this pattern.

Stages of the fashion cycle reflect the work of Everett Rogers, who focused on how innovations are diffused in a society (Rogers, 1962; Rogers & Shoemaker, 1971, 1983). Rogers developed a model in the form of a typical bell-shaped curve representing stages of adoption over time. Rogers proposed five typical categories: (1) *the innovators*, who are the first to adopt a new idea (2.5 percent of the population), (2) *the early adopters* (13.5 percent), (3) *the early majority* (34 percent), (4) *the late majority* (34 percent); and (5) *the laggards* (16 percent). To simplify the curve for our purposes, these can be grouped into three stages (Figure 2–1).

In its first or beginning stage, a fashion is adopted by people who like or can afford to be first with what is new or who are highly motivated by a desire to dress dif-

Figure 2–1

Fashion cycles differ. This figure depicts how the cycle may be different for Fashion X compared to Fashion Y.

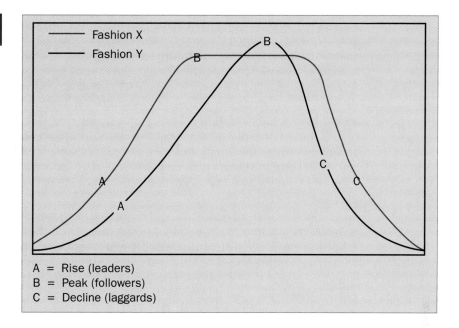

A = Rise (leaders)
B = Peak (followers)
C = Decline (laggards)

ferently from others. These pacesetters are relatively limited in number. In this first stage, the new fashion is often called a "high fashion," as explained earlier in this chapter.

If and when the new fashion idea spreads and is widely imitated by the greater number of people who tend to follow rather than lead, we arrive at the second stage of peak, or mass, acceptance. The fashion is then in such demand that it can be mass-produced and distributed at prices within the reach of many consumers.

Ultimately, each fashion moves into its third or declining stage—usually the result of consumer boredom arising from seeing too much of the same thing. Some consumers will still be wearing it at this stage, but they are no longer willing to purchase it at regular prices. Meantime, other, newer fashions are going through the earlier stages of their cycles.

This pattern of acceptance and decline has been explained thus by sociology professor Neil J. Smelser:

> It is important to (style leaders) to be among the first in order to reap the psychological rewards of being in the forefront of fashion, and it is almost as important to flee from a new style when it is assumed by the masses. Further back in the procession, among the followers, the motivation is more purely sociable—persons adapt to styles to avoid being conspicuously traditional, rather than to be conspicuously original. (Quoted in Ivins, 1976)

These stages of public acceptance tend to occur in all products that are subject to changes in fashion—not just in dress. Similar cycles can be traced in home furnishings, architecture, food, and even vacation spots, but the pattern shows up most obviously in what we wear.

Different fashions vary in their life spans, in the degree of acceptance they attain, and in the rate at which they move through their various stages. The length of time a particular fashion may remain in any of its three stages depends on the extent to which it is gaining or losing public acceptance. Some fashions may endure for a year or more, others for a season, and indeed, some may never get beyond the first stage of acceptance by small groups of people. Therefore, if one were to draw a fashion cycle, it would include the three stages, but its shape would be different for different fashions. The rise and fall may be gradual or sharp; the peak may be narrow or wide. Although no one graph can depict the life story of all fashions accurately, all would have a wavelike appearance.

Scholars of fashion have sought to chart the ups and downs of fashions in an effort to determine the length of time a fashion movement takes to run its course. The time intervals, however, elude measurement. The spread of fashion, as of every new idea, is a complicated social phenomenon. The public's needs and interests do not change like clockwork.

The problem of applying the stopwatch technique to an analysis of fashion movements is also complicated by the fact that price differentials, which at one time tended to mark the different stages of style acceptance, have virtually disappeared. Moreover, although some cycles are in their peaks, their successors are already in the growing stage. Many new fashions often reach full growth without ever entirely displacing those that preceded them. A further complicating factor is that, owing to the evolutionary nature of changes, clearly definable shifts in fashion do not occur at a given time, and it is impossible to pinpoint the exact beginning or end of a specific fashion.

Application to Merchandising Fashions

An understanding of the fashion cycle is basic to successful merchandising of fashion goods, either at wholesale or retail. Because very few concerns, if any, can successfully serve under one roof both the pacesetters and the followers, each firm must have a clear-cut policy on which fashion stages it wishes to deal in.

The main volume of business, in manufacturing and retailing alike, is done in fashions that are widely accepted or well on their way to the top or peak of the fashion cycle. A business that aims to attract a mass-customers audience must concentrate on widely popular fashions or on those that show promise of rising into the mass-acceptance stage. These volume fashions constitute the major portion of the business done by the giant firms in the fashion industry. Conversely, those manufacturers and retailers that concentrate on being the first to carry the newest, the most individual, or the most extreme fashions cannot expect to do a large volume of business. Their appeal is to the limited group of customers who adopt such fashions. Their volume contributes only a small part of the total business done in the fashion industries, but a vital one indeed. Figure 2–2 depicts the relative importance of various stages of the fashion cycle and how merchandising varies for each stage.

Theories of Fashion Leadership

Social scientists explain the follow-the-leader element in fashion cycles in terms of an individual's desire to achieve status by choosing apparel similar to that chosen by an admired individual or group. This association through choice of fashion is a means of bridging the gap between social classes—that is, becoming in one's mind like "them" by wearing what "they" wear. Imitation and conformity in dress are also explained in terms of insecurity, because it takes more social courage than most of us possess to be conspicuously different from others in the appearance we present to the public. Thus, fashion gives expression to two basic human needs: the need for social status and the need to conform (Sapir, 1931; Tarde, 1903).

Figure 2–2	**Stages of the fashion cycle and how merchandising may vary for each stage.**

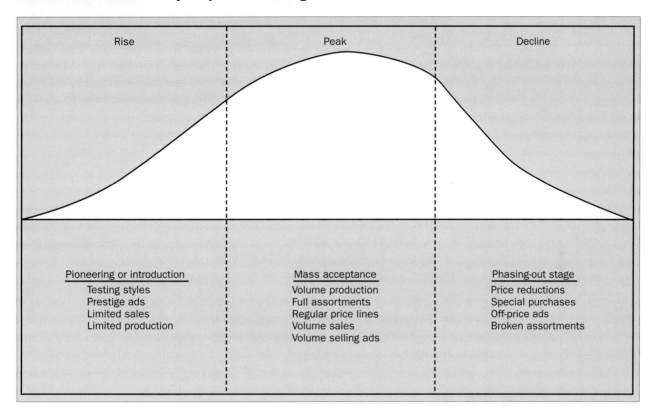

Rise	Peak	Decline

Pioneering or introduction
Testing styles
Prestige ads
Limited sales
Limited production

Mass acceptance
Volume production
Full assortments
Regular price lines
Volume sales
Volume selling ads

Phasing-out stage
Price reductions
Special purchases
Off-price ads
Broken assortments

Three academically accepted theories categorize the admired groups or individuals from whom fashion leadership flows. These theories are "trickle-down," "horizontal or trickle-across," and "bottom-up" (Figure 2–3). Each has its own claim to validity with respect to specific fashions and the fashion cycle.

Trickle-Down Theory

The **trickle-down theory** maintains that new styles make their first appearance among people at the top of a social pyramid and then gradually move down to progressively lower social levels.

Centuries ago, the persons at the top of the pyramid, and therefore the setters of fashion, were royalty. Fashions trickled down through the ranks of the nobility and those of the middle classes who had the means. The lower classes, of course, had neither the means nor the temerity to copy or were even prohibited by law from doing so.

Figure 2–3	
Theories of fashion leadership.	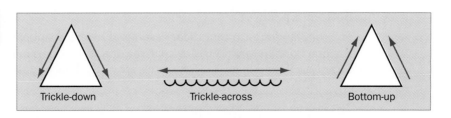

Trickle-down   Trickle-across   Bottom-up

These days, royalty has practically disappeared; however, Princess Diana was an exception in terms of her influence on fashion. With Princess Diana as an exception, the position at the top of the pyramid is held by individuals at the top of the economic, social, entertainment, and political ladders. Many such people make it their business to dress well, and their activities and appearance are highly publicized. To the large majority of the public, the fashions accepted by the glittering personalities at the top constitute a guide of what to wear, within the limits of their own more-restricted budgets and social activities. For most consumers, innovation is risky, but imitation is safe. Thus, fashions trickle down from higher to lower echelons, just as they did in the days of royalty.

Simultaneously, those at the top seek to dissociate themselves from those whom they consider socially inferior. They abandon a fashion once it has achieved popularity at less-distinguished levels and introduce a new and different idea. This is perhaps why department store buyers will not carry a clothing brand that has become available in discount stores.

This type of social behavior was recognized and its implications for fashion were propounded by such early economists as Thorstein Veblen (1963), John Roe (1834), and Caroline Foley (1893) and by such sociologists as George Simmel, who spelled it out, step-by-step, in a paper published in 1904 (reprinted in 1957).

Behling (1992) reviewed fashion adoption research and constructed a profile of *early adopters* (also called *fashion leaders* or *fashion innovators*) based on the collective findings from the studies.[2] The profile that emerged suggests that the early fashion adopter is relatively young, has a relatively high income and occupation, is not married or has no children (and, therefore, has funds available to purchase clothing and accessories), is likely to be female (although young males are also early adopters), is likely to read fashion magazines, and is mobile. Early adopters tend to be gregarious or social, conforming, and competitive; like or do not object to change; and tend to be exhibitionists or narcissistic.

Trickle-Across Theory

As the 20th century progressed, it became clear that fashion was no longer a matter of imitating any single social or economic class, but of choosing one's own role models—and not necessarily from among individuals with glittering genealogy or fabulous wealth. This phenomenon gave rise to another theory of fashion emulation: the **trickle-across theory**, enunciated by Charles W. King (1963). He observed that fashions spread horizontally within and across homogeneous groups, rather than merely vertically from one social level to another. He believes that each segment of our pluralistic society has its own leader or leaders whom it emulates. For example, a "Big Man" on campus may favor a certain type of jeans or baggy T-shirt and thus set a fashion for them among other students. In the business world, aspirants to the executive office tend to dress as the upper echelons do, be it the gray flannel suit of the 1950s or the colorful neckties of the 1990s. Even in so small a group as a suburban country golf club, the dominant members subtly influence the dress of the other members by the fashions they favor.

Bottom-Up Theory

The third and most recent theory espoused by many students of fashion and by fashion practitioners themselves is that the traditional trickle-down movement has reversed itself, and many fashions now filter up. This **bottom-up theory**, as advanced

---

[2]Behling's review provides a very useful overview of 20 studies based on Rogers's model conducted over three and one-half decades.

by Greenberg and Glynn (1966), maintains that young people are quicker than any other social group to initiate new and different fashions and that fashions filter up, not merely from youth to older age groups, but also from lower to upper economic classes. Typical of fashions initiated by the young and less than affluent are jeans, sneakers, T-shirts, baggy shorts, military surplus and safari clothes, and black leather pants and jackets (see the example in Figure 2–4). In another example, hip-hop apparel began as urban street wear for African Americans. Each of these started

Figure 2–4

Popularity of overalls among trendy, fashionable consumers illustrates the bottom-up theory.

Source: Reprinted courtesy of Cotton Incorporated.

in the streets with young people of modest means and streamed upward to well-to-do middle-aged adults. The male espousal of flowing hair and beards similarly was initiated by the young in the 1960s, and that fashion spread to gray-haired, balding men as well. When younger men became reacquainted with razors, their elders soon followed suit.

Marketing Implications

These three different theories of how fashions spread have major significance for practitioners in the field, because they confirm that there is no single homogeneous fashion public in our pluralistic society. A number of distinctly different groups make up the fashion public, and each has its own leaders and its own perception of fashion. Although we continue to see many new styles introduced at high prices that eventually become fashions, this is less often the case than it once was. One successful new style may originate in the studio of a prestigious designer, but another may come into fashion from the stock of an Army–Navy store.

Leadership in fashion these days has less and less to do with price and high-priced merchandise. Therefore, producers and retailers can no longer look only to an elite group of traditional fashion leaders for incoming trends. They must also look at what people are wearing in the streets. They must be aware that some fashions flow upward and others flow across within special groups. Dominant individuals and dominant influences, wherever they reveal themselves within our society, are important influences on fashion. Success depends on identifying and watching these, not just the patrons of elite restaurants, resorts, and entertainments.

How Fashions Develop

There is no question that it is far easier to recognize what is fashionable at a given time and place than to say why or how it became a fashion. When we search for the influences that brought forth such fashions as the hobble skirts and crinolines of the past or some of the fashions of the present, we are confronted with a complex question indeed. Several things we do know, however. One is that esthetic appeal alone does not produce a fashion. Veblen (1963) made this point when he observed that there is no intrinsic difference between the gloss of a patent leather shoe and the shine of a threadbare garment. People, he observed, are ready to find beauty in what is in vogue; therefore, the shine on the shoe is beautiful, and the garment's shine is repulsive.

Another thing we know is that promotional efforts by designers, producers, or retailers cannot in themselves dictate what customers will accept. If there were such dictators in the past, there certainly are none today. And a third factor that we know is that a fashion does not just happen without a reason. It is in response to many things: attitudes, social changes and movements, major events on the world stage, and new technological developments, for example. Which of these is the most important, no one can say; their relative strengths vary with the times.

The Role of Designers

There are countless styles, each of which has its own distinctive characteristics and most of which have, at one time or another or more than once, been a fashion. It is a common misconception, however, that all have been "created" by designers and only by them.

It is true, indeed, that many new fashions have been introduced by famous designers. Some examples include the boxy jackets of Chanel's 1920 suits, the bias-cut dresses of Vionnet in the 1920s, and Dior's "new look" in the 1940s. More recently, at least two American designers have left a distinct mark on fashion. These include Ralph Lauren's look of casual elegance and Donna Karan's bodysuits.

Often, however, it is a functional garment rather than an individual designer that generates a new fashion. Some examples that have taken the fancy of the public and become fashions in their time are the bomber jackets of aviators, the pea coats of sailors, the trench coats of soldiers, the leg warmers of dancers, and the protective overalls of farmers. Similarly, denim pants, the ultrapractical style created by Levi Strauss in gold-rush days, inspired the jeans that have enjoyed worldwide popularity in the second half of the 20th century. And let us not forget that many examples of "street fashions" started among young people and moved out to a wider following. A classic case is the miniskirt: the miniskirt and boots that London working girls adopted in the 1960s attained widespread popularity before being shown in Paris by Courreges.

Designers who acquire a reputation for "creating" fashion are simply those who have been consistently successful in giving tangible expression to the shapes, colors, fabrics, styles, and looks that are wanted and accepted by a substantial number of customers. The fact that a style may be widely heralded as a new fashion does not make it one. Even among the greatest of designers, it is recognized that it is only when customers accept a style, new or old, that the particular style becomes a fashion. Paul Poiret, one of the greatest Paris couturiers, once told an American audience the following:

> I know you think me a king of fashion. It is a reception which cannot but flatter me and of which I cannot complain. All the same, I must undeceive you with regard to the powers of a king of fashion. We are not capricious despots who wake up one fine day, decide on a change in habits, abolish a neckline or puff out a sleeve. We are neither arbiters or dictators. Rather we are to be thought of as the blindly obedient servants of woman, who for her part is always enamored of change and a thirst for novelty. It is our role and our duty to be on the watch for the moment at which she becomes bored with what she is wearing, that we may suggest at the right instant something else which will meet her taste and her needs. It is therefore with a pair of antennae and not a rod of iron that I come before you, and not so much as a master that I speak, but as a slave . . . who must divine your innermost thoughts. (Quoted in Bell, 1947)

Poiret was at his peak in the early decades of this century, but designers today still see things as he did—although they express themselves in less flowery language. Halston, an important designer for a part of this century, commented similarly: "I have always felt that all the designers can do is suggest; it is the consumer who accepts or rejects and is the ultimate maker of fashion" (*RAM Reports to Retailers*, 1977).

Fashions Reflect Their "Times"

Fashions in clothing have always been more than merely a manner of dressing. A study of the past and a careful observation of the present will make it apparent that fashions are social expressions; they document the taste and values of their era just as painting, sculpture, and other art forms do. Fashions are a fact of social psychology. They reflect the way people think and live and are therefore influenced by the same environmental forces that act on any society (Table 2–1). Every fashion seems completely appropriate to its era and reflects the spirit of an age as no other symbol of the

Table 2–1 Fashions Reflect the Times

1920s

Events	Entertainment	Looks
Prohibition	*The Jazz Singer*	Short skirts
The Charleston	*The Sheik*	Flapper chemises
Art Deco	*City Lights*	Bobbed hair
Bootleg liquor	"Tea for Two"	Powdered knees
Showboat on Broadway	"Ol' Man River"	
The Cotton Club in Harlem	"Swanee"	
	"The Man I Love"	
	"I'm Just Wild about Harry"	

1930s

Events	Entertainment	Looks
Hollywood glamour influences fashion	*Gone with the Wind*	Streamlined silhouettes
Café society	*The Wizard of Oz*	Body-conscious shape
Our Town on Broadway	*It Happened One Night*	Bias cut
Jazz	*42nd Street*	Shirtwaists
	"10¢ a Dance"	Draping and shirring
	"I Got Rhythm"	Halters and hip wraps
	"Night and Day"	Hats and gloves
	"Putting on the Ritz"	Fox-trimmed coats

1960s

Events	Entertainment	Looks
Woodstock	*2001: A Space Odyssey*	Ironed hair
Pop art	*The Sound of Music*	Nehru jackets
Psychedelics	*Bonnie and Clyde*	Love beads
The Beatles	*The Graduate*	Teased hair
Flower children	*Z*	Go-go boots
Hair on Broadway	"Let the Sun Shine In"	Miniskirts
	"Strangers in the Night"	Dark eyes, pale lips
	"Moon River"	Pillbox hats
	"I Want to Hold Your Hand"	Prints

1970s

Events	Entertainment	Looks
Roller skating	*The Godfather*	Granny dresses
Disco	*The Great Gatsby*	Platform shoes
A Chorus Line on Broadway	*Annie Hall*	Message T-shirts
	Rocky	Midis
	Butch Cassidy and the Sundance Kid	*The Great Gatsby*
	Cabaret	*Annie Hall*
	"Send in the Clowns"	Hot pants
	The Way We Were	Designer jeans
	"Losing My Mind"	Punk
	"Killing Me Softly"	

1940s	1980s
WW II ends	MTV
Nylon stockings available	New wave music
Death of a Salesman and *A Streetcar Named Desire* on Broadway	Michael Jackson
	Postmodern art and architecture
Casablanca	Cats on Broadway
Citizen Kane	Madonna
Adam's Rib	Heavy Metal
Born Yesterday	*Phantom of the Opera*
Notorious	*Les Miserables*
The Red Shoes	
"So in Love"	*Rambo*
"If I Loved You"	"Born in the U.S.A."
"Some Enchanted Evening"	*Flashdance*
"Moonlight Serenade"	"We Are the World"
	Eraserhead
Short hemlines to long	*Murphy Brown*
Dior's "New Look"	*thirty-something*
Hepburn pants	*LA Law*
Sarong drape	*Cosby Show*
Peplum jackets	*Golden Girls*
Uniform-style suits	*Wheel of Fortune*
Hats with veils	*Batman*
Platform shoes	
	Menswear
	Sweaters
	Preppy
	Leggings
	Punk hairdo
	Torn jeans
	Sweat clothes
	Athletic shoes
	Earrings
	Bodysuits

1950s	1990s
Television	Globalization
The "Beat" generation	Computerization
Abstract expressionism	Information age
Sock hops	Satellite TV
My Fair Lady on Broadway	Cellular phones
	The Internet and cyberspace
Rebel without a Cause	NAFTA and GATT/WTO
Some Like It Hot	Environmental concerns
Gigi	AIDS/HIV grows
Singing in the Rain	Cautious consumer spending
Psycho	Gulf War
High Society	Oklahoma City bombing
"Hound Dog"	Asian/global economic crisis
"Three Coins in a Fountain"	Health and fitness craze
"I Love Paris"	Political correctness
"Standing on the Corner"	Deaths of Princess Diana and Versace
	El Niño
The trapeze	Attack on affirmative action
The chemise	*Lion King* on Broadway
The shirtdress	
Penny loafers	Compact discs
Bobby sox	*Jurassic Park*
Capri pants	*Seinfeld*
Ponytails	*The Simpsons*
The sheath	O. J. Simpson trial
Saddle shoes	*ER*
Princess dresses	*NYPD Blue*
	90210
	Friends
	Titanic
	South Park
	Janet Jackson
	Casual wear everywhere
	Grunge or post-industrial thrift shop look
	Retro looks
	Dress-down Fridays
	Baseball caps—men and women
	'70s revival
	Big platform shoes and squared toes
	Tattoos and body piercing
	Natural fibers
	Wonderbra
	Long, shapeless rayon dresses
	Hip-hop
	Waif (thin) look
	Breast augmentation

times does. This is true both for widely accepted fashions and for those that flourish only within small isolated or counterculture groups. To illustrate: Mennonite attire reflects Mennonite ideals; punk dress and hair styles reflect the attitudes of punk rockers.

Teri Agins, a senior writer at the *Wall Street Journal* who covers the fashion industry, writes about how consumer lifestyles and preferences have changed the entire nature of the industry. In her book, *The End of Fashion* (1999), Agins writes about how consumers—not the forces of fashion—have taken over the power in dictating trends. This includes deciding what we want to wear, when we buy it, and how much we pay for it. She elaborates on major trends of the times that have "sent fashion rolling in a new direction": (1) women let go of fashion and no longer had an interest in what the French couture or other top high-fashion designers dictated; (2) people stopped dressing up as jeans and knit tops became the uniforms of the day, and casual office attire emerged, as personified by Microsoft's Bill Gates; (3) people changed attitudes with regard to fashion, realizing that good-looking clothes could be found at any price and that designer labels were often a rip-off; and (4) top designers stopped gambling on fashion, and those that emerged as most successful were those grounded in reality such as Tommy Hilfiger, Polo Ralph Lauren, and Liz Claiborne—with merchandise that appealed to millions of consumers around the world and "generated the bottom line that Wall Street expects" (p. 14).

Agins refers to consumers' love affair with the most functional and affordable clothes as the **"commodization" of fashion**. This commodization of clothes coincided with the clothing trends of the 1990s: the "classics," "simple chic," and "minimalism." These staple fashion items happened to be the perfect kind of products for production for what had become the new global apparel industry. That is, these more simplified, mainstream styles are easier to execute on a large commercial scale and have fewer chances for errors when produced in far-flung factories in Asia or elsewhere.

Agins concludes that many of the trends of the times, along with competitive market conditions, have sapped the creativity and distinctiveness from fashion. This mass marketing of the apparel business results in what she chose for the title of her book: *The End of Fashion*. All this leads to the "sameness" among products found in the U.S. markets.

Newsworthy Events and Personalities Make Fashions

Fashions are made by outstanding personalities and major happenings in the fields of entertainment, sports, art, and politics. Almost anything or anyone of newsworthy importance in the world of entertainment, from prominent personalities to major television or motion picture productions, has an effect on the fashions of the times. To cite but a few examples from the 1970s and 1980s: the Indian inspired fashions influenced by the widely watched television production of *Jewel in the Crown* and the Indian art exhibits in New York and Washington; the tremendous impact on hair and clothing styles of superstars whose personae are as closely identified with their clothes as with their music; the career fashions that received impetus from a new wave of television and movie productions that starred women in positions as business executives; and the popularity of the black leather look, skull and crossbones imagery, and decorative metal studs resulting from the enthusiasm for "heavy metal" music. Youth of the 1990s, known as Generation X, were influenced by grunge dressing of bands such as Nirvana, leading to popularity of flannel shirts, ripped jeans, Doc Marten boots, Teva sandals, reversed baseball caps, pierced noses, and tattoos.

Many new fashions have also emerged from the public's participation in sports and physical fitness activities. Each activity usually creates a need for different types of functional garments, many of which develop into everyday fashions. For example, sweatsuits and sweatshirts are an outgrowth of the functional running suits worn by joggers. A relatively short-lived fashion for dancers' leg warmers and cutoff T-shirts was generated by the active interest in aerobic dancing. Similar also are the fashions that developed from the brightly printed jams worn by surfers and skateboarders and the skintight bicycle pants of bicycle enthusiasts.

Emulation of personalities in the public eye, whose clothing and activities are featured in the media, also plays a part in the development of fashions. For instance, the pillbox hat and bouffant hair style of Jackie Kennedy, the young and much admired "first lady" in the 1960s, were widely imitated, as were the classic styles of dresses worn by Nancy Reagan in the 1980s, the faux pearls of Barbara Bush, and the classic suits of Hillary Clinton in the 1990s.

Social Movements Create Fashions

Fashions also develop in response to social movements. For example, the focus on career fashions and specialized career shops for women in the 1980s was a direct response to the rise of women in the ranks of corporate executives. Similarly, the antiestablishment fashions of the 1960s—cutoff jeans, long hair, beards, and the "hippie" look—were visible expressions of the antiestablishment attitude that developed as a reaction to the unpopular Vietnam War of the 1960s. The postindustrial thrift shop or grunge look of Generation X in the 1990s perhaps has reflected a spirit of pessimism about their prospects for jobs and the frequent burden of heavy college loans (Zinn, Power, Yand, Cuneo, & Ross, 1992).

In ways uniquely their own, hair styles have reflected social movements. In the gay nineties, women enhanced the luxurious look of their hair with pinned-on puffs, curls, rats, and other devices that have gone the way of tight corseting. In the 1960s, alongside the unkempt locks of the hippies, blacks let their hair grow long and full in the Afro styles that proclaimed that black was beautiful. In the 1970s many blacks, looking back to their roots, adopted cornrow hair styles and dreadlocks—two African hair styles almost impossible for Caucasians to copy. In the late 1970s, Mohawks and spiky pink and green hairdos were part of punk rock's way of thumbing its collective nose at the establishment.

Social Values and Attitudes Create Fashion

There is, of course, no one universal way of life in America today, even among those who constitute the mainstream. Except within fragmented groups, such as those mentioned earlier, our values are varied. Some of us are hedonistic; others are antimaterialistic. Some are conservative; some are futurists. Whatever our values and lifestyles, our dress reflects that choice, consciously or otherwise. As one commentator points out, clothes nowadays are viewed "sometimes with almost mystical fervor, as the most basic expression of lifestyle, indeed of identity itself" (Silberman, 1971, p. 95). Thus, fashions are a language that communicates self-identity and group identity with instant impact. When youth ideas are dominant, there is a tendency for people of all ages to dress, act, think like, and make believe they are young. The expanding use of hair dyes by both sexes and hair transplants by men reflect the desire to appear young, no matter what nature may say to the contrary.

The success of Victoria's Secret and other companies specializing in sensual attire perhaps reflects society's increasingly open attitude toward sexuality. The wearing of pants by women for many occasions is not merely a matter of dressing practically; it is also an expression of their freedom from the conventional restraints that they and their mothers had accepted in earlier years. When women, even those who wear trousers for most occasions, prefer to express their femininity, they move into fashions that are frillier, lacier, and sexier. When ostentation is seen as an expression of success, then rich clothes and elaborate home furnishings are "in." At other times, a revulsion against "conspicuous consumption" will express itself in understated clothes and home furnishings. And so it goes.

Technological Developments Create Fashion

New technological developments often spawn new fashions. So simple a thing as a digital clock, for instance, makes it possible to depart from the round-face design that prevailed for centuries. Some apparel fashions seem to have their origins in the development of new fibers and fabrics, new processes for utilizing familiar ones, and other fruits of the chemist's genius—plus a waiting need for the new or a weariness with the old. For example, the synthetic fibers that made wash-and-wear fabrics possible, and thus influenced fashion, might not have had such a rousing welcome if they had come on the scene early in the century, when domestic help was plentiful and when the stiffly starched, beautifully ironed garment was a symbol of a well-run household. More recently, the development of microfibers has led to a new luxury look in outerwear that resembles silk but has the easy-care features of manufactured fibers. The lofty, lightweight warmth of Polartec fabrics has spawned a fashionably bulky look in casual outerwear.

Other examples abound, such as the popularity of skintight bodysuits and activewear resulting from the rediscovery of stretch fabrics and the proliferation of graphics on T-shirts, which was made possible by the advances in heat-setting technology. Plastics in their infinite variety influenced the development of such fashions as raincoats in bright colors and the leather look of suedelike fabrics that offered the flexibility, easy care, and lightweight qualities of cloth.

The Prediction of Fashion

Analyzing and predicting which styles will become the fashions for coming seasons has been called an occupational guessing game for the fashion industry, with millions of dollars at stake. Fiber, textile, and leather producers must work from 1 to 2 years ahead of the consumers' buying seasons; apparel and accessory designer/manufacturers must prepare their lines from 9 months to a year ahead in order to show them to retail buyers 3 to 6 months in advance of the consumers' wearing season. Without accurate forecasts and projections of what looks, colors, fabrics, silhouettes, and design details are likely to be acceptable to customers, they would not be able to produce and sell the massive quantities of textiles and apparel that they do.

Such forecasts and predictions of fashion, however, are neither guesswork nor a game nor a matter of intuition. Rather, **fashion forecasting or fashion prediction** is one of the most vital activities in the industry. The successful forecaster recognizes that fashion is neither haphazard nor mysterious, but a tangible force whose progress can be charted, graphed, understood, explained, and projected. Basically, what fashion practitioners do is examine past experiences for clues as to what will happen today and then analyze and evaluate today's activities for indications of what may happen tomorrow. In her book, *Fashion Forecasting: Research, Analysis, and Presentation*, Brannon (2000) combines theories of fashion changes with the process of organizing and analyzing the information and synthesizing the data into actionable forecasts.

In Chapter 4, we will focus further on how fashion firms determine their target customers and how they try to serve those target markets.

Recognizing and Evaluating Trends

The logistics of projecting current fashions are relatively simple. Whatever styles have been steadily rising in popularity during the last few months may be expected to continue to rise for a few months more—or at least, not to decline abruptly for some time. Figure 2–5 depicts "looks" that have lasted over several years to characterize a decade in each case. For instance, a rising trend for fur-trimmed coats at the end of a fall season is very likely to be followed by a high demand for fur-trimmed coats at the

Figure 2–5

The looks from the 1920s to the 1990s.

| 1920s | 1930s | 1940s | 1950s |

| 1960s | 1970s | 1980s | 1990s |

beginning of the next fall season. Likewise, whatever has been steadily declining in popularity up to the present offers little favorable prospects for the future. People in the fashion business seem to develop almost a sixth sense for weighing various factors and judging probable ups and downs of trends. Their apparently instinctive skill arises from years of experience in studying signs that may escape the untrained observer, just as a weather forecaster observes signs the rest of us may not have noticed and becomes adept in this work.

Sources of Information

Fashion practitioners base their predictions not only on their own selling records and preliminary sales tests, but also on facts and observations that are available from other segments within the fashion industry.

The fact-gathering procedure, to continue the analogy to weather forecasting, is similar to preparing a meteorological map, with its isobars, temperature readings, pressure systems, and other indicators of present and future conditions. On the fashion forecaster's mental map of present and future customer preferences are the following factors—in addition, of course, to a knowledge of the movement of fashions.

With respect to the firm's targeted customer group, the fashion forecaster calls on the following:

- Careful observation of current events that have captured or are likely to capture the imagination of customers and affect the styles they will prefer
- Awareness of the current lifestyles and dress of those men and women most likely to influence what the firm's own customers will ultimately adopt
- Study of sales trends in various sections of the country, not only for the forecaster's own company, but also for competing companies to whatever extent is possible
- An intimate knowledge of the fashion opinions of sources of supply
- Familiarity with professional sources of information, such as fashion reporting services, fashion periodicals, opinions of consultants, analyses offered by resident buying offices, and the like
- Exchange of information with noncompeting concerns
- Understanding of and constant awareness of the inevitable and evolutionary nature of changes in fashion

Thus, a forecaster, whose official title may be merchandise manager, designer, fashion director, product developer, magazine editor, or store buyer, may decide that brighter and livelier colors will be more acceptable than they were in the previous year, that oversized tops have run their course for the time being, or that sleek hairdos are coming in.

A fashion forecast, once made, whether in one's own mind or in print, is seldom final and immutable. The unexpected can often happen when some new factor enters the picture. In any forecasting, whether it be weather or fashion, all that can be hoped for is a high percentage of successful projections. Even the best-informed and most-successful designers, producers, buyers, and fashion reporting services make errors, resulting in merchandise that must be disposed of in some way—usually unprofitably.

Consumers have given proof often enough that they have minds of their own and will reject a so-called fashion before it can even get going if it does not appeal to them. And if the industry had any doubts about this, it has only to look back a bit. Efforts to induce customers to wear hats when they preferred to go hatless achieved nothing. Similarly, an effort in 1970 to switch customers from miniskirts to the so-called midi, or midcalf length, met with disastrous results.

The importance of the customer in determining the course of fashion was stated effectively by Bill Blass, the American designer whose leadership has been legendary for decades. He said, after the midi fiasco:

> I have never felt for one minute that the designers or the press or the industry could force or impose a new fashion on the customer, and that's never been more evident than now. The designer can only propose; the customer decides. This is a time of great individuality in customer buying, so the store merchant must pay more attention than ever to what his or her customers are looking for, and then find the designers who are making clothes that relate to their customers. (*RAM Reports to Retailers*, 1977)

In summary, fashion is a dynamic phenomenon that drives the industry. Many factors influence fashion trends, but it is the customer who has the final word on whether a fashion lives or dies.

Readings

These readings focus on various trends in fashion and factors that have influenced those trends.

The American Way

From minimal styling to marketing savvy to a host of high-profile posts, American designers are impacting international fashion as never before.

A Century of Change: Jeans

Jeans have been a constant staple in the American wardrobe, evolving from rough, uncomfortable workwear to fashionable, designer-signature jeans.

Gimme a "T": Nearly a Century of T-Shirt Wearing Reveals Something Unique about the Character of Americans

Next to blue jeans, the T-shirt has evolved as a unique form of American expression often symbolizing rebellion, daring, and high fashion.

Marketplace Aesthetic Goes, Like, Totally '80s

"Retro" and "vintage" are important forces in fashion today, with the '80s becoming important. Authors note that the longing for familiarity has traditionally occurred in 20-year cycles.

The American Way

American fashion—once upon a time, those words were considered an oxymoron. But that was then. Today, American themes are embedded deeply in the worldwide fashion vernacular: casual style, minimalism, street chic. All concepts long championed by designers here, they are now dominant themes the world over. From LVMH to Gucci and, this fall, to the hallowed halls of Yves Saint Laurent, an American creative perspective rules some of the most storied addresses in fashion, while around the world, U.S. pop culture continues to influence style at every level.

But then, the mine is rich. Musings on American fashion instantly trigger comments on marketing genius, and rightly so, as over the years, designers here have revolutionized fashion advertising. More than 20 years later, the image of the adolescent Brooke Shields contemplating her Calvins remains iconic, daringly presented not only in traditional print ads but on television. Rosemary McGrotha's Oval Office adventures for Donna Karan celebrated the notion of limitless possibilities for women, while Ralph Lauren's perfect world lifestyle campaigns put his clothes in alluring context, from the American Southwest to Africa.

Marketing genius? Absolutely. But to stop there negates the significance of the fashion itself, and of each designer's brilliance in identifying the moment, and speaking to it with a provocative voice. If there is a common note among those voices, it is the simple notion that form follows function.

Practicality is a deeply ingrained element in American fashion, one that designers have reworked and refined ever since Levi Strauss created the most popular, enduring, and perhaps best item of clothing ever designed. From Claire McCardell to Anne Klein to Michael Kors, a deep-seated respect for the classic and functional has sustained American fashion, and inherent in that, the coexisting notions of practicality and modernity. Bill Blass's upper-crust—and sometimes crusty—antifashion independence was totally American; ditto the grace with which Perry Ellis and Willi Smith infused style with wit. But then, function has range: Stephen Burrows's slinky shapes, Norma Kamali's sweats, Giorgio di Sant'Angelo's groundbreaking jerseys. As for Halston's gloriously danceable dresses, they symbolized the madness of Studio 54, a lifestyle that not only influenced Seventies fashion, but helped trigger the transformation of the American designer from quiet artisan to major celebrity.

Since then, of course, society has become increasingly celebrity-obsessed, and at this point, the fashion-music-Hollywood links are a given. Sarah Jessica Parker picks sit-com frocks from the front row at numerous shows; Tommy Hilfiger touts urban edge and sponsors rock tours; designs compete furiously for their own Oscar winners. Yet none of this is new. Back in the Eighties, David Cameron based a collection around rap style and the look of urban bicycle messengers, and long before that, Arnold Scaasi made for one of the most memorable Oscar moments ever when he dressed Barbara Streisand in twinkly, see-through sailor pajamas at a time when barely there just wasn't done.

The news was that such simplicity could shock. To a large degree, American fashion is, and will always

Source: From Women's Wear Daily, *June 2000, p. 8. Special Supplement:* American Dreamers, 8–9.

be, about such simplicity—minimalism, if you will—which may be why Helmut Lang felt comfortable moving from Paris to Greene Street. Yet the fashion climate here has always been remarkably inclusive. It welcomes flamboyance, whether the high intellectualism of Geoffrey Beene, the fleeting promise of Angel Estrada or the savvy hippie trips of Anna Sui.

There is always room for the fashionably out-there, notably Betsey Johnson, whose wackiness is surpassed only by her durability, and Mary McFadden, ever ready to put world history in the context of polyester pleats. And there has always been a cross-cultural element, from the likes of Pauline Trigère, Carolina Herrera and Oscar de la Renta, who does double duty, bringing a Latin flourish to New York and Yankee practicality to the haute couture.

Of course, today, such globalization, along with a voracious quest for the new, is reshaping fashion. At a time when a guy born in Austin and raised in San Antonio designs for Gucci, a New Yorker holds court at Vuitton and an Irish girl dresses the hip set from her outpost on Bond Street, what exactly defines American fashion—or French or Italian—is more difficult to pinpoint than ever before.

As for the youth search, increasingly, designers such as Nicole Noselli and Daphne Guitierrez of Bruce and Susan Cianciolo are getting major play. But the most dramatic case in point: the frenzy over Miguel Adrover, who last season staged a stunning runway success. Now, he hopes to capture the moment and make a real business of it. Because in the end, the moment is what fashion is all about.

A Century of Change: Jeans

by Molly Knight

Over the century, fashion trends have been a lot like waves, rising and falling with the tides of popular interest. But in all the coming and going, one thing has remained a constant in the American wardrobe—blue jeans. Although they're quintessentially American, blue jeans were conceived of by a Bavarian-born emigre, Levi Strauss. Inspired by the gold rush in 1849, he left New York to find his fortune in California. Making his way across the country as a traveling salesman, Strauss sold dry goods including needles, thread and canvas. By the time he got to California, the only thing he had left to sell was heavy, brown canvas.

Strauss tried to sell the canvas to the gold miners to make tents, but he met with little success. According to legend, Strauss was having a drink at a local bar, possibly to drown away his troubles, when a young prospector approached him with an enterprising idea. Why not make pants with the canvas? Carrying pocketfuls of craggy, heavy gold nuggets, the miners desperately needed durable bottoms to wear.

Strauss liked the idea and in 1850 made America's first pair of blue jeans, which he called waist-high overalls. The pants became so popular, Strauss ran out of canvas, and started using a fabric from France called denim (named for the town of Nimes). As for jeans, the name comes from sailors in the Italian port of Genoa, or Genes in French, who were some of the first to wear denim pants.

Source: From Daily News Record, *May 14, 1999, p. 134. Reprinted by permission.*

The first pairs of jeans were a far cry from the stylish pairs worn today. They were untailored, stiff, unwashed and uncomfortable. They had no belt loops, only suspenders or waist-cinching buckles in the back. Over the years, gradual changes were made to Levi Strauss's jeans. In 1872 Strauss partnered with a Nevada tailor named Jacob Davis and added rustproof rivets as pocket reinforcements. The leather patch was soon added to the back of the waist, then the double orange stitching on the back pockets. Just after the turn of the century in 1902, Levi Strauss died and left a successful jeans business to his brothers. Today, according to the NPD Group, Levi's ranks number one on Americans' list of most recognizable brands.

The next big player in the history of denim was H. D. Lee, an investor from Vermont who sewed together jackets and dungarees for his chauffeur, who was tired of cleaning his uniform. Hence the beginning of the Lee Union-All, a one-piece denim workwear garment. In 1917 the U.S. Army contracted Lee to make as many Union-Alls as possible for official army fatigues. Lee's motto became "The jeans that built America."

In 1922 the reputation of jeans as workwear was made official with the founding of Williamson-Dickie Co., a denim company that made jeans specifically for the working-class American.

Jeans weren't only the uniform of blue-collar workers, they were also the uniform of the American cowboy. In the 1940s a company called Wrangler began making jeans specially for cowboys.

But it was not until the 1950s that jeans became a fashion commodity, largely due to Hollywood icons like Marlon Brando and James Dean. These cool, sexy, rebellious actors represented a breaking-away from social constraints, and young wannabes across the country copied their casual jeans and T-shirt look.

By the 1960s, jeans were moving closer to the fashion market. With the country in political and social upheaval, jeans were the chosen apparel for young people protesting the war in Vietnam or celebrating at Woodstock. The '60s also marked the opening of America's first jeans retailer-turned-manufacturer, The Gap. Founded in 1969 by Donald Fisher, The Gap originally sold only Levi's. When it finally launched its own private jeans label in 1974, denim grew to 98 percent of the company's sales. It wasn't until 1991 that Levi's were dropped entirely from The Gap's jeans offering.

In the late 1970s, jeans sales reached an all-time high. Responding to a consumer demand for denim, designers began making signature jeans. Despite the fact that his Calvin Klein's cost 50 percent more than Levi's, consumers bought 200,000 pairs the first week the jeans were on the market.

By 1980 a whole list of players joined the designer jeans market. Guess, a hot line founded by the French-born Marciano brothers in 1982, was one of the first to pioneer stonewashing in its sexy line of jeans. Marithe and Francois Girbaud were among the first jeans makers to experiment with bleaching. The '90s saw a whole new designer denim decade, as Polo, DKNY, Tommy Hilfiger and Kenneth Cole all spawned jeans collections.

Gimme a "T": Nearly a Century of T-Shirt Wearing Reveals Something Unique about the Character of Americans

by Jennifer M. Kim

*I*f blue jeans are this country's great contribution to fashion, then the white T-shirt isn't far behind.

Through the century, the T-shirt's basic style hasn't changed all that much, but what it stands for has continually evolved. And as commercial fashion goes, the T-shirt has never been a healthier proposition.

"The T-shirt is the backbone of most teenagers' wardrobe today," said David Wolfe, creator director of the New York-based Doneger Group.

At different times, T-shirts have symbolized rebellion, daring and high fashion.

Today, the T-shirt is still affordable and comfortable and worn by most of society, often as underwear and sometimes as sportswear.

As it did when first created, the T-shirt still embodies comfort and ease.

When American John Sharp invented the ring-spinning frame in 1828 along with Isaac M. Singer's perfection of the sewing machine in 1851, it set in motion the combination of the T-shirt and cotton that continues today.

The origin of the T-shirt goes back to around World War I. American soldiers arrived in France in 1917 wearing a wool uniform and "light" wool underwear. When they saw the French wear light, knit cotton underwear, they decided to borrow from the French and rid themselves of their stuffy wool underwear. When the war was over, they brought home some of the shirts. Underwear manufacturers quickly began making copies of the French shirt, some in the "T" shape, and many in the tank style.

Source: From Daily News Record, *September 27, 1999, p. 20. Reprinted by permission.*

By World War II, both the navy and the army had adopted the T-shirt as underwear. GIs slept in it, worked in it, used it to polish brass buttons and wrapped their toothbrushes in it. But through the first decades of the century, the T-shirt was still considered underwear and wasn't considered polite to wear as outer wear in social situations.

The 1920s popularized the union suit. It was also known as the combination suit and came in either long- or short-sleeved styles. Manufacturers and retailers like Munsingwear and Sears, Roebuck offered these long-bodied suits that came to be known as "long johns."

The nainsook suit, a lightweight cloth of strong basketweave construction, also became widely popular. Through technological innovation, new materials were being generated and by 1928 rayon had made its appearance in the cotton- and wool-dominated underwear market.

In the 1930s Hanes and others began producing undershirts with short sleeves and crewnecks for about 24 cents apiece. They began to advertise the T-shirt as a practical item with the role as both inner and outer garment.

A year after the Japanese attack on Pearl Harbor in 1941, the U.S. Navy sent out its official specs to suppliers for an all-cotton shirt with a round, moderately high neck, and short sleeves at right angles to front and back panels. Issued in plain milky white, they became known as "skivvy" shirts. With so many men in T-shirts, WWII had basically generated acceptance of the T as outer wear.

The T saw so much frontline battle action that it became the emblem of manliness. It washed easily and rolled compactly. It also functioned as a towel, shoeshine rag, pillow and bandage. The army adopted the T as a part of the uniform after convincing reports that it protected soldiers against burns and bugs.

When the war ended, men began wearing their T's as outer wear. U.S. Senator John F. Kennedy was photographed relaxing in a T-shirt in his Georgetown townhouse and the T became fully acceptable.

In 1951s *A Streetcar Named Desire*, Marlon Brando wore a white T-shirt while portraying sullen Stanley Kowalski. In a classic scene from the movie, one of his women rips his T-shirt almost completely off, revealing Brando's rippling muscles.

The T-shirt became a kind of Brando trademark as his physique took on a role of its own.

Movies and advertisements adopted the T-shirt because it mixed the spirit of athleticism with military accomplishment. And in the 1950s it got its biggest boost ever when James Dean wore it in *Rebel Without a Cause*.

While the T was once the uniform of farm workers, worn under blue denim overalls, by the '50s the T appealed to all classes and occupations.

When young people wanted to make a statement in the 1960s, they paired T-shirts with blue jeans and overnight it became an anti-establishment symbol for both sexes. T-shirts were further politicized when war protesters turned then into anti-war, anti-establishment billboards to get their story across.

In the 1970s, T-shirts were tie-dyed and later screenprinted with logos, cartoons and jokes.

The 1980s saw such modifications as the half-shirt muscle T, torn T-shirts, rolled-up-sleeve shirts, neon T-shirts and more. Michael Jackson and Arnold Schwarzenegger wore variations of these T-shirts onstage and in film.

As licensing boomed in the '80s, a wide array of products displayed athletic team logos from every sport imaginable. In the '90s, stores like The Gap have commercialized their simple white T-shirt as Hollywood stars announced to teens that it's the hip thing to wear. The simple fact is that T-shirts are cheap, fun and comfortable. Status designer labels and T-shirts advertising everything from beer to rock concerts have been major themes for the '90s. Ralph Lauren, Abercrombie & Fitch, Nike and Reebok have all turned a simple workout shirt into chic activewear.

Cross Colours made its T-shirt fashion statement with its bright-colored T's, displaying phrases such as "Post Hip-Hop Nation, Academic HardWear and Ya Dig."

"T-shirts will become more and more important," said Doneger's Wolfe, "in a more modern way for the millennium because it is so comfortable and it's about individuality. It's the perfect garment for the millennium," he added.

Marketplace Aesthetic Goes, Like, Totally '80s

by Anne Cashill and Rachel Matteson

Retro, retro, retro. All we hear is "retro this" and "vintage that." What's new in fashion seems to be what's old. The futuristic concept of men and women walking around in tight-fitting, shiny coverall suits tucked into boots a la "Star Trek" hasn't happened. Instead, designers and consumers are preferring to design, wear and buy things that look familiar.

The trend toward retro or vintage looks certainly isn't new. However, it continues to grow and is a dominant force in creating and selling consumer products today. Old Navy and Abercrombie & Fitch continue to use warm, old-looking graphics on T-shirts and sweatshirts. Adidas, Nike, and Puma all have sneakers reminiscent of the '60s and '70s, and Gucci, Louis Vuitton, and Prada all have the classic "doctor bag" shaped handbags of the '40s in their line. The September [2000] issue of *Bazaar* says that full-on fashion will have to include "a retro silhouette (i.e., a '50s full skirt, a mod '60s jumper and a '70s beaded halter)."

For the first time this in recent years, designers are revisiting the '80s, a decade of inspiration for high-end designers, junior sportswear, accessories, and music. Gold is important in jewelry as well as in clothing; bow and ruffle blouses return, as well as looks from popular '80s rock and punk bands. Vintage stores continue to have good business, and newer stores like Anthropologie, which has a vintage feeling, are gaining in popularity as well.

Volkswagen started the retro trend in the automobile industry with the reintroduction of the Beetle. Chrysler followed suit with the introduction of the PT cruiser, which crosses the muscular '50s hot-rod aesthetic with the dapper good looks of a London taxicab. Meanwhile, Chris Craft, a fine name in boats for the past century, is coming out with a line of boats that look like the classic runabouts from the '40s and '50s. Single-speed bikes are making a comeback, and brands like Dyno, with its Glide model, offer a very classic, retro style. The incredible new popularity of foot-powered scooters is also a blast from the past.

Food products have also gone back to the future. Krispy Kreme doughnuts are in fashion again, despite people's desire to be health-conscious. Coca-Cola bottles in their familiar, small green-glass incarnation are back in vogue, and home-cooking favorites—including macaroni and cheese and meat loaf—are appearing on menus across the country.

Consumers' need to stay in a comfort zone with products that are familiar or have proven successful in the past is one reason for the continuing popularity of retro and vintage looks. It would also seem that in a world with so much newness and change in technology, people long for some things to remain the same.

This longing for familiarity has traditionally happened in a 20-year cycle. As each generation gets closer to middle age—about 40 years old—they tend to think back to a time that was simpler, when they didn't have kids, bills, or even careers. For most, that means looking back at the time they were in college, which explains the 20-year time period. If this theory holds true, then the first decade of the new millennium will be about the '80s in the same way that the '90s looked back at the '70s, the '80s reflected the '60s, and the '70s looked back to the '50s.

By taking cues from the past and incorporating the latest technological advances for performance, comfort, and convenience, designers are able to keep capturing the attention of consumers while simultaneously making them feel right at home.

Chapter Review

Key Words and Concepts

Define, identify, or briefly explain the following:

Avant garde	Fashion	Mass fashion
Bottom-up theory	Fashion cycle	Style
Classic	Fashion forecasting	Style number
Commodization of fashion	Fashion-forward	Trickle-across theory
Design	Fashion prediction	Trickle-down theory
Evolutionary	Fashion trend	
Fad	High fashion	

Review Questions on Chapter Highlights

1. Give examples of each of the following: style, fad, classic, design, fashion, fashion trend. Explain the differences and relationships between these terms.
2. "The only thing constant about fashion is change." Explain why fashions change and cite examples.
3. Provide examples of products other than apparel and accessories that are currently being affected by fashion.
4. Do you agree or disagree that there are different fashions for different groups of people? List examples to prove your answer.
5. Does your current wardrobe represent one or more stages of the fashion cycle? Which stage or stages and why?
6. Explain the following statement: "There are three accepted theories that categorize the admired groups from which fashion leadership flows." Give examples.
7. Do designers originate all fashions? Support your opinions.
8. Explain how fashions reflect their "times" and cite specific current examples.
9. Describe the factors that must be considered by fashion professionals in predicting coming fashions.

References

Agins, T. (1999). *The end of fashion.* New York: William Morrow and Company, Inc.

Beaton, C. (1954). *The glass of fashion.* Garden City, NY: Doubleday.

Behling, D. (1992). Three and a half decades of fashion adoption research: What have we learned? *Clothing and Textiles Research Journal, 10*(2), 34–41.

Bell, Q. (1947). *On human finery.* London: Hogarth Press.

Brannon, E. (2000). *Fashion forecasting: Research, analysis, and presentation.* New York: Fairchild.

Foley, C. (1893). *Economic journal,* Vol. 13. London: publisher unknown.

Greenberg, A., & Glynn, M. (1966). *A study of young people.* New York: Doyle, Dane, Bernbach, Inc.

Ivins, M. (1976, August 15). The constant in fashion is the constant change. *The New York Times.*

King, C. (1963). *Fashion adoption: A rebuttal to the "trickle down" theory.* Reprint Series 119. Reprinted from American Marketing Association Winter Conference, by Purdue University, Krannert School of Business Administration.

Lane, A. (1994, November 7). The last emperor. *The New Yorker,* 82–88.

Nystrom, P. (1928). *Economics of fashion.* New York: Ronald Press.

RAM reports to retailers (1977).

Powers, M. (1996, Fall). *In the eye of the beholder.* Human Ecology Forum, pp. 16–19. Ithaca, N.Y.: Cornell University.

Riemer, B., Zinn, L., & Dapner, F. (1991, April 22). Haute couture that's not so haute. *Business Week,* 108.

Roe, J. (1834). *The sociological concept of capital.* London: Macmillan.

Rogers, E. (1962). *Diffusion of innovations.* New York: Free Press.

Rogers, E., & Shoemaker, F. (1971). *Diffusion of innovations* (2nd ed.). New York: Free Press.

Rogers, E., & Shoemaker, F. (1983). *Diffusion of innovations* (3rd ed.). New York: Free Press.

Sapir, E. (1931). Fashion. *Encyclopedia of Social Sciences, VI.* New York: Macmillan.

Silberman, C. E. (1971, March). Identity crisis in the consumer markets. *Fortune,* 95.

Simmel, G. (1957, May). Fashion. *American Journal of Sociology, 62,* 541–558. Reprinted from the *International Quarterly, 10,* (October 1904), pp. 130–155.

Sproles, G., (1981, Fall). Analyzing fashion life cycles—principles and perspectives. *Journal of Marketing, 45,* 116–124.

Sproles, G. & Burns, L. (1994). *Changing appearances: Understanding dress in contemporary society.* New York: Fairchild Publications.

Tarde, G. (1903). *The laws of imitation.* New York: Henry Holt & Co.

Veblen, T. (1963). *The theory of the leisure class* (mentor edition). New York: New American Library of World Literature.

Zinn, L., Power, C., Yand, D., Cuneo, A., & Ross, D. (1992, December 14). Move over boomers: The busters are here—and they're angry. *Business Week,* 74–82.

Selected Bibliography

Adburgham, A. (1966). *View of fashion.* London: Allen & Unwin.

Agins, T. (1999). *The end of fashion.* New York: William Morrow and Company.

Arthur, L. (1999). *Religion, dress and the body.* Oxford, UK: Berg Publishers.

Anspach, K. *The why of fashion.* (1967). Ames: Iowa State University Press.

Barnes, R. & Eicher, J. (Eds.). (1993). *Dress and gender: Making and meaning.* Oxford, UK: Berg Publishers.

Batterberry, M., & Batterberry, A. (1977). *Mirror mirror: A social history of fashion.* New York: Holt, Rinehart & Winston.

Beaton, C. W. H. (1954). *The glass of fashion.* Garden City, NY: Doubleday.

Behling, D. (1992). Three and a half decades of fashion adoption research: What have we learned? *Clothing and Textiles Research Journal, 10*(2), 34–41.

Bell, Q. (1976). *On human finery* (2nd ed.). London: Hogarth Press.

Bergler, E. (1953). *Fashion and the unconscious.* New York: R. Brunner.

Boehn, M. von. (1932). *Modes and manners.* Philadelphia: J. B. Lippincott.

Boucher, F. (1967). *2,000 years of fashion.* New York: Harry Abrams.

Brannon, E. (2000). *Fashion forecasting: Research, analysis, and presentation.* New York: Fairchild.

Broby-Johansen, R. (1968). *Body and clothes: An illustrated history of costume.* New York: Reinhold.

Brydon, A., & Niessen, S. (1998). *Consuming fashion: Adorning the transnational body.* Oxford, UK: Berg Publishers.

Carter, E. (1980). *Magic names of fashion.* London: Weidenfeld & Nicolson.

Celente, G., & Milton, T. (1991). *Trend tracking.* New York: Warner Books.

Coleridge, N. (1988). *The fashion conspiracy.* New York: Harper & Row.

Contini, M. (1965). *Fashion: From ancient Egypt to the present day.* New York: Odyssey.

Craik, J. (1994). *The face of fashion: Cultural studies in fashion.* New York: Routledge.

Cunningham, C. W. (1979). *Why women wear clothes.* New York: Gordon Press.

D'Assailly, G. (1968). *Ages of elegance: Five thousand years of fashion and frivolity.* London: MacDonald.

Damhorst, M., Miller, K., & Michelman, S. (1999). *The meaning of dress.* New York: Fairchild.

Davis, F. (1994). *Fashion, culture, and identity.* Chicago: University of Chicago Press.

DeLong, M. (1998). *The way we look: Dress and aesthetics* (2nd ed.). New York: Fairchild.

Everyday Fashions of the Twenties as Pictured in Sears and Other Catalogs. (1981). New York: Dover.

Eicher, J., Evenson, S., & Lutz, H. (2000). *The visible self: Global perspectives on dress, culture, and society* (2nd ed.). New York: Fairchild.

Fairchild, J. (1989). *Chic savages.* New York: Simon & Schuster.

Fiore, A. (1997). *Understanding aesthetics for the merchandising and design professional.* New York: Fairchild.

Flugel, J. C. (1966). *The psychology of clothes.* New York: International Universities Press.

Gamber, W. (1997). *The female economy: The millinery and dressmaking trades, 1860–1930.* Urbana: University of Illinois Press.

Harris, C., & Johnston, M. (1971). *Figleafing through history: The dynamics of dress.* New York: Atheneum.

Haynes, M. (1998). *Dressing up debutantes.* Oxford, UK: Berg Publishers.

Hollander, A. (1994). *Sex and suits.* New York: Knopf.

Jobling, P. (1999). *Fashion spreads.* Oxford, UK: Berg Publishers.

Johnson, K., & Lennon, S. (1999). *Appearance and power.* Oxford, UK: Berg Publishers.

Kaiser, S. (1996). *The social psychology of clothing* (2nd ed., rev.). New York: Fairchild.

Kaiser, S., Nagasawa, R., & Hutton, S. (1995). Construction of an SI [symbolic interactionist] theory of fashion: Part 1: ambivalence and change. *Clothing and Textiles Research Journal, 13*(3), 172–183.

Khornak, L. (1982). *Fashion, 2001.* New York: Viking Press, 1982.

Klensch, E. (1995). *Style.* New York: Berkley.

Kohler, C. (1963). *A history of costume.* New York: Dover.

Lagner, L. (1959). *The importance of wearing clothes.* New York: Hastings House.

Laver, J. (1938). *Taste and fashion.* New York: Dodd, Mead.

Laver, J. (1950). *Dress.* London: J. Murray.

Laver, J. (1964). *Women's dress in the jazz age.* London: H. Hamilton.

Laver, J. (1969). *Modesty in dress.* Boston: Houghton Mifflin.

Laver, J. (1983). *The concise history of costume and fashion* (Rev. ed.). New York: Oxford University Press.

Laver, J., & Provert, C. (1983). *Costume and fashion* (Rev. ed.). New York: Oxford University Press.

Lurie, A. (1981). *The language of clothes*. New York: Random House.

McDowell, C. (1985). *McDowell's directory of twentieth century fashion*. Englewood Cliffs, NJ: Prentice Hall.

Lynch, A. (1999). *Dress, gender and cultural change*. Oxford, UK: Berg Publishers.

Milbank, C. R. (1990). *The evolution of American style*. New York: Harry Abrams.

Moore, J. (1988). *Perry Ellis: A biography*. New York: St. Martin's Press.

Murray, M. P. (1990). *Changing styles in fashion: Who, what, why*. New York: Fairchild.

Nystrom, P. F. (1928). *Economics of fashion*. New York: Ronald Press.

Roach, M. E., & Eicher, J. B. (1965). *Dress, adornment and the social order*. New York: John Wiley & Sons.

Roach-Higgins, M., Eicher, J., & Johnson, K. (1995). *Dress and identity*. New York: Fairchild.

Rubinstein, R. (1994). *Dress codes: Meanings and messages in American culture*. Boulder, CO: Westview Press.

Rudofsky, B. (1971). *The unfashionable human body*. New York: Doubleday.

Schnurnberger, L. (1991). *Let there be clothes: 40,000 years of fashion*. New York: Workman.

Solomon, M. R. (1985). *The psychology of fashion*. Boston: D. C. Heath.

Sproles, G. (1981, Fall). Analyzing fashion life cycles—principles and perspectives. *Journal of Marketing, 45*, 116–124.

Sproles, G., & Burns, L. (1994). *Changing appearances: Understanding dress in contemporary society*. New York: Fairchild.

Steele, V. (1997). *Fifty years of fashion*. New Haven, CT: Yale University Press.

Tortora, P., & Eubank, K. (1994). *A survey of historic costume* (2nd ed.). New York: Fairchild.

Tozer, J. (1985). *Fabric of society: A century of people and their clothes, 1770–1870*. New Jersey: Laura Ashley.

Trachtenberg, J. A. (1988). *Ralph Lauren: The man behind the mystique*. New York: Little, Brown.

WWD century: One hundred years of fashion. (1998, September). New York: Fairchild Publications.

Trade Associations

American Apparel and Footwear Association (AAFA). 1601 N. Kent Street, Suite 1200, Arlington, VA 22209.

Council of Fashion Designers of America (CFDA), 1412 Broadway, New York, NY 10018.

The Fashion Association (a division of AAFA), 475 Park Ave. S., 9th Floor, New York, NY 10016.

The Fashion Group, 597 Fifth Ave., New York, NY 10017.

International Association of Clothing Designers, 7 E. Lancaster Ave., Ardmore, PA 19003.

Trade Publications

DNR, Fairchild Publications, 7 W. 34th St., New York, NY 10001–8191

Women's Wear Daily, Fairchild Publications, 7 W. 34th St., New York, NY 10001–8191

*G*lobalization of the Fashion Industry

*T*oday's fashion industry is being reshaped by **globalization**. In his book, *The Lexus and the Olive Tree*, award-winning *New York Times* author Thomas L. Friedman defines globalization as:

> . . . the inexorable integration of markets, nation-states and technologies to a degree never witnessed before—in a way that is enabling individuals, corporations and nation-states to reach around the world farther, faster, deeper and cheaper than ever before, and in a way that is enabling the world to reach into individuals, corporations and nation-states farther, faster, deeper, cheaper than ever before. (p. 9)

Globalization has changed where fashion goods are made, where they are sold, and how each company fits into a network that includes both competitors and partners beyond U.S. borders. Not since the Industrial Revolution has anything affected the fashion industry as dramatically as globalization. Global shifts in where garments are made may represent the decline of an industry in one country and a boost to the industry in another region halfway around the world (see Figure 3–1). Workers lose jobs in one country as the population in another gains those jobs. Because globalization has become such a basic aspect of the fashion industry, this chapter is considered early in the book. Chapter 9 will provide additional information as we look at fashion producers in other countries.

Most firms in the fashion industry have found it necessary to restructure their organizations and their operations—either to be a part of global activities—or to adjust because of the effects of globalization. Although trade among nations has been a fact of life for centuries, today's globalization of business occurs with speed and intensity that transforms the industry in ways never seen before.

Imports and **exports** have long been a major consideration of nations. Each country tries to sustain and expand its economy by exporting products it has in abundance or can produce efficiently and importing those it needs or cannot produce efficiently. As far as fashion merchandise is concerned, international trade in the United States dates back to the country's beginnings. As far back as the 18th century, the in-

Figure 3–1

Figure 3–1

Fashion merchandise is produced under a wide range of conditions around the world. Here we see Indian women making sweaters on small knitting machines in very primitive conditions.

Source: Photo courtesy of International Labor Organization.

ventories of our sailing ships listed silks from China, woolens and calicos from England, damasks and velvets from Italy, and embroideries and fine laces and fabrics from Paris. In the 19th century, dolls dressed in the latest French fashions were imported by American dressmakers to be used as models of the garments they would create for their wealthy clientele. When advanced printing techniques made possible illustrated magazines, dressmakers turned to such early European magazines as *Peterson's* and *Mrs. Demarest* to see what was being worn in London and Paris—and copied what they saw. Early American fashion retailers, such as Lord & Taylor of New York and Marshall Field of Chicago, bought the models of leading Paris designers, such as Worth and Doucet, as well as the European fabrics and trimmings needed to copy couture styles in their workrooms.

This chapter provides an overview of how globalization affects the U.S. fashion industry, why this has occurred, some of the issues involved, and the importance of being prepared to function in a global economy. The readings focus on topics related to globalization of the fashion industry. The chapter that follows deals with producers in other countries and regions that are important partners and competitors in the industry.

Overview of Globalization

Although **trade** among nations occurred for centuries, it was a slow and often dangerous matter, particularly in early times. In the earliest days, there were no ways to communicate with people in distant countries. Adventuresome merchants simply took their wares to other countries or went to buy, embarking on long and dangerous trips by sea. Even after the development of postal services and telephones, communicating with individuals in other countries was slow by mail or costly by telephone. Although airplanes were developed in the early 1900s, their early use was limited in areas of trade.

In contrast, advances in modern communications have grown phenomenally in the past decade. Computers and fax machines facilitate instant and inexpensive communication among buyers and sellers on different continents. Jets that travel 500 to 700 miles per hour have made it easy, in most cases, to travel to far corners of the globe to conduct business. Other developments have contributed to a global economy. International banks can transfer currency electronically and exchange one country's currency for another with ease. Additionally, international trade bodies develop and oversee rules to guide trade among nations.

All of these advances have led to an **interconnected global economy**. Today, many U.S. fashion firms in all segments of the industry use these technologies to communicate daily with their partners in Europe, Asia, or South America. For apparel manufacturers and now many retailers, product lines may be developed in the firm's U.S. headquarters. Sketches and markers may be transferred electronically to facilities where garments are cut and sewn to meet the U.S. firm's expectations. Garment specifications and other details can be sent online between countries. If a problem occurs as the product is being made, this is handled through calls, faxes, and electronic mail. For example, if the manufacturer in Thailand believes the neckline is too low, sketches can be faxed back and forth until the issue is resolved.

As noted in Chapter 1, the growing logistics industry helps facilitate this globalization in the fashion industry. These firms coordinate and track clients' shipments throughout the world. Services may include importing or exporting fabrics, coordinating the pickup of finished garments in another country and delivery to the U.S. client or to the client's customer. Some of these firms have special containers for hanging garments so they are ready to go on the retailer's sales floor when they arrive. For a logistic firm to provide their array of services and to assure fast and accurate deliveries, these companies must also rely on electronic technologies.

Fashion merchandise can be **global products** in a more complex way. A garment may be made of Taiwanese fiber woven into fabric in China and then shipped to the United States. A U.S. firm may cut the garments and send them to the Dominican Republic for sewing operations. After garments are finished, they are reexported back to the U.S. market for sale. These interlinked stages of production result in products whose origins are hard to identify. These global products result from manufacturing operations in several countries, as shown in Figure 3–2.

Figure 3–2

Global products result from manufacturing operations in a number of different countries.

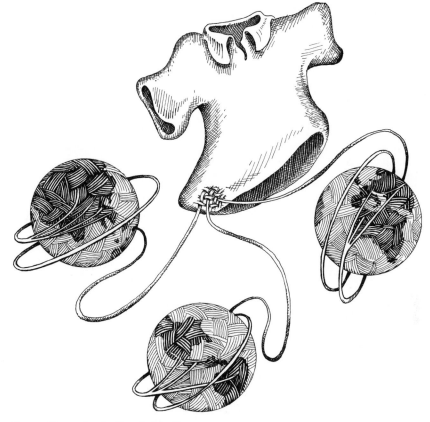

Source: Illustration by Dennis Murphy.

All Industry Segments Are Affected by Globalization

Every segment of the softgoods chain has taken on more global ways of doing business. That is, global activities are taking place in virtually all segments shown of the industry identified in Figure 1–3 (see page 9). Although examples given refer to the U.S. market, similar patterns exist for companies in many other regions. Table 3–1 gives a summary of some of the positive and negative aspects of globalization for the major players.

- **Textile producers** may buy their components from other countries that can supply these at lower costs than those from local firms. Many large textile weaving and knitting mills import the yarns needed to make fabrics. For example, a U.S. textile knitting company may use cotton yarns from Pakistan to reduce the costs in making fabrics. In a survey of textile companies, more than half reported they were using imported components (Hooper, Dickerson & Boyle, 1994).

  In another example, textile firms in more-developed countries often provide the fabrics to apparel firms in **Third World** countries that are not yet producing fabrics for the garments they make to export. Examples here are those U.S. firms that supply the fabrics for the apparel firms in the Caribbean or Mexico; garments are made from those fabrics and sent back to the U.S. market. For example, Cone Mills has a partnership with Cia. Industrial de Parras SA in Mexico and produced about 100 million square yards of denim in 1998 to supply the region's 350 jeans factories (Millman, 1998).

| Table 3–1 | | | The Impact of Globalization on Segments of the Softgoods Chain |

Textile Industry		Apparel Industry	
Positive	**Negative**	**Positive**	**Negative**
Cheaper components such as yarns	Domestic job loss; workers in some regions hard hit	Lower costs of production	Domestic job loss; workers in some regions hard hit; protest by unions
Able to sell in other countries	Protest by unions	Less investment in physical facilities (factories)	Greater risks on quality and delivery times
Build factories in other countries that produce apparel	May reduce investment in domestic mills	Greater production flexibility	Must beware of sweat-shops and child labor
		Can sell brand name merchandise in other countries	Longer lead times required

Retail Industry		Consumers	
Positive	**Negative**	**Positive**	**Negative**
Able to offer customers variety, good prices	Alienates domestic suppliers	More variety in products—including those not available from domestic producers and hand-crafted items	Domestic job loss (i.e., workers are consumers)
Essential to most private-label programs	Less control over quality and delivery times		Import prices include tariffs and shipping costs (but usually still lower)
Imports generally permit higher markups	Longer lead times required	Generally lower price (if retailer passes savings on to consumer)	Some want to support domestic industry
	Must beware of sweat-shops and child labor		

- **Apparel firms** have garments produced in countries where they find a large labor force in need of jobs and where wages are lower than in the United States. Firms such as Liz Claiborne, Esprit, Nike, Jockey, and Levi Strauss have their garments made in dozens of countries around the world. Global companies such as these have extensive networks throughout the world and communicate regularly with overseas partners through e-mail and faxes. A number of apparel firms have no production facilities of their own (and cannot, in a strict sense, be called "manufacturers") but rather have all their garments made in factories from Asia to Central and South America.

  In another form of globalization for apparel firms, a number of high-profile apparel firms have also discovered that their products are popular with consumers in other countries. Nike, with annual sales of more than $9 billion, is pinning its future on global sneaker and apparel markets. The company believes that its domestic sales, which average an astounding $20 for each American, may be reaching its limit. Thus, Nike's goal has been to have more than half its sales originate from other countries in the early 2000s, compared to about 40 percent previously. Although different in both products and approaches, Ralph Lauren, Calvin Klein, and Tommy Hilfiger have developed successful businesses selling their lines in other parts of the world. These companies may have their own stores or may have in-store shops in major department stores. Calvin Klein has opened stores in Hong

Kong and Milan and has plans to open some 100 stores in other parts of Europe and later the Middle East (Ozzard and Forden, 1997; Thurow, 1997).

- **Retailers** are also very active global players. Retailers have been actively participating in the global economy for many years as they traveled to other countries to buy product lines for their stores. Now, however, most major retailers have taken this a step farther. For their **private-label** lines, retailers are now assuming many of the roles once associated with manufacturers. In these arrangements, retailers' product development divisions develop their own designs for the line, coordinate details related to making the garments (fabric, garment assembly specifications, details for trims and other components, etc.) and then have the garments produced in a broad array of countries throughout the world. As for apparel firms, using **contractors** elsewhere generally occurs because of lower labor costs in **less-developed countries**.

  The Limited and The Gap have nearly all the merchandise for their stores produced in this manner, and other retail firms have a growing share of their fashion goods made in a similar way.

  Retailers are becoming global in another important way—opening stores in other countries. The Gap has an active expansion program in Europe, Asia, and the Americas with stores in Bermuda, Canada, France, Germany, Hong Kong, Ireland, Japan, the Netherlands, Singapore, and the United Kingdom. Wal-Mart is opening stores at a rapid pace in other countries, with several hundred now in operation.

- **Consumers** are another active link in the global fashion industry, although they may not be aware of it. For years, consumers have been buying merchandise produced elsewhere in the world, and this will only grow as the industry itself continues to be more and more global. About 60 to 70 percent of the apparel sold in the United States is made in other countries, and the import portion is expected to grow.

  Additionally, many products have a global appeal. In earlier years, the so-called global brands tended to be luxury products that were appreciated and bought by the wealthy. These included Rolex watches, Chanel purses, and Mont Blanc pens. Today, however, satellite communication systems have expanded television audiences to include consumers around the world. From Paris to Peoria, teenagers may want similar products: Cokes, Big Macs, Diesel or other popular jeans, T-shirts, and Nikes. Even in faraway places, the odds are great they are watching *Friends*, seeing the same movies, and listening to the same music popular with U.S. teens. This trend means that a global market with a broader base of consumers interested in similar products has emerged, much of which is based on U.S. popular culture.

  These trends mean that fashion now travels more widely and more quickly. Whether it's the high-fashion apparel from the European runway shows or the latest fads in U.S. movies or television, consumers around the world see and want these new items much faster than in the past, when it might have taken two years for the new trends to reach the masses.

  Additionally, the time has arrived when consumers just about *anywhere* in the world can order products from companies on another continent. Three developments are making this possible: (1) the "plasticization" of business—that is, the ability to use credit cards to pay for just about any product from anywhere; (2) the Internet permits both apparel firms and retailers to sell to consumers anywhere in the world where they can log on; and (3) worldwide delivery services such as United Parcel Service and Federal Express have global distribution systems that can deliver an order almost anywhere. As an example of the potential growth in this form of global retailing, Amazon.com, perhaps the most successful Internet retailer, reports that 20 percent of the company's sales are to customers outside the United States (Cable News Network [CNN], 1999).

- **Auxiliary enterprises** for the fashion industry have also become more global. Although fashion publications have long functioned globally by scouring the markets in other countries and then reporting on trends to readers, other operations that support the industry were less global. Today, trade associations have to function more globally and keep members informed of important global issues that will affect their businesses. Advertising agencies now have to be in tune with global markets. Consultants in the industry may find that issues related to globalization account for a large portion of the services they provide to manufacturing and retailing firms in the fashion markets. Even property management firms have become very global. For example, the Los Angeles-based firm Mart Management, Inc. plays an active role in managing TradeMart Singapore as well as similar trade marts in Germany and Turkey.

Brief Background of Globalization of the Fashion Industry

Although trade in textiles has occurred for centuries, the most dramatic changes have occurred in the second half of the 20th century. The controversial aspects of this trade began in the 1930s, when Japan started selling significant amounts of its textile and apparel products in the European and U.S. markets. At the time, Japan was a low-wage **developing country** that began its economic development by emphasizing textile and apparel production. The trouble began when the nation wanted to earn **foreign exchange** by selling those products outside its own market. Japan began to export a substantial amount of textile goods. Although much of Japan's industry was destroyed later in World War II, the country soon rebuilt the industry and began exporting again. By the 1950s, textile producers in the United States and Western Europe were worried that Japanese producers were a threat to their businesses. A significant point was that, at that time, Japan had low wages. This meant Japanese products could be sold for less than those made in the United States and Europe. Beginning at that time, a series of trade policies was developed to attempt to "protect" the United States, Canadian, and European manufacturers from competition from imports made in countries with low wages (Dickerson, 1991, 1999).

Other less-developed nations saw Japan's success in building an economy with the textile/apparel industry, particularly to export the products to **more-developed countries**. The less-developed countries had little capital or technology to start other industries and had large populations desperately in need of jobs. Many other Asian countries followed Japan's pattern. The newcomers—such as Taiwan, South Korea, Hong Kong, India, and Pakistan—also wanted to export their products to the United States and the countries of Western Europe. These two markets were attractive because of the large number of consumers with enough disposable income to have fairly extensive wardrobes (at least compared to the rest of the world). Canada and Australia were the other two attractive markets.

As this pattern continued, almost every country in the world developed at least a simple textile and apparel industry. Many nations and individuals built their dreams for a better life around the prospects of making and selling textile/apparel products in the wealthier nations. Textile and apparel firms in the more-developed countries feared, however, that imports would drive them out of business. As a result, textile/apparel trade became very contentious. Complex trade policies were initiated to "manage" this sticky area of trade. Exporting and importing nations had diametrically opposed positions. The less-developed countries wanted to ship their products to the more-developed nations. Textile/apparel producers in the more-developed countries wanted to do whatever they could to keep out the imports they saw as damaging their industry.

As other countries set their sights on the U.S. market, domestic manufacturers began more and more to feel the impact of this competition. Until the 1970s, U.S. manufacturers had a fairly large, captive market to themselves. Consumers bought what U.S. manufacturers produced. As imports made inroads into the market, they were no longer just a threat. Imports had become serious competition, taking an increasing share of the U.S. market. Firms found it hard to compete with products made in countries where wages were a fraction of U.S. wages. Many companies went out of business when they were unable to respond to the competition. Many other firms restructured to become more efficient and better positioned to compete (Dickerson, 1991, 1999).

Who Imports and Why

There are three major categories of fashion merchandise imported into the United States:

- The first consists of components, such as fabrics or the yarns to weave or knit fabrics.
- A second type is ready-to-wear fashion merchandise that is totally designed and produced by foreign manufacturers and, for the most part, is purchased by retail buyers for resale to their customers.
- The third type is the merchandise that is contracted out to overseas factories for all or part of the production process and is then returned to the United States.

Whenever the domestic market is unable to meet a fashion need, whether due to lower prices, variety and innovation, production capabilities, or whatever, imports have become a means of supplying the need. Each source of supply in another country contributes to the import stream according to its specialized capabilities and its particular area of expertise.

The reasons for the high growth rate of imports are many and varied. Among them are:

- *Lower prices:* On the price front, the domestic industry has a twofold disadvantage. U.S. labor costs are much higher than in the low-wage countries around the world, and the domestic producer does not enjoy the tax exemptions, rebates, preferential financing schemes, and other profit cushions that many foreign governments provide their exporting entrepreneurs.
- *Availability of hand labor:* Many countries have hand-production capabilities and expertise that the United States may not possess. For example, many foreign countries have generations of skills behind them in such hand operations as laces, embroideries, beading, hand-finished buttonholes, hand-loomed fabrics, and hand-knitted sweaters, to name but a few. They also have a large pool of handicraft workers.

Hand labor is very expensive in more-developed countries. Therefore, low-wage, less-developed countries can produce products that involve hand labor, whereas countries such as the United States are unable to produce affordable garments with this detailing.

- *Product voids in the United States:* In the category of merchandise that American producers either cannot produce at all or cannot do as well are the cashmeres of Scotland and China, the soft-as-butter leathers of Spain, the linens of Belgium, and the silks of Italy (Figure 3–3) and China. Another example of a product void is the absence of domestically produced full-fashioned sweaters, which is such a labor-intensive process that the American knitwear industry cannot produce them at a salable price.

- *Producers in other countries are more adaptable or cooperative:* Many users of imports feel that foreign producers are more cooperative and responsive to their needs than domestic suppliers. For example, an executive of a major apparel firm explained that the firm makes 35 different styles of blouses, which it is able to do overseas without the snafus that would be encountered in the United States.

Figure 3–3

Italian silk production in Como, Italy.

Source: Photo by Kitty G. Dickerson.

"Here," he said, "they want to mass-produce one style of blouses and factories tell us what their needs are and what we should be doing instead of letting us design and telling them what we want. In the Orient, they are more flexible and less insistent upon large mass cuttings" ("Asia's Lure," 1988).

And as Art Ortenberg, the former cochairman of Liz Claiborne, explained it, "When we show a new design to a Japanese sweater knitter, he says, 'Oh, how simple' but the American knitter says 'Oh, how complicated' " ("Asia's Lure," 1988). Many designers also verbalize that it's much easier to work, buy fabrics, and get things done in Europe and the Orient. According to Isaac Mizrahi, Europe has a more nurturing approach toward its talent, and Marc Jacobs says, "It's much easier to work in Tokyo where everyone wants to work with you. Here you go into a fabric company and they give you minimums. How can a young designer be creative here with that kind of attitude? A lot of times I see great fabric but I can't have it because the minimums are so high" ("Asia's Lure," 1988).

- *Exclusive rights:* Foreign purchases also give U.S. companies an opportunity to avoid sameness—assortments that are too much like those of their competitors. Retailers are always in search of new and different merchandise to which they can get exclusive rights, particularly if they can secure these rights without making the massive purchases often required by large, volume-minded U.S. apparel producers. The exclusive items, not available in competing stores, permit the retailer to generate storewide excitement because the merchandise is free from competition. Similarly, it has been almost impossible for apparel producers to obtain exclusivity of fabrics from U.S. textile producers without committing themselves to the purchase of huge runs far in advance of their selling season. Non–U.S. producers of apparel or textiles, which often are not as large as U.S. manufacturers, do not need or demand big commitments.

- *Fashion cachet of Europe:* Not to be underestimated as a reason for importing fashion goods is the glamour associated with European fashions and labels. From its inception, the U.S. fashion business has been influenced by European fashions and has found inspiration across the Atlantic. It is true that today a circle of American designers get adoring treatment from U.S. retailers and their customers, yet what comes from the European fashion centers will probably always have a special cachet just because of its origin.

Imports by Retailers

A retail firm's success ultimately rests on the strength, balance, and competitiveness of its merchandise assortment. A major responsibility of retail buyers and merchandise managers is, therefore, to seek ideal assortments wherever they can find them. In many situations, imports are an essential ingredient of the retail product mix because they can provide distinctive, competitive, and profitable merchandise.

Import Buying Methods

Not all foreign purchases by retailers are made in a single manner. Procedures vary and may involve anything from sending representatives abroad to placing an order with a foreign source at a showroom in the United States. Among the most common means are the following:

- *Foreign trade shows in the United States.* Many producers from other countries exhibit their collections in the United States. Such showings may be at international trade shows staged in this country or in single-nation shows sponsored by a particular country to court foreign buyers. Buyers who are unable or unwilling to make trips overseas do their buying at such shows. For example, as Turkish apparel producers have attempted to increase their sales in the U.S. market, they have used this strategy.

- *Foreign producers' showrooms in the United States.* Many large overseas producers maintain individual sales forces in showrooms in New York, as well as in major regional apparel marts, for the convenience of retailers.

- *Store-owned merchandising/buying offices.* Most large retailers maintain offices, independently or in conjunction with their buying offices in the United States, in major cities of Asia and Europe, such as Paris, London, Hong Kong, Singapore, and Tokyo. These offices keep their principals updated on new producers, important new products, and fashion developments. Even more important today, they place orders as requested and handle the forms and other procedures that are involved, such as **letters of credit**, quality control checks, and follow-through on shipping arrangements and delivery dates. Retailers that maintain such offices include, for example, Sears, J. C. Penney, Wal-Mart, Kmart, May Company, and Saks Fifth Avenue. Previously, independent merchandising/buying offices, such as Frederick Atkins and the Associated Merchandising Corporation (AMC), maintained offices in major overseas regions to assist their retail clients. However, today major retailers have developed their own offices so effectively that these longtime services have had to close their doors.

  Today, both the store-owned and independent offices located in other countries to serve retailers have evolved from being only buying offices to now assuming more merchandising and product development activities. Frequently, the representatives in those offices are closely involved in the manufacturing process for the retailer's lines. This will be discussed further in the following section on securing products for private label lines and in Chapter 11.

- *Foreign commissionaires and agents.* Retailers, particularly those of smaller size that are not represented by their own foreign offices in a particular country, use **commissionaires** and agents. These functionaries assist store buyers when they make direct visits to the countries concerned. In return for a fee (i.e., a commission), they direct visiting buyers to suitable producers, handle the necessary export forms, and follow through on delivery and shipping arrangements (Figure 3–4).

- *Foreign trade showings.* Practically every European country and several Asian fashion centers hold seasonal group showings. These shows are attended by thousands of visiting buyers from all over the world who come to buy, to observe new devel-

Figure 3–4

Ad by foreign commissionaire.

Hong Kong Buying Office

Our overseas buying office has been representing manufacturers of women's leisurewear and sportswear in Hong Kong, Singapore, and Korea for 20 years. We are expanding and looking for additional clients. For information, contact:

More Fashions Far East Ltd.
11111 900th St., New York 17777
212-111-0000

opments in foreign fashions and products, or both. Purchases are followed up by either commissionaires or the foreign buying office serving the store concerned. These shows, which are both national and international in nature, are discussed in Chapter 9.

Securing Products for Private-Label Lines

As noted earlier, retailers are now using sewing factories in other countries to produce their **private-label** merchandise. These store brands give retailers a chance to have their own distinctive merchandise in addition to national brands. Such private-label goods, more often than not, are made overseas by producers that offer favorable comparative values in terms of styling, price, or sometimes both. Nearly all private-label merchandise is made to the specifications of the importing retailer (or retail buying group). In **specification buying**, the buyer/merchandiser plans the styles and designs to be produced (Figure 3–5). This is sometimes done by describing the garment and sometimes by supplying an actual sample for copying or adaptation. The merchant may even supply the fabric, not necessarily from the country in which the garment is to be made. Also specified by the purchaser are the garment's measurements, its trimmings, the quantity, and the negotiated wholesale price. In effect,

Figure 3–5

Private label manufacturing.

YOUR Designs or Ours...

BOOTHS 2058/2060

A variety of individual and collective PRIVATE LABEL FASHION PROGRAMS for small, medium & large buyers.

Junior, missy, petite & large size sportswear, dresses, lounge wear, scarves and handmade sweaters... Also, men's shirts and sportswear in cottons, rayons, silks, linen and rami-cotton blends.

INDIA IMPORTS
OF CALIFORNIA
P.O. Box 1026, Providence, CA 92901-1026
(999) 272-8600, Telex: 211071INDIARI

NEW YORK SHOWROOM
1400 BROADWAY, SUITE 473, (212) 555-4942

the retailer fulfills many of the same functions as many apparel firms categorized as "manufacturers," and the foreign producer functions as a contractor. Today, many large retail firms have extensive product development staffs who develop lines in much the same way the merchandising staffs in apparel firms do. Moreover, the retailers' representatives are actively involved in the manufacturing process. In this way, U.S. retailers can enjoy both exclusive styles and the favorable prices that are possible when merchandise is made to specifications by lower-cost producers in Asia and elsewhere. Private-label lines will be considered further in Chapter 10.

Imports by Manufacturers

Even if all retailers were to purchase exclusively from domestic sources, imports would still be a major factor in their merchandise assortments, because U.S. manufacturers also import. The retailer that purchases these imports does so not necessarily because they are imports, but because they satisfy a need in the merchandise assortment and can be sold profitably at a price point attractive to the store's customers.

Direct Imports by Manufacturers

Manufacturers do direct importing of textiles and apparel for the same reasons that apply to retailers—price advantage, exclusivity of product, foreign expertise, and any other fashion or quality factors that may be absent from domestic markets. Fabric mills import yarns not readily available in this country. Fabric jobbers and apparel manufacturers import silks and certain luxurious fabrics that are not produced here. Many sportswear apparel companies import sweaters or leather items to coordinate with their domestically produced skirts, slacks, and other separates. There also are some U.S.–based companies that specialize in importing finished products, such as dresses and skirts, and market them domestically under their own labels (Figure 3–6).

Offshore Production

Despite their outcry over the amount of direct importing done by retail buyers, American producers have been steadily increasing their own import practices by hav-

Figure 3–6   **Imports from India and South America.**

Pisces Fashions Ltd.
India
Looking for importers/wholesalers for woven sleep and loungewear production. We have 10 years experience with top corporations in U.S. market.
NY contact: 999-555-1234. Overseas: 25 W Gandhi Arena, Delhi, India. 555-5454 TELEX: 22-7114.

TEE SHIRTS IN SOUTH AMERICA
Large tee shirt manufacturer, high-volume production, offers high-quality services in manufacturing or silk-screening tee shirts on any textiles. Contact Tee-Shirts, 8454 Elk St. Broadhead, NY 00068

ing their merchandise produced abroad. For example, all of Liz Claiborne's merchandise is produced by contractors, mostly Asian manufacturers.

To manufacture overseas, domestic producers send electronically the designs, markers, and production specifications, which must be exact and clear. Of course, today's communication advances permit easier and faster information exchanges than in the past. The three basic methods used when producing overseas are as follows:

1. **Production package:** In this method, everything but the design is supplied by the contractor, including the fabrics, all of the production processes, finishing, labeling, packaging, and shipping.
2. **Cut, make, and trim (CMT):** In this method, the domestic producer that supplies the designs buys the fabric and then has it shipped to a contractor to be cut and sewn according to specifications. The fabric supplier and the contractor may very well be in different countries.
3. **Offshore assembly:** In this method, fabric is made and cut[1] in the United States and then sent elsewhere for sewing as specified. It is then sent back to the originating company, possibly for some finishing and for shipping.

Imports Versus Domestic Production

Although competition from imports is a problem shared by all consumer-oriented domestic manufacturing industries, the fashion industry has been among those most affected by imports. Since 1970, imports have increased faster than domestic output, which means imports account for an increasing share of fashion goods bought by U.S. consumers.

According to the U.S. Bureau of Economic Analysis (2001), U.S. consumers spent about $319 billion on apparel and footwear in 2000. Of total purchases, about half were made in other countries. Figure 3–7 shows components that constitute the value at retail for both imported and domestic apparel. It is important to note that although imports cost less initially, duties and other charges are added to those costs.

The level of **import penetration** varies a great deal from one product to another. Because wages are a major factor in determining where garments are made, items requiring more labor input (meaning they are **labor-intensive** products) are more likely to be produced in less-developed countries. For example, bras require a great deal of intricate sewing (i.e., are labor-intensive); this garment category has a high import penetration level.

Textile and Apparel Trade Deficit

A **trade deficit** is the amount by which the value of imports exceeds exports. In 2001, the United States imported $59.4 billion of apparel and $15.7 billion of textiles, a combined total of more than $75 billion. Although U.S. firms are making a greater effort to export now than in the past, the total value of exports is still relatively small compared to imports. Exports were $6.5 billion for apparel and $10.1 billion for textiles. The

---

[1]Under 807A, manufacturers do not have to face quota limits on products if garments are made of U.S.-made and U.S.-cut fabrics. Consequently, this form of offshore assembly has been more popular in recent years than the original 807/9802 production.

Figure 3–7

The U.S. Apparel Market

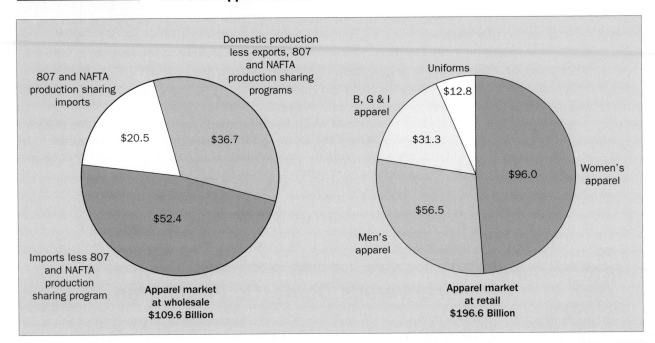

Source: From *Focus: An Economic Profile of the Apparel Industry* (p. 4) by the American Apparel & Footwear Association, 2000, Arlington, VA: Author. Adapted by permission.

Figure 3–8

U.S. imports of textile and apparel products.

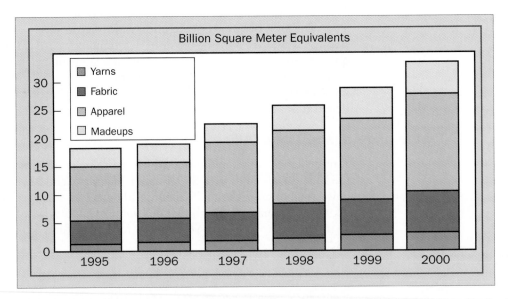

Source: From *Textile HiLights* (March 2001) (p. 27). Reprinted by permission of the American Textile Manufacturers Institute.

trade deficit for textiles and apparel combined was $58.5 billion, the highest in history (Office of Textiles and Apparel, U.S. Department of Commerce online source). The growth of the textile and apparel trade deficit is illustrated in Figure 3–8.

For many years, U.S. fashion producers were in the enviable position of having a large market of consumers who bought their products. Under these desirable conditions, most companies gave little or no thought to trying to sell their products in other countries. In recent years, however, many companies have awakened to the possibilities of selling their products in other parts of the world. Many U.S. fashion products, particularly those with recognizable designer or brand names, appeal to consumers in other countries. The "American look" of jeans, T-shirts, and other casual wear can be observed on every continent. Levi's jeans have long been popular in many countries. High-profile fashion goods names such as Calvin Klein, Ralph Lauren, and DKNY are bought by upscale customers in many countries from Europe to Asia. Tommy Hilfiger has become a popular brand. Consequently, many U.S. firms have started to become more global by selling their products beyond U.S. borders. Exporting textile and apparel products helps offset the high trade deficit in these merchandise areas. However, exporting is a fairly new activity for most U.S. firms in the industry. Therefore, these efforts must grow a great deal from the present level to significantly impact the very large trade deficit.

The Global Trade Battle

Globalization, and especially the growth of imports in the U.S. fashion business, has given rise to a highly vocal battle between advocates of protectionism and proponents of free trade. **Protectionism** means the reduction, limitation, or exclusion of merchandise from other countries. **Free trade** means avoiding protectionist measures and letting goods flow freely among countries.

On the protectionist side are U.S. producers of apparel, accessories, and textiles; the major industry union—Union of Needletrades, Industrial & Textile Employees (UNITE); and many of the manufacturing industry's trade associations. All have a record of continuously lobbying in Washington for more protection from imports. On the other side are the retailers and importers, their trade associations, apparel firms with production in other countries, and some consumer groups.

Officially, at least, the United States supports a free trade position, which means that restrictions on imports are kept to a minimum. This "official" position suggests that excessive restrictions on foreign goods will lower our standard of living (and, as noted in some of these points, affect our relationships with other countries) for the following reasons:

- Trade barriers mean high prices for consumers. Consumers do not benefit from competition among countries that leads to the best values in what they buy. Decreased competition may allow domestic firms to charge higher prices.
- Domestic producers that cannot successfully compete in the world market are not entitled to special protection from imports by the government.
- Nations whose textile and apparel merchandise is restricted on entering the United States may retaliate against what they consider to be American protectionism and thus damage the export prospects of other U.S. companies. Jobs may be saved in one industry only to be lost in another when foreign countries retaliate by buying less from the United States.

- U.S. firms that rely on imports would be less able to compete and would lose business.
- Erecting barriers to restrict the products of other countries creates political ill will with countries with whom we may need to work on other matters. For example, if the United States wants to maintain a military base in a country, the local government is likely to be less cooperative if their products are restricted from U.S. markets.

As noted earlier in the chapter, all segments of the industry are affected by globalization of the industry. Table 3–1 summarizes some of the pros and cons for each of the major groups of players involved in or affected by this globalization.

The World Trade Organization (WTO)

In 1947, the United States and other major trading nations entered into a new agreement to reduce trade barriers that countries were erecting against products from other nations. This trade pact, the General Agreement on Tariffs and Trade, was known as **GATT** and administered by the GATT Secretariat in Geneva, Switzerland. By its active participation in GATT, the United States publicly supported a free trade philosophy of not placing restrictions on trade (Dickerson, 1999). In reality, however, a free trade position for textile and apparel trade did not result, as we shall consider later.

In 1995, the members of GATT made significant changes in its agreement that oversees world trade. The GATT was replaced by the **World Trade Organization (WTO)**; the headquarters of the WTO remain in Geneva. Under GATT and now the WTO, a number of basic rules for international trade exist. However, a special and unique agreement has existed for the textile and clothing trade. As part of the 1995 changes for GATT/WTO, this agreement for textiles and apparel is changing, too.

The Multifiber Arrangement (MFA)

A few countries, particularly Japan, became proficient cotton product exporters in the 1950s and 1960s. Japanese cotton goods became a concern for a number of U.S. and West European industry leaders, who feared the Japanese shipments would take away sales in U.S. and European markets. U.S. and European textile and apparel leaders applied political pressure and were successful in getting a variety of trade agreements approved by GATT that limited Japanese cotton imports.

Until the 1970s, however, the dollar volume of textile and apparel imports coming into the U.S. market was relatively insignificant and therefore created little or no real disruption of domestic textile and apparel industries. As imports began to swell, U.S. industry leaders (and their counterparts in Western Europe) became alarmed, believing the domestic industry could not survive if imports continued at that pace. Consequently, domestic industry leaders were able to persuade policy makers to secure trade agreements that would protect them from imports from low-wage countries. European and U.S. leaders pressed for, and obtained, a new policy under GATT designed to control the flow of textile and apparel imports.

By the early 1970s, manufactured fibers had been developed, and limiting only cotton imports was no longer enough. Producers in other countries had cleverly avoided the restrictions on their cotton exports by switching to those made of manufactured fibers. Thus, in 1974, the **Multifiber Arrangement** (multifiber, to go beyond just cotton products), commonly known as the MFA, was implemented under the auspices of GATT.

The MFA established general rules for the kinds of actions countries might take to protect their industries from being hurt by rising imports. Under its provisions, the United States (or other importing nation) might control "disruptive" imports by entering into **bilateral** (two-country) **agreements** that established import **quotas** for that country. For example, the United States could negotiate an agreement that set a limit (quota) on the textile and apparel products from India, another agreement with Hong Kong, another with South Korea, and so on. Quotas established under those bilateral agreements governed the volume of products each country could ship to the U.S. market. In Western Europe and Canada, the other major markets for products from low-wage countries, the systems worked very much the same (Dickerson, 1991, 1999).

Restrictions were applied almost entirely to the products from less-developed countries because of the dramatic differences in wages. That is, U.S. manufacturers who paid their workers the minimum U.S. wage felt their products could not compete fairly with those made by workers in less-developed countries who earned, in many cases, only a few cents per hour (Figure 3–9). Examples of those wage differences are shown in Figure 3–10.

As a growing number of less-developed countries around the world began producing more and more textile and apparel products, shipments into the United States, Europe, and Canada mushroomed. Each time the MFA was renewed, the restrictions on imports from low-wage countries became tighter and tighter. A trade tug of war resulted. Basically, the less-developed countries wanted to send increasing volumes of products to the more-developed countries. These exporting countries were most interested in shipping to the same countries where textile leaders tried hardest to restrain those imported products from coming in.

In short, almost no countries liked the MFA. The less-developed countries felt their exports met with too many harsh barriers under the MFA quota system. These countries became very impatient. After all, the MFA existed under the sponsorship of

Figure 3–9

Garment workers in many less-developed countries, like this young woman in China, work for very low wages.

Source: Photo by Kitty G. Dickerson

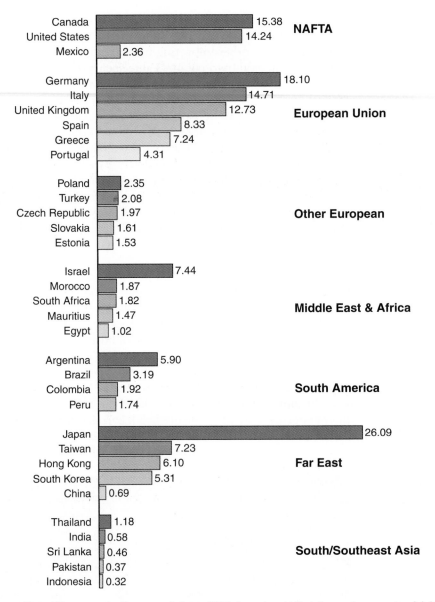

Figure 3–10

A comparison of wages in the textile industry in various parts of the world. Figures are in U.S. dollars and include social benefits and fringe benefits.

Canada	15.38	**NAFTA**
United States	14.24	
Mexico	2.36	
Germany	18.10	
Italy	14.71	
United Kingdom	12.73	**European Union**
Spain	8.33	
Greece	7.24	
Portugal	4.31	
Poland	2.35	
Turkey	2.08	
Czech Republic	1.97	**Other European**
Slovakia	1.61	
Estonia	1.53	
Israel	7.44	
Morocco	1.87	
South Africa	1.82	**Middle East & Africa**
Mauritius	1.47	
Egypt	1.02	
Argentina	5.90	
Brazil	3.19	**South America**
Colombia	1.92	
Peru	1.74	
Japan	26.09	
Taiwan	7.23	
Hong Kong	6.10	**Far East**
South Korea	5.31	
China	0.69	
Thailand	1.18	
India	0.58	
Sri Lanka	0.46	**South/Southeast Asia**
Pakistan	0.37	
Indonesia	0.32	

Note: Wages are for Summer–Autumn 2000, based on U.S. dollar exchange rate of July 25, 2000.

Source: Werner International data sent online to author.

the GATT—an international body formed to eliminate trade restrictions. These exporting nations believed their products were being unfairly "choked off" by the quota system.

At the same time, industry leaders in the wealthier importing countries thought the agreement had not done an adequate job of keeping imports out of their markets. Imports grew phenomenally under the MFA quota system, at a faster rate than the growth of the domestic industry, thus taking a disproportionate share of the market. Additionally, the quota system set limits on the quantity of imports brought into the United States rather than the value (cost) of the merchandise. This meant producers in other countries shifted to higher priced items (known as **upgrading**) to maximize the value of what is shipped under the quota limits. Imports had once been limited to lower priced product lines; however, upgrading meant imports became a threat at upper price points, too (Dickerson, 1991, 1999).

The MFA has been a highly controversial trade agreement. Although it was sponsored by the GATT, it contradicted many of the basic free trade goals of GATT. The less-developed exporting countries fought hard to have this peculiar trade policy phased out. After all, no other industry had this kind of special protection provided by GATT.

Eventually, MFA opponents prevailed. In 1995, when GATT officially became the WTO, the clock started ticking toward an eventual phaseout of the MFA and the quota system. Over a 10-year period, quotas on textile and apparel products will be phased out in three stages. By 2005, all products are expected to be traded freely, with no remains of the quota system in place.

Quotas and Bilateral Trade Agreements

The United States has negotiated separate bilateral agreements with each of the textile/apparel exporting nations whose products have been regarded as a threat. These bilateral pacts establish country-by-country quotas, or annual maximums, on hundreds of categories in cotton, wool, and manufactured fiber textiles and apparel. For example, the bilateral agreement with Indonesia might allow 500,000 dozen men's cotton knit shirts to be shipped to the United States in a year. A different limit would be placed on men's cotton woven shirts, or manufactured fiber knit shirts. Also, the limits on each product category would be different *from one country to another*. Each bilateral agreement established the quota level on a category-by-category basis, specifies the amount the category can grow in the year, and provides for establishing new quotas in cases that the bilateral agreement does not cover.

The chief U.S. textile negotiator, in the Office of the U.S. Trade Representative, negotiates the bilateral agreements on behalf of the United States. The U.S. Customs Service is responsible for keeping track of import levels and quota levels. When more goods are presented for entry into the United States than the quota level allows, that merchandise is denied entry and is warehoused at the port of entry, at the expense of the importer. For example, if J. Crew ordered 100,000 women's cotton sweaters from China for a holiday promotion, but China's quota had been completely used for the year in this product category, the sweaters would be stopped by U.S. Customs and warehoused at J. Crew's expense until the new quota year began. Of course, the season for which J. Crew ordered the sweaters would be over.

Quotas, which vary for different merchandise categories and for different countries, are specified in **square meter equivalents (SMEs),** and all apparel items can be translated into SMEs. For example, customs authorities can convert every dress, shirt, or pair of slacks into square meter equivalents to monitor shipments to be sure the exporting country does not exceed its quota limits.

Under the bilateral agreements, the U.S. government grants each trading partner (nation) designated quota levels. Then, each exporting country administers its own quota and makes allocations to individual producers based generally on their past export performance. Allocations can be lost if they are not used within the designated quota year. Manufacturers, however, can and do sell unused quotas to other companies and thus maintain their export rights for subsequent years. Each exporting country has its own system for distributing quotas among its manufacturers. In some cases, a board of government and/or industry representatives makes the decisions. In

Hong Kong, quotas may be bought and sold from one company to another. In earlier years, when quota was in high demand in Hong Kong, a manufacturer who had large quota allotments might have made as much from selling part or all of its quota as from actually producing apparel.

A manufacturer in another country who plans to export products having quota limits must have available quota to be able to ship products into the U.S. market. For example, the Fabulous Frocks company in Indonesia must hold adequate U.S. quota for those product categories the company plans to produce and ship to the U.S. market. If Fabulous Frocks wants to ship to a West European country, the company must hold adequate European quota[2] to cover the shipment. Documentation to prove this "ownership" of quota must accompany shipments or they will be stopped in the port of entry by customs authorities.

U.S. fashion firms, whether manufacturers or retailers, that have products made in another country must be certain they are working with companies holding adequate quotas to cover the products being made for the U.S. firm. Without the quota, the merchandise cannot be delivered to the U.S. company ordering it. This applies, of course, only to those countries and products with quota limits.

Several areas in the world, however, have had no quota restrictions on their products for entering the U.S. market—for example, the **European Union (EU)**. Exemptions are based on the assumption that (1) these are high-wage industrialized countries whose products are not price-competitive with U.S. goods, (2) our exports to these countries balance our imports from them, and (3) their import penetration is not large enough to cause harm to the U.S. industry.

Mexico and Canada are exempt from the quota limits as a result of the **North American Free Trade Agreement (NAFTA),** which permits free trade among the three countries in North America. As a result of this agreement, Mexico has become the major source of apparel imports in the U.S. market. This group of countries exempt from quotas will increase if the United States enters into additional free trade agreements in the Americas.

Also exempt from U.S. quotas are other countries in the Caribbean Basin and in Central America (for most product categories) under the Caribbean Basin Initiative, which is discussed in a following section. These countries have been given special treatment in the past because the United States has felt a responsibility to aid many of these very poor countries in their economic development. Additionally, many U.S. government leaders have considered it important to assist with economic opportunity to avoid political uprising in nearby countries. Many countries in Africa that are not yet industrialized or even on the road to development are exempt as well. All of these exempt areas are in marked contrast to the quota restrictions placed on more than 90 percent of the textile and apparel products imported from Taiwan, Hong Kong, South Korea, and China. This group, known as the "Big Four," has been the biggest source of supply to U.S. markets over the past two decades.

The 10-year phaseout of the MFA means that quotas are expected to become a thing of the past by 2005. Figure 3–11 shows the progressive removal of quotas during the 10-year phaseout. However, until that time, a good deal of world trade in tex-

---

[2]This major group of West European countries is now called the European Union (EU) and consists of 15 countries that operate as one unit in trade with the rest of the world. Quotas, for example, are designated by the European Union rather than by each specific country (much as the U.S. government would do for all 50 states). Earlier, this West European group (when it consisted of fewer countries) was known as the European Economic Community (the EEC) and later the European Community (EC).

Figure 3–11

MFA quota phaseout schedule.

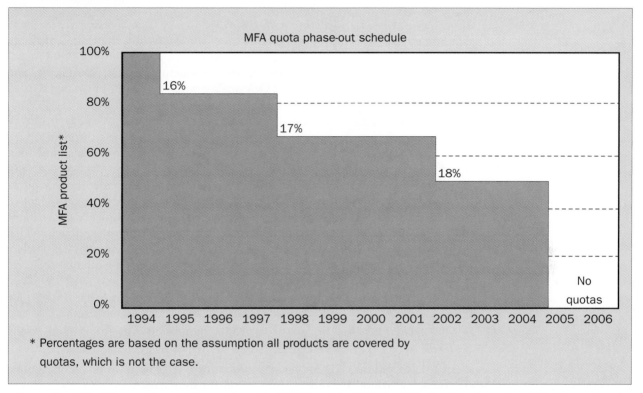

MFA quota phase-out schedule

* Percentages are based on the assumption all products are covered by quotas, which is not the case.

Source: From *The U.S. manufactured fiber market under NAFTA and the WTO* (p. 10) by P. O'Day, September 1994. Presented to the 33rd International Man-Made Fibres Congress. Dornbirn, Austria. Reprinted by permission of Paul O'Day and the American Fiber Manufacturers Association, Inc.

tiles and apparel will be governed by the quota system. Therefore, it is important for those working in the fashion field to understand the quota system and its impact on nearly all segments of the industry, from manufacturing to retailing.

Getting Around the Quotas

As might be expected, many producers in other countries have devised ways to "get around" the quota limits imposed by the United States. When an exporting country has used all its quota but is determined to continue shipping products to the U.S. market, foreign producers have been very enterprising. Examples of these strategies follow:

• *Moving production to countries where quotas are not a problem*. Often production has been transferred to countries with unused or excess quotas or to countries without quotas (those that are underdeveloped or that may have a preferential arrangement with no quota). An example of moving production has been when some of the Big Four Asian countries have set up garment production in Caribbean or African countries that are free from U.S. quota limits. They produce and ship fashion goods to the U.S. market without the quota restrictions placed on them in their homelands. In one example, more than 20 South Korean firms have production in Honduras alone. Taiwanese textile firms are starting to build factories in Central America so they can supply fabrics to apparel makers that ship to the U.S. market.

- *Moving operations to a location with the market where a foreign supplier wants to sell.* Some have even moved operations to a location within the United States to avoid quotas. For instance, Hong Kong-based Odyssey International Pte. Ltd. acquired Cal Sport in Yuma, Arizona, a firm producing skiwear, sportswear, and camping equipment. This launched Odyssey's strategy to build or buy a total of 10 to 12 manufacturing facilities in the United States.

- *Transshipment.* In addition, **transshipment** has been a common strategy. In this illegal practice, countries with used-up quotas transship products through a third country with quota availability. The countries with available quotas are sometimes called "quota havens." For example, China has the ability to produce a volume of garments far in excess of what the country is permitted to ship under the U.S. quota limits. To get around this problem, Chinese manufacturers have frequently shipped their merchandise to other places, such as Macau, that have plenty of available quota. The garments bear "made in Macau" labels, and when they arrive in U.S. ports, they appear to have been made in Macau. The U.S. government has cracked down on these illegal practices and on occasion has penalized China by reducing quota in certain product categories.

When the U.S. Congress passed a sub-Saharan (below the Sahara) free trade bill to give quota-free and tariff-free treatment to African countries, the U.S. textile industry opposed this. Their main concern was that Asian countries would transship goods to the U.S. market via the African countries.

In a sense, quotas created *opportunities* of export growth for many of the low-wage countries around the world. As demand for inexpensive imports grew, manufacturers and retailers from many countries have of necessity sought sources beyond the quota-limited facilities of the Big Four Asian countries. Many of the most underdeveloped countries would not have the equipment, the know-how, and the market contacts to start up garment production on their own. Start-ups in these poorest countries have required the investment and assistance of industry representatives from more-developed countries who are looking for low wages and quota-free production sites. In many cases, as the newest countries become proficient at making garments, quotas were then imposed. Then, manufacturers and retailers sometimes move on to yet another developing country without quotas.

As long as the quota system lasts, it is likely that some producers in exporting countries will try to find illegal means of shipping beyond their legal limits to the more-prosperous market countries such as the United States. By the same token, as long as the quota system exists, industry representatives working with producers in countries covered by quotas will find it critically important to be sure their international partner has legal access to quota before signing business contracts.

Country-of-Origin Rules

To curtail quota evasion by transshipment through second countries on categories covered by quotas, new **country-of-origin rules** were established by the United States in 1985. The rules set up criteria for determining which country was truly the country of origin for incoming merchandise—and thus which country's quota was used.

Traditionally, it had been accepted as legitimate practice for two or more foreign countries to contribute to the making of some apparel categories. For example, in the case of a knitted sweater, yarn could be spun in one country; dyed in another; knit into panels for back, front, and sleeves in a third; and then finally assembled into a garment, labeled, and exported in a fourth. Hong Kong, for instance, has functioned as the assembler and shipper for much of its knitwear, using panels knitted in mainland China.

The 1985 rules required that the country where "substantial transformation" occurred determined the garment's origin.[3] This was, generally, the first manufacturing stages. In the case of garments that were cut from fabrics, the country where the cutting occurred determined the country of origin. In the case of the sweaters cited earlier, the sweaters came to be regarded, under the 1985 ruling, as having originated in China and would be counted against China's quota, even though Hong Kong did the finishing and shipping. The complication was that China had very limited quota. But, after all, that was the reason U.S. manufacturers had been able to secure this protection—to stop shipments that were mostly made in China.

By the 1990s, Taiwan, Hong Kong,[4] and South Korea had become much more advanced nations. Wages in their countries had risen, and it became increasingly difficult to find workers for their garment factories. These countries began to invest and move their own garment production to less-developed, low-wage Asian nations such as Indonesia, China, Malaysia, Thailand, Bangladesh, and Vietnam. Operating under the 1985 rules of origin, if Hong Kong manufacturers cut garments in their Hong Kong factories, these garments could be sewed in mainland China, where wages were much lower. Then, when garments were brought back to Hong Kong, they were shipped under Hong Kong quota. This strategy of sending out the cut parts to low-wage areas for the sewing operation is called **outward processing trade (OPT)**. (Many U.S. manufacturers use a similar strategy, which will be discussed in a later section.)

Soon, however, U.S. manufacturers who opposed imports began to realize that OPT was another way of interpreting the rules to export more products to U.S. markets. The biggest concern was that the United States had very restrictive quotas on products from mainland China. However, under the OPT arrangements, a great many products were actually being made in China for shipment to the United States, but the products were legitimately labeled as made in Hong Kong.

By 1996, U.S. country-of-origin rules were changed again to limit the OPT arrangements taking place in Asia, particularly in China. Under the new rules, the country of origin is the country in which the garment assembly occurs. The intent was to require that China's quota be used if production of items occurred in China.

Changes in regulations such as the country-of-origin rules make a dramatic difference in how U.S. fashion firms participate in international aspects of business. A partnership with a company in another country can be working smoothly one day and changed totally by the next day. A retail buyer may suddenly discover it is impossible to do business with an established partner in China or elsewhere because the trade policies have changed. For the fashion goods industries, the trade rules affect where production occurs, what can be produced, and to whom it may be shipped.

---

[3]This is a very simplified description of a complex set of rules, which often required a U.S. Customs ruling to settle each case in question.

[4]Since June 1997, Hong Kong is once again part of China; however, for textile and apparel trade, Hong Kong is still treated as a separate area.

Therefore, it is critical that professionals in the field learn about and try to understand these rules and the changes in rules as they occur.

Taxes on Imports: Tariffs/Duties

In addition to the restraints imposed by import quotas, most fashion goods are subject to an import tax. This tax on imports, known as a **tariff** or **duty**, is established and regulated by the U.S. government, paid by the retailer/importer, and collected by the U.S. Customs Service. In the end, it is the consumer who pays this added tax when it is passed on in a selling price. The amount varies for different categories of merchandise, but it is generally *ad valorem*, or a percentage of the **first cost** (invoice cost). Its primary purpose, of course, is to increase the eventual selling price of imported goods, and thus protect domestic industries (Figure 3–12). For many fashion products from the low-wage countries, however, even with the addition of tariffs and shipping costs, the final **landed cost** in the United States is often considerably less than for domestically produced apparel of equal quality.

As part of the 1995 WTO agreement on textiles and apparel, tariffs on imports coming into the U.S. market will decline over the 10-year phaseout period for quotas. However, by 2005, when quotas are to be fully removed, tariffs on textile and ap-

Figure 3–12

The effects of tariffs on the price of fashion merchandise.

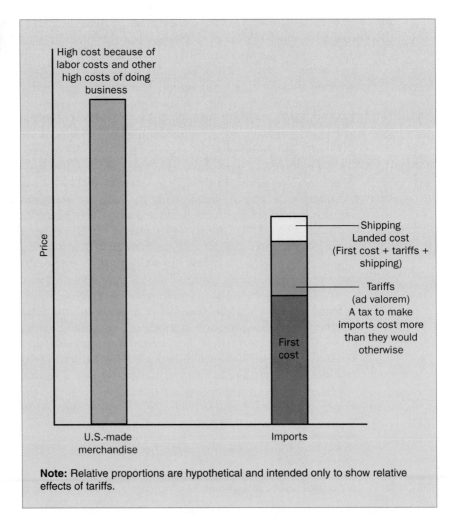

Note: Relative proportions are hypothetical and intended only to show relative effects of tariffs.

parel goods will remain. In the GATT/WTO negotiations, the U.S. government retained higher tariff levels for textiles and apparel than is generally true for other industries. Similarly, the U.S. textile and apparel industries have more tariff protection from imports than their counterparts in the European Union.

Although many countries that have exported their textile and apparel products to the United States have complained about the quota restraints on their products, many of those countries make it very difficult for outsiders to sell in their markets. Because many less-developed countries rely so heavily on their textile and apparel industries to support their economies, they do not want products from elsewhere to compete in their markets. Some have very high tariffs; some have other trade barriers; and a few will permit only products that do not compete with their own. This has been a sensitive matter for U.S. and EU manufacturers who would like to sell in those countries. In recent years, many of these less-developed countries have started to permit products from elsewhere in their markets. For instance, India had a closed economy until the early 1990s but has since opened the country's market slightly to products from other countries. As a result, fashion manufacturers elsewhere began to consider India as a potential market for their products, particularly to appeal to India's growing upper-income groups who would have the means of buying imports.

Preferential Programs:
Exemptions from Tariffs or Quotas

The U.S. government also has a number of programs that exempt products from other countries from tariffs or quotas, or in some cases both. Some of these programs are designed to stimulate the economy and encourage trade for less-developed countries around the world.

- **The Multifiber Arrangement (MFA).** As noted earlier, other more-developed countries including those in the European Union are exempt from quota restrictions. This exemption is primarily because the EU is at a similar stage of economic development, and wages are comparable to those in the United States. Many of the less-developed countries, whose products have been subject to tight restraints, have resented the preferential treatment that the EU and the United States provide one another. Tariffs are, however, levied on textile and apparel products traded between the two.
- **The North American Free Trade Agreement (NAFTA).** Under NAFTA, the United States, Canada, and Mexico moved toward open trade with one another, trade that is free of quotas, tariffs, and most other trade barriers.

    Free trade among the countries in the Americas may continue to expand in NAFTA-like arrangements. In late 1994, President Bill Clinton led an effort in which 33 countries signed an agreement called "Free Trade of the Americas," to be completed by 2005. Protectionist forces have resisted this, and President Clinton's personal problems reduced his ability to lead on this. Even today, many nations in Central and South America have free trade among themselves. If the United States does not participate, it risks being left out altogether.
- **The Generalized System of Preferences (GSP).** In 1974, Congress passed the Trade Act, which among other things authorized the Generalized System of Preferences (GSP). The 1984 Trade Act extended the GSP. The purpose of this segment of the act was to give special trade privileges to more than 130 developing countries in

Central America, Africa, Asia, the Caribbean Basin, and the Far East. Some 4,000 products made in these designated countries are permitted to enter the United States duty-free. Not surprisingly, most exceptions are in the textile/apparel sector. This has mattered little, however, because even with tariffs added, textile/apparel products made in low-wage, less-developed countries are still less costly than those made domestically. The exclusion of textile and apparel products from the GSP illustrates the special protection given the U.S. textile/apparel sector.

- **Special Tariff Provisions: 807/9802 Production.** Under the former U.S. tariff schedule, a special provision permitted U.S. apparel firms to have their garments assembled in other countries, much like the outward processing trade (OPT) described earlier. Under this earlier tariff provision, Item 807.00, apparel firms were permitted to send U.S.–cut garments to low-wage countries for the sewing to be done and then brought back into the United States. Tariffs were charged only on the value added in the production process. Under this provision, garments were still subject to quota limits. Fabrics used in garments could be from any source; only *cutting* in the United States was required (Dickerson, 1991, 1999).

  In 1989, a new Harmonized System of tariff schedules was implemented to give all participating countries the same tariff system. At that time, Item 807 officially became Item 9802. However, in the industry, this strategy for having garments assembled elsewhere is still commonly called 807 production (Figure 3–13).

- **The Caribbean Basin Initiative (CBI).** The CBI is a preferential program developed by the U.S. government to promote economic development in 27 countries in the Caribbean Basin region. Although the CBI provided duty-free access to most products made in those countries, tariffs remained on textile/apparel products as a measure to protect the U.S. industry. Basically, the CBI *per se* had no effect on textiles and apparel, except to illustrate again that the industry had special protection.

- **The Caribbean Basin Textile Access Program** (known as **807A production** or "Super 807"). Under this 1986 agreement, Caribbean apparel products are given a more liberal quota system for access to the U.S. market if fabrics are both made and cut in the United States. This provision increased U.S. quota allotments—known as **guaranteed access levels** or **GALS**—to CBI countries. In short, if garments met the requirements noted, adequate quota for shipping to the U.S. market was virtually assured. As might be expected, this agreement was more popular with U.S. textile makers because it required the use of U.S. fabrics. The Caribbean Basin Textile Access Program was the provision that led to the greatest growth of apparel production (i.e., assembly) in the region.

- **Trade Development Act of 2000 (TDA).** This includes two separate policies: (1) *The U.S.–Caribbean Basin Trade Partnership Act (CBTPA).* Following the passage of NAFTA, U.S. apparel firms with production in the Caribbean were at a disadvantage compared to those with production in Mexico. Like the Caribbean, Mexico had low wages but also duty-free access to the U.S. market. U.S. firms with production in the Caribbean fought for **parity** (equality), so they could have duty-free trade access similar to that provided Mexico under NAFTA. The CBTPA provided many of the advantages the apparel industry wanted but these are still not equal in all respects.

  (2) *Africa Growth and Opportunity Act (AGOA).* This policy gives preferential trade advantages to 48 countries in sub-Saharan Africa. This was a measure sought by Congress to provide trade benefits to this troubled part of the world for political reasons. Although apparel production may be a prospect at some future time, the logistics of getting U.S.-made fabric to that region for the production of garments is too costly for the freight at this point in time.

Figure 3–13   How the 807 (9802) and 807A in the CBI countries works.

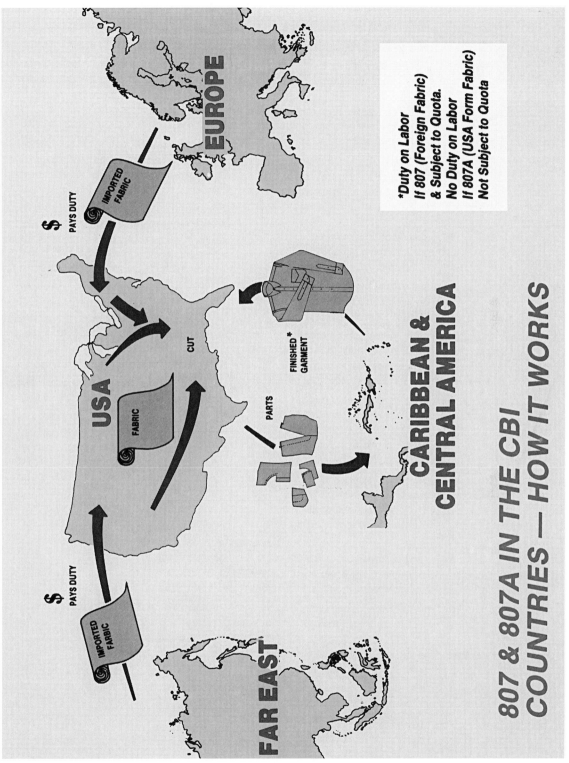

EUROPE

IMPORTED FABRIC

PAYS DUTY $

FAR EAST

IMPORTED FARBIC

PAYS DUTY $

USA

FABRIC

CUT

PARTS

FINISHED* GARMENT

CARIBBEAN & CENTRAL AMERICA

*Duty on Labor
If 807 (Foreign Fabric)
& Subject to Quota.
No Duty on Labor
If 807A (USA Form Fabric)
Not Subject to Quota

*807 & 807A IN THE CBI
COUNTRIES—HOW IT WORKS*

Source: From *Bobbin* (p. 81), November 1989. Reprinted by permission of *Bobbin*. Copyright © Bobbin Blenheim Media. All rights reserved.

The Politics of Textile and Apparel Trade

Most of the trade agreements that govern textile and apparel trade have developed for political reasons as well as economic reasons. A major reason for this has been that the textile and apparel industries are so vitally important to nearly every nation's economy. Production has increased in a majority of less-developed countries. At the same time, the industry remains a major manufacturing sector in the more-developed countries to which the less-developed countries wish to export. In both the United States and the European Union, the combined textile-apparel-fiber sectors represent the largest manufacturing employers in each. This means that the countries that have been recipients of most of the world's imports have many jobs at stake. In the United States, the combined industry employs about 1.4 million workers; in the EU, numbers are similar. Thus, jobs become the main point of argument in trade debates.

In the United States, the textile sector is relatively concentrated in the Southeast. Apparel manufacturing occurs in every state. Because of the large number of workers and the geographic spread, the combined industry has a great deal of power in Washington. Virtually no member of the U.S. Congress is without production in his/her district. Consequently, a large number of U.S. political leaders, from presidents to legislators, have found it necessary to take note of the trade problems affecting the industry. In the last four decades, industry leaders[5] have lobbied for protection from imports. These leaders have been very successful in parlaying their clout into special trade agreements to limit imports.

As an example of the strength of the textile/apparel lobby, the industry nearly succeeded in having acts of Congress passed to protect the domestic industry. On three different occasions, when the textile/apparel **lobby** felt U.S. trade policies provided too little protection, members of Congress from the major textile/apparel-producing states introduced bills that would have provided special import protection specifically for these sectors. On three occasions,[6] textile/apparel trade bills failed to pass Congress by only a few votes. This near success reflected the power of the textile lobby (Dickerson, 1991, 1999).

At the same time that some manufacturers lobbied to keep imports out, retailers and importers began to lobby to eliminate barriers to imports. Both retailers and importers have grown increasingly dependent on imports for their lines. Therefore, as some manufacturers tried increasingly to limit imports through political avenues, retailers and importers also became politically active to protect their own interests. Each side exerted pressure to protect the interests of its members.

In addition to their lobbying efforts, both sides exhort the general public to add its voice. Statements have been made in newspapers and on TV, petitions are circulated, demonstrations are held, and consumer surveys are made. Both sides have employed consultants and professional lobbyists. Collectively, a great deal of funding and energy has been spent on the political fray.

In recent years, as a growing number of U.S. apparel firms have moved their production outside the country, the apparel industry has been less vocal in fighting

---

[5]Previously, the textile and apparel industries had a very strong anti-import coalition that worked together to secure protection for the industry. The coalition included a large number of industry associations, unions, and cotton producers.

[6]These "textile bills" were introduced in Congress in 1985, 1987, and 1990.

imports. This has weakened the previously tight-knit coalition of textile and apparel producers that secured so much protection in the past.

Additionally, as U.S. manufacturers face the reality of ending import quotas, many have changed their strategy. A growing number have begun to think more globally and to look to the markets in other countries as places to sell their products.

The politics of textile and apparel trade have changed; however, this sector will probably never be totally free of politics. The reason: too many people have too much at stake. The dilemma over textile and apparel trade will continue and will require many compromises to satisfy retailers, importers, domestic textile/apparel/accessory producers, workers, labor unions, the governments and producers in other nations, global trade officials, U.S. legislators—and the consumer.[7]

Promotion of Domestic Products

In an effort to offset the deluge of imports coming into the U.S. market, domestic textile and apparel manufacturers developed a campaign to draw attention to domestic products. Financing from textile and apparel firms permitted the industry to form the Crafted with Pride in U.S.A. Council. The Council launched a labeling and promotion campaign to heighten consumer awareness of the advantages of U.S.-made apparel. An easily recognized certification mark identified domestically made garments on labels and hang tags (Figure 3–14). A multimedia campaign featured famous personalities who encouraged viewers to buy U.S.-made garments.

Figure 3–14

The certification mark used by U.S. manufacturers in a voluntary labeling campaign to call attention to U.S.-made products.

Source: Reprinted courtesy of Crafted with Pride in U.S.A. Council, Inc.

---

[7]For further consideration of the positions of each of these groups, see *Textiles and apparel in the global economy* (1999) by K. Dickerson.

Council members also tried to educate retailers on the bottom-line advantages of domestically produced goods. These advantages include timeliness (i.e., quick response), reduced shipping costs, geographic proximity, flexibility in reordering, and having investment tied up in shipments for much shorter time periods.

Later stages of the multimedia campaign emphasized job losses resulting from imports. TV commercials featured families who had to move because the breadwinners lost their jobs as a result of imported merchandise.

Selling U.S. Products in Other Countries

U.S. textile and apparel producers have been unable to match their exports to the rising tide of imports. Many factors account for this. An important reason discussed earlier is the difference in production costs, resulting largely from different labor costs. Another reason for the trade deficit is that many of the countries that have exported extensively to the United States have been unwilling to accept U.S. products into their markets. Although this has begun to improve in many of these countries in recent years, much room for improvement still exists.

An important factor in limiting U.S. textile and apparel shipments to other countries is that many domestic firms simply did not think about it or try it until the mid-1990s. Although a number of companies have sold their products in other countries for years, many others had been content to sell only in the U.S. market. Many spent more time complaining about imports than thinking about how to export. Companies simply have not had an export mentality. Few have had staffs with the multilingual and multicultural skills necessary to work in other countries. These comments could apply to most U.S. industries, however, and were not unique to the textile and apparel sector.

A number of U.S. textile and apparel producers have penetrated the markets in other countries in a variety of ways described briefly in the following sections. Some large companies (e.g., Levi Strauss & Co. and Sara Lee) have used various strategies from one country or region to another. Through various strategies, Sara Lee, for example, has become a leader in intimate apparel and hosiery in Europe, Asia, and Mexico. Similarly, Nike has used a variety of strategies to gain significant market share on six continents. Nike's shoes are manufactured and sold in more than 90 countries.

Licensing Agreements

Licensing is a relatively uncomplicated way for a domestic manufacturer to cultivate foreign markets, and it is the least costly. The U.S. company enters into a legal arrangement that gives the right to use its brand name (trademark), manufacturing process, or both to a foreign producer. In return, it receives a fee or royalty percentage on sales.

The foreign producer gains production expertise and the use of a well-known name, or both. The licensing U.S. firm gains entry into a foreign market with little risk or financial investment. In some countries that will not accept imports of U.S. products, this may be the only way to penetrate the market. Often, the foreign producer simply wants to be able to produce and sell a well-known brand. For example, Jockey International was one of the early leaders among U.S. firms in having its products sold in more than 100 countries. In many cases, this occurred through licensing agreements. Producers in other countries were able to make and sell this respected brand. Jockey was able to establish its name in many foreign markets where it would have been unable to sell otherwise.

Pierre Cardin is another widely licensed name. In fact, the name has been licensed for so many products that it has lost some of its cachet. Many U.S. cartoon characters have been licensed around the world. When the author visited the Singapore zoo, more than half the children there were wearing clothing with U.S. cartoon characters. In short, enormous amounts of clothing and accessories are produced and sold in other countries that bear well-known American or European designer or brand names. Much of this has occurred under licensing agreements—or, in some cases, companies in those nations have illegally used labels or brand names.

Direct Exporting

When a company is involved in direct exporting, this means it is selling products in other markets directly from the home base. In other words, the company does not have a production base in the region where it is selling. This strategy is one of the most common, and it is less complicated to implement than some others. Direct exporting may be limited, however, by the fairly high cost of U.S. products and the trade barriers in other countries. For example, if a country imposes a tariff as high as 60 or 70 percent on a U.S. product, the increase makes the merchandise very costly to consumers in that market. Nevertheless, many consumers in other countries are attracted to products that are uniquely American, and they covet the "Made in USA" label. For example, when Levi first began to open stores in India, the company reported running out of merchandise.

Direct exporting may require modifying products for another consumer market. For example, U.S. apparel firms may have difficulty selling garments sized for U.S. consumers in Asian markets, where people are smaller and have a slight body build. Sensitivity to cultural differences is important, both in the products sold and how they may be marketed. For example, suggestive Calvin Klein advertisements would be poorly received in conservative Muslim countries.

Although U.S. textile and apparel exports have increased in recent years, these are still very small compared to the volume of imports. To attempt to improve the balance of trade (imports versus exports), the U.S. Department of Commerce has a program to assist U.S. firms in exporting. Staff in the Textile and Apparel Export Expansion Program[8] help U.S. manufacturers increase the amount of direct exporting for the sector. Staff coordinate the showing of U.S. merchandise at major trade fairs around the world. For example, merchandise from a number of U.S. apparel firms may be shipped to a trade fair in Europe. The U.S. booth or pavilion at the trade fair features the U.S. garments for viewing by retail buyers from several European countries (Figure 3–15). This provides exposure for the U.S. companies' lines and leads to ongoing business for the companies that exhibited.

In addition to the overseas trade fairs, the U.S. Department of Commerce has established an extensive online Export Data Base to help U.S. firms gain additional information on the markets in other countries where manufacturers might wish to

---

[8]This program is part of the Office of Textiles and Apparel (referred to as OTEXA) in the U.S. Department of Commerce.

Figure 3–15	The Market Expansion Division of the Office of Textiles and Apparel (OTEXA) in the U.S. Department of Commerce coordinates exhibits for U.S. manufacturers who wish to participate in trade fairs in other countries. Exhibiting in a trade fair gives the company an opportunity to show its lines to potential buyers in other countries with hopes of developing long-term relationships.

Source: Courtesy of Market Expansion Division of OTEXA. Reprinted courtesy of U.S. Department of Commerce.

sell their products. Among other types of information, the database provides information on trade policies and other factors that may affect doing business in that country. (The URL for the U.S. Office of Textiles and Apparel [OTEXA] is: http://otexa.ita.doc.gov)

Success in exporting may vary greatly depending on **currency exchange rates**. When the dollar is weak relative to other currencies, it is easier to sell U.S. products than when the dollar is strong. When the dollar is weak, this means foreign currencies are strong against the dollar and U.S. merchandise is a better value to foreign retailers and consumers. However, when the dollar is strong against other currencies, customers in those countries cannot as easily afford U.S. products. For example, a number of U.S. fashion firms had begun to develop a successful business in Korea, but when the Korean won dropped to about half its previous value (in relation to the U.S. dollar) as a result of the Asian economic crisis, Korean consumers could buy only half as much U.S. merchandise as they could before the crisis.

Joint Ventures

International **joint ventures** are partnerships between a domestic company and a company in another country. Joint ventures are yet another way of entering an overseas market that can penetrate import barriers. A few countries still limit the percentage of ownership a foreign manufacturer may own in that country. For example, until 1994, Indonesia did not permit an outside firm to own more than 49 percent of a firm located there.

Joint venture partnerships may take various forms. The outside investor firm often provides the technology, expertise, and much-needed capital. The host-country firm provides the local knowledge and marketing skills. For an apparel firm, for instance, the investor firm may provide the capital, the production equipment, the expertise to produce the products, and the brand name. The local firm may provide the workforce, at least some of the management, the knowledge of the country's market, and expertise to sell in that market.

A notable example is the U.S.-based firm of Esprit, which has established Esprit Far East in Asia with a partner in Hong Kong. The Asian partner owns half the company and serves as its managing director. Esprit Far East is a major exporter of women's and children's casual apparel. Ninety-five percent of its merchandise is produced in Asia. Some of the merchandise is produced in Hong Kong, with the remainder contracted out to factories in other parts of Asia where wages are lower. The U.S. company, however, is involved in every operational step, from design to patterns, to fabric, to quota, to shipping arrangements. Most of the elements that constitute the garments are purchased in Asia—even zippers, labels, and buttons. Esprit Far East also operates its own shops in the region.

Sara Lee's hosiery business in the Asia-Pacific region was boosted by a joint venture with Shanghai Vocal, which markets sheer hosiery, opaque stockings, and socks under the Vocal brand in China. This is a way for Sara Lee to penetrate the very large Chinese market, which accepts few U.S. apparel imports.

Direct Ownership

Another way to penetrate a foreign market is by a 100 percent investment in a foreign-based operation. This may be just an assembly or production facility, or it may be the ownership of a company complete with production and marketing. Some foreign countries, for economic reasons, offer investment incentives to U.S. companies to establish wholly owned subsidiaries within their borders. As in the case of most joint ventures, the foreign-owned facility provides employment to the host-country's labor and often uses at least some local materials.

For example, DuPont owns more than 20 production facilities in other countries. Plants are located in various regions to make DuPont's fibers available to textile customers there—the weavers, knitters, and carpet producers who make fabrics, carpeting, and other products to sell in local markets. DuPont's plants are located in these areas to serve regional markets and to avoid trade restraints and other costs associated with exporting. Many U.S. apparel firms are now establishing their own plants in Mexico to take advantage of NAFTA. In another case, Sara Lee Corporation has an extensive strategy to penetrate other markets. By buying firms in other countries, the company not only gets to sell the products of the firms purchased but also has almost instant access for its familiar U.S. brands to be sold through channels of distribution used by the acquired firm. For example, owning the European company that produces Dim products also gives Sara Lee access to distribution for Playtex, Bali, Hanes, and other company products in those markets.

Figure 3–16   **Forward-thinking companies are combining a global view of the industry and the newest technologies to expand their markets.**

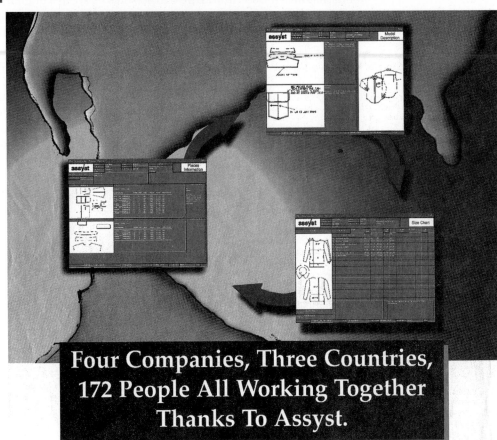

Source: Reprinted courtesy of Assyst-Bullmer, Inc.

The Importance of Preparing for Globalization

Globalization is a reality today. Companies and individuals can no longer think in terms of only a domestic market. Those who do will be left behind. Like it or not, technological advances have propelled us into an era in which globalization is a part of everyday business. Today, our business partners may be in another state or, just as readily, in another country. We can communicate with our overseas partners more quickly and more cheaply than we could have exchanges across state lines only 10 years ago. Forward-thinking companies are combining a global vision and new technology to position themselves to serve a world market. Many suppliers for the fashion industry are thinking of a global industry and have geared up to serve this sector wherever it goes. See Figure 3–16.

Individuals who plan to enter any segment of the fashion industry must prepare for this globalized era. This includes having an open mind toward our neighbors in other countries and keeping in mind that the "American way" is not the only acceptable way of doing things. It means respecting the different cultural backgrounds of our global neighbors. U.S. residents must improve on geography skills that have been sorely lacking. Staying abreast of news events, including global news events, is critical to being the kind of informed citizen needed to function in a global arena. And, finally, having foreign language skills is more valuable than ever before.

Readings

Globalization is a fact of life for today's fashion industry. Regardless of the segment of the industry in which one is involved, it is important to follow major trends related to trade and trade policies. The following articles highlight examples of important changes a person in the industry needs to follow in trade publications.

Streetwear Brands Take to the Streets of Europe

Fashion today knows no boundaries. Just as U.S. music has been adopted by young people in other parts of the world, various types of casual clothing are also popular. Just as hip-hop music has gone global, so has American streetwear. This article reports on the popularity of streetwear at a European fashion fair.

Wal-Mart Plots Big Global Expansion

Retailing has become global, and Wal-Mart is one of the major companies moving fast and hard in its global expansion. This article describes some of Wal-Mart's bold plans to take advantage of opportunities in many countries.

Streetwear Brands Take to the Streets of Europe

by Molly Knight

Cologne—Hip-hop is going global. Not just music—but also apparel.

That's the message from a handful of American streetwear companies exhibiting at the Inter-Jeans trade show that ended its three-day run here in Cologne on Saturday. And if you want to go global, Cologne is the place to be.

"A lot of streetwear companies don't take Cologne seriously," said Ronnie Comia, sales representative for Virginia Beach-based RP55. "What they don't realize is that it's a potential gold mine." Both RP55 and Karl Kani are represented in Cologne by Urban Trends & Trading Co., the European distributor for both brands based in the Netherlands.

One streetwear company for which Cologne has proved extremely profitable is Fubu. In its four years exhibiting at the show, Fubu's European sales have grown so much that the company just hired an international sales representative, Brent Ullman, formerly vice-president of Donna Karan International, and signed the lease on a European headquarters in Amsterdam. At the Cologne show, Ullman estimated the company would write upward of $5 million in orders from European headquarters.

Although it might be hard to imagine streetwear hitting the streets of quaint European cities, the size of the crowd at Fubu's booth spoke vol-

umes. While waiting to attend hourly line presentations, retailers participated in free-throw contests on the basketball half-court the company set up at its booth. After the contest, a troupe of Fubu-clad dancers put on a show to the sound of booming rap tunes.

"At this point, Fubu's not just a hip-hop brand, but a global brand," said Ullman.

Fubu isn't the only streetwear brand with a presence at the Cologne show. In its third year exhibiting there, Maurice Malone also makes Cologne a priority on its list of trade shows to attend.

"Cologne is really important because Europe is the next big market for Maurice Malone," said Ezra Hanz, director of the company's European distribution. "You get such wide exposure by being here."

For Maurice Malone, denim is the biggest hit in the European market. For the show, the company wrapped its booth in swathes of denim fabric. "It's all about denim for us," said Hanz.

Instead of writing orders, Pelle Pelle exhibits in Cologne in order to keep in touch with European retailers. "It's important for us to be here to talk to retailers and know what they're thinking," said Marinko Vinkesevic, managing director of Pelle Pelle in Europe.

Creating an oasis for retailers with its island-themed booth, Pelle Pelle invited guests to come in and relax in wicker chairs, listen to reggae music and browse the fall collection. While Vinkesevic said nothing is confirmed, the company is in negotiations to open a freestanding store in Prague. With its fall

Source: Daily News Record, *February 11, 2000, p. 65. Reprinted by permission.*

collection, Pelle Pelle is showing more sophisticated, dressy looks than in previous seasons. New to the line are leather jackets and iridescent jeans called "Black Shark."

According to the majority of exhibitors, one of the driving forces behind streetwear's popularity in Europe is the music industry.

"It all starts with music," said Hanz. "Hip-hop is no longer considered ethnic. It's now becoming what rock-and-roll was in the '50s. It's all over the world, and with it are the clothes."

Vinkesevic agreed: "Streetwear has come to Europe because of the music industry. At the end of the '80s it was techno. Now it's hip-hop."

Wal-Mart Plots Big Global Expansion

by David Moin

*L*as Vegas—Growing fast, with an estimated $33 billion in non-U.S. sales by the end of this year, Wal-Mart International hasn't even scratched the world's surface. Lots of countries are on Wal-Mart's hit list, including the U.K., where its first supercenter will open in July and where the giant retailer already has a huge supermarket stake through its ownership of Asda. Turkey is also on the "radar screen," and Wal-Mart might even enter Africa one day.

Yet according to John Menzer, president and chief executive officer of Wal-Mart's international division, China poses the really big expansion opportunity, with mind-boggling potential for volume growth. Wal-Mart currently has six stores there under a joint venture agreement.

"China is the country of the future. Wal-Mart could double its size just with expansion in China, but it may take 20 or 30 years," Menzer on Tuesday told a crowd of 2,000 real estate developers, mall operators, retailers, brokers and suppliers at the annual convention of the International Council of Shopping Centers here.

Last year, Wal-Mart posted $165 billion in sales and $5.4 billion in net income. This year, the retailer is poised to become the world's largest company and is expected to soon surpass General Motors. The international division posted $23 billion in sales last year.

"China is a market largely untapped by modern retailers," Menzer said, adding that so-called modern retailers account for only 4.4 percent of retail sales in China. Currently, Wal-Mart officials are spending a lot of their time fostering government and public relations in China and other countries.

"Anywhere you go, it is very important," Menzer said of developing local relationships. To lock in sites, for example, Wal-Mart often seeks approval from both local governments and provinces.

Regarding other key foreign markets, Menzer characterized Germany as a "work in progress," with profitability in that country on a three-to-five-year timetable, similar to what Wal-Mart experienced in Canada.

The international division was launched in 1991 with a joint venture in Mexico, and that country remains "one of our favorite emerging markets," Menzer said, where over half the population is under 21 years old and where Wal-Mart operates a variety of formats, including Sam's Clubs, supercenters, grocery stores, Suburbia apparel stores and even restaurants.

But Wal-Mart had a tough time in Indonesia in the Nineties and has pulled out of that country.

In response to a question from the audience, Menzer said, "We have Turkey on our radar screen. Someday, we may be there. We have a lot of countries on our radar screen."

Other markets seen as growth opportunities are Puerto Rico, which has nine Wal-Marts and six Sam's Clubs; Argentina, which has 10 supercenters; Brazil, which has nine supercenters and six Sam's Clubs, and Korea, which has five units.

However, as Wal-Mart grows abroad, it is confronted with unusual real estate challenges requiring

Source: Women's Wear Daily, *May 25, 2000, p. 10. Reprinted by permission.*

creative store designs and some higher costs. Consequently, Wal-Mart is feeling a little lonely far from its home base of Bentonville, Ark., and is looking for partners.

"Not many developers are competing in overseas markets. We would love to have some help," Menzer told the audience during a "blockbuster" session. "Where is everybody? Why don't you join us, because it is exciting."

Menzer said that in many countries, there are old factories and other available real estate that could be converted to stores. The retailer has even gone underground, choosing to build a subterranean unit in China, below a soccer field and stadium.

But Wal-Mart is no expert in property development. Instead, said Menzer, as it continues to grow overseas, the company wants its focus to remain on the consumer and running one store at a time.

Decisions on locations in different countries, and how stores are merchandised in different markets, are made on a decentralized basis. Menzer noted that every Friday, the company conducts conference calls to discuss the best practices seen around the world at Wal-Mart and its competitors.

During the same session, Joe Ellis, a limited partner at Goldman Sachs & Co., said that there are two areas where "globalization is moving quickly." The first is hypermarkets, which are generally referred to as supercenters in the U.S. He described them as the fastest-growing mass-merchant format, with enormous potential for American growth; there were 1,107 such stores in the U.S. at the end of 1999, most of them concentrated in the West and Midwest regions.

The other format for rapid retail globalization is apparel specialty chains. Ellis cited Zara, H&M, Mango and French Connection as some of the European chains fated for big futures in the U.S. Other possibilities are Club Monaco, Bebe and Banana Republic for foreign expansion beyond North America.

Chapter Review

Key Words and Concepts

Define, identify, or briefly explain the following:

Ad valorem tariffs
Africa Growth and Opportunity Act (AGOA)
Bilateral agreements
Caribbean Basin Initiative (CBI)
Caribbean Basin Textile Access Program
Caribbean parity
Commissionaires
Contractor
Country-of-origin rules
Currency exchange rates
Cut, make, and trim (CMT)
Developing country
Duty
807/9802 production
807A production
European Union (EU)
Exports
Foreign exchange

First cost
Free trade
GATT
Global products
Globalization
Guaranteed access levels (GALs)
Import penetration
Imports
Interconnected global economy
Joint ventures
Labor-intensive
Landed cost
Less-developed countries
Letters of credit
Licensing
Lobby
More-developed countries
Multifiber Arrangement (MFA)
North American Free Trade Agreement (NAFTA)

Offshore assembly
Outward processing trade (OPT)
Private label
Production package
Protectionism
Quota
Specification buying
Square meter equivalent (SME)
Tariff
Third World
Trade
Trade deficit
Trade Development Act of 2000 (TDA)
Transshipment
Upgrading
U.S.-Caribbean Trade Partnership Act (CBTPA)
World Trade Organization (WTO)

Review Questions on Chapter Highlights

1. Why must we now think more about globalization than in the past?
2. Why has the traditional international trading policy of the United States been based on the principle that excessive import restrictions will lower our standard of living?
3. How has the United States departed from that principle for textile and apparel trade? What led to that departure?
4. Why have the less-developed countries become major textile and apparel exporters?
5. List the regulations that pertain to imports. Explain each one.
6. Do you feel it is appropriate to have quotas on products from some countries and not on others? Explain your answer.
7. Why do you think it is said that textile and apparel trade policies have developed more because of political reasons than economic reasons?
8. What types of domestic companies import goods and why?
9. Describe the various methods used by retailers to buy foreign merchandise.
10. What is private-label production? How is it done, who does it, and why?
11. Name several major U.S. apparel firms who produce "offshore," and explain why they have their garments made in other countries rather than in the United States.
12. How have U.S. textile and apparel producers tried to draw attention to their domestically made products?

13. Are you a "protectionist" or a "free trader"? What are your reasons for your position?

14. In view of the production capacity and the creative talent in the U.S. fashion industry, why is our textile and apparel trade deficit so large?

15. Some of our textile and apparel producers have found ways to penetrate foreign markets. List those ways, explain each one, and give an example of a company using that strategy.

16. How do you think your future career will be affected by globalization? What are you doing to become prepared to function in a global fashion industry?

References

American Textile Manufacturers Institute (2000). *Textile highlights, 2001.* Washington, D.C.: ATMI.

Asia's lure continues. (1988, February 24). *Women's Wear Daily.*

Cable News Network (CNN). (1999, January 1). *Headline news.*

Department of Commerce, Bureau of Economic Analysis (various years). *Survey of current business.* Washington, D.C.: Department of Commerce.

Dickerson, K. (1991). *Textiles and apparel in the international economy.* Upper Saddle River, NJ: Merrill/Prentice Hall.

Dickerson, K. (1999). *Textiles and apparel in the global economy* (3rd ed.). Upper Saddle River, NJ: Merrill/Prentice Hall.

Friedman, T. (2000). *The Lexus and the olive tree.* New York: Anchor Books.

Hooper, C., Dickerson, K., & Boyle, R. (1994). A new course in world trade. *America's Textiles International, 23*(4), 52–56.

Millman, J. (1998, July 21). Mexican textile makers find a protector in NAFTA, *Wall Street Journal,* p. A9.

Office of Textiles and Apparel (OTEXA), U.S. Department of Commerce, online (http://otexa.ita.doc.gov).

Ozzard, J. & Forden, S. (1997, March 19). Calvin's 5-year plan: A Milan store today, then Europe, Mideast. *Women's Wear Daily,* pp. 1, 12–13.

Thurow, R. (1997, May 5). In global drive, Nike finds its brash ways don't always pay off, *Wall Street Journal,* pp. A1–A10.

Suggested Bibliography

American Apparel Manufacturers Association (1997). *The dynamics of sourcing.* Arlington, VA: Author.

American Apparel Manufacturers Association (1998). *Sourcing without surprises.* Arlington, VA: Author.

Balkwell, C., & Dickerson, K. (1994). Apparel production in the Caribbean: A classic case of the new international division of labor. *Clothing and Textiles Research Journal, 12*(3), 6–15.

Bonacich, E., Chang, L., Chinchilla, N., Hamilton, N., & Ong, P. (Eds.). (1994). *Global production: The apparel industry in the Pacific Rim.* Philadelphia: Temple University Press.

Caribbean/Latin American Action. (annual). *Caribbean Basin databook.* Washington, DC: Author.

Cline, W. (1990). *The future of world trade in textiles and apparel.* Washington, DC: Institute for International Economics.

Dickerson, K. (1991). *Textiles and apparel in the international economy.* Upper Saddle River, NJ: Merrill/Prentice Hall.

Dickerson, K. (1997). Textile trade: The GATT exception. *St. John's Journal of Legal Commentary, 11*(2), 393–429.

Dickerson, K. (1998). Apparel and fabricated textile products. In *U.S. Industry & Trade Outlook '98* (pp. 33-1 to 33-14). Lexington, MA: DRI/ McGraw-Hill and U.S. Department of Commerce.

Dickerson, K. (1999). *Textiles and apparel in the global economy.* Upper Saddle River, NJ: Merrill/Prentice Hall.

Ernst & Young (2000, January). *Global online retailing.* A special report for *Stores* magazine. Washington, DC: Author.

Fairchild Publications. (1995, May 4). Made on the planet earth: The facts, the issues, the future of globalization (special "Infotracs" supplement in both *Women's Wear Daily* and *DNR*). New York: Author.

Friedman, T. (2000). *The Lexus and the olive tree.* New York: Anchor Books.

The GATT agreement. (1994, February). *Textile Horizons,* pp. 16–23.

GATT/WTO. (annual). *International trade*. Geneva, Switzerland: Author.

Grunwald, J., & Flamm, K. (1985). *The global factory*. Washington, DC: The Brookings Institution.

Hamilton, C. (Ed.). (1990). *Textile trade and the developing countries: Eliminating the Multifiber Arrangement in the 1990s*. Washington, DC: World Bank.

Khanna, S. (1991). *International trade in textiles*. New Delhi, India: SAGE.

Locker, S., Good, L., & Huddleston, P. (Eds.). (1998). *Softgoods to the world*. (ITAA Monograph #9). Monument, CO: International Textile and Apparel Association.

Naisbitt, J. (1994). *Global paradox*. New York: Avon.

Naisbitt, J. (1996). *Eight Asian megatrends that are shaping our world*. Old Tappan, NJ: Simon & Schuster.

Ohmae, K. (1990). *The borderless world*. New York: Harper Business.

Onkvisit, S., & Shaw, J. (1993). *International marketing* (2nd ed.). Upper Saddle River, NJ: Merrill/Prentice Hall.

Porter, M. (1990). *Competitive advantage of nations*. New York: Free Press.

Rodrik, D. (1997). *Has globalization gone too far?* Washington, DC: Institute for International Economics.

Shim, S. (1998). The changing marketplace in the global economy: Implications for future research. *Family and Consumer Research Journal, 26*(4), pp. 444–461.

Sternquist, B. (1997). *International retailing*. New York: Fairchild.

Textile Institute. (1991). *The globalization of textiles*. Manchester, UK: Author.

Textile Institute. (1994). *Globalization: Technological, economic, and environmental imperatives*. Manchester, UK: Author.

Thurow, L. (1996). *The future of capitalism: How today's economic forces shape tomorrow's world*. New York: William Morrow.

Toyne, B., Arpan, J., Barnett, A., Ricks, D., & Shimp, T. (1984). *The global textile industry*. London: George Allen & Unwin.

United States International Trade Commission. (annual). *U.S. imports of textiles and apparel under the Multifiber Arrangement*. Washington, DC: Author.

Trade Associations

American Apparel and Footwear Association, 1601 N. Kent Street, Suite 1200, Arlington, VA 22209.

American Textile Manufacturers Institute, 1801 K St., N.W., Washington, DC 20006.

Camara Nacional de la Industria del Vestido (National Chamber of the Apparel Industry), Tolsa No. 54, 06040 Mexico, D.F.

Camara Nacional de la Industria Textil (National Chamber of the Textile Industry), Plinio No. 220, Col Polanco, 11510 Mexico, D.F.

Canadian Apparel Federation, 130 Slater St., Suite 605, Ottawa, Ontario K1P 6E2, Canada.

Canadian Textile Institute, 280 Albert St., Suite 502, Ottawa, Ontario K1P 5G8, Canada.

Caribbean/Latin American Action, 1211 Connecticut Ave., N.W., Suite 510, Washington, DC 20036.

The Textile Institute, 10 Blackfriars St., Manchester M3 5DR, U.K.

Trade Publications

Apparel International, The White House, 60 High St., Potters Bar, Herts EN6 5AB, U.K.

Canadian Apparel Manufacturer, 1 Pacifique, Saint Anne de Bellevue, Quebec H9X 1C5, Canada.

DNR, 7 W. 34 St., New York, NY 10001-8191.

International Business, 500 Mamaroneck Ave., Suite 314, Harrison, NY 10528.

International Textiles, 23 Bloomsbury Square, London, WCIA 2PJ, U.K.

Textile Asia, P.O. Box 185, California Tower, 11th Floor, 30–32 D'Aguilar St., Hong Kong.

Textile HiLights, American Textile Manufacturers Institute, 1801 K St., NW, Suite 900, Washington, DC 20006.

Textile Horizons, 23 Bloomsbury Square, London WCIA 2PJ, U.K.

Wall Street Journal, 200 Liberty St., New York, NY 10281.

Women's Wear Daily, 7 W. 34th St., New York, NY 10001–8191.

World Clothing Manufacturer, Perkin House, 1 Longlands Street, Bradford, West Yorkshire BD1 2TP, U.K.

World Trade, 500 Newport Center Dr., 4th Floor, Newport Beach, CA 92660.

The Consumer

The fashion business exists for one reason only—the CONSUMER. Although the industry makes important contributions to the economy and provides a host of fascinating jobs, these reasons alone do not justify the existence of this large, diverse sector. Jobs and profits occur only because they are part of the process through which the industry produces and sells products and provides services for people—the customers.

Textile producers are in business because the consumer buys the end products. Apparel manufacturers would not survive without the consumer to buy their products. Retailers would have no need to carry merchandise or, for that matter, even open their doors each day, were it not for the consumer. The whole industry must keep its eye on the consumer and have a strong service commitment to that consumer to survive and to thrive.

Business conditions in recent years have made it more important than ever for companies to have a strong emphasis on the consumer and on service. If one company doesn't serve customers well, another will. Similarly, some segments of the industry itself have customers within the softgoods industry (before products reach the end consumer) whom they must serve well. For example, the textile company that makes fabric for apparel must think of the apparel firm as its customer, as well as the person who later purchases the finished garment.

In contrast to the free spending of the 1980s, the lackluster economy of the early 1990s created cautious consumers who have changed their buying habits. Another factor that may have influenced consumer spending is that the bulk of the population is older. Whatever the reasons, consumers have changed, and their expectations have changed. Companies are learning that they gain in the end by satisfying customers first.

In short, the 1990s were dubbed the "Decade of the Consumer." Some sources refer to the consumer as "King Customer." Figure 4–1 depicts this en-

Figure 4–1

(1) Today companies realize they must seek to please the consumer. (2,3) Smart companies research consumer needs and build their product lines around what the consumer wants. (4) Problems are seen as opportunities to serve the consumer even more effectively. (5) Increased consumer satisfaction results in growing sales. (6) Consumers must feel the company wants to continue to hear how they feel about the products.

Source: Illustration by Dennis Murphy.

hanced interest in satisfying the consumer. In his book *Why We Buy*, Paco Underhill (1999) observed:

> The era of the visionary retailer or the manufacturer king is over. In the twenty-first century the consumer will be king. Just as fashion now comes from the street up, the world of retail is about following shoppers where they are going. (p. 240)

Articles at the end of this chapter focus on various ways in which the industry is attempting to understand the needs of consumers and respond effectively to those needs. Forward-thinking companies know this is an important ingredient in being successful.

Background: Never Take the Consumer for Granted

Through the 1960s and into the 1970s, U.S. manufacturers in all industries experienced the luxury of a booming economy. This strong economy, plus a growing population and only limited competition from imports, meant that manufacturers could sell just about anything they could produce. Consequently, many began to focus their attention on the *production* part of the business—how to make products faster and most cost effectively. Many began to emphasize winning a greater share of the market. Manufacturers who had this approach thought of the "market" as a collection of competitors, not customers. Many companies forgot about the customer after the sale (Phillips, Dunkin, Treece, & Hammonds, 1990).

The fashion industry has always been very competitive because of the large number of companies competing for the same business. However, like industry in general, the 1960s and early 1970s were a prosperous time for segments of the softgoods industry. Compared to most of the rest of the world, the U.S. market is a very large and affluent collection of consumers who spend a great deal of their incomes and save very little. A combination of the large market and the thriving economy caused many companies in this industry to begin to take the consumer for granted. They even took their intermediate customers in the industry for granted. For example, the textile industry often provided apparel firms with the fabric selections the *textile mills wanted to produce* rather than what the *garment companies wanted*. The textile firms had, after all, invested heavily in high-technology production equipment so they could efficiently produce thousands of yards of the same fabric.

By the mid-1970s, market conditions began to change for U.S. textile and apparel firms. Imports provided the first stimulus for the softgoods industry to begin to think more seriously about its customers' needs. Although imported products had been entering the United States earlier, these garments filled a small part of the market. By the 1970s, however, products from other countries began to be seen as a serious threat by domestic producers. Parts of the U.S. industry actually fostered growth of imports. Apparel firms, tired of the take-it-or-leave-it attitude of many textile mills, often found that companies in other countries were willing to provide what they wanted and worked hard to please. Retailers, too, began to turn increasingly to imports for part of their fashion merchandise.

By the mid-1980s, various segments of the industry began to realize that all could benefit by working together to serve the customer. New partnerships developed between textile and apparel manufacturers and between apparel firms and retailers. A new **customer orientation** began to emerge in the industry. Apparel manufacturers began to work more closely with retailers to develop and make products that were based on customer preferences. This information was in turn fed back to textile producers, who tailored production around what the customer wanted. The consumer began to have more influence in determining what would be available. **Style testing, focus groups,** and various other strategies became increasingly important in gauging consumer likes and dislikes.

The sluggish economy of the early 1990s added to the need to be more sensitive to the customer. A new emphasis on value and service emerged. Consumer confidence plummeted, and many people no longer felt optimistic about the future. Higher taxes, medical costs, housing, and other costs of living left consumers with less

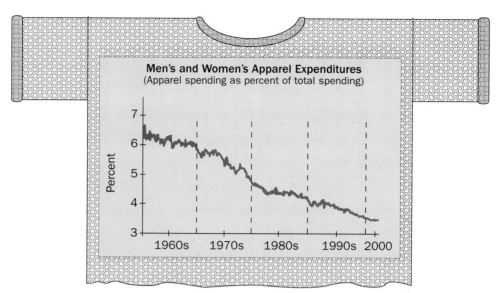

Figure 4–2

Decline in apparel expenditures as a percent of total consumer spending.

Men's and Women's Apparel Expenditures
(Apparel spending as percent of total spending)

Source: U.S. Department of Commerce.

to spend on apparel (Figure 4–2). Sobered by recessionlike conditions and widespread job layoffs related to "downsizing" of companies, consumer spending changed dramatically. Shopping at prestigious stores and wearing designer-label clothes became less important. Priorities changed. Consumers began to place greater emphasis on personal fulfillment than on material status. As a result, consumers became more value oriented and price conscious. All segments of the fashion industry felt the impact of the slowdown in spending, the shift in the types of products bought, and where they were being bought. Another new phenomenon has been the emergence of a new breed of consumer called the **cross-shopper**. These are the consumers who may want prestigious items in some product areas but look for bargains when buying other items. This customer may go to prestigious stores for suits and to discount stores for hosiery.

In the late 1990s, the U.S. economy was booming and consumer confidence was high. Although spending increased, consumers spread their purchases across other categories such as travel, home furnishings, and home computers. Additionally, consumer debt has reduced Americans' spending potential. And, finally, many consumers are simply less interested in fashion than was once the case (Agins, 1999; Cotton Incorporated, 1998).

Sociocultural trends have a major impact on how consumers view fashion and spend. Table 4–1 summarizes some of these trends for recent decades.

Fashions of the 1970s (particularly street fashion of the counterculture) represented the protest mood of that decade. In the 1980s, when Wall Street and Main Street were bustling, consumers used certain looks to project images of success—the "dress for success" approach. Fashion manufacturers experienced healthy demand for their products, and retailers opened stores at a very rapid pace. The 1990s was a time for greater introspection and emphasis on authenticity, as people concluded that "a good design in the '90s is one that cares for people, for their body, their soul, their health, and their comfort" ("Who Are Tomorrow's Consumers?," 1992, p. 3).

Table 4-1 Sociocultural Trends That Affect Consumers' Fashion Spending

1960s & 1970s	1980s	Early 1990s	Late 1990s & Early 2000s
Focus on Self	**Focus on Status**	**Focus on Economic Worries**	**Authenticity; Postmaterialism**

• Individualism took an expressive form
• Duty to self
• Self-expression ruled
• Old inhibitions cast off
• Pleasure, choice
• Living for today
• Seeing no need to sacrifice
• Protest against "the establishment"
• Collapse of confidence
• Collapse of institutions
• Sexual freedom seen as healthy and normal
• Birth of consumerism in the 1970s
• Emerging emphasis on efficiency and convenience
	• Individualistic, in a "look-at-me-I-made-it" sense
	• Accomplished individuals wanted to excel in several domains at once
	• Narcissistic, eclectic
	• Development of the individual in all facets
	• Assertiveness
	• Two-tiered society forming:
	  (a) the "haves":
	    status, yuppies
	  (b) the "have nots":
	    beat the system
	• New economic concerns, cynicism
	• Stress, anger, anxiety
		• Corporate-downsizing
		• Economic uncertainties as a result of massive layoffs in many large firms
		• Opportunities in question
		• Feelings of being out of control
		• Low consumer confidence
		• Stress and pressure
		• Adversarial behavior
		• Fear, anger
		• Worries about the future
		• Belief in economic ceiling
		• Disparity increases in two-tiered society
		• Growing ethnic pride
			• Focus on enjoyment
			• Less emphasis on economic agenda; we survived
			• More emphasis on longer-lasting and deeper concerns
			• Concern for comfort, health, and soul
			• Time, intimacy, and responsibility are growing values
			• Search for meaning and spiritual content
			• Looking beyond the superficial appearance
			• Conveying our unique personhood rather than conforming to a "look"
			• Terrorist acts have a sobering effect

Fashion	**Fashion**	**Fashion**	**Fashion**
• Street fashion of the counter-culture • Fashion reflected protest mood of the era • Fashion reflected emphasis on self	• "Dress for success" attitude (i.e., desire to be perceived as more than one might be, thus appearance was important) • Fashion was vital • Certain "looks" required for various situations	• Growing emphasis on value; consumer demands to get more quality for the price • Desire to buy brands at a discount • Cross-shoppers emerge in larger numbers	• Fashion reveals the unique person • Fashion conveys inner beauty • Emphasis on comfort, products that adapt to the consumer's lifestyle • Desire for easy purchase and care of products

118

The Power of the Consumer

The success or failure of the fashion industry depends on consumers' purchases of its products. To illustrate the power of the consumer, we might think of the whole fashion pipeline as a train (Figure 4–3). Different cars in the train represent various segments of the fashion industry: the fiber producers, fabric manufacturers, apparel makers, and apparel retailers. The train goes nowhere without an engine, however, and the consumer represents that engine.

The consumer provides the momentum to make things happen for the rest of the train. Consumer demand for products creates sales for the retailer, who then needs to buy more garments from the apparel manufacturer. As the garment firm produces more merchandise to send to the retailer, more fabric is needed from the fabric producer. As the fabric mill fills orders, it requires more fiber from the fiber producer. When consumer spending occurs at a healthy pace, the whole fashion pipeline experiences prosperous times. When business conditions are favorable, the segments of the chain usually respond and work together with remarkable speed. It is, after all, an industry that must move its products quickly because of the importance of fashion timing.

A few decades ago, various segments of the industry kept large inventories on hand so they could respond readily at each stage to fluctuations in consumer demand. Changes in the economy and the costs of doing business have changed that practice, however. Retailers, apparel firms, and textile companies have experienced having large inventories on hand when spending dropped sharply, leaving companies at all these levels stuck with inventories that could not be sold in the next fashion season. Companies took great losses as they disposed of these inventories by selling them very cheaply just to clear them out. Companies have also become sensitive to the high costs involved in having huge investments tied up in inventories that sit in a warehouse. Because of these changes in the economy and in ways of doing business, retailers, apparel producers, and textile firms all work with much smaller inventories than in the past. Fewer keep large inventories in warehouses awaiting orders. Instead, firms are now more inclined to match their orders to consumer demand. Because the large

Figure 4–3

When the consumer spends, all segments of the fashion industry move with healthy momentum.

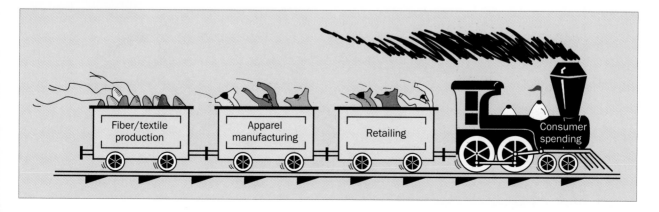

inventories may not be on hand to accommodate demand, this means that the segments of the industry (the cars of the train) must work together closely to keep the train moving (to respond to the consumer).

Sometimes, however, conditions change. The train may not move along smoothly. Changes in the economy or in consumers' needs may influence consumer spending patterns and create conditions that cause the industry to lose its momentum. Just as consumer demand keeps the train moving, a slowdown in consumer spending reduces activity throughout the fashion pipeline. An abrupt slowdown in spending results in the braking effect we see in Figure 4–4.

A number of factors may cause this abrupt stoppage or slowdown in fashion business activity. Sometimes these are widespread occurrences that affect the entire industry. For example, a downturn in the economy may dampen consumers' spending patterns. This type of change tends to affect the industry broadly, as witnessed in much of the early 1990s and again in the early 2000s. Nearly everyone involved in the industry is affected by this kind of slowdown—all the way back to the fiber suppliers, fabric producers, and of course, the apparel firms and retailers. Other suppliers to the industry are also affected—those who provide zippers, buttons, threads, hangers for new garments, or transportation services for merchandise. Workers may experience layoffs or reduced workweeks.

Sometimes a slowdown in fashion spending occurs when the population reaches a stage where consumers begin to emphasize spending for areas other than apparel. For example, a widespread interest in building or refurnishing homes often results in reduced apparel spending in many households.

Momentum in certain segments of the industry (that is, our "train") is affected when the industry miscues seriously in having products that consumers want in a season. These changes can affect specific segments of the industry or companies, with a ripple effect back through the pipeline. For example, manufacturers may introduce their lines with only very short skirts, and many women avoid purchases altogether because they find nothing they feel is suitable for them. Firms that offer a variety of skirt lengths may have more customers than those offering only very short skirts. In other cases, fashion trends may shift business from one group of producers to another. Firms that produced only traditional tailored menswear felt this slowdown in spending when men began to wear more casual office wear.

| Figure 4–4 | **When consumer spending slows, this causes a slowdown in the whole fashion industry.** |

Sometimes the industry is not prepared to move as quickly as the consumer expects. We might think of this as a train with an engine that is moving so fast that the rest of the train has difficulty keeping up. Sara Lee's Wonderbra of the early 1990s created this kind of consumer demand when it was first introduced. Customers actually waited in long lines to buy the bras. Although the company had expected healthy sales, they simply had not anticipated the incredible consumer demand that followed. Sara Lee scrambled to manufacture bras quickly enough to keep them in stock in stores, and as might be expected, other bra companies quickly developed their own versions.

Organizing the Industry Around the Consumer

Old industry strategies that focused just on improving manufacturing processes or gaining an increasing share of the market may have been fine in their time. However, in the 1990s, companies were forced to think about how their business structures and strategies were organized to serve the new independent, sophisticated consumer.

Mackey McDonald, president of VF Corporation, the world's largest publicly held apparel firm,[1] spoke on the increasingly important role of the consumer:

> Business as usual is not an option, because the consumer is now in control. For some years now, the retailers have been calling the shots. That has ended now. The consumer is really the center of the decision-making process for the textile, apparel, and retail industries. Consumers have changed. They are time-poor, aging, have less money, are very, very value- and quality-driven, seek personalized products and, what is very important, are faced with a lot of shopping alternatives. (Maycumber, 1995, p. 9)

As these consumers asserted themselves in the marketplace, forward-thinking companies in the fashion industry began to grapple with how to serve this new independent customer. For many firms, old strategies did not work anymore. Many began to realize that they needed to be more customer focused. For some, it was much harder to understand that the organization itself generally needed to change. Management consultants and authors of a plethora of new books have made a specialty of helping companies learn to serve the customer more effectively.

Like companies in all industries, many firms in the fashion industry have, in fact, become more sensitive to satisfying customers. Leading companies gave customer *service* a top priority in their business strategies—with the ultimate commitment for this coming *from the top*. Some companies have restructured their entire firms around giving customers what they want. Some have tried creative ideas to learn more about service. For example, a few executives have tried a stint answering complaint calls to learn more about what customers are saying. A mail-order firm learned a great deal from analyzing the customer returns. More importantly, customer returns became seen as a source of information rather than just a bother.

The author recalls an experience with a leading apparel firm that functioned under the old mentality when customer returns were a nuisance. The shoulder pads in her name-brand jacket failed miserably after the first dry cleaning. The dry cleaner

---

[1]Sara Lee is also a very large publicly held apparel firm, but because the company produces many other products, it frequently is not listed among the apparel firms per se.

felt responsible and made an honorable attempt to substitute new shoulder pads. However, because of a particular shoulder design, it was deemed that only the manufacturer could remedy the problem. Together, the dry cleaner and the author determined the original shoulder pads were faulty anyway. Believing the manufacturer would welcome feedback to prevent further use of this type of shoulder pads, the author went to great effort to find the New York address of the apparel firm, drive across town to the UPS shipping point, and pay the costs of returning the jacket to the company. The package included a letter indicating that the primary purpose of the return was to let the company know of its problem. Replacing the shoulder pads was secondary. A few days later, the company returned the jacket—same shipping box and all—with a terse letter that the garment should be returned to the retailer where it was purchased. Such a return was no easy feat—the jacket had been purchased in another state while on a business trip. Today's consumers will no longer tolerate this sort of callous response; they will take their business elsewhere. Manufacturers, retailers, or any other components of the fashion industry who are indifferent to consumer feedback will lose in the end.

For companies who are seriously committed to service, such strategies have meant training and rewarding employees who fulfill their roles well. It often involves giving employees the power to handle customer problems on the spot. For example, Montgomery Ward customers were frustrated in the past by having to wait for store managers to approve checks and merchandise-return problems. To solve this, the company's chairman authorized all salesclerks to handle these transactions. To reward good service, companies are linking performance reviews and bonuses to customer-satisfaction ratings. Many of Wal-Mart's earliest sales associates became millionaires through the company's profit-sharing plan, which gave employees a stake in doing a good job of creating and keeping faithful shoppers.

If we think of the fashion industry as one that is becoming increasingly consumer centered, we might envision the entire pipeline as revolving around those consumers (Figure 4–5). As this illustration depicts, all segments of the industry must try to remain close to the consumer. This means that although the fiber producer does not sell directly to the end-use consumer, it is important to know what that consumer wants in terms of aesthetics, comfort, and performance of garments made from that company's fiber. Fabric producers also must be sensitive to what the consumer likes and dislikes in fabrics for different purposes. If consumers are frustrated by pilling (formation of small "balls" on the surface of a fabric after repeated wear and laundering), textile firms must resolve this problem if they want repeated business. Every player in the industry has a stake in creating products that satisfy the consumer.

A survey of U.S. textile company CEOs indicated that textile firms are placing a high priority on serving the end-use customer. CEOs ranked the consumer *first* among the groups with whom they wished to improve business relationships. This is particularly significant because in most cases the end-use customer is relatively far removed from the textile firm. One might expect textile executives to place greater emphasis on an industry segment with which their companies work more directly. This emphasis on the end-use customer, however, likely reflects the industry's growing marketing orientation in recent years (Dickerson, Hooper, & Boyle, 1995).

When a company has a true service orientation, this is evident to all who do business with that firm. This commitment will be evident in the way the textile mill works with the apparel firm or how the apparel firm works with the retailer on matters of what will be produced, quality, prompt deliveries, and handling of problems that arise. Producers of intermediate components have another important reason to

Figure 4–5	**The entire fashion industry must be consumer centered. All segments of the industry must revolve around consumers' needs and wants.**

Source: Illustration by Dennis Murphy.

treat their business customers well. For many parts of the industry, the only way a company gets its products to market is through companies in another stage of the industry. Many segments are far removed from actual sales to the consumer. For a fabric producer to get its fabric to the consumer, an apparel firm must make it into garments. Consequently, treating the business customer well is as important as how the end-use consumer is served.

The Marketing of Fashion

Most of our discussion so far in this chapter has actually dealt with the shift toward a **marketing orientation** for the fashion industry. This is a change from the earlier **production orientation**, when apparel firms and others in the industry "thought of their business and markets in terms of *what their plants could produce*" (American Apparel Manufacturers Association [AAMA], 1982, p. 55).

Import competition caused U.S. firms to develop more thoughtful marketing plans. Increasingly competitive conditions no longer permitted the losses that accompanied a less-focused, hit-or-miss approach used by some. The fashion industries were slow to awaken to the marketing approaches that sparked growth in many other sectors. In recent years, however, there has been a major change in fashion marketing philosophy. Sophisticated marketing research techniques have been applied to the study of consumer wants.

These marketing activities take place at all levels of the fashion industry—from the producers of fibers, fabrics, and apparel to the retailers of fashion merchandise. A basic difference is that producers are concerned with what to manufacture, whereas retailers are concerned with what to select and purchase for resale. (However, in recent years, as a number of retailers develop and contract production for many of their own lines, they are also concerned with what to *manufacture*).

The Marketing Approach

When companies have had a production orientation, they relied on "persuasive salesmanship" to move as much of the company's goods as possible. Such production and selling focused on the needs of the seller to produce goods and make profits. The distinction of a few terms may be useful here:

- **Marketing** identifies the customer and determines what products to offer that customer and how to do so while meeting the financial return objectives of the company.
- **Merchandising** is the process through which products are planned, developed, and presented to the identified **target markets**.
- **Sales** operations implement marketing and merchandising activities by physically selling the line to retail customers according to marketing plans (AAMA, 1982; Kunz, 1998).

Marketing focuses on the needs and wants of the consumer, and the customer-centered approach is known as the **marketing concept**. This concept is based on the philosophy that achieving the company's goals depends on determining the needs and wants of customers and delivering the desired satisfactions more effectively and efficiently than competitors do. A firm's **marketing strategy** will look at customer needs and that company's ability to satisfy them. This approach means that all parts of a company function with the customer at the *center* of its activities (Kotler & Armstrong, 1994).

The model shown in Figure 4–6 shows marketing's role and activities in a company. This model summarizes the whole **marketing process** and the forces influencing company marketing strategy. Components of this marketing process will be discussed in sections that follow.

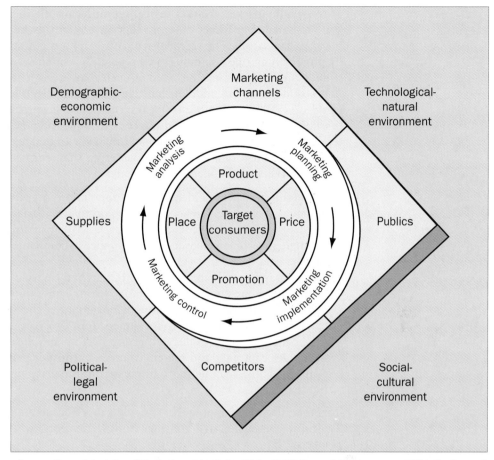

Figure 4–6

Factors influencing a company's marketing strategy. In this model, we see that the company's target consumers are the center of all the firm's activities.

Source: From *Principles of Marketing*, 6th ed. (p. 43) by D. Kotler and G. Armstrong, 1994, Englewood Cliffs, NJ: Prentice Hall. Reprinted by permission of Pearson Education, Inc., Upper Saddle River, NJ.

Target Customers

Given what we have said so far, it is logical that the **target market** (this could also be customers that are companies at various stages in the fashion pipeline) is at the center of the model in Figure 4–6. Whether one is designing, producing, or selling, the first step is to have a clear picture of the customer market segment that constitutes the firm's targeted customers. Because no business can be all things to all people, it must identify a group of customers as its target. For a high-fashion business, this group may be very small and homogeneous. For a mass-marketing company, this targeted group of consumers will be large and quite diverse. Everything that follows in the marketing process is then geared to the target group or market segment. In general terms, a **market** means a meeting of people for the purpose of buying and selling. Such a meeting is not necessarily physical or personal. Specifically, a market for fashion merchandise refers to people with money (some more, some less) and with an inclination to buy fashion-related goods. Fortunately, the potential fashion market in the United States is so large that there is enough business for a company to operate successfully by satisfying even a small percentage of that market.

Just as there can be no universal weather forecast, but only one that is specific as to time and area, the fashion firm must identify its market segment—that is, its part of the whole market. **Market segmentation** means dividing the heterogeneous market into smaller customer divisions that have relatively homogeneous characteristics the firm can satisfy. The segment will consist of a group of customers (not necessarily physically in one community) who react in a similar way to a given set of market stimuli. The segment may be based on such characteristics in common as income level (high, middle, upper middle), lifestyle (suburban, city), fashion preferences (*avant garde*, classic), special interests (jogging, aerobic dancing, disco), sizes (extra large, petite, junior, misses), occupation (career executive, homemaker), and so on. The potential categories are many more than can be illustrated here, and the kinds and types within each category are also more numerous than our necessarily limited examples. Target markets can be identified by analyzing:

- **Demographics**, which identifies the population in groups based on demographic variables such as age, gender, income, occupation, education, religion, race, family size, or stage of the family life cycle. Much of this information is available through government sources, and a number of companies sell their services to identify the data desired.
- **Psychographics**, which identifies lifestyles and lifestyle classifications that appear to influence consumers' buying motivation. These dimensions include attitudes, activities, interests, and opinions. Consumers in the same demographic groups can vary a great deal on these dimensions. For example, one consumer in an upper-income, highly educated group may be an outdoors person with interests in hiking, camping, and the environment. Another person with the same demographic profile may be more interested in the arts, visiting museums, and reading the classics.

Together, these two approaches provide a more-complete look at consumer markets. Typically, companies will consider both dimensions when identifying their target markets.

Usually, a market segment includes a combination of two or more of such characteristics as were mentioned here. The individuals who constitute a segment may differ in other respects, but they have a commonality of interests and wants that makes each one a potential customer for the business concern that is courting that particular market. A market segment can even be large and powerful enough that producers and retailers prepare whole new categories of clothing for it. For example, in the 1980s, as the baby boomers born in the 1950s and early 1960s entered the workforce, they created a market segment for executive career apparel.

If a business, either manufacturing or retailing, is large enough, it may cater to several different market segments at once, creating separate divisions or departments for each. An obvious example is the special shops, both freestanding and within department stores, for "big is beautiful" women and for extra-tall, extra-large men.

It must be realized that segments do not always remain static. One of the costliest errors a business can make is to take its market for granted. Economic and social conditions change; competitors develop new market strategies; new products arise and affect consumer purchasing patterns. The only way for a business to expand or even maintain its market position is to keep up with—or even ahead of—such changes. Products, services, and pricing policies must continuously be reevaluated in terms of changing market influences.

The need to target consumer groups is threefold: (1) to identify consumer characteristics most suited to the goals and capabilities of the firm, (2) to provide a basis for formulating and, if necessary, adjusting the firm's policies and products to satisfy these characteristics, and (3) to pinpoint consumer characteristics that affect patterns of buying behavior.

Market segmentation in itself will not ensure success in the fashion business, as it is only one of a combination of many factors in the equation. Not to segment, however, is to choose a sure way to failure. The principle of segmentation is based on the fact that people are different and that, to make the point again, no one company can be all things to all people. A choice must be made as to which segment of the market a particular business or division or department can most effectively serve.

With a specific targeted customer group in mind, the next step is to collect all the facts one can get. What are they buying this season? What are the activities and occasions for which they need clothes? What are their priorities? Are they innovators or imitators? What people, periodicals, or environmental influences will affect their choice? And so on. The more answers one has to such questions, the clearer the picture becomes, and the easier it is to forecast.

Marketing Mix

After the company identifies its target market, it then designs a **marketing mix** made up of factors under its control—product, price, place, and promotion—shown in the middle ring in Figure 4–6. The company finds its own combination of these factors that will do the job it wants to do in serving the identified market. The marketing mix is determined by management as they go through marketing analysis, planning, implementation (putting the marketing plan into action), and control (evaluating strategies and making adjustments to be sure marketing efforts are doing what they intended). These management functions are shown in the outer ring of the model (Kotler & Armstrong, 1994). Elements of the marketing mix are:

- *Product* refers to the fashion items and services that a company will offer its target market. Company history may play a major role here; many firms have a long-standing record in producing specific lines. For example, jeans makers may venture into related sportswear lines but will not usually decide also to make and sell bras or evening gowns.
- *Price* refers to what customers who buy the product will be charged. Firms in the fashion industry have had to think carefully about prices of their products aimed toward today's consumer. Consumers have resisted paying inflated prices for so-called prestige label merchandise. Instead, they expect good value for their money and even like to boast about their ability to get quality they like for cut-rate prices. Many manufacturers have felt squeezed on prices in recent years. As the prices of cotton and other fibers increased, the apparel firms' cost of materials have risen dramatically, but apparel firms found it difficult to pass these higher costs on to consumers, who balked at paying higher prices for garments.
- *Place* indicates where the product will be sold. Companies may produce products to be sold only in department stores or only in discount stores. Large apparel firms may make various lines geared at specific channels of distribution, with the intent of covering all major retail channels. For example, Sara Lee sells its L'eggs hosiery in supermarkets and discount stores, its Hanes Silk Reflections in department stores, its Donna Karan line in upscale specialty stores, and several acquired international brands in other countries (e.g., Dim in Europe). For a retailer, *place* may mean that certain products may be sold in some of its branch stores and not in others. For example, a Dillard's store may not offer its Ellen Tracy collections in stores located in predominantly blue-collar sections of a city.
- *Promotion* includes all the efforts of a company to establish the identity and enhance the demand for specific brands and designer name products or to encourage buying from certain retailers. The fashion industry has spent vast amounts to achieve these goals.

The Marketing Environment

The **marketing environment** includes all the factors that affect how a company is able to meet its goals in developing and maintaining successful business relationships with its target customers. As Kotler and Armstrong (1994) note, these can be either opportunities or threats. A company must monitor these environmental factors at all times to be able to respond by changing its marketing strategies. If we refer back to the marketing model in Figure 4–6, we see that these environmental factors are of two types.

1. The **microenvironment**, which consists of the forces *close to the company* that influence its ability to serve its target market—suppliers, marketing channel firms, customer markets, competitors, publics, and even other parts of the company. We might consider each of these briefly. *Suppliers* affect the availability of certain fabrics and trims, thus influencing what a company can produce. *Marketing channel firms* might include ways to ship and store merchandise. *Customer markets* refers to determining the type of customers the firm will serve and studying the characteristics of those customers; the customers may be end-use consumers, businesses, government sources, those who may resell the product, or buyers in other countries. For *competitors*, a firm must position itself to gain certain advantages over others to win the customer's business; for example, Levi Strauss & Co. must be able to persuade consumers that their jeans have superior points to Lee jeans (and vice versa). Examples of *publics* are the financial community, the media, and the general public. *Other parts of the company* refers to all the other divisions that must cooperate and be supportive in order to implement the marketing plan (Kotler & Armstrong, 1994).

2. The **macroenvironment**, which consists of factors in the larger societal setting in which the company functions—demographic-economic influences, technological-natural factors, political-legal environments, and social-cultural forces (Kotler & Armstrong, 1994). In the next section, we shall consider some of these influences.

Macroeconomic Factors That Affect Consumption of Fashion

Let us consider some of the macroeconomic forces that affect the fashion business. Although we might easily have a chapter on just this topic, space permits us to consider just a few of these important factors.

The growth of the fashion business in the United States directly reflects the vast social and economic changes that have taken place in this country's lifetime. As one noted social commentator expressed it, "Few societies in history have been as fashion conscious as the American, and there have been few in which styles and clothes changed so often. Students of human society know that changing fashions are an index of social change within a society" (Lerner, 1957).

Keeping up with the changing social and economic trends is not a onetime or a once-in-a-while research project for fashion professionals. Instead, it is necessarily as much a part of their day-to-day activity as keeping sales and inventory records. The fashion industry must be aware of the various macroeconomic factors that influence the needs and wants of consumers; it must also be aware that, as consumers react to these influences, their fashion needs and wants change. The industry must constantly fine-tune its awareness of these changes and its responses to them.

The consumer market is the source of all ultimate demand. Significant changes that take place in the consumer market have had and will continue to have a significant impact on the fashion industries. For example, the age mix of the population, both present and projected into the future, has a definite bearing on the current fashions and those to come (see Table 4–2). The baby boom that followed World War II gave us the rise of the "Yuppies"—or young, upwardly mobile urban professionals—who became a major economic and fashion force in the 1980s. Marketers in all areas of business have followed population demographics, watching the **baby boomers** go through changing stages of their lives, with attempts to respond to this group at various stages because it represents a very large potential market for all kinds of goods and services.

Baby boomers began the strong thrust of women in the workforce and especially into executive positions. This trend not only changed the status of women but also affected the way they dress. By the same token, the younger men of this age group increasingly participated in home and leisure activities, and accordingly adopted more varied styles in dress. Early generations, it is true, had working wives and husbands who participated in home activities, but not in the numbers or with the impact of this group. The rise in the number of dual-income households was accompanied by a decrease in time available to shop, as shown in Figure 4–7.

Now the baby boomers are aging. Many are growing wealthier—not only from their own earnings, but also from substantial inherited wealth. Many have become what some writers are calling a new development in American sociology—the "overclass." Although the United States has always had a wealthy segment of the population, the new elite in the "overclass" are different. Members of this group share a common culture and interests and are different from the "underclass," with the obvious difference that no one is trying to get out of the "overclass." This group places great value on competitive achievement and has a tendency to judge people on "merit," as defined by a continual and strenuous accumulation of academic and professional credentials. For many in this group, success began by graduating from Ivy League schools and then scrambling up the merit ladder through intense work. They lead a lifestyle that might be called "Yuppie taste updated" to take into account their increased affluence and sophistication. The "overclass" are prominent in the upper 5 percent group of U.S. incomes, which are $125,000 and up. Members of this group want prestigious private schools even for their preschoolers; they often want housing that separates them from the middle class and below;

Table 4–2	U.S. Population Groups
Group	**Dates Born**
Maturers	1909–1945
Baby Boomers	1946–1963
First Wave	1946–1955
Second Wave	1956–1963
Generation X	1963–1973
Generation Y	1972–1982
Generation Z	1982–1992

Note: Although various sources have conflicting views on birth years for these groups, these are the typical range of dates.

Figure 4–7

The rise of dual incomes and the decline in shopping time. As this graph indicates, dual incomes increase spending potential but greatly reduce the amount of time available for shopping.

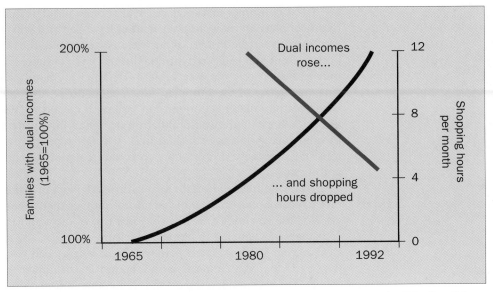

Source: From *Vision for the new millennium . . . evolving to consumer response* (p. 3) by Kurt Salmon Associates, Inc., 1995, New York: Author. Reprinted courtesy of Kurt Salmon Associates, Inc.

they eat gourmet food and drink gourmet coffee. Members of this group are obvious prospects for the upscale end of the fashion business, both for themselves and their children. As an example, Bloomingdale's, Neiman Marcus, Nordstrom, and Saks tap their vast customer databases to identify their most profitable customers. Some of these retailers extend special perks and shopping services to this group (Adler, 1995; Bird, 1995).

Another related significant socioeconomic trend is that there is a growing gap between the incomes of the richest and the poorest Americans. Middle-class income is growing slowly, incomes of "the poor are stagnating, and the rich are getting richer, very rapidly" (Adler, 1995, p. 43). This pattern, too, has important implications for the fashion industry. We must keep in mind, however, that the upper-income group represents a relatively small percentage (5 percent) of the population. Despite high spending potential of the affluent, the majority of the fashion market is not in this group.

Although the economy was robust in the late 1990s, consumer debt and personal bankruptcies grew to staggering proportions. Credit card debt skyrocketed to all-time highs. More than 1.34 million bankruptcies were filed in 1997, with more than 95 percent of these personal bankruptcies. This meant that one in every 80 U.S. households filed for bankruptcy that year. Consumer debt in 2000 exceeded $1.5 trillion, compared to $132 billion in 1970—a 1,047% increase. Consumer debt includes auto loans, mobile home loans, credit card debt, student loans and other. Mortgage debt is a separate category; in 2000, this was approximately $5.178 trillion (source: *2001 Economic Report of the President* online at http://w3.access.gpo.gov/eop/). This trend has a very significant impact on consumers' ability to spend on fashion products (Silverman, 1997; Young & Seckler, 1998).

A generation that followed the baby boomers—given labels such as the twentysomethings, **Generation X**, slackers, and baby busters—have moved into the mainstream of American life. This group represents the second-largest group of young adults in the country's history, some 46 million of them. Zinn, Power, Yang, Cuneo, and Ross (1992) describe this group as follows:

> Busters are the first generation of latchkey children, products of dual-career households, or, in some 50 percent of cases, of divorced or separated parents. They have been entering the work force at a time of prolonged downsizing and downturn, so they're likelier than the previous generation to be unemployed, underemployed, and living at home with Mom and Dad. They're alienated by a culture that has been dominated by boomers for as long as they can remember. They're angry as they look down a career path that's crowded with thirty- and fortysomethings who are in no hurry to clear the way. And if they're angry and alienated, they dress the part, with aggressively unpretty fashions, pierced noses, and tattoos. (pp. 74–75)

Generation X launched the "grunge" look consisting of "slovenly, asexual, antifashion fashion" and embraced antiheroes like Nirvana's Kurt Cobain. Variations of the look include items suggesting a "postindustrial thrift shop look": baggy clothes, faded flannel shirts, clunky work boots, ripped sweaters, old jeans and corduroys, long flowing skirts, body piercing, and tattoos—perhaps making a statement on the materialism of their elders.

Generation Y, successors to Generation X, represent a massive growing market. These "Echo Boomers," the children of boomers, are also called the digital generation, generation wired, and millennials. These eager consumers entered their teen years in the early 1990s, ending a 15-year decline among the teen population. When the bulge of teenagers reaches its peak of 31 to 35 million teens in 2010 (Figure 4–8), this group will exceed the baby boom teen explosion of the 1960s and 1970s both in size and duration. Many companies in the industry were slow to recognize the potential of this group, whose annual spending is estimated at $100 billion (Black, 1998).

The Generation Y group is a powerful force in fashion markets, and companies that have catered to this group are profiting handsomely. Echo Boomers have already made their preferences known for Steve Madden Shoes, surfwear, wraparound sunglasses, Nike products, baby tees, and sassy-colored makeup. Gadzooks, The Buckle,

Figure 4–8

Growth of U.S. teen population compared to overall U.S. population growth.

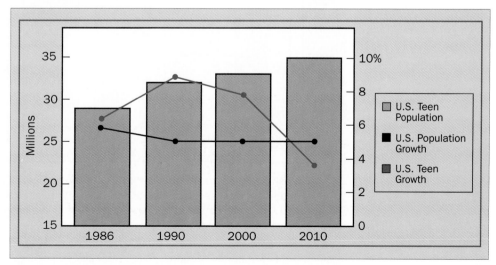

Source: U.S. Census Bureau.

Pacific Sunwear, and Urban Outfitters, to name a few retailers, are doing well from catering to this group. Delia's Inc., a company that targets teens, gets between 3,000 and 5,000 unsolicited requests a day for its catalog. Among manufacturers, Quicksilver sales and profits have soared by responding to this generation's needs both in the United States and abroad. Fashion and beauty companies clamor for a chance to advertise in *Seventeen* magazine. Malls are trying to cultivate a loyal following among this group so they keep coming back (Munk, 1997; Neuborne & Kerwin, 1999).

Generation Y represents the most educated and affluent teenagers in history; they are the first generation of "cybercitizens" weaned on computers and the most ethnically diverse group ever. They want to live for today and focus on short-term goals. They enjoy being teenagers. They earn an average of $64 to $70 per week and spend even more, with help from parents and gifts. Collectively, they spent about $84 billion of their own money in 1997. "Teenagers are sophisticated, savvy and decisive consumers. They want to make their own statements, but within the realm of what's dictated by their peers and friends." Marketers must study this group constantly because trends change on a daily basis. "You can't define 'cool'—it's impossible because it's constantly changing" (Silverman, 1998, p. 9).

Generation Z is another group of teenagers that follows on the heels of Generation Y. While Generation Y rediscovered consumerism, Generation Z may tend to be very antiestablishment and anticonsumerism. Generation Z will be more jaded and suspicious of the establishment and harder to exploit. One industry expert said, "The only way to become successful in approaching them will be to infiltrate their ranks" (Romero, 1997).

Figure 4–9

50 and Over, a Growing Force

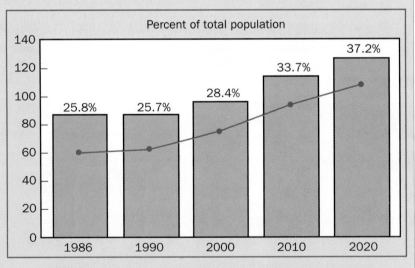

Line shows projection to the year 2020 for the number of people in the U.S. 50 years old and older, starting with an estimate for July, 1986, in millions. Bars show the percent of the population 50 years old and older.

Source: U.S. Department of Commerce; U.S. Census Bureau.

At the same time, an increasing portion of the U.S. consuming population is growing older. An estimated 10,000 Americans are turning 50 every day—one every seven seconds—according to the U.S. Census Bureau (1995). This represents more than 3.6 million consumers a year! The over-50 population will expand by 56 percent between 1998 and 2011. The growing mature market is viewed by many as an economic bonanza with a collective spending power of more than $900 billion a year. Companies that fail to cater to this group will be losers. New products and new approaches are needed in selling to this group. Some companies are gearing up to meet these needs. For example, Talbots has updated its fashion image to appeal to the 35-to-50-year-olds. J.C. Penney bought Eckerd Drug in the late 1990s to serve this population's growing health needs (Brookman, 1998; Silverman, 1998) (see Figure 4–9).

First, there is the "middle-age" group, with a larger percentage in the 50-plus group than ever before. As baby boomers have entered their fifties, many are attempting to defy the aging process through "exercise, diet, and dye." Efforts seem to be paying off because this "middle-age" group looks, feels, and acts younger than previous generations did. Most Americans will have more years of adult life *after* their children leave home than they spent parenting. For many, the fifties is the most productive and rewarding decade of their lives. At this age, consumers generally have their highest spending potential, and their continued interest in remaining active and youthful bodes well for the fashion industry. Fashion companies have found they need to adapt products for the effects of aging such as spreading girth. However, it can be deadly to sales to make any sort of age reference in the labeling or advertising. People don't want to be reminded they are getting older.

Second, the so-called "senior citizen" group accounts for a growing proportion of the population, as Figure 4–10 indicates. Today, about one in eight Americans is 65 years or older, compared to one in 25 at the turn of the century. The 85-and-over group is growing especially fast. By 2030, *one in five* Americans will be elderly, and senior citizens will live longer. People who used to be considered old at 65 are usually still in their prime at that age today. Healthier lifestyles mean that older consumers are leading active, vital lives and retain their interest in being well dressed. Studies also show that mature consumers want comfort, convenience, and value.

Lifestyles are another important macroeconomic factor affecting purchases of fashion goods. Family life has been turned inside out by the rush of married women, many of them mothers, into the workforce. Households made up of single individuals, once a rarity, are commonplace today; so are single-parent households, in which the unmarried or divorced parent leaves the child at a day-care center and spends the major part of the day in the business world, rather than in the nursery and the kitchen. Customers have changed from the conventional mother-at-home shopping during the week in downtown or suburban stores to the working woman, the senior citizen, and the single adult, each with his or her preferences in clothing, food, and lifestyles in general.

Changing lifestyles affect fashion purchases in other ways, too. The health and fitness craze in recent decades provides terrific boosts to athletic and other activewear manufacturing and sales. As baby boomers began to age and have demanding careers, many have adopted a lifestyle known as *cocooning*. This means they are spending more time at home, often taking advantage of food delivery and other in-home services. This trend affects demand for clothes, shoes, and home products that create a comfortable environment. Moreover, it means that catalogs and online shopping services appeal to this group. When these consumers do shop in stores, they want quick, convenient, affordable shopping. Consumers are frustrated by the dizzying array of indistinguishable products, and many women are moving toward a "male" pattern of

Figure 4–10

As the population ages, the percentage of the young decreases.

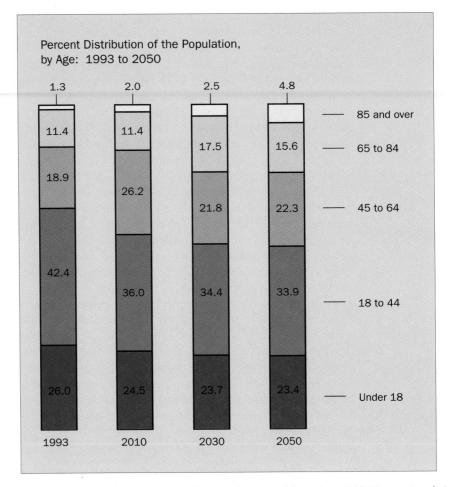

Percent Distribution of the Population, by Age: 1993 to 2050

Source: From *How we're changing—demographic state of the nation: 1995* (Current Population Reports, Special Studies, Series P-23, No. 188) (p. 1) by Bureau of Census, December 1994, Washington, DC: U.S. Dept. of Commerce.

shopping. Men tend to avoid haphazard or confusing shopping environments. Consequently, retail stores, mall developers, and others must attempt to respond to these concerns.

Fashion marketers must also take into account that the U.S. population is becoming more ethnically diverse, with new target markets that are growing in explosive numbers demographically and socially. The recent census provided data that sparked all consumer product marketers to think of the growing importance of minorities. The U.S. minority market of 84 million people represents an estimated annual buying power of $600 billion and spends more on some categories of apparel than Caucasians. The minority population is growing much faster than that of whites (see Figure 4–11).

Asians, Hispanics, African Americans, and other nonwhite groups could soon represent 47 percent of the total population. The Asian/Pacific Islander group is the fastest-growing segment of the population; their numbers are expected to increase fivefold to roughly 12 percent of the population by 2050. Moreover, a surge of the Hispanic and Asian groups are expected to affect total population projections, be-

Figure 4–11

**Share of U.S.
Population by
Race/Ethnicity**

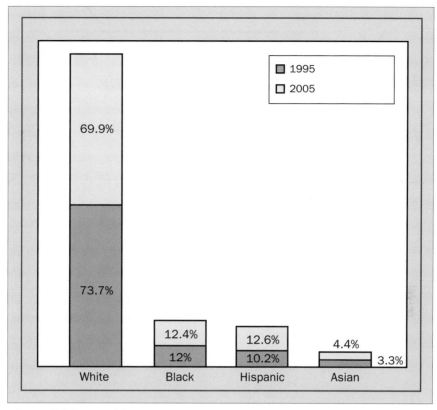

Source: U.S. Bureau of Census.

cause those groups tend to have larger families. African-American consumers represent a growing percentage of the U.S. population and have increasing collective economic clout.

Up to now, most companies have only made modest efforts to develop and market products specifically for various ethnic groups. As these groups' spending power increases, companies will find that it is increasingly important to stop regarding them as "dark-skinned white people" (Mallory & Forest, 1992, p. 70). Many members of these ethnic groups do not want to assimilate with the rest of the population. They are proud of their ethnic heritage, want products of their own, and are willing to spend to get them.

Some fashion companies have recognized the importance of serving these important ethnic markets. For example, J.C. Penney is now advertising in Hispanic magazines such as *Latina*, in African-American publications such as *Essence* and *Black Entertainment TV*, and in radio campaigns geared for the Asian consumer. Some manufacturers are offering lines specifically for women of color, with bold, vibrant colors and in sizes more suitable for ethnic groups who need styles that fall between misses' and petites. Sears has been offering African Village, a line of "ceremonial loungewear" for holidays like Kwanzaa. Levi, Nike, and Tommy Hilfiger are other companies that see the advantage of directing marketing toward various ethnic groups. Fashion companies have found they must avoid stereotypes in advertisements.

Analysis of Customers' Fashion Preferences and Trends

An important part of the fashion marketer's job is the analysis of what customers are actually buying. In the fashion industry there is a constant flow, back and forth, of information about these purchases. The systems that producers and retailers have today for this purpose are extremely rapid and accurate, thanks to the development of the computer. In most retail stores, a record is kept of the styles, colors, fabrics, and so on that have been purchased for resale. On this record are also entered the store's day-to-day sales. Every garment bought by a consumer thus becomes a ballot cast by the customer for the desired size, color, fabric, silhouette, and style. Computerized registers provide this important **point-of-sale (POS) data** from every purchase made. Bar coding provides this data (Figure 4–12).

From the point-of-sale records, retailers can discern sudden or gradual changes in the preferences of their own customers. These changes become apparent whether the same customers are turning to different fashions, or whether there is a change in the kind of people who make up the store's clientele. In either case, the proprietor or buyer sees that there is less demand for Item A and more for Item B.

These variations in what consumers are buying at that store are then reflected in what the store buys from the manufacturers of fashion merchandise. Multiply that store's experience by the hundreds or even thousands of stores that buy from one manufacturer, and you see that producers have a relatively broad spectrum of consumer response as represented in the rate at which their various styles are sold. If they have countrywide distribution, they may see that certain areas are buying certain colors, styles, or fabrics faster or more slowly than others. If they have no reason to believe that this is due to special effort (or lack of effort) on the part of their retail outlets in those areas, they can assume that a regional difference is influencing sales. Typical of such differences are the West Coast's quickness to accept what is new, and especially what is casual and relaxed, or the Midwest's fondness for shades of blue to go with the blue eyes that predominate among the German and Scandinavian groups who have settled there.

From the manufacturer of the finished garment, information about customer preferences, as expressed in customer purchases, flows in several directions. One flow is back to the retail stores, by means of the manufacturer's salespersons, to alert them to trends they may not have noticed themselves. Another flow is to the fabric producers, in the form of the garment maker's reorders for the most accepted fabrics and colors.

The POS data provide the basic information needed for Quick Response (QR) systems to operate. As these electronic linkages among producers and retailers have become more prevalent, a number of large apparel manufacturing firms are actually connected to retailers' computer systems. When retailers sell certain products, this information informs the apparel firm that it should replace those items in the retailer's supply of that apparel firm's lines. For some mail-order firms, orders for certain products will be sent *directly* to the manufacturer, who ships the product to the customer. In those cases, the mail-order retailer may hold none of the apparel firm's product in the retail inventory.

A new strategy known as **data mining** is being used to go far beyond analyzing POS data to help manufacturers and retailers analyze consumers' wants, needs, and

<table>
<tr><td>Figure 4-12</td><td>**Analyzing fashion purchases at point of sale (POS). Retail sales ticket showing manufacturer, style number, classification, season, size, and price. This information is fed into a POS register, and the data appear on sales and inventory reports. POS data are also being used to enable replacement of merchandise as it is sold.**</td></tr>
</table>

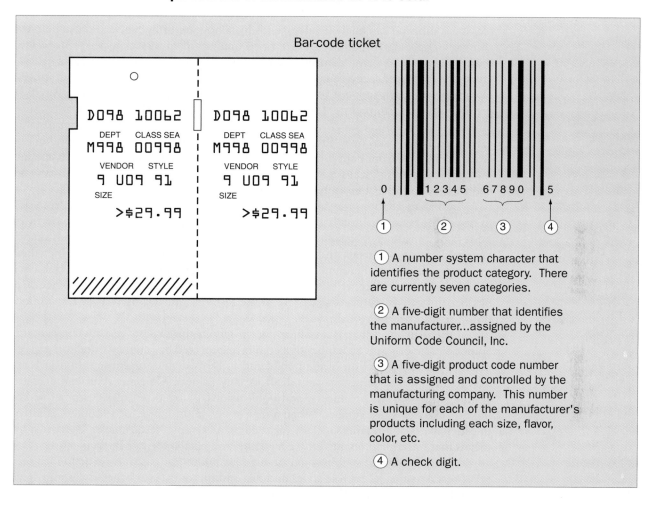

Bar-code ticket

① A number system character that identifies the product category. There are currently seven categories.

② A five-digit number that identifies the manufacturer...assigned by the Uniform Code Council, Inc.

③ A five-digit product code number that is assigned and controlled by the manufacturing company. This number is unique for each of the manufacturer's products including each size, flavor, color, etc.

④ A check digit.

spending patterns. It has been relatively easy for companies to identify which customers are spending money with them or which products are selling. However, technical difficulties and the high cost of software and data storage have caused many companies to muddle along with only rough approximations of what is selling and to whom.

Data mining offers the possibility for manufacturers and retailers to work together to forecast consumer demands. Today, retailers are out of stock (known as **stockouts**) of 20 to 30 percent of the items consumers want almost all the time. Both manufacturers and retailers lose when this is the case; thus, data mining allows these two segments of the industry to work together to reduce stockouts by making available the sizes, colors, and styles consumers want while at the same time eliminating markdowns and **chargebacks**. Data-mining tools allow a company to slice and dice—that is, to "drill"—through large databases seeking trends and building very specific customer profiles. For example, Sara Lee Corporation licenses casualwear for the NBA, NFL, and NCAA and had difficulty forecasting sales if demand was off slightly. Data mining recommends seasonal profiles and identifies which colors, sizes, and styles belong in each profile group; it can also do this for any specific league or team to see exactly who is buying what.

Data mining permits a company to go very "deep" for information. For example, Liz Claiborne can analyze sales trends by silhouette or by fabric and can help the company analyze profitability by size or to analyze inventory that performs well at the regular price. A manufacturer can determine if sales are down for a particular retailer and whether certain items are not selling at certain types of retail stores. Companies can determine if some customers cost more to lure than they're worth in profitability and can pamper those more-faithful spenders. Mail-order retailers such as Victoria's Secret are narrowing their mailing lists to focus on the most profitable catalog recipients and drop those who order little from the company. Joseph Fink of Guess? noted that the data-mining approach—not the data—is new. "We're just improving our analysts' access to it where they can quickly ask questions, get an answer, and then ask another question based on the first answer" (Hill, 1998, p. 80).

Information about the customer and the balloting that he or she does from day to day at the retail cash register is also collected by other people in the fashion field. Editors of consumer magazines, for instance, check regularly on trends with manufacturers of raw materials and finished products. They do this to see whether their own previous editorial judgments of fashion trends have been right and to establish a basis on which to select styles to be featured in future issues. What the customer does or does not buy is watched as closely in the fashion industry as Wall Street transactions are watched by stockbrokers.

Often the customer is a guinea pig on whom the experts test their judgment. Sometimes he or she is a member of a committee formed by retailers or editors to represent a particular section of the public and to be available for consultation or reaction to new ideas, or just to sound off on any subject. Consumer surveys are also conducted by stores, producers, and publications. More often, the customer serves unknowingly as a test subject. When a new style, color, fabric, or silhouette is introduced, makers and retailers usually proceed on a "sample, test, reorder" system. This means that only small quantities are made up and placed for sale in retail stores. This approach is known as style testing. At the first inkling of customer reaction, the retailer reorders the acceptable styles and discontinues whatever other styles may have evoked little customer enthusiasm. The manufacturers, meanwhile, are watching the retail reorders to see which styles they should cut in quantity and which ones should be discontinued.

No one, least of all the customers, may fully understand why one style is chosen in preference to another, but everyone in the fashion industry is observing their selections, which determines what the current fashions are, and evaluating their degree of popularity and their directions.

Quick Response as a Marketing Strategy

Although the industry's Quick Response program encompasses production operations and uses new computer technologies in a range of activities to fulfill its promises, the *objectives of the QR effort rely on a marketing concept: getting the right merchandise to market at the right time.* Even more fundamental, QR is based on the marketing principle of *serving the customer more effectively by focusing on the customer's needs.* The apparel industry is concerned with serving more effectively both the retail customer and the end-use customer, and QR provides an important strategy for doing that.

Push System

Quick Response represents a dramatically different marketing strategy from that used by most apparel manufacturers in the past. Traditionally, the apparel industry expected merchandisers to be able to predict a year in advance what the consumer would want in the next year's selling season. Given the transient nature of fashion and the fickle tastes of the apparel consumer, choosing styles, colors, and other aspects of a line that far in advance was risky. Despite the risks and inconveniences, the softgoods chain was structured to support the **push system**. The push system depended on force-feeding a product line through the multistage production and marketing process in hopes that the consumer would like the end product. If the consumer did not like it, markdowns resulted (Figure 4–13). Whether planned or forced, markdowns are said to approach 25 to 30 percent of total U.S. apparel sales.

Figure 4–13	**The push system is based on force-feeding a product line through the manufacturing and marketing process in hopes the consumer will like it.**

Source: Reprinted with permission from *Bobbin*. Copyright © Bobbin Blenheim Media. All rights reserved.

Pull System

In contrast, the **pull system** is based on observing the consumer and translating the consumer's wishes back through the pipeline to determine what will be produced. The pull system relies on using retailers' point-of-sale data to record consumer reactions and preferences. Consumer preferences, as indicated through purchases of introductory lines, are transmitted quickly back through the information pipeline so that merchandise is produced promptly to respond to what the consumer wants (Figure 4–14).

The entire QR system is based on tracking, analyzing, understanding, predicting, and responding to consumer demand. The system depends on electronic communication systems for transmitting data through the softgoods chain, a willingness of retailers and suppliers to share information, and a cooperative spirit among members of the production and marketing chain.

Another reference to the earlier train analogy may be useful in considering the push/pull systems. Under the *push system*, the engine (consumer) ran the train, but the train (fashion pipeline) was not geared to respond quickly and effectively to the engine's activity. The cars had tried to second-guess the path of the engine, and on occasion, the back cars tried to divert the engine to where the cars wanted to go. Under the *pull system*, the train recognizes that the engine is in control. Rather than try to second-guess the engine or divert it, the train responds to the path being charted by the engine (Dickerson, 1991).

Figure 4–14	The pull system is based on determining the consumer's needs and wants and basing production on that information.

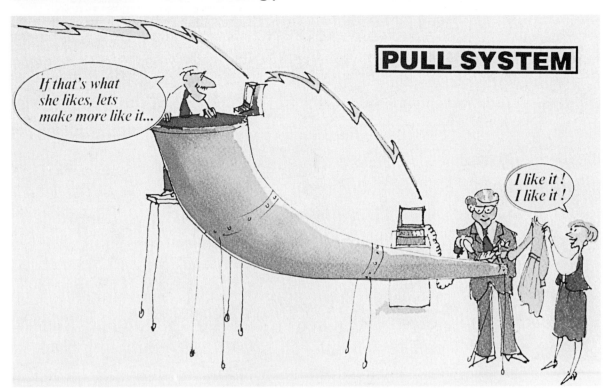

Source: Reprinted with permission from *Bobbin*. Copyright © Bobbin Blenheim media. All rights reserved.

The Marketing Concept and Manufacturing/Distribution

When an apparel company adopts the marketing concept as a vital part of company philosophy, this provides a focus for the firm and serves as a guide for the company's production and distribution of its lines—both domestically and globally. The manufacturer must understand the markets and the firm's role in those markets. Furthermore, as the company develops a marketing strategy, this targets the firm's customers, providing a focus so the company can concentrate on serving that customer or group of customers. Obviously, a company must take the firm's capabilities into account in making these plans. The marketing strategy may also provide guidance on which markets to avoid because of oversaturation, excessive import competition, or other reasons.

In short, the marketing strategy helps the firm identify who it is and what it does, and then it keeps the company on target as it proceeds with production and distribution. The marketing strategy determines the manufacturing strategy—including sources of production—rather than the reverse. The marketing strategy will take into account a full range of production alternatives, including manufacturing in the firm's own plants, contracting, or perhaps **offshore production**. Or, a company may use a combination of production alternatives suitable to serving its customers well. For example, it may produce more fashion-oriented merchandise in its domestic plants so that it can deliver time-sensitive lines to the retailer and consumer quickly. When timing is not as critical, the company's lines of a more "staple" nature might be made in another country to take advantage of lower production costs.

A number of U.S. apparel firms have placed added emphasis on marketing and service while deemphasizing manufacturing. This means that some apparel firms have little or no manufacturing base; instead, products are manufactured to a company's specifications by independent contractors both in the United States and other countries. In these firms, a product development team generally develops the lines, selects fabrics, and makes other specifications on how garments should be made. All of this occurs with the target market in mind. The production then occurs elsewhere. Finished garments are sent to the firm's distribution center and from there are shipped to the apparel firm's retail customers. A growing number of apparel firms are having their garments made in this manner.[2]

Distribution operations play a very important role in customer-centered firms. The company's distribution area is responsible for getting the right merchandise to the retail customer in a timely fashion so that it is available for quick-turn fashion trends, promotional sales, to replenish the retailer's inventory, or for other needs. Distribution operations monitor the company's available inventories to be sure a supply is available to respond quickly to the customer. Distribution areas of a firm often handle returns and other service matters related to the retail customer.

Logistics (refer back to Chapter 1), which is becoming the key aspect of the distribution, is providing an increasingly important role in helping companies achieve the **five Rs** in the marketing concept—delivering to the consumer the right product

---

[2]Today many retail firms are engaged in contracting the production of their lines, just as apparel firms are. This means that the retail firms' marketing strategy will determine how and where garments will be produced, just as it does for apparel firms.

of the right quality in the right quantity at the right time and at the right price (see Figure 4–15). Logistics plays a critical role in helping companies coordinate their far-flung production and distribution networks, whether global or within the country. Through computer information technologies, logistics experts are able to track production and shipments of products anywhere in the world.

Logistics help a company pace its inventory supply so that items get to the retail floor on time. This means that *logistics play a vital role in moving a company from the push system to the pull system.* In the push system, companies stocked warehouses with large inventories they thought the consumer wanted. In contrast, a pull system operates more closely to consumer demand and reduces the backlog of costly inventories sitting in warehouses in anticipation of what the consumer *might* want. By being able to track sales and shipments of finished products on a daily basis, companies can gauge what they need to produce and to do so more closely to what the consumer is buying. That is, logistics help ensure that inventory levels are maintained at the right levels throughout the production-distribution chain.

Professor Sundaresan Jayaraman of Georgia Institute of Technology summarized the growing importance of logistics in the softgoods industry as follows:

> While the customer is the visible driver that sets the goals for a company's performance, logistics can be viewed as the invisible driver that truly governs a company's performance in keeping its customers and stockholders pleased. . . . In the future, profitability will come from improvements in logistics and not from the shop floor. (Jayaraman, 1998, pp. 68, 70)

Serving Consumers in the Next Millennium

Kurt Salmon Associates (KSA), a leading consulting firm for the fashion industries, has identified a number of anticipated visionary changes in how these sectors will serve their customers in the year 2000 and beyond. These experts predict that the

Figure 4–15

Increasingly, logistics management has become critical in having the softgoods industry serve the consumer efficiently.

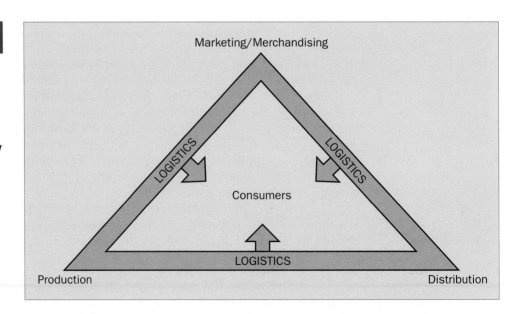

production-distribution chain with its distinct segments, as we know it today, will give way to a more integrated, interlocking complex with the consumer as the focal point. Companies will develop differentiated competitive business expertise, focus on their core businesses, and link with other companies without regard to ownership. Products will be more customized rather than mass-produced where one or a few sizes are expected to fit all.

Today, many retailers expect manufacturers to send merchandise to them **floor-ready**, with packaging and ticketing ready to move directly to the sales floor. The KSA team predicts that links directly between the producer and the consumer will grow, with a shift to **consumer-ready** manufacturing. According to KSA predictions, retail stores will become the shopping "theater" in which the consumer makes buying decisions, and customized products will be sent directly from the manufacturer to the consumer.

KSA experts have coined a term to describe a new replenishment model based on the consumer: Automatic Consumer Replenishment[SM]. KSA calls this the "next generation of relationship marketing" (Kurt Salmon Associates [KSA], 1995, p. 10). This takes the customer-centered company a step closer to the consumer compared to today's automatic replenishment schemes that replace garments in the retail store as soon as they are sold. In KSA's visionary model, new relationships between producers and consumers will permit automatic replenishment of a variety of items on a regular periodic basis: toiletries, food, underwear, hosiery, dress shirts, and activewear. The producer might approach the customer in the following manner: "Mrs. Johnson, you normally order 10 pair of Hanes panty hose, style 485, size B, color black, from us about every 3 months. Would you like us to send those to you, automatically, on a regularly scheduled basis?" (KSA, 1995, p. 7). For consumers who are increasingly pressed for time to shop, this convenient, timesaving approach is likely to be very well received, particularly in certain product areas.

Federal Legislation Affecting the Fashion Business

Under the American systems of government and economy, businesses enjoy certain rights and freedoms. Although business in America originally operated in a *laissez-faire* economy (i.e., noninterference by government), the emergence and abuses of trusts and monopolies in the late nineteenth century, which minimized competition and made it difficult for small business to survive, created the need for regulation. Two basic categories of federal legislation affect the fashion industry: (1) laws that regulate competition and (2) labeling laws designed to protect consumers. In essence, those laws that regulate competition help consumers also by assuring market conditions that provide competitive prices and other conditions to serve them fairly.

Federal Laws Regulating Competition

Sherman Anti-Trust Act—1890: This was the first law enacted in the United States to restrain unfair competition. It outlawed monopolies and practices that restrained competition.

Clayton Act—1914: This law reinforced the Sherman Act by spelling out some specific restraints pertaining to price fixing, price discrimination, and interlocking directorates.

Federal Trade Commission (FTC) Act—1914: This law created the **FTC** to serve as a "policing" agency to enforce the Sherman and Clayton acts, to investigate alleged unfair methods of competition, to conduct hearings, and to issue cease-and-desist orders. This law was amended by the Wheeler-Lea Act of 1938 and gave the FTC authority to prohibit fake advertising and made it an additional offense to injure the general public.

Robinson-Patman Act—1936: According to this law, which was aimed primarily at giant retailers, large purchasers of goods may not be given so large a discount as to give them monopolistic advantage. This act makes price discrimination between purchasers of like grade or quantity illegal (e.g., it outlawed "phony" advertising allowances).

Celler-Kefauver Act (or Antimerger Act)—1950: This law made it illegal to eliminate competition by creating a monopoly through the merger of two or more companies.

Product Labeling Laws to Protect Consumers

In addition to regulating business to promote competition, the federal government has enacted various product labeling laws intended to protect consumers by requiring that the materials used be listed, that they be safe and accurately identified, that the percentage of natural and synthetic fibers be shown, and that clear instructions to consumers about the care and maintenance of articles be provided. Examples of these labeling laws are as follows:

Wool Products Labeling Act—1939; amended in 1984
Fur Products Labeling Act—1951
Flammable Fabrics Act—1953
Textile Fiber Products Identification Act—1966; amended in 1984
Fair Packaging and Labeling Act—1966
Care Labeling of Textile Wearing Apparel Act—1972; amended in 1984 and again in 1997. The last amendment permitted manufacturers to use symbols on their labels to reduce the need to write care instructions in other languages. Changes resulted initially for selling in the Mexican and Canadian market, but Federal Trade Commission staff believe this may be the first step to a global label that can be used around the world.

Readings

Competitive conditions in the fashion industry have made companies increasingly interested in understanding consumers, learning their needs, and focusing on how to best serve those consumers' needs. These articles focus on specific consumer market segments that are becoming increasingly important in the U.S. marketplace

Latina Fashionistas

Livin' la vida loca? Well, if you're a marketer or retailer who isn't paying attention to the skyrocketing Hispanic population in the United States, you just might need to do so.

Reaching the Aging Boomers

As the baby boomer generation enters middle age, companies have a task in serving this very large segment of the U.S. market—who see themselves as healthy and in the prime of their life.

Commit to SINS, Win Lifelong Customers

The "Single Income, No Spouse" (SINS) consumers are young adults in the 25 to 45 age range with money to spend on self-indulgences, including fashion, because of their lack of family responsibilities. This consumer market has doubled in the past 30 years.

Latina Fashionistas

*L*ivin' la vida loca? Well, if you're a marketer or retailer who isn't paying attention to the skyrocketing Hispanic population in the U.S., you just might need to be.

Hispanics comprise 12 percent of the nation's population, two-thirds of whom are under 35. By 2050, one out of every four people in the country will be of Latin descent, according to Editorial Televisa, a Miami-based publisher of 40 Spanish-language magazines that include *Cosmopolitan, Elle, Harper's Bazaar* and *Marie Claire*.

Young Hispanic women are major trendsetters ready to be courted by fashion marketers: they love to shop, don't hesitate to buy those must-have items, and spend more on fashion and beauty than most other market segments. In fact, the Cotton Incorporated *Lifestyle Monitor*™ reports that 38 percent of Hispanic women aged 25–34 spent over $100 in the last month on clothes, compared to 21 percent of Caucasians in that same age range (only African Americans, at 47 percent, spent that much on apparel in the last month). And they shop more too: 2.1 times per month, versus Caucasians 1.8.

Christy Haubegger, president and publisher of *Latina* magazine, doesn't mince words. "Retailers who need to succeed in the major U.S. markets— LA, New York, Miami—cannot ignore the fact that these cities are 40 percent, 30 percent and 60 percent Hispanic, respectively. To ignore the 12 million Hispanic trendmakers in those three cities alone

Women between the Ages of 25 and 34

	Hispanic	Caucasian	African American
Loves shopping	25%	20%	33%
Spent over $100 on clothes in last month	38%	21%	47%
Number of times shop per month	2.1	1.8	2.3
One of first to try new styles	33%	28%	46%
Believes it's important to keep wardrobe updated	59%	41%	63%
Will sacrifice comfort for fashion	47%	31%	41%

would be foolish at best, considering the competitive retail and fashion environment."

"We are geographically concentrated in urban markets and originate trends in both fashion and beauty," says Haubegger. "Long before Chanel packaged Vamp nail polish, Latina girls in LA and New York were layering black and red nail polish to achieve that look—the return to color we've seen on the runways in the last few years reminds me of the fearlessness with which Latin women have always worn color."

It's a big mistake to assume that most Hispanics are recently arrived immigrants with weak spending power and a low appetite for fashion, point out multicultural marketers. Thirty percent of Hispanic

Source: Cotton Incorporated. Reprinted by permission.

households earn at least $50,000 annually, reports Editorial Televisa.

"Brand names are extremely important to Hispanic women, regardless of income," says Enrique Perez, international advertising director of Editorial Televisa. "Upper-income women are the same all over the world. They want the brand names connected to luxury goods—Louis Vuitton, Gucci, Armani, Calvin Klein, Ralph Lauren, Donna Karan, you name it. And then the medium and lower income women go after the more affordable brand names."

Cynthia Vincent, an LA-based designer of Latin heritage, observes that in the past five years Hispanic women have become even more educated and aware about brands, and keep a keen eye on high-end trends. "Even if they can't afford it, they follow what Versace and Gucci are doing."

The Monitor reveals that Hispanic women aged 25–34 are the ethnic group most willing to sacrifice comfort for fashion. "It's tradition to look your best," explains Fernando Quintero, senior producer at Latino.com. "It's about being respectful to your family and your community. We have so many events—church, baptisms, birthdays, weddings—and you always want to look your best." *Latina*'s Haubegger emphasizes, "Keep in mind that we communicate a great deal with our appearance. We believe that it is a reflection of not only our achievements and success, but we hope to reflect well on our families also."

In terms of advertising aimed at these fashion-savvy shoppers, Haubegger says, "Most of the time, we don't need a different message. We may just need to know that the invitation to other consumers is being directed toward us as well." How to do that? Make sure that models of color are included in the ad. "Any message can be improved and strengthened through the representation of a wide spectrum of beauty," she points out. "After all, we range in skin color from Daisy Fuentes to Salma Hayek to Celia Cruz."

One major retailer, J.C. Penney, has made a concerted effort to reach Hispanics who prefer speaking Spanish while making a purchase. Store managers can create Spanish-language in-store signage in heavily populated areas such as California, Arizona and Texas; customers can place phone orders with Spanish-speaking associates; and ads appear on Spanish-language TV and radio and in magazines. "It behooves anyone in the consumer goods and services industries to pay attention to this segment," remarks Manny Fernandez, manager of multicultural marketing at J.C. Penney.

Fernandez also points out that a considerable portion of the female Hispanic population is petite. "We know that it's very important to serve them both in the store and through our catalogue," he says. "We have extensive petite offerings and are expanding even more next year—to reach both Hispanic and Asian women."

Reaching the Aging Boomers

by Susan Reda

After keeping up with all the twists and turns of the baby boomers—from bell-bottoms to designer suits, from station wagons to minivans, from Pepsi to cafe latte and from acne medication to anti-aging creams—retailers are struggling with how to reach this huge generation as it enters the latest and perhaps most perplexing stage of its life as consumers.

While the oldest members of this 76-million-strong group are already into their 50s, there is widespread agreement that the marketing and merchandising strategies that worked with their parents as senior citizens will be ineffective or even alienating for baby boomers. But over the long term, at least, retailers that refuse to change their approach to this affluent segment in its 50s and beyond may find themselves going the way of the Me Decade.

Analysts expect the graying of the boomers to alter the retail landscape in other ways as well. Vitamin retailers and service-oriented companies seem perfectly positioned for success in the coming years, for example, while apparel and music stores will have to be alert to avoid sinking under a tide of generational disinterest.

Are baby boomers empty-nesters, finished with mortgage payments and college tuition, or new parents? Are they looking forward to retirement, or putting the finishing touches on a new business plan, perhaps for a second or even third career? Are they buying vitamins, or indulging in fine cigars? The answer is: all of the above.

"Baby boomers hovering around age 50 defy precise definition, except to say that they are healthy people who see themselves as being in the prime of life," says Myra Stark, director of knowledge management at Saatchi & Saatchi. "One thing is sure: Boomers will go kicking and screaming into old age. They are not ready to accept growing old."

The task for companies planning to mine this target market is to appeal to boomers with items suited to their age-defying lifestyle, and to find a way to market these products and services without the negative connotation of "mature" or "graying" customers. Figuring out how to reach these customers with a relevant message that will lure them to a particular store or brand remains the challenge.

Gene Wright, industry director of Andersen Consulting's Retail Place, encourages retailers to re-tool their marketing and merchandising strategies with an eye toward understanding boomers' shifting priorities and changing definition of value. He argues that the rise of different segments of retailing in recent decades has been closely tied to the changing spending patterns of baby boomers.

"When they were in their 20s and early 30s, they spent a disproportionate amount of money on clothes. As they moved through their 30s they married and set up homes, driving the home furnishings and consumer electronics businesses," explains Wright. "By the time they hit their mid-40s, attention shifted to more luxury items and financial investments. The trick is to figure out how they're going to spend it next."

Some safe bets, Wright suggests, are vitamins, travel, home improvement products, new experiences and nostalgia. "And it's fair to say that the

Source: From Stores, *March 1998, pp. 22–26. Reprinted by permission.*

biggest grossing rock tour of 1997—the Rolling Stones' 'Bridges to Babylon'—can be unequivocally linked to the nostalgia of baby boomers," says Wright.

Other analysts, by contrast, are convinced that retailers can continue for many years to reach boomers by using the same tactics that worked when that generation was young. One is Ken Gronbach, a leading generational expert and forecaster who urges businesses to reject the "graying of America" theory.

"The fact of the matter is that targeting anything designed for graying boomers will first gain importance for this market in the year 2025," he says. "And if that product even remotely conjures up an image of old age, it will be instantly rejected by the boomer."

Gronbach also uses the example of the Rolling Stones to prove his point. "Anyone who believes that the boomer is suddenly going to embrace old age at 50," he says, "also believes that Mick Jagger is going to play Big Band."

Still, while there is clearly no one-size-fits-all approach to targeting aging boomers, most industry watchers feel that modifying marketing and merchandising methods to be more in sync with the lifestyles, needs, interests, and opinions of this group is a giant step in the right direction.

"It all boils down to giving them something to buy," says David Wolfe, creative director of the Doneger Group. "Designers need to create clothes that are kinder to bodies that are no longer 16 years old. This is a shopper with lots of disposable income and she has demonstrated over and over again that if you give her something appropriate to buy, she'll buy it."

Roger Blackwell, professor of marketing at Ohio State University, asserts that apparel retailers targeting baby boomers must come to grips with the distinction between fashion and style.

"Fashion is a risk reducer," he points out. "Consumers—especially young ones—rely on fashion to reduce the risk of dressing wrong. By the time a person is 45 or older, though, they've developed a sense of style. They know what looks good on them and they make purchases that coordinate well with what's already in their closets. They tend to be brand loyal and they buy brands to reduce time."

One apparel retailer that has managed to span generational boundaries is the Gap, which offers a classic American style that has struck a chord with consumers of all ages.

Commit to SINS, Win Lifelong Customers

by Anne Cashill and Rachel Matteson

The influx of designer advertisements in consumer fashion books and the re-emergence of the infamous interlocking C's, alligator logos and more all indicate one thing for the consumer-savvy merchandise buyer: the return to a status level the industry hasn't seen since the '80s. Many status icons of the decade of conspicuous consumption, such as Gucci, Chanel, Louis Vuitton and Fendi, are making marketing comebacks with the anticipation of big sales increases.

The question is: Who might be spurring this on? We say it's the SINSs—as in "Single Income, No Spouse": This group is comprised of the late baby boomers and early generation X'ers, ages roughly 25 to 44. Over the past 30 years, the number of people in this age group living alone has more than doubled, and the number of persons who have never been married has risen to 28 percent of the total population. This figure increases to 35 percent of the people in the age group of 25 to 34. The individuals in this group also are part of the growing number of people in the new "child-free movement," as it was labeled in a recent article in the *New York Times*. The article cites an organization called No Kidding!, which had two chapters five years ago and now has 47.

In the new millennium, there has been a redefining of the traditional family. Not only are there same-sex parents, single parents and grandparents raising children, there are also childless families and SINSs. For the SINSs, their new families become the tight groups of friends they hang out with or co-workers at the office. Popular television shows like "Friends," "Sex and the City," "Will & Grace" and "Ally McBeal" all reflect the SINS lifestyle. Because the focus for this group isn't on saving money for children's education, they find themselves with more money to spend on self-indulgences like designer fashion, status cars, adventure travel, and spa/beauty products and services.

A product of the '80s, this group grew up with influences from television shows like "Dallas" and "Dynasty." They are highly educated and have been motivated to work and earn money. Their careers are demanding and may be the reason they are SINSs. It also may be that a majority of SINSs came from the one in two marriages that ended in divorce while they were growing up, which has affected their attitude toward traditional families. A third factor may be the view SINSs have of friends or family who have traditional homes, yet appear to be unhappy and dissatisfied. Whatever their motivations, this is a group of consumers to watch.

With the attention being given to brand-building and positioning in the past several years, it would seem logical that this group of high-income, high spenders would return to the status brands they have known and trusted. "Super brands will grow in status as we rely on chosen favorites to do the thinking and designing for us," wrote Alan Mitchell in an article in *ViewPoint* titled "Contradictory Consumer." Because they are a busy group, time is valuable, and making purchases that don't last is a waste of that limited resource. If this consumer was pleased with those brands when they were purchased in the '80s, then they more than likely will be pleased again.

Source: Apparel Industry Magazine *61, (9), September 2000, pp. 74–76. Copyright Bill Communications, Inc.*

Only now, it won't break the bank to purchase one alligator-enhanced shirt; they are able to afford to buy more of what any of those brands have to offer.

Also affected by this new family are the restaurant, travel and pet industries. SINSs look at friends and co-workers as family, and the time spent with family is often out for dinner or drinks at the newest places. According to the U.S. Census Bureau, sales in the "Eating/Drinking Out" category have increased $2 billion in the past year to become a $25 billion-plus industry.

Travel is also a key place for SINS to spend money: Magazines such as *Travel and Leisure* cater to this part of the SINS life. Since this group is childless, pets—particularly dogs—become a focus of attention and spending. Witness all the increases in pet-supply aisles at discount stores and grocery stores and the increase in pets-only stores, such as Petfood Warehouse and Pets.com online.

The SINS are also searching for personal fulfillment and meaning. They seek out yoga classes, Pilates workouts, meditation and "life coaches." Life coaches are experts who combine career counseling, psychotherapy, sex therapy and personal counseling all into one, helping people understand their priorities, achieve balance and reach goals.

With the increase in status levels and sales of designer brands, the impact on this segment of the apparel market is pretty obvious. However, it is harder to predict or advise on the impact to non-branded, non-status apparel. As Mitchell wrote in "Contradictory Consumer," ". . . retailers should focus on these things, . . . not competing on price . . . but by developing the loyalty and enjoyment factor with their customers." If SINSs are purchasing status brands because of trust and ease, creating enjoyment for a purchase of a non-status brand could be very profitable. This group is busy, but also searching. If a retailer can make purchasing entertaining and simple, and a source of fulfillment in a SINS life, they will gain the loyalty of that consumer for the future.

Chapter Review

Key Words and Concepts

Define, identify, or briefly explain the following:

Baby boomers	Generation Z	Merchandising
Chargebacks	Market	Offshore production
Consumer orientation	Market segmentation	Point-of-sale (POS) data
Consumer-ready	Marketing	Production orientation
Cross-shopper	Marketing concept	Psychographics
Data mining	Marketing environment	Pull system
Demographic	Marketing macroenvironment	Push system
Five Rs	Marketing microenvironment	Robinson-Patman Act
Focus groups	Marketing mix	Sales
FTC	Marketing orientation	Stockouts
Floor-ready	Marketing process	Style testing
Generation X	Marketing segmentation	Sherman Anti-Trust Act
Generation Y	Marketing strategy	Target market

Review Questions on Chapter Highlights

1. Why is it important for a company to place serious emphasis on serving the consumer well?
2. What role have textile and apparel imports played in causing the U.S. fashion industry to think more about satisfying the customer?
3. How is the consumer of today different from the 1980s consumer? What implications does this difference have for the fashion industry?
4. How does the consumer play a powerful role in affecting the whole fashion pipeline? Give an example of how this role can affect a textile firm, an apparel manufacturer, and a retailer.
5. What does it mean to "organize the industry around the consumer"?
6. What does it mean to say that a company's whole organizational structure could be restructured around giving customers what they want?
7. Contrast what is meant by a "marketing orientation" and a "production orientation."
8. Distinguish between marketing, merchandising, and sales.
9. What is the marketing concept? Why is this concept important for the fashion industry?
10. Give examples of consumers who might be identified by a fashion firm's market segmentation efforts.
11. What are the elements of the marketing mix? Think of a fictitious product and define how you would identify elements of the marketing mix for your product.
12. Contrast the marketing microenvironment with the macroenvironment. Give examples of each.
13. List examples of current social and economic factors that affect the consumption of fashion.
14. What are some of the demographic factors that affect the business of fashion? Why?
15. Why have marketers in all industries followed the baby boom generation?

16. How is either the growing teen population or the increased number of senior citizens likely to affect the fashion industry?
17. Give an example of marketing fashion products to minority markets.
18. How do marketers follow consumer preferences and buying trends?
19. Contrast the push system with the pull system used in industry.
20. How is the fashion industry likely to serve its customers in the year 2010 and beyond?
21. Why does federal legislation exist that may affect the fashion industry?

References

Adler, J. (1995, July 31). The rise of the overclass. *Newsweek*, 32–45.

Agins, T. (1999). *The end of fashion*. New York: William Morrow and Company.

American Apparel Manufacturers Association (AAMA). (1982). *Fashion apparel manufacturing: Coping with style variation*. Arlington, VA: Author.

Bird, L. (1995, March 8). Department stores target top customers. *Wall Street Journal*, pp. B1, B4.

Black, P. (1998, June). Firms capitalizing on "Echo-Boomers" come out ahead. *Bobbin*, 54.

Brookman, F. (1998, June). Aging boomers, booming sales. *Women's Wear Daily*, p. 8.

Cotton Incorporated. (1998, August 20). The big picture: What the barometers are telling us, Lifestyle Monitor, *Women's Wear Daily*, p. 2.

Dickerson, K. (1991). *Textiles and apparel in the international economy*. Upper Saddle River, NJ: Merrill/Prentice Hall.

Dickerson, K., Hooper, C., & Boyle, R. (1995, April). A new approach for manufacturers. *America's Textiles International (ATI)*, 28–32.

Hill, S. (1998, August). "I see a tall, dark man in Wal-Mart, looking for wide-leg jeans . . ." *Apparel Industry Magazine*, 78–81.

Jayaraman, S. (1998, October). Logistics: The invisible driver. *America's Textiles International (ATI)*, 67–70.

Kotler, P., & Armstrong, G. (1994). *Principles of marketing* (6th ed). Upper Saddle River, NJ: Merrill/Prentice Hall.

Kunz, G. (1998). *Merchandising: Theory, principles, and practice*. New York: Fairchild.

Kurt Salmon Associates (KSA). (1995). *Vision for the new millennium . . . evolving to consumer response*. New York: Author.

Lerner, M. (1957). *America as a civilization*. New York: Simon & Schuster.

Mallory, M., & Forest, S. (1992, March 23). Waking up to a major market. *Business Week*, 70–71.

Munk, N. (1997, December 8). Girl power. *Fortune*, 132–140.

Neuborne, E., & Kerwin, K. (1999, February 15). Generation Y. *Business Week*, 80–88.

Phillips, S., Dunkin, A., Treece, J., & Hammonds, K. (1990, March 12). King customer. *Business Week*, pp. 88–94.

Romero, E. (1997, October 8). Dressing things that go "Echo Boom," *DNR*, 10, 11.

Silverman, D. (1997, August 1). Consumer debt builds a house of cards. *DNR*, 10–18.

Silverman, D. (1998, May 11). Malls have that teen spirit again. *DNR*, 8, 9.

Underhill, P. (1999). *Why we buy: The science of shopping*. New York: Simon & Schuster.

U.S. Census Bureau. (1995, December). *How we're changing—demographic state of the nation: 1995* (Current Population Reports, Special Studies, Series P-23, No. 188). Washington, DC: U.S. Department of Commerce.

Young, V., & Seckler, V. (1998, February 4). House gets bankruptcy bill. *Women's Wear Daily*, p. 21.

Zinn, L., Power, C., Yang, D., Cuneo, A., & Ross, D. (1992, December 14). Move over boomers. *Business Week*, 74–82.

Suggested Bibliography

Agins, T. (1999). *The end of fashion*. New York: William Morrow and Company.

Anderson, W. (1992). Retailing in the year 2000: Quixotic consumers? Exotic markets? Neurotic retailers? In R. A. Peterson (Ed.), *The future of U.S. retailing: An agenda for the 21st century* (pp. 27–84). New York: Quorum Books.

Baker, S., & Baker, K. (1995). *Desktop direct marketing*. Hightstown, NJ: McGraw-Hill.

Barrett, J. (1999, October). Market research wins in the marketplace. *Textile World,* 57–61.

Boutilier, R. (1993). *Targeting families: Marketing to and through the new family.* Ithaca, NY: American Demographics.

Celente, G., & Milton, T. (1991). *Trend tracking.* New York: Warner Books.

Dunn, W. (1993). *The baby bust: A generation comes of age.* Ithaca, NY: American Demographics.

Dychtwald, K., & Gable, G. (1990). *The shifting American marketplace.* Emeryville, CA: Age Wave.

Esquivel, J. (1995, January). Theme for 1990s: Dress for survival. *America's Textiles International,* K/A 2–K/A 10.

Evans, C. (1993). *Marketing channels: Infomercials and the future of televised marketing.* Upper Saddle River, NJ: Prentice Hall.

Feather, F. (1994). *The future consumer.* Buffalo, NY: Warwick.

Gale, B. (1994). *Managing customer value.* New York: Free Press.

Guber, S., & Berry, J. (1993). *Marketing to and through kids.* New York: McGraw-Hill.

Hines, J., & O'Neal, G. (1995). Underlying determinants of clothing quality: The consumers' perspective. *Clothing and Textiles Research Journal, 13* (4), 227–233.

Hughes, A. (1991). *The complete database marketer.* Chicago: Probus.

Hughes, A. (1994). *Strategic database marketing.* Chicago: Probus.

Kantrowitz, B., & Wingert, P. (with Springen, K., Figueroa, A., & Joseph-Goteiner, N. (1999, October 18). The truth about Tweens. *Newsweek,* 62–72.

Kincaid, D. (1995). Quick Response management system for the apparel industry: Definition through technologies. *Clothing and Textiles Research Journal, 13*(4), 245–251.

Kotler, P., & Armstrong, G. (1994). *Principles of marketing* (6th ed). Upper Saddle River, NJ: Merrill/Prentice Hall.

Kunz, G. (1998). *Merchandising: Theory, principles, and practice.* New York: Fairchild.

Kurt Salmon Associates. (1995). *Vision for the new millennium . . . evolving to consumer response.* New York: Author.

Leeming, E., & Trip, C. (1994). *Segmenting the women's market: Using niche marketing to understand and meet the diverse needs.* Chicago: Probus.

Longino, C. (1995). *Retirement migration in America.* Houston, TX: Vacation Publications.

Mallory, C. (1991). *Direct mail magic.* Menlo Park, CA: Crisp Publications.

Mergenhagen, P. (1994). *Targeting transitions: Marketing to consumers during life changes.* Ithaca, NY: American Demographic.

Meyers, G. (1993). *Targeting the new professional woman: How to market and sell to today's 57 million working women.* Chicago: Probus.

Morgan, C., & Levy, D. (1993). *Segmenting the mature market.* Chicago: Probus.

Mowen, J. (1992). *Consumer behavior* (4th ed). Upper Saddle River, NJ: Merrill/Prentice Hall.

Nystrom, P. (1929). *Economics of consumption.* New York: Ronald Press.

Ostrow, R., & Smith, S. (1987). *The dictionary of marketing.* New York: Fairchild.

Perna, R. (1987). *Fashion forecasting.* New York: Fairchild.

Peterson, R. (1992). A context for retailing predictions. In R. A. Peterson (Ed.), *The future of U.S. retailing: An agenda for the 21st century* (pp. 1–25). New York: Quorum Books.

Popcorn, F. (1991). *The Popcorn report.* New York: Bantam Doubleday Dell.

Popcorn, F. (1995). *Clicking.* New York: Harper Business.

Reda, S. (1998, March). Reaching the aging boomers. *Stores,* 22–26.

Ritchie, K. (1995). *Marketing to Generation X.* Greenwich, CT: Lexington Books.

Rossman, M. (1994). *Multicultural marketing: Selling to a diverse America.* Saranac Lake, NY: AMACOM Books (American Management Association).

Smith, D. (1992, Spring). Changing U.S. demographics: Implications for professional preparation. *Journal of Home Economics,* 19–23.

Smith, T. (1995, January). Marketing in 2004. *Textile Asia,* 107–110.

Stanley, T. (1993). *Networking with the affluent and their advisors.* Burr Ridge, IL: Irwin Professional Publishing.

Templeton, J. (1994). *The focus group.* Chicago: Probus.

Underhill, P. (1999). *Why we buy: The science of shopping.* New York: Simon & Schuster.

U.S. Census Bureau. (annual). *How we're changing— Demographic state of the Nation (annual)* (Current Population Reports). Washington, DC: U.S. Department of Commerce.

Vavra, T. (1992). *After-marketing: How to keep customers for life through relationship marketing.* Burr Ridge, IL: Irwin Professional Publishing.

Weinstein, A. (1994). *Market segmentation.* Chicago: Probus.

Who are tomorrow's consumers? (1992). *Textile Horizon*, 12 (10), 3.

Trade and Consumer Associations

American Council on Consumer Interests, 240 Stanley Hall, University of Missouri–Columbia, Columbia, MO 65211.

American Marketing Association, Suite 200, 250 S. Wacker Dr., Chicago, IL 60606–5819.

Direct Marketing Association, 1120 Ave. of the Americas, New York, NY 10036–6700.

Direct Selling Association, 1776 K St., NW, Suite 600, Washington, DC 20006.

Consumer Federation of America, 1424 16th St., N.W., Suite 604, Washington, DC 20036.

Consumers Union of the U.S., Inc., 101 Truman Ave., Yonkers, NY 10703–1057.

International Organization of Consumers Unions, Emmastraat 9, 2595 EG The Hague, The Netherlands.

Trade and Consumer Publications

American Demographics, P.O. Box 2888, Boulder, CO 80322–2606.

Consumer Reports, Consumers Union of the U.S., Inc. 101 Truman Ave., Yonkers, NY 10703–1057.

Marketing Communications Magazine, 475 Park Ave. S., New York, NY 10016.

Marketing News, Suite 200, 250 S. Wacker Dr., Chicago, IL 60606–5819.

Journal of International Consumer Marketing, Haworth Press, Inc., 10 Alice St., Binghamton, NY 13904–1580.

Sales and Marketing Management, Bill Communications, Inc., 355 Park Ave. S., New York, NY 10010–1789.

CHAPTER 5

The Materials of Fashion

T*he expression of every* fashion in the form of a garment or accessory owes as much to the fabrics, furs, or leathers that are available as it does to the idea that inspires its birth. As Christian Dior once said, "Many a dress of mine is born of the fabric alone" (Dior, 1953, p. 35).

To grasp the importance of the producers of the raw materials in the business of fashion, one must recognize that many of the changes are primarily variations in colors, textures, or fabrics rather than changes in style.

This chapter is concerned with the components industry that provides the fibers, fabrics, leathers, and furs that enable designers to give substance to their ideas. The text discusses the most important segments of the components industries and indicates how each of these influences fashion and is influenced by it. The readings that follow illustrate the operations of select companies and developments in the field.

From Fiber to Fabric

The making of fabrics involves a great many processes, uses machines of many different types, and employs the skills and knowledge of a variety of producers and processors.

No matter what the end result, every textile product originates as fiber. Fibers fall into two main categories: (1) **natural fibers**, such as cotton, wool, ramie, silk, and flax, which come from plant and animal sources and have been used for thousands of years, and (2) **manufactured fibers**, previously known as "manmade" fibers, which are basically chemical products and whose development and utilization are twentieth-century phenomena. Whether fibers are natural or manufactured, however, they undergo the same basic fabrication processes in the course of their transformation into textile products: the spinning of fibers into yarns, the weaving or knitting of yarns

Figure 5–1

In today's modern textile plants, computers are used extensively to maintain quality and efficiency.

Source: Photo courtesy of Burlington Industries, Inc.

into fabric, and the finishing of fabric to impart color, texture, pattern, or other characteristics. *Weaving* is the interlacing of two sets of yarns, vertical and horizontal. *Knitting* involves machines that make fabric by interlooping of either vertical or horizontal sets of yarns.

Before being made into a fabric, fibers must first be spun into yarns. **Yarn** is produced by twisting together strands of fiber into a continuous thread or filament. This may be as coarse as rug backing or finer than sewing thread. To manufacture cloth, the yarns are knitted or woven together. Figure 5–1 shows a modern textile facility.

Some natural fiber yarns are dyed before being made into fabric. This is particularly true of wool, but sometimes manufactured fibers receive similar treatment. In the latter case, the fibers are **solution-dyed**, which means that dye is introduced into the chemical "dope" from which the fiber is made. In **yarn dying** the yarn is first spun, then put on cones, then dyed on the cone prior to the fabric production process. More commonly, however, yarns are used in their undyed state to produce **greige goods**, which is undyed, unfinished fabric that is later dyed in the piece and subjected to a variety of finishing processes. At every step of the way, from fiber production to finished product, fashion is the primary influence in determining what materials will be used, how they will be treated, and what the end product will be.

Fiber Producers

Much of the fashion industry's ability to respond promptly and accurately to changes in consumer preferences for apparel and accessories is due to the immense variety of textile products available for use. In turn, the textile industry can more readily present an impressive range of textures, colors, weights, lusters, and other characteristics because the fiber producers are also aware of and responsive to fashion's requirements. That responsiveness, this far back in the production process, was slight in the days when only natural fibers were available, but it has reached enormous proportions now that manufactured fibers have opened new doors in the industry.

The U.S. fiber industry employed almost 143,000 persons by the late 1990s. Of this number, nearly 49,000 were the manufactured fiber industry, nearly 63,000 were wool growers, and more than 31,000 were cotton growers (American Textile Manufacturers Institute [ATMI], 2000).

Suppliers of Natural Fibers

The natural fibers are cotton, wool, silk, ramie, and flax. The amounts and qualities available at any given time and place are influenced by environmental conditions, such as climate and terrain suited to the animals and plants that are their source. Suppliers of natural fibers are many, are located all over the world, and are often relatively small in size. They generally sell their products in local markets to wholesalers who, in turn, may sell them anywhere in the world. In the case of cotton and wool, commodities dealers may buy these fibers from central wholesalers throughout the world and sell them on the global market. Thus, it is possible for an American textile producer to create a shirting fabric from Egyptian cotton, or a Japanese knitter to offer a sweater of Australian lambswool. In a bid to boost wool's global profile, the Woolmark organization (Figure 5–2) has a new service to assist U.S. apparel manufacturers in finding sources internationally for wool fabrics. Woolmark will use its extensive contacts around the world to help U.S. apparel manufacturers find fabrics—either in the United States or elsewhere—of the cost and quality they need (Chirls, 1998).

Before the entrance of manufactured fibers, the suppliers of natural fibers were scarcely a part of the fashion industry. Their traditional role was only to produce and sell their raw materials. They were not concerned with the making of these raw

Figure 5–2	WOOLMARK

The Woolmark Certification Mark

PURE NEW WOOL

Source: Woolmark logo courtesy of Wool Bureau, Inc.

materials into yarns for weaving or knitting fabrics, and they had no relationship with the garment makers or ultimate consumers. They certainly were not attuned to fashion. All of this changed with the entrance of manufactured fibers into the business of fashion.

The need to compete with manufactured fibers forced the cotton and wool growers into reevaluating their marketing procedures. They were impelled to take a more aggressive role and become proactive in reaching the textile producers, the garment makers, and the ultimate consumers. In addition to improving the desirable properties of their fibers, the suppliers of wool, cotton, and other natural fibers each began efforts to compete more favorably with the manufactured fibers. For example, the wool people talk of more lightweight, more comfortable, and easier-to-care-for fabrics. Wool researchers are working on development of wool fleece, permanent creasing, and all-wool products that may be machine washed and tumble dried, as well as new blends with fibers such as spandex (Reichard, 1997).

Today, natural fiber producers, through their trade associations, act as a source of information about the fabrics processed from their respective fibers and about fashion in general. They also promote their fibers to the trade and to the general public by directing attention to the virtues of their product. Figure 5–3 shows an example of a natural fiber logo.

For example, there is an International Wool Secretariat supported by wool growers from all over the world. Their headquarters, which is located in London, is staffed with fashion specialists who advise fabric manufacturers of new developments in weaves, patterns, and colors. This association also publicizes wool in all media and by all means—films, fashion presentations to the trade and to the press, and cooperative advertising programs with makers and sellers of wool garments.

Similarly, Cotton Incorporated, previously headquartered in New York City and now in Raleigh, North Carolina, acts as an information and promotional center for cotton. They prepare and distribute advance information about fashions in cotton and cotton-blended fabrics to designers, manufacturers, the fashion press, and retail stores. They also advertise cotton fashions in consumer and trade publications. In ad-

Figure 5–3

Mohair Council Logo

Source: Courtesy of Mohair Council of America.

dition, both associations encourage producers and retailers to use their distinctive logos (a ball of yarn in the one case, a cotton boll in the other) in the advertising for fashion garments made of their particular fibers. The promotional activities of their trade associations have drastically changed the part played by natural fiber producers in the world of fashion.

Manufactured Fiber Producers (NAICS Subsector 325)

As defined by the Textile Fiber Products Identification Act, manufactured fiber is "any fiber derived by a process of manufacture from any substance which, at any point in the manufacturing process, is not a fiber." This is in contrast to the term *natural fiber*, meaning a fiber that exists as such in the natural state.

As we noted in Chapter 1, all U.S. industries are classified by a number system, the North American Industry Classification System (NAICS),[1] which replaced the Standard Industrial Classification (SIC) system that designates what each does. Manufactured fiber companies tend to be part of large chemical complexes that in some cases produce chemical components for everything from fertilizers to aspirin. Because of the nature of manufactured fiber production, this industry is part of the chemical products sector (Sector 32), rather than with other textile or apparel products.

For hundreds of years, humans have toyed with the possibility of duplicating the work of the silkworm by mechanical or chemical means. These small creatures feed on mulberry leaves and are able to produce a thick liquid, which they force out through tiny openings in their heads in the form of silk fiber. Thus, in 1855, a Swiss chemist named Audemars attempted to produce synthetic silk by using the fibrous inner bark of the mulberry tree.

It was not until 1891, however, that the French Count Hilaire de Chardonnet built the first "artificial silk" plant in France. He eventually earned the title of "father of the rayon industry" when, in 1924, artificial silk was renamed *rayon*: "ray" to suggest sheen and "on" to suggest cotton. Rayon was followed by a deluge of manufactured fiber experiments and developments in the 1920s and 1930s. A giant breakthrough came with the first public showing of nylon hosiery, introduced by DuPont, at the 1939 Golden Gate Exposition in San Francisco. Not only did nylon hosiery immediately become one of the most wanted articles of feminine apparel, but nylon itself played a significant role in World War II for such uses as parachutes and uniforms.

With the development of manufactured fibers, the importance of natural fibers declined dramatically, whereas the growth of the manufactured fiber industry was phenomenal. These figures illustrate the point: At the end of World War II, manufactured fibers accounted for only 15 percent of all fibers used in the textile mills of the United States. By 1965, the manufactured fiber industry was providing 42 percent of the nation's fiber needs, and by 2000, manufactured fibers accounted for 71.6 percent of total fiber consumption (this includes interior and industrial uses for manufactured fibers). Figure 5–4 gives a graphic comparison of these trends (Fiber Economics Bureau, U.S. Department of Commerce, ITA, D'Andrea, 2000).

---

[1]The U.S. NAICS manual, *North American Industry Classification System, United States*, 1997, was released in July 1998. For information on the manual, call 1-800-553-6847 or visit the NTIS NAICS website at: http://www.ntis.gov/naics. For more information on NAICS call the Census Bureau at 1-888-75NAICS or visit their website at http://www.census.gov/naics.

Figure 5–4

U.S. total fiber consumption in 1950, 1980, and 2000 (percentages based on weight). Figures include textiles used in interior and industrial markets, as well as apparel.

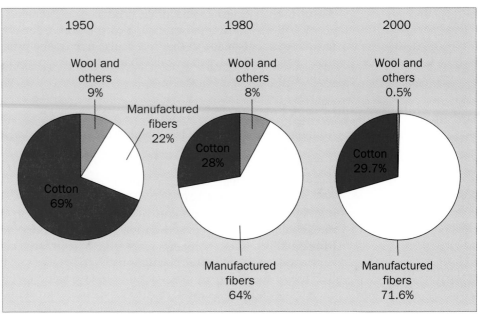

Source: Fiber Economics Bureau; 2000 data from personal contact with Paul O'Day and Frank Horn of American Fiber Manufacturers Association.

Impact of Chemical Fiber Producers

The continuing development of an unending procession of new manufactured fibers took place and continues to do so in the laboratories of giant chemical companies such as DuPont. The entrance of chemical producers into the fashion industry brought about many changes in the fashion business, along with a whole new world of textiles. Because few in the textile industry knew how to handle new synthetic fibers, the manufactured fiber producers had to teach and guide spinners, weavers, and knitters in the processing and fabrication of new fibers. They also had to create a demand among garment producers for the fabrics made with their fibers and provide them with guidance and encouragement. Finally, they had to educate and create a demand among consumers as well. In short, they not only supplied their fibers to yarn makers, but with their enormous facilities for financing and research, they assumed a dominant role in how these fibers were used in yarns, fabrics, and fashion apparel. Unlike the suppliers of natural fibers, the manufactured fiber producers made fashion their business from the start.

The entrance of giant chemical companies into the business of fashion has added new dimensions to the fashion industry. The concept of creating whatever kind of fiber is needed or wanted to develop new and different fabrications opened up a whole new world of textiles such as "stretchable," "wash and wear," "durable press," "heat-set pleats," and "wrinkle resistant," with more to come. The promotional funds provided by manufactured fiber producers to help finance the advertising of fabrics and/or garments that feature their fabrics generate more fashion advertising than would otherwise be possible. The financial resources of giant chemical companies are such that they can support continuing research and development of new concepts in technology, merchandising, and fashion, the results of which are made available to fabric and apparel producers.

Flexibility of Manufactured Fibers

Two basic types of manufactured fibers are used for apparel: cellulosic and noncellulosic. Cellulosics are produced from cellulose, the fibrous substance found in plants such as softwood trees, and are made with a minimum of chemical steps. They include rayon, triacetate, and acetate. Noncellulosic fibers are made from chemical derivatives of petroleum, coal, natural gas, air, and water. Fiber chemists link the molecules from these sources into long chains called polymers. In this category are nylon, acrylic, and polyester fabrics.

Manufactured fibers have been improving the quality of fashion goods by offering a variety of characteristics unavailable in natural fibers. Their production, moreover, is not affected by the vagaries of weather or other natural conditions. For example, in 1998 the scorching heat and drought in Texas and the El Niño downpours and cool temperatures in California stunted cotton crops in the nation's two largest cotton-producing states. Manufactured fibers, by contrast, can be produced in quantities as large or as small as anticipated demand requires, and they can be endowed with desirable characteristics not necessarily found in natural fibers. For example, triacetate can be used to produce fabrics that are washable and wrinkle resistant, or with pleats that are heat-set for permanency; it can also be used in fabrics with brushed or napped surfaces and textured effects. Acrylic fibers can be used in pile fabrics that are used in fleecewear and that simulate furs. Modacrylics, inherently flame resistant, are excellent for use in children's sleepwear, upholstery, blankets, and draperies.

An example of how a fiber can constantly be improved to meet changes in consumer demand is offered by nylon and polyester. Today, high-filament nylon is blended with stretch fibers such as spandex to create new swimwear, exercise wear, and dance clothing. DuPont's spandex fiber, Lycra, has been a bonanza for the company.[2] The massive marketing and advertising campaign has been tremendously successful, fostering a whole new look in sleek activewear. Lycra now has a strong global presence and is even being used in combination with leather in shoes (Monget, 1998). Nylon reflective yarn is used in clothes that reflect the headlights of oncoming cars when worn by nighttime joggers and bicycle riders. In the home, nylon has become the leading fiber for carpets; 99 percent of all domestic carpets are made of it.

In the early 1990s, new **microfibers**, filaments of less than one denier—two or three times thinner than a human hair—were introduced, leading to the creation of yarns and fabrics with greater softness and silklike characteristics than previous fiber filaments provided. Although DuPont developed the technology to produce microfibers in the 1960s, the Japanese first introduced these to the markets. By the early 1990s, DuPont first introduced microdenier polyester, with a number of other companies not far behind, some of which applied microdenier technology to other types of fibers besides polyester. Development of microfibers opened the door to a range of new "looks" for manufactured fibers. Because the filaments are so fine, many more are combined to form the yarns used in weaving and knitting fabrics; this gives fabrics a much more natural look than the shiny, "plastic" effect sometimes associated with manufactured fibers. Not only do the fabrics look more elegant, they also feel better. They have more breathability and better performance characteristics than previous products from manufactured fibers (Brunnschweiler & Hearle, 1993; Maycumber, 1991).

In today's quest for things that are faster, stronger, lighter, and safer, textile researchers have developed a new group of **high-performance** and **temperature-**

---

[2]DuPont is now using the term *elastane*, which is the European and international term for spandex.

resistant fibers. To understand these, we must first consider that fibers are either **commodity fibers** or high-performance fibers. *Commodity fibers* are typically those used in a highly price competitive environment, in large-scale, high-volume production; most fiber production today for apparel and interior uses fall into this category. Within the high-performance group, the *high-temperature-resistant fibers* are formally defined as a manufactured fiber with a continuous operating temperature ranging from 375 to 600 degrees F. Temperature-resistant fibers such as DuPont's Nomex and Kevlar or Akzo's Twaron are used in fire-resistant apparel for firefighters and others with similar needs for protection. The definition of *high-performance fibers* is less specific, but they are generally driven by special technical functions that require specific physical properties unique to these fibers. They usually have high levels of at least one of the following properties: tensile strength, operating temperature, limiting oxygen index, and chemical resistance. These are usually technically driven, specialty oriented and made with smaller batch-type production. Of the estimated 19 billion pounds of manufactured fibers produced globally, less than 1 percent would be in this group. Many of these fibers have to be blended with other fibers to be usable in fabrics. Still in relatively limited use, these fibers have potential for many additional areas such as the military, general aviation, the automotive industry, and a whole array of fabrics yet to be developed (Smith, 1998, pp. 53, 55).

Additionally, companies are creating specialty versions of existing fibers to create new fabrics, particularly for activewear. Examples include DuPont's specialty polyester business, which has led to creation of new fabrics such as CoolMax and ThermaStat. CoolMax is used in activewear to wick moisture away from the body, and ThermaStat is a base fabric that gives insulation value. Optimer's Dri-Release™ is a blend of a specialty polyester with a small amount of cotton to give excellent wicking ability that does not wash out.

Emphasis on Brand Names

Under the Textile Fiber Products Identification Act, the Federal Trade Commission establishes generic names for synthetic fibers. A **generic name** is one that designates a general group of fibers with similar chemical composition and properties. Of the more than 20 generic names established, however, relatively few are used for apparel fabrics. Polyester, nylon, and rayon, in that order, are the most widely used for clothing; other fibers used include acrylic, acetate, modacrylic, and triacetate. Within any of the basic broad categories, fiber producers can modify the basic chemical and physical composition to produce a new fiber. Although the same generic names may apply to the newer creations, these *variants*, as they are called, are usually identified by a **brand name** given them by the manufacturer (Table 5–1).

From the first, the producers of manufactured fibers have been very aggressive in promoting their brand names. A *brand* is a device, sign, trademark, or name that is used to identify and distinguish products as a means of building a market for them. Each company uses its brands to build recognition and acceptance of its product, to differentiate it from other similar products in the customer's mind, and to lessen price competition. To accomplish these ends, producers of manufactured fibers advertise their brands in trade and consumer magazines and in other public media either under their own names or in conjunction with fabric firms or makers of finished products. Anything from a multipage advertisement in a trade paper to an elaborate fashion presentation on TV may be used. In addition, their cooperative advertising money pays for much of the trade and consumer advertising of the textiles and apparel in which their branded fibers are used and identified. They also arrange or participate in

Table 5–1	**Manufactured Fiber Groups and Examples of Trade Names**

Fiber Type	Trade Names	Fiber Type	Trade Names
ACETATE	1. Celanese 2. Chromspun 3. Estron 4. MicroSafe	NYLON 6 *(cont.)*	13. Anso Soft 14. Anso Solution 15. Anso Total Comfort 16. Anso Vibrance 17. Caprolan
ACRYLIC	1. Acrilan 2. BioFresh 3. Bounce-Back 4. CFF Fibrillated Fiber 5. Conductrol 6. Creslan 7. Cresloft 8. Duraspun 9. Evolutia 10. Ginny 11. MicroSupreme 12. Pil-Trol 13. So-Lara 14. The Smart Yarns 15. Wear-Dated 16. WeatherBloc		18. Dry Step 19. Eclipse 20. Hardline 21. Hydrofil 22. Matinesse 23. Micro Touch 24. Nylon 6ix 25. Powersilk 26. Shimmereen 27. Silky Touch 28. Softglo 29. Sportouch 30. Stay Gard 31. Tru-Ballistic 32. Ultra Touch 33. Zefsport 34. Zeftron 200 35. Zeftron 2000 36. Zeftron 2000ZX
ARAMID	1. Kevlar 2. Nomex		
BICOMPONENT	1. AXXEL 2. Resistat	NYLON 6.6	1. Antron 2. Antron Advantage
FLUORO	1. Teflon		3. Antron II 4. Antron Legacy
LYOCELL	1. Fibro 2. Galaxy 3. Lyocell by Lenzing		5. Antron Lumena 6. Assurance 7. Avantige 8. Cantrece
MELAMINE	1. Basofil		9. Comforlast
MODACRYLIC	1. SEF Plus		10. Cordura 11. Durasoft
MODAL	1. Micro-ProModal 2. MicroModal 3. Modal by Lenzing 4. Modal Sun 5. ProModal		12. Duratrek 13. DyeNAMIX 14. Enka Nylon 15. Hytel 16. Meryl 17. Meryl Nexten
NYLON 6	1. Anso 2. Anso AllSport 3. Anso Caress 4. Anso Choice! 5. Anso Color Solutions 6. Anso CrushResister III 7. Anso CrushResister III ACT 8. Anso CrushResister III Select 9. Anso CrushResister TLC 10. Anso HTX 11. Anso Premium 12. Anso Replacement Plus		18. Meryl Satiné 19. Meryl Souple 20. MerylMicrofibre 21. Micro Supplex 22. Natrelle BCF 23. No Shock 24. OPTA 25. Stainmaster 26. Stainmaster Luxra 27. Stainmaster XTRA Life

Continued

Table 5–1	**Manufactured Fiber Groups and Examples of Trade Names *(continued)***

Fiber Type	Trade Names	Fiber Type	Trade Names
NYLON 6.6 *(cont.)*	28. Supplex 29. Tactel 30. Tactel Aquator 31. Tactel Ispira 32. Tactel Micro 33. Tactel Strata 34. Traffic Control Fiber System 35. Ultramirage 36. Ultron 37. Ultron 3D 38. Ultron VIP 39. Wear-Dated 40. Wear-Dated Assurance 41. Wear-Dated Freedom 42. Wear-Dated II	POLYESTER *(cont.)*	13. Easy Dye Fibers 14. ESP 15. Fiberbrite 2000 16. Fillwell 17. Fillwell II 18. Fillwell Plus 19. Fortrel 20. Fortrel BactiShield 21. Fortrel EcoSpun 22. Fortrel EcoSpun2 23. Fortrel MicroSpun 24. Fortrel Plus 25. Fortrel Spunnaire 26. Fortrel Spunnese 27. Hollofil 28. Loftguard 29. Loftguard Xtra 30. Microloft 31. MicroMattique 32. Microselect 33. Microtherm 34. Nature Tex 35. Polyguard 3D 36. Polyguard Classic 37. Polarguard Home 38. Polyguard HV 39. Quallofil 40. Qualloform 41. Sensura 42. Serelle 43. Serene 44. Securus 45. Stay Gard 46. Substraight 47. Tairilin 48. Thermastat 49. Thermax 50. Thermolite 51. Thermoloft 52. Wellene
NYLON 6 or 6.6	1. Wellon 2. Wellstrand		
OLEFIN	1. Alpha BCF 2. Essera 3. Impressa 4. Innova 5. Marqesa Lana 6. Permafresh 7. Spectra 1000 8. Spectra 900 9. Spectra Fusion 10. Spectra Guard 11. Spectra Shield 12. Spectra Shield Plus 13. SpectraFlex 14. Telar 15. Trace 16. Trace FR		
PBI	1. PBI Logo		
PELCO	1. Securus		
PEN	1. Pentex		
POLYESTER	1. A.C.E. Polyester 2. Avora FR 3. Celbond 4. Colorfine 5. Comforel 6. ComFotrel 7. CoolMax 8. CoolMax Alta 9. Corebond 10. Dacron 11. Diolen 12. DSP	RAYON	1. Fibro 2. Galaxy 3. Viscose by Lenzing 4. Viscose FR by Lenzing
		SPANDEX	1. Cleerspan 2. DC-100 3. DC-700 4. Dorlastan 5. Lycra 6. Glospan

Source: Fiber Economics Bureau.

fashion presentations staged by textile firms that identify their fibers, and they distribute free educational booklets to both retail employees and consumers to acquaint people with the properties and names of their fibers. Some branded fibers are sold under a licensing arrangement that restricts the use of the brand name to products that comply with standards set by the fiber producer. An example of such a brand is Fortrel. At the other extreme are fibers that are sold as unbranded products, with no specified or implied performance standards or restrictions on their end use.

Restructuring in the Manufactured Fiber Industry

As in other segments of the softgoods industry, a great deal of restructuring has occurred in the manufactured fiber sector. For example, one of the largest polyester producers in the world that makes Trevira was originally Celanese. This was bought by the German conglomerate Hoechst and known for a time as Hoechst-Celanese. For a while this business was called Trevira Fibers, was later Hoechst Fibers, and was finally sold to other international firms. Hoechst didn't want to be in the fiber business, largely because of low-cost Asian competition. Once the U.S.'s largest acrylic producer, Monsanto spun off both its acrylic and nylon business to form a separate company, Solutia. Some experts believe these recreated, spin-off fiber companies will result in a more stable fiber industry than when these were part of larger chemical complexes (Maycumber, 1998).

Textile Component Producers (NAICS 313, most relevant to the fashion industry, and 314)

The textile components sector, commonly known as the **textile mill products** industry, is a broad term that describes fabrics and yarns made from fiber by any of a number of different methods. First, fibers are made into yarns. Then, thousands of yards and millions of pounds are produced annually in the United States, in infinite variety: fabrics include wovens and knits, polka dots and stripes, reds and blues, chiffons and seersuckers, and on and on, in every kind and color and texture fashion can demand. In providing the materials with which to express the designers' ideas, textiles are the very essence of fashion. Without denim, for instance, the fashion for jeans could not have come into being. Nor could there be sweat suits and jogging outfits if the appropriate sweatshirt materials were not available.

All textile component and textile mill products fall into NAICS 313 and 314 grouping. For the NAICS system, Sector 31 is manufacturing, and the additional digits after the first two for the group designate the specific segments of the industry. Subsector 313 includes the textile mills more relevant for the fashion industry, whereas 314 is primarily interior and industrial products. Vertical knitters, which are generally considered "textile" companies, are classified under NAICS 315, the apparel category (see Table 5–2).

All government data-collection agencies use the NAICS system to report industry data; this officially began with the 1997 Census of Manufacturers. The NAICS categories are very useful in studying the performance of any segment of the textile industry. For example, we might look at government data and determine the sales, number of employees, and so on for any specific part of the industry, using these numbers. If we were employed in a specific segment of the industry, we could see what

Table 5–2	NAICS Codes for Textiles Used in Apparel
31	**Manufacturing**
313	**Textile Mills**
3131	Fiber, Yarn, and Thread Mills
31311	Fiber, Yarn, and Thread Mills
313111	Yarn Spinning Mills
313112	Yarn Texturing, Throwing, and Twisting Mills
313113	Thread Mills
3132	Fabric Mills
31321	Broadwoven Fabric Mills
31322	Narrow Fabric Mills and Schiffli Machine Embroidery
313221	Narrow Fabric Mills
313222	Schiffli Machine Embroidery
31323	Nonwoven Fabric Mills
31324	Knit Fabric Mills
313241	Weft Knit Fabric Mills
313249	Other Knit Fabric and Lace Mills
3133	Textile and Fabric Finishing and Fabric Coating Mills
31331	Textile and Fabric Finishing Mills
313311	Broadwoven Fabric Finishing Mills
313312	Textile and Fabric Finishing (except Broadwoven Fabric) Mills
31332	Fabric Coating Mills
Manufactured Fibers	
325221	Cellulosic Organic Fiber Manufacturing
325222	Noncellulosic Organic Fiber Manufacturing

Source: Federal Register. (1996, November 5). Office of Management and Budget. Economic Classification Policy Committee; Standard Industrial Classification Replacement: The North American Industry Classification System. Proposed Industry Classification Structure. Part II.

portion of the total our company represents. We could also compare the production of any subsector with its counterparts in Canada or Mexico. For example, if one's company produced men's and boy's underwear, it would be possible to see how much is produced in the United States, Canada, and Mexico. If a growing portion is being produced in Mexico, that would tell a company that it is a good place to source or it might identify competitors.

Economic Importance

The basic function of the textile mill products segment of the fashion industry is the transformation of fibers—natural or manufactured—into yarns and then into finished fabrics. At one end of the industry spectrum are thousands of manufacturing plants that perform one or more of the three major processes involved in the production of fabrics: spinning fibers into yarns, weaving or knitting yarn into fabric, and finishing fabric to provide color, pattern, and other desirable attributes. At the other end of the spectrum are the sales offices that market the finished cloth to apparel and accessories producers, fabric retailers, and the home furnishings industry.

The textile industry plays a vital role in the economy of the United States. It encompasses companies operating more than 5,800 plants and employs about 558,000 people. Its output was valued at the manufacturing level at nearly $83 billion in 1997 (ATMI, 2000, based on latest data from U.S. Census Bureau, Census of Manufacturers).

Although the bulk of the manufacturing facilities are on the East Coast, some phase of textile activity is carried on in nearly every state of the union, with the largest concentration in the Southeast. Marketing, styling, and design activities are centered in New York City as the number one location, with Los Angeles second, but selling activities reach into many other major cities.

The textile industry consumes fibers and dyes, machinery and power, services and labor to produce cloth that finds its way into a myriad of end uses—fashion apparel and accessories, to be sure, but also such diverse products as inflatable buildings, tire cord, space suits, sheets, carpets, heart valves, and diapers. Clothing and accessories take up more than one-third of the industry's output, with products for the home ranking second and increasing rapidly. Some textile companies are well known for producing specific fabrics, such as Guilford Mills' lingerie and swimsuit fabrics (Figure 5–5).

Figure 5–5

Many textile companies specialize in specific types of products. In this case, Guilford Mills is well known for its lingerie and swimsuit fabrics.

Source: Courtesy of Guilford Mills.

History and Growth

Although the U.S. textile industry today is one of the largest in the world, textile production by factory methods had its beginnings in England. During the eighteenth century, while the United States was establishing its own identity and struggling for its independence, a series of inventions, each a closely guarded trade secret, mechanized the spinning of yarn and the weaving of cloth in England and moved production from the home to the factory in that country. The American colonies were, as England intended, a dependent market for one of the mother country's major products.

Colonial America imported most of its fashion materials: silks from Italy, China, and France; woolens, calico, and cashmere from England; and feathers and artificial flowers from France. Prosperous settlers took full advantage of such imports; those who were less prosperous produced their own crude materials with which to clothe themselves. The men raised and sheared sheep, grew flax, tanned leathers, made shoes, and cured furs. Women did the spinning, weaving, dyeing, cutting, and sewing of the family garments.

Eighteenth Century: From Hand to Machines

The transition from handcraft to factory production of textiles had its start in the United States when the first cotton **spinning mill** was built in 1790 at Pawtucket, Rhode Island, by **Samuel Slater** (Lewton, 1926). Slater was a young Englishman who had worked in one of England's leading mills and memorized the machinery his country refused to export. Declaring himself a farmer, rather than a mechanic, he was allowed to emigrate to the United States, carrying his knowledge in his head to build the spinning equipment and a mill. In 1793, Slater expanded his plant to house all the processes of yarn manufacture under one roof. That same year, Eli Whitney introduced his cotton gin, a machine that pulled fibers free of seeds and helped to make a bountiful supply of cotton available to Slater and other early American textile producers.

Slater's spinning mill, now a textile museum, not only was the first successful spinning or yarn-making plant in this country but was also considered to have started the **Industrial Revolution** in America. His contribution to the industrialization of this country was recognized by President Andrew Jackson, who called him the "Father of American Manufacture" (American Textile Manufacturers Institute, *Textiles—An industry, a science, an art*, date unknown).

Rapid Growth in the Nineteenth Century

The nineteenth century saw a period of great development in textile manufacturing activity. The country was growing rapidly, and the continuing improvement of textile machinery and factory methods made it increasingly economical to produce textiles outside the home. Fundamental to this development was the introduction and perfection in 1814 of the power loom by **Francis Cabot Lowell**, a Boston merchant, importer, and amateur scientist, who visited England and memorized the system in factories there. Lowell's factory in Massachusetts was the first in America to handle all operations from raw cotton to finished cloth under one roof. Before Lowell, spinning mills contracted out the weaving of yarn into cloth to individuals or small groups of workers. Spinning was thus a factory industry and weaving a cottage industry before Lowell. The nineteenth century also saw the rise of a domestic wool industry as a result of the introduction of Merino sheep into America early in that century. By 1847, more Americans worked in textiles than in any other industry (American Textile Manufacturers Institute, *All about textiles*, 1996). Textiles was clearly the leading industry prior to the Civil War, with nearly all the industry centered on cotton (Poulson, 1981).

Additional impetus was given to the industry by the Civil War, which made great demands on American mills for fabrics for soldiers' uniforms, over and above the country's normal requirements. By the end of the war, the textile industry was firmly established, and mass production of fabrics, although not yet of top-quality goods, was well on its way. As late as 1858, England and France were still our sources for better-grade textiles, notably fine broadcloth, and the New York Chamber of Commerce reported "that American wool, when used alone, cannot produce cloth of equal quality and finish as that made of foreign wools" (Heaton, 1929, p. 147).

By the end of the nineteenth century, however, woolens became available in a great variety of patterns and in great quantities, and cotton fabrics were even more abundant and variegated. In the relatively small silk industry, in which imports dominated the market as late as the 1860s, domestic production provided the overwhelming share by the turn of the century (Alderfer & Michl, 1957).

The Evolution of an Industry

Spurred on by the booming postwar economy in the late 1940s and an increasingly affluent consumer market, leading firms in the industry began to expand by means of mergers and acquisitions and to "go public" by offering shares in their companies on the stock exchanges. For some companies, the objective was diversification, such as by acquiring carpet and hosiery mills in addition to those that produced garment fabrics. Burlington Industries, for example, originally specialized in weaving rayon fabrics. In 1939, it moved into hosiery production. During World War II it made nylon parachute cloth. After the war, it continued to expand, acquire new plants, buy up other companies, and diversify. Later, another company tried to take over Burlington, which had become the world's largest textile firm. To fend off the hostile offer, the company resorted to a leveraged buyout to go private. The company had to sell off major divisions to pay for these moves. For several years, Burlington's future was shaky and uncertain. In recent years, however, the company has recovered and has once again become a publicly held firm. At present, as one of the largest textile producers, it produces many different types of fabric and is a vertically integrated operation.

The drive toward integration and diversification that began in the 1940s continued in the 1950s and 1960s. Between 1955 and 1966, when acquisitions were perhaps at their height, the Federal Trade Commission reported that about 365 textile companies were acquired by other companies (U.S. Department of Labor, no date). In the 1970s, the Federal Trade Commission moved against excessive mergers and acquisitions, in this and many other industries, to avoid the lessening of competition that could result.

From the mid-1980s on, there was a total restructuring of the American textile industry. Many public companies went private either through leveraged buyouts, or as a result of acquisitions by other textile companies or major investment companies. Of the top 15 U.S. textile companies that were publicly held in 1981, only a handful among them (Springs Industries, Guilford Mills, Burlington Industries, Westpoint Pepperell, and Fieldcrest Cannon) remain recognizable as descendants of the original firms.

Acquisitions, Mergers, and Consolidation

Merger mania in the textile industry has been encouraged in part by the flood of imports of fabrics and also by a desire on the part of many companies to increase market share and gain access to capital. For example, small companies may be unable to borrow the additional capital needed to modernize. Companies often acquire or merge to gain complementary product lines. Some are purchasing companies to vertically integrate, such as an apparel firm buying a textile business so it can produce its own fabrics. Some companies are selling off noncore divisions—that is, shedding divisions or plants that produce something the company no longer sees as part of its future success. The consolidations and other restructuring have resulted in an industry that is better equipped to meet competitive challenges.

In the late 1990s, a flurry of mergers and acquisitions took place, many among very large companies. For example, Polymer Group, Inc. acquired Dominion Textile, a major apparel fabrics firm, for $698 million. Not too many years ago, Dominion had purchased Swift Textiles. Avondale acquired Graniteville for $225 million. Bibb Company announced its intentions to get out of the apparel business in order to focus on its profitable home textiles division. Tultex bought a Champion Finishing Company plant. Stonecutter Mills bought Doran Textiles' organic cotton division, and the list goes on (Chirls, 1997; Morrissett & Dawson, 1998; Morrissett & Smyth, 1997).

U.S. textile firms are increasingly investing in foreign manufacturing facilities. Companies based in other countries may also own facilities or portions of a U.S. company. Polysindo, an Indonesian-based textile group that has been aggressive in making investments in U.S. textile companies, owns a 23 percent stake in Dyersburg and an 11 percent stake in Texfi.

Sara Lee, one of the largest firms in the industry today, was never thought of as a player in the textile industry little more than a decade ago. Through acquisitions of the Hanes Group, Pannill Knitting, Champion, and a number of other companies, Sara Lee—through its Knit Products Division—became a major force in the industry. Then in 1997, Sara Lee suddenly announced that the company was getting out of the manufacturing business for its apparel lines and becoming a marketing firm. Consequently, many other companies have purchased production facilities previously owned by Sara Lee's various divisions.

Consolidations have changed the nature of the textile industry from a manufacturing-driven industry into a more marketing-driven sector, with huge market shares now in the hands of fewer and stronger players. For example, four firms dominate the denim market (Cone Mills, Avondale, Burlington, and Thomaston). Only two independent texturizers (providing texturized yarns to weaving and knitting operations), Unifi and Madison, dominate this segment of the industry, compared to 200 to 250 independent texturizers in the early 1980s. Although concentration and specialization have helped many firms stay competitive, this strategy is no guarantee for success, however, as shown by the bankruptcy of Crompton and Co., the largest corduroy and velvet/velveteen fabric producer in the United States (Finnie, 1992).

Most textile companies have seen the marketing advantages of specializing in either home furnishings and domestics or apparel textiles and of becoming a more important presence in one or the other. Milliken and Dan River remain the major holdouts that continue to market in both areas.

The 1970s, 1980s, and early 2000s were difficult indeed for the textile industry. Some companies went out of business; some drastically restructured; and some new ones even emerged. As a result of these changes, the textile industry remains an important manufacturing sector whose productivity or other measures of performance often surpass those of manufacturing in general. Most companies have been transformed to meet changing markets, and those efforts have paid off. The largest U.S.-based textile firms are identified in Table 5–3.

Table 5–3	Major U.S.-based Textile Firms[a] (by sales)
Company	**1999 Sales[b] ($ in millions)**
Shaw Industries	4,108
Milliken & Company	3,200[c]
Springs Industries	2,200
Westpoint Stevens	1,883
Burlington Industries	1,651
Unifi	1,251
Galey & Lord	953
Wellman	935
Guilford Mills	857
Dan River	629
Cone Mills	616
Dixie Yarns	580
Delta Woodside	314
Johnston Industries	264
Texfi	187[c]
Thomaston Mills	168

[a]Some of the textile components produced by these firms also go into interior furnishings products. For example, Springs Industries focuses primarily on the home textile market.
[b]Except as noted below.
[c]1998.
Source: From "Company Profile Display," *Business & Company Resource Center* (online), part of the Gale Group, March 2001, and company websites, March 2001. Reprinted by permission of the Gale Group.

Geographic Location

Throughout the nineteenth century, the industry was located principally in New England, where it began. Cotton, however, was grown in the warm southern states, and the transportation northward to the mills was slow, inconvenient, and costly. Industry leaders began to turn their eyes southward, but although there were small textile mills in virtually every southern state in the early nineteenth century, they were not especially welcome. Plantation owners found industrialization repugnant, perhaps seeing it as a threat to their way of life and as competition for slave labor.

After the Civil War, however, southern leaders recognized the need for industrialization and offered textile companies special inducements, such as low taxes and utility rates, if they would build plants in the South. The movement of cotton manufacturing plants gained momentum after World War I, and by 1920, more than half the spinning and weaving capacity of cotton textile manufacturing was found in the South (Adams, 1957). Woolen and worsted plants, attracted by an improved spinning system developed in the South for woolen manufacture, followed suit shortly after World War II. Today, the three southern states of North and South Carolina and Georgia are the largest employers of the textile industry's labor force.

Along with the growth of the industry came changes in the sale and distribution of its output. Merchants who had originally started as importers of European fabrics gradually became selling agents for the domestic mills or bought their goods outright for resale. The expansion of domestic output after the Civil War stimulated the establishment of a textile center in downtown Manhattan, on and near Worth Street, that became the heart of the textile trade. The name *Worth Street* became synonymous with the body of textile merchants on whom American mills depended for their orders and often for the financing. After World War II, however, when fashion's impact hit the industry, the textile showrooms began moving uptown, where they are still located, right on the doorstep of the women's apparel industry.

Today, the textile mills are largely situated along a broad arc reaching from New England through the Southeast, but their designing, styling, and sales activities are heavily concentrated in New York City.

Different Types of Textile Producers

In its early history, the U.S. textile industry was highly fragmented. Different companies specialized in different stages of production, each of which required different machines, processes, and skills. Spinning mills bought fibers, which they spun into yarn. Fabric mills purchased such yarns and performed the weaving or knitting into cloth. Much of what the fabric mills produced was greige goods, or unfinished cloth. At this point, finishing plants took over, doing the dyeing, printing, or whatever other treatments were required. In the case of yarn-dyed fabrics, commonly woolen cloth, the fabric usually required less finishing than piece-dyed fabrics.

Today, more and more fabric producers seem to be utilizing a wider range of fibers or combinations of fibers, and more companies are producing more-diversified product lines.

Vertically Integrated Firms

During and immediately after World War II, problems of scarcity and price made the prewar production and marketing procedures of fragmented operations infeasible. The industry began to become more integrated. In some cases, fabric mills ceased to rely on spinning mills, selling agents, and finishing plants and acquired or set up their own operations. Burlington Industries was one such company. In other cases, independent selling agents such as J. P. Stevens acquired textile mills and finishing plants. In still others, converting firms such as Cohn Hall Marx bought mills to be sure of having fabrics to sell.

Today the textile industry includes companies that engage in all processes of production and distribution—spinning, weaving, knitting, finishing, and selling. This all-encompassing operation is called **vertical integration**, and it enables a company to control its goods through as many processes as are potentially profitable. Russell Corporation and Fruit of the Loom were two well-known firms that have had high levels of vertical integration. Even in these integrated firms, however, operations were specialized in their different plants, each of which performed a single function in the production of fabric, and different products were distributed by their different specialized marketing divisions. However, both these companies have initiated major restructuring efforts that have sold or closed U.S. plants to shift production to lower-cost countries.

Specialized Firms

There are still, however, many more companies that specialize in a single phase of production. Some are large firms that employ hundreds of workers, such as spinners like Dixie Yarns and Wintuk Yarns; weavers such as Dan River; giant converting companies such as Concord Fabrics; and printers such as Cranston. There are also many small firms, some of which limit themselves to narrow product lines, such as velvets and velveteens, or to such dressy fabrics as chiffons, taffetas, and silk failles. Other firms deal only in knits, brocades, metallics, or novelty fabrics. Their limited specialization seems to make some of the firms less attractive acquisition targets for very large firms.

Converters

Converting is a specialized textile operation whose function it is to style greige goods and arrange to have them finished. The unfinished goods are contracted out to finishing plants for processing as ordered by the **converter** (i.e., dyeing, printing, waterproofing, etc.). The finished goods are then sold by the converter to apparel and home furnishings manufacturers or to fabric retailers. The converter may be either a division of a vertically integrated textile company or an independent company that owns neither fabric mills nor finishing plants but serves as a middleman between these two stages of production. In that capacity, the converter specifies all aspects of the finished fabric, such as design, color, and other treatments considered necessary to make the goods salable to apparel producers or fabric retailers. Independent converters are usually relatively small operators, but there are big names among them, such as Concord, Loomskill, Erlanger Blumgart, and Pressman-Gutman.

There are three basic types of converting organizations, each of which performs essentially the same functions. One is the *independently owned converting company*, which has contractual relationships with the mills from which it purchases greige goods, the finishing plants it uses, or both. A second is the *converter-jobber*, also independently owned, who does not have any contractual arrangements. The third is the *integrated converter*, which is a division of a vertical textile firm. Such a converter works primarily with greige goods from mills of the parent organization and, as a general rule, has the finishing done in its own plants. It may also use outside sources, however, for greige goods or finishing.

Converters fulfill an important function in the textile industry. Because they enter the fabric production process in its end stages, they can work quite close to the time of need and adjust quickly to changes in fashion. Converters (either company or independent) keep in contact with clothing producers, seeking indications of colors, patterns, and finishes that are likely to be wanted. For this reason, most of them are located in major apparel markets, with more than 90 percent represented in New York City. The successful converter is a keen student of fashion, observes trends, anticipates demand, and is one who senses and responds to fashion directions.

Fashion Research and Development

Apparel designers say that fabric is the designer's creative medium, just as pigment is the painter's. A good designer responds to new fabric and searches for the quality that will make it—and his or her designs—come alive. To make possible fabrics that will evoke such response and that will ultimately be acceptable to the consuming public, fiber and textile producers must keep many fashion steps and several years ahead of the design and production of apparel. By the time fashions are featured in stores and magazines, they are old hat to textile designers and stylists, because these are the people who created these patterns and colors at least a year earlier. And probably two years before the public sees the fashions, the fiber companies and their associations were working with fabric mills on the kinds of cloth to be presented. At that time or even earlier, fiber companies were working on color projections and fiber variants for seasons still further ahead.

Specialized Fashion Staffs

Fiber and textile producers invest a great deal of time and money in fashion research to guide the development of salable fabrics, blends, textures, colors, finishes, and whatever other properties are expected to be wanted. All of the large producers, textile as well as fiber, maintain specialized fashion staffs in menswear and women's wear to research and report on trends in fashion.

Although their individual responsibilities and titles—fashion merchandisers, creative directors, fashion coordinators, stylists, and others—vary from one company to another, the recommendations of these fashion experts guide their company's design and production activities. These fashion specialists tour the world fashion centers looking for fashion inspiration and direction; observe what fashion leaders are wearing; exchange ideas with apparel designers, manufacturers, and fashion editors; and generally use every resource available to anticipate what will be wanted by their customers and eventually by the public. At the same time, many large producers conduct market research to analyze consumer attitudes and their ever-changing tastes and preferences as to performance characteristics. Thus armed with their research findings about the performance and fashion features that are likely to be wanted, producers design, develop, and produce fibers and fabrics long before they become available to ultimate consumers.

Early Color Decisions

Fashion decisions in the primary markets begin with color. Color is a sensation—a mood—and one of its attributes is that it helps sell clothing. Fairly typical of the procedures followed in determining the colors to be used are those described by Ed Newman, then vice president and creative director of Dan River, Inc., in the comment:

> When putting together a color line we review the best and worst sellers of the last season, check computer readouts, have informal discussions with manufacturers and check the racks of department and specialty stores. We think of what colors have been missing from the palette for a while and which shades seem "new again." Many colors make the natural progression through the seasons; a wine becomes purple, the purple moves to magenta and the magenta to a pink. No mystery—just logic. The final choice of a color line is logic, research and "gut feeling." With it lies the success or failure of your next season. (Newman, 1981, p. 92)

The Color Association of the United States (CAUS), a major force in guiding industry color decisions, has been issuing color projections for textiles and apparel for more than 80 years and has been forecasting home furnishings and appliance colors for nearly 35 years. It is a nonprofit service organization whose board of directors consists of top industry executives, each from a different industry, and all of whom donate their time. Seasonal forecasts for women's wear, menswear, children's wear, and the interior design industries are developed by committees of experts from each industry segment from fiber producers to retail. These forecasts are arrived at by committees of volunteers who evaluate what they call the "color climate." To arrive at their decisions, they consider everything from politics to the economy to cultural events and movements. Among the members of their committees are such distinguished persons as Mary McFadden, the well-known fashion designer, and Jack Lenor Larsen, a famous textile designer.

CAUS makes its predictions at least two years in advance and sends them to 1,500 subscribers, including design companies, textile mills, and paint manufacturers. The choice of colors will rule everything from women's fashions to desktop accessories.

Intercolor, an association of representatives from the worldwide fashion industry, arranges meetings in Paris twice each year. There, these experts analyze color cycles and the natural evolution of color preferences to determine specific color palettes for their target season two years into the future. Another color prediction service offered to textile and apparel producers is the **International Colour Authority** (ICA). They, too, meet twice a year to establish their color predictions for fiber, yarn, and fabric producers. Six months later, they send a modified version of their selected colors to member apparel producers.

Textile Design

In addition to the color story, fabric stylists must also be aware of the silhouettes coming into fashion, so that the fabrications they recommend will be appropriate. For example, if the trend is toward a tailored or structured look, firm fabrications are necessary, whereas soft, light fabrics are needed for a flowing or layered look.

Once the stylists have their color story set and the fabrications determined, the next step is designing the fabric. Textile designers, unlike apparel designers, are primarily concerned with two-dimensional surfaces, rather than with the three-dimensional human form. A further consideration is the capabilities of the knitting machines or weaving looms to be used. If a printed design is to be applied to the fabric, the designer must also consider any problem the pattern may present to the garment cutter. The pattern, usually a continuous repetition of a motif, is planned so that it does not entail unnecessary waste or difficulties in the cutting of garments.

Textile designers, like professionals in other parts of the fashion industry, rely heavily on computers today to develop their designs. Fabric designs sometimes result from first scanning an existing motif from virtually any source, and from that, the designer modifies and manipulates the design to create a desired look. On high-quality color printers, fabric designs can be printed to resemble the final printed textile piece goods. See Figure 5–6. Computers permit fast manipulation of motifs and colors, saving costly artwork done by hand and the slow trial-and-error process required in the past.

Textile designers tend to specialize in print, woven, or knitted design. Some are full-time employees of fabric mills, converters, or textile design studios. Others work freelance and sell their designs to textile companies.

Fashion Presentations

Fiber and fabric producers have developed considerable skill in utilizing their fashion expertise to sell their products. And through the fabrics they make available and the fashions they promote, they exert an important and continuing influence on the fashion industry's chain of production and distribution.

Large producers (both fiber and fabric) are very active in disseminating the fashion information they have collected to all segments of the industry. Most maintain fabric libraries in their showrooms that contain swatches of fabrics currently available or scheduled for production for an upcoming season. In addition, producers and retailers are invited to visit, inspect, and consult special displays of new yarns and fabrics that are set up periodically. These libraries and exhibits are used by apparel makers and their designers, retailers, and fashion reporters as sources of information about future fabric and color trends.

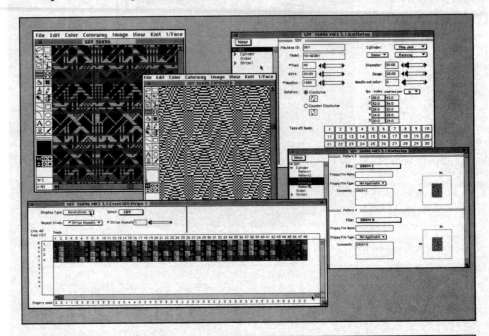
Source: Courtesy of Point Carré.

Some conduct seasonal clinics and workshops at which they visually present their fashion projections and illustrate them with garments they have had made up for this purpose and in which their fibers or fabrics are featured. These clinics are open to all segments of the industry: producers, retailers, and fashion reporters.

Seasonal Lines and Sales Presentations

Once a fabric line is set and sample yardage is in process, the work of the sales and merchandising staff is put into motion. In the fabric and other component suppliers' markets, two new seasonal lines a year are customary. Fabrics for seasonal apparel lines are shown from six to nine months in advance.

The actual selling of piece goods is broken down into two phases. The first of these, called *preselling*, is a presentation by the textile company's merchandising staff to its key accounts—the decision makers. Presentations take the form of color swatches (small fabric samples made on sample machines), croquis (painted samples on paper), color puffs, and sketches set up on story boards for approval. Or, today, many of the "swatches" are computer renditions, which permit the textile firm greater flexibility in quickly and easily modifying designs to meet the needs of the apparel firm. Presentations are made either in the fabric mill's own showroom or in the showrooms of their customers. At this point, all samples shown are **open-line** goods, available for selection. If a customer chooses to have a particular sample "confined" and not available to others and agrees to purchase an amount of yardage considered adequate by the mill, then no other customers may purchase it. Exceptions are sometimes made, however—for example, for a very prestigious designer label.

The second phase of fabric selling is the sales presentation to all other customers, regardless of size. Appointments are made six to eight weeks in advance of these customers' market weeks (selling periods), and presentations are made to apparel designers, stylists, and even the apparel companies' marketing staffs. Sample yardage is then ordered by the apparel producers for use in making up sample garments. After such garments have been shown to retail store buyers, apparel producers decide how much goods to buy and place their fabric orders. By the time this takes place, the textile creators are well into work on the next season's goods.

Textile Trade Shows

American producers participate in trade shows both in the United States and abroad. Held semiannually, these shows are attended by designers, manufacturers, and retailers who come to look at and perhaps buy the new fabrics. At this writing, the most comprehensive of such shows are the **Interstoff** Textile Fair held in Frankfurt, Germany; the **Première Vision** in Paris, France; the **Ideacomo** in Como, Italy; **Texitalia** in Milan, Italy; the **International Fashion Fabric Fair (IFFE)** in New York and the **Canton Trade Fair** in Canton, China. Each host country presents the latest lines of textiles developed within its own borders, along with whatever else producers from other countries choose to exhibit. Other, smaller shows include the Knitting Yarn Fair in New York City, which features new yarns, dyeing, and knitting techniques; and Cotons de France in New York City.

In addition to stimulating sales of fabrics, these shows result in further benefits. First, they make all related industry branches aware of changing fashions. At the same time, they unify and coordinate the thinking of related areas within the industry, so that they change in phase with one another and thereby facilitate the mass production that mass demand requires.

The Technologies Required to Compete

Although we still have a long way to go before we can produce a million yards of fabric by a simple verbal command, the fashion industry has been in the process of modernizing itself with new electronic capabilities that are reshaping its present and its future.

Because the textile industry requires modern technology to stay competitive, the U.S. industry has invested a great deal in state-of-the-art production facilities and equipment, spending upward of $2 billion a year to maintain and upgrade production plants (D'Andrea, 2000). These investments have paid off. Textile mill **productivity**—which is measured by total fiber processed per employee—has more than *doubled* since 1978. These continued investments have made the U.S. textile industry among the most modern and efficient in the world.

Quick Response (QR): Computerized Partnerships

The late 1980s witnessed the introduction of a new industrywide strategy called Quick Response. No recent industry development has created as much interest, publicity, and reams of printed materials as QR.

QR is a strategy whose aim is to achieve quick and precise replenishment of fast-selling merchandise by means of computerized partnerships between fabric suppliers, apparel producers, and retailers. Companies that participate in this strategy are linked electronically to each other so that each can speedily exchange, in computer language, information about the merchandise that is currently being purchased by the ultimate consumers. Its purpose is to considerably shorten the time it takes for currently desired merchandise to arrive in retail stores and to keep inventories at each level in balance with consumers' current needs and wants. Its development was spearheaded by the textile industry in order to meet the competition from apparel imports that involved the use of foreign-made fabrics.

A QR program begins with an agreement among a textile company, an apparel producer, and a retailer to participate in a computerized partnership after the fabric producer has shown its line to an apparel producer, who then prepares and shows his or her line to a retailer. The preparation and presentation of these lines are done many months in advance of a retail selling season. At this point, the retailer decides only on the styles and fabrications to be produced and establishes the quantities that will be needed for specific time periods, subject to timely revision. Colors and sizes, however, are not yet specified.

After the apparel manufacturer knows the styles, fabrics, and quantities, he or she works with the fabric supplier and establishes the types of fabrics to be used and the estimated quantities of as yet unfinished fabrics to be held in reserve and finished as needed for future use. Before the garments are put into production, the retailer establishes model stocks by style, fabric, size, color, and quantities for specified time periods, all of which are subject to needed revisions. The apparel producer now details the ordered fabrics by the colors and quantities wanted by the retailer for opening inventories and goes into production.

When the merchandise is received by the retailer, it is ticketed with an identification code. When a sale is made, a scanner at the cash register decodes the ticket and records the key elements of the sale, such as the price, the vendor number, and the size, color, and classification. This information is relayed to the store's central computer, where a running inventory of goods on hand is maintained. It is also transmitted through **electronic data interchange (EDI)** to the apparel manufacturer's computer, which enables the producer to replenish the styles, colors, and sizes that are needed, based on planned stock levels. Now that the producer knows which fabrics and colors need replenishing, this information is then quickly transmitted to the textile company's computer; the company will finish and quickly deliver the unfinished goods that have been reserved for the apparel producer.

This preplanning at all market levels makes it possible to stock smaller lots of goods close to the time of consumer purchases, thereby eliminating heavy inventories of untested goods at all market levels. The advantages to all participants are increased sales as a result of being able to respond quickly and accurately to consumer wants, reduced investments in raw materials and finished goods inventories, and a reduction of markdowns due to a surplus of slow-moving stock.

Expediting the movement of information about consumer purchases back through the production system involves a great deal of computer input and cooperation at each level. Although the concept of Quick Response involves many companion developments such as electronic mailboxes, merchandise information systems (MIS), automatic reorders, electronic message and answering centers, automatic warehousing and inventory controls, and voice activators, its basic components are as follows:

- *Electronic Data Interchange (EDI):* A method of transmitting computer data from one company to another into an electronic mailbox that unscrambles the data and makes it usable by the recipient and vice versa.
- *Bar coding:* A series of 11 black-and-white vertical bars printed on a ticket or label that is attached to merchandise. These bars are a code that identifies the merchandise category, the manufacturer, and the individual item down to the details of size and color.
- *Scanners:* Devices that read the bar code at the point of sale (POS), transform it into numbers, and transmit the product code into a computer. By means of EDI, retailers and producers can instantly keep track of all sales data on individual purchases and thus monitor styles and current or emerging trends.
- *Universal Product Code (UPC):* The Uniform Code Council is a nonprofit trade association that sets standards for transmitting information by computer and administers a Universal Product Code (see Figure 4–12). The UPC is a 12-digit numeric code that identifies the product. The first digit in the UPC code is a number system that serves to key the other numbers as to meaning and merchandise category. The next five digits are the manufacturer's identification number, which is assigned by the Uniform Code Council. The item or product code is the next-to-the-last five digits, which are assigned and controlled by the supplier and are unique to his or her item. The last bar is a checking digit.

This QR strategy, using high-technology data exchange and inventory controls and based on industry-to-industry cooperation and coordination, has proven to be successful. The formation of two industry groups has contributed to its success, and both groups contributed to the development of the third.

TALC/SAFLINC

TALC/SAFLINC is a network of U.S. apparel, sundries, and textile industries that work together to establish and maintain bar coding uniformity, EDI standards, ticket design, and other standards necessary to transmit uniform and accurate information from computer to computer. The group emphasizes Quick Response strategies and partnerships as overall critical business issues. This group resulted from a merger of the Textile and Apparel Linkage Council (TALC) and the Sundries and Apparel Findings Linkage Council (SAFLINC). Many major companies, such as Oxford Industries, Milliken & Company, Levi Strauss & Co., Burlington Industries, and Haggar Apparel, are members.

VICS

Voluntary Interindustry Communications Standards is an outgrowth of the Crafted with Pride organization. This committee includes representatives from Kmart, Sears, Bullocks, Dayton-Hudson, Blue-Bell, VF Corporation, Levi Strauss, Milliken, and Wal-Mart. Their efforts are directed toward improving customer service through voluntary standards for identifying and marking products and for communicating across all industry segments involved in bringing goods to consumers in a more timely manner.

ANSI X 12: American National Standards Institute

ANSI X 12 is the result of a committee, cutting across many major industries, that was formed to apply a set of conventions that establish the format of an electronic document. For electronic data interchange to take place, a format or set of conventions must be uniformly established and accepted by all. This enables all companies, regardless of size, computer type, or computer language used, to accept and understand each other's data. Using a specific set of data keys with its accompanying dictionary, all businesses (both big and small) can receive and interpret the numbers transmitted. For example, the first three-digit number describes the type of document being transmitted (purchase orders, invoice, etc.); the next 10 digits give the sender's identifying code for its own name; and so on through the document. This system has already been accepted by the automotive, electronics, textile, apparel, retailing, and footwear industries, for a total of 44 industries.

Thus, ANSI X 12 is the backbone of QR because it makes the industry capable of both receiving and sending immediate electronic information to its customers, be they General Motors, Levi Strauss, or Wal-Mart.

Computer Aided Design (CAD)

As noted earlier, computers are used in designing textiles. The introduction of computer aided design (CAD) systems in textile designers' studios provides the capability to experiment with weave, color, and yarns directly on a computer monitor. High-definition printers can print on paper full-color fabric designs that are so realistic that they are sometimes mistaken for an actual swatch of fabric. Once a fabric printout is accepted, the computer can prepare and deliver exact instructions for replication in the sample weaving department.

This provides a textile company with the ability to offer an endless supply of new and innovative designs tailor-made to each customer's particular wants and needs.

Computer Aided Manufacturing (CAM)

The computer aided manufacturing (CAM) system is used to guarantee that the colors on the CAD printout of the design are identical to those used in weaving an actual sample fabric, or blanket. A textile industry blanket is a series of preselected color combinations all in the same pattern. Data from dyeing used to calibrate color matching programs can be fed into color simulation computers. (Calibration data defines the dye's coloristic attributes. This, along with the colorant's performance specifications, produces an "electronic shade card.")

Shuttleless Weaving

The high-speed shuttleless loom has increased productivity dramatically, with each new shuttleless loom capable of weaving more than twice as many yards per hour as the old shuttle loom. Figure 5–7 shows an example of a modern weaving facility.

There are different types of these looms, and each offers different benefits.

- *Projectile looms.* These looms weave a broad assortment of fabrics from basic poplins and twills to a variety of fibers and blend levels.
- *Rapier shuttleless looms.* More versatile and less productive than the others, they can take all types of colored yarn for many end-market uses.
- *Air jet shuttleless looms.* The workhorses of all of these types of looms, these are the most productive and widely used shuttleless looms. They cannot weave multicolor or decorative fabrics.
- *Water jet looms.* These looms produce synthetic silklike fabrics for blouses. They are characterized by good productivity and fine quality, but they lack flexibility.

Figure 5–7

An example of a modern weaving facility. Modern textile mills are highly automated and can produce large amounts of fabric with few workers.

Source: Photo by Kitty G. Dickerson.

The next generation of shuttleless looms are likely to be fully robotic, with the ability to insert several different-colored yarns into the weave. When combined with CAD-CAM, the future holds superior fashion styling with shorter required minimum yardage and shorter production times at competitive prices.

E-Commerce for the Textiles Sector

As we have seen, computers are being used in many ways in the design and production of textiles. Today, electronic commerce (e-commerce) and the World Wide Web are propelling the textiles sector into a new era of growth. e-commerce provides new linkages between all stages of the manufacturing and distribution process. A great deal of the e-commerce for the textile sector is of a business-to-business (B2B) nature, because this segment of the industry produces many components rather than finished products that go to the end-use consumer. This fast, low-cost means of communicating has also quickly linked industry segments in many countries to create a truly *global* industry. Today, an apparel firm almost anywhere in the world can shop for the best fabric choices and prices from among suppliers on various continents. Similarly, a textile weaving firm can shop for the best choices in yarns from suppliers in numerous countries. Sales representatives from supplier firms may find themselves competing with company websites that give their longtime customers many more options from which to choose. For example, the weaving company can consider yarns from many more sources than in the past when they purchased directly from yarn company sales representatives. Thus, more of the sales of fabrics, yarns, and other components will occur online. Transactions may take place online, thus reducing the costs of travel to textile exhibitions or other market venues. Examples of some of these **dot-com businesses** include the Asian site shown in Figure 5–8 and the following sites (the reader is advised to keep in mind that a great deal of transition exists within the dot-com industry):

- **FTADirect.com:** Designed to allow fiber makers, yarn spinners, and mills around the world to do business electronically, closely monitoring one another's needs and costs.
- **TextileCo.com:** Primarily Korean textile companies, working with a few U.S. importers, for selling Asian-made cloth to businesses that want to buy imported fabrics but are uncertain how to go about it. This site will also serve as an order consolidator, allowing small companies to pool their fabric orders in order to meet large mills' minimum yardage requirements.
- **Fabria.com:** Links mills and fabric buyers.
- **TextileSolutions.com; Etexx.com:** European-based textile exchanges.
- **Textrade.com:** Another exchange service; an outgrowth of the former Global Textile Network website.
- **EcomTextile.com; Clicktex.com:** Textile exchange services.

Many of these dot-com exchanges have been launched or managed by former high-profile industry executives (Malone, 2000).

Other online sourcing services such as The Apparel Exchange and Fabrics On-Line provide apparel companies with information on the textile firm, general product offerings, and contact names. These services provide mills with a place to present their goods and allow apparel firms to quickly source fabrics through custom

Source: i-textile.com.

searches. To support electronic commerce, the American Textile Manufacturers Institute has developed a set of Fabric and Suppliers Linkage Council (FASLINC) voluntary standards to facilitate electronic business between the textile industry and its suppliers, including suppliers of dyes, chemicals, and natural and manufactured fibers. By providing voluntary standards for bar coding, labeling, and EDI, FASLINC is an integral part of a Quick Response business strategy.

Another group is helping to facilitate electronic commerce as a bridge among the fiber, textile, apparel, and retail businesses. The American Textile Partnership (**AMTEX**) is a collaborative group that includes the textile industry, the U.S.

Department of Energy and its laboratories, other Federal agencies, and universities. AMTEX's main project is the Demand Activated Manufacturing Architecture (**DAMA**), whose purpose is to link the fiber-textile-apparel-retail complex into an electronic marketplace where companies will identify, compare, buy, and sell resources, products, and services in support of innovative business partnerships. Two of the main tools developed by DAMA are: (1) the Textile Industry Data-Sharing Network (**TEXNET**) and (2) the Supply Chain Integration Program (**SCIP**) to foster e-commerce among the various industry segments. TEXNET is a communications infrastructure that has four security features that uses the Internet for supply-and-demand analysis among strategic business partners in the customer-supplier relationship. SCIP enables business partnerships to analyze consumer demand, material availability, and resource capacity to reduce the time to get product to market in the supply-chain pipeline. See readings at the end of the chapter for additional examples of e-commerce applications in the industry.

ISO 9000

ISO 9000 refers to a set of international standards that companies must meet to be "ISO certified." Under the International Organization for Standardization (ISO), this certification program does not focus on product standards; rather, companies must have systems in place to scrutinize quality. Standards are generic and may apply to any industry. Although ISO 9000 is generally not a requirement to do business in the United States, many European companies will not buy products from firms that are not ISO 9000 certified. Although this is a relatively new concern for most U.S. textile firms, as more companies increase **export** efforts, they will find it necessary to be certified, especially if they wish to sell in Europe.

Environmental Issues

Historically, as the textile industry used various chemicals in the production of fibers, dyeing, finishing, and so on, many pollutants were released in the environment. In fact, the largest U.S. rayon producer, Avtex, was forced to close down because of chemical runoff in streams.

Today's textile industry is both sensitive and committed to preserving the environment, as illustrated by the large expenditures on environmental controls to reduce or eliminate contamination of the air, water, or land. New methods of applying dyes and finishing treatments reduce water usage and chemical discharge. Additionally, an industrywide program called Encouraging Environmental Excellence (or "E-3") encourages companies to promote environmental awareness and responsibility. To qualify for E-3 recognition, companies must meet 10 requirements, from having a corporate policy in support of the environment and detailed environmental audits of their facilities to the development of employee education and community outreach programs. Participation also entitles companies to use the distinctive Encouraging Environmental Excellence logo (Figure 5–9) in their communications and marketing

Figure 5–9

The Encouraging Environmental Excellence ("E-3") award is given by the American Textile Manufacturers Institute to textile firms that meet the award criteria.

Source: American Textile Manufacturers Institute (ATMI). Reprinted courtesy of ATMI.

efforts. This distinction may be a plus for companies because of rising consumer interest in environmental responsibility.

Additionally, many companies have been required to rethink their product packaging so they are using materials that are environmentally friendly. Consumers' concern for the environment now influences what many individuals buy. The previously distinctive plastic egg-shaped package for L'eggs hosiery is one example of product packaging that had to change. Landfills can no longer accommodate millions of nondegradable packages like plastic L'eggs "eggs"; therefore, packaging was changed to recycled paper.

Textile firms have responded to environmental concerns in another creative way. A few firms have developed processes to recycle plastic soda bottles to make fiber to be used in textile products. Early efforts produced fibers used in carpets. Now the quality of fiber can be used in apparel, generally in blends.

The Fibers Division of Wellman, Inc., a leader in the recycling movement, introduced Fortrel® EcoSpun™, polyester fiber manufactured from recycled PET (polyethylene terephthalate), including two-liter plastic soda bottles. Fibers are being used in a variety of consumer products: home furnishings, sleeping bags, and apparel. Patagonia, well-known maker of outdoor clothing, was one of the first apparel firms to develop a line using the new recycled fiber. Wellman recycles approximately 2.4 billion PET bottles annually to produce EcoSpun. The oil saved yearly by using these bottles instead of virgin raw materials (petroleum is used in production of polyester fiber) is enough to power a city the size of Atlanta for one year.

Imports and Exports

Global competition has been a difficult matter for many U.S. textile firms. For decades, the industry had a nearly captive market—the large, relatively affluent U.S. market. Compared to most of the rest of the world, U.S. citizens have a fairly high standard of living, with incomes that permit them to buy many things beyond the most basic items for survival. For a long time, the domestic textile industry was in an enviable position of having customers willing to buy almost anything they produced. The only competition was from other U.S. producers.

By the late 1950s and 1960s, the textile industry's captive market began to erode. Textile and apparel items appeared in the U.S. markets from Japan, Hong Kong, Taiwan, South Korea, and a number of other countries where wages were low. Because of the low production costs, merchandise from these other countries was being sold at prices below those the U.S. industry could offer for similar products. Consumers bought the imported goods because of the affordable prices.

Over the years, **imports** continued to grow. Many more *types* of textile and apparel products were being imported, compared to just a few in the earlier years. Merchandise came from a *growing number* of low-wage countries. Many retailers soon came to see other countries as good places from which to secure merchandise for their stores. Additionally, some apparel manufacturers began to assign their own production to low-wage countries as a way to reduce manufacturing costs. And, for all these reasons, the percentage of the U.S. textile and apparel market being filled by imports continued to increase, as shown in Figure 3–8.

U.S. textile leaders were very successful over the years in securing government support for trade policies to restrict imported textile products from the domestic market. Despite these restrictive measures, imports have continued at very significant rates. In 2001, $75.2 billion in textile and apparel products were imported into the U.S. market, while $16.7 billion was exported. This means the textile/apparel **trade balance**, or in this case **trade deficit** (imports minus exports), was $58.5 billion for the year (U.S. Department of Commerce, OTEXA online trade balance report[3]).

Textile producers have felt they are losing their markets in many ways. First, they have seen many of their industry customers buying imported textile components. For example, weavers and knitters may buy imported yarns. Second, when garments are imported, textile manufacturers feel they lose the market for their fabrics—compared to the past, when domestically made garments were made from U.S. fabrics.

In the mid-1990s, the U.S. textile industry embarked on a very different plan to counter the growing loss of its domestic markets. For many years, industry leaders had been preoccupied with fighting imports, and most had given little attention to the prospects of selling *their products* in other countries. The change was that many com-

---

[3]For annual updates, check this Internet site: http://www.ita.doc.gov/industry/textiles/

panies adopted an **export orientation** for the first time. This means many of the companies began to think about products that would sell in other markets, started opening offices to represent their firms in other regions of the world, and began to think of their global neighbors as their potential *customers* instead of competitors.

Expansion of Business into Mexico

As noted earlier, textile firms have lost a good deal of their market to other countries because imported garments, particularly from Asia, are made of Asian fabrics. Since NAFTA was passed, several U.S. textile firms are busy putting a new strategy into place—building plants in Mexico.

In the late 1990s, a consortium of U.S. textile companies, along with financial support from the Mexican government, developed an industrial complex for textile and apparel production. The industrial park, known as **NuStart**, is located in the Mexican state of Morelos. Leadership in developing NuStart came from Chuck Hayes, Chairman and CEO of Guilford Mills, who felt the Mexican apparel industry was not flourishing as rapidly as he envisioned after the passage of NAFTA. Other participating companies include Burlington Industries, DuPont, and Akra, a division of Alfa, the largest yarn producer in Mexico. A goal of NuStart is to bring textile and apparel production from Asia to the Western Hemisphere.

The unusual aspect of these U.S. textile companies' Mexican operations in Mexico is that they are going into *apparel* production. In NuStart, these textile firms are building *cutting and sewing* facilities—very much a new twist on the role of *textile* producers. The reason: the textile firms are providing the apparel production as a service to their customers—apparel firms that have become marketing entities and no longer have production facilities of their own. Large U.S. apparel firms have sophisticated global sourcing operations of their own; however, many smaller apparel firms do not have the contacts or know-how to have garments made in Mexico. However, these textile producers must be careful that their major customers, the large apparel firms, do not come to see them as competitors.

Furs and Leathers

Furs and leathers were used for garments long before textiles were developed, and they are still major raw materials in the fashion industry. Both materials share certain basic qualities: they utilize the skins of animals; the natural habitat of the individual animal determines the part of the world in which the material originates; high degrees of skill are required in selecting, treating, and making garments and accessories of the material; there can be great variations over the years in the availability of a particular animal skin; and there has not yet been a way to produce truly equivalent materials in laboratory or mill.

The qualities with which nature has endowed both furs and leathers make them uniquely desirable in today's sophisticated, mechanized age, just as they were in the dawn of history. In the fashion field, dominated by textiles and other machine-made products, each of these two materials occupies a small but important place. Although both materials require skilled handling and slow processing, the fashion industry curbs its appetite for speed when dealing with fur and leather. It has no real choice.

The Fur Industry

The wearing of fur as a status symbol goes back to the ancient Egyptian priests, if not further. Present-day use of fur for prestige and fashion is evidenced most clearly in the parade of sable, chinchilla, mink, and other expensive furs on such occasions as inaugural balls, opera openings, and other gatherings of the socially and financially elite.

Nature of the Industry

Sales of fur garments within the United States reached a historic high of $1.8 billion in 1986 to 1987. In the years that followed, sales declined but have risen again in recent years. Sales for 2000 were $1.69 billion. More than 60,000 jobs are provided by the fur industry. This includes retailers, manufacturers, buyers, brokers, dealers, fur farmers, skin buyers, and trappers. Slightly less than 300 U.S. firms produce fur garments today (Fur Information Council of America, 2000; Wilson, 1998).

In recent years, animal rights groups have sought media attention and have attempted to defame the fur industry. Two groups, the Friends of Animals and the People for the Ethical Treatment of Animals (PETA), have staged demonstrations at fur showings in the United States and other countries. For example, activists from the United States and Britain staged protests outside the Hong Kong International Fur & Fashion Fair, one of the largest for fur sales. Activists, half stripped and wearing a banner that read, "We'd rather go naked than wear fur," were arrested (Sung, 1994).

The fur industry responded to activists by establishing various trade associations to promote fur apparel: the Fur Retailers Information Council, the American Fur Industry, and the Fur Information Council of America. These associations have set about to educate consumers on the industry's philosophy, which encourages the use of fur as long as animal species are not endangered (Vryza & Hines, 1994).

Fur industry leaders believe the impact of antifur activists has been vastly overblown. Many question this assertion, however, because many mink ranchers have gone out of business in certain areas. Furriers insist that their lean years had little to do with the antifur campaign. One industry group says its research shows that fur sales reflect the state of the economy rather than the impact of the animal activists. Other sources believe the economy does not play a major part in sales, citing that the industry's best year ever was after the stock market crash in 1987. One industry representative summed this up in saying, "People with money always have money." As might be expected, warm winters are detrimental to sales.

Manufacturing of Fur Garments

At every step of the way, from the living animal to the finished fur garment, the industry requires specialized knowledge, plus skills that are acquired through a long learning process (Figure 5–10). In many phases of the work, hand operations prevail. Mass-production methods have little application.

The process begins with a trapper who obtains animals in the wild by methods that do not damage the **pelts** or with a breeder who raises certain species under controlled conditions on a fur ranch. According to the Fur Information and Fashion Council, about 80 percent of the furs used in the United States are from ranch-bred animals, notably mink and fox. The fur business is necessarily worldwide in scope, with each country offering pelts of animals indigenous to its area. To secure desirable pelts, fur traders attend auctions all over the world: in Russia and Finland; Oslo, Norway; Montreal, Canada; and Frankfurt, Germany.

Once purchased, the raw skins are prepared for use by *dressers*—firms that prepare skins for use by the garment producer. These companies first immerse skins in a

Figure 5–10

Fur Industry Flowchart

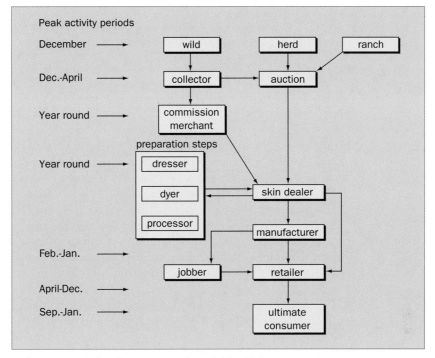

Source: Reprinted with permission of Fairchild Publishing Company.

saltwater solution, then scrape off excess fat and flesh from the hide. Next, the pelts go into revolving, sawdust-filled drums that remove grease and dirt. Oils are then added to keep the skins soft and pliable. Finally, the fur itself is combed and blown to raise its pile. Only after the furs become part of a finished garment is the last step taken—glazing, to add to the natural luster by drawing the oils to the surface.

To enhance their natural beauty, some furs are subjected to other steps. Beaver or nutria, for instance, may be plucked to remove the guard hairs and enhance the underfur. On furs such as beaver or nutria, shearing may also be used to clip the fur into an even pile.

Colors, too, may be subjected to change. White furs may be bleached to remove stains or discolorations, at least until a few years of exposure to air causes them to yellow. Other furs may be given a dye bath to change the color entirely. In such cases, a federal law, the Fur Products Labeling Act, requires appropriate labeling. Other beauty treatments are tip dyeing or blended color. The latter is a matter of brushing dye over the fur to even out the color or give additional color depth. All this is done before the making of a garment begins!

Production of the actual garments involves a number of skills. First comes the selection and matching of bundles of pelts for each individual garment. Then the skins are cut individually by hand, sewn together in garment sections, and wetted, stretched, and nailed by hand, fur side down, to a board and allowed to dry in the desired shape. Only then are the sections sewn together to complete the garment.

For some expensive furs, such as sable and mink, the expensive **letting-out** process precedes the garment construction. Again, this is a hand operation that requires great skill. Each skin is cut in half through the dark center stripe. Diagonal cuts are then made down the length of the skin at intervals of one-eighth to three-sixteenths of an inch apart. When the resulting strips are sewn together at a different angle, a longer, narrower skin is formed, presenting the striped effect that is wanted, for example, in mink garments.

Marketing Fur Garments

There is one major market period when fur garment producers present their wares to retailers—the period from May 15 to June 15—in New York City. Showings are usually held in the manufacturers' showrooms, generally on live models in the larger companies. The majority of fur wholesalers are located on or near Seventh Avenue, between 27th and 30th Streets. In that area, messengers carrying thousands of dollars worth of furs and fur garments stroll through the streets as casually as if they were bringing a bag lunch to the office.

There are approximately 1,200 fur retailers in the United States (Wilson, 1998). Because of the huge investment in merchandise required to present an adequate assortment to the consumer, the practice of consignment selling is common in the fur trade. This means that the manufacturer ships a supply of garments to the retailer and is paid for them only when they are sold; unsold garments are returnable at a specified date.

Department stores and large specialty shops almost universally lease out their fur departments, thus calling on the capital and the expertise of the lessee. Under such an arrangement, the lessee supplies stock, hires and trains salespeople, and pays for the advertising. All activities are subject to store policy and approval. The lessee benefits by the drawing power of the store's name and location and pays a percentage of sales plus rent.

In addition to the advertising done by retailers, the industry launches advertising and publicity through its trade associations, many of which concentrate on a single type of fur—for example, EMBA (the Eastern Mink Breeding Association), GLAMA (Great Lakes Mink Association), SAGA (Scandinavian mink and fox breeders), the Canadian Majestic Mink Association, and the British-Irish-Dutch conglomerate.

The Impact of Fashion

Many factors influence the fashion for furs. When there is a fashion for opulence, furs are "in." When there is a revulsion against ostentation or against wanton killing of animals for their skins, people swing away from furs. When the fashion world, as it has done in the past, goes overboard for an exotic fur to the point that the animal involved is threatened with extinction, the conservationists and sometimes the government itself will bring pressure to bear against the use or importation of such furs. This happened with leopard, which zoomed into prominence in the 1960s, causing such indiscriminate slaughter that by 1969, the animal was an endangered species. Similarly, revulsion against the use of certain types of seal fur, for which trappers kill very young pups, curtails the market to some extent—but not enough to stop the annual slaughter. These days, a retailer may add a footnote to the store's advertising, stating that no endangered species are among its offerings.

A fashion development since the late 1970s has been the introduction of major American apparel designers into the fur business. Through licensing arrangements with major fur producers, Valentino, Oscar de la Renta, and Adolfo, among others, now have their names on a variety of high-priced fur garments. Where formerly terms such as *quality* and *luxury* got major emphasis in the industry, today a new fashion dimension has been added—designer names.

The fur industry realizes it needs to be more innovative and not rely on the basic, classic designs year after year. They believe there is a need now to respond more to fashion trends and new lifestyles. Now that people are dressing down, they need coats they can wear with jeans and sneakers. Furriers have learned to offer lower price ranges in the past decade to market to young working women.

The rise in popularity of **fake fur** in recent years suggests that the animal rights activists may have been successful. Many consumers appear to like the look of fur but choose a substitute of manufactured fiber, many of which are very realistic, perhaps because of costs and/or in support of the activists' campaign.

Imports and Exports

U.S. fur sales account for one-third of the world market. In the world fur market, the United States ranks behind only Italy. Once a fur garment gets into the channels of trade in the United States, it is not easy to identify its source. The Federal Fur Products Act requires that a garment be tagged with the following information: the name of the fur in plain English, the country of origin of the pelts, any processing such as dyeing or shearing, and whether full, partial, or pieced pelts were used. In addition, secondhand furs must be marked as such. However, it does not require information about where the garment was made. It could be presented or even labeled "U.S.A.," yet have been made elsewhere.

The Leather Industry

Leather is one of humankind's oldest clothing materials. Long before people learned to plant cotton and make fabrics, they were skilled in the tanning and use of leather for sandals and crude garments. Leather apparel in this country goes back to the Native Americans, who made moccasins and cloaks from deerskin. Renowned frontiersmen such as Daniel Boone and Davy Crockett and other early settlers wore deerskin and buckskin pants, shirts, shoes, and jackets.

Nature of the Industry

The leather tanning and finishing industry is made up of establishments primarily engaged in tanning, curing, and finishing animal hides and skins to produce leather. Also included are leather converters and dealers who buy hides and skins and have them processed under contract by tanners or finishers. Figure 5–11 shows stages of leather production and distribution.

The supply of cattle hides used in the leather industry depends solely on the demand for meat, because the hides are only a by-product of the meatpacking industry and, to a lesser extent, the wool industry. The meatpacking houses derive their primary revenue from the carcass; the hides and skins, which have no food value, are sold to the leather trades. A long-term decline in U.S. consumption of red meat has reduced the hides available to the industry and, furthermore, has discouraged growers from rebuilding cattle herds. Also part of this industry, but of far less importance, are the hides from goats, sheep, lambs, horses, fish, birds, and reptiles.

Industry shipments of leather and leather products were about $3.3 billion in 1999. The U.S. tanning industry has decreased and consolidated, dropping to about 300 companies. About 14,700 people worked in the tanning and finishing segment of the industry, and the output from this segment was valued at $3.3 billion in 1999. Fewer than 100 establishments of any size are involved in the wet-processing part of

Figure 5–11

Leather Industry Flowchart

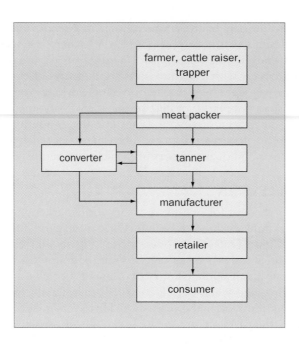

the industry that turns hides and skins into leather (Byron, 2000; Byron, 1998; U.S. Department of Commerce, 1994).

Processing of the hides and skins is done largely in small plants located mostly in the north-central and northeastern states. Three major types of companies are involved: (1) converters, who buy the hides and skins from meatpackers and contract them out to tanneries for finishing; (2) contract tanners, who finish skins but do not market them directly; and (3) regular or complete tanneries, which purchase and process skins and hides and sell finished leathers.

Like the fiber and fabric producers, the leather industry promotes and sells its products to manufacturers of apparel and accessories. Yet, unlike fiber and fabric companies, the tanning companies do not make their names known to the consuming public. Advertising for leather garments and accessories may include the name of the fashion designer, the manufacturer, and the type of leather, but never the name of the producer of the leather.

Hides and Skins

These terms, used interchangeably by the layperson, have very specific meanings within the leather industry. **Hides** come from animals whose skins weigh more than 25 pounds, such as cattle, horses, and buffalo. These hides are so thick they are frequently split into two or more layers, called **splits**. Under Federal Trade Commission regulations, the under pieces must be identified as splits and cannot be called genuine leather or genuine cowhide. **Kips** is a term applied to skins weighing between 15 and 25 pounds. The term **skins** designates still smaller skins, from such animals as calves, pigs, sheep, and goats (Tanners' Council of America, date unknown).

Processing of Leathers

There are three basic steps in processing leather: pretanning, tanning, and finishing. **Pretanning** is basically a cleansing process in which the leathers are soaked and rid of all flesh, hair, and dirt. Next is **tanning**, which both preserves the skin and improves its natural physical properties. The varied tanning methods use such substances as oil, vegetable substances, alum, formaldehyde, zirconium, and, most commonly used in the United States, chrome. The technical term "in the blue" refers to hides, skins, or kips that have been chrome-tanned but not yet finished. Final steps after tanning include dyeing and a variety of finishes. Among these is aniline, the most expensive, used only on the finest, smoothest skins to impart a highly polished surface. Other finishes include embossing, which presses a pattern onto the leather, often to simulate expensive alligator or snakeskin; also sueding and napping to raise the surface; or pressing, to give a shiny glazed finish. That last, called glacé leather, is often used for accessories.

Leather Marketing

Because of the length of time required to purchase and process its raw material, the leather industry is among the earliest to research and anticipate fashion trends. Its decisions as to colors, weights, and textures are reached early and are presented early. The industry as a whole participates in this process through its strong association, Leather Industries of America (LIA). The LIA offers color seminars semiannually and sells swatches of its colors to industry members at nominal cost, some 18 to 24 months in advance of the season concerned. As experienced observers of fashion signals and early forecasters of trends, the leather industry is looked to for guidance by other segments of the fashion industry.

At least one to one and a half years before the ultimate consumer sees the finished products in retail stores, there are leather trade shows at which tanners show and sell their latest products to professional buyers. For example, the *Semaine du Cuir* is a long-established major annual show in which tanners from around the world participate and to which buyers come from all over the world, along with the fashion press. This show is held in Paris, usually in September.

The Hong Kong International Leather Fair is a more recently established trade show. It is held in June in Hong Kong and attracts buyers and sellers from many countries, including the United States. The Tanners' Apparel and Garment (TAG) Show is held in New York City in October of each year and attracts garment manufacturers, suppliers, and retailers, among others.

Imports and Exports

U.S. imports of leather products increased about 4 percent in 1996, to about $16.4 billion (this figure includes shoes, luggage, gloves, etc., as well as apparel). Most of the imports come from developing countries, accounting for 85 percent of the total imports—of which 48 percent came from China. Lower wages in those countries mean that it is less costly to make products there.

Although the U.S. leather industry exported $1.8 billion in leather products in 1999, imports are much greater. In 1999, leather imports exceeded exports (a trade deficit) by about $16.2 billion. The United States is the world's largest *hide* exporter, but many of these are shipped back in the form of finished products (Byron, 2000).

Environmental Concerns

The Environmental Protection Agency (EPA) develops and administers environmental regulations affecting the tanning industry. The EPA has established standards to control wastes that tanners discharge so that dangerous chemicals do not enter publicly owned waste-treatment facilities. Most tanners meet these federal standards;

however, some state and local restrictions are more stringent and have forced some tanners to cease production or confine it to the processing of "wet-blue" or crust leathers, which produce fewer pollutants. The recycling of materials, new processes that reduce the chemicals used, and the installation of new equipment have reduced the tanning industry's impact on the environment. These new processes have also lowered costs, helping to make U.S. leathers more competitive in global markets (Byron, 1998, 2000).

Readings

The textile industry provides the basic component for putting together a fashion line. The following articles reveal some of the strategies being used by select companies or segments of the industry.

Color Forecasting: From Runway to Real World

Color forecasters provide an important role in identifying trends that will be used by textile firms in producing fabrics for future seasons.

Dot-Coms Are Making the Textile World Go 'Round

A number of business-to-business (B2B) e-commerce sites have formed to connect the large, fragmented global textile industry and make companies more accessible to one another.

Burlington Launches Super Fabrics

Using nanotechnology and a Silicon Valley joint venture company, Burlington aims to bring new, "intelligent" fabrics to market.

Color Forecasting: From Runway to Real World

by Mary McCaig

With rumblings from distressed manufacturers saddled with fabric inventory dating back to last season, last year and beyond, the question arises: are forecasters' color choices just a matter of whim?

According to Roseann Forde, fashion director and color marketer for DuPont Fibers in New York and a member of the Color Association of the United States (CAUS), "When a color forecaster makes a decision about colors for a particular season, these decisions are based on reality—where we see the world going." Forde says she bases her own forecasts on several factors. "It helps that I have years of experience. I also travel a lot, and am a keen observer of trends. I go to Europe and my decisions are somewhat influenced by what's happening there with fashion. I buy fabric in Europe and bring it back to interpret. But I don't take European trends at face value—I reinvent them to fit the American market.

"I have to take what I see, and also ask myself what are people buying now, what's already in their closet, and what will they want?" Forde adds. "Silhouettes usually stay somewhat the same from year to year, so what makes them more interesting are the new colors that come out."

The Color Marketing Group (CMG), founded in 1962 and based in Alexandria, Va., is an international, not-for-profit association of 1,500 color designers who forecast color directions one to three or more years in advance for a variety of industries, manufactured products and services, including apparel. Members of the CMG meet twice a year to compile each season's color card.

"When it comes to settling on the trends our [apparel] committee presents to the rest of the CMG, we have our own meeting and [hash things out]," says Lynne DeVaney, director of design and fabric development with Tapetex, a fabric converter, and co-chair of the CMG's apparel committee. "People will write reports and drag in information from around the world, keep notebooks of design influences, color chips, magazines, books—whatever trends anyone sees, they bring to the table. We look at what's happened in the past and what's evolving, decide what's influencing us and what's making colors evolve one way or another. Typically, we have to agree on 12 colors, and let me tell you, we get into some pretty fierce debates. People will fight to the death to support colors they believe are really 'it.' And naming them—naming is entirely another issue."

Tracy Hazzard, a member of the CMG, says, "We do debate, but our members seem to bring in many of the same ideas for the directions colors are taking." Hazzard has a background in textiles, having worked in the past for Milliken and Quaker Fabrics.

Once each CMG committee agrees on a color palette, the committee heads meet and look for overlapping color ideas. From these colors, a final palette is compiled and developed into the CMG's color cards, which support all industries represented. "The CMG sees our input as a guideline, and puts together a final color marketing palette, and under each color sample, they'll put a symbol—a star for a fashion color, a little car for transportation colors, or several symbols if they fit more than one category,"

Source: From Apparel Industry Magazine, November 1999, pp. 12–15. Copyright Bill Communications Inc. Reprinted by permission.

says DeVaney. "The CMG really represents the biggest influence for all industries."

Hazzard emphasizes that the colors presented on CMG palettes are not designed to be copied, per se. She offers an analogy of a paint company and an apparel designer each taking direction from a forecast of warmer yellows, and adapting that information to their individual markets. "Our palettes are to be used as an idea for gauging directions. Our customers want to know if their industry can support what we forecast," she says. "So the paint company may take our direction for a warmer yellow, and whiten it a bit to fit their market, where the apparel designer can go with a brighter, warmer yellow."

The CMG works almost three years in advance for contract and commercial colors, but forecasts consumer colors about 18 months out. DuPont's Forde says she works on colors 18 to 20 months ahead of season. "The closer you play to the vest, the better your chance of making a correct analysis," she says. "The longer you can hold back and wait to see what's happening, the better your interpretation will be."

Whether a forecast is as far out as three years or as recent as 18 months, a forecaster's color card will typically hold a minimum of 30 to 35 colors, most of which will be workable for the market.

Designers, manufacturers, and retailers who must make color decisions do typically opt to hear presentations from several forecasters. Then, they may sit down with all of the color cards spread across a table and begin to pick colors from there. "First they may look at the overall messages sent by the color cards to see if they agree—our cards will not be all that different. And then they may pick, say, a red from Cotton Inc., a blue from DuPont, and maybe a green from a paid color service," Forde says.

But is it truly necessary to follow the predictions of color forecasters? On CMG's Web site, (www.colormarketing.com) the first message readers see is that, "Forecast colors are color 'directions,' not directives." And Los Angeles-based color forecaster Fran Tesser-Sude of Design Options uses the slogan, "Colors are not about rules, they're about options." Without direction, how else does a manufacturer choose from a seemingly endless palette of colors for upcoming lines?

"Usually, you as a manufacturer have got to have forecasted colors to start out with," says CMG's DeVaney. "Patagonia and L.L. Bean, for example, will have colors from each season's trends, but they also have a couple of staple colors they sell season after season.

"The bottom line is that a designer, manufacturer or retailer is going to interpret the forecasted colors for their own needs—whether they're looking at pants, which will be more neutral; or tops, which will have more color. Junior wear, children's wear and accessories will be more in tune with an active color palette, too, versus a neutral palette.

"But then your higher priced lines, such as Armani, will probably stay with neutral and softer colors because a consumer who is paying $4,000 for a suit generally does not want a color to scream at them, nor do they want a color that will be out of style any time soon," says Forde.

A Look at How Color Has Evolved over the Past Century

1900s
"You can have it in any color as long as it's black." Henry Ford

1910s
Modern art and the Ballets Russes influence the bright colors and simple furnishings that replace the dull brocades of the previous century.

1920s
Color is in full swing and nothing is sacred from color improvement. Even Niagara Falls is enhanced by "Tutti Frutti" lights in 1926.

1930s
The depression is reflected in colors that cause this era to be described as "The Taupe Age" and "Color at a Standstill."

1940s
Like a World War II battlefield, the wartime palette is full of heavy grays, somber teals and thick reds.

1950s
The war is over, and color explodes into bright pastels. Who could forget appliances sold in aqua, pale yellow and pink? Another favorite color is chartreuse.

1960s
Color televisions outnumber black and white, while Avocado Green and Harvest Gold take over homes across America! The yellows and oranges of Andy Warhol permeate the culture.

Source: the Color Marketing Group www.colormarketing.org

1970s

Consumers take a respite from vibrant colors and discordant patterns. Earth tones dominate.

1980s

Known as the "Color Conscious Decade," color takes on a sophistication. Gray edges out beige as the new neutral. Light blues catch on, and "The Mauve Age" begins.

Early 1990s

Consumers clamor for color, and product colors get rich with jewel tones. However, you can't talk about the '90s without talking about green—in countless variations from teal to sage to hunter.

Late 1990s

Consumers become confident shoppers, buying corals, soft yellows and yellow-greens. Effects such as pearlescent, iridescent, holographic and metallic are changing the future of color. They have a bigger impact on color than color itself.

Dot-Coms Are Making the Textile World Go 'Round

by S. Gray Maycumber

New York—Most of the excitement in the textile industry these days is being generated by the surge of new B2B e-com companies being formed, almost weekly, to serve it and its customers.

Several textile-related B2B e-coms have already announced their start-ups or plans to do so, and there are more coming. Some are U.S. based; others are in Europe and Asia.

Some also have the glitter of a former top textile executive in management—Textiledge has named Bill Harris (former head of Hoechst-Celanese Fibers) as its CEO, and TDAdirect.com has Nick Hahn (former CEO of Cotton Inc.) as chairman. Click-Tex recently named former Burlington PerformanceWear senior vice-president Bob Getto as vice-president of operations.

Now two more textile-related e-com companies are in the process of launching, with very well known textile executives in top positions: Fabria.com and Ecom-Textile.com.

Fabria.com, a New York-based launch, has named David Tracy as its vice-chairman. Tracy is best known for his past stints as president of Fieldcrest, where he pioneered designer bed and bath lines, and as vice-chairman of J. P. Stevens, then one of the biggest and most diverse textile companies in the world.

His role there was to surmount archaic family management and bring the company into the 20th century before the 21st arrived. He tried valiantly,

Source: From Daily News Record, *July 5, 2000. Reprinted by permission.*

including getting Ralph Lauren to design for the company's bed/bath line, but since you haven't heard of J. P. Stevens lately, you can guess what happened.

"The textile industry is a natural for a B2B e-com company. It needs the huge global network the Internet can provide because the textile industry is massively fragmented. It is not a simple business. It has a high product differentiation, high vendor costs and high sourcing costs. Our mission is to develop a system that will solve all that. It won't be just an online sourcing site," Tracy told DNR.

Fabria.com, in addition to Tracy, has an outstanding management staff and will be online later this month, it says. CEO Vikas Luthra has a Wall Street background in derivatives at Bear Stearns.

Its angel financing was $2 million, and it is now working on the second round, which will come soon, Luthra said. Fabria will soon name another key senior executive, he added.

One of its advisors, Pete Scotese, former CEO of Springs Mills, is well known in the textile industry.

EcomTextile.com has named John Adams CEO. Adams is the former chairman, president and CEO of Russell Corp. He also served as president of the American Textile Manufacturers Institute and chairman of the American Apparel Manufacturers Association and as a director of the National Cotton Council.

EcomTextile.com, which is based in Fullerton, Calif., is a B2B marketplace for small-to-large businesses in the textile, apparel, related-machinery and sewn-products industries that offers global supply chain solutions and services.

"I feel good about our status now, and I think we can be in business in late July," Adams told DNR.

"It has an informational Web site now. We will start data testing after the Fourth of July." An Atlanta office would be set up around the first of the year.

A spokesman at the Fullerton office said the company was currently looking for its first round seed capital and that this should be completed soon.

FTAdirect, located in New York's Empire State Building, was one of the earliest to get financed and build an organization. It continues to expand and add people and partners. According to Frank Baker, CEO, it expects to have its site ready for live trading in early August or maybe even sooner.

It recently acquired FiberMatch.com of Spartanburg, S.C., and named its owner, Alfred Shirk, as FTA president. FiberMatch was formed as a fiber trading site. Shirk's background includes being the founder of e-Chemicals, a B2B exchange for the chemicals industry that provides end-to-end supply chain solutions.

FTA's Hahn told DNR that he will be announcing some of the top industry partners for the company in about a week.

ClickTex.com, one of the first to actually go online for B2B trading in textiles, continues to make advancements. In addition to adding Getto, it is opening a new office in Seoul, Korea. But perhaps its most important move is to offer free unlimited Internet access to anyone in the textile industry through 1stUp.com.

Two important new textile dot-com companies from Asia focusing on the U.S. market are i-textile.com and TexWatch.com, both based in Hong Kong.

I-Textile is a vertical B2B e-commerce company targeting the textile and garment industry. It features a strong network of fabric/yarn suppliers in China, Korea and Taiwan.

According to Paola Poon, marketing director, in Hong Kong, "We strongly believe that with our online search engine and exchange, we can help the apparel manufacturers in the U.S. to source and trade more effectively and efficiently."

I-Textile's Global Online Marketplace was launched last December. Its co-managing directors are Benjamin Mok and Wing Chan, both former executives with McKinsey & Co. In addition to its Hong Kong headquarters, it has offices in Shanghai and Guangzhoul, China, and Seoul, Korea.

TexWatch.com was started in June 1999 by garment and textile executives, and is dedicated to efficient and flexible supply chains in the global apparel industry, according to its CEO, Vincent Chan.

Back in New York, TexTrade.com is planning to launch its trading site in mid-August. According to Jeff Silver, CEO, it will also move up to 37th Street, in the heart of textile country, about that time also.

Burlington Launches Super Fabrics

by S. Gray Maycumber

The fabrics of Burlington Industries have sometimes been derided by its competitors for "having whiskers." Well, that term is soon to be one the company expects to be proud of, as it launches a major new, extremely high-tech fabric initiative that involves changing a fabric at the molecular level to create "nano-whiskers" that will produce new properties.

These fabric properties, revealed to DNR last week by Burlington Industries' chairman and CEO, George Henderson, at a meeting in his New York office, include breathability, stain resistance, water repellency and wrinkle resistance.

All are created by permanent molecular hooks, or whiskers, about 1/1000 of the size of a conventional cotton fiber that are imparted to the fabric through nanotechnology. They change the fabric and pass on the features permanently, unlike topical coatings or bulky laminated fabrics that have traditionally been used for this purpose. The whiskers are actually hydrocarbons added to the fabric's fibers by dipping it in an aqueous solution, Henderson said.

Burlington moved into textile nanotechnology quickly (for it) and in the traditional American way of the early 21st century, with a jump from Greensboro, N.C., to Silicon Valley. Burlington invested $35 million in the start-up of an Emeryville, Calif., high-tech company, AvantGarb Inc., in February 1999 and increased its ownership to 51 percent in November.

Source: From Daily News Record, *July 5, 2000. Reprinted by permission.*

According to Henderson, the company, which changed its name last week to Nano-Tex LLC, now forms "the core of Burlington's technology arm. It will introduce the textile industry to nanotechnology."

The technology of Nano-Tex will eventually be available to other textile companies on a licensing basis, he added.

The company was founded by David Soane, who has a Ph.D. in chemical engineering from the University of California and a B.S. in chemistry from National Taiwan University. He has already founded two other high-tech firms in the late '90s: ZMS, a specialty polymers company, and Alnis LLC, a biotechnology company pioneering in molecular recognition. He continues as chairman of both.

While Soane entered the textile arena with some trepidation, he told us he was excited by the prospect. Unlike traditional textile researchers, he feels that "we don't know what can't be done, so we do things." He said Nano-Tex is "a combination of a new-economy small company with an old-economy big company."

A very important aim in the formation of Nano-Tex, Henderson said, was to "attract talented young people into the textile industry. The good young people have been heading into other industries. This kind of company can attract them."

Nano-Tex has a modest staff of about 12 but will be adding more in the near future. One of the attractions will be that an IPO is planned for the company, but Henderson wouldn't say when.

Henderson noted, "We don't have a commercial product yet. It should be in the market in about six months."

However, Soane had a test garment on hand, a men's shirt, made with fabric from the nanotechnology process. He gleefully poured water and coffee on it, and the liquids ran off (onto Burlington's boardroom table) without being absorbed by the fabric. But he noted that pressure would cause the liquid to pass through the fabric. He demonstrated that the hand was soft, the fabric very wrinkle-resistant and the processing undetectable. He said the shirt had endured 30 washings and noted that the nano-whiskers create a "peach fuzz effect."

Technically, the nanotech aqueous solution "reduces the aperture size in the fabric to create a surface energy that inhibits the water molecule from passing through." It is said to work with cotton, wool and synthetics.

Soane added that he didn't see "any difference in breathability from regular cotton fabric, but there may be some." They are working on the perspiration angle and where it will go. The fabric, in addition to being hydrophobic, is oleophobic (highly resistant to oil stains) as well.

Soane feels that nanotechnology will also work with leather and "keep shoes looking good in rain."

Another fabric under development, he said, uses a synthetic core fiber with a cotton-like sheath around it.

As for markets, Henderson said, "We believe that these intelligent fabrics will be the way the better fabrics of the future will be made. It is like putting a microchip in a fabric. We hope to create a whole now category of fabrics, called intelligent fabrics."

In the licensing business model he described, "the chemical manufacturers would mix the chemicals to our specifications and sell them to licensed mills. The mills would sell the fabrics."

As far as pricing, he said, "We will work with the branded partners on this. The fabric will be branded and has to be hang-tagged. Right now there are very few branded fabrics. We want to establish a Nano-Tex fabric brand. This will require a lot of work. We have to beef up the company (Nano-Tex) to more than 12 people. In marketing, Burlington will help, but Nano-Tex will have its own marketing people."

When will Nano-Tex go public? "When our financial advisors tell us to," Henderson concluded.

Chapter Review

Key Words and Concepts

Define, identify, or briefly explain the following:

AMTEX	IFFE	QR
Bar coding	Imports	Scanners
Brand name	Industrial Revolution	Skins
CAD	Intercolor	Samuel Slater
CAM	International Colour Authority	SCIP
Canton Trade Fair	Interstoff	Solution-dyed
Commodity fibers	ISO 9000	Spinning mill
Converter	Kip	Splits
Converting	Letting-out	Tanning
DAMA	Francis Cabot Lowell	Temperature-resistant fibers
dot-com business	Manufactured fibers	TEXNET
Electronic data interchange (EDI)	Microfibers	Textalia
Export(s)	Natural fibers	Textile mill products
Export orientation	NuStart	Trade balance
Fake fur	Open-line	Trade deficit
Generic name	Pelt	Universal Product Code (UPC)
Greige goods	Premiére Vision	Vertical integration
Hide	Pretanning	Yarn
High-performance fibers	Productivity	Yarn-dyed
Ideacomo		

Review Questions on Chapter Highlights

1. Give examples of current and past fashions that prove the following statement: "Many of the changes in fashion are primarily variations in colors, textures, or fabrics rather than changes in styles."
2. In their correct sequence, name the steps in the production of fabrics.
3. Explain the statement, "Unlike the suppliers of natural fibers, the manufactured fiber producers made fashion their business from the start."
4. What was Samuel Slater's role in the Industrial Revolution in the United States?
5. How is the textile industry involved in environmental concerns?
6. How has the domestic industry met the competition of imports?
7. What are the competitive advantages and disadvantages of a vertical operation?
8. Describe a converter's function and explain the various ways in which different types of converters perform the same function.
9. Discuss the various fashion activities of the textile industry.
10. What are new technological developments in the textile industry, and what are their advantages?
11. Discuss the controversy associated with fur fashions. Take a position on this and defend your position.

12. What is there about the processing of leather that causes the leather industry to be among the earliest to research and anticipate fashion trends?
13. What are some of the new technologies being used in the textile industry?
14. How is e-commerce being used in the textile industry? How do you think e-commerce will change the way business takes place in the fiber-textile-apparel-retail chain?
15. Select one or more of the readings in this chapter, and explain its relationship to the content of this chapter.
16. Discuss and explain the relationships between apparel producers and the textile producers.

References

Adams, W. (1957). *Structure of American industry.* New York: Macmillan.

Alderfer, E., & Michl, H. (1957). *Economics of American Industry* (3rd ed.). New York: McGraw-Hill.

American Textile Manufacturers Institute (ATMI). (2000, March). *Textile HiLights.* Washington, DC: Author.

American Textiles Manufacturers Institute. (1996). *All about textiles.* Charlotte, NC: Author.

American Textiles Manufacturers Institute. (date unknown). *Textiles—an industry, a science, an art.* Charlotte, NC: Author.

Brunnschweiler, D., & Hearle, J. (1993). *Tomorrow's ideas and profits: Polyester 50 years of achievement.* Manchester, England: The Textile Institute.

Byron, J. (1998). *U.S. industry and trade outlook '98*, Chapter 34: Footwear, Leather, and Leather Products. New York: DRI/McGraw-Hill and Standard & Poor's and U.S. Department of Commerce.

Byron, J. (2000). *U.S. industry and trade outlook 2000*, Chapter 34: Footwear, Leather, and Leather Products. New York: DRI/McGraw-Hill and Standard & Poor's and U.S. Department of Commerce.

Chirls, S. (1997, January 21). Big consolidation ahead, KTA told. *Women's Wear Daily.*

Chirls, S. (1998, September 29). Woolmark offers sourcing aid. *Women's Wear Daily,* p. 9.

D'Andrea, M. (2000). Textiles. *U.S. Industry and Trade Outlook 2000.* Washington, DC: U.S. Department of Commerce.

Dior, C. (1953). *Talking about fashion.* New York: G. P. Putnam's Sons.

Fiber Economics Bureau. (various years). *Textile Organon.*

Finnie, T. (1992). *Textiles and apparel in the U.S.A.: Restructuring for the 1990s.* London: The Economist Intelligence Unit.

Fur Information Council of America (FICA). (2000). http://www.fur.org.

Heaton, H. (1929, November). Benjamin Gott and the Anglo-American cloth trade. *Journal of Economics and Business History,* 2, 147.

Lewton, F. (1926). Samuel Slater and the oldest cotton machinery in America. *The Smithsonian Magazine.*

Malone, S. (2000, July 25). Dot-Com parade continues in August. *Women's Wear Daily,* p. 11.

Malone, S. (2000, July 25). *FTADirect's aim: Market efficiency.* Women's Wear Daily, pp. 10, 11.

Maycumber, G. (1991). Microfibers—what they are and what they are not. *Daily News Record.*

Maycumber, G. (1998, June 26). Industry structure of man-made fibers turn to turmoil. *DNR,* pp. 1, 11.

Monget, K. (1998, August 5). Lycra's global leader, *Women's Wear Daily,* pp. 36, 37.

Morrissett, B., & Smyth, J. (1997, March). Industry consolidation continues. *Textile World,* 140–143.

Morrissett, B., & Dawson, C. (1998, May). Pace of mill mergers is quickening. *Textile World,* 50–54.

Newman, E. (1981). Development of a fabric line. *Inside the fashion business* (3rd ed.). New York: John Wiley & Sons.

Poulson, B. (1981). *Economic history of the United States.* New York: Macmillan.

Reichard, R. (1997, January). Do positive signs point to prosperity? *Textile World,* 31–38.

Smith, W. (1998, October). High-performance fibers protect, improve lives. *Textile World,* 53–64.

Sung, V. (1994, April). Rather nude than furred. *Textile Asia,* 128.

Tanners' Council of America. (date unknown). *Dictionary of leather terminology* (4th ed.). Publication location unknown.

United States Department of Commerce, Bureau of the Census. (1994). *M-3.* Washington, DC: Author.

United States Department of Commerce, Bureau of the Census. (1996). *M-3.* Washington, DC: Author.

United States Department of Commerce, International Trade Administration (ITA). (1994). *U.S. industrial outlook.* Washington, DC: Author.

United States Department of Labor. (date unknown). *Technology and manpower in the textile industry of the 1970s*, Bulletin No. 1578. Washington, DC: Author.

Vryza, M., & Hines, J. (1994). The use of fur for apparel: An attitudinal study. *Journal of Family and Consumer Sciences*, 86(3), 45–50.

Wellman, Inc. (1995). *Wellman, Inc. profile*. Unpublished material.

Wilson, E. (1998, May 12). Furriers stress fashion over function. *Women's Wear Daily*, pp. 8–9.

Selected Bibliography

American Textile Manufacturers Institute. (quarterly). *Textile HiLights*. Washington, DC: Author.

Berkstresser, G., Buchanan, D., & Grady, P. (Eds.). (1995). *Automation in the textile industry: From fibers to apparel*. Manchester, England: The Textile Institute.

Bona, M. (1995). *Textile quality*. Manchester, England: The Textile Institute.

Brackenbury, T. (1992). *Knitted clothing technology*. London: Blackwell Science.

DRI/McGraw-Hill and Standard & Poor's and U.S. Department of Commerce (annual). *U.S. industry and trade outlook (year)*, relevant chapters. New York: Author.

Ewing, E. (1981). *Fur in dress*. England: Batford.

Feitelberg, R. (1995, May 23). Fur week sets stage for rebound. *Women's Wear Daily*, p. 7.

Harris, J. (Ed.). (1993). *Five thousand years of textiles*. London: British Museum.

Hearle, J., Hines, T., & Suh, M. (Eds.). Global marketing of textiles. *Journal of the Textile Institute* (special issue).

Higginson, S. (Ed.). (1993). *World review of textile design*. London: I.T.D.B./Textile Institute.

Hudson, P., Clapp, A., & Kness, D. (1993). *Joseph's introductory textile science* (6th ed.). Niles, IL: Harcourt Brace.

International leather guide (1993). Kent, England: Benn Publications.

Jerde, J. (1992). *Encyclopedia of textiles*. New York: Facts on File.

Kadolph, S. (1998). Quality assurance in textiles and apparel. New York: Fairchild.

Kadolph, S. (1998). *Textiles* (8th ed.). Upper Saddle River, NJ: Merrill/Prentice Hall.

McIntyre, J., & Daniels, P. (Eds.). (1995). *Textile terms and definitions* (10th ed.). Manchester, England: The Textile Institute.

Matsuo, T., & Suresh, M. (1998). The design logic of textile products, *Textile Progress*, 27(3) (special edition).

Montgomery, F. (1984). *Textiles in America 1650–1870*. New York: Norton.

Textile Institute. (1992). *Tomorrow's fabric, tomorrow's people*. Manchester, England: Author.

Textile HiLights. (quarterly). Washington, DC: American Textile Manufacturers Institute.

The textile industry: An information sourcebook. (1989). Phoenix, AZ: Oryx Press.

Thornton, A. (1994). *Index to textile auxiliaries*.

Tortora, P., & Collier, B. (1997). *Understanding textiles* (5th ed.). Upper Saddle River, NJ: Prentice Hall.

Tortora, P., & Merkel, R. (1995). *Fairchild's dictionary of textiles* (7th ed.). New York: Fairchild.

Walton, F. (1953). *Tomahawks to textiles: The fabulous story of Worth Street*. New York: Appleton-Century-Crofts.

Trade Associations and Other Groups

American Association of Textile Chemists & Colorists, P.O. Box 12215, Research Triangle Park, NC 27709.

American Association for Textile Technology, Inc., P.O. Box 99, Gastonia, NC 28053.

American Fiber Manufacturers Association, 1150 17th St., NW, Washington, DC 20036.

American Printed Fabrics Council, 45 W. 36th St., New York, NY 10018.

American Textile Manufacturers Institute, Inc., 1801 K St., NW, Suite 900, Washington, DC 20006.

American Wool Council, 6911 S. Yosemite St., Englewood, CO 80112.

American Yarn Spinners Association, Inc., P.O. Box 99, Gastonia, NC 28053.

Canadian Textile Institute, 280 Albert St., Suite 502, Ottawa, Ontario K1P 5G8, Canada.

The Color Association of the United States, 409 W. 44th St., New York, NY 10036.

Cotton Incorporated. Marketing offices: 488 Madison Avenue, New York, NY 10022. Corporate headquarters: 6399 Weston Parkway, Cary, NC 27513.

Fiber Economics Bureau, Inc., 1150 17th St., NW, Washington, DC 20036.

Fur Information Council of America (FICA), 655 15th St., NW #320, Washington, DC 20005.

International Silk Association, U.S.A., 200 Madison Ave., New York, NY 10017.

Knitted Textile Association, 386 Park Ave. S., Suite 901, New York, NY 10016.

Leather Industries of America, 1000 Thomas Jefferson St., NW, Suite 515, Washington, DC 20007.

Mohair Council of America, 499 Seventh Ave., 1200 N. Tower, New York, NY 10018.

National Association of Hosiery Manufacturers, 200 N. Sharon Amity Rd., Charlotte, NC 28211.

National Cotton Council of America, P.O. Box 12285, Memphis, TN 38182.

Northern Textile Association, 230 Congress St., Boston, MA 02110.

Textile/Clothing Technology Corporation [TC]^2, 211 Gregson Dr., Cary, NC 27511.

The Textile Institute, 10 Blackfriars St., Manchester, M3 5DR, U.K.

Textile Distributors Association, 45 W. 36th St., New York, NY 10018.

Textile Fabric Association, Inc., 36 E. 31st St., New York, NY 10013.

Wool Bureau, Inc., 330 Madison Ave., New York, NY 10017-5001.

Trade Publications

America's Textiles International (ATI), 2100 Powers Ferry Rd., Atlanta, GA 30339.

Canadian Textile Journal, 1 Pacifique, Ste. Anne de Bellevue, Quebec H9X 1C5, Canada.

DNR (Daily News Record), 7 W. 34th St., New York, NY 10001-8191.

Journal of the American Leather Chemists Association, Leather Industries of America Research Laboratory, Campus Station, Cincinnati, OH 45221.

Journal of the Textile Institute, 10 Blackfriars St., Manchester, M3 5DR, U.K.

International Leather Guide, Miller Freeman U.K. Ltd., Sovereign Way, Tonbridge, Kent TN91RW, United Kingdom.

International Textiles, 23 Bloomsbury Sq., London WC1A 2PJ, U.K.

Knitting International, 23 Bloomsbury Sq., London WC1A 2PJ, U.K.

Knitting Times, 386 Park Ave. S., New York, NY 10016.

Leather Industry Statistics, Membership Bulletin, 1000 Thomas Jefferson St., NW, Suite 515, Washington, DC 20007.

Leather, International Journal of the Industry, Sovereign Way, Tonbridge, Kent TN9 1RW, U.K.

New York Connection, 1 Times Square, New York, NY 10018.

Textiles, 10 Blackfriars St., Manchester, M3 5DR, U.K.

Textile Horizons, 23 Bloomsbury Sq., London WC1A 2PJ, U.K.

Textile News, 9629 Old Nations Ford Rd., Charlotte, NC 28273.

Textile World, 4170 Ashford-Dunwoody Rd., Suite 420, Atlanta, GA 30319.

World Textiles, Regency House, 34 Duke Street, Norwich NR3 3AP, United Kingdom.

CHAPTER 6

The Women's and Children's Apparel Industry

Although the apparel industry works closely with the textile industry, the two are really quite different in nature. The apparel manufacturing sector consists of far more firms, many of which are very small, and employs far more people than the textile industry. Also known by terms such as the *garment trade*, *the needle trades*, and the "*rag trades*," the clothing-producing industry is a sizable force in our nation's economy. The apparel industry is also a major employer worldwide—almost no country in the world is without a garment industry that contributes significantly to the local economy through the jobs it provides. Although we will focus on primarily the U.S. industry, the apparel sectors in many other countries have similarities.

As we noted in Chapter 1, the development of the U.S. **ready-to-wear** industry meant that fashionable clothes were mass-produced and affordable to a large portion of the population. As Kidwell and Christman (1974) noted in quoting William C. Browning, a clothing manufacturer near the end of the 1800s, "abundant clothing at a moderate cost for all classes of citizens . . . [is] essential to the self-respect of a free, democratic people" (p. 15).

This chapter deals with the development, location, operations, and economics of the women's branch of the apparel industry, including the subdivision concerned with children's wear. Much information in the early sections of the chapter applies also to the men's and boys' industry covered in Chapter 7. The readings following the text discuss topics related to significant new developments in the apparel industry.

Economic Importance

By any of a number of yardsticks, the importance of the women's fashion business is clear. In terms of how consumers spend their money, it is estimated that in 1999, the outlay for men's, women's, and children's clothing and accessories, exclusive of

210

shoes, was $184 billion at retail price (American Apparel Manufacturers Association, 2000). In terms of the value of its production, the women's fashion industry also ranks high. In 2000, the estimated value of factory shipments of apparel, accessories, and fabricated textiles for men, women, and children was over $73 billion. Another yardstick—employment in the apparel industry as a whole (men's, women's, and children's wear combined)—was about 670,000 in mid-1990 (Tucker, 2000). The women's and girls' segment of the apparel industry accounts for well over half the total figures for clothing expenditures, employment, and value of factory shipments.

Numbers alone, however, do not tell the full story of the importance of the fashion industry as an employer. Historically, the industry has been a haven for women, the foreign-born, and minorities in search of work; it is a source of jobs in all parts of the country for semiskilled labor; and it is notable for hiring and training unskilled workers.

Not only is the women's apparel industry, with which we are primarily concerned here, of considerable size itself, but its activities have great influence on many other business areas. Its production facilities, as is discussed later in this section, are distributed throughout the United States. It provides an outlet for the talent of gifted, creative individuals. In addition, it is an industry that has changed fashion from what was once for the privileged few to something within reach of all but the most deprived women in this country. It was in the United States that the development of mass markets, mass-production methods, and mass distribution of fashion merchandise was most rapid. It is to this country that manufacturers and retailers from many other countries turn for the know-how to make and sell fashionable ready-to-wear merchandise.

NAICS Groupings for Apparel

The North American Industry Classification System (NAICS) designates certain categories for apparel; these are shown in Table 6–1.

- *The first two digits* define the industry sector (Sector 31, manufacturing is one of 20 sectors under the NAICS system).
- *The third digit* defines the subsector. In this case, 315 is apparel manufacturing.
- *The fourth digit* defines the industry group. Group 3151 is apparel *knitted* in textile mills. Group 3152 defines cut-and-sew garments, and 3159 defines apparel accessories.
- *The fifth digit* refers to the NAICS industry. For example, 31522 defines men's and boy's cut-and-sew apparel, and 31523 is women's and girls' cut-and-sew apparel.
- *The sixth digit* gives national industries in Canada, Mexico, or the United States an opportunity to use this digit if desired for further designations within each country.

The NAICS category concept is important to understand, because all industry production, employment, and trade are tracked by these codes. Further, members of NAFTA can follow the industry segments in the three member countries, using these categories.

Table 6–1	NAICS Codes for Apparel
31	**Manufacturing**
315	**Apparel Manufacturing**
3151	Apparel Knitting Mills
31511	Hosiery and Sock Mills
315111	Sheer Hosiery Mills
315119	Other Hosiery and Sock Mills
31519	Other Apparel Knitting Mills
315191	Outerwear Knitting Mills
315192	Underwear and Nightwear Knitting Mills
3152	Cut and Sew Apparel Manufacturing
31521	Cut and Sew Apparel Contractors
315211	Men's and Boys' Cut and Sew Apparel Contractors
315212	Women's and Girls' Cut and Sew Apparel Contractors
31522	Men's and Boys' Cut and Sew Apparel Manufacturing
315221	Men's and Boys' Cut and Sew Underwear and Nightwear Manufacturing
315222	Men's and Boys' Cut and Sew Suit, Coat and Overcoat Manufacturing
315223	Men's and Boys' Cut and Sew Shirt (except Work Shirt) Manufacturing
315224	Men's and Boys' Cut and Sew Trouser, Slack and Jean Manufacturing
315225	Men's and Boys' Cut and Sew Work Clothing Manufacturing
315228	Men's and Boys' Cut and Sew Other Outerwear Manufacturing
31523	Women's and Girls' Cut and Sew Apparel Manufacturing
315231	Women's and Girls' Cut and Sew Lingerie, Loungewear and Nightwear Manufacturing
315232	Women's and Girls' Cut and Sew Blouse and Shirt Manufacturing
315233	Women's and Girls' Cut and Sew Dress Manufacturing
315234	Women's and Girls' Cut and Sew Suit, Coat, Tailored Jacket and Skirt Manufacturing
315238	Women's and Girls' Cut and Sew Other Outerwear Manufacturing
31529	Other Cut and Sew Apparel Manufacturing
315291	Infants' Cut and Sew Apparel Manufacturing
315292	Fur and Leather Apparel Manufacturing
315299	All Other Cut and Sew Apparel Manufacturing
3159	Apparel Accessories and Other Apparel Manufacturing
31599	Apparel Accessories and Other Apparel Manufacturing
315991	Hat, Cap and Millinery Manufacturing
315992	Glove and Mitten Manufacturing
315993	Men's and Boys' Neckwear Manufacturing
315999	Other Apparel Accessories and Other Apparel Manufacturing

Source: Federal Register. (1996, November 5). Office of Management and Budget. Economic Classification Policy Committee; Standard Industrial Classification Replacement: The North American Industry Classification System. Proposed Industry Classification Structure. Part II.

History and Growth of the Women's Industry

Until the midnineteenth century, ready-made clothing was virtually nonexistent, and fashionable clothing was something that relatively few people in the United States wore or could afford. The wants of these few were supplied by custom-made imports, usually from England or France, or by the hand labor of a small number of custom tailors and dressmakers in this country. The dressmakers worked at home, in the homes of their customers, or in small craft shops. The fabrics they used for their wealthy clients were generally imported from Europe.

Ready-to-Wear in the Nineteenth Century

From colonial times to the end of the 1800s, the majority of American women wore clothes made at home by the women of the house; every home in modest circumstances was its own clothing factory. Aiding these home sewing operations were the instructions for constructing garments printed in such early American women's magazines as *Godey's Lady's Book* and *Graham's Magazine*. And in 1860, Ebenezer Butterick developed paper patterns that provided the home sewer with help with styles and sizes. Home dressmaking continued to prevail.

Early Ready-to-Wear

In contrast to custom-made apparel, which is constructed to the exact measurements of the garment's wearer, the term **ready-to-wear** applies to apparel made in standardized sizes and usually produced in factories. An advertisement for early ready-to-wear is shown in Figure 6–1.

Figure 6–1

An early advertisement for women's ready-to-wear.

Source: From a city directory, circa 1855. Courtesy of the Bettmann Archive.

As we shall note in the chapter on menswear, the first ready-to-wear clothing in the United States was produced for men. Not until the U.S. Census of 1860 was the commercial manufacture of women's ready-to-wear deemed worthy of enumeration. In that year, mention was made of 96 manufacturers producing such articles as hoop-skirts, cloaks, and mantillas. What was available was of poor quality and completely lacking in good design. Although the industry grew rapidly once it started, home dressmaking continued until into the early twentieth century, and it was not until well into the 1900s that the term *store clothes*, applied to early ready-to-wear, was used in other than a derogatory manner.

The women's ready-to-wear business in the United States is indeed young, and its early beginnings were anything but fashion inspired. In not much more than a century, the industry that once served only the lowest income levels of society has worked its way up to acceptance by the very richest of women.

From Hand to Machine Production

The major event that opened the way to ready-to-wear production was the development of the sewing machine by **Elias Howe** in 1845. Howe's machine was further perfected by **Isaac Singer**, whose improvements made it suitable for use in factories. Singer also promoted it aggressively, thus bringing it to public attention. These machines, first operated by foot power with a treadle and later by electricity, revolutionized production by making volume output possible in machine-equipped factories.

Immigrants: A Source of Manpower

A plentiful supply of labor is essential to growth of any industry. This is especially true of an industry such as apparel production, which was, and still is, heavily dependent on hand-guided operations such as machine sewing. Workers to perform those tasks became available in vast numbers, beginning in the 1880s, in the person of immigrants from Central and Eastern Europe. Many of the newcomers were Jews, fleeing Czarist persecutions and bringing tailoring skills with them; others, without a trade and with no knowledge of the language, were ready and willing to master the sewing machine and work at it to survive in their new country. Hundreds of thousands of immigrants came each year, and the stream never slackened until restrictions were placed on immigration in 1920. This influx of immigrant labor, both skilled and unskilled, made possible an accelerated pace of industry growth.

Developments in the Twentieth Century

During the first two decades of the twentieth century, a number of developments combined to give additional impetus to the industry. In the 1920s, the industry came of age, and the output of apparel passed the billion-dollar mark, representing one-twelfth of the country's total output of manufactured goods (U.S. Department of Commerce, 1966).

Improvements in Technology and Retail Distribution

Continuing improvements in textile technology in both Europe and America made available a wide variety of fabrics. Improvements in machines for sewing, cutting, and pressing made garment production faster, easier, and cheaper.

Along with the improvements in textile and apparel production technology, there were advances in mass distribution. Retailers began to learn the ready-to-wear business. Dry goods merchants learned to sell apparel; department and specialty stores that prided themselves on their custom-made operations began to establish ready-to-wear departments. Continuing innovation in retail salesmanship and advertising stimulated the demand for the industry's products and contributed to further expansion of women's apparel manufacturing.

Increasing Need for Ready-to-Wear

As manufacturing improved, ready-made clothing overcame the stigma of inferiority and cheapness that had originally been attached to it. It became an acceptable answer to a growing need for reasonably priced and respectably made apparel.

An important reason for this need was the changing role of women. Prior to 1900, there were relatively few women who looked beyond the confines of home and family. Many of those who did work held miserably paying domestic or farm jobs. To be well dressed was primarily the privilege of the wives and daughters of well-to-do men.

At the turn of the century, a whole new breed of busier and more-affluent women began to emerge: women in colleges, women in sports, women in politics, and women in factories, offices, and retail stores. World War I further gave many women their first view of an occupation outside the confines of their homes and stimulated the need for ready-made clothing. Their expanding interests and activities made ready-to-wear for themselves and their families a great convenience and thus accelerated its acceptance among nearly all classes and incomes.

Recognition of American Designers in the 1940s

In the early years of the twentieth century, the American apparel industry had demonstrated an awareness of fashion but had not yet reached the point of sponsoring or participating in its development. Instead, producers and retailers looked to Parisian couture designers for inspiration. Twice a year, heads of apparel-producing firms went to view the Paris collections and bought samples for copying or adapting into mass-produced garments. At the same time, buyers from leading retail stores also bought lavishly from the Paris collections and arranged for manufacturers to copy or adapt the garments chosen. American fashion publications also concentrated their publicity almost solely on what was being shown in Paris. The phrase *Paris inspired* was the key to fashions and their promotion.

Inevitably, however, American design talent had been attracted to the industry. By the 1930s, many capable and creative designers were at work in the trade, but so great was the enthusiasm for Paris that their names were rarely mentioned in the press or by the stores. In the war-ridden years of the 1940s, with Paris blacked out by the German occupation, Dorothy Shaver, then president of Lord & Taylor and an outstanding fashion merchant, smashed the tradition of idolizing Paris designers. Her store, for the first time in retail history, advertised clothes designed by Americans and featured their names: Elizabeth Hawes, Clare Potter, Vera Maxwell, Tom Brigance, and Claire McCardell, considered by many to have been the first true sportswear designer. The rule that only French-inspired clothes could be smart had been broken.

Publicly Owned Versus Privately Owned Apparel Firms

Development of publicly owned giants in the 1960s.   Until the 1950s, the women's apparel industry consisted almost entirely of relatively small, privately owned, single-product businesses, each concentrating its efforts on its own specialized product. Large or publicly owned firms were virtually nonexistent. In the late 1950s and throughout the 1960s, however, the situation changed, and huge, publicly owned, multiproduct corporations made their appearance in the apparel field, usually by means of mergers with and acquisitions of existing companies (Table 6–2). Many influences contributed to this phenomenon. Among them was the increase in consumer apparel spending resulting from an expanding economy. Another factor was the need to become large enough to be able to deal successfully with ever-larger textile suppliers, on the one hand, and enormously large retail distributors, on the other.

The rise of publicly owned giants in the apparel field during the 1960s is reflected in the fact that, in 1959, only 22 such publicly owned firms existed in the women's apparel field but, by the close of the 1960s, some 100 multiproduct apparel companies were listed on the stock exchanges and inviting public investment as a source of capital for further expansion.

Going private in the 1980s: Leveraged buyouts. In the mid-1980s, the trend toward going public began to reverse itself for a time, and some large manufacturing firms began to "go private" again through **leveraged buyouts**. In a typical leveraged buyout, a group of investors, aided by an investment firm specializing in the field, buys out a company's public shareholders by leveraging or borrowing against the company's own assets. The investors put up between 1 and 10 percent of the total price in the usual case. The rest of the purchase price, up to 99 percent in some cases, is financed by layers of long-term loans from banks and insurance companies. The company's assets and cash flow are then used to pay back the loans, with or without the sale of bonds. The company's management has reclaimed their autonomy, albeit

Table 6–2	Women's Apparel[a] Producers: Selected Examples
Company	**1999 Sales (in $ millions)**
Sara Lee Branded Apparel	7,440
Calvin Klein Inc.	5,552
Jones Apparel Group	3,129
Liz Claiborne, Inc.	2,806
Kellwood Company	2,151
The Warnaco Group	2,114
Donna Karan	662
Guess? Inc.	599
Norton McNaughton	408
Esprit Holdings, Inc.	387 (est)
St. John's Knits	300
Chic by H.I.S.	238
Byer California	210 (est)
Leslie Fay	194
Bernard Chaus Inc.	188
Carol Little	180
Donnkenny	174
Jessica McClintock	145

[a]Some produce other products, but are for the most part women's apparel firms.
Source: "AIM's Global 150." (June 2000). *Apparel Industry Magazine,* 18–38. Copyright Bill Communications, Inc.

with a load of debt and interest payments, but without the need to submit their operating decisions to the review of outside stockholders. Some examples of leveraged buyouts were those of Levi Strauss, Leslie Fay, and Puritan, among others.

Additional companies go public.   In the early 1990s, a number of privately held companies decided to go public. Companies generally choose this strategy so they can sell shares in the company, and through those sales they can generate capital for the company's growth. When stock is sold for the first time, this is called an **initial public offering (IPO)**. Examples of well-known companies that issued stock in recent years were Ralph Lauren, Donna Karan, Tommy Hilfiger, Danskin, and Haggar Corporation.

Wall Street observers report that the greatest successes with investors are those that have a strategy for growth, management with the experience to execute the plan, and a hot brand. Companies that produce classic fashions rather than cutting-edge designs seem to appeal more to investors (Seckler, 1998).

Industry Restructuring

The apparel industry has faced many challenges that have forced changes—changes that cause today's industry to be very different from that of 20 years ago. Competition from imports has created difficulties for many companies. However, the business climate is tough for firms, even if imports were not considered because of the large number of U.S. companies competing in the market. Additionally, sluggish consumer spending has hurt companies.

Because of the challenges, the apparel industry has restructured in many ways in recent years. Many small companies were trying to survive without adequate capital to keep them afloat. As a result, a number of companies and apparel plants have gone out of business. Others have merged, and some have acquired smaller companies. Some have sold off unprofitable parts of their businesses. In general, these changes have resulted in larger and stronger firms with funds to hire professionals to manage the businesses.

Development of the Unions

In the early days of the women's apparel industry, working conditions, as in many other industries of the period, were generally extremely bad. Men and women worked 12 hours and more a day, seven days a week, in damp, disease-breeding places, referred to in disgust as **sweatshops**, such as the one shown in Figure 6–2. The hourly wage was five cents. Some provided their own machines and paid for thread and needles, for the water they drank, and sometimes even for the "privilege" of working in the factories. Work was also taken home to dark, unsanitary tenements that often doubled as sweatshops and in which children worked long hours side by side with their parents. It was in this environment in the early 1900s that the International Ladies' Garment Workers' Union (**ILGWU**) developed. At that time, the union represented fewer than 2,000 workers and was founded after two decades of desperate struggle.

But the union did not achieve strength until after several major strikes and the monumental disaster of the **Triangle Shirtwaist Fire** of 1911. This tragic event took place in a factory where 146 persons lost their lives because of locked exit doors, inadequate fire escapes, and one fire escape that actually ended in midair. The shock of the holocaust was the turning point in the sweatshop era, because it awoke the public conscience to labor conditions in the garment industry.

Figure 6–2

An example of an early sweatshop in the garment industry.

Source: Courtesy of the Bettmann Archive.

Since the 1920s, industrywide strikes and lockouts have been all but nonexistent. Reports vary as to the proportion of apparel industry workers in unions, with the range generally between 20 and 60 percent (anonymous union source). Unionized workers are more likely to be in the Northeast, in major metropolitan areas, and on the West Coast—but are not commonly found in the South. After all, many firms located in the South to take advantage of less-costly labor. Wages of unionized workers are generally somewhat higher than those of nonunionized workers.

In 1995, the ILGWU merged with the Amalgamated Clothing and Textile Workers Union (ACTWU)[1] to form one union with 355,000 members. The merger gave birth to the **Union of Needletrades, Industrial & Textile Employees (UNITE)**, which became one of the largest unions in the United States. The unions combined their strengths to gain more power to fight imports and the rash of sweatshops that have developed in recent years in several major U.S. cities. UNITE also represents its members on wage and other labor issues of concern (Friedman, 1995a).

---

[1]The ACTWU included apparel workers who produced men's and boys' wear. Also included were employees in men's tailored wear firms that later produced women's tailored garments. The small portion of textile industry workers who were unionized were in this union.

The Organization of an Apparel Firm

As garments go through the process of design and production, many of the processes are similar from one company to another. A great deal of difference exists, however, in *how* the processes are organized and *how* they occur within the industry. For example, the way a company is organized affects how designs are developed and sewn.

Apparel manufacturing firms must perform a certain number of basic functions regardless of the size of the firm or the product being made. Kunz (1995) has developed the following model to depict the functional areas within a modern apparel firm: executive management, merchandising, marketing, operations, and finance. Figure 6–3 illustrates the necessary interaction of these main areas and the fact that activities of a company must be built around the needs and demands of the target market. All this must occur in a way that produces a profit.

Kunz (1995) provides the useful summary of each area's responsibility in the following list. Following this summary, each area will be covered somewhat more in detail.

Figure 6–3

Functional areas and interactions within a modern apparel firm.

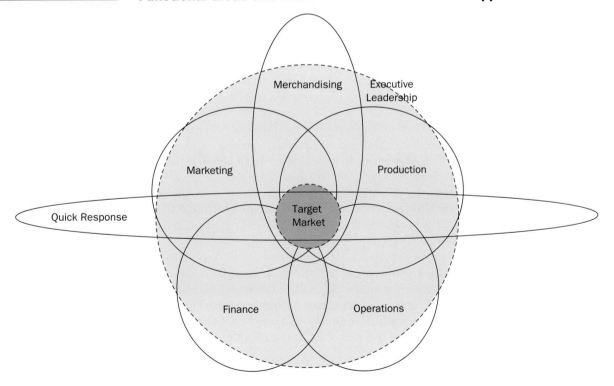

Source: From Apparel Manufacturing: Sewn Product Analysis, 3rd ed. (p. 19) by R. E. Glock and G. I. Kunz © 2000. Reprinted by permission of Pearson Education, Inc., Upper Saddle River, NJ.

Executive	Establishes the firm's goals and administers activities to achieve them
Merchandising	Plans, develops, and presents product lines
Marketing	Defines target customer(s) and develops positioning and promotion strategies
Operations	Manages people and physical property
Finance	Manages financial resources (p. 257)

- *Executive management* sets the direction for a company and oversees the running of the company. This group makes decisions on such basics as the target markets to serve and product lines to produce. Position titles include chairman, president, chief executive officer (**CEO**), chief operating officer (**COO**), vice presidents of the major areas, director, and manager (Kunz, 1995).
- *Merchandising* in a manufacturing firm is more specific than marketing, concerning itself with the development, execution, and delivery of the product **line**. With its close ties to the market segment it serves, the merchandising function is not only able to adjust to market variations rapidly, but is capable of anticipating and helping to create market changes (Frank, 1985, p. 10). In short, merchandising includes directing and overseeing the development of product lines from start to finish. Position titles in this area may include designer, product development manager, merchandiser, product manager, and merchandise manager (Kunz, 1995, p. 256).
- *Marketing and sales.* Marketing focuses on (1) defining a company's market and identifying new opportunities for growth, (2) establishing the position of a company's products in relation to its competitors, and (3) determining advertising and promotional plans to reach sales goals. The sales division provides the link to get products to the retail customer and to give feedback on merchandise to appropriate personnel in the company. Position titles in this grouping may include market researcher, advertising manager, manufacturer's representative, sales manager, and sales representative (Frank, 1985; Glock & Kunz, 1995; Kunz, 1995).
- *Operations* manages people and physical property. These include human resources, physical facilities and equipment, inventories, and quality control. In many companies, operations is responsible for all activities associated with getting garments made and ready for the customer. Among the range of position titles are personnel manager, inventory controller, receiving manager, plant manager, apparel engineer, line manager, and sewing machine operator (Kunz, 1995). Sewing operators are the backbone of the company—the people who transform everyone else's plans into products to be sold (Figure 6–4).
- *Finance* personnel manage the financial aspects of the apparel firm to be sure enough profit is earned and to assure the company's financial future. This includes setting financial goals, monitoring financial performance, borrowing and spending money, managing **accounts receivable** and **accounts payable**, and keeping others in the company informed on financial matters. Among position titles often found in this area are controller, treasurer, accountant, and financial auditor.

In a very large apparel firm, experienced and more-specialized staffs (usually teams) carry out these functions. In a smaller company, one individual may be responsible for a whole area or even multiple areas.

An Industry Reshaped by Computer Technology

Computers are dramatically transforming the apparel industry in ways not seen since the invention of the sewing machine. Nearly every aspect of the industry now incorporates some form of computerization. These will be discussed in sections that follow. Today apparel firms can source fabrics and other components through business-to-business websites from companies around the world.

New technology enables the industry to speed up the product development process, preassembly operations, manufacturing processes, and finishing operations while reducing labor time per garment. Computers also contribute in these other areas: production planning, marketing, sales, financial management, inspection of fabrics, costing, programmable sewing machines, unit production systems that move garments in a conveyor manner from one operation to another during the sewing process, and state-of-the-art automated warehouse facilities. For many companies, the computer makes possible easy communication and transfer of information from one company location to another—even when some facilities are located halfway around the world.

By capturing sales data at the checkout counter, EDI computer linkages help both retailers and manufacturers reduce the large investments and risk each must make in goods that might sit idly in distribution centers. In their book, *A Stitch in Time*, Harvard researchers Abernathy, Dunlop, Hammond, and Weil (1999) write about lean retailing and the accompanying transformation of manufacturing—which reduce inventory risk, reduce costs, and increase profitability while being more responsive to customers. Computers are also used extensively in logistic and distribution operations that bring garments to the U.S. market from overseas and then distribute them to retail stores where they are sold.

Early computer applications for the manufacturing segments of the industry focused mostly on a single aspect of the product development or production process. Computerization in one activity was not linked to that in others. Data had to be reentered at each stage. Today, the goal is to integrate multiple computerized activities, a concept known as **computer integrated manufacturing (CIM)**.

Large apparel firms have an advantage over smaller ones in being able to buy and use the range of new technologies. A company must have adequate capital to be able to buy costly equipment and to employ specialists who can operate it.

Quick Response

As described in a previous chapter, **Quick Response (QR)** is an industrywide strategy for quick and precise production and replenishment of merchandise. First, we will give an overview of the QR strategy in the industry and, in sections that follow, will give more specific details on how QR initiatives are used throughout the stages from product development through distribution.

Today, many apparel companies are participating in computerized partnerships with retail customers and fabric suppliers, which is enabling them to accelerate their manufacturing process and provide customers with more timely delivery of currently wanted merchandise. By means of electronic data interchange, participating apparel producers receive an instant and continuing flow of information about what their "retail partners" are selling by style, sizes, and colors and what needs to be replenished. This information enables them to predetermine production plans and schedules more precisely by discontinuing slow-moving styles and concentrating on best-sellers, thereby reducing costly markdowns and increasing turnover. Also, by receiving retail reorders and giving fabric reorders directly into their interlocking computers, they can bypass the manual order entry process. For apparel producers, the implementation of a QR program requires a change in their traditional operational strategies and production planning, which formerly focused on the reduction of production costs and is now focusing on the reduction of production time. It also requires a clear working relationship with their retail customers and their fabric suppliers.

The first QR partnerships were between large-volume producers and retailers, each of which had the capital to invest in the necessary but costly electronic equipment. For example, the Wrangler division of VF Corporation, which has a computer-to-computer network with the giant Wal-Mart retail company, affixes identifying bar code labels on its merchandise and provides elaborate software services to track the sales in its stores. Dillard's, one of America's largest department store chains, is linked to major suppliers with which it electronically shares information to place reorders and to pinpoint trends. Among its suppliers are Sara Lee's Hanes Hosiery and Haggar. These and other QR participants claim that the program has increased their sales tremendously.

Fast delivery (through Quick Response) is one of several added expectations retailers have of their apparel suppliers in recent years. Retailers now prefer to place smaller orders for apparel, with the expectation that they will be able to get quick replenishment from the manufacturer as items sell. Some companies refer to this as their **rapid replenishment** program. Retailers prefer this method over previous strategies in which they purchased much larger amounts of merchandise early in a season. Retailers like this approach because they have less money invested in inventory and they are relieved of some of the risk if items do not sell as expected. Manufacturers often have to assume more burden for carrying inventory in some of their relationships with retailers.

Because manufacturers have worked in Quick Response partnerships with retailers, much shorter planning cycles have changed the whole concept of apparel merchandising. Instead of planning and committing for a season, manufacturers and retailers work much closer to the actual selling season. This is known as **real time merchandising (RTM)**—which is at the core of successful Quick Response systems. Having merchandise tied up in the production pipeline for months is becoming a thing of the past. Instead, manufacturers and retailers are operating in *real time*. That is, lines are continuously updated to reflect consumer preferences closer to and during retail selling seasons. RTM is the continuous analysis of fashion direction, consumer style testing results, and current retail sales. Under real time merchandising, the line planning calendar becomes a flexible and more responsive tool for merchandisers, not a strait jacket (Brown, 1989). Figure 6–4 depicts the basic steps in real time merchandising.

Industry consultants Kurt Salmon Associates (KSA) (1985) predict that Quick Response, as the industry knows it today, someday will not exist as a chain with its distinct functions (i.e., different segments in the softgoods chain). Instead, we will have an interlocking complex that revolves around the consumer. Speed, electronic linkages, and strategic alliances among companies will be "givens" in the future. KSA concludes that companies *will have to be quick to survive*.

Another strategy, called **agile manufacturing**, was introduced to the industry by the Textile/Clothing Technology Corporation, [TC]^2. [TC]^2 is an industry/

Figure 6–4

Quick Response Real Time Merchandising

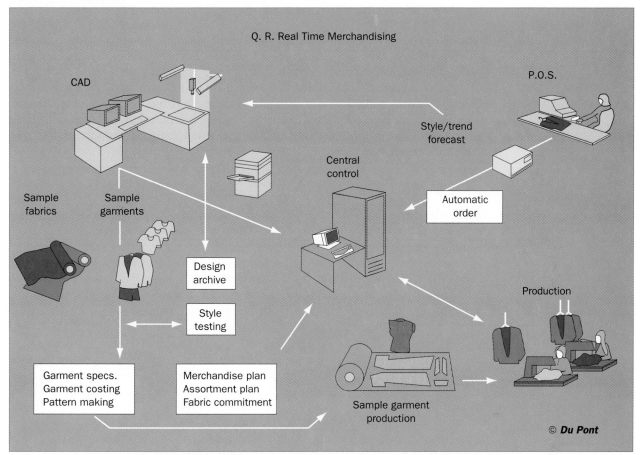

Q. R. Real Time Merchandising

CAD

P.O.S.

Style/trend
forecast

Central
control

Sample
fabrics

Sample
garments

Automatic
order

Design
archive

Style
testing

Production

Garment specs.
Garment costing
Pattern making

Merchandise plan
Assortment plan
Fabric commitment

Sample garment
production

© *Du Pont*

"Real time merchandising" starts with analysis of what is selling, proceeds to consumer style testing of sample designs, and follows with short-lot production of styles that proved most popular in consumer tests. Initial sales, monitored by size and color, guide production for fill-in stock and provide styling guidance for following seasons.

Source: Reprinted by permission of DuPont.

government-funded program that develops leading-edge competitive strategies for the apparel industry. *The agile manufacturing concept might be considered Quick Response with a higher rate of flexibility, or QR made-to-order.* It is considered a strategy for twenty-first-century manufacturing, which may go from the cash register to design, to cut fabric, to screen printing, to assembly, and to shipping in a matter of hours. As former [TC]^2 managing director Joe Off noted:

> In an agile . . . world, we need to be able to design and deliver new products very quickly. Products are designed to evolve. Patterns on shorts today, for example, are not selling well tomorrow. We can immediately redesign that pattern and start shipping a new product in a day's time. It's designed to evolve so it's produced to order." (Clune, 1993, p. 8)

From Design Concept to Consumer

Figure 6–5 gives a very simplified overview of the major steps in producing a garment. Following this, a more detailed discussion on the various steps is given, including the way in which QR computer technologies are involved at various stages.

The next sections consider the fundamental processes an apparel firm goes through in developing products and taking them from the design stage to the consumer. When retailers produce their private-label lines, they perform essentially these same steps (Table 6–3). In sections that follow, details are given about each of these major process areas.

Line Development—Preadoption Steps

In the women's apparel industry, producers have traditionally prepared and presented (or "opened") new **seasonal lines** to be shown to retail store buyers. A line is a collection or group of styles designed for a specific season. In the women's apparel industry, four to six new lines or collections have been customary in the past: Spring, Summer or Transition, Fall I, Fall II, and Resort or Holiday. The opening dates and number of new lines have varied from one segment of the industry to another, but as a general rule, higher-priced lines have been presented before lower-priced lines.

However, computer technology has revolutionized the whole idea of developing new lines. Now, because of computers, apparel firms can learn quickly from retailers what is selling. This permits the apparel firm to continually update its lines. This strategy means that companies are thinking less and less in terms of discrete seasons and are moving toward a seasonless continuum of introducing new lines closer to the selling season.

Table 6–4 gives the basic steps in the **preadoption** product development process. Preadoption includes early stages of development up through review and selection of items in the line that will be produced. Table 6–4 also indicates how computer technologies are involved in each of these steps. Most of these computer applications are tied to QR strategies. The various steps are discussed further in sections that follow.

Designing the Line

In today's apparel industry, many variations exist regarding who does the designing and other aspects of developing a line. The size of the firm, the nature of the apparel produced, and the fashion orientation of the company influence how lines are developed.

In high-fashion apparel firms, designs may originate on the drawing board of its **designers**, who create new ideas and execute new lines four to six times per year. In these companies, the designer's ideas are made into sample garments by expert seamstresses known as **sample makers**. Revisions are made during these stages to give the effect the designer wants.

Designers: Owners or Employees.   The authority, position, and name recognition of the designer vary greatly from one firm in the industry to another. In the majority of apparel firms, the designer is simply a hired talent, perhaps only one of several responsible for developing lines that will be presented under the manufacturer's firm name or brand name. Manufacturers generally hesitate to build up the name of a designer who could be working elsewhere next season. Therefore, the vast

Figure 6–5

Major steps in producing a garment.

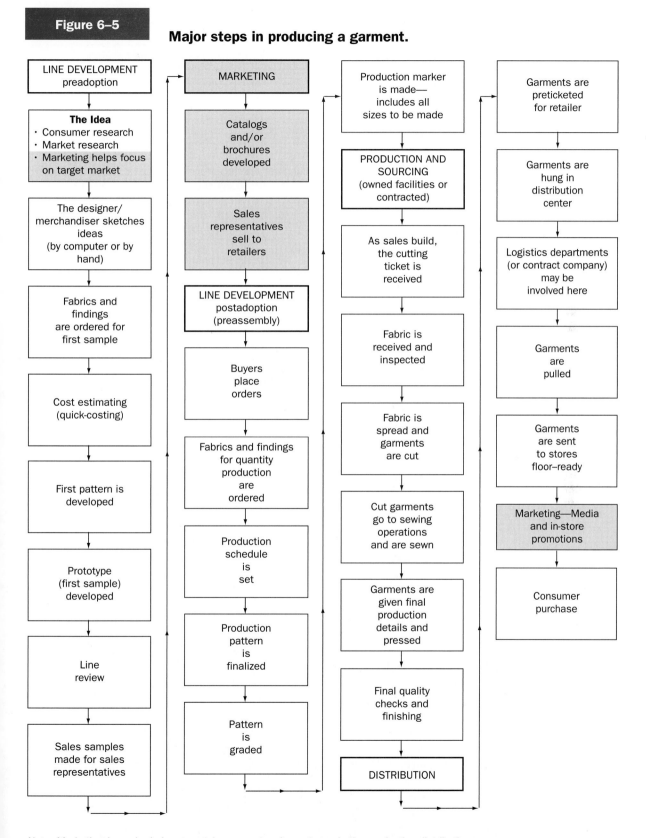

Note: Marketing (see shaded segments) occurs at various stages in the production-distribution process.

Table 6–3	Fundamental Processes of an Apparel Firm

Process	Segments and Activities Included
1. **Line development** (also called product development) • Preadoption • Postadoption	From concept to the production stage.
2. Product sourcing and production	From the development stage through production and into a stage ready for distribution.
3. Product distribution	Servicing customers (for apparel firms, this is mostly retailers) from the time the order is received until payment is received.
4. Marketing	First, positions the firm to produce for a defined target market. Then creates marketing, promotional programs for the finished line.

majority of the industry's designers are nameless as far as the public is concerned. Also in the industry are many small firms that do not even employ designers but rely on freelance design services or on a patternmaker with a good sense of fashion.

Today the number of American designers whose names are well known to the public has increased. This is because they have become owners, partly or completely, of their own producing companies, operating in their own names, and featuring their names on labels, in national advertising, and in the fashion press. Among the best known and most successful are the companies of Calvin Klein, Ralph Lauren, Tommy Hilfiger, Bill Blass, Oscar de la Renta, James Galanos, Nicole Miller, Adrienne Vittadini, Arnold Scaasi, Donna Karan, and Liz Claiborne.

Typical of the way a designer wins recognition by operating his or her own company is the story of Liz Claiborne. During the many years she worked for Jonathan Logan, she was unknown to the consuming public. In 1976, in conjunction with several partners, she formed her own company under her own name and became well known among manufacturers, retailers, the apparel-buying public—and even among investment strategists who take a lively interest in trading shares in her company, which has a sales volume of about $3 billion a year.

Terri Agins (1999), fashion writer for the *Wall Street Journal*, described Ralph Lauren and Tommy Hilfiger as the "masters of the fashion universe, galloping lengths ahead of the rest of the fashion pack" by establishing their names as synonymous with classic American style. Most of all, she notes they became the "haute couturiers of marketing" (p. 83). Agins believes they remained ahead of the fashion curve by largely ignoring it, and Lauren in particular made fashion history through his "lifestyle merchandising" as seen in advertisements and in the ambiance of in-store shops.

High-fashion designer-name firms generate relatively small sales volume, because their products are aimed and priced for a limited, affluent group of customers. Their importance, however, goes far beyond the dollars in their respective tills, because of the impact of their ideas on the fashion business and the fashion consumer. They are like the icing on the cake—a small but important part of the whole, and a part without which the cake would have little appeal.

Table 6–4	The Line Development Process (Preadoption) and Use of Computer Technologies

Steps in Line Development (Preadoption)	Use of Computer Technologies
1. *Line planning and consumer research* Based on knowledge of the apparel firm's target market. • Determine sales trends • Development of what consumer wants	• Analysis of POS data to understand consumer base • Use of consumer profile data • Use of data-mining tools to analyze sales trends and consumer information
2. *Concept development* Based on line planning, shopping the market, and consumer research, a well-targeted product assortment is developed. • Design may be original or may draw on fabric and silhouette libraries stored in computer. • CAD systems permit trial and error in developing concepts for approval without having to sew physical samples early in the process. • Fabrics and **findings** are identified (tentatively, at this stage). • As initial fabric and production sources are identified, the firm will want to be sure these resources can respond to the volume needed for production.	• CAD system may be used to create new silhouettes and fabric, and/or • Use of company's historical database of designs stored in computer • B2B websites permit apparel firm to consider fabrics and findings from sources around the world. • EDI links with textile mills and other component suppliers to assure fast, dependable delivery of materials when needed.
3. *Quick costing* This is an initial **cost estimating**, sometimes also known as precosting. More-extensive costing occurs later if a concept is actually chosen to be put into production.	• A quick costing software program helps merchandisers or designers calculate rough costs for the materials and labor. This catches early any designs that will be too costly for the retail price anticipated.
4. *Pattern development* This is the **first pattern**, which may be modified later during the fit process. Initial patterns may be done manually or with computer programs. Computers aid greatly in speed and accuracy, as well as integrating with other stages of production.	• Use existing, similar block patterns in computer, or • Use CAD to make original pattern on computer, or • Digitize an existing pattern (or disassemble a garment) into the computer.
5. *Making samples* • A **prototype** garment (**first sample**) is made either by the apparel company or a contractor. • If a contractor is used, making the samples may be a good test of whether that contractor can do a good job of producing the line.	• Computerized sample cutters may be used to cut samples. • A database of contractors (possibly through B2B website) can provide information on a contractor's performance.
6. *Line reviews* At this stage, the merchandiser, designer, production engineer (and perhaps others from manufacturing), a representative of the sales department, and possibly someone from upper management meet to review the line. Garment samples are available, and **fit models** may try on the garments. • Garments are reviewed for cost, production, styling, and other considerations.	• Software may be used to support line review. • Computerized concept groupings can be rearranged as styles are eliminated. • At this stage, most companies will develop a computer-automated, enterprisewide merchandising calendar, with key deadlines, for everyone in the company to follow. • Catalogs or brochures may be developed from line concepts developed on the computer.

(continued)

Table 6–4	The Line Development Process (Preadoption) and Use of Computer Technologies *(Continued)*

Steps in Line Development (Preadoption)	Use of Computer Technologies
• Styles are pulled together into coordinated groups. • Some styles will be eliminated. • Target prices and **gross margins** will be established. • At this stage, leading companies use software that sales representatives may use later to present a picture of the line visually and financially.	• Software described at left.
7. Fabrics, trims, buttons, zippers, etc. needed to make style samples for sales representatives are ordered.	• B2B computer connections expedite these orders to assure that supplies will be available for prompt delivery.

Note: Feedback is given back at each stage, and this feedback may influence line development.

In large apparel firms, **merchandisers** are responsible for developing new lines. Merchandisers plan the overall fashion direction for the coming season and give directions to the design staff about seasonal themes, types of items to be designed, and colors. A **product development** team is responsible for the planning and development of a particular product, product line, or brand. In the product development team, designers are primarily responsible for the creative aspect of product development. In a smaller company, the owner or sole designer may perform these tasks.

In a very large company a merchandiser plans the overall fashion direction for the coming season and gives directions to the design staff about seasonal themes, types of items to be designed, and colors and fabrics to be used. In a smaller company the owner or the designer will fulfill this function. Among less-original manufacturers, designs often start life in the form of someone else's merchandise that has been sketched or purchased for copying.

Responsibilities of Designers/Merchandisers

The designer or merchandiser is expected to develop a group of new designs in advance of a marketing period—which, in turn, is in advance of the consumer buying period. In many instances, because fashion is basically an evolutionary process, each seasonal collection may include "new" designs that are simply updated versions of the current or past season's best-sellers. Also included may be copied or revised versions of some other company's best-sellers.

The designer's or merchandiser's responsibilities go beyond ideas alone, and there are many practical obstacles to overcome. In addition to creating styles that will fit into the firm's price range and type of merchandise, the designer is responsible for the selection of fabrics and must give consideration also to the availability and cost of materials, the availability of production techniques, costs of labor, and the particular image that the company wishes to present. Great designers/merchandisers are those who can apply their creative talents and skills to overcome business limitations and produce salable merchandise.

For most firms these days, designing takes place on computers that store many basic styles, including designs from previous lines (Figure 6–6). **Computer-aided**

Figure 6–6

(a) Pattern making with computer speed and accuracy are provided by pattern design systems, such as Gerber Garment Technology's AccuMark™ shown here. Patterns are easily drafted from scratch or modified from existing styles. (b) Computer systems such as Gerber Garment Technology's Product Data Management (PDM) system automate the entire product development cycle. PDM organizes fabric, sketches, patterns, sizing data, and labor and costing information. The information is available on a central database and can be accessed from any geographical location.

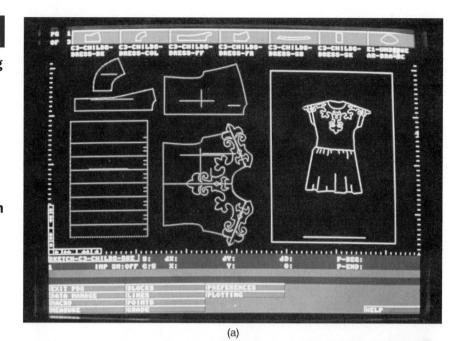

(a)

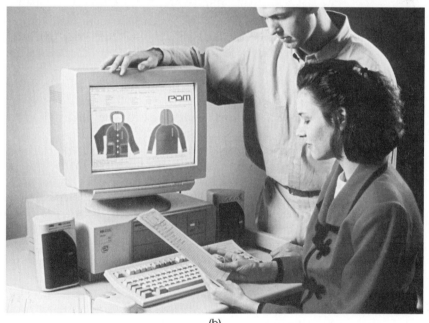

(b)

Source: Photos courtesy of Gerber Garment Technology, Inc.

design (CAD) systems have led to many changes in the development of a design. When creating new ideas for a line, the designer/merchandiser can sketch new garments on the screen and manipulate lines, silhouette, fabric patterns, color, and other design features. Although new designs will be made into samples and perfected through that process, the computer permits shortcuts for a significant portion of many companies' lines.

Many companies today store a large portion of their basic patterns in the computer's memory. In the product development stage, a company can modify an existing pattern for many new styles without having to start from the beginning. Additionally, patterns made by more traditional ways can be entered into the computer by digitizing or scanning them into the computer. Then, the designer can manipulate and modify those patterns on the computer. Designs stored in the computer can be modified without having to go through the time-consuming process of making sample garments for every design idea. By not having to go through the sample-making stage, a great deal of time is trimmed from the schedule for developing a line. Additionally, the computer sketches can be printed for use in meetings with company executives and retail buyers or for use in printed materials showing the line.

After tentative designs are developed, whether by computer or by the more traditional way, key teams in the company review first-sample garments for cost, production feasibility, **sourcing** for production, fabric requirements and availability, and profit potential. The decision is made at this point whether the garment will be accepted as part of the new line. Again, in small companies, one or two individuals may make these decisions.

Line Development—Postadoption

Once the final selections from the line have been designated for production (i.e., **postadoption**), the next steps occur. Generally known in the industry as **preproduction operations** are those steps between the stage when a style is accepted in the line and when the cut garment pieces are sent to the sewing floor (Glock & Kunz, 1995). These might even more accurately be called "*preassembly* operations." If production is contracted, some of these operations—as well as the sewing process—may be performed by the contractor.

Once a garment is approved for the line, styling and fit are perfected. Then, production-related steps occur.

Making the production pattern. If a design is to be produced, it moves to the next stage of having a **production pattern** made for the garment. Traditionally, a highly skilled pattern maker made the master production pattern for the garment—in one size only (whatever size the firm used for its samples). Some high-style design houses may still use this traditional method. Other firms may use this only in the very early stages of developing patterns for designs for which no similar pattern exists in the computer's memory.

Again, computers have revolutionized this stage for much of the industry. See Table 6–5.

Style samples are made. After designs are selected for the line, duplicate samples (in the sample size) are produced for sales representatives. Samples are shown to buyers in showrooms in New York and/or some of the regional marts, or sales representatives may take samples with them on the road as they call on retailers. Orders placed with sales representatives determine the quantity of various styles to be produced.

Pattern grading. After a basic pattern is perfected, **grading** occurs to produce a pattern for that garment in all the sizes in which it will be offered. Traditionally, pattern graders were highly skilled individuals whose tedious work made a great deal of difference in how wearers felt about the fit of garments. Grading is equally important now, but computers expedite this task greatly in most firms.

Body scanning technology, already in use to a limited extent, will permit manufacturers to scan the customer's body and generate a pattern uniquely sized for that person's body. When this process is more commonly available, pattern grading may seem old fashioned.

Table 6–5	The Line Development Process (Postadoption) and Use of Computer Technologies

Steps in Line Development (Postadoption)	Use of Computer Technologies
1. *Styling and fit are perfected* At this stage modifications can be made before making the final pattern.	• Modifications may be made by computer
2. *Create production pattern*	• Database holds patterns in a well-organized, easy-to-copy format, or • CAD software speeds the development of production patterns
3. *Style samples are made* Samples of garments from the line are made for sales representatives to use in showing the line at market.	• Samples are made from patterns developed manually or with the computer. Samples may be cut with a computerized sample cutter.
4. *Production patterns are graded* Patterns are developed in all the sizes to be produced for a style.	• Patterns are graded by computer. Few companies now do this manually.
5. *Production marker is made* (Particularly if a line is contracted for production, this may occur later as part of the production process.)	• Computer programs aid in efficient fabric utilization. From this, a marker is made by computer.
6. *Order production fabrics and supplies* Quantities of fabrics, trims, buttons, zippers, etc. are ordered based on sales orders.	• B2B websites (and/or EDI) link with textile mills and other suppliers.
7. *Final arrangements for production (garment assembly) are made* If production is to be contracted, final arrangements are made with contractors. If made in company-owned plant, plant staff are advised of production schedule and other details.	• EDI or other electronic linkages are often used between the merchandising staff and the factory.
8. *Specifications are developed* for • Styling • Fit • Fabrics and components • Assembly methods • Quality standards	• Database holds specifications. • Programs such as Gerber's PDM system organize this data.
9. *Final costing*	• After all decisions have been made, final costing is done with computer programs designed to do this.

Note: Some of these steps may occur simultaneously, and the exact sequence may vary from company to company.

　　　Marker making.　　The next step after grading is **marker** making. The marker is made according to the ratio of orders. The marker is a long paper diagram that shows placement of all of the various pattern pieces for all the sizes produced as they should be laid out in order to cut the cloth economically and with bias and straight **grainlines** where each is needed. Computers generate most of today's markers because of the great savings in fabric achieved through more efficient markers (Figure 6–7).

Figure 6–7

Computer technologies permit efficient marker making. The placement shown on the screen is transmitted to a printer that prints the marker in full scale for manual cutting or transfers it to a computerized cutter with this layout stored in its memory.

Source: Photo courtesy of Gerber Garment Technology, Inc.

Ordering of production fabrics and supplies. Up to this point the apparel firm's staff will have already been in touch with textile mills and vendors of trims, buttons, zippers, and other components. Today, apparel firms are likely to consult Internet textile exchanges or websites for textile and findings companies in a variety of countries. Up to this point, the company probably ordered only enough to make the samples. After the sales force shares information on the orders received for various items in the line, the final order is placed for the **production fabrics** and **findings**.

Final arrangements for garment assembly are made. The apparel firm will have determined long before this stage whether garment assembly will occur in the firm's own factories or if it will be contracted. At this stage, final arrangements must be made with the staff in the sewing plant regarding matters of scheduling, delivery of fabrics and other supplies, and completion date expected.

Final specifications are developed. **Specifications** are brief written descriptions or guidelines for how the garment should be produced and standards for the finished item. This includes standards for the materials used, how assembly should occur, and details for what is expected in the final garment. Although many of these will have been determined along the way in developing the garment line, the final specifications must be developed at this stage before the garments go into production in the factory.

Final costing. Although a quick precosting occurred early in the preadoption stage and costing issues were considered throughout the product development process, a final costing occurs in the postadoption stage before production begins. This is detailed costing to provide an accurate picture of what actual costs are going to be and to find ways to minimize costs wherever possible.

Product Sourcing and Production

Prior to this point, an apparel firm will have decided where the production of the garments will take place. As noted earlier, this can be in the firm's own facilities or in a contractor's facility. Facilities for each of these may be in the United States or in another country. Major steps in product sourcing and production are shown in Table 6–6 and discussed in further detail in sections which follow.

Marker making. When contractors are used to make the garments, markers may be developed by the contractor at this stage.

Spreading. In preparation for cutting, layers of fabric are rolled out on long tables, often as many as 100 or more plies high. In the past, spreading occurred manually as workers moved fabric rolls from one end of the cutting table to the other. Now, automatic spreading machines are available to perform this step.

Table 6–6	Steps in Product Sourcing/Production and Use of Computer Technologies

Steps in Product Sourcing/Production	Use of Computer Technologies
1. *Identify production facility* In earlier stages, the facility would have been identified and arrangements made for the start of the production.	• A database of contractors (possibly through a B2B website) will provide capabilities of various plants as well as the timing and quality records of each. • Markers, production instructions, and specifications may be sent electronically to plants. • In **computer integrated manufacturing (CIM)**, patterns, markers, cutting, and other steps are integrated so that data are transferred from one step to the next without having to reenter data.
2. *Coordination of delivery for fabrics and other supplies* This must occur well before the cutting and production are to begin.	• B2B website and/or EDI linkages between the apparel firm and suppliers assure timely deliveries.
3. *Spreading*	
4. *Cutting*	• This may be done manually or with computerized cutters.
5. *Garment assembly* (sewing)	• **Unit production systems (UPS)** are computerized overhead transport systems that move garments to sewing operators. Bar codes permit computerized tracking of **work-in-process (WIP)**. • Computerized production systems permit computer tracking of work-in-process.
6. *Quality control* Both in-line and final inspections assure that finished garments meet quality standards.	
7. *Finishing*	
8. *Pressing*	
9. *Ticketing* • Hang tags, price tags, care labels	• These may be computer generated. If the retailer's price tags are attached, these usually include bar coding necessary to capture POS data that will be used in repeating the product development–production cycle for reorders or next season's lines.

Cutting.   Cutting occurs next, with the marker providing the cutting plan. The number of orders received or realistically anticipated determines the number of garments to be cut at this stage. The decision on the number of units to be produced must fit the company's broad business plan—that is, the number of units that must be produced to meet the company's financial goals. A **cut order** will have been sent to the plant to determine the quantity of garments to be cut in various sizes (the **cutting ticket**). Risk is a concern. Companies do not want excessive inventory left over if they produce too many units in the line. In recent years, firms have tended to be conservative on the number to cut at this stage. Instead, they test the market with a limited number of units. Unless items are basic, the company is more likely to make garments according to orders received rather than making them to have in stock.

Firms vary on the minimum number of garments they will cut. For example, producers whose dresses retail at medium to higher prices say that they require orders of 100 to 500 units of a number before cutting. On the other hand, one producer whose coats use carefully hand-cut leather in their designs and whose retail prices are very high stated that he will start production with orders for as few as 10 units. For manufacturers that are producing for mass distribution, the number of units considered a minimum for a production order may be counted in the thousands. Each producer has to work out its own minimum, in terms of how many units can be expected to be sold to customers and how much must be realized in profit on the sales of a given number to offset the costs of putting it into production, in addition to other costs.

For actual cutting, layers of fabric are rolled out on long tables. The way in which cutting occurs depends on the size of the company and the extent to which it spends money to buy modern timesaving equipment. In traditional methods, the marker is placed on top of the layered fabric. In these cutting methods, a person called a cutter uses electrically powered portable knives and follows lines on the marker to cut through fabric layered several inches deep.

Newer cutting technology automates and expedites the cutting step. Among these, the most common is the computerized cutter, which has the marker stored in its memory; therefore, the paper marker is not required (Figure 6–8). An automated cutting head quickly moves about, cutting multiple layers of fabric and stopping from time to time to resharpen the cutting blades. Laser cutters are also available, and although these do excellent precision cutting, most types cannot cut through thick layers of fabrics. High-tech cutting equipment is very costly, frequently placing it out of the reach of smaller companies.

Production: Garment Assembly.   The cut parts of the garments are then collected, identified, and passed along for the sewing operation. This is done in the firm's own plant if it is an **inside shop** or to a contractor—either in the United States or another country—for the sewing. If it is an **outside shop**, in some instances, contractors do the cutting, working from the marker and continuing on from that point.

Firms vary in the type of production systems used to sew the garments. The basic types follow.

- *Single operator.* In this system, sometimes known as the tailor system, a single operator does all the machine sewing on a garment. This system is used for expensive or customized garments that require highly skilled workers.
- *Progressive bundle system.* In this system, workers generally sew one part of the garment in an assembly line manner. The name for this system comes from the cut bundles of garment pieces that are distributed to operators who sew their part and then pass the item on to the next operator. In this system, workers are usually paid by the number of items they produce (also known as the *piece rate* system).

Automated cutters, such as this GERBERcutter®, cut garments with precision and speed.

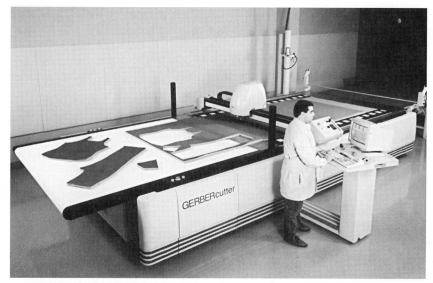

Source: Photo courtesy of Gerber Garment Technology, Inc.

- *Unit production system (UPS).* Using a computerized overhead transport system, garments are moved one at a time to sewing operators. This reduces the amount of handling time for operators.
- *Modular production system.* In this system, small teams of operators work in a group to produce garments from start to finish. Workers in the module generally are able to perform more than one task. They often have autonomy to set their own production goals. Many companies have shifted from the bundle system to the modular approach. Pay systems vary, but often bonuses are given to the team based on quality, productivity, and meeting deadlines.

Inspection. Garments are inspected after final assembly. This occurs either in the module or in a separate inspection department for the progressive bundle system. This stage is a final check to be sure garments meet the quality standards expected.

Finishing. After inspection, workers trim loose threads and prepare the garment for pressing.

Pressing. Garments are pressed to give a pleasing appearance to shoppers who will view finished items. Many retailers now want garments ready to put on the floor without additional pressing in the store.

Ticketing. As more and more retail stores are demanding that garments be **preticketed** by the manufacturer, the price tag and other hang tags may be attached at this stage.

The End Result: A Finished Garment for Sale

As our discussion has indicated, a great many decisions and activities are part of the apparel development and production process. Each step is important in producing merchandise customers will find in their favorite stores. The women's apparel industry is distinguished by the rapidity with which it produces and distributes its goods. In a business that must keep up with changing fashion, it is vital to surmount time and distance factors by speed and flexibility in production. The industry maintains an impressive record in doing so.

Figure 6–9   **Behind the Price Tag of a $73.00 Skirt**

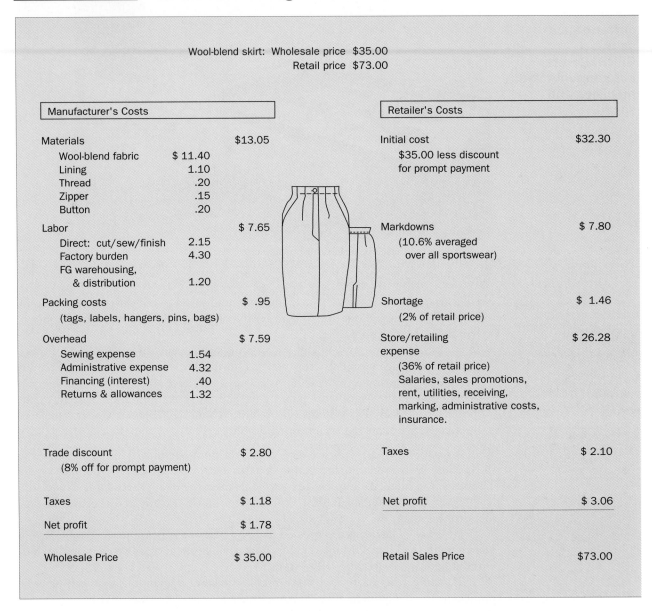

Wool-blend skirt: Wholesale price $35.00
Retail price $73.00

Manufacturer's Costs		
Materials		$13.05
Wool-blend fabric	$ 11.40	
Lining	1.10	
Thread	.20	
Zipper	.15	
Button	.20	
Labor		$ 7.65
Direct: cut/sew/finish	2.15	
Factory burden	4.30	
FG warehousing,		
& distribution	1.20	
Packing costs		$ .95
(tags, labels, hangers, pins, bags)		
Overhead		$ 7.59
Sewing expense	1.54	
Administrative expense	4.32	
Financing (interest)	.40	
Returns & allowances	1.32	
Trade discount		$ 2.80
(8% off for prompt payment)		
Taxes		$ 1.18
Net profit		$ 1.78
Wholesale Price		**$ 35.00**

Retailer's Costs	
Initial cost	$32.30
$35.00 less discount	
for prompt payment	
Markdowns	$ 7.80
(10.6% averaged	
over all sportswear)	
Shortage	$ 1.46
(2% of retail price)	
Store/retailing expense	$ 26.28
(36% of retail price)	
Salaries, sales promotions,	
rent, utilities, receiving,	
marking, administrative costs,	
insurance.	
Taxes	$ 2.10
Net profit	$ 3.06
Retail Sales Price	**$73.00**

Note: These calculations vary from firm to firm. <u>Assumptions for the **manufacturing** portion of this example</u>: returns and allowances = 3.8% of wholesale price, total costs of goods sold (materials, labor, factory burden, FG warehousing and distribution) = 70.1% of wholesale price, and net profit = 5.8% of wholesale price. <u>Assumptions for the **retailing** portion of this example are</u>: markdowns = 10.6% of retail price, shortages = 2% of retail price, store expenses = 36% of retail price, taxes = 40% of gross income, and net profit = 4.1% of retail price.

Source: The author wishes to express appreciation to the following executives at Kellwood Company who provided updated calculations for this figure: John Turnage, Deane Thompson, Roseanne Grady, and John Henderson (formerly with May Department Stores). These figures reflect business conditions for both industry sectors in the 1990s.

Although consumers usually do not understand all the steps involved in getting a garment to the sales floor, many people have contributed in important ways to produce and deliver that garment. Figure 6–9 provides an estimate of the cost of each of these aspects that go into making and selling a garment.

Distribution

Product distribution is the process of servicing customer orders from receipt to receiving payment. The goal behind this process is to provide what consumers want, when they want it, in the most cost-effective manner.

Shipping. Garments are prepared for shipping to retail customers or to the apparel firm's **distribution center (DC)**, previously called warehouses. Sometimes items are shipped in boxes, but increasingly, retailers now demand that garments be shipped in hanging form so they are ready for the sales floor.

Today, forward-thinking apparel firms view shipping and DC management as critical to the success of the company. Many firms use third-party logistics firms to bring finished contracted garments from other countries. These companies use

Figure 6–10	**Customer Order Processing**

An integrated customer order processing system.

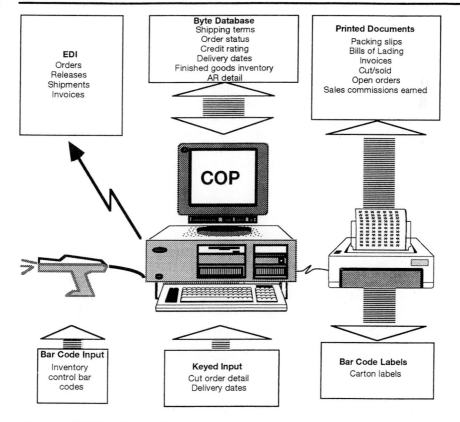

Source: © 1993 Byte Systems, Inc.

sophisticated global positioning technologies that permit tracking a shipment anywhere in the world.

Modern apparel distribution centers use computerized storage and picking systems that rely on bar coding for storage and retrieval of garments when needed to fill orders.

Today, computer systems permit integration of many of the ordering and distribution processes. An example from Byte Systems Inc. is shown in Figure 6–10. In this **customer order processing (COP)** software, orders are entered into the computer, and the COP system produces bar code labels that when scanned can produce packing slips, bills of lading or invoices, or transmit the same information in an EDI format. This system can stand alone or can be integrated with the apparel production and/or inventory control systems. Systems such as these reduce administrative costs and assure more accurate delivery of products to the customer.

Marketing Procedures

The marketing divisions of successful apparel firms are involved from the time a line is conceived. In the early stages, marketing helps to determine that a line is suitably aimed at the company's target market. Marketing is also involved in developing sales plans, sales goals, and necessary gross margin goals for the company to make a profit on the line. Marketing will be concerned about the **sell-through** of a line—the extent to which it moves through the marketing channel to reach the consumer. Marketing operations are involved at several stages in promoting and selling the line.

Over the years, the women's apparel industry has established a pattern of selling directly to retailers, supplementing the efforts of producers' salespeople with advertising and publicity. This practice of direct selling, from producer to retailer, is related to the need for speed in the marketing time for ever-changing fashions. Because timing in fashion is of utmost importance, there is no real place for wholesale middlemen in the marketing of fashion goods. Such middlemen would have to buy, warehouse, and sell—distribution procedures too time consuming to be practical except for staple items such as basic hosiery and undergarments, and any other articles in which fashion change is fairly slow.

Presentation of Lines

The methods of introducing new lines to buyers vary. Some firms show their new collections accessorized, dramatized, and professionally modeled in elaborate fashion shows. These shows may be staged in ballrooms, chic restaurants, discos, and other "in" locations. Other companies simply have their lines ready in their showrooms, where the garments are on racks, to be taken down and shown to individual retail buyers for inspection and possible purchase. Some firms stage press previews of their new collections, to which they invite fashion editors in order to get publicity to the consuming public. Others show their lines only to publications in which they are eager to have a "credit"—an editorial mention of one of their numbers. The method and timing of presenting new lines varies from firm to firm and from one branch of the industry to another.

The initial presentation of a line, however, is only the beginning of a manufacturer's selling effort, because relatively few retail store buyers will be present at the opening. For the benefit of latecomers, the line will continue to be shown at the company's headquarters or showrooms, although without the initial fanfare and probably without live models. For the benefit of retail store buyers who may not have seen the line while in the market or who may not have come at all, the firm may send it out with traveling sales representatives or exhibit it at regional showrooms and trade shows, or it may do all of these.

Beginning in 1992, nearly all major U.S. designers banded together to centralize and unify their fall and spring fashion showings. Today, most leading U.S. designers are collaborating and staging their opening seasonal runway shows under large tents in Bryant Park, which is next door to New York's Public Library. The Bryant Park showings are under the auspices of "**Seventh on Sixth,**" a nonprofit organization put together for the seasonal shows by the Council of Fashion Designers of America. Important cogs in this event are corporate sponsors that underwrite costs in addition to rental fees from the participating designer companies, which range from $15,000 to $30,000, depending on showing time and seating capacity of the tents.

Reliance on a Sales Force

By and large, women's apparel producers rely on their own salespeople to bring the products to the attention of retail store buyers. Most firms maintain selling staffs in their showrooms to wait on visiting retail store buyers and to build a following among retailers who are potential customers. Some firms also employ road salespeople who travel with sample lines to show their merchandise to retailers within their assigned territories. These men and women may also set up temporary displays in any regional trade shows that take place in their territories. In addition, many of the larger firms supplement their headquarters showrooms with regional showrooms.

For those manufacturers who do not have their own sales staffs or regional sales offices, there are independent selling representatives that maintain permanent showrooms and represent several noncompeting lines in given areas.

The industry usually pays its salespeople on a commission basis, except for those who staff the showroom in the headquarters office.

Advertising and Publicity: National and Trade

Before the 1960s, the names of American designers and garment manufacturers were not generally well known to customers; apparel was purchased by a combination of approval of a garment's appearance and confidence in the retail seller. The source of a garment or accessory was considered the retailer's trade secret; the store's label was of paramount importance.

The rise of giant apparel firms in the 1960s gave impetus to the development of brand names and their promotion by national advertising campaigns. This advertising was aided by the **cooperative advertising** funds made available by the giant producers of manufactured fibers such as Dacron (by DuPont) and Kodel (by Eastman). These were (and still are) arrangements under which the manufacturer and fiber company share the cost of advertising, which is run in the manufacturer's name and features the fiber brand in order to promote it to the consumer. The national advertising of "names" became increasingly important when designers of higher-priced merchandise went into business for themselves, either alone or with partners, and established the manufacturing companies that today bear their names. The amount of brand- and designer-name national advertising done by the apparel industry today is very impressive in comparison with this almost nonexistent type of industry advertising prior to the 1960s, but it is still small alongside what is spent by such other major industries as food, drugs, autos, and electronics. In addition to the national advertising done by large brand- or designer-name companies, all fashion manufacturers make widespread use of trade publications as advertising media to bring their names and products to the attention of retailers. The small and specialized circulation of these publications ranks their advertising rates far below those of consumer publications, and thus an apparel producer does not have to be large to make good use of them. Among those widely used are *Women's Wear Daily, California Apparel News*, and *Body Fashions/Intimate Apparel*. All of these are supported by the advertising of small and large producers.

Also common in the apparel business are cooperative advertising arrangements, between retailers and apparel manufacturers. In these arrangements, the advertising appears under the store's name and features the manufacturer's name or brand. In such an arrangement, the retailer enjoys more advertising space than is paid for out of pocket; the manufacturer enjoys advertising that is run in conjunction with the name of a locally known and respected retail store, which is usually backed up by the store with a substantial stock of that maker's goods. The retailer, moreover, as a large and consistent purchaser of space in the local papers, pays a much lower rate for this space than the manufacturer could obtain for its occasional insertions. "Co-op" money buys the producer more space for less cost.

Other promotional techniques include providing retailers with selling aids: customer mailing pieces and newspaper advertising mats and photographs for use in store advertisements, for example.

Many of the larger firms also employ publicity agents. It is through their efforts that many of the fashion articles that appear on the lifestyle pages of newspapers have their origin. Press releases, often accompanied by fashion photographs of high quality, are sent directly to newspaper editors or, in some cases, to local stores for forwarding to the editors.

Designer Trunk Shows

Another marketing technique used by many well-known designers is the **trunk show**. A trunk show is a showing by a manufacturing company of its complete line to consumers assembled in a major retail store. A key company salesperson is in attendance, and often the designer makes a personal appearance. There are also live models to exhibit the garments. Such shows are backed by heavy local advertising and publicity. The consumer has the opportunity not only to see the manufacturer's complete line, but also to order through the store any styles, sizes, and colors not available in the store's stocks, as it is usually impossible for any store to stock an entire line. Designers get a firsthand view of consumer reaction; retailers observe consumer response to style numbers they did not select as well as to those already chosen for resale; producers and retailers gain sales from the impact of the promotion. Many designers say there is nothing like a trunk show for stimulating interest in and sales of their merchandise.

New Technology

New computer and communication technologies provide many new ways to view a line. These might include fashion shows via communication satellite, viewing a line on the Internet, or a compact disc.

Apparel Manufacturers' Relationships with Retailers

Retail consolidations through buyouts and mergers have resulted in larger and more-powerful retail firms. This concentration of power and clout has many advantages as retailers respond to difficult business conditions. However, the massive buying power of the retail giants permits them to demand very competitive prices on merchandise. These competitive prices permit the megamerchants to offer merchandise to their customers at attractive prices and to improve their own profit margins. Industry experts predict that this retail consolidation will continue.

Retail consolidations create challenges for manufacturers who sell to the new breed of giant merchants. As retailers get larger, they are positioned to make increasing demands on their suppliers, the apparel manufacturers. As retailers have experienced profit difficulties, they tend to squeeze suppliers. The consolidation means that the suppliers now have fewer potential retail customers. The remaining retailers buy very large quantities of merchandise; therefore, manufacturers generally want part of that business. Of course, powerful retailers know this.

Figure 6–11

An example of how retailers' chargebacks affect apparel firms (or designers).

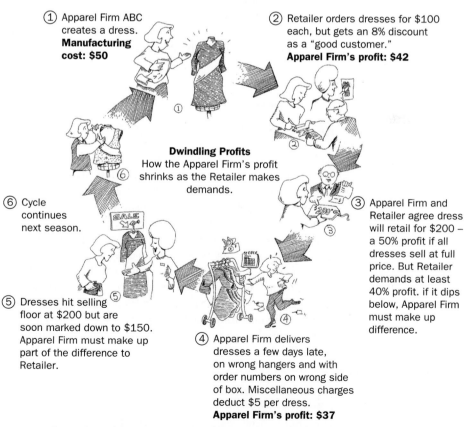

① Apparel Firm ABC creates a dress. **Manufacturing cost: $50**

② Retailer orders dresses for $100 each, but gets an 8% discount as a "good customer." **Apparel Firm's profit: $42**

③ Apparel Firm and Retailer agree dress will retail for $200 – a 50% profit if all dresses sell at full price. But Retailer demands at least 40% profit. if it dips below, Apparel Firm must make up difference.

④ Apparel Firm delivers dresses a few days late, on wrong hangers and with order numbers on wrong side of box. Miscellaneous charges deduct $5 per dress. **Apparel Firm's profit: $37**

⑤ Dresses hit selling floor at $200 but are soon marked down to $150. Apparel Firm must make up part of the difference to Retailer.

⑥ Cycle continues next season.

Dwindling Profits
How the Apparel Firm's profit shrinks as the Retailer makes demands.

Source: Adapted from the *Wall Street Journal.* Illustration by Dennis Murphy.

Consequently, large, powerful retailers continue to press suppliers to give better and better prices and to provide more and more services to the retailer. For example, retailers often want suppliers to guarantee their stores' profit margins and expect rebates if those goals are not met, also expecting the suppliers to cover the heavy discounts and markdowns on their own selling floors. Stores now expect manufacturers to preticket merchandise, to ship it floor-ready, and to hold the extra inventory. Retailers continue to demand more **chargebacks**, financial penalties imposed for transgressions ranging from errors in purchase orders to failure to deliver merchandise floor-ready. Stores may fine the supplier for violations of ticketing, packing, and shipping rules. Figure 6–11 shows how chargebacks occur. All of these demands are devastating to the profits for apparel suppliers (Bird & Bounds, 1997).

A number of retail giants have added another difficult dimension for manufacturers. Several retailers have concentrated their purchasing with a limited group of vendors, in a strategy called **matrix buying**. This preferred vendor list, called the *matrix*, consists of suppliers who can provide the products, service, and pricing that retailers need to execute their particular strategies. For large powerful retailers, this is likely to consist of manufacturers who give attractive prices on merchandise that fits into the store's merchandising plan and provide the services the retailer demands.

Increasingly, it is the largest apparel manufacturers who can meet the demands of the giant retailers. For example, if retailers want the supplier to hold the bulk of the inventory and send replenishment items as needed, this **Quick Response** strategy may not be possible for small suppliers. Quick Response requires sophisticated electronic data interchange (EDI) technology that small apparel firms are not likely to have. Considering the consolidations in both the retailing sector and the manufacturing sector and the proficiencies each requires of the other, it is possible there will be a time when "the elephants dance only with the elephants."

Manufacturers into Retailing

Today, many apparel-producing companies, dissatisfied with the capabilities of their retail customers to efficiently market their products, are taking an increasingly active role in retailing their own merchandise. Instead of depending exclusively on retail accounts to buy and sell their products, more and more apparel manufacturers are also selling directly to the consumer through company-owned retail shops, factory outlets, and their own separately run shops within the retail stores that buy their merchandise. Some reach the consumer directly through catalogs, the Internet, or television home shopping. Usually, these retail activities represent a small portion of the company's total sales, and there appears to be no intention on the part of these producers to abandon manufacturing in favor of retailing. Their aims are to seek a larger share of the consumer market, to "showcase" their entire line, and to be less dependent on retailers to buy and distribute their merchandise.

Manufacturer-Owned Retail Stores

The manufacturer-owned retail stores have long been an established channel of distribution in the menswear industry, as is discussed in Chapter 7. In the women's apparel field, however, the trend toward company-owned retail stores accelerated in the 1980s as more and more women's apparel manufacturers moved into their own retail operations in ever-increasing numbers. These company stores are located in prime shopping areas, carry a large and complete stock of the firm's products at regular prices, have an attractive environment, and offer many customer services.

Some industry observers believe that these company-owned stores essentially bring them into direct competition with their retail accounts. For many retailers, this trend is very distressing.

The relatively new company stores that have been discussed should be distinguished from the manufacturers' underselling factory outlets that have been around for decades. These older factory outlets were usually sparsely located, in out-of-the-way factory town locations and were stocked with an incomplete assortment of irregulars, seconds, and excess out-of-season merchandise—an inevitable by-product of mass-produced ready-to-wear that was unsalable at regular prices. Today's newer factory outlet developments, however, generally carry a good deal of new, first-quality merchandise. The current proliferation of factory outlets is discussed in the retailing chapter.

Manufacturers' Shops within Stores

Producers with strong images are further playing an increasingly active role in the presentation and sale of their own merchandise by means of their own separate "named" (i.e., brand or designer) shops within the large retail stores to which they sell. In cooperative operations such as these, the retailer provides the "real estate" (the space within the store) and is credited with the sales volume of the department. Although financial arrangements vary, the vendors participate in the design and fixturing of their department and pay all or part of the cost for setting them up as well as the costs of advertising. The department's selling personnel either are employed and paid by the manufacturer directly or are the retailer's employees whom the manufacturer has specially trained. The quantity and quality of the merchandise assortment, as well as its presentation, are determined by the manufacturer.

In order for manufacturers to be given their own department within a store, their merchandise must appeal to the store's targeted customers, and the vendor must guarantee the retail company that it can provide continuity as well as a minimum amount of sales on which the retailer will achieve a required gross profit. The ability to provide enough merchandise to keep the shop filled and to keep that merchandise moving is also a vital consideration for the retailer.

The companies of Tommy Hilfiger, Liz Claiborne, and Ralph Lauren have been leaders in this "in-store shop" concept with their creation of "Hilfiger Shops," "Liz Shops" and "Polo" shops. Their success encouraged other manufacturers to follow suit. In recent years, however, as these in-store shops have proliferated, some major retailers feel they have lost control of their own store space and are taking steps to reclaim it.

Nature of the Industry

Apparel producers vary widely as to size, product, and type of operation. Small companies coexist with giant firms. Specialists rub shoulders with firms that, through their various divisions, can dress a person from the skin out and for every conceivable occasion. Self-contained operations and plants that perform no more than a single step of the production process, publicly owned giant companies and small privately owned firms, fashion creators and flagrant copiers—all are found in the industry.

Different Types of Producers

Apparel manufacturers do not always handle the entire production of a garment in their own factories; they may contract out some of the work. The U.S. Census of Manufacturers, therefore, divides the industry's firms into three classifications according to the comprehensiveness of their production activities: manufacturers, apparel jobbers, and contractors. Common usage, however, uses different criteria and terminology.

Manufacturers

Classified as **manufacturers** by the census are those firms that buy fabric and do the designing, patternmaking, grading, cutting, sewing, and assembling of garments in factories that they own. In the industry, factories that are wholly owned by a manufacturing company are known as **inside shops**, whether or not all steps in production are performed on the same premises. A major advantage of such an integrated operation is that there is complete control over the production quality of the product. A disadvantage is that the necessary factory facilities and machinery require large capital investments.

In reality today, however, few large firms commonly considered "apparel manufacturers" would qualify under the census terminology as *manufacturers*. In common usage, firms considered apparel *manufacturers* in the 1990s by industry executives, trade associations, industry publications, Wall Street analysts, and others who follow the industry may actually perform a very limited number of the tasks in the census definition. For example, in a summary of the top U.S. apparel firms' sales for 1999 in *Apparel Industry Magazine* ("AIM's Global 150," 2000), a leading trade publication for the industry, all of the top 10 companies are actively involved in contracting production outside the respective firms' own facilities. Some use domestic contractors, and nearly all of them use extensive overseas contracting. For example, the Liz Claiborne company invariably appears on the list of apparel manufacturers in industry sources; however, all production is contracted outside the firm's facilities—and a very large portion of that production is performed by overseas contractors.

Therefore, the term *manufacturer*, as it is generally used within the industry today, has a much broader interpretation than the census definition. Industry use of the term refers to any firm that develops garments, controls production, sells to retailers (and, in some cases, directly to end-use customers), and ships and bills merchandise. Firms may or may not buy the fabrics to be used; in some cases, the contractor may even place the fabric orders. Today, mostly only smaller apparel companies conform to the limited census definition for apparel manufacturers.

Retailers as Manufacturers. In today's fashion industry, a number of the largest fashion retailers have private-label divisions that function much the same as today's firms that are more commonly considered "manufacturers." In its 2000 overview of the largest apparel companies, *Apparel Industry Magazine* listed The Limited and The Gap as the top two apparel "manufacturers," with 1999 sales at $9,723 million and $9,055 million respectively. Including retail firms on the "manufacturers" list indicates how clearly the distinctions between these two industry segments have blurred.

Apparel Jobbers

What the census defines as an **apparel jobber** is a firm that generally handles all processes but the sewing, and sometimes the cutting, and that contracts out these production processes to independently owned outside contracting facilities. The majority of women's apparel firms, both small and large, high priced and low priced, contract out their sewing and often their cutting, as well as any other highly specialized production processes, such as embroidery, quilting, and pleating, that require special machinery. One advantage of using outside facilities in this way is that minimal capital investment is required. A disadvantage is that there is less quality control.

The Contracting System: Outside Shops

There are independently owned factories that own their machinery and employ operators to sew and often cut goods from the designs, materials, and specifications of the apparel jobbers that hire them. Both the census and the industry refer to such factories as **contractors**.

The contracting system evolved early in the history of the industry. Prior to 1880, the manufacture of women's apparel was generally accomplished, in all its steps, under one roof. However, as ready-made clothing began to be produced in volume, it became common practice to perform in one place only such key operations as designing, patternmaking, grading, cutting, inspection, selling, and shipping. Most of the sewing tasks were contracted out to individual women who worked in their homes. This was a "cottage industry" procedure in which women added to the family income by doing piecework sewing at home. Eventually, this production shifted to privately owned factories that were devoted entirely to such work. This system of employing outside production facilities—the contracting process—continues to play an important role. The burden of seasonal idleness and production peaks can be shifted to entrepreneur contractors, along with the investment in sewing machines and the dealings with labor.

Contractors are used by both small and large firms, and a large individual company may use hundreds of different sewing shops at the height of the producing season (Figure 6–12). Even firms with their own "inside" production facilities hire independent contractors for extra capacity in busy periods; still others subsidize contracting shops. This system of using outside production facilities also enables manufacturers to diversify their product mix to meet changing consumer demands. For example, sportswear producers may one season need jackets in their lines and the following season need sweaters. The contracting system makes it possible for them to adjust and change their lines without making large dollar investments in new equipment. Most contractors specialize in a particular category of merchandise. Some of them work only for one company; others do contract work for several different firms.

Today, the women's clothing industry is a maze of inside and outside shops, of contracting and subcontracting and contracting beyond that. This system makes it possible for newcomers with salable ideas but limited capital to swing into large-scale production almost overnight, through the simple device of hiring the contractor's plant, labor, and production know-how. Contractors need not be located in the major market centers. Nowadays, they are located not only in every section of this country, but almost everywhere in the world where labor is abundant, facilities are available, and wages are reasonable.

Not all contractors abide by accepted labor standards of how workers are treated and paid. Unfortunately, in the past this has meant no one is looking after the welfare of the workers employed in these shops.

Figure 6–12

Examples of the Contracting System

Contract Work Wanted

ATTN: MFRS

Long est. contractor in NYC doing business w/K-Mart, Limited, Express, etc. Exp in all phases of sewing & finishing. Production capacity 2000 dozen/week. Quick turn. Specialize in knits.　　　　　608-555-1240

America's most advanced contract service for all apparel

Contract Apparel Network

555-488-9122
FAX 319-555-9141

CUT & SEW FACTORY

In Dominican Republic is looking for long term 807 relationship. We can handle small or large programs.
515-555-8070

CUT & SEW

Small orders. Will pick up & deliver. Or you cut, I sew. Call (608)555-3266

Immediate Production - Private Label Program. Sportswear - Outerwear.
Ph: (312) 555-1834　　　　Fax (608) 5554910

L. I. Cutting Service. Large & small lots, markers & copies. Good prices.
319-555-1795.

Contractors Wanted

Children's Activewear

Mfr seeks contractors in NY/NJ, Carolinas area. Please contact Russell
515-555-4551

Size of Apparel Companies

In matters of size, as in almost every other characteristic, the apparel industry presents enormous variety. There are huge companies that devote themselves entirely to the women's wear business; there are other enormous companies that have one or more divisions in this field; and there are the small fry. Despite the emergence of giant firms, the trend toward consolidation, the presence of conglomerates, and all the other indications of bigness, the women's apparel industry remains a stronghold of small business—more so perhaps than any other major industry.

Dominance of Small Specialized Firms

The U.S. apparel industry consists of more than 24,000 establishments, two-thirds of which employ fewer than 20 workers (American Apparel Manufacturers Association, 1998).

Many of these firms are contractors whose very existence makes it possible for an enterprising and creative person with a flair for fashion and selling ability to set up an apparel company and hope to prosper. Except for the purchase of fabric, little else is needed in the way of capital outlay, because the cutting and sewing can thus be farmed out. The key to success is in producing styles that will find acceptance. In that respect, the small firm is viable and has an equal chance with a large one. The small entrepreneur has the further advantage of being able to move quickly to exploit sudden fashion shifts. On the other hand, a single poor season can wipe out a small, undercapitalized firm—and often does.

Today, small reputable specialized producers continue to set the fashion pace for the industry, as some of the country's leading designers give splendid proof of how a small firm can flourish. The companies such as those of Bill Blass, Anne Klein,

Geoffrey Beene, and Oscar de la Renta, for example, are relatively small; their individual sales volume figures exclusive of licensing royalties are in most cases less than $100 million. Although their target customers are women who spend a great deal on a single garment, their combined spending for fashion is a drop in the bucket compared with the volume done by moderate-priced apparel companies that cater to the great mass of American consumers. Dollar volume alone, however, does not measure the importance of the designers and their firms. The publicity they generate in the news media, plus the impact of the fashion news embodied in their garments and their licensed names, constitutes a major element in keeping the general public aware of fashion and the American fashion industry.

No matter how much the future holds for further merging and giantism in the apparel industry, one can be sure that there will always be a pool of small manufacturers that are innovative and flexible and have a clear view of what their small, special target customer group wants. As an element in the apparel industry, the small producer will survive. Those who fall by the wayside are sure to be replaced by newcomers.

Multiproduct Giant Companies

Although the greatest majority of apparel companies have an annual sales volume of less than $100 million, today there are some multiproduct giant companies involved in the production of apparel whose sales volume is far in excess of that figure. All have expanded either by diversification or by acquiring other companies. Three outstanding examples of giant companies that have diversified their product mix are Sara Lee Branded Apparel, with sales of over $7 billion; VF Corporation, with sales over $5.5 billion; Jones Apparel Group, with sales over $3 billion; Liz Claiborne, with sales around $3 billion; and Kellwood Company, with sales of $2.2 billion ("AIM's Global 150," 2000; Black, 1998; Company reports, 2000). Liz Claiborne, who began her business in 1976 as a sportswear producer, expanded into dresses, menswear, and accessories. Kellwood went from a producer of moderate-priced apparel primarily for Sears, Roebuck, and Co. to one that now sells merchandise to all retail levels from upscale to discount stores.

A second type of diversified giant company is exemplified by Warnaco and Vanity Fair, each of which started as undergarment producers and moved into new fields by acquiring other companies already active in the area in which they wished to function. For instance, under the $5.5 billion corporate umbrella of VF Corporation (which evolved from Vanity Fair) one will find the following separate divisions: Lee Jeans, Wrangler Jeans, Jantzen, and Healthtex, among others (Table 6–7). VF's companies are positioned to serve different types of retailers. In the table, we see how both VF's jeans brands and its lingerie brands are targeted to span the distribution spectrum. VF Corporation owns additional companies besides those shown in the table.

A third type of giant company is composed of conglomerates whose business activities involve companies operating in widely diversified fields. For example, Sara Lee, originally a food company, owns Hanes, Playtex, L'eggs, Bali, and Isotoner. For many years, Coach (leather products) was part of the Sara Lee family.

Giant apparel companies, however, are actually multiproduct aggregates of small and medium-sized business divisions, each of which concentrates on a range of products targeted to a specific consumer market segment and operates quite autonomously. Conglomerates such as VF Corporation, Sara Lee, and Kellwood are each a "family" of companies held under a corporate umbrella. In such setups, each

Table 6–7	**VF Brands and Their Distribution Channels**		
Category	**Department Stores**	**Discount Stores**	**Specialty Stores**
Jeans	Lee Joe Boxer	Wrangler Rustler Riders Brittiana Timber Creek	Wrangler Western Wrangler Rugged Wear Red Kap Bulwark
Intimates	Vanity Fair Jansport Jantzen	Vassarette Wolf Creek	private label
Knitwear	Lee Sport private label	private label	
Playwear	Healthtex Nike		

Source: Company reports and trade publication sources.
Note: Some of these are licensed agreements for specific lines (e.g., Nike and Joe Boxer).

specialized product division draws on the parent firm for financing and for policy decisions, but each one has its own name, its own clearly defined product area, its own design staff, its own contractors, its own selling force, and even its own advertising.

Specialization by Products and Prices

Traditionally there has been a high degree of product and price line specialization among industry firms. Small companies generally limit themselves to a particular category of garments such as sportswear, evening wear, bridal dresses, coats, or suits within a narrow range of prices and also in particular size ranges, such as juniors, children's, misses, women's, and the like. Even multiproduct giant producers and retailers tend to follow this pattern by maintaining separate divisions or departments for different categories of merchandise. Although specialization still continues, over the years producers have tended to broaden their assortments as a result of changes in fashion. Many of the giants mentioned earlier have a broad range of products, but their member companies or divisions may be quite specialized.

Product Specialization

The following are typical products in the women's apparel industry in which companies or divisions of multiproduct companies specialize:

- Outerwear—coats, suits, rainwear
- Dresses
- Sportswear and separates—activewear, pants, tops, sweaters, jackets, blouses
- After-five and evening clothes
- Bridal and bridesmaid attire
- Uniforms and aprons—career (other than office) apparel, daytime dresses
- Maternity
- Swimwear and beachwear
- Intimate apparel—foundations, lingerie, robes
- Blouses
- Sweaters and knitwear

Price Specialization

Within the wide spectrum of wholesale prices for garments, there are *price ranges* in which individual manufacturers specialize. Elements in the price of a garment are (1) the quality of workmanship, (2) the cost of labor, and (3) the quality and amount of fabric and trimmings. The women's apparel industry generally divides itself into the following five price ranges (or groups of individual prices per garment):

1. *Designer* (highest-priced merchandise). This includes the lines of American name designers such as Calvin Klein, Bill Blass, Oscar de la Renta, Donna Karan, Ralph Lauren, and Geoffrey Beene.
2. *Bridge* (high prices but lower than designer). This includes the lower-priced or secondary lines of designers such as Anne Klein II and Donna Karan's DKNY. It also includes such lines as Ellen Tracy, Adrienne Vittadini, Dana Buchman, David Dart, and Maggy London.
3. *Better* (medium to bridge prices). The lines of Liz Claiborne, Jones New York, Chaus, and Ciao would fall into this price range.
4. *Moderate* (or lower than better but higher than budget). This includes such lines as Koret, White Stag, Russ Togs, Jantzen, Norton McNaughton, Alfred Dunner, and Sag Harbor.
5. *Budget* (the lowest prices in which one would find advertised brand names). This includes firms such as Rustler jeans, Cape Cod women's wear, and the Kathie Lee line.

Prevalence of Style Piracy

Apparel designs cannot be copyrighted; therefore, copying the work of creative designers is standard operating procedure for many firms, both large and small. Design and styling are such important competitive weapons in the fashion industry that **style piracy**, against which U.S. laws provide no protection, is considered a way of life in the garment business. In the language of the industry, however, a design is rarely considered "stolen"; it is "knocked off." It is copied, adapted, translated, or even pirated, but the **knock-off** is never considered as having been "stolen." A few high-profile cases are exceptions. This is not hypocrisy but simply the garment trade's way of acknowledging that copying dominates the industry; it is done openly and without apology. The late Norman Norell, who produced garments in very high price lines, indeed, and who was considered in his day the dean of American designers, expressed his philosophy about style piracy: "I don't mind if the knock-off houses give me a season with my dress. What I mind is if they bring out their copies faster than I can get my own dresses to the stores" ("He's a," 1964).

Aside from the absence of copyright protection for apparel designs, there are several reasons for this copying practice. Plunging into a fast-selling style, regardless of whose design it was originally, is one way to make a modest investment work to the limit. Another reason style piracy is rife is the highly specialized nature of the firms themselves. If, for example, a dress intended to retail at $200 has features that would make it a fast seller at a lower price, the originator of the style is in no position to produce or market inexpensive versions. The originator's entire purchasing, production, and distribution are geared to customers who are willing to pay for the particular grade of fabric, workmanship, and details in which he or she has specialized. In addition, apparel firms' labor costs may be established by the union, based on the companies' normal wholesale price lines, and they cannot be reduced. On the other hand, a maker specializing in garments to retail at $75 has much lower labor costs, enjoys access to sources for much less expensive fabrics, knows how to cut corners in production, and has established distribution among retailers catering to the price-conscious consumer. And if a style can be copied down to a still lower level or can be marketed at some intermediate levels, makers specializing in those levels are likely to step in.

Occasionally, the copying process is reversed, and a style that originates in the lower-priced lines will have features that make it desirable for higher-priced manufacturers to adapt. Normally, however, the procedure is for a style that originally retailed for hundreds of dollars to be "knocked off" at successively lower prices, if it shows signs of popular acceptance by customers.

Proliferation of Industry Licensing Agreements

The 1970s witnessed the burgeoning of the "name game"—the licensing by prominent American apparel designers of their names for use by manufacturers of accessories and of lower-priced clothing. **Licensing** is a legal arrangement covering a specific period of time, during which a manufacturer of goods in a particular generic category is given exclusive rights to produce and market a line of merchandise bearing the name of a licensor. For this privilege, the **licensee** pays a **royalty fee**—that is, a percentage of the wholesale sales of the goods concerned. Royalty fees for apparel average 7.3 percent, ranging from 4 to 12 percent. In addition, a guaranteed minimum payment is usually specified.

The **licensor**, however, is not required to confine his or her name to only one product category. For instance, a licensing arrangement with a jewelry manufacturer does not preclude similar arrangements with producers of jeans, sunglasses, shoes, bed linens, scarfs, hosiery, fur coats, perfume, swimwear, or any other product that can profitably become part of the name game (Figure 6–13). Apparel and accessories, nevertheless, are a major field for such arrangements. It is estimated that in 2000 licensed apparel and accessories represented 21 percent of all licensed name products sold at retail, out of a total of $73.75 billion a year, an amount still on the rise (*The Licensing Letter*, January 1, 2001, p. 4).

Licensing arrangements are not new to European couture; some of the most famous among them have long had income of this sort from American manufacturers and stores. For American designers, however, this is a relatively new development and one that has grown enormously. Today, some designers are receiving royalty fees that equal and in some cases even exceed the total sales volume of their own apparel enterprises.

The proliferation of licensing by both American and European designers has arrived at the point that their names now appear on apparel priced well below the high price level of the merchandise for which they became famous. Past examples included the Calvin Klein jeans line manufactured by Puritan Inc.[2] and the Halston name marketed by J.C. Penney, to name but two. Some of the top licensed names in fashion are Guess, Calvin Klein, Donna Karan,[3] Tommy Hilfiger, Liz Claiborne,[3] Ralph Lauren, and B.U.M.

Apparel producers do not necessarily limit themselves to licensing one designer's name alone. They may have several arrangements during the same period. For example, Fairbrook Enterprises, a prominent coat producer, makes coat lines under licenses with Perry Ellis, Anne Klein II, and Calvin Klein, while at the same time manufacturing other branded lines of their own.

[2]Calvin Klein now owns Puritan, Inc.
[3]A very small percentage of sales based on these designers is licensed.

Figure 6–13

Licensing: Sales of Licensed Products by Category

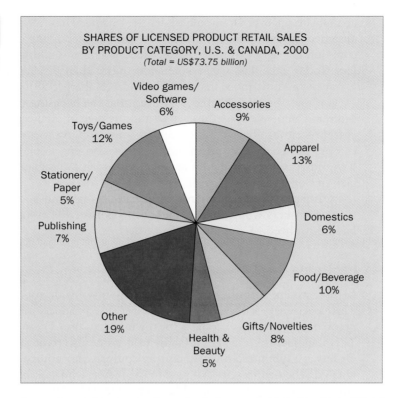

SHARES OF LICENSED PRODUCT RETAIL SALES BY PRODUCT CATEGORY, U.S. & CANADA, 2000
(Total = US$73.75 billion)

- Video games/Software 6%
- Accessories 9%
- Toys/Games 12%
- Apparel 13%
- Stationery/Paper 5%
- Domestics 6%
- Publishing 7%
- Food/Beverage 10%
- Other 19%
- Gifts/Novelties 8%
- Health & Beauty 5%

Source: From *The Licensing Letter* (p. 1), January 1, 2001, New York: EPM Communications, Inc. © Copyright 2001 EPM Communications, Inc., 212-941-0099.

The practice of licensing in the apparel industry is not limited to designer names. There are organizations or firms whose company names are so well known that they are able to license them to makers of other products. For example, the National Basketball Association (NBA) has developed its own line of apparel and may license its name. Also into the licensing act today are legions of widely recognizable names such as cartoon characters, sports figures, movie and television idols, and corporate names and logos. For example, the Halmode division of Kellwood Company and Wal-Mart signed entertainer Kathie Lee Gifford for a line of clothing to bear her name. Among the foremost is the licensing of the different characters of Disney Enterprises and those of Looney Tunes. Although cartoon and story characters are the most popular licensing group, at the height of his career, Michael Jordan had replaced Mickey Mouse as the single most popular licensed name.

The major value of a licensing arrangement to the licensees is that the merchandise carries a highly recognizable, presold name. To consumers, the name often symbolizes status, achievement, and quality. To the licensors, of course, it means additional income from royalty fees and extended name exposure without the hassles and high cost of having to produce and market the goods themselves.

Among the most active American designer-name licensors are Bill Blass, Anne Klein, Calvin Klein, Ralph Lauren, and Oscar de la Renta. The designer's input varies. For example, the Anne Klein company supplies its 28 licensees with color, fabric, design, and display ideas, and it retains final approval on all merchandise bearing its name. Others merely "edit" their licensed collections, reserving the right to approve such factors as color, quality, and design approach. With a few exceptions, very few actually design every item sold under their name. These items are more often than not designed by the unknown designer of the licensed company. What they all have in common is a very profitable royalty fee income amounting to many millions of dollars. Today Bill Blass licenses generate more than $750 million annually at retail, Oscar de la Renta more than $500 million (Haber, 1999).

It must be remembered, however, that the licensing value of a designer's name is directly dependent on the success and prestige of the licensor. Almost any designer entrepreneur can have an unsuccessful collection. A series of unsuccessful collections can put any such firm out of business and also put an end to licensing, as licensees have no reason to renew an arrangement with a designer whose name has lost its glamour or status. No licensing agreement is forever.

Today, with the thousands of licensed names and licensed products plus the licensing brokers who serve as the liaisons between licensors and licensees, licensing has almost become an industry unto itself.

Financing by Factoring

Many garment manufacturers rely heavily on outside sources for operating capital. This is necessary for many companies because products must be made and delivered before the apparel firm collects for the merchandise. These sources are called **factors**. The manufacturer engages a factor to become its credit and collection department. Orders are submitted to the **factoring** company for approval and are shipped as designated. The invoices are assigned to the factor, who supplies immediate cash, usually equal to 90 percent of receivables' net value. (The 10 percent reserve of outstanding receivables is usually held to cover returns, allowances, etc.) The factor then proceeds to collect payment from the manufacturer's customers and takes the credit risk. For their services as a credit and collection department and guarantor of credit risks, factors receive a fee known as a factoring commission, as well as interest on money loaned out before collecting on the receivables.

A highly publicized example illustrates the role factors play in the industry. When Sarah Phillips designed the Presidential Inaugural Ball gown for Hillary Clinton, she was a 37-year-old designer who had opened her own shop just three years earlier. Although she had worked for Yves St. Laurent, Ralph Lauren, and Christian Dior, she was a relative unknown at the time. Although the inaugural gown brought Sarah Phillips into the limelight, like most starting designers who wanted to develop her business, she was operating on a shoestring. Becoming the first lady's couturiere didn't attract the seed money Phillips needed to grow her business. She needed equity capital of several million dollars to go forward. Phillips was able to expand her business through the assistance of a factor. The factor (in this case a prefactor because Phillips's business was still in early stages) supported her on a purchase order basis to help in the initial financing. This provided the funding to buy the fabrics and other components as well as to support production facilities. That is, the factor approves the credit and loans money to the client before collecting on receivables (i.e., collecting from retailers for the products they buy from the client). Although factors generally work with more established companies than Sarah Phillips, this example helps illustrate the role of factors.

Twenty or 30 years ago, a manufacturer used a factor only for financial assistance, but today, many manufacturers realize that factors provide additional services. The factor becomes an extension of the manufacturer, providing expert staff, industry expertise, and the latest technologies to handle the increasingly complex accounts receivable process. As retailing continues to consolidate, they become more powerful

Figure 6–14   **An example of an advertisement by a factoring firm.**

Nicole Miller, President and Head Designer, Nicole Miller

For Nicole Miller, smart financing is always in fashion.

When world-renowned fashion designer Nicole Miller was searching for financing to support her retail expansion, she turned to CIT. The company needed a financing partner who understood the apparel and retail business, appreciated the complexities of the fashion world, and had the flexibility to meet the company's short-term needs with the depth of resources to support its long-term goals. For Nicole Miller, the choice was obvious. CIT.

Today, with CIT, Nicole Miller has more than just a lender. Her company has a true business partner it can trust to help achieve its vision for the future.

If you and your business could use a financial partner that understands what it takes to reach your goals, call us at 1-800-248-3240 or visit us at CIT.com. Discover why today's business leaders put their trust in today's financing leader.

CIT.com

Source: Reprinted courtesy of The CIT Group, Inc.

and make competition more difficult for manufacturers. Factors can help companies manage problems such as retail chargebacks. They can also help apparel firms calculate the risks of selling to retailers that may go into bankruptcy and default on paying the manufacturer (Sakany, 1999a).

Factoring is a very large business in itself, and it is very global. For example, the Factors Chain International (FCI), the global network of 125 factoring companies in 48 countries, reported that factoring volume grew to $396 billion in 1996. Textiles and apparel represent a majority of the total U.S. factoring market.

The largest factor worldwide is Heller Commercial Services, with offices in more than 20 countries. Another large U.S. factoring firm is The CIT Group, which acquired Barclays Commercial and Congress Talcott from First Union Bank (Figure 6–14). The top five or fewer factors now account for a majority of the business.

Global factoring allows exporting firms to have credit lines in place for customers and speed up response time for orders and reorders, be covered against credit losses, avoid long delays in negotiation of letters of credit, and improve cash flow by fast collection and remittance.

Location of Fashion Market Centers

Although some phase of apparel production (i.e., contracting and subcontracting) can be found in many states of the Union, the design and marketing activities of domestic apparel companies are concentrated in relatively few major cities throughout the United States. It is in these cities that one finds an enclave of apparel companies, also known as **vendors**, that produce and sell merchandise at the wholesale level to retail buyers. Known as **market centers** in the trade, these centers are the very heartbeat of the industry because they are the marketing link between apparel manufacturers and retail distributors.

New York, the Leading Market Center

The oldest, largest, and best-known wholesale fashion center in the country is located in the heart of New York City. Whereas other sections of the country have been whittling away at its base, insofar as women's and children's ready-to-wear is concerned, it is still the U.S. fashion capital.

It is not entirely an accident that New York occupies this dominant position. When Elias Howe first perfected his sewing machine, factory production of garments was not limited to any one city or area. But then came the great wave of immigration, as mentioned earlier in this chapter. New York was a major port of entry for newcomers, eager to find work in the city where they landed. Their assimilation into the garment industry there was often immediate, with some manufacturers and contractors actually meeting incoming vessels to recruit whole families for work in their factories. This pool of labor, growing out of the steady stream of immigrants, was the circumstance that enabled New York to leave its rivals behind in the production of apparel.

New York had the further advantage of being close to both the cotton mills of the South and the woolen mills of New England. It was also the nation's largest city and the center of fashionable society. Once New York had gained dominance, it became a magnet, attracting such auxiliary businesses as embroidery, pleating, and trimmings, as well as textile showrooms, consumer and fashion periodicals, trade associations, and the like. With these advantages, the city became the hub of the women's garment industry.

Today, New York still remains and will probably continue to remain the dominant center of the U.S. fashion industry. It is only in that city that one can find the showrooms of an estimated more than 5,000 apparel firms, the showrooms of all major fiber and fabric producers, the headquarters of consumer and fashion magazines, and the offices of many major trade associations. Add to that the countless opportunities for fashion practitioners to engage in New York's other important activity—"shop talk" with suppliers, friends, competitors, editors, and other sources of fashion information—and it becomes clear why the city retains its position as the hub of the fashion industry. Most of the leading American fashion designers work in New York-based firms because, as Donna Karan explained it: "Everything is here . . . you have to commute to see what kinds of clothes are needed for commuting and working. You have to live through the seasons to design clothes for the seasons. New York is just like fashion: dirty and clean, casual and uptight, alive and changing" ("The City," 1976).

Although the Garment District in Manhattan is undergoing changes, it is expected to remain an important hub for the industry. However, as real estate prices have soared in recent years, the *manufacturing* part of the industry is being squeezed out and replaced by other businesses. A good deal of manufacturing continues in the outer boroughs, but showrooms, corporate offices, and the fashion press are likely to remain in the district. Separating operations takes away much of the convenience of earlier days, however (Sakany, 1999b).

Seventh Avenue

So much of New York City's garment and accessories business is concentrated within a distance of one block east or west of **Seventh Avenue (SA)**, from West 41st Street south into the low West 30s, that the term *Seventh Avenue* has become synonymous with the women's fashion industry. The street itself was renamed Fashion Avenue in 1972. Within this area, there are literally thousands of showrooms presenting every known type and price line of women's ready-to-wear and accessories. These showrooms include not only those of New York firms, but also those of many producers whose headquarters are in other parts of the country and even in other parts of the world. There are other apparel centers elsewhere in the country where women's garments are produced and sold, but to those in the fashion business, no other center has the color, tension, activity, or merchandise variety of Seventh Avenue.

Individual buildings within the garment center tend to be specialized, each housing producers of more or less the same categories of merchandise and wholesale price ranges (Figure 6–15). For example, 1410 Broadway (the next street east of Seventh Avenue) is the market for moderate-priced sportswear, sweaters, and budget apparel; 1407 and 1411 Broadway house the showrooms of more than 2,000 sportswear companies; 1400 Broadway is the main building for medium-priced misses and junior dress firms; 1375 houses many bridal and evening dress firms; and 1350 contains many producers of lower-priced apparel, of the type sold by the dozens, sometimes called "daytime" dresses.

The upper end of Seventh Avenue has a range of coat and suit firms and higher-priced designer-name companies, with the overflow spilling into West 39th Street. Coat and suit firms are in 500 and 512 Seventh Avenue. Designer-name companies like Bill Blass, Trigère, Ralph Lauren, Geoffrey Beene, and their peers are in 530 and

Figure 6–15

New York's Garment District

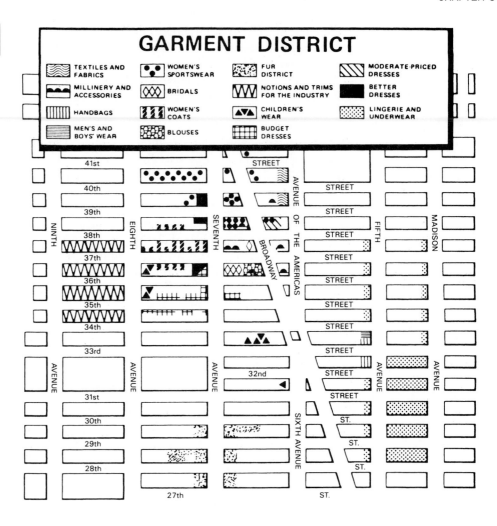

550 Seventh Avenue. At the lower end of Seventh Avenue are makers of lower-priced apparel whose names are generally unknown to the public. Children's wear showrooms are mostly on the south and west fringes of the area, with many of them concentrated in a specialized children's wear building at 112 West 34th Street. The garment center's tenants, however, have been pushing out its boundaries. For example, two buildings on West 35th Street have attracted many young designer firms, and 1441 Broadway now houses three floors of the Liz Claiborne company and other better-sportswear producers.

Decentralization of Production

At one time, practically every New York-based firm had its design, showroom, production, and shipping facilities in the garment district, and even all in the same building. Increasingly in recent years, apparel firms locate their cutting and, to a larger extent, their sewing operations in areas outside the city, and even outside the country, whether these production facilities are owned by the companies or simply contracted. This trend is noticeable not only in New York, but in other large cities as well. The high cost of rent, the unavailability of space that can be adapted to newer methods and equipment, the rising cost of taxes and labor, the almost unbelievable traffic congestion on city streets—all these have encouraged the establishment of factories in small towns in New York State and the surrounding states, in the Southeast, and in other countries—Mexico, the Caribbean, or Asia, for instance. No matter where the goods are produced, however, the finished garments are generally sent back to the parent firm for selling and distribution. Seventh Avenue remains the nerve center of the design, marketing, and management operations, regardless of how far afield the production facilities may be.

Secondary Fashion Centers

There are other regional market centers outside New York City. Although some of these are very important, no one of them can compare with New York in terms of the number of companies based there or the variety, quantity, and dollar sales. Each of these other centers tends to be fairly specialized as to the types and price ranges it produces. Many of the manufacturers in these **secondary fashion centers** have sales representation in New York City.

Los Angeles

Los Angeles, following close on the heels of New York City, has emerged as the second-most-important design and manufacturing center, known for its "California look." Once limited mostly to swimsuits and active sportswear, it now turns out a wide range of garments, including blue jeans, "trendy" junior-sized garments, and boutique items.

California has greatly surpassed New York in the number of persons employed in the industry. Los Angeles manufacturers have some advantages over New York: less-expensive and abundant space and a large pool of Mexican workers. Unfavorable factors include a shortage of the small specialized fabric and findings firms that are plentiful in New York. California manufacturers, however, have developed their own "look" and are noted for their creative innovations in sportswear styling and colorations. Particularly in the casual wear areas, California designs have influenced the entire country.

Miami

Miami's major role in the apparel industry today is that of being the "gateway to the Caribbean." Under U.S. **tariff** rules (formerly 807 of the tariff regulations, now 9802), apparel manufacturers send cut garments to other countries to have them sewn and pay tariffs on only the value added during those operations. To use this strategy, still commonly called **807 production**, much of the garment cutting occurs in Miami and the sewing takes place in various low-wage Caribbean countries. Then finished garments are sent back to the U.S. markets through Miami, completing the cycle that has made Miami a major hub of industry activity in recent years.

Miami has a relatively important children's wear industry, resulting from early relocation there in the 1940s. In the 1960s, some 30 children's wear firms founded the Florida Children's Wear Manufacturers Guild, which sponsors a successful trade show each year for retail buyers. Additionally, a number of leisure and activewear firms are located in Miami.

Like New York, Miami became an important apparel center because of immigrants. Whereas European immigrants were instrumental in founding New York's industry, Cuban immigrants contributed similarly in Miami. In the 1960s, many Cuban immigrants fled the Castro regime and needed jobs when they arrived in Miami. As one children's wear manufacturer put it, "The Cuban immigration of the Sixties was the catalyst that allowed us to grow. Once we got the Cuban labor working for us, we could take orders from major stores and know that we could deliver the merchandise" ("More than," 1985). Today, many Cubans have moved from positions as machine operators to become principals in their own companies—a modern parallel to the European immigrant saga in New York.

Dallas

Once a design and production center primarily for lower-priced polyester knit garments distributed through large-volume apparel chains, Dallas has changed. Most of the manufacturers headquartered in Dallas have made a shift to a mix of moderate-priced dresses and sportswear in a greater variety of fabrications to meet the changing demands of a large segment of mainstream customers. In recent years, a cadre of young designers who live and work in Dallas are breathing new life into their local industry and are becoming known for their creative and innovative designs. To date, the best-known Dallas-based designer is Victor Costa.

Chicago

Chicago has changed. At one time it had a reputation for conservatively styled and well-made dresses for misses and women, at higher than moderate prices. But here is how an article describes the Chicago market:

> Gone are the days when traditional and polyester were the fashion watchwords here. Gone are the days when moderate-priced volume manufacturers and their multi-million dollar business along the crowded banks of the Chicago River were the ONLY game in town. Today Chicago is fashion. From the fresh young talent not long out of design school, like Richard Dayhoff, Kate Jones, and Peggy Martin, to the long established designers rapidly gaining a national reputation, like Maria Rodriguez, Mark Hester, and Gina Rossi, Chicago is making a new fashion statement.

Other Fashion Design Centers

Some other secondary design centers, even more distant from New York in terms of both the value of output and the variety of merchandise, are Boston, whose local manufacturers have developed a reputation primarily for well-made, moderate-priced classic sportswear and rainwear; and Philadelphia, for moderately priced sportswear and children's wear.

Apparel Marts: Regional Selling Centers

An industry development that began in the late 1960s is the marketing importance of **apparel marts**, or large regional selling centers. Located in major cities throughout the United States, their purpose is twofold: (1) to reach out for and sell to small fashion retailers in the surrounding areas and (2) to serve as a wholesale selling facility for apparel producers, wherever the headquarters of the companies may be.

In addition to the lines of local producers, these marts house **regional showrooms** of hundreds of apparel firms from other parts of the country and even those of some foreign fashion producers. The showrooms bring the current and incoming seasons' lines of these companies within easy reach of the area's small retailers, most of whom do not have the time or money to go to New York more than once or twice a year, if that often. Buyers for nearby large retail organizations also find the marts a convenience, as it is often more practical to fill some of the special or urgent needs from a nearby source of supply.

Showrooms are leased both on a year-round basis and for temporary use during major seasonal buying periods. The temporary showrooms are particularly convenient during regional **market weeks**. Such weeks are scheduled periodically as a means of introducing the new lines of hundreds of out-of-town producers to the retailers of the area at the start of a buying season. Separate market weeks are usually held for different categories of merchandise and range in number from two to five a year. Merchandise categories include accessories, sportswear, intimate apparel, infants' and children's wear, and dresses, among others. A typical calendar of market weeks in major marts is shown in Figure 6–16. These schedules appear in trade periodicals such as *Women's Wear Daily*.

Los Angeles, Dallas, Atlanta, and Chicago have emerged as important regional selling marts, challenging what was once New York's exclusive domain. To attract buyers to market weeks, these marts stage many special events, such as fashion shows, merchandising seminars, and entertainment galas. As the fashion industry has evolved in recent years, however, the regional marts have been affected. Mergers in both retailing and manufacturing have resulted in giant firms whose business is conducted at the top executive level. That is, there are fewer small firms—both in retailing and manufacturing—that need this kind of "middleman" operation the regional mart showrooms provide. Some of the marts have struggled to keep tenants.

The Dallas International Apparel Mart

The Dallas International Apparel Mart[4] is part of the Dallas Market Center. The total 125-acre complex ranks as the world's largest wholesale apparel and merchandising complex, with approximately 7 million square feet of space in six buildings. In addition to the Apparel Mart, the complex boasts the International Menswear Mart, a separate facility for the menswear industry.

The Dallas International Apparel Mart has 1,200 showrooms and is home to more than 10,000 apparel and accessories lines. In a year, about 27,000 stores will have shopped in the Apparel Mart, writing orders for more than $2.5 billion in business from the mart tenants. To maintain a flow of customers for the exhibitors, the mart spends millions on promotion. The Dallas Mart was one of the first to open a site on the Internet to disseminate information about the complex to retailers and to permit retailers to place orders with the mart tenants via computer. The Dallas Mart has encouraged major chain retailers to shop there by offering them free offices in the building; retailers must pay taxes and utility bills (Haber, 1995; Williamson, 1994).

Although large Texas retailers such as Neiman Marcus may shop this mart, the typical and best customers of any mart are not the buyers from the major stores, but a host of small independently owned specialty store retailers from the surrounding areas. Dallas draws these customers primarily from Arkansas, Louisiana, Oklahoma, and Texas, with these states accounting for 78 percent of the mart's traffic. Another 17 percent comes from other states, 4 percent from Mexico and other Latin American countries, and about 1 percent from the rest of the world (Williamson, 1994).

The CaliforniaMart

Located in downtown Los Angeles's garment district, the California apparel center, known as the CaliforniaMart, contains some 1,200 permanent showrooms, plus 300 or so that are available for temporary rentals. This mart is not only a regional selling facility for New York manufacturers but also the showcase for West Coast producers

[4]The Dallas Apparel Mart added "International" to its name to reflect increasing efforts to draw international buyers, particularly those from Mexico and other Latin American countries.

Figure 6–16   # Market Week Schedule

Location	Summer	Fall I	Fall II	Resort	Spring
Atlanta (Atlanta Apparel Mart)	Jan. 25-29	April 11-15	June 13-15	Aug. 22-26	Oct. 24-28
Birmingham (Birmingham Jefferson Civic Center)	Jan. 21-22	March 24-25	June 9-10	Aug. 18-19	Oct. 13-14
Boston (Bayside Expo Center)	Jan. 14-17	April 14-17	June 16-19	Aug. 18-21	Oct. 13-16
Charlotte (Charlotte Merchandise Mart)	Jan. 19-23	March 22-26	June 7-11	Aug. 16-20	
(children's market)	Jan. 19-22	March 22-25	June 7-10	Aug. 16-19	Oct. 11-14
Chicago (Chicago Apparel Center)	Jan. 26-30	March 29-April 2	May 31-June 4	Aug. 16-20	Oct. 25-29
Dallas (International Apparel Mart)	Jan. 18-22	March 21-25	June 6-10	Aug. 15-19	Oct. 17-21
Kansas City (Kansas City Market Center)	Jan. 13-15	April 13-16	June 22-24	Aug. 24-27	Oct. 26-29
Los Angeles (California Apparel Mart)	Jan. 12-16	April 19-23	June 21-25	Aug. 9-13	Nov. 1-5
Miami (Miami Merchandise Mart)	Jan. 14-17	March 16-19	May 31-June 3	Aug. 9-12	Oct. 12-15
Minneapolis (Hyatt Merchandise Mart)	Jan. 21-24	March 10-12	April 14-17	June 9-11 Aug. 11-14	Oct. 20-23
New York (For New York updates, contact Fashion Calendar, 212-289-0420)	Jan. 8-19	Feb. 19-March 1	March 25-April 12	July 29-Aug. 9	Oct. 28-Nov. 15
Pittsburgh (Monroeville Expo Mart)	Jan. 21-23	April 14-16	June 9-11	Sept. 8-10	Nov. 3-5
San Francisco (The Fashion Center)	Jan. 6-9	April 13-16	June 15-18	Aug. 17-20	Oct. 19-22
Seattle (Seattle International Trade Center)	Jan. 20-23	March 30-April 2	June 8-11	Aug. 3-6	Oct. 26-29

The 1996 general women's and children's apparel market weeks at the various regional marts and in New York are listed above. In addition to these general markets, various specialized events are held throughout the year at some of these venues. Dates are subject to revision, and individual marts should be contacted for confirmation and more information.

Source: From *Women's Wear Daily* (p. 15), January 18, 1996. Reprinted by permission.

whose merchandise is not exhibited in other marts or even shown in New York. Retail buyers are drawn from the Southwest, the whole of California, Washington, Oregon, and New York.

Various incentives are offered to retail buyers to attract them to the mart: rebates on airfare or gasoline, free meals, and other inducements. Attendance is also promoted by means of a newsletter, a calendar of special events, and market directories. As a service to exhibitors, the mart also publishes a buyer registration list, which manufacturers can use as a mailing list.

By the early 1990s, managers of a number of showrooms became disenchanted with CaliforniaMart for what they considered poor service, high rents, and facilities that lacked contemporary appeal. Under new management since late 1994, these concerns have been addressed.

The Atlanta Apparel Mart

The newest of these apparel selling centers is the Atlanta Apparel Mart, which opened in 1979 with seven floors of showrooms. The Apparel Mart is part of a larger complex, the Atlanta Market Center, which draws heavily from southeastern states. In 1987, the Center announced a major $43 million expansion of the Apparel Mart. This expansion, completed in 1989, consisted of adding seven additional floors on top of the original seven (Lloyd, 1994).

Apparel Mart managers planned the expansion during the boom years of the 1980s. However, by the time it was finished, the economy took a nosedive. Many specialty stores in the Southeast went out of business, and retailing was restructuring in other ways. As the Apparel Mart was in the process of expanding, retailing was changing in ways that meant fewer users for the Mart. Department stores throughout the United States were consolidating, many of these in the Southeast. Longtime names disappeared when companies merged, including Loveman's, Cain Sloan, and Ivey's. Macy's closed its buying offices in the South. All these changes resulted in reduced traffic from retailers who had been customers for the Mart's tenants. Consequently, in the mid-1990s, the Apparel Mart was only about half leased, and efforts were made to increase use of the mart (Lloyd, 1994).

The Chicago Apparel Center

The Chicago Center is a 25-story building, opened in 1977. It has 11 floors of showrooms, plus a hotel and a 140,000-square-foot exhibition hall. There is also a 3,000-square-foot exhibit, set up as a modern retail store, to offer ideas for store plans, fixturing, color effects, and the like.

At its peak, some 4,000 resources were represented on a year-round basis. These spanned all price levels and covered a wide spectrum of manufacturing firms from all over the world. Well-known tenants have been Oscar de la Renta, Geoffrey Beene, Yves St. Laurent, and others of similar stature. As in other marts, there are several hundred showrooms available for temporary rentals.

Industry changes have affected the Chicago mart, just as it has its counterparts. The decline of small retail stores and the mergers of large retailers has resulted in much less traffic for market weeks and for year-round showroom business. Consequently, future demand for showroom space is uncertain (Sharoff, 1994).

Other Merchandise Marts

In addition to the four major apparel marts described, there is a smaller specialized apparel mart in Boston and a new Fashion Center in San Francisco. There are also general merchandise marts in other cities that have several floors devoted to apparel showrooms. Like the specialized marts, these more general ones aim to promote their local industries and house both permanent and temporary showrooms for local, national, and international producers. And like the apparel centers, the general merchandise marts hold regularly scheduled market weeks that are attended mostly by smaller retailers from the surrounding regions. Some examples are the Miami Merchandise Mart, the Carolina Trade Center in Charlotte, North Carolina, the Kansas City Trade Center, and the Radisson Center in Minneapolis.

Future of New York as a Fashion Center

Although a good deal of the buying and selling action has moved to regional apparel marts, New York is still firmly entrenched as the key marketplace of the United States because it offers buyers their choice of more than 175,000 lines of goods, an amount that no other area can ever begin to match. It still remains to be seen whether the proliferation of regional marts will affect the frequency with which buyers for major stores throughout the country shop the New York market. Some New York-based manufacturers feel that market weeks at the regional marts detract from the business that could be done in New York. They feel there is an "overkill" of market weeks.

The manufacturing segment of the New York apparel industry has declined over the years because of the high costs of doing business there—real estate, labor, utilities, and so on. However, a core group of manufacturers, particularly makers in the higher-end market, are committed to keeping their production in the city. For many, having production there is an integral strategy enabling them to respond quickly to hot trends and to meet the demands of retailers who want to buy close to the season.

Realizing the economic importance of its apparel industry, the City of New York has funded special projects in recent years to boost the long-term health of the industry. The mayor of New York has been involved in various efforts to promote the city's industry. Civic and industry leaders have launched a "Made in New York" campaign to promote New York-made fashions (Friedman, 1995b). Efforts are also being made to entice buyers from other countries, particularly those whose customers are attracted to upscale merchandise.

Children's Wear

In the not-too-distant past, when children were expected to be seen but not heard, they were dressed in miniature versions of adult apparel. Parents chose their clothes. Today, largely as a result of their exposure to television, children have become customers in their own right and have definite opinions about the toys they want, the foods they eat, and the clothes they wear. This "liberation" of children has had a direct effect on the styling of children's wear.

Nature of the Industry

The development of the children's wear segment of the industry and its methods of operation, as far as the presentation of seasonal lines and the production methods used, follow much the same pattern as the women's sector. However, the children's industry has a relatively small volume of output and many fewer companies, is less competitive and less aggressive in its marketing practices, and puts emphasis on the ages of the ultimate consumers.

Table 6–8	Top Children's Apparel Producers
Company	**1999 Sales (in $ millions)**
Oshkosh B'Gosh	432
William Carter Co.	424
Gerber Childrenswear, Inc.	277
Garan Inc.	229

Source: "AIM's Global 150," June 2000, *Apparel Industry Magazine*, 18–38. Copyright Bill Communications Inc.

There are fewer than 1,000 companies that produce children's wear. The total value of output is more than $4 billion.[5] With the notable exception of a few giant firms such as Oshkosh, Carter, and Healthtex, the majority of companies are small (Table 6–8). Most manufacturers produce three seasonal collections per year—Spring/Summer, Fall, and Holiday. Many children's wear firms are located in New York City, but there is a substantial contingent in the Miami fashion industry, many of which maintain sales representatives in New York.

Some large-scale multiproduct producers of adult apparel have entered into some phase of children's wear. Among them are such companies as Levi Strauss, Lee, Russ Togs, Guess, and Esprit. As explained previously, these large producers set up separate divisions for each of their product categories, and their children's wear is no exception. The design, production, and marketing of children's products has its own division in these firms.

Industry Specializations

As in the women's wear industry, manufacturers tend to specialize by price range, sizes, and types of merchandise. In terms of price levels, most companies fall into low-, moderate-, or higher-priced categories. In regard to type, the most common specializations are by age or size groups rather than by merchandise categories. Children, it should be understood, have different body proportions at different stages of growth, and their garments must be designed accordingly. For example, two girls of the same height and weight may require garments from different ranges, because one still has toddler proportions and the other has small-girl proportions.

Thus, the size ranges are related to the age or stage of growth. The following sizes are the same for girls and boys:

Infants: 3 to 24 months
Toddlers: T2 to T4

From children's size 4, the sizes for the two sexes diverge. Children's sizes for girls go from 4 to 6x, then go on to girls' 7 to 14, and preteen 6 to 14. Boys' wear is sized 4 to 7 and 8 to 12, and their garments are made in the children's wear industry. When they pass this age and size, however, the boys move into the menswear industry, wearing boys' sizes 14 to 20, and going on to young men's and students' wear.

In a large retail store, each age or size grouping is often in a section of its own, usually within the infants' and children's department, and usually under one buyer

---

[5]The exact output is difficult to determine because some NAICS categories (e.g., undergarments) have women's and children's apparel in the same grouping.

unless the store is quite large. Clothes for boys who have outgrown the children's size ranges are generally bought, displayed, and sold with or near menswear.

Marketing Activities

Marketing practices are similar in many respects to those of the women's wear industry. For example, seasonal lines are presented in showrooms, at company headquarters, and sometimes also at regional marts. The merchandise, however, is not

Figure 6–17

An advertisement for the International Kids Fashion Show, a trade event that shows products for retailers who cater to young customers.

Source: Reprinted by permission of MAGIC.

usually dramatized and accessorized as is done in the women's industry. Advertising and sales promotion are relatively minor, with the exception of the few very large firms, which have made their names well known through national advertising. Most producers in this industry leave consumer advertising to the retail stores.

The industry has its own specialized publications: *Earnshaw's Infants-Girls-Boys Wear Review* plus a periodic section in *Women's Wear Daily*. These focus on trade and product news and carry advertising to the retail trade.

There are three trade shows a year, held in New York; more than 300 lines are usually exhibited at each (Figure 6–17). These are the International Kids Fashion Shows, which are in addition to the Florida Children's Wear Manufacturers' Guild Show, an annual trade show held in Miami.

As in the women's industry, the licensing "name" game is very prevalent. Character licensing is a practice so rampant in the industry that very few T-shirts, sweatshirts, sleepwear, and similar items are without the licensed names of a Mickey Mouse, Star Wars, Lion King, Looney Tunes, Snoopy, Pocahontas, and ad infinitum. Also important is the licensing of sports figures and designer names. Today, many children's wear manufacturers have licensing agreements with both European and American designers. European luminaries such as Christian Dior, Pierre Cardin, Yves St. Laurent, and Givenchy have licensed their names to producers of higher-priced children's wear, as have some well-known American designers such as Ralph Lauren and Tommy Hilfiger.

It is interesting to note that in recent years many large retailers of adult apparel have gone into the children's wear business such as The Limited, Abercrombie & Fitch Co., Gap Kids, Benetton's 012, and Laura Ashley's Mother and Child.

Both manufacturers and retailers of children's wear (including teens) have made more effort to serve this market, recognizing its huge buying power. In the past, this group of young consumers reported, however, that their special needs are often ignored by retailers. One researcher found that aggregate spending by or on behalf of children ages 4 to 12 roughly doubled every decade in the 1960s, 1970s, and 1980s. It more than tripled in the 1990s (Bannon, 1998).

Children have become more opinionated in their choices for all kinds of products. More than that, they exert their power in purchases made. Some experts believe this increased power among children is related to the fact that dual-career parents are giving their children more choices. Child psychologist Dr. Sylvia Rimm notes, "The style of child-rearing today is to empower very young children and give them choices about everything. . . . When you give small children power, they act like adolescents" (Bannon, 1998, p. 1; Frastaci, 1999).

Readings

Not only has the apparel industry experienced radical changes in the ways it goes about its business, but many changes are also taking place in the manner in which the industry markets its products. The following articles address examples of both types of these changes.

Apparel E-Commerce: Online and Kicking

Sale of apparel through e-commerce channels is exceeding what expectations had been. This article gives an overview and also tells how five major apparel firms are using the Web.

VF Extends Its Mass Appeal

Through a series of acquisitions, VF Corporation has fashion products to appeal to a range of target markets. This article focuses particularly on VF's strategy in the jeans market.

Improving Product Development with E-Commerce Tools

New business-to-business (B2B) e-commerce tools are allowing the softgoods industry to dramatically improve the product development process.

Apparel E-Commerce: Online and Kicking

by Kathryn Kelly, Arthur Andersen Consulting

With everyone from pet stores to public trading companies jumping onto the .com scene, it's no wonder that apparel manufacturers should want their own slice of the online pie. In fact, the past year has revealed that ever-increasing numbers of people are shopping and purchasing apparel online. While most analysts do not expect Internet sales to reach 5% of all apparel sales before 2005, the Internet remains an explosive force—ignored at a retailer's own peril. Surprisingly though, many major apparel manufacturers have not even taken that first essential step toward establishing Web sites. Not only are these manufacturers missing out on the opportunity to advertise and sell products online, but they are rapidly being left behind in the e-tailing race.

Web Shopping Growing, Barriers Remain

Many apparel manufacturers believe that apparel shopping on the Web will never be significant enough to merit joining the e-commerce revolution. While e-commerce channels are still dwarfed by brick-and-mortar stores, the growth this year was far ahead of expectations and has the industry reconsidering e-commerce as a viable channel. Apparel sales, estimated to be about $700 million in 1999, are expected to reach $5 billion by 2003 according to a study by Xceed Intelligence.

Source: From Apparel Industry Magazine, *March 2000, pp. 48–50. Copyright Bill Communications, Inc. Reprinted with permission.*

Barriers—returns, security, cost, and the inability to touch, feel or try on clothing—are on the decline, becoming less and less important to consumers. Several surveys, including those by Cybershopper, shop.org, and Greenfield Online, show that consumers are becoming more comfortable using the Web as a shopping and purchasing medium. The CyberShopper survey, for example, showed that about 21% of respondents were concerned about security—about half of those that were concerned in 1997. A Greenfield Online survey done in July 1999 reported that 56% of shoppers would not buy apparel because they were worried about not being able to touch and see the product; this percentage had declined to 41% by December 1999. And based on sales figures from this past holiday season, it is clear that the Internet is now a viable and growing shopping channel for apparel.

Why Should Apparel Manufacturers Establish a Web Presence?

If the growth in apparel sales doesn't prove that it is worthwhile to establish a Web site, the sales growth spurred by online research should. Many online shoppers do an extensive amount of research on products and fashion trends before purchasing through any medium. To drive additional sales, businesses can no longer ignore the Web as a marketing, promotion and even selling channel. We at Arthur Andersen have outlined various shopping behaviors uncovered through market research and have developed strategies to consider when designing a Web site.

What Are Apparel Manufacturers Doing on the Web?

After reviewing the *AIM* Top 100 apparel manufacturers to see what they were doing on the Web, we see that many in the industry have not yet joined the online world, while a relatively small percentage of others have embraced it with fervor.

Surprisingly, the largest group—over one third—of apparel manufacturers do not have a Web presence at all. Another 10% had a working URL but the Web site did not have any significant content or was under construction at the time of our review. Apparel manufacturers that have sites, 56% in our study, are pursuing a variety of strategies from providing basic company information to providing a full-service site where users can learn about the company, review product information, order items, check availability and track orders.

Web Site Profiles

To illustrate how apparel manufacturers are using the Web, we have profiled five companies that have taken different approaches. These profiles are designed to help apparel manufacturers learn from others in the industry. These sites include: Bugle Boy Industries (www.bugleboy.com); DELiA*s (www.delias.com); Liz Claiborne (www.lizclaiborne.com); Nike (www.nike.com); and The North Face (www.thenorthface.com).

Bugle Boy Industries—Bugle Boy, a $500 million manufacturer of casual clothing and accessories for the whole family, provides an example of a site that has embraced e-commerce wholeheartedly. The site features company information, product promotion, online shopping. One of the less common features of the site is that the company has linked its ordering functionality with inventory data to allow customers to check availability before they buy. Type in the Web address and you can see the items the company features as promotional items. Registered users receive targeted information on special promotions, reminders for gift items and new products through e-mail. The virtual store previews various items for sale. Before selecting a size, check out the size charts to make sure that you're ordering one that fits, read the product detail and check out the washing instructions. Once you select an item you can put it in your shopping cart, check availability and then buy it once you're ready to check out. Regular customers can check their order history on the site. Knowing that some customers search the Web to learn about items and then buy in a brick-and-mortar store, Bugle Boy has included a store locator so customers can find nearby stores that stock its products.

DELiA*s—Most teenage girls likely already know about DELiA*s. This $150 million vertically integrated apparel manufacturer and retailer has gone on the Web in a big way. The site boasts many features to keep its teenage targets clicking away, and does a thorough job in creating a sense of community designed to appeal to its target market. When we visited the site we could get a free CD with an order, figure out what our favorite color says about our personality and weigh in on the "freak-o-meter" and that was only on the homepage. Click through and customers could read about movies and makeovers on the "gurl pages." You could also get "gurl mail" as your free e-mail account and create your own Web page. If you want to shop, the site is easy to browse through and is equipped with a useful customer information section. If you're sure about buying the item you can put it in your shopping cart. If you're too young to have a credit card, you can add it to your wish list. In order to make gift giving just a little easier the site offers gift wrapping. In an attempt to create that collaboration that goes along with teenage shopping, you can e-mail items to friends and get their opinions before buying.

Liz Claiborne—This is one of the only sites profiled where you cannot shop online or even link to online shopping. Why did we profile it? Because it is good example of the full-featured promotion that can be done on the Web when a company has made the strategic decision not to pursue an e-commerce strategy. The site features attractive graphics and extensive promotion materials. Liz Claiborne's ad campaigns are prominently displayed and the site allows you to create the looks that you have seen in the campaigns through providing detailed product and store locator information. Each of the company's major divisions are featured on the site. To create a sense of community, the site hosts live chat events, promotes goodwill through providing information on what the company is doing to help women, and creates excitement through a variety of contests.

The site is one of the more highly integrated we have seen. Instead of needing to go through layers of pages to get complete information, there are a great many links on the page to help the visitor get the information they need with a minimum of clicks. When a visitor is researching an item, they can view the size information, product details, fabric information, they can also locate a retailer near their home or office where they can purchase the item. If they need a personal touch, the site also lets them make an appointment with a personal shopper. In a section of the site called "LizMatch" you can create the looks you have seen in Liz's ad campaigns. One interesting feature is a fabric glossary to educate consumers on the fabric of the garments.

Nike—Sports stars and mass customization shake hands on the Nike Web site. Nike has created a site with online shopping, a great search engine where you can find products by gender, sports activity as well as special size considerations. The site is linked to inventory information that lets you know whether the product you are interested in is available. If this information is not enough, the site contains a great deal of customer service information on it. With special events, live chats with your favorite sports stars and the ability to create and send a customized sports clip, sports enthusiasts will visit this site more than once. Most unique, however, is the "Nike ID" section where you can design your very own sneakers. This was the only site of those we reviewed where we saw a company allow for mass customization.

The North Face—The North Face has decided not to implement e-commerce. The company's strategy is to rely on its online and brick-and-mortar retailers to sell its product. While many apparel manufacturers have done this, North Face was one of the few companies that built a Web site to promote its product and provide links to help its customers find out where to purchase products. Many other manufacturers that rely on online malls for their online presence did not have Web sites of their own. At the North Face Web site, users can research and view selected products. The site lists brick-and-mortar stores where North Face products can be found and links to online stores, such as REI, mGear and PlanetOutdoors.

VF Extends Its Mass Appeal

by Scott Malone

New York—VF Corp. now has enough jeans in its closet.

After picking up two mass-market jeans labels in recent months, as part of a series of corporate acquisitions, VF's mass-market jeanswear unit is focusing on integrating those new brands into its operations.

As reported, last week VF agreed to acquire the Gitano brand from bankrupt Fruit of the Loom. That announcement came two months after the company bought the Chic jeans brand, and marked the end of an extended search, according to Angelo LaGrega, president of mass-market jeanswear for the Greensboro, N.C.-based company.

A year-and-a-half ago, LaGrega explained, VF officials sat down to analyze the mass-market segment and determine how to broaden its consumer reach. Realizing that its Wrangler and Riders brands were targeted towards customers in search of comfortable jeans, the company decided to increase its offering of fashionable jeans.

However, the company figured that introducing more fashion-forward jeans under its existing brands would only confuse shoppers. That meant acquisition was the way to go.

"Most companies, to keep on growing their businesses, keep on stretching their core brands so greatly that you lose the point of what the brands really stand for," said LaGrega. "We believe very strongly in having very specific brands highly targeted to different consumer profiles."

While the company's four mass-market jeans brands all appeal to shoppers of a similar age group—25 to 55—they satisfy very different needs, he said.

"When you look at the women's market, you have to drill down so much deeper" to determine what shoppers in that age group want, he said. "Wrangler, Riders, Gitano and Chic all do a good job of covering that group, but they all resonate differently."

LaGrega said he feels the division now has a wide enough variety of brands to satisfy its customer base.

"Right now, we feel very good about the portfolio we have. We're going to focus on these four brands and make sure the marketing elements are executed at the highest level."

On a scale from least to most fashionable, the brands run Wrangler, Riders, Chic and Gitano, LaGrega said.

The Wrangler customer "dresses very much for herself," LaGrega said. "She doesn't run over to the mirror first, to say, 'Do I look thinner?'"

For the Riders customer, looks are a little more important, he said, noting, "She wants to look good in the product, but wants a certain degree of comfort."

With Chic, comfort is a second priority to the look provided by the brand's distinctive fit.

"It's for a customer that is into figure enhancement. She wants to look 20 pounds smaller, she wants to wear a size 6 when she used to wear a size 8. She wants to be attractive. A good hair day is important to her."

Source: From Women's Wear Daily, *June 22, 2000. Reprinted with permission.*

At Gitano, the look is also key, and the shopper wants a more fashion-forward design. Describing the brand image as "junior fashion for missy sizing," LaGrega said that touches like boot-cut legs and sandblasted fabrics would make their way into the Gitano line, while those elements would be a touch too forward for the other three brands.

VF's mass-market jeans business has been consistently touted as a top performer by company executives of late. Observers said this performance is clearly tied to the mass sector's strong gains recently in selling fashionable apparel—with chains like Target and Kohl's attracting the attention of fashion shoppers.

LaGrega didn't dispute that point.

"There's definitely an acceptance by more and more people to buy softline products in the mass channel. There's not a stigma of buying a jean at a big box, as long as it's the right brand and the right product that meets their need. The better job we do of meeting their emotional and rational needs, the bigger chance we have of attracting people who already are shopping in the channel for other things, when they see fashionable, contemporary product that they didn't expect under a recognizable brand."

Neither Gitano nor Chic have been perceived as hot brands lately.

When VF bought Chic for an undisclosed amount, LaGrega admitted that its sales had been "declining aggressively" in recent years. Similarly, Gitano's volume had shrunk to around $150 million over the past decade, allowing VF to pick it up for $18 million. But Gitano retained a place in shoppers' psyches, registering as the 54th most recognizable brand in the 1999 Fairchild 100 survey.

And, sources said that the two brands' histories, and mass-marketers' prowess in promotions, could still make them powerful names in the channel.

"I would have never thought that Cherokee was worth a nickel, and it's going to do over a billion dollars at Target," said Dick Gilbert, president of the Mudd juniors line. "Target and Wal-Mart can make anything work if they want to. If they take anything with a modicum of notoriety, they can make it work."

Five years ago, after emerging from bankruptcy, Cherokee Inc. re-engineered itself, eliminating all its manufacturing operations and setting itself up as a licensing operation. Target is the company's largest licensor.

Analyst Jack Pickler of Prudential Securities said he also believes that VF could score a hit with the Gitano and Chic brands.

"The Gitano brand was once a huge brand," he said. "A decade or a decade-and-a-half ago it probably did between $500 million and $1 billion at retail. That is one brand that had some pizzazz in the past and certainly was nowhere near that point with Fruit of the Loom. The same with Chic. That was a strong brand, particularly in Kmart, and it had a very definable niche because of the fit."

Chic jeans are cut in several inseam lengths for each size, rather than in just one length, allowing women to find jeans that fit both around the hips and at the ankles.

Pickler added that VF has plenty of room to develop its women's jeans business at the mass channel. He said the company believes it has a 40 percent share of the mass market men's jeans business, but a substantially smaller chunk of the women's business.

VF certainly believes the business has room to grow.

"We've identified the female as a high-growth segment," said LaGrega. He said that the Wrangler and Riders brands have enjoyed substantial growth of late, adding, "We have a lot of accounts running up 20 to 30 percent with our current brands."

The division's high rate of organic growth, coupled with these acquisitions, will mean a substantial boost in women's jeans sales, he feels.

He declined to provide sales volume figures on the women's business. Analysts expect VF's overall jeanswear sales—including The Lee Co.—to come in at around $2.8 billion this year.

"These two new brands will give us a 20 percent incremental business, on top of businesses that were running 20 to 25 percent ahead already," he said. "Probably this will bring us to a 40 to 45 percent increase in our total female [mass-market] business over last year."

At the moment, the company is gradually taking over control of production and distribution of the two lines, LaGrega said. That transition is being overseen by Franz Van Zeeland, formerly of VF's international jeans operations, who last year was named vice president and general manager of the mass-market jeans business.

A month ago, VF began shipping Chic product. For the next 30 to 60 days, Fruit of the Loom will be shipping Gitano product under VF's direction, a situation LaGrega described as unusual but necessary.

"What we were very concerned about was the critical back-to-school period," he explained. "We didn't want goods to be on trucks and not getting to the retail shelves. It's not the way we would have liked it, but we're making sure they work on getting the flow of goods from the Fruit warehouses to the retailers."

After the b-t-s season is passed, he added, VF will take over distribution and probably begin shipping its own Gitano product in October or November.

"We have a lot on our plate, and now the key is execution, making sure that we solidify the brand position. Getting goods to market is the most critical element we have right now."

While the results of its recent shopping spree may have satisfied the mass-market jeans segment, VF as a whole has given no hint that its acquisition run is over.

In addition to the jeans labels, the company this year bought outdoor-apparel and equipment maker The North Face Inc., backpack maker Eastpak and the HIS brand, which was owned by the same company that owned the Chic brand.

Observers suggested that there are a few areas where VF might seek additional acquisitions.

"The intimates business has been in some turmoil, and that is a business they have had some significant success in for a couple of years. There may be more effort to broaden their presence there," said Prudential's Pickler.

He said he wouldn't expect further buys in the backpack category, but suggested that the company might be interested in a traditional luggage brand.

Pickler also suggested that the company might want to expand its presence in the casual bottoms market, where it has very limited operations.

"I've been surprised that they haven't gotten a bit deeper in the casual slacks business, the core khakis," he said. "They do have a business there, but not a huge business relative to their denim business. It would make a lot of sense for them to have more."

Improving Product Development with E-Commerce Tools

by David Bassuk, Kurt Salmon Associates

The product development process has never been more critical than it is today, and more and more sewn products firms are looking to Web-based tools and services to help them improve this function within their organizations.

Just how important is product development? Consider these findings of the most recent annual Consumer Outlook Survey from Kurt Salmon Associates (KSA):

- Even when consumers have a clear idea of what they want to buy, only 51 percent actually make the purchase.
- Of the consumers who choose not to buy, 63 percent say the store does not have their size in stock, and 42 percent say they cannot find the item in the store.
- The No. 1 reason consumers walk out of stores empty-handed is because they do not like the styles offered.

The key to making the customer happy lies in product development. Fortunately, opportunities to improve the inefficient product development process abound. In fact, KSA's recent study also identified an opportunity to reduce nearly $7 billion in inefficiencies from the soft goods supply chain through enhanced collaboration in product development.

By adopting collaborative business practices, companies have improved their market responsiveness; introduced more innovative, fashion-right products; and increased the effectiveness of their de-

velopment teams. In short, such practices are allowing companies to:

- stay abreast of trends by designing closer to market;
- improve forecast accuracy by committing to production quantities with more information; and
- reduce work-in-process inventory levels by improving efficiencies.

These developments translate into increased sales, reduced costs and ultimately, market share improvements.

Design and Development Complexities

Many apparel and soft goods companies rank the product development process as the most complex part of their business. The complexity of coordination required throughout the process—among the departments and the systems housing the ever-changing information—is unparalleled.

Consider the following example. A popular women's wear company attempts to reduce its cycle time by creating an integrated calendar of all activities. The problem is that each time it identifies the need for a new activity—a focus group, an additional fitting, a new sample or another meeting—the affected departments request more time. So, rather than reducing time to market, the company now faces longer and longer processes. In the final tally, the company has identified 250 product development activities, including more than 40 that occur simultaneously. How can all of this be managed?

It is not just the processes that are challenging. Coordinating people and information through the processes is not an easy task. The manufacturing department needs to know what the design department is creating. Pattern graders need to know what the designers are thinking. The specification technician needs to be aligned with the bill of materials and costing groups. As a result, the number of meetings, both formal and informal, that take place just to get one season to market can potentially add up in the hundreds.

Now imagine a world in which these frustrations are reduced. Samples are on time. Costs and margins are within the plan. Manufacturing is able to produce the garments as design has intended. Why has this been so difficult to achieve before? It is because the ability to share real-time information with all required parties throughout the process has been limited.

Different companies' objectives for improving the product development process vary. Some fashion-oriented companies attempt to improve their rate of "hits," or new styles that are successful, by doing everything they can to gather inputs that will improve the chances of bringing a hot product to market. Other companies focus on improving their time to market so they can react to market trends in season, or simply beat their competitors to market. However, many firms attempt to make both improvements at the same time. This often results in opposing directives.

The good news is that both objectives can be accomplished more successfully with effective sharing of information during the process. If key customers are able to view designs prior to receipt of a sample, for example, they can give valuable input prior to raw material commitment dates. Likewise, if manufacturing representatives view designs and specification details as they are created, they often can identify problems before delivery is delayed.

New Web-enabled business tools can help make this possible. Following is an overview of some business-to-business (B2B) e-commerce solutions that can be used to improve the product development process.

E-Commerce Tools for Product Development

Collaborative development portals allow authorized users to collaboratively develop things such as designs, specifications, bills of materials and costs in real-time, shared online environments. Utilizing such tools, each party in the product development process still maintains its own deadlines, but can now perform its function with the benefit of this shared, real-time information.

Companies using such portals report that departments no longer feel left out, and they do not need to add buffer time to their tasks because they are no longer forced to start late. Instead, departments work simultaneously to complete tasks. Depending on the type of product and the number of fixed dates in the process, collaborative (or parallel) tasking has allowed some companies to improve cycle time by 30 percent to 50 percent, and hit rates have seen similar improvements. In addition, manufacturing problems have been minimized to enhance the ability to deliver goods on time.

Web-based showrooms enable firms to feature photos of prototype products on the Web, and invite retailers to search for products to complete their assortments. The results can give the apparel firm's designers more understanding of the potential success of their designs while they are still in the prototype stage.

For instance, one footwear supplier is using the information gathered from a Web-based showroom to revise its planned assortments, improving sell-through of its overall line. In apparel, a major branded women's wear wholesaler has used online showrooms not only to feed information to design and merchandising to improve hit rates but also to automate its order management process.

Fashion information providers are Web-based sites and services that provide daily coverage of fashion shows, fashion trends, pop culture and the latest hits in the fashion world. They are key ingredients in supplementing trips to fashion shows and events, store shopping and market research. In addition, they provide opportunities for everyone in the development process to play a part in creating the final product.

Web-based "event management" technologies can enable companies to better adhere to their development schedules by maintaining a product development line calendar that is accessible to relevant parties online. Internal departments and authorized trading partners can view and update the status of their respective tasks in real time, and manage their workloads and commitments accordingly. By simply placing renewed focus on calendar deadlines and enabling realtime management of line calendars, some companies have been able to shorten cycle times by as much as 15 percent.

Making It Work

The benefits of these new Web-based collaborative applications are substantial. Making the tools work for your company, however, is not a simple task. First, an organization must prepare for new information and understand how to integrate it into its processes. Next, it must determine who will be responsible for gathering, understanding and managing the data. Additionally, someone in the organization must be responsible for piloting the new concepts with a small number of designs before launching the technologies across the business. After all, the success and delivery of a full season's line cannot be risked.

In conclusion, Web-based collaborative technologies provide new ways to eliminate inefficiencies from the soft goods supply chain and reduce time to market. Collaboration also improves customer service by reducing stock-outs, giving consumers what they want when they want it and creating the opportunity for significant results to top line sales and bottom line profits.

Chapter Review

Key Words and Concepts

Define, identify, or briefly explain the following:

Accounts payable
Accounts receivable
Agile manufacturing
Apparel jobber
Apparel marts
Body scanning
CEO
Chargebacks
Contractor
COO
Cooperative advertising
Computer-aided design (CAD)
Computer integrated manufacturing (CIM)
Cost estimating
Customer order processing (COP)
Cut order
Cutting ticket
Designers
Distribution center
Elias Howe
807 production
Factoring
Factors
Findings
First pattern
First sample

Fit model
Grainline
Grading
Gross margin
ILGWU
Initial public offering (IPO)
Inside shop
Isaac Singer
Knock-off
Leveraged buyout
Licensee
Licensing
Licensor
Line
Manufacturer
Marker
Market center
Market weeks
Matrix buying
Merchandisers
Modular production system
Outside shop
Postadoption
Preadoption
Preproduction operations
Preticket
Product development

Production fabrics
Production pattern
Progressive bundle system
Prototype
Quick Response (QR)
Rapid replenishment
Ready-to-wear
Real time merchandising (RTM)
Regional showroom
Royalty fee
Sample makers
Seasonal line
Secondary fashion centers
Sell-through
Seventh Avenue (SA)
"Seventh on Sixth"
Sourcing
Specifications
Style piracy
Sweatshop
Tariff
Triangle Shirtwaist Fire
Trunk show
UNITE
Unit production system (UPS)
Vendor
Work-in-process

Review Questions

1. Explain the economic importance of the women's and children's apparel industry to the United States.
2. Why is the NAICS system useful to one who is studying the apparel industry?
3. In chronological order, list the major developments that contributed to the growth of the women's ready-to-wear industry and explain the importance of each.
4. What forms of industry restructuring have we seen in recent years?
5. What changes have occurred for the industry's union?

6. Describe the five major functional areas of an apparel firm, as covered in this chapter.
7. List the major steps involved in the development and production of apparel. Be familiar with how computer technologies are involved in the various steps.
8. Identify as many ways as you can that computers have drastically changed the apparel industry.
9. Contrast the progressive bundle system of production with modular production. If you were a sewing operator, which would you prefer? Why?
10. Describe the overall role Quick Response has in today's apparel industry.
11. What is real time merchandising?
12. Discuss the strategies that may be used by an apparel producer to market a line to retailers.

13. Discuss the methods by which manufacturers are selling directly to consumers and give an example of each.
14. Explain the difference between a manufacturer, an apparel jobber, and a contractor. What are the advantages of each?
15. Is the practice of style piracy good or bad for the fashion industry? Why?
16. Why is licensing so prevalent in the fashion industry?
17. Explain why New York developed into the fashion capital of the United States. Do you think it will retain its present status?
18. What is the role of regional marts in the marketing of apparel?
19. Find an article in a current trade publication that relates to the information in this chapter. Explain how your article relates to the new information you learned.

References

Abernathy, F., Dunlop, J., Hammond, J., & Weil, D. (1999). *A stitch in time: Lean retailing and the transformation of manufacturing.* New York: Oxford University Press.

Agins, T. (1999). *The end of fashion.* New York: William Morrow and Company, Inc.

AIM's global 150. (2000, June). *Apparel Industry Magazine,* 18–38.

Abend, J. (1993, June). Factors report vigorous business. *Bobbin,* pp. 70–73.

American Apparel Manufacturers Association. (2000). *Apparel market monitor, annual 1999.* Arlington, VA: Author.

American Apparel Manufacturers Association. (annual). *Focus: Economic profile of the apparel industry.* Arlington, VA: Author.

Apparel manufacturers' results for the fourth quarter and year. (1996, March 4). *Women's Wear Daily,* p. 22.

Bannon, L. (1998, October 13). Little big spenders: As children become more sophisticated, marketers think older. *Wall Street Journal,* pp. A1, A6.

Bird, L., & Bounds, W. (1997, July 15). Stores' demands squeeze apparel companies. *Wall Street Journal,* pp. B1, B12.

Black, P. (1998, June). The *Bobbin* top 40. *Bobbin,* 48–63.

Brown, P. (1989, February/March). Quick Response: Fashion's quickening pulse. *Fairchild supplement: Retailing technology & operations.* New York: Fairchild.

The city that dresses a nation. (1976, February 15). *New York Sunday News.*

Clune, R. (1993, October 5). [TC]²'s agile manufacturing to give preview of 21st century production. *Daily News Record,* p. 8.

Dallas, the business of fashion. (1985, October 15). *Women's Wear Daily.*

Factoring volume grows worldwide. (1997, May). *ATI,* 22–24.

Feitelberg, R. (1994, December 13). NY gripe: Regional schedules. *Women's Wear Daily,* pp. 21, 22.

Frank, B. (1985). *Profitable merchandising of apparel* (2nd ed.). New York: National Knitwear and Sportswear Association.

Frastaci, M. (1999, November). The children's wear market grows up. *Apparel Industry Magazine,* 44–49.

Friedman, A. (1995a, February 21). Apparel unions "UNITE." *Women's Wear Daily,* pp. 10–11.

Friedman, A. (1995b, May 25). New York gives push to private label plan, cuts funding to GIDC. *Women's Wear Daily,* pp. 1, 10.

From Michael to Mickey, licensed products show broad appeal. (1995, June). *Stores,* pp. 34–37.

Glock, R., & Kunz, G. (1995). *Apparel manufacturing: Sewn product analysis* (2nd ed.). Upper Saddle River, NJ: Prentice Hall.

Haber, H. (1995, May 25). Dallas Market Center getting @ address. *Women's Wear Daily,* pp. 2, 14.

Haber, H. (1999, February 16). Bill Blass gets set to call it a career at the millennium, *Women's Wear Daily,* pp. 1, 12.

He's a fashion purist with the golden touch. (1964, September 12). *Business Week.*

Kids feel ignored by retailers. (1995, April). *Apparel Industry Magazine,* p. 16.

Kidwell, C., & Christman, M. (1974). *Suiting everyone: The democratization of clothing in America.* Washington, DC: Smithsonian Institution Press.

Kunz, G. (1995). Behavioral theory of the apparel firm: A beginning. *Clothing and Textiles Research Journal, 13*(4), 252–261.

Kurt Salmon Associates. (1995). *Vision for the new millennium . . . evolving to consumer response.* Atlanta: Author.

Levi Strauss & Co. (1995, February). *NewsWatch.* San Francisco: Author.

The Licensing Letter. (1995). New York: EPM Communications, Inc.

Lloyd, B. (1994, November 8). Marts face uphill battle in muddled market: Atlanta Apparel Mart. *DNR,* 8, 10.

More than just kid stuff. (1985, May 26). *Women's Wear Daily.*

Reda, S. (1995, June). When vendors become retailers. *Stores,* pp. 18–21.

Sakany, L. (1999a, August). Factors reap rewards of industry consolidation. *Apparel Industry Magazine,* 46, 47, 61.

Sakany, L. (1999b, August). Is New York evicting manufacturing? *Apparel Industry Magazine*, 24–28.

Sakany, L. (1999c, November). The children's wear market grows up. *Apparel Industry Magazine*, 44–49.

Seckler, V. (1998, May 11). Wall Street's runaway: Why some stocks fly and others don't. *Women's Wear Daily*, pp. 1, 6, 7.

Sharoff, R. (1994, November 8). Marts face uphill battle in muddled market: Chicago Apparel Center. *DNR*, pp. 8, 10.

Thornton, M. (1993, January). Factoring: Which service is best for you? *Apparel Industry Magazine*, pp. 71–76.

Tucker, J. (2000). Apparel and fabricated textile products. *U.S. Industry and Trade Outlook 2000*. Washington, DC: U.S. Department of Commerce.

U.S. Department of Commerce. (October 1966). *Long term economic growth 1860–1965*. Washington, DC: Author.

Vargo, J. (1994, November 8). Marts face uphill battle in muddled market: Dallas Market Center. *Women's Wear Daily*, pp. 8, 11.

Williamson, R. (1994, September 26). Mart's keys for growth. *Women's Wear Daily*, pp. 22–23.

Select Bibliography

Abernathy, F., Dunlop, J., Hammond, J., & Weil, D. (1999). *A stitch in time: Lean retailing and the transformation of manufacturing*. New York: Oxford University Press.

Agins, T. (1999). *The end of fashion*. New York: William Morrow and Company, Inc.

American Apparel Manufacturers Association. (annual). *Focus: Economic profile of the apparel industry*. Arlington, VA: Author.

Brown, P., & Rice, J. (2001). *Ready-to-wear apparel analysis* (3rd ed.). Upper Saddle River, NJ: Merrill/Prentice Hall.

Burns, L., & Bryant, N. (1997). *The business of fashion*. New York: Fairchild.

Carr, H., & Latham, B. (1994). *The technology of clothing manufacture*. Oxford, England: Blackwell Science.

Carr, H., & Pomeroy, J. (1992). *Fashion design and product development*. Oxford, England: Blackwell Science.

Chuter, A. (1995). *Introduction to clothing production management*. Oxford, England: Blackwell Science.

Chuter, A. (1995). *Quality management in clothing and textiles*. Oxford, England: Blackwell Science.

Cooklin, G. (1991). *Introduction to clothing manufacture*. Oxford, England: Blackwell Science.

Cooklin, G. (1997). *Garment technology for fashion designers*. Oxford, England: Blackwell Science.

Craig, J., & Horridge, P. (1995). Characteristics of successful and less-successful manufacturers of women's and children's apparel. *Family and Consumer Sciences Research Journal*, 24(2), 139–160.

Dickerson, K. (1999). *Textiles and apparel in the global economy* (3rd ed.). Upper Saddle River, NJ: Merrill/Prentice Hall.

Dubinsky, D. (1977). *David Dubinsky: A life with labor*. New York: Simon & Schuster.

Fairchild Publications. (annual). *Fairchild's textile & apparel financial directory*. New York: Author.

Fairchild Publications. (annual). *WWD buyer's guide: Women's apparel and accessories manufacturers*. New York: Author.

Fairchild Publications. (annual). *WWD supplier's guide: Women's apparel and accessories manufacturers*. New York: Author.

Finnie, T. (1992). *Textiles and apparel in the USA: Restructuring for the 1990s*. London: The Economist Intelligence Unit.

Frastaci, M. (1999, November). The children's wear market grows up. *Apparel Industry Magazine*, 44–49.

Gaines, S. (1991). *Simply Halston—the untold story*. New York: G.P. Putnam's Sons.

Geoello, D., & Berke, B. (1979). *Fashion production terms*. New York: Fairchild.

Glock, R., & Kunz, G. (1999). *Apparel manufacturing: Sewn product analysis* (3rd ed.). Upper Saddle River, NJ: Prentice Hall.

Gray, S. (1998). *CAD/CAM for clothing and textiles*. Aldershot, England: Gower Publishing Ltd.

Guber, S., & Berry, J. (1993). *Marketing to and through kids*. New York: McGraw-Hill.

Hunter, N. (1990). *Quick Response in apparel manufacturing*. Manchester, England: Textile Institute.

Kunz, G. (1998). *Merchandising: Theory, principles and practice*. New York: Fairchild.

Kurt Salmon Associates (1997, March). Quick Response mandates today. *Apparel Industry Magazine*, 45–54.

Laing, R., & Webster, J. (1998). *Stitches and seams*. Manchester, England: The Textile Institute.

Lowson, B. (1998). *Quick Response for small and medium-sized enterprises: A feasibility study*. Manchester, England: Author.

Mass, M. (1991). *Fashion designers*.

Morgenson, G. (1992, May 11). The feminization of Seventh Avenue. *Forbes*, 116–120.

Seckler, V. (1998, May 11). Wall Street's runaway: Why some stocks fly and others don't. *Women's Wear Daily*, pp. 1, 6, 7.

Solinger, J. (1988). *Apparel manufacturing handbook* (2nd ed.). New York: Van Nostrand Reinhold.

Stegemeyer, A. (1995). *Who's who in fashion* (3rd ed.). New York: Fairchild.

Stein, L. (1962). *The Triangle fire*. Philadelphia: Lippincott.

Tate, S., & Edwards, M. (1990). *Inside fashion design*. New York: Harper Collins College.

Textile Institute. (1997). *Restructuring manufacturing*. Manchester, England: Author.

Ulrich, P. (1995). "Look for the label"—The International Ladies' Garment Workers' Union label campaign. *Clothing and Textiles Research Journal, 13*(1), 49–56.

ZuHone, L., & Morganosky, M. (1995). Exchange relationships between apparel retailers and manufacturers. *Clothing and Textiles Research Journal, 13*(1), 57–64.

Trade Associations

American Apparel Manufacturers Association, 2500 Wilson Blvd., Suite 301, Arlington, VA 22201.

American Apparel Producers Network (formerly the American Apparel Contractors Association), Box 720693, Atlanta, GA 30358.

American Coat and Suit Manufacturers Association, 450 Seventh Ave., New York, NY 10123.

Bureau of Wholesale Sales Representatives, 1801 Peachtree Rd., NE, Suite 200, Atlanta, GA 30309.

California Fashion Creators, 110 E. 9th St., Los Angeles, CA 90015.

Canadian Apparel Federation, 130 Slater St., Suite 605, Ottawa, Ontario K1P 6E2, Canada.

Canadian Association of Wholesale Sales Representatives, 1712 Avenue Rd., Box 54546, Toronto, Ontario M5M 4NS, Canada.

Children's Apparel Manufacturers Association, 8270 Mountain Sights, Room 101, Montreal, Quebec H4P 2B7, Canada.

Color Association of the United States, 409 W. 44th St., New York, NY 10036.

Council of Fashion Designers of America, 1633 Broadway, New York, NY 10019.

Ladies Apparel Contractors Association, 450 Seventh Ave., New York, NY 10001.

National Association of Blouse Manufacturers, 450 Seventh Ave., New York, NY 10001.

National Association of Uniform Manufacturers and Distributors, 1156 Ave. of the Americas, New York, NY 10036.

National Dress Manufacturers Association, 570 Seventh Ave., New York, NY 10018.

National Knitwear and Sportswear Association, 386 Park Ave. S., New York, NY 10016.

The Fashion Association, 475 Park Ave. S., 17th Floor, New York, NY 10016.

United Infant's and Children's Wear Association, 520 Eighth Ave., New York, NY 10018.

Trade Publications

Apparel Industry Magazine, 6255 Barfield Rd., Suite 200, Atlanta, GA 30328-4300.

Apparel International, The White House, 60 High St., Potters Bar, Herts EN6 5AB, U.K.

The Apparel Strategist, Apparel Information Resources, 101 E. Locust St., Fleetwood, PA 19522.

Bobbin, 1500 Hampton St., Suite 150, Columbia, SC 29201.

California Apparel News, 110 E. 9th St., Suite A-777, Los Angeles, CA 90079.

Canadian Apparel Manufacturer, 1 Pacifique, Ste. Anne de Bellevue, Quebec H9X 1C5, Canada.

CAMA Review (Children's Apparel Manufacturers Association), 3110, 6900 boul. Decarie, Montreal, Quebec H3X 2T8, Canada.

Chicago Apparel News, Ste. 1045, 350 N. Orleans St., Chicago, IL 60654.

The Discount Merchandiser, 233 Park Ave. S., New York, NY 10003.

Earnshaw's Infants-Girls-Boys Wear Review, 475 Fire Island Ave., Babylon, NY 11702.

Fur Age Weekly, P.O. Box 868, Glenwood Landing, NY 11547.

International Colour Authority, 23 Bloomsbury Square, London WCIA 2PJ, U.K.

Kid's Fashions, Larkin Group, 100 Wells Ave., Newton, MA 02159.

The Licensing Letter, 160 Mercer St., 3rd Floor, New York, NY 10012-3212.

Outerwear, 19 W. 21 St., #403, New York, NY 10010.

Private Level Development, 19 W. 21st St., #403, New York, NY 10010.

Sourcing News, 110 W. 40th St., New York, NY 10018.

Women's Wear Daily, 7 W. 34th St., New York, NY 10001-8191.

World Clothing Manufacturer, 23 Bloomsbury Square, London WC1A 2PJ, U.K.

T*he Menswear Industry*

U*ntil the 1950s,* the average man's wardrobe consisted of one or more dark suits with vests, white shirts, subdued colored ties, highly polished shoes, an overcoat, and a hat. Whatever changes in fashion did take place usually expressed themselves in little more than variations in the width of lapels, the number of buttons, the style and flap of a jacket pocket, and the location of a vent in the suit jacket. The industry that produced men's garments did not consider itself to be in the fast-changing business of fashion.

Change came dramatically after World War II. Surfeited with khaki drabness, many of the younger men yearned for color, even in undershirts. Suburban living, the shorter workweek, and the trend toward family oriented leisure activities set up a demand for sports and leisure wear and resulted in a much freer style of dress, even during business hours. By the 1960s, the presence of a large and highly visible generation of young adults sparked a demand for greater variety, faster change, and new opportunities for expression of individuality. Through the 1970s and on into the 1980s, the winds of fashion change continued to blow up a storm in the men's field. From the late 1980s and into the new millennium active sportswear has created a casual dress code that has revolutionized and revitalized the menswear industry. Special-purpose wardrobes abound in the closets of fashion-conscious males who want to make a "statement" about themselves, with different wardrobes for work, sports, evenings out, shopping, and just hanging out. (The same is true for females, but this trend is relatively new for males.)

Today men's interest in fashion has become increasingly pronounced, and the industry that serves them has responded accordingly. Obviously then, no book about the fashion business would be complete without a discussion of the menswear industry—the subject of this chapter and the readings that follow it.

Economic Importance

The menswear industry's importance as a segment of the U.S. fashion business is demonstrated by such figures as these: More than 2,500 separate companies are engaged in the production of men's and boys' clothing and furnishings. They employ more than 200,000 people, the majority of whom are engaged directly in production activities. Factory output was estimated at about $20 billion (wholesale value) for 2000 (Tucker, 2000).

Consumer expenditures in 1999 for men's and boys' clothing and accessories were about $70 billion, exclusive of shoes. Not all of this was domestic production, of course, nor did all of the domestic industry's output necessarily go to consumers in this country (American Apparel Manufacturers Association, 2000).

Men's and boys' clothing has been the bright spot in the apparel industry in recent years, outperforming the apparel industry in general. Although the women's and children's wear industry sales have generally been somewhat sluggish at times, sales in the men's and boys' segments have been strong. Many in the apparel industry have taken special note of this and made special efforts to capitalize on this strong business and to serve those related to that business.

A number of factors are credited for the strong menswear market. An important one has been men's and boys' increasing interest in clothing—a trend to be discussed further in this chapter. Other explanations include the trends toward casual "office wear," the appeal of wrinkle-resistant apparel, and a move toward European styling in the suit and coat areas.

History and Development

The U.S. ready-to-wear apparel industry started with clothing for men; it was born in the early 1800s, almost half a century before women's ready-to-wear had its beginnings. Until that time, all men's apparel in this country either was custom tailored, for those who could afford this service (Figure 7–1), or was made at home for those less affluent.

Early Beginnings in the Nineteenth Century

Like so many other segments of the fashion industry, menswear manufacturing began with the efforts of some enterprising individuals who saw a need and proceeded to fill it. In this case, the need was to supply clothes for men who either had no access to the then-customary source of supply—the housewife's nimble fingers—or could not afford custom-made clothing.

Development of Men's Ready-to-Wear

In such port cities as New Bedford, New York, Boston, Philadelphia, and Baltimore, a few venturesome tailoring shops conceived the idea of producing and selling cheap ready-to-wear trousers, jackets, and shirts for sailors who needed to replenish their wardrobes inexpensively and immediately during their brief stops in port.

Figure 7–1

An early advertisement for men's tailored clothing.

The Cut of The Coat

Tells the taste of the tailor. The garment that strikes your fancy may not be the one that you should wear. In the mirror of the retail clothier you cannot see yourself as others see you. Is it safe to trust your appearance to the judgment of the ready-made salesman; biased by the necessity of fitting you to the clothing rather than the clothing to you? Individuality and character are subtly expressed in every garment I make. Years of experience in serving the best dressers guarantee that clothing made by me is perfect in style and finish, and is of the color and cut best suited to the wearer's complexion and figure.

BLENHEIM

Tailor of Taste

Source: Courtesy of the Bettmann Archive.

These clothes were poorly made in low-quality fabrics. The cutting was done in the dealers' shops, and the garments were then sent out to local women for hand sewing.

This early ready-made clothing was referred to as "**slops**," a term from which the word *sloppy* developed, with the same connotation then as now. It was remarked that these garments "could be readily recognized about as far as the wearer could be seen. Hence, there was a sort of shame in the purchase and wear of such clothing, and it was considered almost disreputable to wear it; it was at once a reflection upon a man's taste and a supposed indication of his poverty" (Kidwell & Christman, 1974). Nevertheless, the market for ready-made clothing soon expanded to serve bachelors who had no one at home to sew for them and plantation owners who needed cheap clothing for their slaves.

From Tailors to Manufacturers

Because no firms then existed that produced clothing for others to sell, these early shops functioned as both retailers and manufacturers. Some of the proprietors were custom tailors who produced ready-made garments from cheaper grades of cloth in addition to carrying on their primary business of made-to-measure clothing. Others cut the cloth on store premises and contracted to have the sewing done outside by people who worked at home.

As industrialization developed in the early nineteenth century, cities grew, and a new mass market began to emerge among middle-class or white-collar city dwellers. To attract these customers, some of the more resourceful shop owners offered higher-priced and better-made garments. The quality of "store clothes" improved, and their acceptance increased. By 1830, the market for "store-bought" apparel had expanded so greatly that there were firms specializing in the manufacture of garments for others to sell at retail. The first steps in the establishment of the men's clothing industry as we know it today had been taken. By 1835, some manufacturers in New York City, then the nation's leading center for ready-made men's clothing, reportedly employed from 300 to 500 workers (Cobrin, 1971). Boston, Philadelphia, Newark, and Baltimore also progressed rapidly as manufacturing centers, as did Rochester and Cincinnati, toward the middle of the century. Impetus was gained when the sewing machine was developed in the middle of the 1800s.

Among the early producers of men's ready-mades was one of today's most famous and prestigious retailers of men's apparel—Brooks Brothers. Founded in 1818 as a custom-tailoring shop, the company got its start in ready-to-wear during the early period of industrialization. By 1857, it employed 78 tailors who worked on the premises and more than 1,500 outside workers (Kidwell & Christman, 1974).

Work Clothes for Laborers

A development that contributed in a special way to the growth of the menswear industry was the Gold Rush of 1848, which drew thousands of men to the West to pan or dig for gold. Anticipating that these prospectors would need tents to shelter them, a man named Levi Strauss went to California with a supply of heavy fabrics from which to make tents. Among these fabrics was one from France, then called *de Nime*, later Americanized to *denim*. Seeing a need for work clothes, he used his fabrics not for tents but to make work pants that featured large back pockets to hold mining tools. When he added metal rivets to the pockets to hold them securely, the success of his pants was ensured. The menswear industry grew in a way typical of American frontier life—with work clothes for laborers. Aside from Levi Strauss's contribution, the industry grew generally as a result of the westward migration. The men who pushed the frontier westward, not just in California but in the prairies and the mountain states, became a promising market for ready-made clothing. Plants to produce such clothing developed in Chicago and St. Louis to meet the demand.

Standardization of Sizes

The manufacture of ready-to-wear is based on **standardized sizes** in sufficient variety so that almost any figure can be accommodated by one of them. In the early years of the industry, each manufacturer worked out its own set of sizes and made garments to its own specifications, hoping to fit as many people as possible. The fit of these early garments was far from perfect.

One of the biggest boosts to the men's ready-to-wear clothing industry came from government orders for soldiers' uniforms during the Civil War. Because hand sewing could not keep pace with the Army's needs, factories had to be built and equipped with the then-new sewing machines. Also, in order to facilitate the production of its uniforms, the Army surveyed the height and chest measurements of more than a million recruits, and thus provided the first mass of statistical data on the form and build of American men. After the war, the results of the Army study were made available to producers of men's civilian clothing. This put the sizing of men's ready-to-wear on a scientific basis and, by making improved fit possible, hastened the change from homemade and custom-made to factory-made garments.

Twentieth-Century Developments

By the time the menswear business entered the twentieth century, it was no longer an industry of small entrepreneurs; it had its share of large enterprises. As the twentieth century progressed, there came such developments as unionization, public ownership, and in time, a return to private ownership on the part of some of those who had earlier gone public.

"The Amalgamated" (ACTWU)—Now UNITE

Like the women's garment industry, the men's clothing industry presented a dismal labor picture at the beginning of this century, with sweatshops prevalent. Producers contracted to have the sewing of garments done outside their plants, either by individuals who did the work in their tenement homes or by contractors who gathered sewing hands together in equally uncomfortable and unsanitary lofts.

In 1910, a strike that started at the Hart, Schaffner & Marx plant in Chicago spread and eventually drew 35,000 workers from their jobs. Settlement of the dispute brought improved working conditions, reduced working hours to 54 hours a week, and set up machinery for adjusting grievances. A few years later, in 1914, the craft union that formerly represented the men's clothing workers yielded its place to the Amalgamated Clothing Workers of America, an industry union, and one that has established a record of labor peace and pioneering effort.

"The Amalgamated" worked for arbitration and industrywide bargaining; it sought stable labor relations with management as a means of keeping its people employed. It has encouraged scientific techniques in industry management, and it has provided extensive and innovative social welfare services to its members. The union points with pride to its relationship with that same Hart, Schaffner & Marx, at whose Chicago factory a strike triggered the events that led to the Amalgamated's birth. For more than 50 years, that plant, now the world's largest in the men's clothing field, did not have a strike.

In the 1970s, the Amalgamated merged with the Textile Workers of America and the United Shoe Workers of America to form the Amalgamated Clothing and Textile Workers Union (ACTWU). In 1995, this union merged with the International Ladies Garment Workers Union to form the Union of Needletrades, Industrial, & Textile Employees (UNITE). Virtually all factories in the United States that produce men's tailored clothing (suits, tailored sports coats, formal wear, top coats, etc.) are unionized today. This is not true, however, of other segments of the men's apparel industry, such as sportswear. In that respect, the union does not have control over its industry. In part, this situation arises because production of men's apparel is widespread throughout the United States, and in part, it is due to the varying patterns of production in the different segments of the industry.

Public Ownership in the 1960s

Until the 1960s, publicly owned firms were the exception rather than the rule in menswear. Just as was the case in women's apparel at that time, most concerns were individually owned enterprises, partnerships, or closely held corporations. During the 1960s, many firms in the men's field went public, for much the same reasons as prevailed in the women's field. In some instances, it was a way for a proprietor with no family successor to ease his way into retirement; in others, it was a need for expansion capital. The lure of expansion capital is a strong one. Without it, firms can expand only to the extent that they plow back the profits of their operations year after year. Drawing on the public's invested capital is a faster way.

Private Ownership in the 1980s

Like the women's industry, in the ultracompetitive atmosphere of the 1980s, some major men's apparel producers began to see public ownership as more of a liability than an asset. Publicly owned companies have a responsibility to shareholders, and this includes public disclosure of new marketing plans and strategies to the extent that swift, silent changes of course are difficult to execute. Some firms, therefore, decided to go private—that is, to buy back their corporation's stock. **Levi Strauss & Co.** took this step. By returning a company to private ownership, a firm is freer in decision making; it is no longer in the spotlight turned on public companies by investment experts and is protected from the possibility of hostile takeovers.

Nature of the Industry

The menswear industry, which also includes garments for boys and youths, resembles the women's wear industry in some ways and differs from it in others. Their points of resemblance include the following: (1) manufacturers usually specialize in clearly definable categories of garments, (2) producers in the various industry branches present seasonal lines, and (3) designer names are featured. Still another point of resemblance is the importance of collections that feature complete, coordinated groups of merchandise, all of which are produced, sold, and ultimately displayed in retail stores under a single brand or designer name. A still later development is the growing importance of classification (pants, T-shirts) merchandising to avoid excessive markdowns sometimes caused by buying complete collections. This development mirrors a prior development from decades ago in women's sportswear as the sportswear market was growing and expanding.

Points of difference from the women's field are numerous: (1) the larger firms account for a larger share of the men's industry's total output; (2) manufacturers' brand names have been long established, may be better known, often are more important to the consumer, and frequently are more influential in marketing than they are in the women's field; and (3) the contracting system, so much a part of the women's field, is somewhat less common. On the last point, however, the growing importance of sportswear is increasing the use of the contracting system.

Like other parts of the apparel industry, the men's and boys' segment has become increasingly global. Various lines, even for some of the leading firms, may be produced by overseas contractors. Similarly, a number of retailers may develop their own men's and boys' lines and contract production just as U.S. manufacturers do.

Men's and Boys' NAICS Groupings

Just as the women's and children's apparel industry has North American Industry Classification System (NAICS) categories for firms by garment type, so does the men's and boys' wear industry. Categories for firms in the men's and boys' wear industry are shown in Table 6–1 (see page 212). Most men's and boys' cut and sew apparel manufacturing is in category 31522. For apparel made in knitting mills, no distinction is made by gender.

In the lexicon of the men's apparel industry, the term **tailored clothing** refers to structured or semistructured suits, overcoats, sports jackets, and separate slacks, the production of which may involve some hand-tailoring operations. This division at one time so dominated the industry that, to the consumer, the term *men's clothing* was synonymous with tailored clothing. Not so today, as we shall discuss later in this chapter.

Types of Firms

Many of the largest menswear firms began as just that. They produced garments for men, and sometimes boys. In recent years, however, many firms have expanded into women's wear, either by creating or acquiring women's divisions. Some of these major firms are shown in Table 7–1.

Levi Strauss & Co. expanded from a men's jeans firm to one that later produced jeans for women and children, and later still other apparel for both men and women. Today, few people would think of this company as a "men's" company because of the large volume of sales to women and children. Ralph Lauren also started in menswear, expanded into women's wear and boys' clothing, and then expanded further into retailing by opening his own stores and franchising stores to sell Ralph Lauren, Polo, and Chaps products.

Geographic Locations: Decentralized

Menswear firms are not heavily concentrated but rather are widely distributed throughout the United States. The industry's largest, Levi Strauss, is headquartered in San Francisco. **Hartmarx**, a major producer of tailored clothing, is headquartered in Chicago. Philadelphia is headquarters for Greif & Company, After Six, and Pincus Bros. Maxwell. In the Pacific Northwest are White Stag and Pendleton. Haggar and Farah are in Texas. Oxford Industries is one of the many companies in the South. Production facilities, as well as headquarters offices, are so widely scattered that the industry is truly national, and there is scarcely a state that is not involved in menswear. All the firms mentioned, however, have showrooms in New York City, as do many, many others.

Importance of New York

New York City is the hub of the industry's marketing efforts and houses the sales office of virtually every important producer in the United States. In just a single building, 1290 Avenue of the Americas, several hundred menswear firms have their offices.

Table 7–1	Major Menswear Producers[a]: Selected Examples	
Company	**Sales (in $ millions) 1999**	**Principal Menswear Products**
Levi Strauss & Co.	5,140	Jeans, sportswear (all products in total)
Tommy Hilfiger Corp.	1,923 (op. revenue)	Casual wear, relaxed dress clothing
Phillips-Van Heusen	1,271	Shirts, sportswear (includes retail stores)
Oxford Industries	839.5	Shirts, sportswear
Hartmarx	681	Tailored clothing (and office casual wear)
Williamson-Dickie Mfg. Co.	644	Sportswear, industrial wear
Haggar Corp.	438	Slacks, casual wear
Savane International Corp. (formerly Farah, Inc.)	277	Slacks, casual wear
Joseph and Feiss Co. (Hugo Boss, U.S.A. subsidiary)	108	Suits, casual wear

[a]Although menswear is a major focus of these firms, in nearly all cases, they also have women's wear divisions that account for a significant portion of annual sales.
Source: Business & Company Resource Center (online), Company Profile Data: http://galenet.galegroup.com/servl. Feb. 2001. Reprinted by permission of the Gale Group.

As the industry has grown, its showrooms have spilled over into surrounding office buildings on 51st, 52nd, and 53rd streets, from Fifth Avenue to Seventh Avenue. Farther downtown, in the Empire State Building at 34th Street and Fifth Avenue, there are sales offices for a major share of the men's furnishings companies. Meantime, the area around 23rd Street and Fifth Avenue, which was once the heart of the industry, has been abandoned to retail and housing uses.

What draws merchants to New York City is the presence of showrooms, showrooms, and more showrooms. The typical retailer has little need or desire to visit production facilities. A few, however, such as L.L. Bean and Lands' End, make frequent visits to work out details of production of products specifically for their respective companies and to monitor quality.

Centers of Production

The production of menswear, as has been mentioned, takes place all over the United States. Certain areas, however, are more important than others for specific types of apparel. Tailored clothing is produced primarily in the Northeast, with New York, Pennsylvania, and Massachusetts being the major areas. Together with Georgia, these states produce more than 50 percent of all domestically made tailored clothing.

As to other categories: A large percentage of men's and boys' shirts and nightwear are produced in North Carolina, Alabama, Georgia, and Tennessee; almost three-fourths of separate trousers are produced in Georgia, Texas, Tennessee, and Mississippi; and the main U.S. production of all men's and boys' neckwear takes place in New York, North Carolina, California, and Louisiana.

Increasingly, U.S. menswear manufacturers are having their lines produced in other countries. Certain regions and countries have established extensive menswear industries, particularly in making tailored apparel. Canada has a tradition of producing high-quality tailored wear. Eastern Europe and Mexico have become centers for production of more moderate-priced men's tailored apparel.

Design and Production Procedures

The procedures in the design and production of men's tailored clothing and in the design and production of men's sportswear differ greatly. In tailored clothing, changes are simple and subtle; in sportswear, changes tend to be more rapid, more drastic, and more trendy. Throughout the entire menswear field, however, men remain slower and less willing than women to accept radical fashion changes in their wardrobes. What has been changing, however, is men's attitudes toward their bodies, with emphasis on health. Exercise became a fact of life in the 1980s. Fitness, says designer Bill Blass, "is a major preoccupation of people in our time" ("The Impact," 1985).

This new body awareness manifests itself in menswear in a number of ways. There is, of course, the demand for jogging suits, tennis and running shorts, and workout outfits. So strong is the interest in athletics and athletic clothes that the warm-up suit became known as the leisure outfit of the 1980s. At the same time, men's tailored clothing has changed to reflect the interest in fit bodies. Shoulders are wider, waists are narrower, and the drop has increased. The **drop** is the difference between the chest measurement and the waist measurement. Traditionally, this was six inches, but nowadays manufacturers are changing their specifications to seven or eight inches.

Tailored Clothing

The tailored clothing segment of the menswear industry presents a completely different picture from what prevails in other branches, and certainly a picture utterly unlike the one that prevails in the women's fashion industry. Production is slow and painstaking; highly skilled operators are required; handwork is still a factor; sizing is complex; emphasis is on selection of fabrics rather than styles alone; and styles change slowly and gradually. With all these elements to consider, it is not surprising that this segment of the industry operates on the basis of only two seasons a year.

Seasonal Lines

The tailored clothing industry, with its long and complex production methods, traditionally presents its lines to retailers only twice a year. Fall/Winter lines are shown to the trade in December and January; Spring/Summer lines are shown in July and August. This long-established calendar prevails today and continues to do so because the apparel concerned remains largely classic in style. If fashion changes were swifter and more marked in this field, necessitating more frequent introduction of new styles, the calendar might change—and the industry's methods of operation would undoubtedly have to change along with it.

Development of a Line

The development of a tailored clothing line starts with a decision as to the bodies, or basic styles, that will be featured for the coming season. Each major suit and coat manufacturer uses at least one master tailor/designer whose job is to make the subtle changes in last year's bodies that may be needed to produce this year's new shape. Changes may include adding or subtracting length in the jacket and lapels; bringing the garment closer to or farther from the body; making the shoulders fuller or less so; choosing between flap and patch pockets; deciding on whether there will be side vents, a back vent, or no vent; and so on.

Once the newly modified bodies are ready, the designer, the piece goods buyer, and the principals of the company set to work to choose the fabric assortment. These assortments are quite extensive, as retailers expect to see a broad range when they come in to make their selections for a major season. Finally, sample garments may be made up in a few of the fabrics, so that the bodies can be shown in plaids, stripes, and solids. However, with today's computer technologies, not all variations may need to be made into sample garments. This is the line that is shown to the retailer, along with a swatch book of additional fabrics that are available.

Production of Tailored Clothing

The process of producing men's tailored clothing is long, complex, and quite different from the procedures followed in women's apparel or in other divisions of menswear. Many hand operations are involved in the construction of structured garments, the sizing system is more complicated, and it is fabric rather than shape or silhouette that differentiates one tailored style from another (Figure 7–2). The manufacturer commits itself in advance to 100 fabrics or more. These are presented to the retail customers, and the retail buyers select those they want and the basic bodies in which they want them made up. To that extent, the retailer designs its own exclusive line. The producer, moreover, may offer PGR (Piece Goods Reservation), a system whereby the manufacturer sets aside fabric for a specific retailer during or

Figure 7–2

Tailored Menswear

Source: Courtesy of *MR Magazine.*

immediately after showing the line. The manufacturer does not begin production until sufficient orders have been accumulated for a fabric to justify a cutting ticket. A quality maker will put a fabric into production if it has been ordered in one or several different models and runs of sizes, as long as there are at least a minimum number of garments to cut. Each producer sets its own figure, of course.

Even after the cutting has been done, production goes slowly. The hand operations involved in tailored clothing are time consuming; as much as an hour or more may be needed for the pressing operation alone. Quality control is maintained throughout the construction of tailored clothing—a factor that explains why many producers in this division of the industry are inside shops, using their own production facilities rather than those of outside contractors. This is in sharp contrast with the men's sportswear field, where style and design features are emphasized rather than exact fit and meticulous workmanship.

Complex Sizing

The dual-sizing system that prevails in tailored clothing is a further factor in making production procedures slow and cumbersome. Men's suits are cut in different chest measurements, each one of which is combined with different figure types. This is in sharp contrast with the situation that prevails in the women's apparel industry, in which each producer tends to concentrate on a single figure type, such as misses, junior, or half-size, and cuts possibly five or six sizes for that figure type. A tailored suit producer, however, has to cope with all these sizes for any one number in the line:

- *Short.* 36, 37, 38, up to 42 chest measurement
- *Regular.* 36, 38, 39, 40, up to 46 chest measurement
- *Long.* 38, 39, 40, 41, up to 48 chest measurement
- *Extra Long.* 40, 42, 44, up to 48 chest measurement
- *Portly.* 39, 40, 41, up to 50 chest measurement

Even in the case of separate slacks, the sizing is not simple. Many in the tailored category are sized by waist alone, it is true, depending on the retailer or the customer to measure off the inseam length and hem the garment. But there are also many men's pants that are sold finished at the hem, and these are sized in waists from 26 to 42 for the most part, and in inseam lengths of 29 to 36 inches.

This enormous variety of sizes is important to the retailer seller, because many menswear stores continue to alter men's suits to fit individual customers and to absorb the cost of such alterations. This, too, is changing, as the mix of stores selling men's tailored clothing has changed to include discounters and others who charge for alterations. Also, stores that have traditionally provided free alterations now charge for some types of alteration in order to keep expenses down. Even Brooks Brothers now charges for some alterations.

The enormous variety of sizes stocked by retailers that desire to have a presence in the tailored clothing marketplace has necessitated huge investments of capital in slow-turning stock. Consequently, the broad range of sizing in men's tailored wear makes this a complex and expensive segment of the industry for both manufacturers and retailers.

The custom of doing free alterations goes back to the made-to-order beginnings of menswear, when accurate fit was expected by the consumer. (In contrast, women, who are supposed by tradition to be competent seamstresses, have nearly always had to pay for any needed alterations.) To minimize alterations, menswear retailers have sought to carry stocks that permit almost any size or figure type to be fitted with a minimum of adjustments. Although it is unlikely that any one style will be carried in all sizes, the average number of sizes bought in one garment ranges from 15 to 25, depending on the type and size of the store and the importance placed on the model and fabric in relation to the total inventory.

Simplifying Sizes

The growing importance of young men as suit buyers is slowly leading the way into S/M/L/XL sizing, introduced at the MAGIC show in 1986 to poor results, to replace the myriad of sizes carried in traditional tailored clothing departments today. This trend to date is confined to makers that market to the customers who desire a more formal version of the contemporary soft suit, but do not want fully constructed clothing. However, traditional manufacturers such as Southwick, Lanvin Studio by Greif, Joseph Abboud, and Bill Robinson, among others, are producing soft-construction tailored clothing.

At the base of this S/M/L/XL sizing, which can be done in regulars and longs, is "Small," which has a 40 shoulder and a 38 body; "Medium," which has a 43 shoulder and a 41 body; and "Large," which has a 49 (or equivalent) shoulder and a 44 body. In a way, this is another way of responding to the desire for increased "drop" in tailored clothing. It may also be the retailer's way to respond to the desire to keep inventories as lean as possible without giving up the tailored clothing business.

Hand Tailoring

The production of men's tailored clothing traditionally has involved many hours of hand tailoring. In the past, tailored clothing was given *grades* from 1 to 6+, based on the number of hand operations that went into the production. In recent years, the practice of identifying suits by grades has disappeared, due to technological developments. Today, many hand-tailoring processes have been eliminated because there is machinery that simulates hand stitching of lapels, turning of pockets, or finishing of buttonholes. Such procedures speed up production and reduce costs. However, top-quality men's suits still involve a great deal of hand tailoring.

Custom Tailors and Tailors-to-the-Trade

Because men's apparel required a more precise fit than women's clothes, custom tailoring remained important in the men's field longer than custom dressmaking did in women's wear. Most of the men's tailors who did custom work in this country in the early years of this century had been trained in Europe under the apprentice system; they could design a suit, sponge the fabric to preshrink it, cut the garment, run up the seams, sew on buttons, make buttonholes by hand, and supply the fine stitching on lapels. Until the 1920s, a man could enjoy the excellent fit of a made-to-order suit at prices and in qualities that compared very favorably with ready-made clothing.

The supply of custom tailors, however, began to dwindle in the 1920s and 1930s. Immigration had been restricted and, as the older European-trained tailors died or retired, very few new ones crossed the Atlantic to take their places. Work in the factories of this country did not produce craftsmen capable of making complete garments. Efficient methods of operation required some men to specialize in cutting, others in sewing, and still others in the hand finishing.

Today, about 600 **custom tailor** shops, also known as **bespoke tailors**, still exist in the United States, principally in large cities and at the upper end of the price scale. Clients are a "who's who" of the rich and famous—screen stars, diplomats, industry magnates—who are willing to pay between $2,500 and $8,000 for a suit. Clients such as these who pamper themselves with luxury sometimes buy four or five suits at a clip. These celebrities trust their public image to the hands of bespoke tailors, who know how their clients should dress for the good life. One bespoke tailor, Maurizio noted, "We're the Maseratis of the business. What billionaire wouldn't like to look at one in his driveway?" (Gellers, 1998, p. 15).

Behind these hefty price tags is an arduous, painstaking process of creating the bespoke suit, with endless handwork that is reminiscent of early years when this was a common practice in the tailoring trade. Exacting measurements, handmade patterns, hand-basting, tacking and felling, hand-sewn padding on the collar and hand-stitched linings endure. Several fittings may be required to fine-tune the perfect fit expected in the final suit. As one industry writer noted, "Understandably, fashion moves slowly at these prices." Thus, most of these businesses are relatively small, with annual sales averaging $1 million. Immigrant tailors continue to provide the skillful workers for this segment of the industry. In the past, many workers were from Italy, but now many come from Asian or Latin American regions (Gellers, 1998, p. 14).

In addition to the custom tailors, who produce a complete garment on their own premises, there are also **made-to-measure firms** or **tailors-to-the-trade**. These are prestige clothing makers that specialize in cutting individual garments according to the exact measurements of customers who place their orders through retail stores serviced by these firms. Bookings often occur through in-store trunk shows.

Made-to-measure suits begin with the same basic process of taking body measurements that bespoke tailors use—but the similarities end there. At $1,500 and up for these made-to-measure suits, the customer has choices from fashion books and swatches that he consults in the retail store to select fabrics and features such as side vents. Then, his selection and his measurements are relayed to the factory; and in due course the garment is made up.

Better specialty retailers are reporting fast growth in made-to-measure sales. Although 30 or fewer prestige apparel firms produce for this market, this market appears to have a promising future. Approximately 35 percent of Oxxford's (as distinct from Oxford Industries) sales are made-to-measure, and Brioni, Hickey-Freeman,

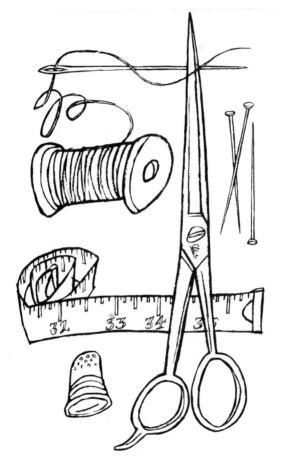

Made-to-Measure
at no extra charge

B A R N E Y S
N E W Y O R K

Source: Courtesy of Barneys New York Advertising.
Art by Robert Clyde Anderson, permission granted.

and Zegna all have thriving programs. An example is Barneys New York (Figure 7–3). The store's customer list has included such names as Cary Grant, Paul Newman, Walter Hoving, and some of New York's leading politicians.

Casual Office Wear

A major new trend in men's dressing has resulted from what started as a perk in computer companies—casual dress on Fridays. As the idea spread, a new term in the fashion industry vocabulary developed: **Friday Wear**. Men discovered what women had known for some time—one can be properly dressed but still comfortable. Large numbers of *Fortune* 500 and smaller companies developed some form of alternative dress code for at least part of the workweek. In 1995, even IBM, known for its formal dress codes, relaxed its expectations for employees' clothing, resulting in marketing efforts directed specifically to men at that long-held bastion of proper attire.

As men in many U.S. companies enjoyed the freedom and comfort of Friday Wear, many decided to extend the trend to other days of the week, leading to what some have called **Everyday Wear**. By whatever name or when it is worn, this trend has had a major impact on the menswear industry. Tailored menswear firms have felt the change in business. Many have introduced new lines of softly tailored, relaxed apparel, such as that shown in Figure 7–4, to fill this need. Retailers, too, felt the effect of shifts toward more casual wear in the workplace (Courter, 1995; Gellers, 1994).

Figure 7–4

With its roots in tailored clothing, this example illustrates the dressed-down relaxed look many men began to wear to the office in the mid 1990s.

Source: Courtesy of *MR Magazine.*

Confusion surrounded the definition of casual wear for the workplace. A number of menswear manufacturers helped customers by introducing coordinated lines with flexibility in mixing and matching jackets, slacks, shirts, and accessories. To help the befuddled shopper, some apparel makers provide guidance on labels to tell when and how to wear the garment. For example, a Pepe Jeans sleeveless lumber jacket label reads, "This shirt must be worn as an overshirt." A "relaxed dress shirt" by Joseph Abboud comes with a booklet that states the shirt "can be worn with jeans or without a tie, perfect for a relaxed day at the office" (Brown, 1994, p. 158).

Sometimes companies have been embarrassed by their employees' overinterpretation of casual wear. Although jeans, T-shirts, and running shoes may fit the California lifestyle or in the development laboratories at computer firms, most companies had something less casual in mind for employees.

At any rate, this fast-growing category of menswear, somewhere between formal business attire and leisure wear, has represented new opportunities for apparel firms. For example, Phillips-Van Heusen created a "Corporate Casual" program that has proven very successful. Hartmarx, Greif, Haggar, and Farah have responded with new lines. Arrow makes "Friday shirts," and Brooks Brothers has a whole line called "Soft Classics" (Brown, 1994). Textile firms benefit from the trend, too, because many of the casual work wear lines incorporate fabrics with increased texture and other design interest.

Sportswear Design and Production

It was only a few decades ago when men's sportswear emerged from the dark ages. The mod explosion of the 1960s transformed the business. The old-furnishings-oriented (ties and shirts) business-clothing-only look gave way to the jeans generation of baby boomers.

The designer revolution of the 1960, which brought names like Oleg Cassini, John Weitz, Pierre Cardin, and Yves St. Laurent to the forefront, later swept in Ralph Lauren and Calvin Klein in the 1970s and Perry Ellis, Alexander Julian, and Giorgio Armani in the 1980s. Joseph Abboud, Donna Karan, and Jhane Barnes are important names today.

From California came the young men's revolution and Brittania (later to become Generra) and Union Bay. The active boom brought in names such as Nike, Wilson, and Adidas to the apparel industry. Names once important, such as Merona, Bruce, and McGregor, lost their luster and gave way to names such as Nautica, Guess, Tommy Hilfiger, and Levi's/Dockers.

The demand of male customers for a more fashionable look—for clothes suited to the multifaceted multidimensional lives they lead—has made the sportswear segment of the men's clothing industry increasingly important. Clothes for activity, the outdoors, casual evening dressing, biking, hiking, running, and working out all require appropriate clothing. Even "hanging out" needs the right clothes, depending on where you do your hanging out. These clothes do not require careful shaping and hand operations; the shape is supplied by the wearer. What is required is more fashion awareness and producers that can quickly respond to changing customer demands.

Seasonal Lines

In men's sportswear, the quickening desire of consumers for fashion newness has resulted in a quickening pace of style change. Because of its ability to respond to changes in silhouette, pattern, color, and trend, sportswear provides faster inventory turnover.

In the quickening fashion pace of the men's sportswear market, the need has developed for more newness more often. Instead of the three seasons that were prevalent just six short years ago, sportswear now has four seasons. Fall (shown in March) is delivered in August; Holiday (shown in June) is delivered in November; Spring (shown in October) is delivered in February; and Summer (shown in January) is shipped in April or May. Claiborne, the menswear division of Liz Claiborne, offers five men's lines a year: Fall I is shown in March for June delivery; Fall II is shown in June for September delivery; Holiday/Pre-Spring is shown in August for November delivery; Spring I is shown in October for January delivery; and Spring II is shown in January for March delivery. The menswear industry is gradually becoming "seasonless" in much the same way as women's apparel, with a constant stream of new products offered.

Development of a Line

The preparation of a sportswear line differs a great deal from the development of a tailored clothing line. In sportswear, as in women's wear, the producer has already preselected the fabrics for the various numbers in the line, and the emphasis is on offering a selection of styles rather than a choice of fabric (Figure 7–5).

Figure 7–5 | **An example of a men's sportswear line, illustrating potential for mixing and matching various pieces in the line.**

In preparing a line of coordinated sportswear, or of men's separates (such as trousers, shirts, or sweaters), there are both similarities and differences between one company and another. Where a designer's name is involved, the designer usually oversees the sketching, selection of fabrics, making of samples, and selection of colors. A company that specializes in separates, such as Haggar, uses house designers who prepare a line of pants by adding or removing front pleats, narrowing or widening pants legs, or making whatever other modifications are needed to achieve the new season's look. Fabric selection is usually handled by the designer, working with the company's principals and the sales manager, each of whom contributes his or her special expertise to the final selection. Pricing is usually done by the same group, but with the production manager replacing the designer on the team for this task.

Production

Because no hand tailoring is involved in the production of sportswear, the sewing (and often also the cutting) is likely to be farmed out to independent contractors (domestic and overseas), much as is done in the women's apparel industry. However, in addition to using outside shops, many large producers such as Haggar, Oxford Industries, and Levi Strauss also handle some of the production in their own plants.

With fashion changes, the scope of a line expands or contracts. There may be more or fewer sweaters, fewer T-shirts, more or less activewear, and so on. In such cases, it is necessary merely to find new contractors for the expanded categories and to drop those no longer needed for fading areas of demand. And, as in the women's industry, both international and domestic contractors are used.

Simplified Sizing

The sizing in some sportswear categories is fairly simple; in others, it is becoming so. Men's sweaters are usually sized Small, Medium, Large, and Extra Large. Sports pants are sold by waist measurement in inches. Some trousers carry both waist and length sizes, in inches, such as 29/30, 29/31, and so on. In these designations, the first figure is the waist measurement and the second is the inseam, or length from trouser rise to hem. More-expensive trousers often come without hems, so that the leg length can be adjusted for the individual customer.

Sport shirts are produced in only four sizes: Small, Medium, Large, and Extra Large. Sleeve lengths are standard for each size. Makers of men's dress shirts have been following the lead of the sport shirt makers in simplifying their sizes, but with limited success. Dress shirt manufacturers had been accustomed to making their entire lines with neck sizes ranging from 14 (inches) to 17 1/2 or even larger. For each neck size, they produced sleeve lengths ranging from 31 to 37 inches, at one-inch intervals. Such a wide range of sizes represented a slow production process for the manufacturer and a formidable inventory problem for both retailer and manufacturer.

To permit quicker response to fashion change and to permit lower inventories, shirt producers have sought to pay less attention to fit and increased attention to fashion. They simply produce a very large percentage of their styles with average rather than exact sleeve lengths. This system of producing only average sleeve lengths (ASL) has not been too well received by some customers. Today, major men's shirt retailers carry both types—fashion shirts in average sleeve lengths only and classic dress shirts in the customary collar and sleeve length sizing.

Importance of the Collection Concept

In the past, male shoppers in professional careers tended to build their wardrobes around tailored clothing and regarded such items as sweaters or sport trousers as merely extra purchases. Today, they may very well make all their purchases in sportswear departments, where they can achieve a look that is properly put together, even if the fabrics in the various garments are different. This has become possible because of the **collection concept.**

Originally in the realm of licensing designers such as John Weitz, Giorgio Armani, and Allan Flusser, the collection concept has grown to the point that it encompasses almost all menswear, whether designer sponsored or manufacturers' brands, and at all price levels. A menswear retailer nowadays buys and presents a collection from a company that produces jackets, trousers, shirts, sweaters, and even ties and belts, thus ensuring that the customer will be offered a variety of items, all of which can be worn together and are color coordinated.[1]

For example, Henry Grethel, a New York designer licensed by Hartmarx, designs a complete clothing collection including trousers, jackets, shirts, sweaters, and T-shirts, all geared for weekend wear. Perry Ellis America produced by Manhattan Shirt Co., a division of Salant Corp., creates complete coordinated collections, as does Andrew Fezza for GFT America. Other designer collections include those by Barry Bricken, Jhane Barnes, Jeffrey Banks, and Claiborne. Giorgio Armani does three collections, each geared to a separate target market by price and lifestyle: Armani Couture, the highest-priced and most elegant; Armani Boutique, moderate to high priced, geared to the man on his way up the corporate and fiscal ladder; and Mani, the most fashion-forward line in department store price ranges. Similarly, Hugo Boss has three distinct groupings targeted toward different consumers: the classic consumer, the "fashion aware," and the *avant garde* (Silverman, 1995).

Increase of Classification Merchandising

Because of the growth of the menswear customer today who has confidence in his own fashion expertise and taste and because retailers want the freedom to pick and choose from a line to satisfy their target market, we see a return to classification buying and merchandising. This approach lowers potential markdown, lowers stock investments in slower selling classifications, and speeds inventory turns.

Marketing of Menswear

The way to achieve growth is to find new markets or to win business away from competing companies. Thus, there is greater emphasis on marketing, instead of on production alone, and this in turn has speeded up the industry's use of contractors to facilitate quick response to the changes in demand. As the apparel industry develops and emphasizes marketing strategies rather than production capabilities alone, the field of menswear becomes an ever more important area of potential growth. Today's menswear customer, at every age and economic level, is more

---

[1]Similarly, a number of retailers may produce their own coordinated collections by contracting directly with domestic or overseas producers.

interested and involved than ever before in the building of a wardrobe and in the process of selection. Fashion shopping is no longer for women only; it has truly become an activity for both sexes.

Manufacturers' Brands

Brand names in the men's field are older and better established—and have been longer promoted—than those in the women's field. Men have been conditioned for generations to purchase apparel in terms of grade, quality, fit, and durability rather than style alone. Thus, until a dozen or more years ago, consumers gravitated to brand names that were associated in their minds with quality: Arrow and Manhattan shirts, Hickey-Freeman and Society brand suits, for example, and such stores' labels (private brands) as those of retailers such as Brooks Brothers, major department stores, outstanding menswear shops, chains, and mail-order companies.

Some of the brand names still prominent in menswear date back to the beginning of the twentieth century or earlier. Hart, Schaffner & Marx, now known as Hartmarx, began promoting its name through national advertising in 1890. In 1901, Joseph & Feiss (now owned by Phillips-Van Heusen) embarked on a national campaign to sell its "Clothescraft Clothes," retailing for $10 and upward, by telling their retail customers that "the wearer will be brought to you by judicious advertising. We pay for it" (Cobrin, 1971). This, of course, was an early and simple form of cooperative advertising.

Responding to a vastly different department and specialty store climate created by mergers and acquisitions on the part of retailers, manufacturers are developing new marketing strategies to maintain consumer awareness of their brand names. Greif companies, which include licensed labels such as Chaps by Ralph Lauren and Colours by Alexander Julian among others, has added a new layer of service people who will act as liaison between the retailers and the company to provide marketing intelligence for themselves and their customers, thus keeping their brand names highly visible. For example, Levi Strauss spends millions of dollars a year to advertise just one style of jeans, and Guess spends millions each year to promote what it describes as "image advertising."

Targeted Customer Approach

As menswear purchases in apparel changed from replacement purchases to impulse fashion purchases, manufacturers had to develop much more knowledge about their customer. A very focused and targeted approach is developing and replacing the commodity thinking that was prevalent in the menswear industry. Major producers such as Hartmarx have developed customer profiles for different divisions of their company, as shown in Table 7–2. Similarly, Generra has separated its business into a young men's market (the 15-to-24 age range) and a men's market (geared to men in the 25-to-45 age range). As noted earlier, Hugo Boss has developed lines for three distinct market segments.

Designer Labels and Designer Licensing

Fashion in menswear took on new importance in the mid-1960s. For the first time, designers gave serious attention to menswear—and consumers noticed. Up to then, men tended to look for favorite brands, placing their confidence in stalwarts like Arrow, Van Heusen, and Palm Beach. These national brands contributed to market

Table 7–2	**Hartmarx Brand and Product Segmentation**		
Upper*	**Upper Moderate***	**Moderate***	**Popular***
Suits $675+	Suits $450–$675	Suits $325–$450	Suits Under $325
Sportcoats $450+	Sportcoats $300–$450	Sportcoats $200–$300	Sportcoats Under $200
Dress Slacks $125+	Dress Slacks $75–$125	Dress Slacks $50–$75	Dress Slacks Under $50
Casual Slacks $90+	Casual Slacks $60–$90	Casual Slacks $40–$60	Casual Slacks Under $40
Classic			
Hickey-Freeman Tailored Clothing *Bobby Jones* Blazers and Slacks	*Hart Schaffner & Marx* Tailored Clothing Slacks Womenswear *Jack Nicklaus* Blazers and Slacks	*Sansabelt* Slacks Tailored Clothing *Barrie Pace* Women's Career Apparel *Palm Beach* Tailored Clothing	*Hawksley & Wight* Women's Separates *John Alexander* Tailored Clothing Slacks Allyn Saint George Tailored Clothing
Traditional			
	Tommy Hilfiger Tailored Clothing Slacks *Austin Reed* Tailored Clothing Women's Separates Women's Tailored Knitwear *Society Brand, Ltd.* Tailored Clothing	*Wimbledon by Racquet Club* Tailored Clothing *Claiborne* Tailored Clothing	*Evan-Picone* Tailored Clothing
Fashion			
	KM by Krizia Tailored Clothing Slacks *Kenneth Cole* Tailored Clothing	*Perry Ellis* Tailored Clothing Slacks *Nino Cerruti* Tailored Clothing	*Daniel Hechter* Tailored Clothing *Henry Grethel* Tailored Clothing *Confezióni Risèrva by Luciano Franzoni* Tailored Clothing *Pierre Cardin* Tailored Clothing Slacks
Furnishings & Accessories			
Hickey-Freeman Dress Shirts Neckwear	*Austin Reed* Women's Accessories		*Hawksley & Wight* Women's Accessories

(Continued)

Table 7–2	Hartmarx Brand and Product Segmentation *(continued)*		
Upper*	Upper Moderate*	Moderate*	Popular*
Sportswear & Outerwear			
Hickey-Freeman	*Hart Schaffner & Marx*		*Desert Classic*
Sportswear	Sportswear		Men's Golfwear
Rainwear	*Nicklaus*		
Bobby Jones	Men's Golfwear		
Sportswear	Women's Golfwear		
Men's Golfwear			
Women's Golfwear			
Robert Comstock			
Sportswear			
Outerwear			

*Men's apparel retail price ranges only.
Source: From *Hartmarx Annual Report 1997* (p. 15) by Hartmarx, 1998, Chicago: Author: Reprinted by permission.

growth for many apparel companies but did not provide the market excitement that designer lines added. Important early designers whose work influenced the menswear industry included John Weitz, Pierre Cardin, Hardy Aimes, Oleg Cassini, and Bill Blass. Menswear companies worked with many of these designers under various arrangements, often licensing the designers' names (Gellers, 1995). Bearing a designer's name, sometimes ordinary garments took on a special aura and customer appeal. The designer influence launched an excitement in the menswear industry that continues today.

Some designers whose names were well established in the women's wear industry took the logical step of moving over into the menswear area. The first steps were made by designers such as Calvin Klein, Pierre Cardin, and Yves St. Laurent, soon followed by Perry Ellis, Christian Dior, and others who signed licensing agreements with various menswear tailored clothing and sportswear producers for the use of their names. Only occasionally did the name designer have much input into the actual designing of the line. Soon celebrity sports and entertainment names such as Johnny Carson and Bobby Jones, both licensed by Hartmarx, entered the menswear arena. In addition, names such as Indiana Jones and Batman come and go as the movie industry grinds out new licensable heroes. These licensing agreements, of course, have added a great deal of additional income for the designers and, hopefully, luster to the apparel producers' products.

Although designer names continue to be important, the consumer's response is only as strong as the continued importance of the designer's name. The designer business has become "more *business* than designer" (DiPaolo, 1988).

Retail Channels of Distribution

In the past, the largest percentage of the retail menswear business was done in the strictly masculine confines of the men's specialty stores. As men became more interested in presenting an appearance that reflected both the current fashions and their own personalities, and as they sought alternatives to the conventional business suit, they began to shop in other types of stores. And to enjoy shopping! At the same time, that bastion of men's privacy, the menswear store, began to solicit female customers. Examples include Brooks Brothers, Hastings, Paul Stuart, and Barneys.

A parallel development has occurred in the traditionally feminine environs of the department store and women's specialty shops. Department stores have become more aggressive in menswear. For a time, they were losing ground to mass merchants. Retail analyst Steidtmann noted, "Bill Clinton [was] the comeback kid of politics and the department stores are the comeback kids of [menswear] retailing" (Palmieri, 1994, p. 30). Most major department stores have responded to men's growing fashion awareness and have arranged their stores to be more appealing and convenient to male shoppers. Many have devoted prime floor space to men's areas, whereas in the past, menswear was less likely to occupy key spots. Neiman Marcus now devotes a large part of the main floor of its flagship Dallas store to menswear. At Bloomingdale's in New York, menswear gets nearly half the main floor, plus another area that was once a low-priced basement sales area. Department stores are devoting more space and more attention to menswear because these have become some of the most profitable areas. Because of competition from off-price menswear retailers such as Men's Wearhouse and Today's Man, department stores are offering suits at prices that compare favorably with some of the off-pricers. This, in turn, is bringing back customers, in some cases at the expense of off-price retailers.

Branded concept shops (also known as in-store shops) have been another popular strategy in department stores to promote high-visibility, major lifestyle labels in menswear. Tommy Hilfiger, Nautica, and Ralph Lauren have been opening their branded shops within stores at a rapid rate in recent years, with plans to roll out hundreds more. Nautica has about 1,400 men's in-store shops. Ralph Lauren has nearly 1,500, and Tommy Hilfiger has about 1,200. The menswear companies consider these concept shops a windfall because their signage, fixtures, marketing, and **merchandisers** (or **brand managers,** who supervise how products are displayed and sold through frequent store visits) give these lines an advantage over smaller vendors whose budgets do not permit them to match this visibility. Retailers like these shops because they get exclusive use of hot labels, and sales results have mushroomed.

At the same time, those specialty chains, whose units are primarily located in malls, are appealing to young men who shop with young women for the fun of it. Both sexes watch MTV and both react to the same fashion images. Nevertheless, there are still many small men's specialty shops that are an important outlet for men's clothing.

Men's specialty shops, large or small, remain important for several reasons. For one, many men still hesitate to enter the predominantly feminine confines of the department store or feel so uncomfortable there that even special entrances and special elevators do not entirely break down their reluctance. Another reason is that men's specialty shops are usually arranged in such a way that furnishings and clothing are placed near one another, and a single salesperson can escort the customer throughout the entire store and assist him in all his purchases. Such procedures save time for the customer and make suggestion selling of second, third, fourth, or add-on items infinitely easier. Still another reason is the convenience of location; men's shops can be found everywhere and anywhere—in business districts, residential areas, and shopping centers.

Figure 7–6

Menswear Sales by Type of Retail Channel

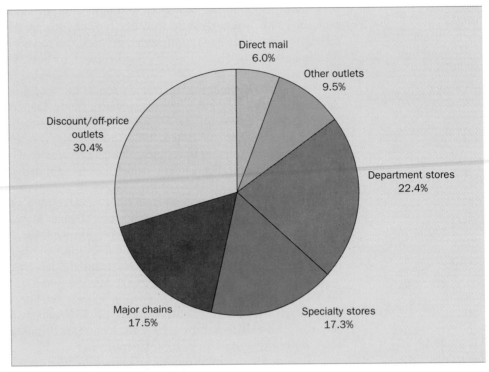

Source: Based on data from *Apparel Marketing Monitor* (pp. 7–8), by American Apparel & Footwear Association, 2000, Arlington, VA: Author. Adapted by permission.

The menswear business pie, once heavily weighted toward men's specialty stores, is now giving a slightly larger slice to the discounters, with department stores, specialty stores, and chains each holding its own share, as illustrated in Figure 7–6.

Menswear Marketing at Apparel Marts

As the menswear market has grown, the regional apparel marts have given increasing emphasis to this segment of the business. In some marts, specific floors are designated for men's apparel and accessories. **Menswear weeks** are scheduled at select times of the year; Figure 7–7 offers an example of the Chicago Apparel Center's promotion for menswear shows. These shows are held when menswear retailers know they can find manufacturers' new lines and can place orders for the coming season.

Manufacturer-Owned Retail Stores: Dual Distribution

Firmly entrenched in the menswear field is the **dual-distribution** system, whereby some large menswear manufacturers own and operate retail stores through which they sell their products—the same products that they also sell to other independent retailers for resale. Manufacturer-owned stores include in their assortments merchandise produced by other apparel makers—men's furnishings, for example, and women's wear. A prominent example is Phillips-Van Heusen, the giant shirt company, which owns many stores. Hartmarx previously owned nearly 500 stores but has sold those to concentrate on its manufacturing business. Many manufacturer-owned stores are given names that do not identify them to the public as belonging to the producer concerned.

Figure 7–7   **An example of a promotion for menswear market weeks.**

Chicago's the market
for all your men's wear needs

Photography: Andrew Martin

February 5-7	**A**pril 7-11	**A**ugust 6-8	**N**ovember 3-7
Chicago Men's Wear Collective,™ Fall Market	Ultra Show of America™ **April 9-11** Men's Show	Chicago Men's Wear Collective,™ Holiday/Spring Market	Men's, Women's & Children's Spring Market **November 5-7** Men's Show
Experience the nation's premier fall specialty store show.	Find everything for fall at this ultimate, all-inclusive men's, women's & children's market.	Return to the national specialty store market for an impressive showing of first-rate resources.	Shop the season's most comprehensive selection of resources at one incredible show.

CHICAGO APPAREL CENTER
Call 800/677-6278 for Market details and registration or 800/528-8700 for travel discounts.

Source: Reprinted courtesy of Chicago Apparel Center.

Marketing Activities by Trade Associations

An important point of difference between the menswear and women's apparel fields lies in the role of trade associations. In menswear, several trade associations are actively concerned with the marketing of the merchandise, acting more or less as go-betweens for producers and retailers. In the women's field, trade associations generally work only at single levels of distribution—that is, retail organizations work only with their retail members, and industry associations only with producers, as far as marketing is concerned.

Clothing Manufacturers' Association

The oldest trade association in the menswear field is the **CMA**. This was formed originally in 1933 by producers of tailored clothing to represent manufacturers in negotiations with the union—"the Amalgamated." Although it still performs this function with UNITE, the CMA's activities have been greatly expanded. CMA is the tailored clothing industry liaison with the federal government on labeling and other matters. The association coordinates and publicizes the two New York market weeks each year: the January/February showings for Fall/Winter and the August/September showings for Spring/Summer. Twice a year, in January and July, the association publishes, in cooperation with *Newsweek* magazine, a trade periodical for international distribution. Appearing in three languages—English, French, and German—it undertakes to inform retailers about major fashion trends in tailored clothing. Another association function is to compile and distribute periodically to its members statistical and technical reports on developments in tailored clothing. And, of course, like most major trade associations, it is the lobbying voice of its industry.

NAMSB/Vibe Style

A second trade association that has been very active in marketing menswear is the National Association of Men's Sportswear Buyers (**NAMSB**). This organization was founded and is financially supported by store buyers of menswear as well as owners of men's stores. It was founded in 1953 to give status and identity to a then-new category of menswear—sportswear. In its early years, it helped give direction to the styling of men's and boys' sportswear by recommending themes and colors the retailers considered most likely to succeed.

Although the NAMSB, as an industry association, will continue to provide services for its members, the major trade show it sponsored for 43 years has been taken over by VIBE/SPIN Ventures. The show, which will continue to be held in New York's Javits Convention Center, is now known as **Vibe Style.** VIBE/SPIN is the company that publishes *Vibe*, *Spin*, and *Blaze* and is producer of the late-night TV show known as *Vibe*. The Vibe Style trade show "offers today's hippest fashion voices in a new forum for retailers who want to reach young trendsetters"(Romero, 1998, p. 6).

At each of these **trade shows**, exhibit booths are set up on several floors for the use of manufacturers in showing their lines. The show includes a wide range of men's and boys' apparel and furnishings, including accessories and shoes. At each show week, more than 1,200 exhibitors buy space. The opportunity to view so many lines draws more than 25,000 countrywide retailers from establishments of every size and type. Because show weeks attract more menswear buying power than any menswear trade event, they have become a key marketing tool not only for domestic producers and retailers, but also for importers, producers from other countries, and groups of overseas suppliers exhibiting under sponsorship of their governments.

The Fashion Association (TFA)

Until the early 1990s, **TFA** was known as the Men's Fashion Association of America (MFA). In many ways, this association's development paralleled that of the menswear industry. A few promotional activities for the menswear industry began in the 1950s, but it was the expanding interest in men's apparel in the 1960s that launched the MFA. The group served as the public relations arm of the menswear industry, organizing press shows, providing press kits, sponsoring design awards, and coordinating a range of activities to promote men's apparel and accessories (Parola, 1991).

The Fashion Association is no longer limited to menswear. Rather, it continues the same activities as in earlier years but promotes the whole apparel industry. It is funded by members drawn from fiber, mill, apparel manufacturing, and retail organizations, and its purpose is to make fashions newsworthy and to provide information on the subject to the press. Press previews are held twice a year—in an area near New York City in June and on the West Coast in January or February. Each preview entails three-day seminars, supplemented by elaborate press kits, to acquaint the media with upcoming trends in fashions. In addition, material is supplied to the press from time to time as the seasons progress. Activity is not limited to the print media; scripts and slides are also provided to television programs. Further encouragement to the media is the award each year of an "Aldo" for outstanding fashion journalism in various newspaper, television, and radio categories.

The "MAGIC" Trade Show

Another important menswear enterprise has moved into women's apparel also. The Men's Apparel Guild of California, once an association and trade show for West Coast producers, began in 1979 as a national men's apparel show with an emphasis on sportswear. Its "**MAGIC**" designation is, of course, an acronym for the name of this increasingly important industry show held in Las Vegas (Figure 7–8). Factors in its development were the energetic promotion of the "California look" by producers and the growing appeal of sportswear. The MAGIC show has expanded into all men's product lines since those early days. Already the world's largest menswear show, MAGIC fills nearly two million square feet of show space. Attendance has reached more than 75,000 people per show. In 1995, the first MAGIC show for women's apparel took place. MAGIC management's ultimate goal is to position this show as the most important apparel trade show in the world so that a buyer anywhere in the world will want to attend the show.

California International Menswear Market (CIMM)

The latest menswear trade show to make an appearance is **CIMM**, which started in 1988. This show hopes to give major competition to the MAGIC shows. CIMM meets in Los Angeles.

Menswear Trade Showings

In addition to the menswear group trade shows described, menswear manufacturers also have the opportunity to show their wares at fashion trade shows held in various fashion centers around the world. In the United States, the **Designers' Collective**, a trade association, presents seasonal shows in New York City, with emphasis on fashion newness and innovation. Participants are a constantly growing group of menswear designers, both established and newcomers.

Source: Reprinted by permission of MAGIC.

Other trade shows are staged by European menswear trade associations. Among them are the European Menswear Show (SEHM) in Paris, Pitti Como in Florence, the English Menswear Designers' Collection in London, the Scandinavian Menswear Fair in Copenhagen, and the International Men's Fashion Week in Cologne. These are seasonal showings that are presented twice a year for the major seasons—Fall/Winter and Spring/Summer.

Fashion Explosion in Men's Accessories

Great as the impact of fashion has been on men's clothing, the American male still wears essentially the same articles of dress that his father and grandfather did before him: coat, pants, shirts, ties. Color, pattern, line, and other elements may have changed, but not the basic costume. Where men have really broken loose from regimentation, however, is in accessories. Not only do they have their hair styled instead of simply cut, and not only do they use perfumes (whose very presence in the home would have scandalized the earlier generations), but they also have let themselves go in wearing medallions, gold chains, and decorative bracelets, in carrying shoulder and tote bags if they choose to, or in wearing western-look hats and boots if they like the idea. Fashion in neckties has exploded, with designs that include everything from colorful abstract art to cartoon characters, Harley-Davidson motorcycles, and hot chili sauce. Not since the days of Beau Brummel have men indulged so much in creative things to wear and in uninhibited colors (Figure 7–9).

Perhaps the most important development in the total men's market is that fashion has become more important in men's lives than it ever has been before.

Figure 7–9

Examples of the whimsy now found in men's ties.

Source: Courtesy of *MR Magazine.*

Readings

The menswear industry experienced a revolution in the last 40 years, resulting to a great extent from the design pioneers. Moreover, men's attitudes about clothing have changed, with many much more interested in fashion than in the past. Changing workplace dress codes have had a significant impact on the industry but are perhaps more complex than former styles for consumers to follow. These articles focus on new trends influencing the menswear industry.

Help Wanted: Career Counselors Ponder What's Suitable

The new variable workplace dress codes have made it difficult, particularly for men, to know how to dress for job interviews. Campus career-service staff are often called on to provide guidance.

Brooks Brothers: Repositioned for Success

The 200-year-old venerable Brooks Brothers company has gone from stodgy to chic. The consumer evolution and changing lifestyles have sparked a Brooks Brothers revolution, resulting in a techno-savvy, fashion-forward, remerchandised company.

Help Wanted: Career Counselors Ponder What's Suitable

by Annmarie Dodd

New York—Until recently Stanford University seniors were often damned if they wore a suit to some job interviews, and damned if they didn't.

Variable dress codes have caused so much confusion among job-seeking students that Stanford officials enacted a policy last month requiring any company listing its openings, or participating in campus career fairs, to specify in writing its workplace dress code before it comes to campus.

After a four-year investment in a top-flight education, Stanford students often felt a bit uneasy knowing their futures were based not on the training of their minds, but on what they wore to a campus interview, said Sam Rodriguez, assistant director of counseling at Stanford's career development center.

"Dot-com employers came in wearing shorts, and those from investment banks were wearing suits and ties," said Rodriguez. "And each side voiced their displeasure about students being either too casual or too dressed up for their interviews. We couldn't win. Too much was left to chance.

"Employers need to give us parameters. So we've added a category to [job] postings for them to spell out how they want students to dress, and students can prepare," he added.

Virtually every college and university across the country is grappling with the same issue.

Career counselors from Princeton to the University of Texas at Austin and Virginia Tech all expressed the same worries as Rodriguez. And if you think employees have a problem understanding variable dress codes—just think of what students schooled on Gap and Abercrombie & Fitch consider to be casual dress. Career-services staff have been forced to take on the added role of wardrobe consultant, many said.

Beverly Hamilton-Chandler, director of Princeton University's office of career services, said her office asked employers to specify interview dress-code policies last year for the 800 students who utilize the office each year. Dress codes have become a part of a student's company profiling. Suits are always best, she said. Ties can come on and off according to whom men are interviewing with.

Career-service staffers said they advise students on rules of dress in one-on-one consultations and use university-sponsored Web sites to spell out business dress for men and women. There are actually stories—perhaps campus versions of urban myths—of students who've had their ties shockingly cut off by interviewers and tossed into a fishbowl with other severed ties to sell the point that formal business dress is not part of that workplace.

Virginia Tech's Web site reminds students: "You are not trying to stand out for your cutting-edge look but for your good judgment in a business environment. If you show up to an event and realize you are not as well dressed as you should be, make a quick apology and make a good impression with your interpersonal skills and intelligent questions."

For men, they advise, "it never hurts to overdress; by dressing nicely, you pay a compliment to your host."

No, university staffers did not ask for the job of ad hoc student stylists. Nor did they think it

Source: From DNR, *June 19, 2000, p. 4. Reprinted by permission.*

would be something they would be forced to research and teach like resume writing and interviewing skills. It just happened.

"This is one of the cultural impacts of business casual," said Princeton's Hamilton-Chandler. "Changing attire changes the interview process. An interview seems a little more social. If interviewers are laid-back, then students don't know where their boundaries are.

"We constantly have to remind them that an interview is an interview, no matter what the dress code is," she said. "You are still being evaluated and judged. Given the news of business casual spreading to banks and law firms, clearly this has become more of an issue to us in the last year."

Retailers from Nordstrom, Brooks Brothers and Men's Wearhouse have made offers to sponsor student wardrobing workshops. A number of career-service centers and Alpha Kappa Psi, a professional business fraternity of more than 140,000 students nationwide, have sponsored on-campus fashion shows for job-seeking seniors.

Business casual, however, is not an unwelcome word and a workplace environment for many college students. In today's rich and healthy economy, students can target their search to workplaces with variable dress codes if they so choose, said Ken Ramberg, cofounder of jobtrack.com, a Los Angeles-based job-listing site aimed at graduating seniors. The site tracks more than 35,000 hits each day.

Generation Y's understanding of business casual is a well-debated issue among menswear makers and career-development counselors. While many students have watched their dads don Dockers for a decade, what they deem appropriate for the office is another story, they said. Ramberg points out that record-low-unemployment rates have given many students an upper hand in the interviewing process.

"It's a tough market out there for employers," he said. "They have to focus on skills and experience.

"We've asked many employers about what they are looking for when it comes to dressing, and the general response from them is that as long as a candidate is well groomed and prepared for the interview, it doesn't much matter if he's dressed in a full suit or business casual."

Overall, students are advised to err on the conservative side in interviews and the early days of a job. If dress codes are not specified, wear a suit. If business casual is preferred, they are told to wear pressed khakis and a dress shirt. Maybe a tie.

But even that advice might not be appropriate. Business casual will mean more than easy-wear khakis and a polo knit, even if Ralph Lauren, long an advocate of better dressing, is running an ad campaign showing a young man in a polo shirt and pinstriped trousers over the text: The New Power Suit.

It's clear that a new, modern suit has a role for the college crowd, as suit separates have become the new graduation suit. Another answer for new grads may be seven easy pieces of sportswear and tailored clothing to prepare them for variable workplace dress: a sport coat, two pairs of trousers, a dress shirt, a woven sport shirt, a cashmere V-neck sweater and a polo knit.

Donna M. Panko, principal of Image Works Wonders, a Chicago-area consulting firm, is often called in to "de-program" students of their campus wardrobe habits. She said new grads often need to be told to lose the eyebrow ring, cover up the tattoos, tuck in their shirts.

Panko stresses clothing is an investment, same as an education and other job skills. Ignore this at career peril, she said.

Not all students are in the dark. Bert Hand, Hartmarx's chairman and CEO, said that after a recent University of Illinois business seminar, he sidled up to the sole grad student in the audience who wore a suit and asked him why he chose to sit through the meeting in a coat and tie.

"He told me, 'I can't make a mistake wearing a suit,' " said Hand. " 'I borrowed a bunch of money for college and grad school. I cannot put myself at risk.' "

Brooks Brothers: Repositioned for Success

by Stacy Baker

Inside the stylish four walls of Fifth Avenue's newest high-traffic retail offering, stark white walls adorned with artsy photos of moody, indifferent youth in celebrity poses make a statement of classic meets cool. Tables with the season's hottest tops and bottoms in trendy hues of gray, pumpkin and blue—and of course the $25 must-have black logoed T-shirt—cry out to shoppers spanning all generations who poke, touch—and buy. While Ella Fitzgerald and Louis Armstrong rock through the sound system, corner-store, floor-to-ceiling glass walls give you a bird's-eye-view of the foot traffic on Fifth and 53rd. Is this Banana Republic? The Gap? Nope. Actually, it's a few doors north of The Gap and across the street from Banana Republic, and it's Brooks Brothers' new flagship. It has refitted and remerchandised itself to speak to a 21st century lifestyle—for the whole family.

The Basic Premise of the Golden Fleece

The sea of change that's come over Brooks Brothers is more than skin deep, but it has preserved the company's nearly 200-year-old values and even enhanced them. "Since the time we were founded, quality has always been at the heart of our business—as has value," CEO Joe Gromek says. "Those two factors are critical to our success. Today we like to throw in a few other adjectives with that: 'modern,' 'current' and 'very relevant.'

Source: From Apparel Industry Magazine, *December 1999, pp. AS17–AS24. Copyright Bill Communications Inc. Reprinted by permission.*

"The relevancy is key because change is important to our business. We've got to entice customers to buy something new and different each season. That's what fashion's all about.

"We have a vision for Brooks Brothers, which is really—in the eyes of our shareholders, in the eyes of our associates, and in the eyes of our customers—to be the leading international brand. That's really very different from where we are today. It means moving from being an American-based specialty retailer toward becoming an international brand. That's where we see ourselves going over the next decade."

In its new incarnation, Brooks Brothers exhibits all the qualities of a branded apparel manufacturer and marketer, *and also* the versatility and flexibility of a first-rank specialty store likely to triumph in the new millennium. In the past half-decade, venerable Brooks Brothers has gone from stodgy to chic. The company—now the shining light in the UK-based Marks and Spencer empire—has repositioned itself as the mass customization apparel emporium for (although no "Baby Brooks" yet) the whole family.

The prime movers behind all this change are Gromek and his mod squad management team, including Derek Ungless, vice president of merchandising, Joe Dixon, senior vice president of manufacturing, and executive vice president and design director, Jarlath Mellet. Gromek joined the business four-and-a-half years ago. "Brooks Brothers was really somewhat stuck in its roots and had stopped evolving for a period of time," Gromek notes. "Part of the mission that was handed to me by Marks & Spencer was to add a new dimension, to recruit a new team and to push the business forward. We've

313

survived the past 180 years and now for us to continue to succeed, we've got to move with our customer—that's not always easy. There's a casualization of America happening today. We've got to address your lifestyle and move along with you. There's an evolution going on, and we'll be part of it."

Behind Brooks' own evolution lies Gromek's untraditional ways of serving consumers. His respect for the company's historical attention to quality, an ever-changing attention to consumer needs and an embracing of cutting-edge technology has Brooks Brothers well positioned for success across generations.

Style Evolution at Brooks Is Old Hat

Brooks Brothers' long history is chock full of innovation: the company brought consumers the peg suit, suiting separates in the United States, button-down collar shirts, and stretch fabric as far back as 1971, to name just a few. Executive vice president and design director Jarlath Mellett believes Brooks Brothers is still thriving today because of this strong role in American history and its adherence to a tradition of quality, style and innovation—concepts that will continue to play a role in the company's next 200 years.

"Tradition can be defined in various ways," Mellett says. "One way that I look at it is that tradition is classic, so a great pair of gray, flannel trousers is traditional. However, if you make them in a much lighter wool, that has a little mechanical stretch, it's modern, it's innovative. It's for the next century, but it's still traditional. It still looks great. And you adjust the fit for the customer today.

"The other part of tradition," Mellett says, "is just to realize who we are. We're Brooks Brothers. We've been around for 200 years and have created a lot of tradition: we created American sportswear, we created the button-down shirt, we created madras, we created seersucker."

Entering a new era, Brooks Brothers is moving to the beat of a dramatically different consumer with much broader apparel needs. Both Gromek and Mellett agree that their newest challenge is moving away from dressing the gentleman's 9-to-5 needs, five days a week, to dressing today's men and women 24 hours a day, seven days a week. This involves catering not only to consumers' workplace needs, but also their lifestyles, with a wide array of quality products, Mellett said. "Quality products,

quality of customer service, quality of our stores, it's all very important," Mellett emphasizes. "It's almost a design attribute—so from a design point of view we get to use the most beautiful yarns, beautiful details, and top-quality fabrications."

Today's Brooks customer, according to Mellett, is well educated, savvy and extremely media aware. Today's Brooks customer "could be 30 or could be 65 and basically wear the same product," Mellett says, "because they are either older consumers who are young in spirit or younger consumers who like what we are doing." In sum, a typical Brooks consumer is today's modern man and woman.

"Along with challenges of the changing face of retail and e-commerce, we have to find out what the customer needs and adjust to that. Day to day, we're looking at what's happening with fabrication and innovations—we are also looking at what consumers need, what they are doing in their lives and how is that changing. They don't need a suit seven days a week—they need a suit two days a week. They need things that pack easy; they need things that aren't heavy; they need things that are functional, yet look correct," Mellett says. "Ten years ago, it was a formula you just kept doing season after season, year after year. Now it's a very different ball game, even from the fabrics standpoint—how fabric is changing and how garments are changing. The customer definitely appreciates change and quality and newness."

Mass Customization Pioneers

Brooks Brothers' lines, both new and old, are made by a handful of outstanding U.S. men's wear private labelers, including the Pietrafesa Corp., Martin Greenfield, English-American, Southwick Clothing, Burlington Menswear, Pincus Brothers Maxwell, Corbin Ltd., Hagale Industries, and ARB, as well as Alessandro and Magashconi. Brooks Brothers makes its own prestigious dress shirts, in two separate factories based in North Carolina.

Brooks Brothers' two factories are an example of the company's divergent approach to the modern market. Factory A cuts and sews stock shirts in traditional bundles. Factory B makes custom shirts with state-of-the-art equipment. Measurements taken by sales personnel who type the numbers into a foolproof electronic form are transmitted to the plant from the stores via the Internet. The resulting savings are enormous—now hand-done alterations, which were free, are no longer necessary, and the customer has his own custom-cut, individualized shirt delivered to his home in days.

According to Scott Pearson, manager of special orders, Brooks Brothers' typical made-to-measure customer is an affluent man in his mid-40s whose primary reason to buy is selection and the ability to get exactly what he wants. A growing market, special order currently represents 5 percent of Brooks' total shirt sales.

According to Michelle Garvey, executive vice president of MIS, Brooks is leveraging its recent investment in ERP and expects to see continuous improvement in supply chain areas, such as POS, allocation, replenishment, warehouse management and datamining, creating an IT environment well advanced over what existed just five years ago at Brooks.

"Systems previously in place were difficult to maintain," Garvey says, "not to mention non-current hardware platforms and often defunct vendors. We now have the Retek application suite in place and it's a robust foundation for continued developments."

Brooks is among the companies that have extensively retooled their legacy platforms with integrated systems and will continue along the path of integration and convergence," Garvey notes. "We believe our efforts have paid off in a platform that is robust and scalable, and will provide the foundation for continued process improvements throughout the supply chain. We'll continually pursue integration of information with our suppliers to mutually focus on opportunities for improved sales and margins, while reducing inventory costs."

A true pioneer, Brooks Brothers launched body scanning—with its custom suit "e-measure" initiative. Partnering with suit maker Pietrafesa, Brooks Brothers communicates customer measurement data and style selections to Pietrafesa via computer stations outfitted with Imageware software at retail.

The technology behind this innovation allows Brooks to track client lists and consumer measurements, as well as style preferences and personal data. It also sends automated notices to customers notifying them of new suit styles and updated merchandise selections. Pietrafesa Corp. has actually evolved coding to move measurements straight into its Gerber patternmaking software. Martin Greenfield cuts mostly by hand, but is also downloading measurements via Imageware. Brooks' other vendors, including English-American, also are beginning to ramp up similar programs. While it's too early to tell in terms of sales how the made-to-measure suit program is doing, feedback from consumers has been very positive, and the technology has generated much excitement.

"Mass customization is cutting edge right now," Gromek says, "yet it's at a very early stage in its development. Take our Fifth Avenue store, for example. It has several million dollars worth of inventory to allow us to sell in specific sizes, etc. If we didn't have to carry all this inventory, but could do the same amount of volume, it would be a beautiful thing," Gromek says.

The key, Gromek says, isn't just style and fit. "Being able to select fabrications from a wide variety is very interesting. To have it fit you perfectly is also a very exciting prospect. But for me, the key to all of this—and it is going to happen—is to make it exciting. Make it entertainment not a challenge and not a negative experience. When I can stand here while you scan me and suddenly have all of my dimensions and then you immediately go make anything I want, that's going to be a revolution in our business."

Brooks is ideally positioned for mass customization, has a strong base of customers raised on tailored clothing and a growing audience of Gen-Whatevers who embrace the marriage of technology and high fashion.

"We are in a market segment where our customers demand something a little bit more special than just something that is off the rack," says Joe Dixon, senior vice president of manufacturing. "We offer great tailoring, great alteration services for ready-to-wear product, but imagine going the extra mile of asking the customer 'How would you like to take part in designing this product? This is something we are going to develop specifically for you.' It has enormous potential and power. We will need to market directly to customers one-on-one. Today's customers are extremely busy—you need to reach out and connect, and then keep that connection."

Dixon adds that the pricetag for a body-scanned, custom-designed suit will be no greater than that of the special-order suits Brooks already makes. "Of course it will cost more than an off-the-rack suit," says Dixon. "But eventually, this technology will help lower the price of our special-order suits below what they cost now."

Brooks' empire of retail stores, flagships, factory outlets, direct mail, e-commerce and an international business that includes 73 stores in Japan, six in southeast Asia, and blueprints for European expansion is, Dixon believes, the result of a well-established brand and a heritage of excellence. "By definition we are global. Today, you have to be.

Brands must travel continents from a manufacturing and sourcing perspective, and they must go to the centers of excellence. We believe we have located most of the markets and as these new technologies come up we must investigate them, develop them and bring them to market," Dixon says.

Once-Stodgy Brooks Surfs Net

Techno-savvy Brooks undoubtedly has joined the ranks of the dot.coms with a consumer-direct Web site in September 1998, where the offer is special discounts, e-mail updates on product offerings and promotions, and access to corporate dressing and affinity programs. www.brooksbrothers.com is accessible worldwide from your laptop or from stations in the retail stores.

And it has provided the company with some serious surprises. There was, for example, little expectation that anyone would buy tailored clothing via the Internet, so suits and sport coats weren't offered until January 1999. Now, Brooks Brothers sells hundreds of units in all sizes a month, ranging from seersucker to poplin to wool in prices starting at $299 (on sale) to $598.

"Last Christmas was the first time that serious business was done through e-commerce and we were there. We've totally revamped our Web site and added new technology and more capacity—our business is going up about four times this year. We think next year it will increase four or five times again, so we've got to prepare for that," Gromek says. "We made our Internet business a freestanding division and I think we're positioned very well to move forward, understanding that this channel changes every day, and just when you think you're current, somebody else has raised the bar."

Brooks is in a position of advantage with its Web site thanks to its successful catalog business. The back end of its operations includes established inventory and fulfillment systems. However, while Internet sales aren't cannibalizing store sales, they are affecting its catalog. The Brooks Internet shopper spends an average of $150 per purchase, slightly less than the catalog consumer does, but "there is significant falloff from our catalog business," Gromek says. "On the other hand, between the two, catalog and e-commerce, we're coming out well ahead. Not only are half the e-customers new to Brooks Brothers, but we like the age factor. They're in their 30s, which is good, and much to our surprise,

they're buying suits. About a quarter of our business coming off our Web site right now is in the tailored clothing area."

Brooks' Millennium Sales Floor

The stores are already taking advantage of the main difference between the channels: touch. Forget about mahogany vitrines, that tell the customer "hands off." Brooks Brothers' Fifth Avenue store customers touch and hold merchandise stacked everywhere on tables. This prototype store is the pilot for the rest of Brooks' locations. Beyond that, Mellett thinks the Fifth Avenue pilot is truly the store of the future. "The design of the retail store in the millennium will be a cross between traditional and modern. It'll be an experience that is very interactive for the customer, an easy shopping environment," Mellett imagines. "I also think it's a place where you're comfortable and very well served. Customer service still is and will always be top priority."

But Joe Dixon, Brooks' manufacturing maven, feels that mass customization and body scanning, the technologies with the greatest impact, are still a few years away from the retail floor of the future. "The store of the future will be smaller in square footage than today, and significantly more entertaining, with more technology widely employed," Dixon predicts. "There will be people; there will be kiosks; there will be fabric feelers. You will be able to design and develop your own product and then order it from manufacturing sites throughout the world. Retail malls will shrink but they will become more specific, more customer-focused and more high tech."

Not your grandfather's suit maker anymore, Brooks Brothers has effectively changed its business model and shed its tired image, emerging as today's hip retailer for the entire family. "It is about having clear leadership, clear direction, great people and keeping those people focused on job one, which is satisfying the customer," Dixon says. "As long as we continue to do that there is no reason why we should deviate from what we are doing now, and I think we will succeed. The current challenge is to continue to evolve at speed. People talk about change and—while we're certain that we must change—that is not the question. The question is how quickly can we change and can we keep pace with people that are looking to take market share aggressively. You change or you die."

Brooks Brothers and Pietrafesa Corp.: A Marriage of Art and Technology

Pietrafesa Corp. has taken its in-house technology and partnered with Brooks Brothers to provide mass customization in a program they've called e-measure. The system takes measurements from the retailer to develop, cut and sew the product in an automated process. The company implemented the back end more than two years ago before developing the front end, which, after being beta tested in two Brooks Brothers stores (Manhattan's Liberty Plaza and Stamford, Conn.), is now installed in 17 Brooks Brothers sites. Data collected at the point of sale comes through the Web to Pietrafesa Corp.'s CAD systems to create a pattern while the customer is still standing in the store. The suit will be cut the following day from the specially ordered fabric received from suppliers via next-day delivery. CAD system generates the marker needed to make the garment and it goes into a queue.

CEO Richard Pietrafesa notes that suppliers understand the importance of speed of delivery. "Response time is the biggest part of what we're selling. Yes, our fabrics are of the highest quality, but more than that, if they don't have same sense of turn time, it won't work." Pietrafesa emphasizes. "Our suppliers also must have a back-end system that works with ours—they must understand from the onset that our systems need to be congruous. That's not an option."

Pietrafesa's president of e-commerce Bill King says the company's goal is to get delivery down to two weeks, matching the turn time on ready-made garments. "The problem in the beginning is that there was generally a 7 percent to 10 percent remake factor—a consumer would receive a garment only to discover that measurements were taken improperly and now it's two more weeks to fix the mistake," King says. "Now, however, our remake is .01 percent, which is far more remarkable than whether we can turn something in five weeks."

Pietrafesa Corp. has developed a store model to follow that outlines how much a store should produce per week and Pietrafesa says mature sores are hitting projections. Dedicated to seeing its e-measure program work, the company refuses to simply throw a computer in store and leave. "We're very visual and we establish face-to-face visits for training, updating fabric libraries, etc. It's a constant and dynamic process," King notes. "The mutual partnership is the key to success—you need a willing participant that understands the benefits of e-measure to both sides."

"From our point of view, it's worth it because we're increasing sell throughs," Pietrafesa says. "Retailers have no investment, so for them, it's a thing of beauty. This is the most productive section of the store because there's no investment, no alterations, no inventory and you take a deposit up front. The initial margins are maintain margins," Pietrafesa adds. "This is the ultimate business model. We're disciplined about our processes. This was a factory that never made singles—either you're making bulk or you're making in singles, but not both. The system is designed so whether we're making 1,000 pieces or one piece, garments go through our operations the same way."

Pietrafesa agrees with Joe Gromek that technology brings both companies closer to their target markets. "There is enormous fascination with technology," Pietrafesa notes. "It's bringing new customers to this business, and it's broken down the barriers of perception that made-to-measure is elitist. On the whole, the response from consumers has been enthusiastic with great curiosity. They like the entertainment value and they view the retailer—Brooks Brothers—as very forward thinking in an industry that historically considers made-to-measure an art form."

"We found that when we take measurements from a piece of paper from, say, 20 different tailors, we'd have 20 different methods of measuring, which left great room for inconsistency and error," Pietrafesa explains. "E-measure standardizes measurements and gives instructions so we're taking consistent points of measure from each store. There's really nothing left up to judgment. Body scanning will only improve this."

Of course, beyond the exactness and accuracy of having a garment created exclusively for your form is the show biz element of body scanning. "Don't underestimate the marketing dimension of body scanning. This is a unique chance for consumers who are carrying palm tops and driving around with navigators in their cars to interact with technology in a completely new way," Kin adds. "It's all very Star Wars."

Chapter Review

Key Words and Concepts

Define, identify, or briefly explain the following:

Bespoke tailors	Dual distribution	"Slops"
Brand managers	Everyday Wear	Standardized sizes
Branded concept shops	Friday Wear	Tailored clothing
CIMM	Hartmarx	Tailors to the trade
CMA	Levi Strauss & Co.	TFA
Collection concept	Made-to-measure	The "MAGIC" show
Custom tailors	Merchandisers	Trade show
Designers' Collective	Menswear weeks	Vibe Style
Drop	NAMSB	

Review Questions on Chapter Highlights

1. Why were the shops that produced men's ready-to-wear in the early nineteenth century known as "slop shops"?
2. Name two developments of the nineteenth century that contributed to the growth of the menswear industry, and explain their effect.
3. How does the menswear industry differ from the women's apparel industry? In what ways are they similar?
4. How do the procedures of the men's tailored clothing segment of the industry differ from those of the other segments of the menswear industry?
5. If you were the CEO of a major company today, how would you define casual office wear for your employees? How would you handle it if their definition differs from yours?
6. How do the sizes of men's tailored clothing differ from those of men's sportswear? Why?
7. What is the meaning of the "collection concept" (branded concept shop) in men's clothing? Why has it developed?
8. What important changes began to occur in the menswear industry in the 1960s? How has this affected the menswear industry today?
9. What trade associations play an important role in the marketing of menswear? What is their importance?
10. Name and compare two of the major menswear companies discussed in the readings.
11. Why is fashion today more important to men than it was formerly? Is it as important to men as it is to women? Why or why not?
12. Who attends the MAGIC show and why?

References

American Apparel Manufacturers Association. (yearly). *Apparel Marketing Monitor.* Arlington, VA: Author.

American Apparel Manufacturers Association. (annual). *Focus: Economic profile of the apparel industry.* Arlington, VA: Author.

Brown, C. (1994, December 5). Dressing down. *Forbes,* 155–160.

Cobrin, H. (1971). *The men's clothing industry: Colonial through modern times.* New York: Fairchild.

Courter, E. (1995, March 1). Dressing down drives some stores out of biz. *DNR,* p. 4.

DiPaolo, N. (1988, September 1). Quotation in *Daily News Record,* citation information unknown.

Gellers, S. (1994, October 31). Clothing men use soft suit to play hardball. *DNR,* pp. 10–11.

Gellers, S. (1995, January 18). The big brand era. [Special issue: 1965–1995: The Designer Decades], *DNR,* pp. 30, 62, 63.

Gellers, S. (1998, March 27). Sizing up the men of measure. *DNR,* pp. 14, 15.

The impact of fitness on the cut of clothes. (1985, September 5). *New York Times, Men's Fashions of the Times.*

Kidwell, C., & Christman, M. (1974). *Suiting everyone: The democratization of clothing in America.* Washington, DC: Smithsonian Institution Press.

Levi Strauss & Co. (1995). *NewsWatch.* San Francisco: Author.

Palmieri, J. (1994, September 5). Financial analysts give high marks to dep't stores' new emphasis on men's. *DNR,* p. 30.

Parola, R. (1991, April 30). MFA at 35. *DNR,* pp. 3, 11.

Romero, E. (1998, July 22). Curtain falls on NAMSB, replaced by Vibe Style, *DNR,* pp. 1, 6.

Silverman, E. (1995, June 13). *Production, sales, and marketing strategies of Hugo Boss.* Unpublished paper presented at the 11th annual International Apparel Federation meeting, Washington, DC.

Tucker, J. (2000). Apparel and fabricated textile products. *U.S. Industry and trade outlook.* Washington, DC: U.S. Department of Commerce.

United States Executive Office of the President, Office of Management and Budget. (1987). *Standard Industrial Classification Manual.* Washington, DC: Author.

Selected Bibliography

Aldrich, W. (1990). *Metric pattern cutting for menswear: Including computer aided design.* London: Blackwell Science.

Bennett-England, R. (1968). *Dress optional: The revolution in menswear.* Chester Springs, PA: Dufour.

Brown, C. (1994, December 5). Dressing down. *Forbes,* 155–160.

Boyer, B. (1984). *Elegance: A guide to quality in menswear.* New York: Norton.

Carlson, P., & Wilson, W. (1977). *Manstyle: The GQ guide to fashion, fitness, and grooming.* New York: Clarkson.

Chenoune, F. (1993). *A history of men's fashion.* London: Flammarion.

Cobrin, H. (1971). *The men's clothing industry: Colonial through modern times.* New York: Fairchild.

Constantino, M. (1997). *Men's fashion in the twentieth century: From frock coats to intelligent fibers.* New York: Costume & Fashion Press.

Cooklin, G. (1992). *Pattern grading for men's clothes: The technology of sizing.* London: Blackwell Science.

Cray, E. (1979). *Levis.* New York: Houghton Mifflin.

Curan, C. (1997, June 6). Ties of the times: A look back at 50 years of neckwear and the NAA. *Daily News Record,* p. 28.

Dolce, D. (1983). *The consumer's guide to menswear*. New York: Dodd.

Dyer, R., & Dyer, S. (1987). *Fit to be tied: Vintage neckwear of the forties and early fifties*. New York: Ron Abbeville Press.

Edelman, A. (1990). *The fashion resource directory* (2nd ed.). New York: Fairchild.

Feldman, E. (1960). *Fit for men*. Washington, DC: Public Affairs Press.

Flusser, A. (1985). *Clothes and the man*. New York: Villard.

Goldman, D. (2000, April 17). "Dressing down" is just the new form of moving up. *ADWeek*, pp. 16, 19.

Goldstein, L. (1999, November 22). What we wore. *Fortune*, 156–160.

Hollander, A. (1994). *Sex and suits*. New York: Knopf.

Hyde, J. (1990). *Esquire's encyclopedia of 20th century men's fashions* (2nd ed.). New York: Abrams.

Jackson, C., & Luow, K. (1984). *Color for men*. New York: Ballantine.

Laver, J. (1968). *Dandies*. London: Weidenfeld & Nicholson.

Lohrer, R. (1997, September 19). Dressing up the business of men's wear: An industry with a split personality sends a mixed message to men. *Daily News Record*, p. 12.

Martin, R., & Koda, H. (1989). *Men's styles in the twentieth century*. New York: Rizzoli International.

McDowell, C. (1997). *The man of fashion: Peacock males and perfect gentlemen*. New York: Thames & Hudson.

McGrath, C. (1994, November 7). The suit doctor. *The New Yorker*, 91–96.

Molloy, J. (1975). *Dress for success*. New York: P. H. Wyden.

1965–1995: The designer decades. (1995, January 18). *DNR* [Special issue].

Peacock, J. (1996). *Men's fashion: The complete sourcebook*. New York: Thames & Hudson.

Pope, J. (1970). *The clothing industry in New York*. New York: Burt Franklin. (Original work published in 1905.)

Rundles, J. (2000, January). Made to order heralds an industry revolution. *Wearables Business*, 24, 25.

75 years of men's wear fashion 1890–1965. (1965). *Menswear Magazine*. New York: Fairchild.

Shapiro, H. (1956). *Man, culture and society*. London: Oxford University Press.

Stegemeyer, A. (1995). *Who's who in fashion* (3rd ed.). New York: Fairchild.

Tolman, R. (1982). *Selling men's fashion*. New York: Fairchild.

Updike, J. (1994, November 7). The seriousness gap (a review of *Sex and Suits*). *The New Yorker*, 243–246.

Wagenvoord, J. (1978). *The man's book: A complete manual of style*. New York: Avon.

Wilson, W., & Editors of *Esquire Magazine*. (1985). *Man at his best*. Reading, MA: Addison-Wesley.

Winnick, C. (1968). *The new people: Desexualization in American life*. New York: Pegasus.

Trade Associations

American Apparel Association, 1601 N. Kent Street, Suite 1200, Arlington, VA 22209.

Clothing Manufacturers Association of the U.S.A., 1290 Ave. of the Americas, New York, NY 10104.

MAGIC International (has moved beyond its origins as the trade association, Men's Apparel Guild in California), 100 Wilshire Blvd., Suite 1850, Santa Monica, CA 90401.

Men's Clothing Manufacturers Association, 555 Chabanel W. #801, Montreal, Quebec H2N 2H8, Canada.

National Association of Men's Sportswear Buyers, Inc., 500 Fifth Ave., Suite 1425, New York, NY 10110.

The Fashion Association (formerly the Men's Fashion Association), 475 Park Ave. S., 17th Floor, New York, NY 10016.

Trade Publications

Apparel International, The White House, 60 High St., Potters Bar, Herts EN6 5AB, England.

The Apparel Strategist, Apparel Information Resources, 101 E. Locust St., Fleetwood, PA 19522.

Bobbin, 1110 Shop Rd., Columbia, SC 29202.

DNR, 7 W. 34th St., New York, NY 10001–8191.

For Him, Tayvale Ltd., 9–11 Curtain Rd., London EC2A 3LT, England.

Men's and Boys' Wear Buyers, Box 31, New Providence, NJ 07974.

Men's Clothing Retailer, Key Note Publications, Ltd.; Field House, Old Field Rd., Hampton TW12 2HQ, England.

Men's Guide to Fashion (MGF), 805 Third Ave., 28th Floor, New York, NY 10022–7513.

Men's Wear of Canada, Laurentian Media, Inc., 501 Oakdale Rd., Downsview, Ontario M39 1W7, Canada.

Menswear Retailing (MR), Business Journals; 50 Day St., Box 5550, Norwalk, CT 06856.

*F*ashion Accessories, Intimate Apparel/ Undergarments, and Cosmetics

*L*ike a pebble dropped in a lake, every fashion change in apparel creates a ripple of change in the industries that produce fashion accessories and intimate apparel. The total look that the wearer seeks to achieve demands such change. For example, a blazer jacket may invite the use of a tucked-in scarf; a long skirt may require a long slip; short skirts may focus enough attention on the leg to suggest eye-catching patterns in hosiery; shoes may change shape and heel height to become good companions to current styles; belts may be wide and colorful when waistlines are important, and vanish when dresses hang straight. Jewelry, too, must conform, playing to the high or low neckline, the short or long sleeve, or whatever are the important features of the garment. Even precious heirlooms may be consigned to the vault for a time if the prevailing "look" is wrong for the treasured pieces. Accessories conform to and accentuate apparel fashions to be viable; they cannot afford to lag or clash with the dress or coat or other garment that is the star of the show.

In fashion's fickle twists, however, the late 1990s even saw a switch of the traditional belief that accessories should complement the wearer's apparel. In a *Wall Street Journal* article titled "Forget the Clothes—Fashion Fortunes Turn On Heels and Purses," writer Teri Agins noted that accessories often become the stars as consumers go casual. Agins reported that as women choose understated classic sportswear, fashion accessories become the stars, with status in the details. She reported that upscale accessories—for years the industry's wallflowers—were driving sales. In this fascinating fashion twist, consumers reported buying casual sportswear from stores like Banana Republic, The Gap, and Polo, then splurging on status-name accessories that cost hundreds of dollars. Some sources speculated that women are unable to find clothes they like, so they go out and buy an $800 Gucci bag, a $1,100 Fendi bag, or a $1,200 Dior bag (Agins, 1999).

Although changes in men's fashions also require modifications in accessories, the less-dramatic changes in menswear generally mean that accessories vary less from season to season than in women's wear. Ties vary in patterns and width; sometimes suspenders are "in" and other times not; and jewelry—from gold chains to cuff links—varies from one time to another. So, although the men's accessory area has become an important one in the fashion industry, changes are much less noticeable than in women's areas.

Accessories, intimate apparel, and the industries that produce them are an integral part of the fashion business. This chapter discusses the economic importance and methods of operation of each of these industries. The readings that follow are concerned with different aspects of this segment of the fashion business.

The Accessories Industries

When designers show their collections on models, and when retail stores put important fashion garments on display, they "accessorize" each suit, dress, or other featured garment to emphasize the total look that is being presented. Consumers also use **accessories** both to accentuate the important fashion points of their appearance and to give individuality to mass-produced clothes. Jewelry in the newest trend, a color-coordinated scarf, a very special handbag, newly textured hosiery—these and similar touches help each woman feel that the outfit she wears is uniquely her own.

Every fashion in the accessory category changes its look as clothing fashions change. Shoes may go from unadorned flats to elegantly pointed high-heeled styles; scarfs and jewelry may vary in size, color, and materials; hosiery may go from neutral to colorful or from plain to textured—all in terms of what best suits the current apparel fashions. Success in accessories production and sales is a matter of moving quickly and surely in step with apparel fashions. Conversely, no amount of promotion and invention can create acceptance for a particular accessory when it simply does not fit into the current fashion picture.

Many accessories have experienced dramatic ups and downs as fashions changed. Belts, for example, went into eclipse for many years when chemise dresses hung from the shoulder, ignoring the natural curves of the body. Millinery, too, has had its problems, reaping only a thin harvest from its industry promotional efforts at times when women preferred to go hatless. Accessories as a whole have had lean years at times when there was little room for them in the fashion picture.

In recent years the accessories business is being perceived as an ever more vital and important part of the fashion industry. Accessories are considered by some to be the most necessary part of dressing because they define the style and character of the wearer. Another indication of accessories' growing importance is that the licensing concept has flourished, as designers want to increase their share of this rich pie. Examples include Echo Design, which has licensed Ralph Lauren for scarfs, Alpert Nipon for belts and small leather goods, and Sarah Coventry for neckwear; Vera produces Perry Ellis and Anne Klein neckwear; and Victoria Creations holds licenses for Diane von Furstenberg, Givenchy, and Karl Lagerfeld in jewelry. The list grows monthly.

The Business of Accessories

The design, production, and marketing of fashion accessories are not a single business, but several. Each category of accessories is produced in its own industry, and these individual industries are as diverse as the merchandise itself. Some, such as shoes and hosiery, are large and dominated by big producers. Others, such as gloves, handbags, jewelry, scarfs, and millinery, are the domain of small firms. Some of the industries are highly mechanized; others still use hand operations not much changed from those used 50 or even 100 years ago. Some have plants in or near New York City; others are hundreds of miles from that center or even in other countries and merely have showrooms there. This industry has its own trade shows (Figure 8–1). This segment of the fashion industry has its own website; "Accessory Web" (http://www.nfaa-fasa.org) is sponsored by the National Fashion Accessories Association, Inc. and the Fashion Accessories Shippers Association, Inc. for retailers, wholesalers, and consumers.

Figure 8–1

Trade Show for the Accessories industry

Source: Reprinted courtesy of the Fashion Accessories Expo.

The accessories industries as a whole, however, do have several elements in common:

1. All are extremely responsive to fashion and very quick to interpret incoming trends. Their success depends on how well they reflect the look of the apparel with which they will be worn.
2. All present a minimum of two new seasonal lines a year.
3. All domestic accessory manufacturers, as is the case with other segments of the fashion industry, are confronted with increasing competition from imports.
4. Almost all major accessory producers have entered into licensing agreements with leading apparel designers to produce and market styles bearing the designer's name.

Economic Importance

According to *Accessories* magazine, this segment of the women's fashion industry represented a $23.4 billion retail business in 1998. More than $4 billion in sales came from the men's accessories segments. For women, the total sales figure included handbags, small leather goods, scarfs, hosiery, hats, gloves, and jewelry, but does not include shoes and fine jewelry. For men, the categories included were similar where appropriate ("Women's 1999," 2000).

In the last decade, the accessories industry has grown a great deal. For example, in 1978, the women's accessories industry accounted for $7.2 billion in retail sales (inflation accounts for part of what appears to be growth). During the 1980s, retail space devoted to accessories expanded, and a number of apparel firms added accessory lines. Examples have been Tommy Hilfiger, Liz Claiborne, DKNY, Ralph Lauren, and Guess?.

In the 1990s, however, most segments of the accessories industry felt the same consumer reluctance to spend that had plagued the apparel industry earlier in the decade. Despite a booming economy and improvements in disposable income, the accessories business remained generally flat. A few segments fared better than others. Many department stores tried to improve business in the accessories areas by continuing to lower prices. Mass merchants moved into the territories once held mostly by department stores, with about one-third of the sales now coming from mass retailers.

By the turn of the new millennium, the accessories industry began to ride a wave of attention from the buying public that had not been seen in decades. Consumers are choosy, however. Although brand names are paramount, those names have to offer something more than just the fashion trend of the moment. In some way, the brand must connect with the buyer's lifestyle, and the price-to-value equation must be right (Hessen, 2000).

Marketing

Accessories firms have used a number of approaches to attract consumers. Some companies have made a concerted effort to build brand recognition of their products. This approach has been successful in many cases, to name a few: Arias gloves, Monet jewelry, Ray Ban sunglasses, Dooney & Bourke leather goods, and L'eggs hosiery. Another approach has been for an apparel firm to build an accessories line around its established name, such as Esprit, Liz Claiborne, and DKNY. Or, in some cases, an accessories line may be developed around a well-established name in another sector. An example of this is the men's personal leather goods line made by Samsonite. In other cases, a firm may have a licensing agreement with a well-known designer to make the products and sell them under the designer's name. Examples here are Givenchy jewelry, Pierre Cardin sunglasses, or Dior scarfs.

When *Accessories* magazine conducted its first-ever survey on consumer accessories purchases, some results were surprising. In the survey of female consumers between the ages 26 and 44,[1] respondents were asked to identify their favorite accessories brands, designers, or labels (Table 8–1). Most consumers, regardless of age, had trouble naming more than one or two categories. Consumers were most likely to be able to identify brands for pantyhose. Aside from this category, almost all other brands for products were department store oriented. Many consumers named

Table 8–1	**Favorite Accessories Brands by Household Income**			
	$15,000–$30,999	**$31,000–45,999**	**$46,000–$64,000**	**$65,000+**
Handbags	Coach, Dooney & Bourke, Gucci, Rolfs	Coach, Liz Claiborne, Contessa, Craft	Coach, Liz Claiborne, Stone Mountain	Coach, Dooney & Bourke, Stone Mountain, Perlina, Perry Ellis, Louis Vuitton, Capezio, Aigner
Costume Jewelry	Monet	Trifari, Monet, Anne Klein, Liz Claiborne, Express, Limited, 1928	Monet, Anne Klein, Christian Dior	Anne Klein, Monet, Trifari, Liz Claiborne Contempo label, Ralph Lauren, Napier
Pantyhose	L'eggs, Hanes, No Nonsense	L'eggs, Hanes, Hanes Alive, Hanes Ultra Sheer, Liz Claiborne, Donna Karan, Gloria Vanderbilt, Evan Picone	L'eggs, Hanes, Givenchy, No Nonsense, DKNY	L'eggs, Hanes, Hanes Alive, Hanes Silk Reflections, Calvin Kelin
Scarfs	none identified	none identified	Hermes	Liz Claiborne, Vera, Hermes
Belts	none identified	Coach, Marshall's	Ann Taylor, Ellen Tracy, DKNY	Liz Claiborne, Dunn Dee, DKNY, Nordstrom
Sunglasses	none identified	Ray Ban, Gucci, Vuarnet	Liz Claiborne, Ray Ban, Foster Grant	Ray Ban, Serengeti, Anne Klein, Vuarnet, Liz Claiborne
Wallets	Coach, Liz Claiborne, Dooney & Bourke, Lady Buxton	Coach, Liz Claiborne, Princess Gardner	Princess Gardner, Coach, Dooney & Bourke	Coach, Louis Vuitton, Esprit

Source: From 1995 National Consumer Accessories Survey, July, 1995, *Accessories*, p. 37. Reprinted by permission.

[1]Consumers were a random sample of subscribers to *Working Woman* magazine, a consumer publication that targets women in middle and upper management with a median age of 38.

Liz Claiborne as one of the leading brands. Coach was a very popular handbag brand. "Favorite brands," as identified in the survey, included those respondents *aspired* to buy; they may not have actually bought them.

Shoes

If we had no other indication of the importance of the shoe industry, consider the leather industry's estimate that each of us walks the equivalent of twice around the world in the course of a lifetime. No wonder foot protection has always been of prime importance to mankind and shoes take a prominent place in our legends, proverbs, and fairy tales! We are cautioned not to criticize a man until we have walked a mile in his shoes; we grow up on tales of seven-league boots, glass slippers, and red dancing shoes; we tie shoes to the cars of newly married couples as symbols of good luck. Aching feet remind us of the importance of being comfortably shod; a glance into a full-length mirror highlights the importance of shoes appropriate to one's outfit.

The first American shoemaker was Thomas Beard, who landed in the Massachusetts colony on the second voyage of the *Mayflower* and opened his shop to produce made-to-order shoes. Others followed, some of whom became "visiting shoemakers." These men lived with a household until all members had been shod. Leather for the purpose was usually supplied by the farmer or householder and was obtained from the cured skins of animals killed for meat. During the eighteenth century, shoemakers began producing "sale shoes," made without waiting for specific orders and brought to market to be offered for sale. Thus, ready-made shoes were introduced. These, however, were made only in three widths and five lengths. The well-to-do, therefore, almost universally had their shoes custom-made as late as 1880 (Quimby, 1936).

The oldest and still active retail shoe organization in the United States is Thomas F. Pierce & Son of Providence, Rhode Island, established in 1767.

Nature of the Industry

The largest dollar volume of business in the accessories group occurs in the shoe industry. This is an industry dominated by large firms. It is not unusual to find among them companies with many divisions, each of which produces and distributes footwear under its own brand name. For example, the Brown Group manufactures Buster Brown shoes for children, Naturalizer and Airstep for women, and Roblee and Regal shoes for men.

Although most shoes worn in the U.S. are now produced overseas, a few remaining production facilities are found in Maine, Texas, California, Pennsylvania, New York, and Missouri. As with most segments of the fashion industry, the major marketing center for shoes is New York City, and most producers maintain permanent showrooms there. For decades, the 34th Street area was the center of activity for American footwear manufacturers. Headquarters were in the Marbridge Building, at 34th Street and Sixth Avenue, and in the Empire State Building, on the corner of Fifth Avenue. Since the mid-1970s, however, many companies have moved uptown to the 50s, close to the hotels where out-of-town retail buyers stay when they come to attend the industry's semiannual trade showings. Most of those who have remained in the 34th Street area are producers of children's and men's shoes. Companies such as Ferragamo, Golo, and Joan and David prefer the more fashionable 50s.

Development of Athletic Shoes

Not too many years ago, athletically inclined people bought a single pair of sneakers in which to run, jump, bike, or scramble up the side of a hill. Today, all are specialized. There are biking shoes that are stiff enough to direct all the rider's energy into the pedal, cross-country running shoes with spiked soles for traction, high-laced shoes for skateboards, and on and on to a variety of special-purpose sports shoes. Some athletic shoes, such as the models with air pockets, are highly engineered, often incorporating a curious blend of high and low technology.

The phenomenal interest of the American consumer in physical fitness has created an entirely new segment within the formerly traditional shoe industry. This segment has its share of giants, such as Reebok International Ltd., whose subsidiaries include Rockport and Avia, and Nike. Also important, but to a much lesser degree, are Converse, L.A. Gear, Adidas, and Keds.

Economic Importance

The **nonrubber footwear** industry includes production of all footwear that is deemed to contain more than 50 percent nonrubber in the upper part of the shoe. Thus, athletic shoes with more than 50 percent of the shoe itself made of suede, leather, vinyl, or any other fabric are considered part of the nonrubber footwear industry. On the other hand, shoes such as "jellies," or those that are produced by a vulcanizing process, or those that have more than 50 percent rubber in the uppers are classified as part of the rubber shoe industry. With the enormous growth of athletic shoes, these distinctions are increasingly difficult to perceive. However, a tariff advantage is currently granted to imported rubber footwear, and many canvas-topped athletic shoes contain just enough rubber to qualify for this category (Treber, 1990). Shoes consist of a number of different parts, all of which must be joined together with precision to make for a comfortable fit. These parts include the shoe **uppers** (the visible outside material) and linings cut to fit inside the uppers. These two elements are joined and draped over a **last**—the form that gives the finished shoe its size and shape. Also included are the toe box, which protects both the wearer's toes and the shape and contour of the shoe, and the **vamp**, which is the front of the shoe from toe to instep.

The lasting of a shoe is one of the most important processes in making shoes, because it gives the finished shoe proper fit, removes wrinkles, and ensures comfort and good appearance. Each size is made on a different last, and it is not unusual for a shoe manufacturer to have thousands of pairs of lasts in a factory. Originally, lasts were constructed of wood, but today newer lasts are made of lightweight plastic or aluminum.

At the bottom of the shoe is the outsole, the surface that hits the ground with each step. Above this is the insole, the lining on which the foot rests. Between these two layers is sandwiched a shank—a metal, leather, or plastic strip that protects and forms the arch of the foot within the shoe itself. Some shoes also contain additional padding within the two sole layers for further cushioning and comfort.

The method by which the sole of a shoe is attached to the upper varies within the industry. Each method is referred to as a "construction," to identify the process used: stitching, cementing, vulcanizing, injection molding, nailing, or stapling. About 60 percent of shoes made today use the cement process, applying adhesives to attach the sole to the upper with a permanent bond. This construction is found primarily in men's and women's casual and lighter-weight dress shoes. The most expensive shoes are usually of hand-sewn construction and are referred to as "bench made."

Heel heights of shoes vary, of course; the industry builds them and refers to them in terms of eighths of an inch. Flats measure up to 7/8 inch, low heels are 8/8 to 14/8 inch. Medium heels are 15/8 to 19/8 inch; high heels are 20/8 inch and up. Heels are made of many materials, including leather, wood, plastic, and rubber.

A most important distinction in shoe construction is whether the various parts are made of leather or synthetic material. Leather is highly valued, because it molds to the wearer's foot, is supple and resilient, and breathes to allow moisture to evaporate. Thus, leather is generally used in footwear of the finest quality. Shoes are generally labeled to identify the areas in which natural and synthetic materials are incorporated.

Marketing

The shoe industry is extremely fashion and marketing oriented, and each season presents a wide variety of new colors, shapes, and designs, geared to apparel trends. Perhaps this is why many women seem to be intensely susceptible to the lure of new shoes and to buy them as often as or even more often than they buy the other major components of their wardrobes. The industry does not rely on fashion alone to sell its products, however. Major emphasis is also placed on manufacturers' brand names in selling and in trade and consumer advertising.

Seasonal Showings

New lines are brought out twice a year. Because shoe production is a slow process, manufacturers develop and show their seasonal lines in advance of ready-to-wear. Fall/Winter lines are shown in January/February and Spring/Summer lines in August. In addition to presenting their lines in their own showrooms, manufacturers participate in semiannual cooperative trade shows, such as the National Shoe Fairs held in New York. These shows attract thousands of shoe store owners and buyers from all over the country, not only to see the new merchandise but also to attend merchandising clinics and discuss new fashion trends with the fashion directors of the participating manufacturers. A regular feature of the New York shows is fashion presentations, at which retailers see how the new shoes coordinate with apparel fashions. All this is done six months before so much as a pair of the new shoes is likely to turn up in a retail store. In addition, there are other, less-elaborate regional showings and clinics throughout the country.

Leased Shoe Departments

Because of the expertise needed to fit and sell shoes, and also because of the tremendous inventory needed to stock a shoe department, department and specialty stores have traditionally leased out some or all their selling space to experts in the field. Many of these are manufacturers of well-known national brands, such as the U.S. Shoe Company, which uses leased departments to stock and sell its Cobbie, Red Cross, and Pappagallo lines, and the Brown Shoe Company, whose leased departments feature its Buster Brown, Regal, and Naturalizer shoes. Other leaseholders are simply shoe merchants, who operate their departments as they would operate free-standing stores, with as many or as few brands as they deem appropriate.

Many of the leased shoe departments, manufacturer-owned or otherwise, also stock related accessories, such as handbags, hosiery, and small leather goods, which they purchase for resale from producers in these various industries.

Manufacturer-Owned Retail Chains

As has happened in the apparel industry, the growth of manufacturer-owned stores has been a fast-developing trend in the accessories area. The shoe classification, as the largest segment of the accessories industry, was the first to get into this business and remains in the forefront.

The advantages shoe companies see in this type of operation include creating a stronger brand franchise for their stores, protecting their share of the market in the wake of a diminishing number of mom-and-pop specialty shoe stores, and providing target consumers with a tightly focused assortment to fit their needs.

As a result, many of the leading names in footwear, including U.S. Shoe, Timberland, Nine-West (part of Jones New York corporation), Stride Rite, Jumping-Jack Shoes, and Nike, either are operating their own stores or are aggressively pursuing franchisees to operate stores for them. U.S. Shoe operates about 600 stores nationwide, 80 percent of which are franchised. Brands include Joyce/Selby, Pappagallo, Red Cross, and Cobbie. Stride Rite itself operates 270 stores and additionally has about 400 individual dealers across the country that are licensed to operate a Stride Rite store.

An even newer development is the trend to outfit the targeted consumer from head to toe as shoe manufacturers expand into apparel and activewear. Nike has opened stores where "we're trying to merchandise appropriate footwear and apparel together as a collection, so consumers can see how it coordinates" (McGuire, date unknown). Others such as Reebok, which purchased Ellesse and L.A. Gear, are opening stores to do the same thing.

Extensive Competition from Imports

In 1998, shoe producers in other countries shipped more than 1.2 billion pairs of shoes into the United States. Imports now account for 93 percent of U.S. shoe consumption, compared to only 22 percent in 1968 (Footwear Industries of America, 1999). Increased imports have led to an all-time low in domestic production. Thus, the footwear industries have felt the effects of import competition just as the fashion industries in general do. (Further discussion on trade for the fashion industry is found in Chapters 3 and 9.) Figure 8–2 illustrates that as U.S. consumption has increased, a growing percentage of the market has been taken by imports.

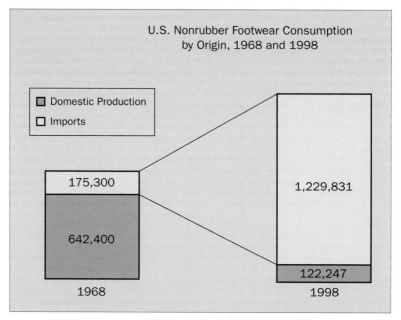

Figure 8–2

U.S. nonrubber footwear consumption by origin, 1968 and 1998.

U.S. Nonrubber Footwear Consumption by Origin, 1968 and 1998

☐ Domestic Production
☐ Imports

175,300

642,400

1968

1,229,831

122,247

1998

Source: From *Current Highlights of the Nonrubber Footwear Industry* (p. 1, online version) by Footwear Industries of America, 1999. Washington, DC: Author. Reprinted by permission.

Like apparel production, footwear manufacturing is a highly labor-intensive process, requiring a large number of cutting, sewing, and stitching operations. This is why most shoe manufacturing has been transferred to low-wage countries. Also similar to apparel, the machinery and equipment for most shoe production does not require large investments, making it easy to move manufacturing operations from one country to another. Thus, Asia—and particularly China—have become the leading shoe manufacturing areas. At least 70 percent of all footwear manufactured in the world comes from Asia. Production has moved from once-important Taiwan and South Korea to low-wage countries such as China, Indonesia, Thailand, India, and even Vietnam (Byron, 2000).

Important competition is also a result of the price appeal of low-wage-labor countries (Figure 8–3). A further complication faced by shoe producers is that other countries are often quick to buy up hides and leather in the United States, where our meat-eating habits make us an important provider of these commodities. Then those producers manufacture shoes and other leather goods in their own countries, at a lower price than is possible here, and ship finished shoes and other products back to the U.S. market.

Figure 8–4 shows where shoes purchased in the U.S. market originated. China now produces more than *seven* times as many shoes for the U.S. market as domestic

Figure 8–3

Shoe making requires a great deal of labor, therefore many shoes are produced in low-wage countries. This photograph shows shoe production in Indonesia.

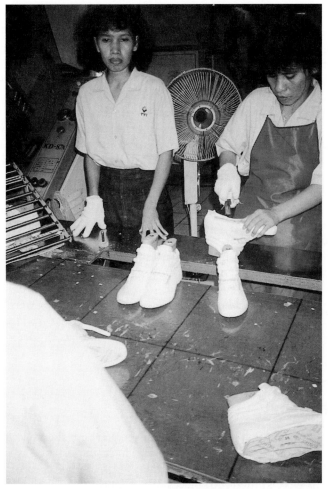

Source: Photo by Kitty G. Dickerson.

1998 percent share of U.S. footwear market by country of origin.

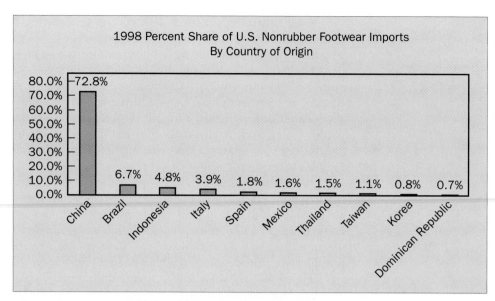

1998 Percent Share of U.S. Nonrubber Footwear Imports
By Country of Origin

Source: From *Current Highlights of the Nonrubber Footwear Industry* (p. 5, online version) by Footwear Industries of America, 1999. Washington, DC: Author. Reprinted by permission.

producers. These figures include shoes imported and resold by domestic manufacturers who find they are unable to compete with high-cost labor in this very labor-intensive industry. A large portion of the imports is contracted or purchased directly by retailers. Payless Shoe buys a large volume of shoes from China. The low-cost production in China and other low-wage countries enables Payless to sell shoes to consumers at very competitive prices.

Some U.S. manufacturers contract their production with offshore producers. The fashion appeal of Italian and other European styling is important; so is their expertise. A few U.S. firms own their own facilities in Italy, Spain, or South America. An example of contracting is the fashion-oriented firm of Joan and David, whose shoes are produced by the Martini factories, among the oldest and finest in Italy.

Although the footwear industry's competition from imports parallel those of the textile and apparel industries, the footwear sector has had far less protection from imports. That is, there are no import quotas. Although the outlook appears grim for the domestic footwear industry, an occasional manufacturer in this country is able, by ingenuity and enterprise, not only to meet foreign competition, but also to sell domestic shoes abroad. More than 27 million pairs of U.S. shoes were exported in 1998. Major countries buying U.S. shoes were Canada, Japan, Mexico, the United Kingdom, and Venezuela (Footwear Industries of America, 1999). Timberland is an example of a company that has exported successfully.

Hosiery

The introduction of nylon stockings in 1938 set the stage for vast changes in hosiery, in the industry that produces it, and in its importance as a fashion accessory. Before nylon, stockings were made primarily of silk and also of wool, rayon, and cotton. Yarns were knitted into pieces of flat fabric, each shaped so that when it was folded in half and seamed down the back, a stocking in the form of a leg resulted. Colors were limited, and fabric surfaces were plain.

Early nylon stockings for women were made much as silks and rayons had been. Except during the World War II years, when civilian use of nylon was ruled out to make way for military needs, nylon has made steady progress in hosiery, to the point that it has virtually crowded out other fibers for dress wear. With continuing technological progress, women's nylon stockings became sheerer, took on more colors, were produced in sandal-foot and other styles, and developed patterns and textures undreamed of in earlier years. In the 1960s, the development and popularity of pantyhose substantially added to the growth and fashion importance of hosiery. Again the development of pantyhose resulted from a change in fashion—women's skirt lengths. When skirts were very short in the 1960s, nylon hosiery that stopped at midthigh was no longer suitable.

Nature of the Industry

The business of hosiery—often called legwear in the industry—is one of chemistry, filaments, yarns, knitting machines, technology, big production, big promotion, and big competition. It is also the second-largest industry in the accessories field, after footwear. And like the shoe industry, it is dominated by large firms. Among the largest are Sara Lee (notably L'eggs, Just My Size, and Hanes), Round-the-Clock, Bonnie Doon, Hot Sox, and Kayser-Roth (No Nonsense). Perhaps it is significant that in national surveys asking consumers to identify the most recognizable brands in all women's apparel, two *hosiery* brands often top the list: L'eggs and Hanes.

Most manufacturing plants are in the Southeast—notably, North Carolina, a state that accounts for more than half the industry's output. Nevertheless, the marketing center for the industry is New York City. There the larger firms have their showrooms and smaller companies also have sales representation. It is there that retail buyers go during market weeks, not only to select merchandise, but also to learn about national advertising programs that producers plan to run and to assess the opportunities for tying in at the local level.

Economic Importance

The hosiery industry (sheer and casual) produced and shipped nearly $4.0 billion (wholesale value) in 1998 ("Women's 1999," 2000). The National Association of Hosiery Manufacturers (NAHM) noted that its member companies contributed $7.6 billion (retail value) to the retail environment in 1999. Of the NAHM retail figure, socks represented the largest category, with $4.9 billion, followed by women's sheer hosiery sales at $2.3 billion. This volume represents the output of 289 companies, operating 345 U.S. plants. Of these, 9 percent, or 24 plants, are in the women's sheer hosiery business, and the other 91 percent, or 316 plants, produce socks. The industry employs 51,100 people in 30 states (NAHM, 2000). Hosiery consumption was estimated at 17.4 pairs per person in 1999, compared to 15.7 pairs in 1979 (NAHM, 1988, 2000).

Hosiery Construction

Hosiery is knitted, either full-fashioned or seamless, in the greige state. Full-fashioned stockings are knitted flat to the desired shape, length, and size; sewn into the shape of the leg; next heat-set or boarded; and then packaged. Seamless hosiery is knitted on a circular machine, at high speed, and then dyed. The same procedure is used for pantyhose, some of which are knitted as stockings and then attached to separate panties. Full-fashioned hosiery had the advantage of a better fit than seamless until the introduction of stretch yarns in the 1960s. With them, the fit of seamless hosiery and pantyhose was greatly improved. Stretch yarns also made possible stretch hosiery, support hose, control tops, and comfortably fitted knee-high stockings.

Automation in hosiery production is constantly increasing, to the point that computerized machines can turn out hosiery that features graphics, patterns, and textures and uses many novelty yarns.

Marketing of Hosiery

As hosiery moved from almost entirely functional purposes toward becoming a important fashion accessory, the marketing strategies of the industry changed along with its product. Manufacturers' brands acquired new influence; producers' advertising took on greater importance to the retailer; fashion became the watchword of the industry. However, as legwear sales have stagnated in recent years, some department stores have moved the legwear department off the main floor to the lingerie department, where real estate is less of a premium, or near the footwear department, to generate multiple sales.

Nationally Advertised Brands

Manufacturers' brand names in the hosiery field are older and better established and have been longer promoted than those in other accessories areas. But whereas women had been conditioned to purchase a brand for its fit and durability, they are now bombarded with advertising that stresses the fashion points of the brands. Major producers advertise consistently in national magazines, on television, and through cooperative advertising with retail stores, in newspapers.

One of the most phenomenal success stories of the entire apparel industry was Sara Lee's quiet movement into the hosiery and intimate apparel business by acquiring well-known brands and building them into commercial successes through high-profile marketing efforts. Through these efforts, nearly all women in the United States would recognize names like L'eggs, Just My Size, and Hanes. More than that, a very large number *buy* those brands. Marketing strategies turned relatively mundane products and brands into megabrands—a strategy that has paid off handsomely for the company. Through wise acquisitions and well-planned marketing, Sara Lee has become one of the largest (or possibly *the* largest) U.S. apparel firms—with women's hosiery as a major component of its business. Additionally, Sara Lee has acquired well-established hosiery and foundations firms in Europe and Latin America—providing access for its U.S. brands in those markets and bringing some of those brands to the United States.

Retailers have capitalized on women's devotion to brand names by not only featuring national brands but also creating their own. These are known as **private labels**. This approach gives them greater price flexibility, removes them from direct competition with other stores in the national brand arena, and creates a certain exclusivity for their stores. Usually, the same manufacturer will produce both the store's private brand and its own national brand that is also carried in the same department. For example, Macy's has its Clubhouse but it carries an impressive array of nationally advertised brands side by side with its own. And in that array, the maker of the house brand is sure to be represented. Its source of supply, however, remains the store's secret. The same situation prevails in discount houses, chain drug stores, supermarkets, and others, except that these latter outlets seldom carry as many brands as department stores and major women's specialty shops.

Impact of Fashion and Designer Names

As hosiery has moved into the fashion spotlight, both retailers and manufacturers have been treating legwear much as ready-to-wear is treated. For example, the industry has changed from two to three market weeks a year: March for the presentation of Fall lines; August for the opening of Holiday and Early Spring lines; and November for Spring lines. This change in the marketing calendar is a natural outgrowth of the increased number of fashion items attuned to the seasonal apparel fashions. More and more emphasis is put on decorative legwear in a wide variety of textures, colors, and patterns. And in response to women's body-building and other exercise activities, the industry produces bodywear in attractive colors to be sold in hosiery departments.

Inevitably, as the total look became important in fashion, leading apparel designers, both European and American, moved into designer-name hosiery—for the most part under licensing arrangements with producers of national brands. For example, Donna Karan hosiery is licensed by Hanes, which is owned by Sara Lee; Round-the-Clock has legwear bearing the name of Givenchy; Bonnie Doon has Geoffrey Beene socks; Kayser-Roth produces the Calvin Klein (cK) line; and Hot Sox has a Ralph Lauren collection. Even when legwear sales have been sluggish, designer brands performed well, most notably cK and Tommy Hilfiger.

Package Marketing

Hosiery, like so many other products, has been affected by packaging and self-service techniques. For decades, it was sold over department and specialty store counters by saleswomen who slipped their beautifully kept hands into the stockings to show how they would look on the leg. Then came packaging, notably L'eggs by Sara Lee. These were pantyhose, folded into egg-shaped containers, for sale from self-service fixtures conspicuously placed near checkout counters in supermarkets and drugstores. With the marketing success of L'eggs, other producers soon followed. Kayser-Roth developed the No Nonsense brand for similar distribution. Presently, the consumer can find a packaged hosiery rack in almost any self-selection store.

The success of these nontraditional channels of distribution has led hosiery producers to seek out more innovative packaging and marketing techniques. Another factor is that consumers have changed in general in terms of *where* they are buying apparel. Together these trends have affected the retail distribution of hosiery. Discount stores have gained at the expense of department stores and national chains (the latter consists of Penney, Sears, and Montgomery Ward). Distribution for all hosiery is shown in Figure 8–5. To compete with the price appeal of discounters, supermarkets, and others, department stores and national chains are using a two-pronged attack. One effort is to push their own brands to meet price competition; the other is to emphasize designer or decorative legwear as a major accessory of fashion.

Global Activities

Pantyhose, hosiery, and basic socks are an area of domestic production that resisted the inroads of import competition until recent years. This was true because the industries involved are capital intensive. Less-costly labor, the competitive edge that many producers in other countries enjoy, has less impact in this segment of the industry compared to most others. However, imports grow each year. Competition also comes from industrialized countries such as Japan, England, and France. These countries produce goods of high quality, have great technical expertise, and use sophisticated dyeing techniques. Despite attempts by the domestic industry to keep imports

Figure 8–5

Retail Distribution Channels for All Hosiery

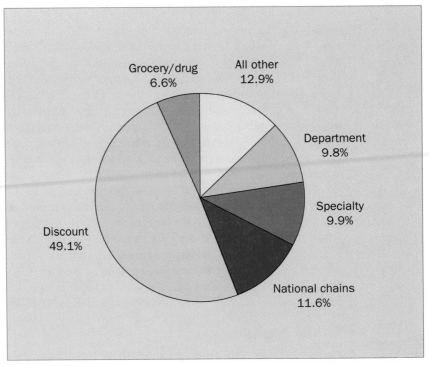

Source: Data from *1999 Hosiery Statistics Annual Report* (p. 31, online version) by The Hosiery Association, 1999. Charlotte, NC: Author.

to a minimum, some manufacturers say they will bring goods in from offshore because of the quality of yarns from some countries, the quality of finishing, and the greater sophistication of dyeing techniques.

In 1999, hosiery imports totaled 94 million dozens of pairs, up 22 percent from the 26 million imported in 1994. Imported hosiery represented 12 percent of the domestic hosiery market in 1999. Sock imports represented 62 percent of the total hosiery imported, pantyhose 30 percent, and tights/opaques 8 percent (NAHM, 2000).

Handbags and Small Leather Goods

From earliest history, people have needed receptacles of some kind in which to carry their various personal possessions and necessities. Quite possibly, a pouch made of skin or leather and suspended from a belt or girdle was used by primitive peoples who had not yet ventured into clothes, much less clothing with pockets. Handbags as we know them are a creation of the twentieth century; before that, women had only a belt from which to suspend housekeeping keys and slit pockets in their voluminous skirts to accommodate whatever a lady wanted to carry with her. As women's activities grew more varied in the twentieth century, and as their garments became slimmer and sleeker, handbags became necessary and developed into accessories that would complement and coordinate with the apparel. Today, most women have a wardrobe of handbags in a variety of materials (leather, fabric, and plastic, for example), and in a diversity of sizes and shapes, such as clutch, envelope, satchel, box, duffle, tote, pouch—and the woman executive's briefcaselike carryall.

Although men do not generally have as many items, they do have wallets, key holders, agenda organizers, toiletry cases, and other pieces. Therefore, this segment is also an important part of the industry.

Nature of the Handbag Industry

For the most part, the handbag industry consists of relatively small specialists, the majority of whom are headquartered in New York—primarily in the 30s, between Broadway and Fifth Avenue. They present their lines in two major showings a year: in May for Fall and in November for Spring and Summer. Supplementary collections, smaller than the main seasonal ones, are shown for Holiday/Transitional in August, for Early Fall in March, and for Summer in January.

The majority of buyers for retail handbag departments also buy other accessory items, such as gloves, belts, or small leather goods. Such buyers demand and usually get coordination in both color and silhouette among the various markets they shop, and they also seek to purchase accessories that will relate well to the upcoming season's ready-to-wear. The handbag industry establishes market dates that dovetail with apparel openings. It also uses its openings as an opportunity to disseminate both industry and fashion information to the retail store buyers.

Economic Importance

In 1998, U.S. manufacturers produced handbags valued at an estimated $4.3 billion at retail. Large quantities of handbags are imported, accounting for about three-fourths of U.S. consumption. U.S. firms (both manufacturers and retailers) with products at all price levels are sourcing a large portion of their handbags from overseas manufacturers. National chains and alternative retailers (off-pricers, mail order, etc.) continue to slowly increase their share of the handbag market at the expense of department stores.

Handbag Construction

Years ago, leather was the principal material from which bags were made. This meant a large amount of hand-guided work and demanded considerable resourcefulness in cutting, as the operator had to work with a natural product, irregular in shape and sometimes with scars to be worked around. Today, vinyl is the leading material used; however, fabrics such as microfiber, gray flannel, and silk shantung have become increasingly important. Vinyl and fabric offer advantages of uniformity in width and quality that vastly simplifies the cutter's task. Cost is, of course, the main reason for using vinyl and fabric over leather. Texture, embellishment, and decorative detailing have also become key selling points.

Today's handbags range from classic, constructed types to unconstructed, unframed bags of leather, canvas, or other materials. The number and difficulty of the operations required varies with the styling. All, however, begin with a design from which a muslin sample is made. From the muslin, a paper or metal pattern is made, and this is used to cut the handbag materials. The actual cutting is done either by hand or with metal dies, depending on the complexity of the design and the quantities to be produced. Each handbag shape, such as the clutch, envelope, tote, and satchel, for example, requires different types of construction and parts. If the design requires a frame, then all of the inside and outside parts must be fitted into the frame; after that, closures and straps are added.

Global Activities

Imported handbags now account for 76 percent of all those sold in the U.S. market. China supplies about 62 percent of those imports (Byron, 2000). Many handbags require a good deal of labor in sewing and other aspects of assembly; therefore, many high-wage countries such as the United States have difficulty competing in this segment of the industry. Most large accessory firms and retailers buy directly from the factories abroad, primarily in the Far East or, increasingly, contract with Asian firms to have lines produced.

Exports increased in recent years, particularly to Mexico. However, these are generally believed to be largely cut parts for handbags, which are being shipped to Mexico to be assembled and then returned to the U.S. market. Other exporting does occur. Coach bags has developed recognition of its quality products in upscale markets in other countries. Coach sells in department stores and operates its own shops in locations frequented by upscale consumers in numerous countries.

Small Leather Goods

Fashion and changing activities of both men and women have had strong impacts on the industry that produces **small leather goods** (sometimes called personal leather goods), such as wallets, credit card cases, billfolds, key cases, jewelry and eyeglass cases, cigarette cases, and similar items for both sexes. Although historically the largest producers of these types of products were Prince Gardner, Buxton, and Swank, the recent addition of Liz Claiborne Accessories, Bosea, and Bond Street has added to the fashion look of these items. Upscale lines such as Coach and Bally are also available.

In today's world of fashion, many women choose to match such items with the handbags they carry. This is especially true of designer-licensed lines, which coordinate the various items by fabric and color. And among women climbing the success ladder in the business world, special needs are developing for which the small leather goods industry is providing some answers: calculator wallets, credit card cases, pocket appointment calendars, work-and-date organizers, notebooks, and all sorts of handbag and briefcase accessories that project both fashion and businesslike efficiency. Professional men are also buying many of these items.

This industry's sales for 1998 were $775 million (retail). This was for women's small leather goods; figures are unavailable for men's. Imports of personal leather goods grew. Leading suppliers of these leather products are China, South Korea, Italy, and India ("Women's 1999," 2000).

Gloves

One can trace the wearing of gloves before and through recorded history. In ancient times, they were worn as protection and adornment—as they are today. Objects in pyramids dating back to Egypt's twenty-first dynasty include gloves. In ancient Rome, ladies protected their hands with gloves. In medieval times, kings and church dignitaries wore richly ornamented gloves, symbolic of their status. A knight wore gloves, or gauntlets, reinforced with armor. When he threw one down before another knight, that constituted a challenge to battle.

Gloves today have many purposes, many of them functional. Foundry workers use insulated gloves to protect their hands from heat; Eskimos need mittens to keep out the cold; racing drivers wear gloves that give them better wheel grip; skiers use waterproof kinds to protect them from frostbite. In fashion, gloves play a role that changes in importance, taking a share of the spotlight when dress becomes elegant and fading out when the look is at a casual extreme.

Nature of the Industry

The glove industry suffered a severe blow during the 1960s and 1970s, when fashion took on an ultracasual look, and gloves became almost obsolete as fashion accessories. The hard times this situation imposed on the glove industry dealt it a blow from which it has not recovered.

Many of today's gloves, especially those made of fabric, are produced by divisions of multiproduct companies that also manufacture small leather goods and handbags, such as Etienne Aigner, or by firms such as Kayser-Roth that produce intimate apparel and hosiery. There are still, however, some specialists that are glovers exclusively. Among these are Aris Glove, producers of a line of fine leather gloves and also the Isotoner glove. Hansen Gloves is another well-known specialist. Other important names here are Fownes and Grandoe, both important producers of fashion gloves, as is LaCrasia, producer of a line of trendy gloves that are unquestionably more fashionable than functional. Companies such as these, which are glovers first and foremost, flourish or suffer according to whether fashion smiles on or ignores the glove as an accessory to the total look.

The plants that produce leather gloves are located principally in the Northeast. Gloversville, New York, was the site of the first glove production facility in the United States, as far back as 1760, and it is where, by 1900, some 80 to 90 percent of American gloves originated. Once the glove capital of the world, Gloversville was home to an estimated 300 companies. Today, fewer than 10 companies are in business there, entrepreneurial spirited makers who believe U.S. production can prosper alongside high-volume importers (Pelz, 1980; Rabon, 1998). Production of fabric gloves, on the other hand, is more widely distributed throughout the country, with 65 percent of the factories being located in North Carolina, Mississippi, Alabama, and Tennessee.

Economic Importance

The glove and mitten industry is largely a business of warm hands and work gloves. That is, the fashion motivation for buying gloves is virtually a thing of the past. The market may vary from year to year—an unusually cold winter can boost sales significantly.

The U.S. leather glove and mitten industry is composed of two product segments: work gloves and mittens, which account for approximately 85 percent of domestic production, and dress gloves, which account for the remaining 15 percent. A shrinking U.S. glove industry produced $96 million worth of gloves and mittens at factory value in 1999. Imports accounted for about 62 percent of the glove/mitten market. Major supplier countries are China, the Philippines, Mexico, and South Korea (Byron, 2000).

Oddly, men's glove sales by type of retail outlet shifted more toward department stores at the expense of the discounters and off-price outlets. The *MR* "Accessories Report" (1995) speculated that department store promotions and markdowns have permitted consumers to buy gifts for friends and relatives at reasonable prices and to do so with the status of a top department store box and wrapping.

Glove Construction

Of all accessories, gloves are among the most labor intensive to manufacture. Although made on an assembly line, they require great skill on the part of production workers and involve many steps, because a glove must fit when the hand is closed in a fist and yet not be baggy when the hand is open.

Gloves are made of numerous small pieces, such as the trank, or hand and finger piece, both front and back; the thumb part, which may be made in any of several ways; the fourchettes, or pieces that shape the fingers between front and back; and quirks, tiny triangular pieces sewn at the back of the fingers to provide flexibility and give additional fit. Only the very inexpensive gloves use few pieces; they consist merely of a front and back sewn together—a procedure that earns them the name of "sandwich gloves" in the trade.

Because there are so many pieces in the usual glove and because they are so small, a great deal of handwork is involved in cutting. This may be done on a table, using a ruler to measure each part, or with the use of a die. The former method is known as table cutting, the latter as clicker cutting. Actual sewing is done on several types of machines and uses lock stitch, chain stitch, and overstitching, depending on quality and style. Because gloves are curved, high-speed production equipment cannot be used.

Because gloves require a great deal of labor to produce, especially high-quality ones, U.S. manufacturers have found it difficult to compete with imports. The lower wages in other countries make production more affordable in those nations.

Glove Marketing

The major marketing center for gloves is New York City, where most glove producers maintain permanent showrooms of their own or use the facilities of sales representatives. These showrooms are usually located in the East 30s, where many of the other accessories industries are also located. Seasonal lines are shown at the same time as the handbag showings. Compared with the promotional outlays and activities of other fashion accessories manufacturers and retailers, the money devoted to promoting gloves is relatively insignificant.

Some of the more aggressive producers, however, have followed the example of the hosiery industry and are packaging "one size fits all" stretch gloves that can be displayed and sold in self-service fixtures. Others are increasing their volume by packaging their gloves with matching hats or scarfs, or both—a combination with strong consumer appeal during cold winter months.

Millinery/Hats

Until the middle of the twentieth century, it was unthinkable for a well-dressed woman to be seen on the streets or to enter a store or office without a hat. Every department or women's specialty store devoted a great deal of prime space to millinery[2] departments, which featured both ready-made and custom-made hats and were usually located adjacent to apparel departments. In the 1950s, there was an enormous exodus from the city to the suburbs and, with it, an emerging fashion for

---

[2]The term *millinery* generally refers to women's hats.

casual living and casual clothes. The outdoor barbecues of the 1950s called for a very different style of dress from the garden tea party of an earlier suburban generation. Country casual dress spread to the city, and the habit of wearing hats declined. The millinery industry, after many years of prosperity when women had whole wardrobes of hats, declined too—from which it has just recently begun to recover somewhat.

Men's hats are also considerably less popular than in earlier decades. Some men are inclined to wear them in colder seasons and cooler climates for functional purposes. However, this industry segment is also very small compared to what it once was.

Nature of the Industry

The millinery industry today is small because of the diminished demand for its wares. It is made up, as it always has been, of small firms, numbering fewer than 100, all of which are specialists in this one field. The industry has been untouched by the drive to bigness and diversification that has affected other areas of the fashion business. Smallness is no handicap in this industry, however, as there is little opportunity to mechanize, automate, or develop huge runs of individual styles. The ability to move quickly on a new idea—the strong point of small operations—is an important asset in the millinery field.

Periodically, the importance of the total look in fashion sparks renewed interest in millinery. Designers dutifully put appropriate headwear on their models as they parade the runways; retailers show millinery with other outer apparel; some customers even buy hats. But one still sees few, indeed, on the streets and in other public places. That tide may turn, as tides often do in fashion. Meanwhile, even the most prestigious of fashion retailers gives only minimal space to millinery departments. The day of the huge millinery department—in which expert salespeople helped women choose the right hats for their outfits or the right hat to enhance their morale for an important occasion—has not yet returned. Until it does, the millinery industry will remain small.

The men's headwear industry generally responds to more functional needs. The industry has some fluctuations as fashions change—but in general the industry is more stable than women's millinery.

Economic Importance

Retail sales of millinery for 1998 were estimated at $842 million ("Women's 1999," 2000). The production of millinery domestically takes place primarily in New York City, although a small number of companies are located in St. Louis, Dallas, and Los Angeles. The fewer than 80 companies operating today represent a continued decline from the more than 400 companies operating in the 1960s, when hats were always worn by a majority of women. However, when hats and caps are added to millinery, 18,675 people were employed in 381 establishments (AAMA, 1999; Millinery Institute of America, 1989).

Today, hats are more casual than in earlier eras. Softer-fabric hats outperform structured styles. Packable hats from fine straw to raffia, which retain their shape after being packed, have grown in sales. The cloche was an important fashion silhouette in turned-up brims; slouchy brims and oversized brims dominated structured straws. These reflect growing concern for sun protection.

Construction of Millinery

Basically, the millinery industry's output falls into two categories: hats and caps, and millinery. The former category can be made by machine or by hand. Millinery-type hats are made by sewing velvet, satin, or other fabric and trimmings over buckram frames, or by shaping and trimming felt or straw bodies. Millinery made by the latter methods involves a great deal of handwork, and the processes lend themselves readily to custom work for consumers or for sale through retail shops. The industry is headquartered mostly on a single street in New York City: West 37th Street, between Fifth and Sixth avenues.

At one time, the industry had its share of well-known designers. Adolfo and Halston, for example, began their fashion careers as milliners. These days, however, the glamorous names bypass the millinery industry and concentrate on the apparel field, where opportunities and rewards are much greater.

Casual hats are often of knit construction. Fewer of these are associated with designer names, particularly because many of these are imported.

Marketing of Millinery/Hats

An unusual factor in the millinery industry is the millinery syndicate of Consolidated Millinery, which operates 250 leased departments. Such a firm leases space for millinery departments in retail stores across the country and provides these stores with a continuing supply of new styles. In order to obtain such styles, the buyers for these firms are constantly in the wholesale markets, not only to seek out actual merchandise but also to find and develop talented new producers and stylists. Help, advice, and sometimes even operating capital will be made available by the syndicate to potentially creative resources.

Unlike other fashion accessories, millinery does not function on two lines a year. Seasonality has its influence, of course, but the life of a hat as an accessory is usually short and, as a rule, the faster a firm gets into and out of a good-selling style number, the better the operation is. In millinery, the important element is an unending procession of new styles or new versions of currently accepted styles. At one time, when millinery was in its heyday, retailers sought to have completely new assortments every three or four weeks, and the term *millinery turnover* was used in retail circles to describe extremely fast-moving merchandise.

Today the millinery market has four specific seasons, currently labeled Fall I, Fall II, Spring I, and Spring II, which roughly correspond to the traditional seasons in ready-to-wear. However, because millinery is such an impulse purchase on the part of most consumers, constant new additions serve to increase the turnover.

The great unknown for millinery today is the customer. It still remains to be seen whether promotion, publicity, and fashion creativity can reverse the trend toward hatlessness and convince women that smart millinery is essential to the total fashion look.

Men's headwear is sold through all major retail channels, including sporting goods stores for caps and casual hats. Mail-order merchants have also increased sales. Industry leaders hope that the baseball cap craze reacquainted a previously hatless American male with the joys of wearing a hat and that this market might continue to grow.

Jewelry

The wearing of jewelry is believed to antedate the wearing of clothes; in fact, among primitive peoples today, even if one sees little that could be called clothing, there is usually a ring or two or ten on the body, the neck, the ears, or the nose. In modern times, jewelry has become a sign of worth and status—and a very important fashion accessory. No fashion costume is complete without it, whether it be the understated string of cultured pearls worn with a woman executive's office clothing, or the exaggerated four-inch earrings hanging from the earlobes of the latest MTV star. More men also wear jewelry today, ranging from gold chains to earrings.

The jewelry industry divides itself into two distinct parts: fine jewelry, made of precious metals and gemstones, and costume jewelry. In recent years, a third category has entered the picture: bridge jewelry, which spans the gap between the other two.

This segment of the fashion industry has its own trade shows. In addition jewelry firms have showrooms in New York and regional marts.

Today, both fine jewelry and costume jewelry are being sold in a variety of ways in addition to traditional jewelry and department stores. Mail order, catalog stores, discount stores, TV home shopping, and now the Internet have become important retail outlets for jewelry. As in other fashion product categories, the consolidation of retailing means that powerful retailers squeeze producers to deliver more for less.

Similar to apparel, the U.S. jewelry industry is faced with increasing imports. Imports now account for more than half the U.S. purchases of fine jewelry and nearly 40 percent of costume jewelry. Jewelry industries have expanded in less-developed countries. Leading suppliers of precious jewelry are Italy, India, Hong Kong (part of China but treated as a special economic zone), Thailand, and Israel. Italy's share of these products dropped during the 1990s as the less-developed countries gained because of low labor costs. Countries accounting for more and more of the U.S. fine jewelry imports are India, Turkey, China, and Oman.

The leading suppliers of costume jewelry are China, South Korea, Taiwan, Hong Kong, and Thailand. China's share of the market has grown to nearly half, at the expense of Taiwan, whose share dropped from 26 percent to 5 percent in the 1990s. Labor costs caused this shift (Harris, 2000).

Precious or Fine Jewelry

The metals used in **fine jewelry** are gold, silver, and platinum, worked alone or in combination with gemstones. The U.S. jewelry industry consists of a large number of fairly small companies. The approximately 2,200 firms operating in this field in the United States produced more than $4.6 billion of merchandise at factory value and employed more than 35,400 people in 1999. Several thousand more work in supporting industries. A majority of the factories are located in New York, Rhode Island, California, and Massachusetts (Harris, 2000).

Gold, the metal of first choice for fine jewelry, is too soft to be used by itself and is therefore usually combined with base metals. The gold content is expressed in terms of carats, or **karats**. Solid gold is 24 karats, or **24K**. The most commonly used alloys are rated 18K, 14K, or 12K and are arrived at by mixing gold with copper (to produce reddish yellow metal), silver (to produce greenish yellow), or palladium or nickel (to produce white gold). Any alloy of less than 10K may not be called karat gold. In the United States, 14K is favored; in European jewelry, 18K is customary.

Platinum, a silvery metal, is rarer, heavier, and more expensive than gold and is a favorite for diamond settings. It, too, is generally alloyed, primarily to reduce its price, with palladium, iridium, rhodium, or ruthenium—all white and hard metals.

Silver, the least-expensive of the precious metals, is usually combined with copper. The term **sterling** may be used where there are at least 925 parts of silver per thousand.

Gemstones

Precious stones include diamonds, emeralds, sapphires, rubies, and real pearls. With the exception of pearls, stones are measured in carats, one carat being the equivalent of 100 points. Pearls are measured in millimeters and length.

Semiprecious stones include amethysts, garnets, opals, lapis, jades, topaz, and aquamarines, among others. Today, fine jewelry uses more of these than ever, because of the high prices of precious stones.

In addition to natural gemstones, wide use is now made of synthetic gemstones. Laboratories can produce synthetic corundum to look like garnets and amethysts and synthetic spinel to look like emeralds, diamonds, and aquamarines, among others.

An important element in the value of a piece of fine jewelry is the workmanship that goes into it. It is a handmade product, with a jeweler creating each setting for each stone at the workbench, one piece at a time. The creativity and skill of the craftsperson are major factors in the cost of the finished piece.

Marketing of Fine and Precious Jewelry

In recent years the fine jewelry industry has seen a major consolidation at the retail level through the steady growth of jewelry store chains. These chains are growing both through internal growth and through acquisitions. Examples here are Kay Jewelers; Peoples Jewelers, a Canadian-owned company; Ratner's Group, a British-owned company; Reeds Jewelers; and Barry's Jewelers, among others.

As noted earlier, new forms of retailing have become important in the jewelry market. TV home shopping has become a particularly important channel of distribution for jewelry, and Internet sales are expected to grow (Figure 8–6).

Bridge Jewelry

With the price of fine jewelry climbing and the demand for jewelry increasing, a new area of jewelry has developed to fill the need. This is **bridge jewelry**, which involves silver, gold-plated metals, or 14K gold, and which uses less-expensive stones, such as onyx, ivory, coral, or freshwater pearls. Much of the fashion leadership comes from designers such as Celia or Karen Sibiri, Elsa Perretti, and M. J. Savitt, who, among others, create handmade and signed pieces. Also important here are items such as gold chains, gold combined with the less-expensive semiprecious stones, and jewelry that sets many small diamonds in a group to create the look of larger stones. Retail prices range from about $100 to $2,000 for these products.

Figure 8–6

Consumer Rights: Jewelry Purchases Via TV and the Internet

The **Federal Trade Commission (FTC) Jewelry Guides** describe the types of jewelry marketing claims the FTC considers false or misleading and provide examples of nondeceptive claims. In 1999, the FTC reported that a review of 100 Internet sites that advertise and sell jewelry had shown that many sites were not providing consumers with information required under the Jewelry Guides. Less than 30 percent disclosed whether the pearls used in their jewelry were cultured or imitation, as is required by the guides. Disclosures for diamonds were better, with two-thirds advertising stone weights correctly. However, among the sites selling gemstone jewelry only 5 percent correctly disclosed gem treatments, whereas 37 percent of auction site sellers correctly disclosed treatments (Harris, 2000).

Costume Jewelry

Costume jewelry is mass-produced to fill the fashion demands of customers who seek relatively inexpensive jewelry to complete the fashion look of their outfits. The materials used may be plastic, wood, brass, tin, glass, lucite, or any other substance that can be manipulated to achieve the desired effect. Retail prices range widely, from items sold in variety stores to those bearing the names of such companies as Kenneth J. Lane and Miriam Haskell.

The costume jewelry trade has deep roots in Rhode Island. It dates back to colonial silversmiths, who hammered out teaspoons and thimbles and who developed a method in the early 1800s for reducing the cost of jewelry by rolling a thin sheet of gold over a cheaper base. Today this is done by **electroplating**, the process for coating materials with a thin layer of gold or silver.

Economic Importance

U.S. costume jewelry producers shipped an estimated $1.2 billion in products at factory value in 1999. The industry consists of about 900 manufacturers, employing 12,200 workers. Imports take an increasing share of the market, amounting to nearly $600 million in 1999. Both imports and exports have increased in recent years (Harris, 2000).

Fashion and sport watches, generally considered to be those retailing under $75, have been a growth area. These have accounted for an additional $2.6 billion in retail sales.

Figures on men's jewelry sales include cuff links, stud sets, and miscellaneous items (key rings, money clips, tie bars, pens, earrings, and pendants). Retail sales of these products are more than $50 million annually. Cuff link sales vary greatly with trends in how men dress. Younger professionals are reported to consider French-cuff shirts as "dated, tight, and impractical"—the opposite of trends toward more relaxed dress.

Some jewelry items, including gold neck chains, earrings, and even fashion/sport watches, may be sold in unisex retail sources. When this occurs, sales of many of these products are difficult to differentiate by gender.

Other Accessories

Other accessories include glasses, sunglasses, scarfs, belts, handkerchiefs, umbrellas, and wigs. Eyeglasses have become very fashionable, sometimes worn by individuals with no vision problems. Optical departments now boast lines by many prominent designers. Sunglasses came into fashion prominence in the 1960s, when then–First Lady Jackie Kennedy wore "shades" constantly. They have remained important in fashion, not only for daytime, functional outdoor wear, but also sometimes as accessories for evening. Wigs, falls, and hairpieces, too, have been important accessories at various times, and to some extent their burgeoning popularity coincided with the decline of millinery. Hair ornaments have been an addition to the well-dressed look. Nowadays some women have an entire wardrobe of watches to wear for different occasions.

Belts gain prominence when waistlines are in fashion. Scarfs and stoles fill in low necklines, provide a bit of warmth, add a touch of color, or can be worn to accent broad-shouldered or slender looks, according to how they are draped and according to current fashion requirements. Handkerchiefs, whose utilitarian functions have been taken over by tissues, pass in and out of the fashion picture, tucked into breast pockets or sleeves if and when they enhance whatever the "in" look may be. Umbrellas, too, have their fashion ins and outs, sometimes carried with a swagger like a walking stick, sometimes brightly colored to liven up drab days and drab rainwear. Utility sells many umbrellas; fashion, when it touches this field, sells more.

Retail sales figures for some of these other categories of women's accessories are: Belts, $600 million; scarves/neckwear, $610 million; hair accessories, $461 million; sunglasses, $1.9 billion; and rainwear/umbrellas, $340 million. Even for items that may seem quite small, total U.S. sales are substantial ("Women's 1999," 2000).

Accessories Designers

"Name" designers in the accessories field are almost exclusively those who have made their mark in the apparel field and who license their names to manufacturers of accessories. The designs themselves may or may not originate with the famous individual whose name is attached to them; they may have come from a design studio run by that luminary, or they may have been created by anonymous employees of the producer and then approved by the licensor.

Very few designers become famous through their work in accessories alone. For the most part, manufacturers have design staffs or use freelancers; in neither case do they feature the names of these designers. Among the distinguished exceptions are Vera, who began many years ago in scarfs; Elsa Peretti, the house designer of jewelry for Tiffany's; Judith Leiber, a handbag designer; and Paloma Picasso and Kenneth Jay Lane, also in the jewelry field. Robert Lee Morris is an important new accessory designer.

Apparel designers moved strongly into licensed accessories in the 1970s, when the total "look" became important in fashion, and consumers began putting together outfits in which the accessories were quite as essential as the apparel if one was to achieve the desired casual or elegant smartness. This trend has brought almost every famous American and European apparel design name into the accessories area. It has also brought glamour and useful promotional tools to the field.

It is interesting to note that Liz Claiborne, Inc., whose name had been licensed to Kayser-Roth for a line of accessories in 1986, discontinued this arrangement and opened a new division, Liz Claiborne Accessories. The decision to do this was explained as follows: "Since there has always been a synergistic relationship between apparel and accessories, we have decided to make that relationship closer" ("Claiborne Buys," 1985). Other designers' companies have followed their lead. Many companies also found that marketing their lines themselves was far more profitable than simply licensing their names to other companies.

Intimate Apparel/Undergarments

The segment of the fashion industry that produces loungewear, nightwear, women's and children's undergarments, and body shapers for women is known as the **intimate apparel industry**. This segment of the industry—by this name—applies for women's garments only. Sometimes, the term **innerwear** is used in the industry. For similar products for men, these are simply **undergarments**. The history of women's products is also a history of society's changing perceptions of modesty and feminine beauty. In the nineteenth century and into the early decades of the twentieth, manufacturers in the United States produced, and women wore, an astonishing variety of devices to shape, distort, and even deform the figure to achieve what was considered fashionable

Figure 8–7

The intimate apparel business has become an important segment of the industry. Special trade shows, such as this important one held in Lyon, France, focus specifically on this industry.

Source: Reprinted courtesy of Lyon, Mode City.

for women. It is a matter of amazement that women of the generations that first fought for suffrage and first entered the business world conducted their activities in garments so constricting that people in the trade referred to them in later years as "iron maidens."

Because undergarments in general come into close contact with the body, they have always had sexual connotations. Even though their appearance to the outside observer is secondary, these garments, other than the actual corsets, have generally been characterized by soft fabrics, a great deal of detailing, and many trimmings (Figure 8–7). The Gibson Girl might have worn a corset of tough fabric reinforced with whalebone, but she wore a dainty camisole and lacy petticoats with it.

Recent years have seen renewed consumer interest in intimate apparel. The industry had hit a low point in the 1960s, when young women burned their bras as a form of protest and declaration of freedom. This was also the era of tight jeans, worn with minimal or no undergarments. In the late 1990s, however, intimate apparel was one of the strongest retail categories and continues to be a money machine for an apparel industry that has been otherwise sluggish at times. Intimate apparel is a highly sought-after business because it is generally a risk-free, high-volume, and commodity-type business that traditionally yields profits even when the economy is down (Monget, 1999, 2000).

Nowadays, the intimate apparel industry is thriving. Women have learned they can be both independent and feminine. Intimate apparel leaders believe that even if a woman is on a limited budget, she most likely can afford to buy a pretty silk chemise or a pair of sexy-looking panties. Many women enjoy the luxurious array of styles and colors provided by the industry today and consider intimate apparel an equally important part of their wardrobes. Lines of practical, special-purpose garments have increased, too. For example, today's concern for fitness has created a need for jogging bras among women who exercise strenuously. Similarly, many types of girdles and other body shaper garments are available for those who want to look more trim and fit than they may actually be.

Although men's undergarments lag far behind women's intimate apparel in terms of design interest and types of products, this segment of the industry has changed, too. The days are gone when men were offered a choice of plain white knit briefs or plain white boxer shorts. Now, men's undergarments come in many colors, fabrics, and patterns. The lower European cut in knit briefs is commonly available. We have seen one notable example of men's undergarments becoming a fashion item that went far beyond the original utilitarian use—namely the popularity of patterned boxer shorts worn by young people in creative layering with the boxer shorts visible.

Industry Segments

The industry's products fall into three major categories:

1. **Foundations**, which include girdles, brassieres, garter belts, and the **shapewear** that nowadays replaces corsets (shapewear is a category of foundation garments that mold and support the body in strategic spots).
2. **Lingerie**, which includes petticoats, slips, panties, camisoles, and sleepwear such as nightgowns and pajamas.
3. **Loungewear**, which consists of robes, negligees, bed jackets, and housecoats. The lines between lingerie and loungewear are not always clear-cut, however, and some in the industry categorize their products as daywear (lingerie and housecoats) and nightwear (sleepwear and negligees, etc.).

Economic Importance

The intimate apparel/undergarment industry is big business in the United States, with total retail sales in 1998 of $11.1 billion. The value of production by some of the categories is shown in Table 8–2. Values given in the table do not add to the total given above because production figures are given in wholesale rather than retail, and breakouts are not available for all garment lines. The largest portion of this total is produced by the women's and children's undergarment segments of the industry, which employs over 38,000 employees and encompasses 372 **establishments**. References to establishments or **plants** include the manufacturing facilities only, and each location is counted separately.[3] The men's underwear and nightwear segment employs approximately 7,267 in 74 plants. Another 2,765 workers in 53 plants produce robes and dressing gowns (AAMA, 1999).

Table 8–2	**U.S. Annual Production in Select Lines of Intimate Apparel and Undergarments (Wholesale Prices)**
Garment Line	**Production in Millions of Dollars, 1998**
Men's and Boys'	
Nightwear and robes*	$95
Undershirts*	497
Undershorts and briefs*	566
Thermal underwear*	125
Woven boxer shorts*	108
Women's and Girls'	
Bras	1,714
Foundation garments	248
Nightgowns	505
Panties	844
Slips and other underwear**	258
Infants	
Underwear	98
Nightwear	344

*Data do not include little boys' garments.
**Data do not include little girls' garments.
Source: From *Focus: An economic profile of the apparel industry* (pp. 23–24) by American Apparel & Footwear Association, 1999, Arlington, VA: Author. Adapted by permission.

---

[3]Plants or establishments are part of a **firm**. A firm may have many establishments (plants) or could have only one. Today, in many parts of the apparel industry, firms may have *no* sewing facilities but simply contract to have all the manufacturing done by others.

Additionally, a significant amount of knit underwear (men's, women's, and children's) is made in plants categorized until 1993 under textile production. Now, these are categorized with other apparel. When knit apparel was categorized in this manner, it meant the garments were made in vertical textile firms. In these firms, products continue to be made from start to finish within a single company, all the way from knitting fabrics to producing finished garments. However, they are now considered with apparel rather than textiles. Approximately 13,000 employees in nearly 70 plants make knit underwear (AAMA, 1997).

Marketing

New York City is the major market center for all segments of the intimate apparel industry, and the showings are timed to mesh with those of ready-to-wear. The buyer of intimate apparel is usually a specialist, not involved with the merchandising of outerwear. Nevertheless, the close relationships between undergarments and outerwear fashions, and between outerwear fashions and the various categories of at-home wear make it essential for the intimate apparel buyer to be guided by what the other segments of the fashion industry are presenting.

The intimate apparel industry, which functioned on two markets a year in the days when its major concern was corsetry, now has five seasonal showings: Early Spring in August, Spring in November, Summer in January, Early Fall in March, and Fall and Holiday in May. Market weeks are also held in important regional centers: the Dallas Mart, the Atlanta Mart, the Chicago Apparel Center, and the CaliforniaMart in Los Angeles.

Competition at the retail level is intense, as intimate apparel titans slug it out for floor space and sales at department stores, national chains, and discounters. Mergers of intimate apparel firms have led to megabrands that edge out smaller brands on the cutthroat retail floor. Once mostly the domain of department stores, national intimate apparel sales are shifting more and more to discounters including Wal-Mart, Kmart, and Target (Monget, 2000).

Impact of Fashion

Even in this industry's purely functional garments, the impact of fashion is felt. For example, the length and fullness of outerwear skirts necessarily determines the length and shape of the slips to be worn under them; figure-revealing silhouettes enhance the demand for body-shaping undergarments, whereas relaxed lines diminish their importance; emphasis on the waistline brings waist cinchers back into production, generally briefly. In recent years, lightweight, less-structured undergarments with fewer seams have been popular with many women. Changes in women's lifestyles and interests, too, affect the industry's output. A notable example, already cited, is the development of special bras for aerobics, in response to the interest in fitness. In loungewear and nightwear, in which looks are more important than function, the relation to fashion is clear indeed. The customer, consciously or otherwise, tends to seek out the same general effects, the same overall looks, that she has been seeing in apparel displays and on smartly dressed individuals in their areas.

Importance of Brand and Designer Names

The brand names of producers in this industry have traditionally been so important that store buyers tend to budget their purchases by resource or vendor rather than by merchandise category. This practice goes back to the days when foundation garments had to be carefully fitted to individual customers. Leading manufacturers, in those days, took a major share of responsibility for planning retail stocks and training sales-people in stores that carried their lines.

Among the best-known names in foundations are Warner (the oldest in the field), FormFit-Rogers, Lily of France, Maidenform, Bali, Olga, and Playtex. In the lingerie area, well-known brands include Vanity Fair, Barbizon, Oscar de la Renta, Christian Dior, Vassarette, Natori, Eileen West for Queen Anne's Lace, and Eve Stillman. However, many of these long-established national names are facing competition by a new breed of megabrands being churned out by corporate creators like Hanes Her Way, Victoria's Secret, and Wonderbra. In the 1990s, apparel giants Sara Lee, VF Corporation, and Warnaco had hearty appetites to acquire or license other brands and high-profile names such as Ralph Lauren Intimates at Sara Lee, Lily of France at the Bestform division of VF, and the Calvin Klein Underwear and Bodyslimmers at Warnaco. Experts believe there are almost no more big-name brands to be acquired (Monget, 2000).

As would be expected in a field where brand names are important, producers advertise widely along three fronts: directly to the consumer in print and television, through cooperative advertising with retail stores, and to retail stores through trade publications. Some companies also provide stores with display fixtures, on which their brand names appear, for use in featuring the particular brand in windows and store interiors. The Internet has added a new medium for marketing and sales, with companies such as Victoria's Secret reaping healthy sales. The company moved cautiously into online sales, anticipating that its provocative merchandise would attract many gawkers (Quick, 1998).

The importance of designer names in marketing fashion merchandise is mirrored in the many licensing arrangements that exist between intimate apparel producers and leading designers of outerwear. Bill Blass, for example, designs robes and loungewear for Evelyn Pearson Company; Christian Dior is licensed to Carol Hochman Designs; and Warnaco licenses Olga, Valentino Intimo, and Ungaro. Jockey produces Liz Claiborne Intimates under a licensing agreement. Previously, Calvin Klein licensed his name in underwear and sleepwear, but now Calvin Klein underwear is part of Warnaco.

According to the designers themselves, their objective is to apply to their intimate apparel collections the interpretation of fashion that they present in their ready-to-wear collections. Thus, the seasons' changes in silhouette and fabrication, as they see them, are reflected in intimate apparel as well as in streetwear.

Global Activities

Globalization has affected the intimate apparel industry as it has every other segment of the fashion industry. Imports generally play their greatest role where production is labor intensive, as in intricately sewn and embroidered loungewear and sleepwear, because of the quality of handwork and the advantageous pricing. Bras, for example, have extensive and intricate sewing. Many U.S. apparel manufacturers have their own lines of intimate apparel produced in lower-wage countries, and retailers have goods produced overseas for presentation under their private labels. Direct import of European-brand bras occurs among some of the prestigious fashion stores, such as Saks Fifth Avenue, which features French bras from Prima and LeJaby and Italian bras from LaPerla. The major offshore bra production center, however, is the Philippines, where such companies as Lovable, Bali, and Warner's have their lines produced. In second place after the Philippines is Costa Rica. For robes and dressing gowns, Hong Kong and China are the major import sources.

The Cosmetics Industry

The cosmetics industry (sometimes called the beauty industry), a companion to the fashion industry, is based on the age-old quest for improving on that which nature gave us. As Baltasar Gracian noted: "Nature scarcely ever gives us the very best; for that we must have recourse to art" (source unknown). Cosmetics provide an important medium for that "art" of enhancing one's appearance.

The cosmetics industry is enormous *worldwide*, with the top 100 companies accounting for over $90 billion in beauty sales. The United States is the leader in volume terms—nearly 40 billion, well over 40 percent of the worldwide total. In some firms, such as Procter and Gamble Co., cosmetic/beauty sales are just a part of a much larger conglomerate; thus, these figures include only the cosmetic segment of the company. In other firms, the entire company may be devoted to cosmetic and beauty products. The 10 largest companies worldwide are shown in Table 8–3.

Many segments of the cosmetics/beauty industry are intensely competitive. The industry has been in existence for so long that an oversupply of competing companies abounds. This means that continuous introduction of new products and product-line extensions are necessary, as well as the development of niches or features that differentiate among products. Short product life cycles, pricing pressures, and shrinking research and development budgets are requiring close collaboration between the industry and its suppliers.

Consumers want value in terms of both price and performance; thus, products must be multifunctional, effective, user friendly, fast, convenient, and preferably, discounted. Consumer concerns for the environment have created demands for products that contain natural ingredients, that are mild and biodegradable, and that minimize impact on the environment—either during the manufacturing process, during use, and of postconsumer product waste. Similarly, many consumers boycott products that require animal testing.

In a notable example, consumer demand has drastically changed the fragrance industry. In the 1970s and 1980s, pricey designer fragrances were developed and promoted widely. As more than 400 new fragrances were launched in the 1980s, hype abounded. Scent strips were placed in magazines, and roving sales staff in white lab coats dispensed samples. Toward the end of this "high fragrance" era in the 1980s, perfumers increased the amount of essential oils to make scents even stronger. Offices, waiting rooms, elevators, and commuter trains were often an overwhelming blend of strong fragrances. One New York restaurant even banned the potent Giorgio fragrance, along with cigars and pipe smoking. Soon, many of these designer fragrances were sold at discounters and other mass-market channels. Upwardly mobile women began to shun the overbearing scents in favor of lighter, more natural fragrances. Fragrance sales slowed. Fashion designers caught the mood and introduced toned-down fragrances. The industry has followed, simply because consumers began to avoid the overpowering scents.

Globalization is surely a fact of life in the cosmetics/beauty industry. Avon products were in Asian markets early on. Avon representatives may travel in boats to make calls on customers deep in the heart of Brazil's Amazon region. Clinique products can be found in major cities almost anywhere in the world. Companies with high-visibility brands such as these can sell a global formula (sometimes with variations to respond to different skin colors or cultural differences) under a universal brand in a

Table 8–3	The World's Top 10 Cosmetics Companies		
Rank & Company	**Sales (1999)**	**Ownership**	**Relevant Information**
1. L'Oréal Group (France)	$11.2 billion	French holding co., Nestlé, and traded on Paris Bourse	In a strong acquisition mode and moving into many new regions of the world. Owns Maybelline (acquired in 1996) and turning it into a global brand. Other brands include: L'Oréal, Lancôme, Garnier, Vichy, Ralph Lauren, Biotherm, Giorgio Armani, Helena Rubinstein, Redkin, and more. Strong in ethnic hair and skin care, acquiring Soft Sheen Products, Inc. and Carson, Inc.
2. Procter and Gamble (Cincinnati, OH)	$7.5 billion (est.)	Traded on NY Stock Exchange	Max Factor, Olay (cosmetics and skin care), Old Spice, Hugo Boss, Noxema, Georgio, Physique, Vidal Sassoon, Head and Shoulders, and many others. Cover Girl expanded line and had TV spots featuring diversity. Introduced Olay color cosmetics. New Pantene products. Helmut Lang signature scent.
3. Unilever (Rotterdam & London)	$6.9 billion	Traded on NY, London, and Amsterdam stock exchanges	In 2000, Unilever created Unilever Cosmetics International to manage its global portfolio of prestige beauty and fragrance brands. Calvin Klein Cosmetics is a division and does very well. Elizabeth Arden line continues to struggle. Chloé, Pond's, Elizabeth Taylor fragrances, Vera Wang, Cerruti fragrances, Helen Curtis, Suave, Finesse, and many others
4. Shiseido Co. (Tokyo)	$4.9 billion	Traded on Tokyo Stock Exchange	Shiseido has had declines in Japanese market (because of Japanese economy) but has an active global expansion program in 60 or more countries—40% of business is outside Japan. Formed strategic alliance with Johnson & Johnson in skin and hair care. Catering to Asia's growing middle class. Opened NY store in 1998. Active multibrand marketing strategy.
5. The Estée Lauder Cos. Inc. (New York)	$4.2 billion	Lauder family owns 70%; the rest traded on NY Stock Exchange	Active acquisition strategy as well as worldwide expansion of existing brands. Estée Lauder, Clinique, Aramis, Tommy Hilfiger, Prescriptives, Donna Karan, Origins, MAC cosmetics, La Mer, Kate Spade, and others. In 1997, entered the mass market with Jane cosmetics and Aveda Corp. Consistent, strong results in fragrances. Developing comprehensive Internet strategy, including a multibrand strategy. Divisions will use gloss.com, which Lauder acquired as a beauty portal.

(Continued)

Table 8–3	The World's Top 10 Cosmetics Companies *(Continued)*

Rank & Company	Sales (1999)	Ownership	Relevant Information
6. Johnson & Johnson (New Brunswick, NJ)	$3.4 billion	Traded on NY Stock Exchange	Major skin care lines include Neutrogena, ROC, Clean & Clear, Johnson's pH5.5, and Johnson's baby skin care. Neutrogena line introduces new products and is very successful. New products introduced under Aveeno banner. Major expansion programs underway to increase sales in Europe and Asia.
7. Avon Products, Inc. (New York)	$3.2 billion	Traded on NY Stock Exchange	Personal Avon representatives (2.8 million of them) sell 98% of sales worldwide. First store opened in NY in 1998, and sales representatives allowed to open kiosks in malls and have their own individual home pages linked to Avon's e-commerce site. New line targeted to teens with affordable, trendy colors. First global advertising campaign launched in 2000.
8. KAO Corp. (Tokyo)	$2.6 billion	Traded on Tokyo and Osaka stock exchanges	Sluggish Asian economy has hurt sales, but strong U.S. sales have offset this. Very successful introduction of Bioré Pore Pack in Japan, creating a new concept in skin care that was an immediate hit in the U.S. Many Bioré extensions of line. In 1998, purchased Bausch & Lomb's skin care business, including Curel skin care and Soft Sense body care. Jergens, Qualité, Trendline, Merit, and others.
9. Beirsdorg AG (Hamburg, Germany)	$2.5 billion	Based in Hamburg, Germany	This company replaced Revlon in the #10 spot in 1999 and moved to #9 in 2000. Strong, growing presence in Europe. Many skin care products and Nivea cosmetics had double-digit gains for 10 years in a row. Many anti-aging products that appeal to aging baby boomers, such as Cellular Lipo-Sculpting Systeme and Age Management Retexturizing Booster.
10. Wella Group (Darmstadt, Germany)	$2.4 billion	Founding family holds majority shares; traded on German, Swiss, and Austrian stock exchanges	Fragrances were consolidated into a new holding company, Cosmopolitan Cosmetics, which includes Rochas, Gucci, Muelhens and many licensed fragrances: Dunhill, Ellen Tracy, Chiemsee, Anna Sui, Mexx and Naomi Campbell. Wella is third in the global hair care market.

Source: Adapted from Keon, T., "The Beauty Top 100," *Women's Wear Daily*, September 1998 (special beauty supplement), pp. 12, 16, 18; and same supplements September 1999, pp. 8, 10 and September 2000, pp. 8, 10.

universal package. It is usually the brand that sells. Because of slow industry growth in the mature markets of the developed countries, such as the United States and Western Europe, companies have entered the markets of less-developed countries where consumer income makes this realistic.

In the United States, the consumer determines the fate of a cosmetics company, and those firms that fail to meet changing needs will be doomed to failure. The consumer is educated, busy, environmentally concerned, and price conscious. The consumer is also aging, and products to help baby boomers resist the impact of the aging process will continue to proliferate in the years ahead. Also, the population has become more diverse. As the proportions of African Americans, Hispanics, and Asians continue to increase, products will have to appeal to the diversity of the population.

The retail market in which cosmetic/beauty products are sold is intensely competitive. Retailers in a broad range of market channels sell these products—specialty stores, department stores, major chains, discounters, and chain drug stores. Some companies are selling directly to the consumer via the Internet. Home pages communicate product information, corporate policies, and product promotions and even provide an opportunity for direct feedback.

Readings

The accessories industries and the intimate apparel/undergarment industries have experienced many significant fashion changes as well as the same competitive pressures affecting other segments of the fashion industry. These articles feature a look back over changes in accessory fashions and consumer shopping patterns in the intimate apparel/hosiery market.

A Century of Accessories

This article provides a brief retrospective by decade of accessory fashions in the last century. Accessory fashions naturally paralleled and complemented broader fashion changes.

Consumer Infidelity

Consumers are no longer loyal to a particular store or type of store. Instead, they have become "cross-shoppers" who look for the best values among all types of retailers, increasingly favoring discounters for intimate apparel.

A Century of Accessories

1900s: The Good Old Days

At the dawn of the 20th century, optimism was in the air. Teddy Roosevelt was in office and the economy had taken a turn for the better. Everyone was in the mood to splurge. Multimillionaires, including the Vanderbilts and the Carnegies, shelled out millions for ornate mansions in Newport, Rhode Island and New York City, while those with less-deep pockets motored around in Model T's, which rolled out in 1908. In search of the latest trends, wealthy women traveled by ship to Paris and other European cities. They brought back hats which became literally huge, both in size and popularity. Styles ranged from dusters to veiled styles that featured feathers and other flamboyant details.

The end of the Victorian Era, marked by the passing of Queen Victoria, had brought a metamorphosis in fashion; everything became more festive. Women, freed from the corset bondage typical of Edwardian full skirts, slipped into slimmer, more linear silhouettes. Because the new, narrower styles made pockets unflattering, handbags became important and women gravitated toward styles that featured gold-plated mesh metal and fancy bead work. Other popular accessories that enhanced the simpler apparel of the day were scarves, intricate hair combs and sterling silver shoe and belt buckles. In stockings, gold and red were favored over black when the hobble skirt, which exposed a full two inches of leg, became popular.

Source: From "A Century of Accessories," Accessories Magazine *(special edition), December 1999, pp. 27, 37, 49, 63, 77, 91, 102, 123, 137, and 153.*

Many accessory looks grew out of the pop culture of the time. The sporty physique of the Gibson Girl (created by illustrator Charles Dana Gibson) was considered the "ideal" for the young American female and was the impetus for accessories like the sailor hat, windsor collar and bow tie. Meanwhile, a more sophisticated image was perpetuated by the Ziegfeld Follies, which debuted on Broadway in 1907. The Follies promoted tall, slender beauties over the buxom girls of the past. This new standard of beauty inspired designers such as Paul Poiret of France to introduce orientalism into fashion, with jewel embroidery, turbans and egret-feather detail.

1910s: A Time of Change

Fashion moved into the limelight when the movie business took off in Hollywood and starlets like Theda Bara and Mary Pickford wore the latest garb. Enhancing public interest in fashion were fashion shows which officially took off in 1910 with Gimbel's infamous Promenades des Toilettes. On film reels and on runways, apparel trends were complemented by elaborate accessories. These included some of the biggest hats in history. Made from beautiful silks and velvets, they were heavily ornamented with flowers, beads, bows and ostrich plumes. Women of the day also fancied beaded and embroidered handbags, large feather fans and jeweled hair accessories.

By the middle of the decade, World War I had pushed fashion out of the limelight as more and more women were forced into service. The turning point occurred in 1917, when the war, which had been raging in Europe for nearly three years, involved the United States. Because women were called onto the battlefields as ambulance drivers, nurses and auto mechanics, and those who stayed at home worked as streetcar conductors and wireless operators and on assembly lines, the fashion order of the day was functional clothing and accessories that allowed for speed and freedom of movement.

Because of the war and the Audubon Society's ban on feathers (egret feathers and those from birds of paradise), hats became simpler; feathers and other embellishments were replaced with scarves and dust-proof veils. And since staying warm was a priority, fur accessories like muffs and collars became fashionable. Wristwatches were also important, but for practical reasons. Although they were invented in 1907 by Louis Cartier, it wasn't until the next decade that a wider selection of styles by makers such as Movado brought them into the mainstream.

1920s: The Flapper Age

Defiance became a popular attitude following World War I, and the flapper emerged as the quintessential image of the decade. She bobbed her hair, bound her breasts, swore, smoked cigarettes, wore bright lipstick and seemed to be everywhere. In knee-length dresses, she did the Charleston in dancehalls across America and was immortalized by F. Scott Fitzgerald in his novel, *The Great Gatsby*. She will always be remembered for her spirit and her accessories, which included long strands of pearls, the cloche hat, black-ostrich-feather and marabou boas, fringed handbags and cigarette holders in ivory and horn.

The flapper's erotic and strange, boylike image became a launching pad for fashion jewelry, a commodity that had been out of place during the previous decade. Fringe and drop earrings and long rope necklaces in beads and pearls became a sign of "good taste," due to the influence of top Parisian designers such as Chanel and Schiaparelli. And as interest in these more novel designs escalated, people paid less attention to the traditional hair combs and shoe buckles that the former decade brought to prominence.

Other accessories favored by fashion-minded women included elegant beaded drawstring bags and the close-fitting cloche, which was often worn pulled down to the eyebrows. In fact, the cloche was part of a strict daily millinery routine that started in the early twenties. The trend called for women to wear a small, chic hat in the morning; a larger-brimmed, decidedly feminine hat to formal afternoon events;

and a more elaborately decorated hat for evening. It's also interesting to note that the discovery of King Tut's tomb in 1922 led to a fascination with Egyptian-style clothing and accessories, from scarab jewelry to velvet and gold-braided hats.

1930s: Rags to Riches

After Black Thursday hit in October 1929 and the stock market crashed, the Roaring Twenties abruptly gave way to the Great Depression. Franklin D. Roosevelt, who was elected president in 1933, had his work cut out for him. A quarter of the labor force was now unemployed and bread lines spanned the country. Nevertheless, it was a great time for the entertainment industry and the "silver screen," which offered an escape from the depressing reality of daily life.

Starlets in glittering jewels—including Marlene Dietrich, Greta Garbo, Joan Crawford and Jean Harlow—reminded women of better days. And as poor little rich girl Barbara Hutton set a trend for orange lipstick, green eyeshadow and Cartier jewelry, Bonnie Parker (girlfriend of Clyde) sparked interest in sleek sweater-and-skirt combos worn with a saucy beret.

These public personalities inspired American women to buy accessories. They bought into artificial flowers, brightly colored chiffon handkerchiefs and beads, which they could drape down the backs of backless dresses. Scarves were big, as well as small, shapely hats, diamond clips, clutch handbags, large studded rings and elaborate strands of pearls. And while the starlets were wearing authentic gems and metals, Coco Chanel made costume jewelry socially acceptable among the wartime crowd used to wearing the real thing.

Art deco jewelry became an important style direction in the thirties, dominating both the costume and real fronts. Characterized by clean lines and angular geometric shapes, designs featured everything from green jade and black onyx to coral and turquoise. Joan Crawford contributed to the deco bracelet's popularity. She not only wore some version of the bracelet on screen, she was known for her personal collection, which featured cabochons and vibrant-colored stones.

As the Depression lifted in the latter part of the decade, those who were lucky could afford real jewelry as well as silk stockings—a luxury that was quickly upstaged by nylon. Nylon was introduced on

October 27, 1938, and touted, "strong as steel yet as fine as a spider's web."

Seeing the value of a textile fiber synthesized entirely from chemicals, Christian Dior would be the first designer to license his name to a collection of nylon stockings during the following decade.

1940s: Moods Swing

The forties began on a somber note, due to the onset of World War II. Women were forced to work in factories and on battlefields and, most of the time, required looser, more-functional clothing and accessories. Styles of the day ranged from WAC uniforms to structured suits and dresses. These tailored styles, popularized by stars such as Joan Crawford, featured sharp angles that exaggerated a women's hips and breasts. Elsa Schiaparelli added another angle to forties-style apparel with shoulder pads.

Although there was a definite forties look in demand, selections at stores were limited, due to fabric and material shortages. Especially in short supply were nylon and silk stockings, which were commandeered by the military. The shortage generated near hysteria among stockingless women, as well as an interest in leg makeup. In fact, it wasn't uncommon to see women with penciled-on seams doing the jitterbug or dancing to the sounds of big bands.

In headwear, practical styles to protect the hair—including bandannas, scarves and turbans—upstaged glamorous hats. Especially in demand were knitted or crocheted snoods, which stylishly held the hair in place at the nape of the neck. Stars such as Katharine Hepburn and Lana Turner increased the popularity of scarves by wearing them around their heads turban style, using them to tie their hair back, and wearing them around their necks.

The war also affected what was happening in jewelry. Because the military had siphoned off more steel than the U.S. could produce, domestic manufacturers turned to plastic as an inexpensive substitute. While sterling vermeil designs were prevalent, bakalite (jewelry made with plastic) became common. Bakalite styles including elaborate enamel flower pins, oversized charm bracelets and pearl chokers surfaced. All were made with trace amounts of metal.

In the heady period that followed World War II, a new prosperity blanketed much of America, and accessories graduated to a new status. No longer just functional pieces, they became luxuries,

and ranged from trendy to designer chic. Teenagers who wore white ankle socks with loafers were called "bobby-soxers," and in 1947, designers reintroduced lower hemlines and opulent fabric to women's fashions. One of the day's most notable designers was Balenciaga; he was well on the road to prominence in the early forties after opening his first shop in Paris.

1950s: Let the Good Times Roll

In the fifties, the postwar boom was in full swing—everyone, it seemed, had a house in the suburbs, two cars in the garage and money to burn. Shopping malls exploded as consumerism flourished like it never had before. And thanks to Dior's New Look, anything French sold, whether it was the designer's signature fit and flare dresses, toy poodles or cuisine. In 1953, Buxton introduced the "French purse" an innovatively-designed framed wallet for women. The company's ad featured a French poodle in the arms of a gloved model, reinforcing gloves as an essential accessory. In fact, gloves and hats became so important they were required at job interviews. Some handbags even featured an attached glove holder. Lucille Ball, the beloved comic of America's first major sitcom *I Love Lucy*, never left home without wearing a hat and gloves.

Meanwhile, teenagers hula-hooped in poodle skirts, saddle shoes and bobby socks. A pin with coordinating earrings were the accessories to wear with the "twinset," a wardrobe staple. In fact, costume jewelry of any kind was all the rage. Plastic beads or "pop" beads were popular in matching earrings, necklaces and bracelets. Pearls, rhinestones and costume jewelry accented with Austrian crystals also gained momentum. The Italians influenced American style by making sunbathing fashionable—hence the growing popularity of Italian leather sandals and sunglasses. The wayfarer sunglass frame, which debuted in 1952, became a perennial sunwear classic and was revived in the '80s. Lucite handbags complemented this Mediterranean resort look.

In Monte Carlo, actress-turned-princess Grace Kelly raised Hermé scarves and handbags to accessory status symbols. Other classic accessories of the moment were handbags by Louis Vuitton and Chanel. When Audrey Hepburn appeared in the movie *Roman Holiday*, her chic style, honed by designer Givenchy, became much imitated. Hepburn also helped bring the all-black Beatnik look into the mainstream. In 1959, pantyhose were invented and marketed by Glen Raven Mills Panty-legs and a new doll from Mattel was born. She was called Barbie.

1960s: The Swinging Sixties

It was the decade of peace, free love and protest. Teenagers went from screaming for the Beatles on the Ed Sullivan Show to smoking pot at Woodstock. The sixties opened with Jacqueline Kennedy looking every bit the first lady in her Oleg Cassini suit topped off with a pillbox hat, Kenneth Jay Lane pearls and a patent leather handbag. In 1965, the miniskirt launched a hemline revolution. It was often paired with white go-go boots and textured knit legwear. Stockings represented 72.7 percent of hosiery business in the mid-sixties, but by the end of the decade, they represented less than 6 percent, with pantyhose taking the lead from then on.

In the later sixties the hippie look came to the forefront. Its hallmarks were bell bottom pants, floppy hats and lots of fringe. The popular TV show *Laugh-In* featured a go-go dancing Goldie Hawn replete with false eyelashes, blue eyeshadow, pale pink lipstick and flower body art. In fact, the power of flowers—and peace signs—was evident on every kind of accessory, from pendants and rings to handbags to scarves. Models Twiggy and Jean Shrimpton redefined beauty with their "Mod" looks while working in Britain, which was where "it" was happening. Meanwhile France grooved on when designers like André Correges, Emmanual Ungaro and Pierre Cardin followed the London lead.

Yves Saint Laurent helped popularize the gypsy look during the turn of the decade with ethnic jewelry, head scarves and long, flowing maxi skirts. Pierced ears also became more common and hair was worn teased or with hairpieces like top knots chignons, falls and braids. Whatever was trending, television helped expedite the wave. The medium became more powerful than ever as historic events were witnessed before the nation's eyes.

1970s: Boogie Nights and Polyester Days

Disco fever gripped the '70s and polyester—whether it was used in a leisure suit or in a jersey knit Diane Von Furstenberg-inspired wrap dress—was the fabric of choice. Even John Travolta's three-piece ensemble in *Saturday Night Fever* stayed wrinkle free as he boogied to the Bee Gees. Halston showed liquid-jersey apparel by day and danced at Studio 54 by night. In fact, American designers began giving the French a good run. Anne Klein (with her assistant Donna Karan), Bill Blass and Oscar de la Renta stressed comfort dressing, which made knitwear chic. Crochet-knit hats and scarves also became popular, thanks to Ali McGraw's look in the movie *Love Story*.

McGraw also promoted the natural look with makeup that was barely visible and hair that was long and straight, not teased or adorned with hairpieces. This natural movement impacted the hosiery industry, too: Girdles all but died, while pantyhose continued to rise thanks to Hanes surprising spokesperson, Joe Namath, and L'eggs Sheer Energy ads promoting comfort and ease in legwear that looked barely there.

Still, some accessories were as bold as a mirrored disco globe. Large handbags (such as those designed by Carlos Falchi), wide, studded belts; dog collars, feather-duster earrings and mesh disco bags were nothing short of over-the-top. Jackie Kennedy Onassis set a trend once again; this time with oversized sunglasses. In 1977, the Annie Hall look—which included menswear vests, ties and fedoras for women—became the epitome of funky chic. The movie's therapy scenes reflected society's obsession with personal growth, which is why the seventies were coined "The Me Decade."

1980s: The Glitzy and Greedy '80s

The era of conspicuous consumption kicked off with a fairy tale wedding between Prince Charles and Lady Diana Spencer, a shy 19-year-old who, as the decade unfolded, blossomed into a confident fashion icon. Whether she was sporting a saucy sailor hat or a pouf dress, the princess possessed a style that was imitated everywhere. Meanwhile, women the world over became more confident as they marched into the workplace—linebacker shoulder pads firmly in place—in record numbers.

Dynasty prime-time divas Linda Evans and Joan Collins who wore over-the-top glitzy faux jewelry epitomized the power and glamour of the times. Designer handbags became the defining status accessory; especially hot were those with a gold chain and a Chanel logo. A Coach or Dooney & Bourke handbag was an essential part of a woman's wardrobe too. In 1983, Swatch came out with a fashion watch in plastic that sold for about $25 and sales skyrocketed. It forever changed the watch market since women began to collect a wardrobe of moderately-priced timepieces. Exercise queen Jane Fonda brought fitness—and leg warmers—to the masses through her videos. Jennifer Beals in the movie *Flashdance* made ripped sweatshirts and bodywear popular. A young women named Madonna took the pop music world by storm with her single "Like A Virgin" and suddenly cross pendants, rosary beads, rubber bracelets and lingerie-inspired apparel were all the rage.

Meanwhile, Nancy Reagan was hosting lavish affairs at the White House wearing red Galanos gowns. American designers like Ralph Lauren, Donna Karan, Calvin Klein and Bill Blass became household names by catering to both career women and "ladies who lunch." Designer names and logos were sought after. Feeding into the "bigger and bolder" fashion message of the era was Donna Karan with contour belts featuring bold gold hardware designed by Robert Lee Morris. Wall Street types benefited from a bull market enabling them to megaspend on megahouses. The whole idea was to look rich, even if you weren't. So women layered on the fake gold chains and pearls while carrying their faux alligator bags. Gordon Gecco, a character played by Michael Douglas in the movie *Wall Street*, summarized the decade's mood in one sentence: "Greed is good." But all this hyperspending came to a screeching halt on October 19, 1987, when the stock market crashed on Black Monday. Soon after, a gloomy recession set in.

1990s: From Minimalism to Embellishment

The early nineties were plagued by recession but by 1997, Wall Street had recovered nicely and was enjoying its longest bull run in history. Fashion also experienced some extremes. First there was grunge, which was epitomized by combat boots paired with slip dresses. Next, the minimalist movement took off, thanks to ready-to-wear designers like Helmut Lang, Calvin Klein and Jill Sander.

By the mid-nineties, minimalism began to subside. Trendier styles like the Y-necklace gave jewelry a boost. Shortly after, Renee Russo popularized a simple pearl necklace, aptly named after the movie in which it appeared, *Tin Cup*. Bridge jewelry made a comeback since women realized they could buy silver jewelry for about the same price as costume jewelry. And, thanks to the neckerchief craze, the scarf industry enjoyed a surge. In 1998, the blockbuster movie *Titanic* created a sudden interest in embellished romantic accessories. Velvet-burnout oblong scarves, embroidered and beaded evening bags and hair jewelry with butterfly and dragonfly motifs were embraced enthusiastically.

Still, the savvy shopper demanded function, which propelled the utilitarian movement. Hands free bags, polarized sunglasses and anything with organizational features—from multifunction belts to pants with cargo pockets—were embraced by consumers in pursuit of simplifying their busy lives.

Contributing to this functional trend were Italian designers from Gianni Versace to Miuccia Prada who made microfiber backpacks fashionable. Hot new designers such as Kate Spade also generated interest in lighter-weight microfiber. When women discovered just how durable and affordable microfiber styles were, leather oftentimes took a back seat.

By the last year of the century, accessories took on a spiritual twist. Message bracelets featuring words like "peace" and power bracelets in semiprecious stones were worn to inspire everything from creativity to success. Eastern Sari looks in handbags and scarves made of raw silk and mirrored accents took this spiritual movement to the next level.

It's clear that accessories during the nineties went full circle. After beginning on a minimalist note, gold chains and bold logos became chic once again. Then, as the economy improved and consumerism was at its height, relief was found in spiritual accessories that seemed to have a calming effect.

As the baby boomer's children—Generation Y and X—come of age, it will be interesting to see what accessories they choose as they make their own mark on the 21st century.

Consumer Infidelity

by Robin Lewis

Women are fickle, if not downright promiscuous, when it comes to where they buy their intimate apparel and hosiery. She'll buy a bra in Wal-Mart, Penney's, Nordstrom, or Victoria's Secret, according to whatever tickles her fancy at the moment. She'll buy sleepwear in Saks, panties in Kmart and hosiery at Ann Taylor, depending on the mood that moves her.

Cross-shopping, or the purchase of different apparel items in different stores or retail channels, is here. Store loyalty for the lifetime apparel needs of any one consumer appears to be a thing of the past.

While department stores once had the lion's share of intimate apparel, their position has been under constant fire, mainly by the discounters and specialty stores, which have been steadily taking chunks of their business.

Discounters, in fact, now control the largest share of the intimate apparel category. In hosiery, the discounters and food/drug outlets dominate and, along with direct mailers, continue to capture more share. Department store share continues to slip.

These shifts are clearly consumer-driven, as consumers exploit virtually unlimited shopping options.

If it's a rush to save time, a consumer might seek the convenience of a specialty store nearby. If the goal is spending less, she might pursue discount store options. Or, if her value requirement is for a more fashion-forward item, the consumer may shop across several department and specialty stores.

This is a consumer who is loyal to no one, who has different value needs at different times and is clearly taking advantage of an overabundance of choice.

However, while the consumer may appear to be promiscuous about where she shops, she's actually more discerning than ever. They buy for very specific reasons. They're also smarter and have a clear idea of what an item is worth. Finally, they know precisely where they can get the best value for the least amount of time and effort.

None of this has to do with having a favorite store, although a shopper may have six favorite stores across all distribution channels. In fact, what some see as promiscuity is really polygamy: the new consumer is discriminately married to many different stores for many different occasions and needs.

The same polygamy exists when choosing between the national brands and private label (which includes store brands). Indeed, in every category except bras, private label is growing in market share while the brands are losing. This indicates both a discerning and more intelligent consumer; she makes a purchase decision based on her own specific value equation, as opposed to being lured simply by the lowest price or the more ephemeral promises of a brand's advertising.

The apparent loyalty to the national brands in the bra category, in addition to the fact that women are willing to pay regular price, merely reinforces the concept of the discriminating consumer. Part of this loyalty obviously stems from the consumers' requirements for fit, function and comfort. However, it also points to the fact that the branded suppliers long ago focused on learning what their consumer wanted in a bra and then painstakingly

Source: From Women's Wear Daily, March 13, 1995, p. 2. Reprinted by permission.

designed, merchandised and marketed their product. Apparently, they are still doing so today. The bra experience provides a clear example of successful strategies that might well be employed by the suppliers and retailers in the other product categories, in order to court the cross-shopper.

As with bras, hosiery brands apparently provide added value over private label. Although the consumer's product requirements are somewhat different than for bras, if she can find those values more conveniently, and at prices she perceives as fair, the type of store she buys from is not a major concern. This is clearly a product category in which the knowledgeable and discerning consumer has a specific set of value requirements and knows the retail outlets that can deliver them.

In many cases, the stores she chooses are brand names themselves, such as Victoria's Secret, which, from the consumers' perspective, provide value equal to the "national brands." Therefore, this form of private labeling will continue to grow. It provides the consumer with branded value and provides the retailer with greater pricing and margin flexibility.

So, as they improve their sourcing skills, retailers will increasingly compete with the national brands. In effect, they will be marketing their stores as brands. And for those that have outlets nationwide, their sheer physical presence is equivalent to a powerful advertising campaign.

Another indication of a more knowledgeable and discerning consumer is the fact that she is increasingly willing to pay regular price in retail channels that are generally recognized for their lower prices. This describes a consumer who has a clear idea of what something is worth, relative to where she's buying it. It also describes a store that understands this consumer's value equation and knows how to deliver it. Therefore, the consumer will seek the product in that store and happily pay what's asked. These discerning shoppers are also increasing their purchases in these stores at the expense of other retailers who have not responded to the value demands of the consumer.

While the largest share of shoppers across all channels spans the 30-to-64-year-old age group, the 30-to-40 segment is growing at a faster clip. There are also higher incomes across almost all channels, which again signals a heightened selectivity, regardless of traditional perceptions of what a store may have represented in the past. In fact, in the discount tier, consumers with incomes over $60,000 comprise the fastest-growing share. This dramatically illustrates that cross-shopping for different values, across all store types, will be with us well into the next century.

Chapter Review

Key Words and Concepts

Define, identify, or briefly explain the following:

Accessories	Lingerie
Bridge jewelry	Loungewear
Costume jewelry	Nonrubber footwear
Electroplating	Plants
Establishments	Precious stones
Federal Trade Commission Jewelry Guidelines	Private label
Fine jewelry	Shapewear
Firms	Small leather goods
Foundations	Sterling silver
Inner wear	24K
Intimate apparel industry	Undergarments
Karats	Uppers
Last	Vamp

Review Questions on Chapter Highlights

1. How do fashions in accessories relate to apparel fashions? List some examples.
2. How would you compare the women's and men's accessories markets?
3. What are four ways that accessories firms have attempted to attract customers?
4. What four factors do all of the accessory industries have in common?
5. What is the difference between rubber and nonrubber athletic footwear? Why is this distinction made?
6. Why do you think imports account for such a large portion of the U.S. shoe market?
7. Why are imports less "threatening" to the hosiery industry than they are to other segments of accessories?
8. Why are more vinyl and fabric handbags sold than leather ones?

9. What types of products are included in the term *small leather goods*?
10. What are your thoughts on the future of the millinery/hat industry?
11. List the three major categories of jewelry and explain the differences among them.
12. How can the customer check on the quality levels of fine jewelry?
13. Give examples of designer licensing in each product area of the accessories industry.
14. Name the three major divisions of the intimate apparel industry and name one well-known brand name in each.
15. What is the difference between a plant or establishment and a firm?
16. What types of factors influence the cosmetics/beauty industry?

References

A century of accessories. (1999, December). *Accessories*, 26–180.

Agins, T. (1999, November 23). Forget the clothes—fashion fortunes turn on heels and purses. *Wall Street Journal*, pp. A1, A13.

American Apparel Manufacturers Association (AAMA). (1999, 1997). *Focus: An economic profile of the apparel industry.* Arlington, VA: Author.

Byron, J. (2000). Footwear, leather, and leather products. *U.S. Industry and Trade Outlook 2000.* Washington, DC: U.S. Department of Commerce.

Claiborne buys its accessories line. (1985, December 23). *Women's Wear Daily.*

Footwear: Concept stores. (1988, August). *Stores.*

Footwear Industries of America. (1999, April). *Current highlights of the nonrubber footwear industry* (online version: http://www.fia.org). Washington, DC: Author.

Harris, J. (2000). Other consumer durables. *U.S. Industry and Trade Outlook 2000.* Washington, DC: U.S. Department of Commerce.

Hessen, W. (2000, January). Dominating the channels. *Women's Wear Daily* (special report, "The Fairchild 100"), pp. 112, 122.

McGuire, P. (date unknown). Comments from McGuire, Director, Nike Retail Division.

Millinery Institute of America. (1989, June 24). Conversations with publicity directors.

Monget, K. (1999, July 12). Solid year on horizon as innerwear vendors count their blessings. *Women's Wear Daily*, pp. 1, 18–20.

Monget, K. (2000, January). Sex and money fuel megabrands. *Women's Wear Daily* (special report, "The Fairchild 100"), pp. 110, 120.

National Association of Hosiery Manufacturers (NAHM). (1988). *1987 hosiery statistics and profile.* Charlotte, NC: Author.

National Association of Hosiery Manufacturers (NAHM). (2000). *Hosiery statistics annual report.* Charlotte, NC: Author.

1995 national consumer accessories survey. (1995, July). *Accessories*, pp. 36–42.

Pelz, L. R. (1980). *Fashion accessories* (2nd ed.). Indianapolis: Bobbs-Merrill Educational Publishing.

Quick, R. (1998, December 29). Gawkers or shoppers? Selling bras on the web. *Wall Street Journal*, pp. B1, B4.

Quimby, H. (1936, December 30). The story of footwear. *Shoe and Leather Reporter, 216* (13).

Rabon, L. (1998, January). Glovers grip new markets. *Bobbin*, 24–29.

Treber, J. (1990). Conversation between Treber (chief statistician of Footwear Industries of America) and author.

Women's 1999 accessory census. (2000, January). *Accessories*, 62–80.

Selected Bibliography

A century of accessories. (1999, December). *Accessories*, 26–170.

Ball, J., & Torem, D. (1993). *The art of fashion accessories.* Atglen, PA: Schiffer.

Becker, V. (1995). *Art Nouveau Jewelry.* New York: E. P. Dutton.

Boehn, M. von. (1929). *Ornaments: Lace, Fans, Gloves, Walking Sticks, Parasols, Jewelry and Trinkets* (reprint of the 1929 edition). New York: Ayer.

Byron, J. (2000). Footwear, leather, and leather products. *U.S. Industry and Trade Outlook*

2000. Washington, DC: U.S. Department of Commerce.

Clark, F. (1982). *Hats*. London: B. T. Batesford.

Cumming, V. (1982). *Gloves*. London: B. T. Batesford.

Dodd, A. (1998, May 1). The underwear boom: What's beneath it all. *DNR*, p. 12.

Friedman, A. (1998, September 24). Liz Claiborne, Jockey sign pact for innerwear. *Women's Wear Daily*, p. 4.

Gray, M. (1982). *The Lingerie Book*. New York: St. Martin's Press.

Greco, M. (1997, September). Intimate apparel: Shaping up the industry. *Apparel Industry Magazine*, 62–70.

Guilford, R. (1999, November). Understanding the challenges of underwear. *Apparel Industry Magazine*, 50–53.

Harris, J. (2000). Other consumer durables. *U.S. Industry and Trade Outlook 2000*. Washington, DC: U.S. Department of Commerce.

Intimate apparel and shapewear (1997, March). *Apparel Industry Magazine*, 66–70.

Jakubiak, I. (2000, January). Rejuvenating a brand: Helen Welsh is the powerful force behind the revival of Liz Claiborne's accessories. *Accessories*, 22–30.

Johnson, E. (1980). *Fashion Accessories*. Aylesbuey, Bucks, England: Shire.

Karp, J. (1999, July 13). Sri Lanka keeps Victoria's Secret. *Wall Street Journal*, pp. B1, B4.

Kedley, L., & Schiffer, N. (1987). *Costume Jewelry, The Great Pretenders*. Westchester, PA: Schiffer.

Keon, T. The beauty top 100. *Women's Wear Daily*, September 1998 (special beauty supplement),

pp. 12, 16, 18; and same supplements September 1999, pp. 8, 10 and September 2000, pp. 8, 10.

Leather Industries of America, Inc. (annual). *U.S. leather industry statistics*. Washington, DC: Author.

Northampton English Museum. (1975). *A History of Shoe Fashions*. Northampton, England: Museum Pub.

Peltz, L. R. (1986). *Fashion Accessories* (3rd ed.). Encino, CA: Glencoe.

Probert, C. (1981). *Shoes in Vogue since 1910*. New York: Abbeville Press.

Rossi, W. (1988). *Profitable footwear retailing*. New York: Fairchild Books and Visuals.

Schiffer, N. (1987). *The Power of Jewelry*. Westchester, PA: Schiffer.

Swann, J. (1982). *Shoes*. New York: Drama Book.

Tice, B. (1985). *Enticements: How to Look Fabulous in Lingerie*. New York: Macmillan.

U.S. leather industry statistics. (annual). Washington, DC: United States Department of Commerce, Bureau of Census, Industry Division (quarterly). Washington, DC: Author.

The Undercover Story. (1982). New York: Fashion Institute of Technology.

Untracht, O. (1982). *Jewelry Concepts and Technology*. Garden City, NY: Doubleday.

WWD buyer's guide: Women's apparel and accessories manufacturers, 2000. (2000). New York: Fairchild Books and Visuals.

WWD supplier's guide: Women's apparel and accessories manufacturers, 2000. (2000). New York: Fairchild Books and Visuals.

Zucker, B. (1984). *Gems and Jewels: A Connoisseur's Guide*. New York: Thames and Hudson.

Trade Associations

Accessories Council, 522 North St., Greenwich, CT 06830.

American Apparel and Footwear Association, 1601 N. Kent Street, Suite 1200, Arlington, VA 22209.

American Leather Accessory Designers, Kleinberg Sherrill, 392 Fifth Ave., New York, NY 10018.

Association of Umbrella Manufacturers and Suppliers, 11 W. 32nd St., New York, NY 10001.

Belt Association, 330 W. 58th St., #413, New York, NY 10019.

Fashion Accessories Association (Scarf Association), c/o Sharretts, Paley, Carter & Blauvelt, 67 Broad St., New York, NY 10004.

Fashion Accessories Shippers Association, 330 Fifth Ave., New York, NY 10001.

Fashion Footwear Association of New York, 768 Fifth Ave., 17th Floor, New York, NY 10019.

Footwear Industries of America (now part of American Apparel and Footwear Association), 1601 N. Kent Street, Suite 1200, Arlington, VA 22209.

Handbag Supply Salesmen's Association, 176 Madison Ave., 3rd Floor, Washington, DC 20006.

Independent Cosmetic Manufacturers and Distributors, Inc., 1220 West Northwest Highway, Palatine, IL 60067.

Intimate Apparel Council, 150 Fifth Ave., Suite 510, New York, NY 10011.

Leather Industries of America, Inc., 1000 Thomas Jefferson Street, NW, Suite 515, Washington, DC 20007.

Lingerie and Loungewear Association, 555 Chabanel St. W., #801, Montreal, Quebec H2N 2H8, Canada.

Luggage and Leather Goods Manufacturers of America, Inc., 350 Fifth Ave., New York, NY 10118.

Manufacturing Jewelers & Silversmiths of America, Inc., 100 India St., Providence, RI 02903.

Millinery Information Bureau, 302 W. 12th St., New York, NY 10014.

National Association of Hosiery Manufacturers, 200 N. Sharon Amity Rd., Charlotte, NC 28211.

National Fashion Accessories Association, 330 Fifth Ave., New York, NY 10001.

National Shoe Retailers Association, 9861 Broken Land Parkway, Suite 255, Columbia, MD 21046–1151.

Neckwear Association of America, Inc., 151 Lexington Ave., 2nd Floor, New York, NY 10016.

Shoe Manufacturer's Association of Canada, 4101 Sherbrooke St. W., Montreal, Quebec H3Z 1A8, Canada.

Sunglass Association, 71 East Ave., #5, Norwalk, CT 06851.

The Cosmetic, Toiletry, and Fragrance Association, 1101 17th Street, N.W., Washington, DC 20036.

The Fragrance Foundation, 145 E. 32nd Street, 14th Floor, New York, NY 10016.

Soap Cosmetics Chemical Specialties, PTN Publishing Co., 445 Broad Hollow Road, Melville, NJ 11747.

Western Shoe Associates, 1040 East Wardlow Rd., Long Beach, CA 90807.

Trade Publications

Accessories Collection, 912 Cheung Sha Wan Road, Kowloon, Hong Kong.

Accessories Magazine, P.O. Box 5550, Norwalk, CT 06856.

American Jewelry Manufacturer, 1 State Street, Providence, RI 02908–5035.

American Shoemaking and American Shoemaking Directory, Shoe Trades Publishing Co., Inc., 61 Massachusetts Ave., Arlington, MA 02174.

BFIA (Body Fashions/Intimate Apparel), 270 Madison Ave., New York, NY 10016.

DNR, 7 W. 34th St., New York, NY 10001–8191.

Fashion Accessories, Trade Media Ltd., GPO Box 11411, Hong Kong.

Fashion Forecast International, 23 Bloomsbury Sq., London WC1A 2PJ, U.K.

Footwear, 7 W. 34th St., New York, NY 10001–8191.

Footwear Forum, Mackirk Publications, 1448 Lawrence Ave., E., Toronto, Ontario M4A 2V6, Canada.

Footwear News, Fairchild Publications Inc., 7 West 34th Street, New York, NY 10001–8191.

Intimate Fashion News, 307 Fifth Ave., New York, NY 10016.

Jewelers Circular—Keystone, 825 Seventh Ave., New York, NY 10019.

Leather and Footwear in Asia, Benn Electronics Publishing Ltd., Sovereign Way Tonbridge, Kent TN9 1RW, U.K.

Modern Jewelers National. Cygnus Publishing Inc., Broad Hollow Road, Suite 21, Melville, NY 11747.

National Jeweler, Miller Freeman, Inc., 1 Penn Plaza, New York, NY 10119.

Shoe Retailing Today, c/o National Shoe Retailers Association, 9861 Broken Land Parkway, Suite 255, Columbia, MD 21046–1151.

Showcase, Luggage and Leather Goods Manufacturers of America, Inc., 350 Fifth Ave., New York, NY 10118.

Travelware, Business Journals, Inc., 50 Day St., Norwalk, CT 06854.

Women's Wear Daily, 7 W. 34th St., New York, NY 10001–8191.

World Footwear, Shoe Trades Publishing Co., Inc., 61 Massachusetts Ave., Arlington, MA 02174.

CHAPTER 9

*F*ashion Producers
in Other Countries

*P*roducers of fashion merchandise have proliferated in almost every country of the world. Many of these are competing for an ever-increasing share of U.S. consumer dollars. Today, however, many are also partners of U.S. apparel firms and retailers. New communications technologies provide quick connections among business partners and customers on many continents. Global participants are not limited to countries with creative design talent and high-quality products; those with only sewing skills to offer have acquired the know-how to become important players in the world fashion market. In this, most have had the encouragement and support of their respective governments. Eager to promote their foreign trade, their governments have developed export incentive programs as well as help in staging international trade shows to attract business from around the world.

This chapter deals with the nature, locations, and fashion operations of the fashion producers in other countries that supply the United States with goods. The readings that follow the text focus on the operations of leading foreign exporting countries and companies.

Different Types of Producers in Other Countries

Fashion producers in other countries fall into three basic categories, each of which is discussed in greater detail further in this chapter.

- *Haute couture houses.* As used in the fashion business, an **haute couture** house refers to a firm whose designer (in French, **couturier** for male or **couturière** for female) semiannually creates and presents for sale a collection of original designs that are then duplicated for individual customers on a made-to-order basis. The important couture houses are located in Paris and Italy. Although men are important leaders in this part of the industry, the business focuses primarily on women's apparel.

- *Ready-to-wear fashion centers in other countries.* Whereas some ready-to-wear was being produced abroad before World War II, it was not until after the war that major ready-to-wear design and manufacturing centers in foreign countries developed and expanded. They did not achieve their present level of design creativity, importance, prestige, and fashion leadership until the 1970s. Paris is still considered a major fashion center in the world; however, there are now other countries whose manufacturers and products have gained recognition as fashion creators and influentials. Italy, England, Germany, Hong Kong, and Japan are prominent among them. U.S. designers have risen in importance, relative to many of these.
- *Contractors in other countries—offshore production.* The system of using independently owned outside production facilities—the **contracting system**—plays a major role in the production of ready-made clothing. Because contractors can be located anywhere in the world where labor is abundant, wages are reasonable, and facilities, machinery, and transportation are available, today there are countless numbers of factories located in low-wage areas such as China, Indonesia, India, Sri Lanka, Vietnam, Mexico, and the Caribbean. They are used by both U.S. and foreign manufacturers and retailers to produce goods from the designs and specifications of those that hire them.

Paris Haute Couture

The fashion leadership of Europe, notably that of Paris, originally derived from a small group of fashion producers known as the haute couture. The founder of the haute couture is generally acknowledged to be Charles Frederick Worth, a brilliant young English designer with a flair for business who was appointed dressmaker to the Empress Eugenie. He established his house (and the Paris couture) in 1858, at about the same time that Elias Howe, in the United States, was busy perfecting his sewing machine.

European haute couture garments are completely different from those of the American firms that produce the high-priced ready-to-wear that is often incorrectly called "couture ready-to-wear." That description is, of course, a contradiction in terms, because *couture* implies clothes made to measure for individual customers, and *ready-to-wear* means garments produced in standard sizes without regard to the individual measurements of the persons who will eventually purchase them. Haute couture garments, moreover, are made of the finest and most luxurious fabrics, use superb needlework and a great deal of handwork, and command astronomical prices. Nothing produced in the United States bears the slightest resemblance to European couture.

Chambre Syndicale de la Couture Parisienne

Shortly after Worth opened his business, a trade association was formed to determine qualifications for a couture house and to deal with their common problems and interests. This was the **Chambre Syndicale de la Couture Parisienne**, founded in 1868. Membership was, and still is, limited to couturiers who met specified qualifications and agreed to abide by a set of rules governing dates of showings, copying, shipping dates, and so on. Membership is reviewed by a commission under the French Ministry of Industry.

To qualify as an haute couture house today,[1] an establishment must do the following:

- Submit a formal written request for membership in the Chambre Syndicale.
- Employ at least 20 people for production in their own studios.
- Present a collection each year for Spring/Summer (in January) and Fall/Winter (in July) to the media.
- Create a collection of 50 ensembles, consisting of both day and evening designs (previously this was 75 ensembles).
- Present the collection to the clientele of the couture house in places that are arranged for that purpose (Fédération Française, 1995).

For the *newly created houses*, during a transitory period of two years, they must:

- Employ at least 10 production people instead of 20.
- Present a collection of 25 ensembles instead of 50.

The revised number of ensembles required of established houses and the less-rigorous requirements for newly created houses reflect the increased financial burden of developing and presenting extensive collections.

Currently, the official Haute Couture is composed of 18 houses. In the late-1990s, the Haute Couture consisted of the houses shown in Table 9–1.

French origin is not a qualification for membership. For example, couturière Hanae Mori is Japanese by birth. Other famous Paris couture designers of the past were not French by birth. For example, Balenciaga was a Spaniard, Dessè was a Greek, Mainboucher was born in Chicago, and Molyneux was an Englishman, as was the founder of the French couture, Charles Frederick Worth.

Chambre Syndicale du Prêt-à-Porter

Originally the Chambre Syndicale limited its membership strictly to haute couture houses. As ready-to-wear operations by couture houses burgeoned in France, the Chambre Syndicale expanded its membership to include some designer-named ready-to-wear (**prêt-à-porter**) companies. Today, there is a subgroup called the Chambre Syndicale du Prêt-à-Porter des Couturiers et des Créateurs de Mode. These are described as "having a brand name image which is in a league with the couturiers" (Fédération Française, 1995, p. 3). Among these fashion designers who have been designated as créateurs are Chloé, Jean-Paul Gaultier, Karl Lagerfeld, Claude Montana, Dorothée Bis, Jacques Esterel, Thierry Mugler, Sonia Rykiel, Balenciaga, Kenzo, and Hermes. Also "held in equal esteem" are Valentino, Romeo Gigli, and Issey Miyake.

The Chambre was developed originally to act in the interests of French fashion houses and designers and to help young designers get their businesses up and running. Chambre presidents have recognized, however, that to keep Paris as the capital of fashion, they needed to show a panorama of what was the best fashion around the world. This does require a great deal of diplomacy to keep French members happy.

In recent prêt-à-porter showings, foreign designers have been present in unprecedented numbers (more than 30). U.S. retailers who shop the French showings

---

[1]Criteria were revised in 1992 to foster the development of young designers for a two-year period.

Table 9–1	**Paris Haute Couture Directory** **(Chambre Syndicale de la Couture Parisienne)**

PIERRE BALMAIN
Chantal Dannaud-Vizioz*
44, rue François-Ier
75008 Paris
Tel. 47-20-35-34

PIERRE CARDIN
Monique Raimond*
82, fg St-Honoré
75008 Paris
Tel. 42-66-92-25

CARVEN
Sophie Favre*
6, rond-point des Champs-
Elysées
75008 Paris
Tel. 42-25-66-52

CHANEL
Véronique Pérez*
31, rue Cambon
75001 Paris
Tel. 42-86-28-00

CHRISTIAN DIOR
Bernard Danillon and
Véronique Bénard*
30, avenue Montaigne
75008 Paris
Tel. 40-73-54-44

CHRISTIAN LACROIX
Laure du Pavillon*
73, fg St-Honoré
75008 Paris
Tel. 42-68-79-00

EMANUEL UNGARO
Patricia Rivière and Pier
Filippo Pieri*
2, avenue Montaigne
75008 Paris
Tel. 42-23-61-94

NINA RICCI
Vanessa Pringle and Sybille
de Laforcade*
39, avenue Montaigne
75008 Paris
Tel. 49-52-56-00

PACO RABANNE
Alexandre Boulais*
6, bd du Parc
92523 Neuilly
Tel. 40-88-45-45

TED LAPIDUS
Elisabeth Caron-Gendry
and Paule Ouahnoun*
35, rue François Ier
75008 Paris
Tel. 44-43-49-50

GIVENCHY
Sibylle de Saint Phalle and
Véronique de Moussac*
3, avenue George V
75008 Paris
Tel. 44-31-50-00

GUY LAROCHE
Catherine Klein, Eric
Fournier, and Jean-Paul
Caboche*
29, avenue Montaigne
75008 Paris
Tel. 40-69-68-00

HANAE MORI
Max Michel Grand and
Véronique Dupard*
17/19, avenue Montaigne
75008 Paris
Tel. 47-23-52-03

JEAN-LOUIS SCHERRER
Alexandra Campocasso
and Valérie Lebérichel*
51, avenue Montaigne
75008 Paris
Tel. 42-99-05-79

LACOANET HEMANT
Kuki de Salvertes*
24, rue Vieille du Temple
75004 Paris
Tel. 43-57-63-63

LOUIS FÉRAUD
Guy Rambaldi, Ghislaine
Brégé, and Astrid Girod*
88, fg St-Honoré
75008 Paris
Tel. 47-42-18-12

TORRENTE
Béatrice Manson*
1, rond-point des
Champs-Elysées
75008 Paris
Tel. 42-56-14-14

YVES SAINT LAURENT
Gabrielle Buchaert*
5, avenue Marceau
75116 Paris
Tel. 44-31-64-17

*attaché de presse
Source: From Chambre Syndicale de la Couture Parisienne. 1996 update provided through the kind assistance of Pascal Morand, Director General, Institut Français de la Mode in Paris.

have noted the French fashion industry is no longer really French. One store president remarked, "Paris is more important to me as an international city than as the home of French fashion." A store owner noted the new internationalism has many advantages. "Having so many designers represented in Paris is not only more interesting, it's more convenient. . . . If all those people weren't in one place, we'd be running all over the world" (Middleton, 1995, p. 18). Although numerous sources believe France's fashion leadership has diminished, a faithful following still consider it the fashion mecca of the world, as noted by one U.S. store president: "Paris is the place where people go to seek and discover. It's where I go to find the concepts, the spirit, and the mood of the season. I don't go to Paris to decide if green is the color of the month. I go to soak up a gestalt. . . . Milan is more commercial, London is more of a party, but Paris is central to my creative process" (Middleton, 1995, p. 18).

Activities of the Chambre Syndicale

The Chambre Syndicale provides many services for both ready-to-wear and couture members. It represents its members in their relations with the French government, arbitrates disputes, regulates uniform wage arrangements and working hours, coordinates the opening dates and times of the collections, issues admission cards for the openings to the press, and registers and copyrights the new designs of its members. Unlike the United States, France considers the copying of a registered design punishable by law.

Designer-Name Couture Houses

The operations of typical couture firms are fairly uniform. Each establishment is known as a *house*, because it operates in a residential building rather than in a commercial neighborhood. The head of the house is generally the chief designer (the **couturier** or **couturière**), who more often than not is the owner or co-owner. The house usually carries the name of its designer, and its reputation is essentially a one-man or one-woman affair. Occasionally, however, as in the case of Chanel and Dior, the well-known name is retained after the death of the founder, but a new hired designer takes over. For example, Gianco Ferre designs for the house of Dior and Karl Lagerfeld for Chanel.

There are usually fewer than 25 dressmaking establishments at any given time that are designated as haute couture, and of these, not all achieve worldwide fashion reputations. Among famous couturiers of the past are Paul Poiret, Vionnet, Schiaparelli, Balenciaga, Dior, Chanel, Molyneux, and, of course, Worth (Figure 9–1). Of those who show collections currently, the best known of all is probably Yves St. Laurent. Among the Paris couturiers, many have made fashion history, each for some innovative contribution.

Semiannual Collections and Showings

Twice a year, the couturiers prepare major collections of sample garments. They work with the most luxurious and expensive materials, some of which cost more than $200 a yard, and trimmings of equivalent quality. Each sample is made to the exact measurements of the model who will show it. In addition, accessories are created for each garment shown—shoes, hats, gloves, perhaps a fur, and generous amounts of jewelry. The cost of preparing such a collection is extreme, as high as $4 to $5 million.

The heavy costs of preparing the collections plus the rise in the costs of labor and materials have skyrocketed the prices of the custom-made couture garments. They range from $2,000 to $3,000 for a blouse, $9,000 to $20,000 for a suit, and up to $100,000 for an embroidered evening gown.

Until 1980, different types of customers, who came from all over the world to attend the openings, included the following:

- Wealthy private customers, to choose styles to be made to their order for their own wardrobes.

- Trade or commercial buyers (i.e., textile producers, designers, apparel manufacturers, retailers), to buy one or several models for the express purpose of having them copied exactly or adapted into ready-to-wear styles to be produced in their respective countries, or both.
- Pattern companies, to buy models or paper patterns to copy as commercial patterns for home sewers.
- Representatives of the press, to whom couture openings were and still are a source of fashion news.

Figure 9–1

Famous Haute Couture Designers

Cristobal Balenciaga de Eisequirre

Captain Edward Henry Molyneux

Gabrielle Chanel

Paul Poiret

Christian Dior

Mme Vionnet

Elsa Schiaparelli

Private customers and the press were admitted without charge, but most houses charged trade buyers a **caution fee** (French for deposit or surety). This right-to-see fee ranged in amount from as low as $500 in some houses to as high as $3,000. In others, the caution took the form of a minimum required purchase, generally one or two models. The caution was then deducted from the amount of whatever purchases were made; if no purchase was made or if purchases did not equal the caution figure, there was no refund.

Trade buyers were traditionally charged more for a garment than a private customer would be asked to pay. The explanation for the higher price was that retailers and producers were actually buying copying rights as well as the garment, whereas the private customer was simply buying for her own use.

Status of Couture Today: Other Sources of Income for Couture Houses

Today, the astronomical prices of couture garments have become prohibitive to all but a relatively few private clients. Trade buyers no longer attend the openings or buy couture clothing for copying. Even the private clientele—extremely wealthy women from all over the world, whose purchases accounted for a sizable majority of couture clothes at its peak—has eroded from 15,000 in the 1950s to about 2,000 (Fédération Française, 1995). Of these customers, about 20 percent are American and 40 percent are from Asia (Agins, 1995).

Annual couture sales reach $50 million (a very small figure compared to the annual sales of major U.S. apparel firms that cater to mass markets), but this is still a losing proposition for even the most successful houses. This amount involves only the sales of the custom-made apparel produced by the members of the Chambre.

Although the semiannual openings of haute couture houses continue to make worldwide fashion news, the sales of couture garments alone have always cost rather than made money for the houses. To survive, therefore, couture houses have expanded into other, more lucrative ventures, making capital of their names to give luster to more profitable activities, including the following:

- *House boutiques.* Most couture houses have established boutiques in or adjacent to their haute couture premises. These boutiques feature very high-priced, high-quality accessories such as handbags, lingerie, jewelry, and scarfs, all manufactured exclusively for the house by outside producers. Often the accessories thus offered are identical to those worn or carried by the models when the haute couture collections are shown. The merchandise that is carried in the boutiques is designed by the couturier or a member of his staff and bears the designer's prestigious label.

- *Prêt-à-porter.* Beginning in the 1960s, the decline in couture sales, combined with growing competition from an increasing number of talented ready-to-wear designers, both French and other Europeans, led haute couture houses strongly into the prêt-à-porter field. Although the ready-to-wear lines of the couture houses are designed by the couturiers, production arrangements vary greatly among the different houses, as do the locations of the manufacturing plants. For example, Ungaro's ready-to-wear is manufactured by an independently owned Italian company that also makes Valentino's ready-to-wear. Givenchy's ready-to-wear is produced under licensing agreements by ready-to-wear manufacturing companies in France. The house of Yves Saint Laurent has a separate ready-to-wear division, St. Laurent Rive Gauche, whose merchandise is produced in France by a manufacturing company in which it has a financial interest. In all cases, however, the sales volume of their prêt-à-porter lines is far greater than their couture sales and yields a far greater profit.

- *Franchised boutiques.* Retail boutiques bearing the name of a couturier and featuring his ready-to-wear merchandise made their appearance in the late 1960s and spread worldwide, opening a far-flung consumer market for couturier-designed ready-made clothing. Some of these "name" boutiques are owned and operated by the couture house itself; others are run by independently owned retail stores under a **franchising arrangement**. Under such an agreement, an independent retail distributor—that is, a franchisee—is given permission by a franchising parent company to sell the producer's product in a store that bears the name of the parent company. Especially noteworthy today are the franchising operations of Yves Saint Laurent. He launched his first Rive Gauche ready-to-wear boutique in Paris in 1966, and it met with such enormous success that he now has a worldwide chain of franchised Rive Gauche boutiques that carry only Saint Laurent's ready-to-wear. Some of these boutiques are free-standing stores; others are specialized shops within large stores that carry other merchandise as well. Among the couture designers who followed his lead into franchised boutiques are Dior, Valentino, and Givenchy, with his Nouvelle Boutiques.

- *Worldwide licensing agreements.* In addition to their ready-to-wear operations, major couture houses also license the use of their names on an enormous variety of products—lingerie, shoes, perfumes, stockings, bed linens, luggage, children's clothing, lower-priced women's and men's ready-to-wear, and anything else that is fair game for a well-known designer's name. As in all such **licensing agreements**, the designer sells different manufacturing companies the right to produce and market specific products bearing his or her name. Although the licensed products are supposedly designed, screened, or edited by the couturier whose name appears on them, it does not always work out that way. However, what does work in all cases is the lucrative royalty percentage of wholesale sales that the licensed manufacturer pays to the designer.

Despite frequent predictions of its imminent demise, Paris haute couture seems destined to remain active in the foreseeable future. Although Yves Saint Laurent, for example, claimed that his couture garments, each of which sold for many thousands of dollars, were a "gift" to his clients, his business managers did not view his haute couture operation per se as a philanthropic venture. As Jean Szware, general director of Yves Saint Laurent, explained it: "As long as the losses align reasonably with the value gained in publicity and image, the couture is worth maintaining. But it is possible, in view of rising costs and declining sales, that a moment could arrive when this is no longer the case" ("Designer's Grumble," 1976). Because Yves Saint Laurent is still continuing haute couture clothing (under designer Tom Ford), it seems evident that "the moment" has not yet arrived.

At the very least, however, it seems apparent that haute couture garments have a new business function: to publicize the name of the house in order to provide a well-known, prestigious label for use in the house's other, more-lucrative business activities. As Pierre Berge, president of Yves Saint Laurent, said, "No, we don't make a profit on the couture, but it's not a problem. It's our advertising budget" ("Voice of," 1984).

Wall Street Journal senior writer Teri Agins examines, in her timely book, the tremendous changes that have taken place in this fascinating industry and how couture houses are affected:

> *The End of Fashion* (1999) traces an arc from the origins of couture and its apotheosis in the early part of this century to the advent of prêt-à-porter post–World War II and the sweeping changes that have taken place

as the century ends. It is an arc from the time when "fashion" was defined by elite French designers whose clothes could be afforded only by global socialites—but whose designs were copied and followed by everyone else—to the point where the rules are set by *consumers* and the designers must follow *them*. From Balenciaga to Banana Republic; from class to mass; from elitism to democratization; from art to commodity. Above all, this is the story of the triumph of marketing. (Front book flap)

Italian Couture

Although other European countries such as Spain and England have at one time had haute couture houses, the only important couture outside Paris is that of Italy. The Italian couture was organized after World War II along lines similar to those of the Paris couture, but on a much smaller scale. Unlike the French, however, the Italian

Figure 9–2

Inspection of Exquisite Woolen Fabrics in a Major Italian Textile Mill

Source: Photo by Kitty Dickerson.

houses are not headquartered in a single city, but are located in three: Rome, Florence, and Milan. The Italian counterpart of the Chambre Syndicale de la Couture Parisienne is the *Camera Nazionale dell' Alta Moda Italiana*. Its membership of some 13 haute couture houses includes such famous designers as Valentino, Audre Lang, Mila Schon, Galitzine, and Gianco Ferre. Like the Paris couture, the Italian houses present two collections semiannually—in January for Spring/Summer and in July for Fall/Winter, one week prior to the Paris showings.

The experience of the Italian couture parallels that of the Paris houses: couture prices too high for all but a dwindling clientele of the ultrarich; no more trade buyers; and a largely unprofitable couture operation that is subsidized by income from ready-to-wear divisions, franchised boutiques, and licensing fees from perfumes, accessories, and other goods to which a designer's name adds prestige. However, industry experts see the Italians as much more proficient in marketing and knowing the customer than the French.

The Italians also have a tradition of producing exquisite fabrics to support the country's prestigious fashion industry. Known for its fashionable silks, premiere woolens, and other luxury fabrics, Italy's textile industry matches the renown of its designers (See Figure 9–2).

Ready-to-Wear Fashion Centers

Today, there is hardly a country in the world that does not produce some type of ready-to-wear fashion merchandise that is of interest to foreign buyers. Even though creative talent and productive capacity abound in this country, hundreds of U.S. textile producers, apparel firms, retailers, and fashion reporters travel regularly to Paris, Milan, London, Munich, Düsseldorf, and other, less-important **fashion centers** in order to observe new trends or buy merchandise for copying or resale. European designers and their designs continue to hold a special cachet for fashion-forward consumers in the United States and in other countries where the elite can afford them. Table 9–2 illustrates a typical European show schedule for this segment of the industry.

French Ready-to-Wear Industry

The production of ready-to-wear has blossomed into a large, full-fledged industry in France. Contributing to its development were such designer-named producing firms as Sonya Rykiel, Daniel Hechter, Dorothée Bis, Cacherel, and Emanuelle Khanh, many of whom had their beginnings as owner-operated retail boutiques. Such designers began to attract the attention of foreign buyers and the press by developing styles and looks of their own, which were quite different and lower in price than the couture garments.

Many other designer-named ready-to-wear firms have since joined their ranks. Among them are Claude Montana, Angelo Tarlazzi, Thierry Mugler, Jean-Paul Gaultier, Rochas, and Azzadine Alaia. As was mentioned earlier, many of these ready-to-wear designers have been designated as *créateurs* by the Chambre Syndicale and have been admitted as members.

Size of the Industry

The ready-to-wear operations of the Paris couture houses and of the designer-named firms that are members of the Chambre represent only a small part of the industry, in both number of firms and value of output. The **Fédération Française du Prêt-à-Porter Féminin**, the trade association that represents ready-to-wear producers other than those who belong to the Chambre Syndicale, reports a membership of some 1,200 companies.

Like the industry in most of the more-developed countries, the French ready-to-wear industry has a large portion of its garments produced outside the country where labor is less costly. A growing percentage of French garments are produced outside the country in low-wage countries of North Africa, Asia, and increasingly, in the former communist countries in Central and Eastern Europe. Nevertheless, French designers have provided the creative input for the lines produced in these other areas.

Innovative fashions and mass production have combined to build a ready-to-wear industry that is a very important resource to the American fashion business. Although the United States dollar purchases of French ready-to-wear amount to only a small percentage of total imports, U.S. adaptations and copies of their styles and ideas have enormous impact.

Semiannual Collections and Trade Showings

Unlike the American industry, French ready-to-wear producers prepare and present only two seasonal collections a year, as do all foreign-fashion manufacturers. Fall/Winter collections are shown in March, and Spring/Summer collections are presented in October. In its efforts to court foreign buyers, the French ready-to-wear industry stages week-long semiannual **trade shows** in Paris, which are attended by thousands of fashion professionals ("lookers," buyers, and fashion reporters) from all over the world (see Table 9–2).

Semiannual prêt-à-porter shows, sponsored and coordinated by the Chambre Syndicale, present the ready-to-wear collections of the couturiers and créateurs. These are held in a central Paris area known as Les Halles—which has developed as a cultural center. A 1995 U.S. film, *Prêt-à-porter*, depicted the colorful activities associated with one of these shows.

The mass-producing ready-to-wear companies stage their own semiannual shows—the Salon International du Prêt-à-Porter Féminin in the Porte de Versailles, an exhibition building larger than the New York Javits Center. Some 1,300 apparel firms, most but not all French, exhibit their seasonal lines there. In 1989, the Fédération Française du Prêt-à-Porter Féminin introduced a secondary and smaller seasonal show called the Collection Privées.

The French menswear industry also stages its own semiannual seasonal trade shows in the Porte de Versailles. Held in February and September, these are run in conjunction with producers of knitwear and children's clothes.

The Fédération Française du Prêt-à-Porter also organizes French participation in international trade shows held in New York, Düsseldorf, Milan, Tokyo, Munich, and Stockholm. It also maintains a permanent office in New York City. This is the French Fashion and Textile Center, whose major purpose is to promote French ready-to-wear in the United States. It represents all branches of the industry except couture and couture ready-to-wear. Additionally, many of the leading couture houses and larger designer-name ready-to-wear companies have established their own offices in New York, along with sales representation at regional apparel marts.

Summing up, it is obvious that the French are not waiting for fashion buyers to come knocking at their doors. They participate in international trade shows, they franchise designer-name ready-to-wear boutiques worldwide, they have global licensing arrangements, and they maintain individual and group sales offices in the United States.

| Table 9–2 | This schedule illustrates typical European ready-to-wear show venues for a season. |

EUROPE READY-TO-WEAR
SHOW SCHEDULES LISTED

MILAN—The schedules for the European designer fall ready-to-wear collections to be shown next month in Milan, London and Paris are as follows.

MILAN
Saturday, March 3

9:30 a.m.	Andrea Sargeant
10:30 a.m.	x Dieci by Luca Coelli
11:30 a.m.	Paola Marzotto
12:30 p.m.	Marina Spadafora
2 p.m.	Harriet Selling
3 p.m.	Massimo Monteforte
4 p.m.	Maurizio Galante
5 p.m.	Emilio Cavallini
6 p.m.	Alma
7 p.m.	Enrica Massei
9 p.m.	Mariella Burani

Sunday, March 4

9 a.m.	Sanlorenzo
10 a.m.	Emporio Armani
11 a.m.	Complice
noon	Chiara Boni
2 p.m.	Max Mara
3 p.m.	Rocco Barocco
4 p.m.	Mario Valentino
5:15 p.m.	Laura Biagiotti
7 p.m.	Gianni Versace

Monday, March 5

9:30 a.m.	Krizia
11 a.m.	Mila Schon
noon	Missoni
1 p.m.	Gianmarco Venturi
2:30 p.m.	Byblos
3:30 p.m.	Salvatore Ferragamo
4:30 p.m.	Erreuno
5:30 p.m.	Blumarine

Tuesday, March 6

9:30 a.m.	Callaghan
10:30 a.m.	Genny
11:30 a.m.	Gianna Cassoli
12:30 p.m.	Basile
2 p.m.	Gherardini
3 p.m.	Sportmax
4 p.m.	Alberta Ferretti
5:30 p.m.	Gianfranco Ferre
7:30 p.m.	Fendi
9:00 p.m.	Filippo Alpi

Wednesday, March 7

9:30 a.m.	Verri
10:30 a.m.	Luciano Soprani
11:30 a.m.	Trussardi
12:30 p.m.	Moschino
2 p.m.	Bill Kaiserman
3 p.m.	Tivioli
4 p.m.	Maurizio Baldassari
5 p.m.	Giorgio Armani
6 p.m.	Giorgio Correggiari

LONDON
Friday, March 9

3:30 p.m.	Caroline Charles
4:45 p.m.	Edina Ronay
6:15 p.m.	Murray Arbeid
7 p.m.	Bodymap

Saturday, March 10

10 a.m.	Red or Dead
Noon	Betty Jackson
12:45 p.m.	Zandra Rhodes
3 p.m.	Workers for Freedom
5 p.m.	Joe Casely-Hayford
6:30 p.m.	Nick Coleman

Sunday, March 11

10 a.m.	Paul Costelloe
Noon	Jean Muir
1:30 p.m.	Bruce Oldfield
3 p.m.	Arabella Pollen
4 p.m.	Ghost

Monday, March 12

10:15 a.m.	Tomasz Starzewski/ Shirin Cashmere
11:30 a.m.	Pam Hogg
5 p.m.	Michiko Koshino
6:30 p.m.	Vivienne Westwood

PARIS
Tuesday, March 13

9:30 a.m.	Claude Barthelemy
11 a.m.	Hiroko Koshino
Noon	Krystyna Bukowska
1 p.m.	Yuki Torii
1:30 p.m.	Corinne Cobson
2:30 p.m.	Kimijima
3:30 p.m.	Emmanuelle Khanh
5 p.m.	Paco Rabanne
6:30 p.m.	Etienne Brunel
7:30 p.m.	Olivier Guillemin

Wednesday, March 14

9:30 a.m.	Barbara Bui
10:30 a.m.	Doby Broda
11:30 a.m.	Elisabeth De Senneville
12:30 p.m.	John Galliano
2:30 p.m.	Junko Shimada
3:30 p.m.	Lolita Lempicka
5 p.m.	Olivier Lapidus
6:30 p.m.	Chantal Thomass

Thursday, March 15

9:30 a.m.	Daniel Hechter
10:30 a.m.	Comme Des Garcons
11:30 a.m.	Angelo Tarlazzi
1 p.m.	Helmut Lang
2:30 p.m.	Yohji Yamamoto

(Continued)

Table 9–2	This schedule illustrates typical European ready-to-wear show venues for a season. *(continued)*

3:30 p.m.	Cerruti	Noon	Hanae Mori
5 p.m.	Jean-Charles de Castelbajac	2:30 p.m.	Christian Dior
6:30 p.m.	Thierry Mugler	4 p.m.	Jin Abe
Friday, March 16		5:30 p.m.	Valentino
9 a.m.	Givenchy	7 p.m.	Lanvin
10 a.m.	Bernard Perris	8 p.m.	Claude Petin
11:15 a.m.	Karl Lagerfeld	**Tuesday, March 20**	
12:30 p.m.	Popy Moreni	9:30 a.m.	Torrente
2 p.m.	Zucca	10:30 a.m.	Guy Laroche
3 p.m.	Chloe	11:30 a.m.	Emanuel Ungaro
4 p.m.	Anne-Marie Beretta	2 p.m.	Frederic Castet
5 p.m.	Jean-Paul Gaultier	3:30 p.m.	Hermes
Saturday, March 17		4:30 p.m.	Lecoanet Hemant
9:30 a.m.	Guy Paulin for Tiktiner	5:30 p.m.	Jacqueline De Ribes
10:30 a.m.	Odile Lancon	7 p.m.	Junko Koshino
2 p.m.	Gres	9 p.m.	Marithe and Francois Girbaud
3:30 p.m.	Balenciaga	**Wednesday, March 21**	
5 p.m.	Issey Miyake	11 a.m.	Yves Saint Laurent
6:30 p.m.	Dorothée Bis	1 p.m.	Michel Klein
8:30 p.m.	Romeo Gigli	**By Invitation**	
Sunday, March 18		Christian Lacroix	
10 a.m.	Matsuda	Claude Montana	
11 a.m.	Enrico Coveri	Kenzo	
12:30 p.m.	Martine Sitbon	**By Appointment**	
2 p.m.	Agnes B	Pierre Balmain	
3:30 p.m.	I.W.S. Woolmark	Carven	
4:30 p.m.	Kansai Yamamoto	Jacques Esterel	
6 p.m.	Sonia Rykiel	Louis Feraud	
8 p.m.	Katherine Hamnett	Nina Ricci	
Monday, March 19		Pierre Cardin	
9:30 a.m.	Jean-Louis Scherrer	Ted Lapidus	
10:30 a.m.	Chanel	Daniel Olivier Favre	

Italy

Today, the most serious challenger to the fashion leadership of Paris is Italy, which has been attracting foreign fashion buyers since the 1960s. Italy's strengths and competitive advantages derive from the superior quality and design of its fabrics, its workmanship, and the innovative, sophisticated styling of its knitwear, sportswear, and accessories—notably leather shoes and handbags. It has also developed a reputation for its interesting and avant garde styling of men's apparel and accessories.

The Italian ready-to-wear industry developed simultaneously with its couture industry and did not depend on Italian couturiers for fashion leadership and design talent. As a result, it started exporting earlier. Today the well-being of the industry relies heavily on its foreign sales efforts, in which it receives encouragement and support from the Italian government.

Semiannual Collections and Trade Shows

When Italy first emerged as a major fashion center, foreign trade buyers went to Florence, where the semiannual collections and showings of ready-to-wear were presented in the luxurious and elegant setting of the Pitti Palace. In the mid-1970s, however, ready-to-wear firms in the north of Italy decided to present their own showings in Milan. The initial handful of firms, among them Basile, Callaghan, Missoni, and Caumont, has grown into an avalanche, and today, Milan has become the major staging ground for Italian ready-to-wear presentations. In fact, many of Florence's ready-to-wear firms have defected to the north and show in both Milan and Florence. Their semiannual showings take place prior to the prêt-à-porter openings in Paris, in early March for Fall/Winter and early October for Spring/Summer. The week-long Milan shows include not only those staged by the country's top ready-to-wear designers, but also Modit, an exhibition at which other countries' apparel manufacturers are invited to show.

Also, like their French counterparts, the Italian industry participates in trade shows in many other countries—among them the New York Pret showings held in early fall and spring. There are many other trade presentations such as Uomo Modo, the semiannual show of menswear manufacturers; an Italian shoe fair staged annually in March in Bologna; the famous textile show, Ideacomo, held in May at Lake Como; and the Mipel accessories show, held in Milan, each January and June. These are but a few of the many trade exhibits staged in Italy.

Leading Designers

Along with those mentioned, some of the best-known ready-to-wear designer companies in Italy are Krizia, Versace, Armani, Prada, Trussardi, Max Mara, and Dolce & Gabbana. All of these have achieved worldwide reputations for their trendsetting fashions. Consider also the names of Gucci and Ferragamo, internationally known for leather products, and Fendi, renowned for innovative fur fashions. Add these names to those mentioned previously in this section and it becomes clear that the fashion story, Italian style, represents serious competition to Paris as the prime source of fashion leadership.

Italy's Fashion Industry

After tourism, the fashion industry is Italy's largest national industry. There are more than twice as many apparel and accessory firms in Italy as there are in France. A significant portion of their annual output is exported, with their largest customers being high-income countries of Europe, Asia, and North America. Italian firms, like those in other high-wage countries, are sending many of their garments elsewhere for production. However, Italian producers were slower to do this than their European counterparts.

It is interesting to note that, because Italian workmanship and fabrics are, on the whole, better and cheaper than they are in France, many French designers are steady customers of Italy. Besides the silks from Como and woolens from Biella, large numbers of sweaters, leather garments, and accessories that come from Italy are sold under French labels.

Like their French counterparts, many Italian companies have established retail boutiques around the world that feature their ready-to-wear. Some of these "name" boutiques are owned and operated by the company itself. Others are owned and operated by franchised retailers. Particularly notable is the worldwide chain of the franchised stores of Benetton. And also, like their French counterparts, many of the Italian companies are involved in worldwide licensing agreements. A case in point is the very large GFT Gruppo Italian clothing manufacturer that has put Armani, Valentino, Ungaro, Dior, and other licensed designer labels into closets from Melbourne to Manhattan.

London

The British have long been famous for their tweeds and their men's custom tailoring, but it was not until after World War II that reverberations from their ready-to-wear industry were heard around the fashion world. Their couture effort, which was keyed to the conservative tastes of royalty and the peerage, did not succeed and is nonexistent today.

Fashion Leadership in the 1960s

The British ready-to-wear industry, unlike their couture, did flourish and made a major impact on both men's and women's fashions in the 1960s. The name *Carnaby Street* became synonymous with colorful, uninhibited, *avant garde* clothes for both sexes. The London streets in that area were filled with boutiques carrying unconventional, trendy fashions by new young designers. Their miniskirted dresses, reflecting the free, young spirit of the decade, sent feminine hemlines soaring to incredible highs all over the world. Especially notable was the work of Mary Quant, a young English designer who understood what many other designers around the world were quite late in recognizing: that the young were setting fashions on their own, and that, instead of the young following their elders, the mature folk were following the young.

Classics in the 1970s

In the 1970s, the mood of the "swinging sixties" changed, as did the ready-to-wear offerings of that period. English fashion houses focused on their traditional and classic high-quality woolen fabrics in men's tailored clothing, the excellent workmanship of their rainwear (notably Aquascutum and Burberry), and the fine cotton products of Liberty of London and Laura Ashley.

Revitalization in the 1980s

Led by Jean Muir, Zandra Rhodes, and Ossie Clark, the British fashion industry was revitalized in the 1980s. All kinds of young, highly individualized, and even outrageous fashion statements began coming out of England. Today, the new and exciting exists side by side with the traditional, conservative, and classic clothing for which England has always been known. There could not be anything more radically different from the romantic cotton prints of Laura Ashley than the industrial cottons and futuristic silks of Katherine Hamnett, the bold prints of Betty Jackson, or the unconventional, inventive styles of such other trendsetting firms as Wendy Dagworthy, Rifat Ozbek, Body Map, Jasper Conran, and Vivienne Westwood, for example. These and other new designer talents are leading the British fashion parade today (Figure 9–3).

Even the retail boutiques in London are as inventive as the designers and the styles seen on the streets. For example, there is a shop called the Warehouse, where one can buy white clothes and dye them on the spot, with the dye and washing machines provided for the customer on the premises. In a shop called Spring, clothes are sold Chinese-take-out style.

Size of the Industry

The British fashions have captured the hearts of both the young and the rebellious and their fashion-conscious elders. What is equally important is that they have also captured the dollars (or other currency) of buyers from outside the country. Representatives of many countries attend the semiannual trade showings in March and October.

Figure 9–3

London Fashion Week

13-17 FEBRUARY 2000

LONDON FASHION WEEK

SPONSORED BY

VS SASSOON

GENERAL INFORMATION
Annette Worsley-Taylor Associates
Tel: +44 (0) 20 7351 2044
Fax: +44 (0) 20 7351 2055
www.londonfashionweek.co.uk

LONDON FASHION WEEK
is organised by:
British Fashion Council
5 Portland Place, London W1N 3AA
Tel +44 (0) 20 7636 7788
Fax +44 (0) 20 7636 7515

LONDON FASHION WEEK IMAGE
PHOTOGRAPHER: MILES ALDRIDGE
MODEL: VIVIEN SOLARI @ MODELS 1
DRESS: HUSSEIN CHALAYAN

Source: British Fashion Council. Reprinted courtesy of the British Fashion Council.

According to the British Apparel and Textile Confederation, industry output continues at a modest, but respectable, rate of growth. Overall wholesale figures for apparel in 2001 was more than $8 billion and more than $11 billion for textiles. Approximately 242,000 individuals are employed in the industry. In recent years, exports have grown and imports have slowed down. In 2001, textile and apparel imports were valued at more than $24 billion and exports at more than $10.5 billion, leaving a negative trade deficit of more than $13 billion (online communication with author, May 2002; conversion from British pounds to U.S. dollars based on the exchange rate in May 2002).

Although British textile and apparel exports to other European Union (EU) countries are three times the level of those to non-EU markets, the latter are growing at a very healthy rate (11 to 16 percent annual growth in recent years). Healthy growth of exports to other markets may be attributed to efforts to promote the industry and its products outside the country and to recent favorable currency exchange rates that made British goods even more attractive.

International Shows in Germany

Germany's apparel industry has long been known for its superior knitting technology and its well-made, moderately priced "middle-of-the-road" clothing. It is only in recent years that a few German companies have begun to make their names and design ideas increasingly felt in the U.S. market. Two companies, Escada and Mondi, are leading their emerging fashion parade, and a number of other companies have begun to follow their lead. Among them is Hugo Boss, who produces a line of fashion-forward clothing for younger men. It is interesting to note that most of these designers have set up their own retail boutiques in the United States and in Europe.

The country's impact on the fashion world, however, arises from a different source. Germany is famous for the international textile and apparel fashion fairs that are staged there and are probably the most impressive events of their kind in the world. For example, in Frankfurt there is a huge textile trade show, **Interstoff,** sponsored by Messe Frankfurt, at which thousands of fabric producers from many different countries exhibit their wares. Apparel producers from every part of the world attend this show, which now occurs as three specialized shows per season (Weisman, 1995a).

In **Düsseldorf** each spring and fall, there is an international women's show, **IGEDO,** reported to draw some 3,000 producers from 41 countries to exhibit merchandise to a worldwide audience of more than 50,000 potential buyers (Figure 9–4).

Each February and August, Cologne offers a week-long International Men's Fashion Week that attracts some 30,000 buyers to see the lines of an estimated 1,000 exhibitors from 27 countries.

In addition to these, there is an annual International Footwear Fair held in Düsseldorf every March, a semiannual international children's fair in Cologne, and semiannual swimwear and underwear shows in Düsseldorf, which are the only trade fairs of their type in the world. And there are still others. Among them is the Overseas Export Fair, held in Berlin every September.

Germany's apparel industry may not be fashion leaders as yet, but its international trade fairs are a major source for new fabric and fashion ideas.

Like other advanced industrialized countries in Europe, the German industry has a large portion of its garments made in lower-wage countries. Turkey has been a popular production site for German firms.

Japan

In the not-too-distant past, a label reading "Made in Japan" was usually associated with cheap and poorly made products that were carried in low-priced stores in the United States. Today, however, the Japanese fashion industry has been transformed. This is partly the result of the postwar aid of the United States and partly the fruit of the Japanese determination to become a major industrial democracy. In the process, that country has become an important fashion center for medium and high-priced goods, thanks to the presence of many bright, talented designers and to the quality of Japanese products.

Figure 9–4 **Publicity on the IGEDO show held in Düsseldorf, Germany.**

DÜSSELDORF
IGEDO DÜSSELDORF 5 - 7 MARCH
THE RIGHT DATE FOR INTERNATIONAL NEW COLLECTIONS

New Collections
new momentum for the current season
just in time
special lines for short delivery
100% safe orders
based on sales made in that season
international attendance
by both exhibitors and buyers

young fashion talents
new international creativity
workshop
young designers who's got what it takes
fashion Swiss made
ambitious, young, and innovative
fair debut
by successful designer Gesine Moritz
wanted romanticism
fashion, wedding, and festive occasions
Creation Cuir
leatherwear collections live and easy
trends on stage
Igedo - the right date for overseas

buyers. Igedo- the fashion fair for

trade buyers who won't miss a single

chance in the fashion market.

Further information
from Igedo Company
Fax: ++49-211/4396-345

Source: IGEDO.

In the 1960s and 1970s, Japan began to be recognized as a significant player in the world of high fashion when designers such as Hanae Mori, Kenzo Takada, Kansai Yamamoto, and Issey Miyake first showed their lines at the Paris prêt-à-porter showings. They became a design sensation overnight, and Tokyo was hailed by buyers and the press as the "worldwide fashion capitol" in coming decades. Although Japan continues to play an important role in the global fashion industry, the country's emphasis on other high-technology industries may have dimmed the prospects for the fashion industry to be the premier global fashion center once predicted.

High wages in Japan have also affected the fashion industry profoundly. In recent surveys of textile industry wages, Japan has had the highest in the world. Because of these high wages, a very large portion of Japan's garment production occurs in other Asian countries with lower wages. First, Japanese companies transferred production to countries such as South Korea and Taiwan. Now, however, as the wages in those countries have risen, Japan's apparel production has shifted to other locations where wages remain low. These include China, Indonesia, Vietnam, and other less-developed Asian countries.

As in the European and North American industries, the creative and marketing aspects of the fashion industry still occur in the home country of the apparel firms (i.e., in Japan). Although garment production may occur in neighboring countries, the Japanese quality standards are still evident in products. Because Japan's consumers are very demanding in terms of product quality, this results in products attractive to consumers elsewhere. In his *Competitive Advantage of Nations*, Porter (1990) found that having demanding buyers in an industry's home market forces local firms to meet high standards of product quality, creating a competitive advantage for a country's industry.

Canada

In recent decades, a number of Canadian apparel manufacturers have developed high-quality, high-fashion lines that have been quite successful in the U.S. market. The sophisticated European styling and quality of Canadian apparel has created a special niche for Canadian producers, whose customers look for distinctive merchandise other than the sameness that characterizes mass-market production. Canadian apparel firms have become experts at producing small runs, making them ideal producers of "limited edition" apparel. Because Canada's population is one-tenth that of the United States and many apparel firms are small, the Canadian Apparel Federation promotes the idea that Canadian firms are well suited to produce for this smaller, high fashion niche. The small Canadian population also accounts for why the country's apparel firms look more and more toward the large U.S. market.

Although the United States and Canada have long been important trade partners, two free-trade agreements encouraged this commerce even more. First, a Canada–U.S. agreement led to a 10-year phaseout of tariffs on products traded between the two countries. The United States and Canada never had quotas on each other's products because the two countries are at similar stages of development. Second, the North American Free Trade Agreement (NAFTA) fostered trade even more and brought Mexico into the partnership.

The United States is the major destination of Canada's textile and apparel exports. Both countries have increased trade with each other in these sectors since the signing of the trade agreements. Canadian shipments of apparel to the United States grew to $1.42 billion in 1998, compared to $146.9 million in 1988, the last year before the Canada–U.S. agreement. Similarly, textile imports from Canada expanded

| Figure 9–5 | The Canadian Apparel Federation provides many services to manufacturers and potential buyers. Also see www.apparel.ca. |

Source: Canadian Apparel Federation. Reprinted courtesy of the Canadian Apparel Federation.

from $212.9 million to $1.33 billion. During this same time, U.S. apparel shipments to Canada jumped from $38.8 million to $709.3 million, and textile shipments soared from $637.7 million to $2.7 billion—for a total increase of 404.6 percent for the decade, or about 40 percent each year (Dunn, 2000; Ostroff, 2000).

The **Canadian Apparel Federation (CAF)** is the national association for apparel manufacturers, contractors, and designers (updates on the Canadian industry may be found at www.apparel.ca). It represents the industry in consultations with the federal government on trade, legislative, and regulatory matters. The CAF provides a variety of assistance to Canadian manufacturers, including marketing and trade expertise, a number of information services, and other support as needed. The Federation can assist in matching the interests of Canadian and U.S. firms (Figure 9–5). The Canadian Textile Institute (CTI) plays a similar role in working with the textile industry.

The Canadian apparel industry requires distinctive fabrics for the types of high-fashion apparel being produced by many of its firms. However, like some apparel firms in the United States, Canadian apparel producers feel the domestic textile industry is often unwilling to make the small production runs necessary for more exclusive garments. Yet, when Canadian apparel firms import fabrics from elsewhere, they must pay tariffs on those fabrics. Tariffs raise apparel firms' costs of doing business and make their products less competitive in the marketplace, especially the U.S. market. Because U.S. apparel wages are less than those in Canada, Canadian firms already are operating at a competitive disadvantage. The tariffs, which apparel firms believe are charged to protect the Canadian textile industry from imports, create further disadvantages.

The apparel industry is one of few Canadian manufacturing sectors that can claim it has companies in every province and territory in Canada. There are between 2,000 and 2,500 apparel manufacturers, employing about 100,000 people (Dunn, 2000). More than half the total Canadian apparel industry is located in Quebec. Thus, Quebec's continued interest in being a separate country, an effort that barely failed in 1995, has potentially serious implications for the Canadian apparel industry. Separatists vowed to continue their efforts. Considering the close 1995 vote, it is feasible that at some point there will be four countries, rather than three, in North America.

Fashion Producers in Lower-Wage Countries

As was explained in Chapter 6, many ready-to-wear apparel firms do not handle the entire garment production process in company-owned factories. Instead, they contract out some or all of their production to independently owned outside facilities that produce according to given specifications. Many of these contracting operations occur in other countries. In a less-common scenario, apparel firms may *own* factories in other countries where wages are lower.

Beginning in the 1970s, apparel firms in the more-developed countries of North America and Europe discovered a strategy for competing with low-cost imports coming into their markets. They began to move their own production to countries where wages were lower than in their home countries. Apparel firms soon developed working relationships with factories in Asia, where ready-to-wear could be produced at a fraction of domestic prices. Today, merchandise produced by **overseas contractors** in low-wage countries around the world constitutes the largest percentage of U.S. imports. The product development and marketing activities have remained in the firm's home country.

Both apparel firms and retailers use overseas contractors in low-wage countries. Many retailers are using this strategy to contract directly with firms in other countries to produce their private label lines, *bypassing* domestic apparel manufacturing firms. When retailers use this approach, it means they are becoming somewhat like apparel manufacturers themselves, rather than buying from established apparel firms. In Figure 9–6, for example, we see that the May Department Stores operates offices throughout Asia. Both apparel firms and retailers use overseas contractors for the same reason: to reduce the price of garments.

As we can see in Table 9–3, many less-developed countries are important sources of U.S. imports. Although European countries provide fashion influence, the bulk of U.S. apparel imports come from elsewhere.

Lower Labor Costs

Apparel production is still one of the most labor-intensive and least-automated industries. Producing three-dimensional garments from two-dimensional limp fabrics requires a great deal of hand manipulation. Thus, labor costs are an important element in the manufacture of clothing. Figure 3–10 provided a comparison of the

Figure 9–6

May Department Stores offices in Asia.

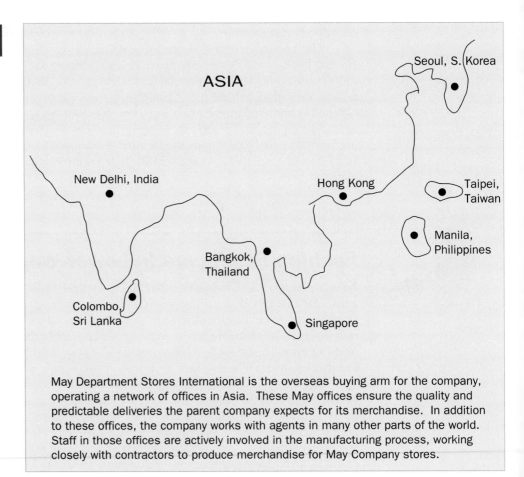

May Department Stores International is the overseas buying arm for the company, operating a network of offices in Asia. These May offices ensure the quality and predictable deliveries the parent company expects for its merchandise. In addition to these offices, the company works with agents in many other parts of the world. Staff in those offices are actively involved in the manufacturing process, working closely with contractors to produce merchandise for May Company stores.

Source: Based on author's discussions with May Department Stores personnel.

Table 9–3	Trends in U.S. Apparel Imports by Major Source (Millions of square meters)[1]			
Country Source	**1984**	**1995**	**2001**	**Change in 2001 over 1984**
Big Four				
People's Republic of China	421	862	975	132%
Hong Kong	848	821	916	12%
Taiwan	808	598	614	−24%
S. Korea	635	343	631	−.01%
Total	2,712	2,624	3,138	15.7%
ASEAN				
Philippines	197	465	553	180%
Indonesia	108	310	594	450%
Thailand	89	244	453	409%
Singapore	107	84	68	−36%
Malaysia	54	152	193	257%
Total	555	1,255	2,451	342%
Other Far East				
Bangladesh	20	519	966	4,730%
India	112	258	403	260%
Sri Lanka	91	281	403	343%
Pakistan	53	154	347	555%
Turkey	13	178	306	2,254%
Total	289	1,390	2,425	839%
CBI				
Dominican Republic	79	632	753	853%
Costa Rica	28	297	350	1,150%
Jamaica	8	225	102	1,175%
Guatemala	2	185	388	19,300%
Honduras	9	329	1021	11,244%
El Salvador	2	239	724	36,100%
Total	208	1,978	3,338	15,048%
Mexico	72	774	2,290	33,720%
TOTAL APPAREL	4,292 100%	9,255 100%	16,103	275%

Source: From FOCUS: Economic Profile of the Apparel Industry (p. 5) by American Apparel & Footwear Association, 1996, Arlington, VA: Author. Reprinted by permission. 2001 update from website of Office of Textiles & Apparel, U.S. Dept. of Commerce (http://otexa.ita.doc.gov), July 2002.

[1] Apparel shipments under MFA agreements.

hourly wages in a number of countries. Many apparel firms in high-wage countries simply could not compete against those odds. Therefore, for the management of many companies, the only means of surviving appeared to be shifting the garment production activities offshore. Although this strategy eliminated many domestic apparel manufacturing jobs, many company executives believe they survived only because they shifted production elsewhere. Those firms were able to maintain in their home countries the management, merchandising, marketing, and other functions that require greater expertise and investment.

An additional factor is that in many other countries, the government offers incentives to producers of textiles and apparel for exports. Some provide **subsidies** of various kinds, despite the fact that these are considered illegal because they create unfair competition. In China, for example, the government provides support for the industry because textile and apparel exports are the top priority for helping the country establish itself as a world economic power. Firms in countries not providing this extra assistance cannot compete against products from other countries where manufacturers have received special support. Even when those products have shipping costs and tariffs added, the **landed cost** of the goods is less than production costs in domestic factories. If a U.S. apparel firm is trying to *compete* in the domestic market with garments made by a Chinese firm that sells to a U.S. retailer, the subsidy is a disadvantage to a U.S. apparel firm. On the other hand, if a U.S. firm contracts with a Chinese producer to make its garments, the U.S. company is also likely *benefiting* from that subsidy.

In many of the low-wage countries, governments also have **free trade zones (FTZs)**, where many incentives are given to attract firms there. The FTZs are special enclaves (usually fenced or otherwise enclosed) where goods can be produced under very attractive financial conditions. Business taxes might be eliminated or reduced, and fabrics or other components brought in are often exempt from tariffs. For example, if Indonesia wishes to attract production to the country, especially to provide jobs, the government might establish an FTZ. Many costs of doing business are reduced in the FTZ to lure firms to the country. Firms from anywhere might locate there, and those from countries with higher wages and/or labor shortages are likely to be attracted. For example, it is common to see South Korean apparel firms located in the FTZs in Indonesia, other parts of Asia, and even Latin America.

Major Countries of Asia

The Newly Industrialized Countries (NICs)

At one time, apparel made in Asian countries was of such poor quality that it was relegated to the lowest price points of the fashion market. This situation no longer holds true. The **newly industrialized countries (NICs)** of Asia,[2] generally considered to include Taiwan, South Korea, Hong Kong,[3] and Singapore, have evolved far from where they were in the 1960s and 1970s. In those days, European, U.S., and Canadian apparel firms had garments produced in these countries to take advantage of low wages. Today, each of these has fashion-forward industries, but the major cities in each case have become centers of finance, product development, and marketing (Figure 9–7). Now, each of these Asian powerhouses send most of *their* production to neighboring low-wage regions, just as the United States and Western Europe have their production sent to lower-cost countries.

Today, the Asian NICs resemble in many ways the countries generally considered to be "more developed." The NICs have advanced to a level that makes them far more interested in being involved in high-technology, **capital-intensive** economic activities than producing garments for other countries. This is not to say the apparel industry has disappeared in the NICs, but the types of activities have changed markedly. Wages have risen dramatically in these countries, and it has become difficult to find sewing operators for the garment industry. The work is hard, and wages in other industries are likely to be higher. Consequently, apparel manufacturers in the NICs have

---

[2]This group is frequently called the "**Asian Tigers**."
[3]Hong Kong was earlier a British colony considered a city-state but became part of the People's Republic of China in 1997. It is still considered a separate economy.

Figure 9–7

Seoul and other major cities in the Asian NIC countries have fashion-forward industries. Offices such as this provide market research and fashion direction.

Source: Photo by Kitty G. Dickerson.

experienced many of the same competitiveness problems as those in Western Europe, the United States, and Canada (Dickerson, 1999).

Although Asia is still a source of lower-priced merchandise, much of it is produced in the NICs' neighboring countries. Major cities in the NICs have become *investment and marketing hubs* for the industry in the region. Apparel firms in the NICs are likely *themselves* to be using overseas contractors in low-wage countries.

Beginning in the 1980s, East Asia has led the world economy in terms of average annual growth rates. This economic growth has resulted in a fast rise in incomes and a rapid increase in demand in consumer markets. *Business Week* authors Engardio, Barnathan, and Glasgall (1993) noted that "East Asia is generating its own wealth on a speed and scale that probably is without historical precedent" (p. 100). Growing affluence, plus high population growth, is making East Asian countries major markets themselves, rather than the source of low-wage apparel products for firms from other nations. Although the Asian economic crisis of the late 1990s played havoc in the short term, most countries are returning to prosperity in the new millennium.

Hong Kong. For decades, Hong Kong has been producing apparel to order—to the order of the garment trade throughout the world. The apparel and textiles industries are Hong Kong's largest manufacturing sectors, accounting for over one-third of its total exports. Hong Kong is one of the world's largest apparel exporters; however, this does not mean all the merchandise is produced there. Many of Hong Kong's apparel exports are made through outward processing arrangements (OPT), especially in Shenzhen, an economic zone in southern China just outside Hong Kong (see Figure 9–8). As noted earlier, Hong Kong and the other Asian NICs have become major marketing hubs for the industry. Business deals are signed and production may be coordinated from these centers—but a large portion of the garment production occurs elsewhere.

Figure 9–8

Many U.S. apparel firms and retailers have garments sewn in factories in the Shenzhen province of China, where wages are much lower than in nearby Hong Kong. The U.S. firms generally have offices in Hong Kong, which coordinate the Shenzhen production on behalf of the American firm.

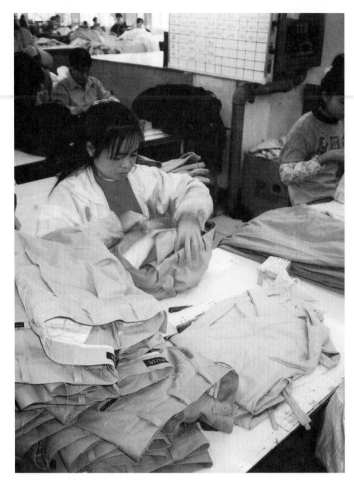

Source: Photo by Kitty G. Dickerson.

Mass-producing firms such as Esprit and Liz Claiborne have offices in Hong Kong but contract out virtually all their production. In addition, almost every important retail store in the United States that offers private-label fashion goods has offices in Hong Kong to coordinate the manufacturing to its specifications. Traffic between Shenzhen and Hong Kong has increased dramatically. Buses now run daily from Hong Kong to take company representatives to check on production in Shenzhen's factories. Trucks line the highways, transporting components into China and finished merchandise back to Hong Kong.

Quota restraints have encouraged Hong Kong to **upgrade** the products shipped to the United States, Europe, and Canada. Quota limits on the physical quantity of exports, but not the value, encouraged Hong Kong to produce garments of higher quality—and higher price. The Hong Kong industry today is noted for its ability to accommodate style changes and for superior workmanship, for which sources generally pay premium prices. Long runs of low-priced staple products are no longer Hong Kong's forte. The Hong Kong industry competes more on the basis of service, quality, and flexibility than on low cost. Leading designers from around the world use Hong Kong for production of high-quality goods.

The **Hong Kong Trade Development Council (HKTDC)** has promoted Hong Kong as a major player on the world fashion stage. This includes presenting Hong Kong designers in U.S. and European trade shows, including those in Düsseldorf and Paris. The HKTDC sponsors an annual fashion week, which is billed as "Asia's Largest Fashion Event." Both exhibitors and buyers come from countries on several continents.

Taiwan and South Korea. Taiwan, for many years a major low-wage contracting center for apparel, was an agricultural area called Formosa until Chiang Kai-shek escaped from China, declared Taiwan to be Nationalist China, became its first president in 1949, and remained its ruler virtually until his death. Within a decade, he had transformed Taiwan into an industrial nation.

Taiwan's textile and apparel industry, which the United States and Japan helped to develop, was the major industry on which the country's economy expanded. During the 1970s and 1980s, Taiwan was among the top three apparel producers in the world. Today, however, Taiwan's emphasis is on high-technology, capital-intensive industries. Many of the early textile and apparel firms have evolved into large commercial conglomerates with other businesses that include real estate, retailing, and chemical complexes. Among Taiwan's wealthiest elite, a majority began in textiles and apparel. Today, those firms still in this industry are more likely to be producing high-technology textile products, including chemical fibers, than assembling garments. All of this reflects the rapid economic and technological advancements in Taiwan.

Although a substantial apparel industry remains in Taiwan, less and less of the production occurs within this island country. Apparel firms' headquarters remain in Taiwan, but much of the labor-intensive garment production is sent to China, Indonesia, or other lower-wage countries.

Taiwan's textile and apparel industry receives support and technical assistance in both its production and marketing activities. The government/industry-supported **Taiwan Textile Federation (TTF)** is an umbrella organization for industry groups representing all segments of the business. The TTF provides marketing and export promotion assistance to companies and sponsors exhibits at trade fairs around the world. A design center keeps apparel and fabric makers informed about the latest fashion trends. The talents of young designers are nurtured. Seminars provide business and trade information. In addition to the TTF, the China Textile Institute (also in Taipei) is a center for technical production assistance to the industry.

South Korea has developed much like Taiwan. The garment industry provided the economic foundation for the country's successful industrialization. Today, South Korea is a bustling, advanced nation whose textile and apparel industries are considered less important than in the past. The electronics industry has become important here, as it has in Taiwan. Still, textiles and apparel represent nearly one-fifth of South Korea's exports. South Korea has moved toward the high-tech segments of the textile sector in preference to garment production. Increased wages plus labor shortages and worker discontent add up to mean that garment producers find it increasingly difficult to be competitive in South Korea. Thus, many Korean apparel firms have taken their production to lower-wage neighboring countries such as Indonesia and other Southeast Asian locations. A number have built factories in the Caribbean nations to be closer to the U.S. market and to avoid the quota limits they face in their home country if they plan to ship to the United States.

Singapore. The description of the industry in the other Asian Tigers also applies to Singapore, except that Singapore has moved out of garment production more rapidly than the others. Like Hong Kong, limited physical space has permitted minimal development of a textile industry *per se*. Singapore has become an important financial and marketing center for Southeast Asia. This is the main role it plays now for the fashion-related industries. Apparel firms are likely to have offices in Singapore to coordinate the production of garment lines in Indonesia, Malaysia, and other countries in Southeast Asia. Similarly, major retailers have offices in Singapore to coordinate the contract work in that region for private-label lines.

Like Hong Kong, Singapore is a major port city and will continue to play a major role in the region's apparel-related industries. Some businesses are eyeing Singapore as an alternative to Hong Kong if conditions become difficult in the latter under Chinese communist rule that was resumed in 1997. Singapore is positioning itself to be a major trade center in the industry, having opened TradeMart Singapore in 1994. This modern trade mart performs the functions normally associated with regional U.S. marts. Additionally, TradeMart Singapore is prepared to assist manufacturers and retailers from other parts of the world in finding Asian contractors to produce merchandise.

The People's Republic of China

Not long ago, the People's Republic of China (ROC), also known as Mainland China or sometimes Communist China, was isolated from the rest of the world. Once a mighty world power, China entered several decades of isolation following its famous Cultural Revolution. Only since the early 1970s has China engaged once again in foreign relations and trade with the rest of the world.

Today, China is a burgeoning economic powerhouse, whose potential far exceeds what this vast country has demonstrated to the world to date. With 1.3 billion inhabitants, or nearly one-fourth the total world population, China is a rapidly growing giant in the global textile and apparel industry. China is clearly the major producer of apparel exports to U.S. markets, even with a very restrictive quota system that has limited China's shipments.

The Chinese government has identified the textile and apparel industries as the top priority sector on which the Chinese economy will be advanced. Textile and apparel exports provide the means for securing badly needed hard currency. Because of the government's priority, the growth of all segments of the textile and apparel industry has been phenomenal. China's enormous population, in need of employment, is willing to work for very modest wages—usually well under 50 cents per hour. These low wages have been a magnet for apparel and retail firms from Western Europe, the United States, Canada, Japan, and other Asian countries seeking low-cost production of garments.

China's manufacturing industries have been aided by investments and technological know-how from Hong Kong in particular. Joint ventures with Hong Kong companies are encouraged by the government in which China supplies the land, facilities, and labor. The Hong Kong partner supplies the machinery, expertise, market access for the products, and often ongoing supervision of production and financial management. Companies from many other countries have similar joint venture or other investment arrangements in China.

China's overwhelming potential has only begun to be tapped. Textile and apparel companies around the world fear the competition that will be unleashed in

China now that this giant is a member of the World Trade Organization and the quota system is eliminated. On the other hand, apparel firms and retailers seeking low-cost production there will be unfettered in their quest for merchandise produced at a bargain.

One thing is certain: Textile and apparel industries in every country around the world will be affected by future developments in China's production and trade. With the strong entrepreneurial spirit of the Chinese, China is still a sleeping giant with the potential to flood apparel markets in every part of the world.

Other Low-Wage Production Centers in Asia

As Japan and the Asian NICs became less competitive (and quota restraints are tightened), particularly in the production of low-priced apparel, many other Asian countries began to fill the void. The more-developed Asian countries have also sought production in neighboring countries where there were fewer quota restraints. Most of the desperately poor nations (often referred to as the **Third World nations**) in Asia welcomed the investments and jobs provided when their more-developed neighbors began to move apparel production to their countries. This shift occurred as the more-advanced nations could no longer produce competitively in their home countries. Firms from European and North American countries also sought less-costly places, other than the NICs, for their contract production. The scenario is nearly always the same as that described earlier: The more advanced nations provide the investment, equipment, technical know-how, and access to markets; the less-advanced nations provide the labor, land, and local contacts. Figure 9–9 shows an example of this production.

A number of other very important countries have made their presence known in global textile and apparel markets. Certain members of the Association of Southeast

Figure 9–9

Managers in a U.S. apparel firm's sourcing office in Singapore consider specifications for garments to be produced in Malaysia.

Source: Photo by Kitty G. Dickerson.

Asian Nations (ASEAN),[4] which includes Thailand, Malaysia, Indonesia, and the Philippines, emerged as major contributors to the global supply of fashion products. Other countries that export a great deal include India, Pakistan, Bangladesh, and Sri Lanka. Newcomers continue to emerge, including Vietnam, Cambodia, and Nepal.

Central and Eastern Europe

In Central and Eastern Europe, a number of countries are placing increasing emphasis on their textile and apparel industries as important cogs in each respective nation's economic development. These countries have a vital interest in the markets of Western Europe and the United States and are making rapid strides in producing for those markets. We shall briefly consider Turkey and the former Soviet bloc countries, reviewing the latter as a group.

Turkey is positioned uniquely between Europe and Asia, with a Middle Eastern heritage similar to its Mediterranean neighbors (Figure 9–10). The textile and apparel industries have been important to the Turkish economy for decades and have made

Figure 9–10   **Up to now, Turkey has been primarily a production site for Western European apparel firms. Now, however, a new breed of sophisticated Turkish designers are able to blend the flavor of the country's Middle Eastern heritage with Western fashion tastes to create fresh new looks.**

Source: Photo by Kitty G. Dickerson.

---

[4]The ASEAN group includes Thailand, Malaysia, Indonesia, the Philippines, Singapore, Brunei, Vietnam, Laos, and Myanmar (formerly Burma). Brunei has little textile/apparel production because of its wealth from oil, and Singapore is an advanced NIC.

great strides in exporting in recent years. For many years, the Turkish garment industry has produced for certain West European markets, particularly Germany. More recently, however, a supportive government and strong industry leadership are positioning Turkey's textile and apparel industry to become an increasingly important player on the world stage. The textile-apparel complex is undergoing world-class modernization, making it even more competitive on a global basis.

The textile-apparel industries are of great importance to Turkey economically, as one of the country's major export sectors. However, rising labor and other costs are hurting Turkey's competitiveness—causing Turkish apparel manufacturers to turn to other neighboring countries, some from the former Soviet Union, for cheaper sources of production labor.

Although most of Turkey's apparel shipments have been directed to the European Union in the past, this country has taken steps to increase its shipments to the United States. In the mid-1990s, Turkey's products accounted for less than 1 percent of the U.S. apparel market, but Turkish industry leaders have taken steps to promote their country's significant future growth in the United States. More recently, shipments have grown about 15 percent per year (for updates see www.tgsd.org).

Many countries of the former Soviet bloc had large textile and apparel industries under the former communist system. However, centrally controlled economies and isolation from the world market resulted in industries out of touch with the rest of the world. The concept of fashion was foreign to garment producers in the region. Factories produced what they were told, regardless of what consumers might have wanted. Because no profit incentive existed, industries were inefficient.

Although the people in the former Soviet bloc countries celebrated the fall of the Berlin wall and an end to communism and isolation, painful transition years followed. Unemployment and declining incomes led to difficult conditions for many. As government-controlled factories were **privatized**, the most basic business skills for competing in a global economy had to be developed. Concepts of quality and fashion had to be learned by workers who had been accustomed to producing merchandise that was not competitive in world markets.

Several of these former communist countries are emerging from the difficult transition years and are becoming important apparel production sites. The apparel industry is playing the same role it has in less-developed countries around the world—it is often the first major industry on which the nations' economies are being built. Moreover, wages are low and many workers need jobs.

Central and Eastern Europe are now important production sites for apparel firms in the more-developed countries of Western Europe. That is, they are becoming Western Europe's "sewing rooms" through outward processing arrangements similar to U.S. 9802/807 operations in the Caribbean. A number of U.S. apparel firms and retailers have contracted production in this part of Europe also. This region is expected to become increasingly important as a site where firms from countries with high wages and labor shortages will seek production of their apparel lines (Dickerson, 1999).

Latin America and the Caribbean

In addition to Asia, many low-wage production facilities have developed in the Western Hemisphere, where labor is abundant and wages are as low or lower than in some Asian countries. Today, the garment industry is a major sector in the economies of the Dominican Republic, Mexico, Costa Rica, Honduras, El Salvador, Jamaica, Guatemala, Colombia, and others.

Figure 9–11

In recent years, apparel produced under 807 and 807A arrangements account for a growing share of U.S. apparel imports.

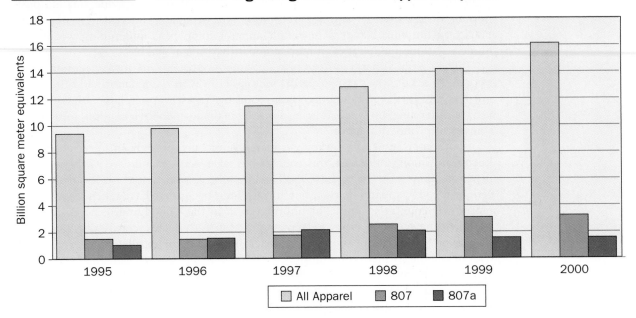

U.S IMPORTS OF APPAREL												
Million Square Meter Equivalents												
	All Countries			*Carribbean Basin Initiative*				*Mexico*				
	Total Apparel	*Total 807/807a*	*% 807/807a*	*Total Apparel*	*807*	*807a*	*Non 807*	*Total Apparel*	*807*	*807a*	*Non 807*	*All Other 807*
1990	6,007.1	788.3	13%	737.4	441.9	141.2	154.3	174.1	46.9	98.0	29.2	60.3
1991	6,149.2	1,011.7	16%	913.3	522.2	195.6	195.5	216.7	63.2	120.5	33.0	110.2
1992	7,078.6	1,260.8	18%	1,140.8	659.2	271.8	209.8	266.6	76.0	155.9	34.7	97.8
1993	7,545.9	1,520.3	20%	1,388.0	799.0	323.4	265.6	321.5	84.1	204.8	32.6	109.0
1994	8,421.5	1,674.8	20%	1,587.9	962.0	341.1	284.8	481.9	NA	NA	NA	NA
1995	9,254.9	2,528.8	27%	2,009.8	1,320.7	404.6	284.5	774.2	52.5	598.8	122.9	152.0
1996	9,658.5	2,957.0	31%	2,259.4	1,221.8	758.0	279.8	1,099.2	113.1	738.5	247.6	125.6
1997	11,349.1	3,862.3	34%	2,842.7	1,450.2	1,079.3	313.2	1,555.0	185.3	1,036.0	333.7	111.4
1998	12,885.5	4,378.7	34%	3,065.7	1,977.0	750.0	338.7	1,984.6	287.2	1,253.9	443.5	110.6
1999	14,102.9	4,775.8	34%	3,415.8	2,449.8	597.7	388.3	2,306.9	414.0	1,168.9	723.9	145.4
2000	16,035.6	4,636.7	29%	3,651.0	2,529.7	476.5	644.8	2,526.8	468.3	1,042.8	1,015.7	119.4
2000: 1st Qt.	3,776.0	1,101.7	29%	864.5	586.6	122.5	155.4	596.1	98.6	263.2	234.3	30.8
2001: 1st Qt.	4,036.6	742.7	18%	856.8	318.7	39.3	498.8	602.9	125.4	227.3	250.2	32.0
% Change 01/00	7%	-33%	-38%	-1%	-46%	-68%	NA	1%	27%	-14%	7%	4%

NOTE: Imports referred to as 807 presently enter the United States under Harmonized Tariff Schedule number 9802. 807A (9802.00.80.01) requires the use of U.S. formed fabric. SOURCE: U.S. Department of Commerce, Office of Textiles and Apparel. Totals may not add due to rounding.
*Correct 1994 807/807A apparel Import data from Mexico were not reported by the U.S. Census Bureau, and thus do not reflect actual trade.

Source: From *Textile HiLights*, September 2001, p. 30. Reprinted by permission of the American Textile Manufacturers Institute.

The Latin American and Caribbean[5] countries have become increasingly important producers for the U.S. garment industry. As retailers have expected faster and faster responses to their orders, many U.S. apparel firms have turned to *neighboring* low-wage countries to produce apparel. Garments can be made and shipped from this region in a matter of days, whereas shipments from Asia by boat can take a very long time. Merchandise from Asia has often taken six to nine months from the time it is ordered until it is delivered. This time lag in getting products from Asia (unless they are sent by costly air freight) ties up the apparel firm's capital for much longer periods of time and does not permit serving retail customers promptly. Consequently, U.S. sourcing in the Americas continues to grow.

In addition, a number of Asian apparel firms have plants in Central America and the Caribbean. Asian manufacturers, plagued by quota restrictions, rising labor costs, and a shortage of labor, have shifted some of their production to the region in order to gain easier entry into the U.S. markets. These Asian producers have also sensed that many U.S. firms prefer the Western Hemisphere over Asia as a place to source production.

For all these reasons, apparel from the Western Hemisphere accounts for a growing percentage of U.S. imports, as shown in Figure 9–11. Since the enactment of NAFTA, this trend has accelerated and is expected to continue (Abend, 1999; Jacobs, 1999; Kessler, 1999).

As we noted in Chapter 3, a number of preferential trade policies have favored garment production in the region, particularly in Mexico and the Caribbean countries. These included (1) NAFTA, (2) the 9802/807 provision of the tariff laws, (3) the Caribbean Basin Textile Access Program (807A or "Super 807" with its virtually unlimited quotas if fabrics are U.S.-made and cut), and (4) the U.S.-Caribbean Basin Trade Partnership Act (CBTPA) of 2000.

Shift of Foreign-Owned Factories to the United States

The drop in the dollar over the past few years together with rising costs of foreign labor and tight U.S. quota restrictions has made direct investment in the United States increasingly attractive to foreign companies. Some foreign producers are establishing a foothold in the U.S. industry and have shifted some of their production facilities to this country. This strategy puts the producers directly into a major market in which they wish to sell and eliminates costly shipping that would be involved when sending goods from great distances. Examples include Hong Kong's Odyssey International's expansion in the United States, which was mentioned in the previous chapter. Tai Apparel Ltd., another Hong Kong apparel producer, bought a 900-employee plant in North Carolina from Burlington Industries. The Kienja Industrial Co. of South Korea opened a sweater factory in South Carolina. A number of Asian textile firms have either bought or built production facilities in the southeast United States. Other Asian companies have established operations in New York's Chinatown district and in Los Angeles.

---

[5]For our discussion, this includes Mexico, the Caribbean, Central America, and some South American countries.

In most cases, the branch factories in the United States are controlled by headquarters in the home country. In some of these cases, designs, fabrics, and other components may be supplied by the home country rather than by segments of the U.S. industry.

Sweatshops: The "Third World" in the United States

The intensely competitive conditions of the apparel sector have led to a shameful dimension of the garment industry. As firms have felt the pressure from low-cost imports, plus the need to respond quickly to market demands, illegal **sweatshops** have sprung up to fill these needs. Found mostly in New York and Los Angeles, these sweatshops frequently prey on new immigrants to provide the workforce. These new immigrants, most often of Asian or Hispanic origin, often lack language or other job skills for other employment choices. They desperately need work to support themselves and their families. Moreover, many immigrants have gained entrance to the United States illegally, which makes them further vulnerable.

Dishonorable entrepreneurs, often of the same ethnic groups they exploit, have taken advantage of this situation by starting sweatshops that provide cheap production for both apparel firms and retailers looking for inexpensive garment contracting. These contractors fill the same role that we have discussed for domestic and overseas contractors. They produce garments on a contractual basis and return finished merchandise to the apparel firm or retailer that contracted with them.

The big difference, however, is that sweatshops operate illegally in a number of ways. Workers are not paid U.S. minimum wages—hence, the attraction to these disreputable firms. Working conditions normally covered by government regulations and benefits expected in the United States today are flagrantly absent. Because workers have few other job options, they are unlikely to report the conditions for fear of losing their only source of income. Many newcomers simply may not know that they should be treated differently; the conditions they suffer in the U.S. sweatshops may be far better than those in the country they left. Illegal immigrants have no option to complain. If they do, they will be deported.

The U.S. public became aware of the sweatshop system in the mid-1990s when authorities discovered a factory in Los Angeles where illegal immigrants from Thailand were being forced to work under slavelike conditions. Tied to an illegal Bangkok operation that promised opportunities to workers to go to the United States, this sweatshop ring isolated immigrants on their arrival and did not permit them to go outside the factory walls. Workers were exploited by receiving wages as low as those in Third World countries. Most of the workers' meager wages were taken to reimburse Thai ringleaders for the costs of transporting them to the United States. Following the disclosure of this operation, U.S. labor and immigration authorities initiated a crackdown on sweatshop operations. Authorities discovered that sweatshops were not unusual in New York and particularly in southern California.

The sweatshop system, closely resembling that in existence in the late 1800s and early 1900s, can be very complex. The contractor for whom the retailer or apparel firm is working may further **subcontract** the work for actual production. That is, the contractor may or may not actually produce the garments. Some contractors in these schemes are simply "middlemen" (or women) who farm out the work to subcontractors. The subcontractors are small sweatshops or even families who produce the garments in their homes. In these arrangements, the individuals who actually do the work are paid woefully low wages to permit those at each stage between the worker and the original owner of the goods to reap profit from the sewing operators' labor.

The contracting system also provides an unfortunate escape route for unscrupulous operators. If the illegal activities are discovered by authorities, each participant claims not to have known about the sweatshop conditions. That is, the manufacturer or retailer claims ignorance of the contractor's illegal activities, and the

Figure 9–12

Members of the Union of Needletrades, Industrial and Textile Employees (UNITE!) stage demonstrations to protest sweatshops in the United States.

Source: Photo by Dwight Burton, courtesy of UNITE!.

Figure 9–13

Is It a WRAP on Poor Working Conditions?

 In introducing the Worldwide Responsible Apparel Production (WRAP) Certification Program at the Bobbin Show, American Apparel and Footwear Association chairman and Kellwood vice-chairman James Jacobsen emphasized the need to speedily implement the program worldwide.

Built on 12 principles based on legal standards for labor practices and factory conditions, WRAP includes bans on forced labor, child labor, and workplace discrimination. It also requires factories' full compliance with all local laws and regulations, including customers and environmental rules.

"This initiative is designed to improve the working conditions worldwide by leveraging the combined strength of apparel manufacturers to ensure all workers are treated fairly," Jacobsen noted.

"The WRAP program has run two pilot inspection efforts and determined that the program is both workable for factory managers and that it uses sufficiently rigorous requirements for factories to demonstrate ongoing compliance," said AAFA then-president Larry Martin.

These Worldwide Responsible Apparel Production Principles are core standards for production facilities participating in the Worldwide Responsible Apparel Production, Certification Program. The Program's objective is to independently monitor and certify compliance with these socially responsible global standards for manufacturing and ensure that sewn products are produced under lawful, humane and ethical conditions. Participating companies voluntarily agree that their production and that of their contractors will be certified by the WRAP CERTIFICATION PROGRAM as complying with these standards.

- **Compliance with Laws and Workplace Regulations—Manufacturers of Sewn Product** will comply with laws and regulations in all locations where they conduct business.
- **Prohibition of Forced Labor—Manufacturers of Sewn Product** will not use involuntary or forced labor—indentured, bonded, or otherwise.
- **Prohibition of Child Labor—Manufacturers of Sewn Product** will not hire any employee under the age of 14, or under the age interfering with compulsory schooling, or under the minimum age established by law, whichever is greater.
- **Prohibition of Harassment or Abuse—Manufacturers of Sewn Product** will provide a work environment free of harassment, abuse, or corporal punishment in any form.
- **Compensation and Benefits—Manufacturers of Sewn Product** will pay at least the minimum total compensation required by local law, including all mandated wages, allowances, and benefits.
- **Hours of Work—Manufacturers of Sewn Product** will comply with hours worked each day, and days worked each week, shall not exceed the legal limitations of the countries in which sewn product is produced. Manufacturers of sewn product will provide at least one day off in every seven-day period, except as required to meet urgent business needs.
- **Prohibition of Discrimination—Manufacturers of Sewn Product** will employ, pay, promote, and terminate workers on the basis of their ability to do the job, rather than on the basis of personal characteristics or beliefs.
- **Health and Safety—Manufacturers of Sewn Product** will provide a safe and healthy work environment. Where residential housing is provided for workers, apparel manufacturers will provide safe and healthy housing.
- **Freedom of Association—Manufacturers of Sewn Product** will recognize and respect the right of employees to exercise their lawful rights of free association and collective bargaining.
- **Environment—Manufacturers of Sewn Product** will comply with environmental rules, regulations, and standards applicable to their operations, and will observe environmentally conscious practices in all locations where they operate.
- **Customs Compliance—Manufacturers of Sewn Product** will comply with applicable customs law and, in particular, will establish and maintain programs to comply with customs laws regarding illegal transshipment of apparel products.
- **Drug Interdiction—Manufacturers of Sewn Product** will cooperate with local, national, and foreign customs and drug enforcement agencies to guard against illegal shipments of drugs.

Source: From the WRAP press kit by the American Apparel & Footwear Association, 1999, Arlington, VA: Author. Adapted by permission.

contractor claims not to know about the subcontractor's illegal operations. In some cases, astute firms truly had not been aware of what happened once they contracted the work, and unfortunately had not inspected production sites.

Following the disclosure of the Thai sweatshop-slavery operation and subsequent sweatshop investigations, a number of major U.S. apparel firms and retailers were identified as having contracted for garments made in those shops. Many respected firms had their images tarnished by participating in these schemes, sometimes unknowingly. In a few cases, businesses were picketed by individuals who called attention to the company's use of sweatshops; pickets encouraged consumers to boycott merchandise from those companies.

As a result of the negative sweatshop publicity, many apparel firms and retailers developed company policies requiring close monitoring of production conditions. Both the U.S. Department of Labor and the U.S. Immigration and Naturalization Service began more active surveillance of the industry. UNITE, the major industry union, became involved, denouncing these conditions, as shown in Figure 9–12. The American Apparel and Footwear Association has developed a program to monitor contractors, both in the United States and abroad. This program, known as **WRAP** (Worldwide Responsible Apparel Production) is discussed in Figure 9–13.

In today's globally competitive apparel industry, it is likely there will always be disreputable entrepreneurs who attempt to profit from the unfortunate conditions of vulnerable workers. Professionals in the industry must be on guard to avoid being part of these schemes, no matter how financially attractive they may seem in an industry characterized by cutthroat competition.

Fashion: A Global Business Today

Today, in addition to shopping European countries for new and incoming fashion ideas and for high-quality products, knowledgeable manufacturers and retailers travel throughout the world seeking low-wage production partners for apparel and accessories. Representatives of these apparel and retailing firms travel from Shenzhen to San José, from Cairo to Calcutta, from Bogota to Bucharest, and from Kuala Lumpur to Kathmandu, with stops in between. Because apparel and accessory production can occur almost anywhere in the world, the world is a stage on which contract or other business arrangements occur. Partners in other countries must be able to provide quality, timely deliveries, and appropriate service for these arrangements to be satisfactory. In other words, contracting production halfway around the world cannot be based solely on low labor costs.

The fashion business has indeed become global in all its aspects—design, production, and distribution. In the process, it has made the whole world into a collection of garment centers. Boundaries, borders, hemispheres—these represent no obstacle if there is an idea or facility the fashion world can use.

Readings

Fashion producers from those in the haute couture to Third World sweatshops are adapting to a rapidly evolving global market. Producers on each end of this production continuum play an important role in providing fashion products for consumers.

Not So Haute: French Fashion Loses Its Primacy as Women Leave Couture Behind

According to this article, the French fashion industry has lost its leadership position, whereas Italian, U.S., and German designers have gained international prestige. The writer suggests the French industry needs to strengthen its marketing efforts to effectively appeal to today's customers.

The Barons of Far East Fashion

Asia accounts for about 40 percent of world trade in textiles and apparel. This article, written by an Asian writer, provides an overview of the industry in key nations.

Not So Haute: French Fashion Loses Its Primacy as Women Leave Couture Behind

by Teri Agins

It was a classic Paris "fashion moment." After Christian Lacroix's *haute couture* show of ornate suits and gowns last month, an exhausted but exhilarated Mr. Lacroix took his runway bow, as ladies leapt from their gilt chairs and tossed carnations at him.

But this effusive response obscured the stark truth: Although Paris has been synonymous with high fashion since the late 1800s, when the first French couture houses began charming European royalty with elegant wardrobes, France's fashion supremacy is now largely mystique.

The couture houses, which turned Pierre Cardin, Yves Saint Laurent, Givenchy and Lanvin into household names during the designer licensing boom that began in the 1970s, have lost their leadership position in a fast-moving global market where savvy fashion houses in Italy, the U.S. and Germany have gained international prestige.

And France's new generation of designers, such as Mr. Lacroix, Jean-Paul Gaultier, Claude Montana and Thierry Mugler, have failed so far to turn their avant-garde styles into commercial hits.

Passages

Retail-industry economist Carl Steidtmann calls the waning French influence a "reflection of what happens in the life cycle of all businesses," akin to International Business Machines Corp.'s troubles when computer upstarts came out with innovative products.

Source: From Wall Street Journal, *August 29, 1995, p. 1, A8. Reprinted by permission.*

"When you look back to the 1950s and 1960s, the Paris designers had an ability to create a fashion look that everyone wanted to have," says Mr. Steidtmann, of the Management Horizons division of Price Waterhouse. "The French felt they didn't need to market to consumers because their brands were very strong. But the focus has shifted away from designing, and if you have enough money and are good at marketing, you can create a strong brand."

Giorgio Armani, Jil Sander, Prada and Donna Karan are among the non-French labels that have redefined modern fashion by steering clear of the rigid couture tradition of sharply tailored suits and gowns, painstakingly sewn for elite patrons largely by hand. The new designers appeal to professional, globe-trotting women, both affluent and middle class, who demand comfortable, understated wardrobes such as the softly tailored jackets and pants by Armani or the simple black nylon dresses from Italy's Prada.

Socialites and countesses interested in carrying the torch for couture are in short supply—and are no longer the fashion role models for most women. Last month, in the ballroom of the Grand Hotel where the final couture show of retiring designer Hubert de Givenchy was held, the famous clients who attended were American women, a lineup that recalled the society columns of the 1980s, including Mercedes Bass, Susan Gutfreund and Lynn Wyatt.

Still Chic

"France is still the capital for servicing fashion—the best place for holding fashion shows," observes Ralph Toledano, a Paris-based marketing consultant who formerly ran the fashion business of Karl Lagerfeld and now is helping Seventh Avenue's Donna Karan expand in Europe. "But the volume of manufacturing of French goods is down, and it is true that French designers are no longer on top."

But the French fashion establishment still considers itself the pre-eminent player. "Before, France was alone in the world, so it had a privileged position," says Jacques Mouclier, president of the Chambre Syndicale, France's main fashion-industry trade group. "It's not so much that France loses its prestige, but we are finding a market that is more competitive than ever."

Haute couture dates back to pioneering Paris designer Charles Worth—an Englishman—who introduced the bustle dress in the 1860s that liberated women from hoop skirts of the era. Paris later spawned legendary designers such as Coco Chanel, Balenciaga and Christian Dior, whose creations caused a ripple effect around the world. In 1947, Dior's radical New Look of sweeping, ankle-grazing hemlines suddenly rendered every woman's wardrobe of short, straight skirts obsolete.

License in Licensing

But the French never developed a strong apparel manufacturing industry. Even during the designer boom years when their labels reached the mass market, the couture houses didn't make the goods. They licensed their names to the hilt and raked in millions in royalties with a flood of "designer" merchandise, including polyester ties and scarves, vinyl luggage, even Yves Saint Laurent cigarettes.

In 1988, Pierre Cardin had 840 licensees, including bidets and frying pans. Christian Dior had 300 and Yves Saint Laurent had 200. "The French houses overlicensed their names and hurt the image," says Richard Simonin, managing director of Givenchy.

While he is confident about Givenchy's prospects, Mr. Simonin believes many of France's 18 remaining couture houses won't survive in the face of growing international competition. Declining to name names, he predicts: "Half of them will close down over the next few years."

Pierre Berge, the managing director of Yves Saint Laurent, vows that the moment Mr. Saint Laurent, 58 years old, retires, the couture part of his operation will close. "Who cares? Nobody cares," Mr. Berge barks. "The money will be better spent to advertise ready-to-wear [collections] and the perfume."

French perfumes have also lost their sizzle. Fashion houses have traditionally depended on high-profit perfume classics like Nina Ricci's L'Air du Temps, which derived their success from the heavily publicized couture shows. But by the early 1980s, American perfumers like Estee Lauder, Giorgio of Beverly Hills and Calvin Klein had begun to upstage the French with their heavily advertised fragrances.

"Fifteen or 20 years ago, half to two-thirds of the top 20 fragrances in the U.S. were French," says John Ledes, editor of Cosmetic World, an industry newsletter. Sales of once-popular scents from couture houses such as Rochas, Nina Ricci and Paco Rabanne "have gone down dramatically," Mr. Ledes says.

The stellar exception is the 83-year-old house of Chanel, which was revived by the German-born Mr. Lagerfeld, a plucky marketer who jazzed up Chanel's tweed suits and accessories and made them appealing to well-to-do women under 30. Buoyed by its enduring Chanel No. 5 perfume, the company is estimated to generate retail sales of nearly $1 billion.

But Mr. Lagerfeld agrees that consumers around the world "are no longer impressed with the prestige of Paris. The Italians are very clever marketers," he says, "and the Americans are making modern and interesting clothes, capturing the right mood of today."

Moi and My Calvins

Indeed, American designers are planning aggressive expansion throughout Europe, particularly in France. Calvin Klein Inc. snared Gabriella Forte, a longtime Armani executive with strong ties in Europe, to serve as president, and will introduce Calvin Klein underwear in Galeries Lafayette department store in Paris next month.

A telling sign of the times: On his first day of office in May, French President Jacques Chirac appeared on the cover of Paris Match magazine sporting an Ivy League look: an oxford dress shirt with a Polo/Ralph Lauren logo.

French investors in fashion businesses are even coming to America to underwrite promising fashion talent. In 1990, Chanel bought a controlling interest in the New York fashion house of Isaac Mizrahi, the charismatic, 33-year-old designer now featured in the documentary "Unzipped."

"The French companies think the American designers are bringing ice to the Eskimos, but what they don't realize is that French consumers are thirsty for something new," says Susan Rice, a marketing consultant based in Paris. And French women are being swayed. "French design is outdated," declares Francoise Aron, president of Paris-based El Dorado advertising agency, whose clients include Hermes, the French purveyor of leather and silk goods, and the Clarins cosmetic company. Ms. Aron says she likes the "simplicity" of designers like Armani, Prada and Donna Karan. As for Mr. Saint Laurent, she concludes: "He reigned all these years, but I find he's less modern, his style is less new, a little old-fashioned."

Better in Italy

The Italian fashion industry poses the most formidable challenge to the French. Italy not only boasts some of the world's finest fabric houses but also a number of top apparel manufacturers such as Gruppo GFT, which makes apparel for, among others, Giorgio Armani and Calvin Klein. It took Gruppo GFT to sell French fashion to Americans: It designs and manufactures Emanuel, one of the few strong French ready-to-wear labels in America, for *couturier* Emanuel Ungaro, under a licensing pact.

"As far as salability, the Italians know how to do it better than the French," says Joan Weinstein, owner of Ultimo, a boutique on Chicago's swank Oak Street. Ms. Weinstein dropped a number of French lines because they were too formal-looking and lacked the variety many women want. "When you are looking for a well-thought-out collection," she says, "there aren't too many of them coming from France."

The French couturiers also took a hard knock when Escada, a 20-year-old German fashion house, beat them at their own game by selling quality French-inspired styles at prices that were still high— $3,000 for an outfit—but lower than the $15,000 made-to-order couture versions.

Escada now operates its fragrance and accessories divisions right in Paris and expects its sales in France to hit $56 million this year, double 1990's.

The French fashion establishment has been slow to change partly because it got a reprieve in new markets in Asia, selling to newly affluent consumers. French fashion companies generate about 40% of their revenue from Asia, up from 25% a decade ago; 20% now comes from the U.S., down from 30%, according to Mr. Mouclier of the French trade group.

This month, French fashion shows in Hong Kong were an "indisputable success," drawing lots of publicity and "all of high society," Mr. Mouclier boasts. The group will put on more fashion shows next year in other new markets like Beijing, Shanghai, Budapest and Belarus.

But most industry experts agree that the French won't dominate such markets for long. "With Japanese consumers traveling abroad and CNN reaching everyone, women around the world are now exposed to the same trends at the same time," says G. Chrysler Fisher, who formerly ran the U.S. division of Hermes. "Strong brands like Armani and Calvin Klein are getting far more attention than Givenchy. Consumers in emerging markets will look to them for leadership."

Vicky Ross, New York liaison for the Hong Kong-based Joyce chain of 49 Asian boutiques, is unimpressed with what she sees in the French showrooms: "It's the same 10 old men doing a boring rehash of what they've already done, like the hobble skirts that are too tight and are too expensive."

So for France's fashion houses, the name of the game is playing catch-up. Last month, Givenchy hired a spirited young designer, British-born John Galliano, 34, to replace 68-year-old Hubert de Givenchy, who is retiring. And both Givenchy and Christian Dior are pulling back licenses in an effort to restore their exclusive images. Dior's U.S. sales have shrunk to about half of the $1 billion level of the late 1980s.

French fans of couture are putting their faith in Mr. Lacroix, the 44-year-old couturier, who is striving to get his business into the black. Several years ago, he made his couture debut with the pouf-skirted dress—a look that became *the* party dress of the late 1980s. But the house of Lacroix failed to turn its early fame into fortune, racking up more than $40 million in losses. It stumbled badly in 1991 when its C'est la Vie! perfume flopped.

Lacroix—which, like Givenchy, is owned by LVMH Moet Hennessy Louis Vuitton—has been expected to break even, according to Robert Bensoussan-Torres, the house's managing director. Last year, Lacroix's new Bazar collection of colorful gypsy skirts, vests and sportswear racked up a respectable $20 million in sales. Next up: Lacroix's first designer jeans. Says Mr. Bensoussan-Torres: "Before we launch another perfume, we have to get women into our clothes."

Soon after Mr. Lacroix's fashion show last month, the house received some 30 orders from women for couture ensembles. Lacroix's Mr. Bensoussan-Torres points to these as evidence that couture—while it loses money—is still a valid enterprise. "Haute couture is the pure exercise of design. It is the best, it is untouchable," he declares. "It makes women dream."

But critics say the real dreamers are the French fashion houses. "We are selling products that nobody really needs," says Chanel's Mr. Lagerfeld. The industry must move on "to advertise, to do better marketing. There has to be a next step, and that is the question mark for the future of French fashion."

The Barons of Far East Fashion

by Josephine Bow

Asia's fashion barons pack a formidable punch. While the region may still lag behind in original fashion design, top-notch manufacturers surge ahead on the retail front—and they sport not only comprehensive technical and production smarts, but important marketing lessons culled from overseas buyers.

The retailing transformation now sweeping Asia leaves no country untouched. Cash-rich Hong Kong, Taiwan and Singapore are studded with modern department stores and exclusive upmarket boutiques, bulging with high-quality Asian-made or -distributed goods.

Developing countries such as Thailand, Indonesia, Malaysia and China are seeing their investment coffers filled. And Asian entrepreneurs, with their particular brand of versatility, creativity and the ability to take calculated risks, are piling up impressive results.

A quick trip around the garment and textile factories of Asia today shows just how rapid the voyage to economic maturity has been. From still-lowly Pakistan to mighty Japan, each country in Asia has climbed the development ladder astride the textile industry.

From nations like struggling Bangladesh, where annual per capita income barely tops US$200, the garment industry has been a lifeline to developing-nation status. In the past 10 years, some 1,600 factories have appeared, and the country hums to the drone of sewing machines.

Countries like Sri Lanka, Nepal and Vietnam tell similar tales. Take the fashionable, impeccably made padded jackets destined for Europe's top shops that are now being churned out, and compare these to the drab Soviet monstrosities Vietnamese factories put together only a few seasons ago, and you understand Asia's astounding growth, both in symbolic and concrete terms.

As a garment-processing country moves up the industry chain, it begins to harness newly developing managerial and financial resources. Local content increases, profits from exports soar, the currency strengthens and then—seemingly overnight—the inevitable occurs: economic factors shift and the country stops being an interesting manufacturing site.

South Korea is one country currently at this crossroads. Garment manufacturers, squeezed by skyrocketing costs and shrinking labor forces, are under pressure from government to move into higher technology sectors. Still some are putting up a good fight to stick with textiles.

Large South Korean companies have gone into lower-cost offshore production, setting up operations in Central America, Indonesia, Vietnam, China and even North Korea. To survive at home, some upmarket South Korean manufacturers have scaled down and done the unthinkable—reduced minimum orders. Production is booked year round, and with consistent quality standards and timely deliveries, buyers aren't complaining over stiff prices.

Taiwan's efforts to save its garment industry haven't seemed nearly as cohesive. So far major companies have set up a hodge podge of overseas operations and seem content to rely on the country's considerable strength in capital and in synthetic textile production.

Source: From Asia Magazine, *33 (K–5), December 2–4, 1994, pp. 9–12. Reprinted with permission.*

Still, Taiwanese investment clout is leaving its mark in joint venture textile industry operations all over the region, and the island nation is exhibiting remarkable retailing ingenuity in China.

Meanwhile, the Philippines, Thailand and Malaysia appear to be floundering. While garments and textiles continue to be substantial revenue earners and provide much needed employment, labour costs are rising, capital backing is lacking and long-term commitment is scarce.

The decade's biggest story of the garment business is China, simultaneously possessing the world's largest manufacturing base and its greatest untapped market. The country's new capitalists are eager to duplicate the successes of their overseas cousins, both in manufacturing and retailing. To this end, massive efforts are underway to modernise the nation's lumbering textile plants.

Another growing force in Asia's garment industry is Indonesia, which has enjoyed the advantage of beginning with a clean slate. Flush with revenue from oil earnings in the 1970s, forward thinkers opted from the start for the latest in technology and management. Today, many of the country's garment factories and textile plants are industry models, attracting a host of eager, well-trained Asian expatriate upper level staff.

In the wings stand two other potential contenders, Pakistan and India. Raw cotton exports already represent 60 percent of Pakistan's economy, although it is still too early to assess efforts to move down the processing chain.

India's industry is similarly cotton dependent and recent dynamic policies aimed at liberalising foreign investment are expected to give the sector a much needed boost.

But Hong Kong is without question the vibrant, pulsating nerve centre of Asia's (and arguably, the world's) garment and textile industry. Second only to Italy for clothing exports, Hong Kong factories employ some 2.5 million workers in southern China alone.

"From Hong Kong you can order garments made anywhere in the world," says David Birnbaum, author of the recently published *Importing Garments from Hong Kong*.

"Hong Kong offers an unequalled level of professionalism, providing access to the world's fabrics, production bases, reliable agents, and the best in modern telecommunications, financial and shipping services, all in one convenient location."

Retailers echo that comment.

"Eventually the Far East will be like a single country," says Jeffrey Fan, chief executive officer of Toppy Ltd. "Regional retail chains will stretch across Asia, with Hong Kong as the trendsetter. Because of greater competition and exposure to the rest of the world, Hong Kong shops will always be the most sophisticated in merchandise, design, and management."

Chapter Review

Key Words and Concepts

Define, identify, or briefly explain the following:

"Asian Tigers"
Canadian Apparel Federation (CAF)
Capital intensive
Caution fee
Chambre Syndicale de la Couture Parisienne
Contracting system
Couturier and couturière
Düsseldorf
Fashion center
Fédération Française du Prêt-à-Porter Féminin
Franchised boutiques
Franchising arrangement
Free trade zone (FTZ)
Haute couture
Hong Kong Trade Development Council (HKTDC)
IGEDO

Interstoff
Landed cost
Licensing agreement
Newly industrialized country (NIC)
Overseas contractors
Prêt-à-porter
Privatized
Subcontract
Subsidies
Sweatshops
Taiwan Textile Federation (TTF)
Third World nations
Trade show
Upgrading
WRAP

Review Questions on Chapter Highlights

1. Name the three categories of foreign fashion producers and explain how they differ.
2. What is a haute couture house, and how do its operations differ from those of a U.S. apparel company? Are there haute couture houses in the United States? Explain your answer.
3. What is the prêt-à-porter division of the Chambre Syndicale de la Couture Parisienne, and why did it come into existence?
4. What are the major sources of income for haute couture houses?
5. What are some other centers of high fashion in the world today?
6. What role do the Canadian and U.S. apparel industries play in each other's home market? How has this changed in recent years?
7. Who does overseas contracting and why?

8. Identify the NICs. Describe how the apparel industry has changed in the NICs and why this is so.
9. What single country has the potential to have a great impact on virtually every apparel market in the world? Why is this country called a "sleeping giant"?
10. Pick one of the other countries discussed in the chapter as an important source for contract production. Locate it on a world map. Go to a library or online reference and learn about the country's economic and political situation. How is the economic situation related to the fact that the country does contract production of apparel?
11. Why are the governments in many other countries so eager to develop the apparel industry in their respective countries?

12. What changes have taken place in Central and Eastern Europe in the last decade? What have these changes meant to the apparel industry there?

13. Why have the Latin American and Caribbean countries become important apparel production sites?

14. Describe how you might envision a sweatshop. Why have these developed in the United States? How can sweatshops be eliminated?

15. What is the WRAP program? Why do you think this was developed?

16. Why should a person entering the fashion business today have a good knowledge of geography?

17. Why are "boundaries, borders, and hemispheres" no longer obstacles for today's global fashion industry?

18. What is one specific step *you* plan to take to be prepared to participate in today's global economy?

References

Abend, J. (1999, November). U.S. mills move south. *Bobbin*, 44–52.

Agins, T. (1995, August 29). Not so haute: French fashion loses its primacy as women leave couture behind. *Wall Street Journal*, pp. A1, A8.

Agins, T. (1999). *The end of fashion: The mass marketing of the clothing business*. New York: William Morrow and Company, Inc.

American Apparel Manufacturers Association. (annual). *Focus: Economic profile of the apparel industry*. Arlington, VA: Author.

British Apparel and Textile Confederation. (1999). *TRENDATA: Key statistics of the UK apparel and textile industry, executive summary*. Unpublished report.

Canadian Apparel Federation. (1999). *Canadian Apparel Federation* (information packet). Ottawa: Author.

Designers grumble but fashion goes on. (1976, July 26). *Women's Wear Daily*.

Dickerson, K. (1999). *Textiles and apparel in the global economy*. Upper Saddle River, NJ: Prentice Hall.

Dunn, B. (2000, January 18). Canada: Heading south. *Women's Wear Daily* (Global edition), pp. 22–23.

Engardio, P., Barnathan, J., & Glasgall, W. (1993, November 29). Asia's wealth. *Business Week*, pp. 100–108.

Fédération Française de la Couture de Prêt-à-Porter des Couturiers et des Creatéurs de Mode.

(1995). *La haute couture et le prêt-à-porter des couturiers et des createurs de mode*. (Unpublished informational piece, translated by L. Divita).

General Agreement on Tariffs and Trade/World Trade Organization (various times). Personal communication with GATT/WTO economist and trade counselor.

Jacobs, B. (1999, November). Regional pacts produce new trade patterns. *Bobbin*, 65–68.

Kessler, J. (1999, November). New NAFTA alliances reshape sourcing scene. *Bobbin*, 54–62.

Middleton, W. (1995, August 21). French fashion now (special feature section on Chambre Syndicale). *Women's Wear Daily*, 18–19.

Ostroff, J. (2000, January 18). U.S.–Canada Free Trade pact great for friends, not for foes. *Women's Wear Daily* (Global edition), p. 19.

Porter, M. (1990). *Competitive advantage of nations*. New York: Free Press.

Voice of the couture. (1984, December). *Vanity Fair*.

Weisman, K. (1995a, September 12). Interstoff to split shows. *Women's Wear Daily*, 21.

Weisman, K. (1995b, October 10). Keeping Paris king. *Women's Wear Daily*, 26.

Werner International. (annual). *Spinning and weaving labour cost comparisons*. New York: Author.

World Trade Organization. (1995). *International trade: 1995 trends and statistics*. Geneva, Switzerland: Author.

Suggested Bibliography

Agins, T. (1999). *The end of fashion: The mass marketing of the clothing business*. New York: William Morrow and Company, Inc.

Balkwell, C., & Dickerson, K. (1994). Apparel production in the Caribbean: A classic case of the new international division of labor. *Clothing and Textiles Research Journal, 12*(3), 6–15.

Balmain, P. (1985). *40 Annés de Creation*. Paris: Musée de la Mode et du Costume.

Bonacich, E., Cheng, L., Chinchilla, N., Hamilton, N., & Ong, P. (Eds.). (1994). *Global production: The apparel industry in the Pacific Rim*. Philadelphia: Temple University Press.

Calliaway, N. (1988). *Issey Miyake*. New York: New York Graphic Society.

Charles-Roux, E. (1975). *Chanel*. New York: Alfred A. Knopf.

Caribbean high-tech dreams. (2000, August 14). *Business Week*, 38.

DeGraw, I. G. (1975). *25 Years/25 Couturiers*. Denver: Art Publication.

DesMarteau, K. (2000, August). Labor conditions— not someone else's problem. *Bobbin*, 1.

Dickerson, K. (1991). *Textiles and apparel in the international economy*. Upper Saddle River, NJ: Merrill/Prentice Hall.

Dickerson, K. (1999). *Textiles and apparel in the global economy*. Upper Saddle River, NJ: Prentice Hall.

Dior, C. (1957). *Christian Dior and I*. New York: E. P. Dutton.

ECHO. (1991). *Textiles and clothing in Eastern Europe*. London: The Economist Intelligence Unit.

Egan, S., & Steinhoff, D. (2000, March). China's WTO entry: Who wins? Who loses? *Apparel Industry Magazine*, 18–20.

Finnerty, A. (1991). *Textiles and clothing in Southeast Asia*. London: The Economist Intelligence Unit.

Giroud, F. (1987). *Dior*. New York: Rizzoli International.

Grunwald, J., & Flamm, K. (1985). *The global factory*. Washington, DC: The Brookings Institution.

Levaux, J. (2001, January). Adapting products and services for global commerce. *World Trade*, 52–54.

Leymarie, J. (1987). *Chanel*. New York: Rizzoli International.

Lyman, R. (Ed). (1972). *Couture*. Garden City, NY: Doubleday.

Milbank, C. R. (1985). *Couture: The great designers*. New York: Steward, Tabori and Chang.

Poiret, P. (1931). *Kings of Fashion*. Philadelphia: J. B. Lippincott.

Porter, M. (1990). *Competitive advantage of nations*. New York: Free Press.

Quant, M. (1966). *Quant by Quant*. New York: Putnam.

Rhodes, Z., & Knight, A. (1985). *The Art of Zandra Rhodes*. Boston: Houghton Mifflin.

Rykiel, S. (1985). *Rykiel*. Paris: Herscher.

Saint Laurent, Yves. (1983). *Yves St. Laurent*. New York: Metropolitan Museum of Art.

Saunders, E. (1955). *The Age of Worth*. Bloomington, Indiana: University Press.

Scheines, J. (Ed.) (1998). *Sourcing without surprises*. Arlington, VA: American Apparel Manufacturers Association.

Schaparelli, E. (1954). *Shocking Life*. New York: E. P. Dutton.

Skrebneski, V. (1994). *The art of haute couture*. New York: Abbeville Press.

Steele, P. (1990). *Hong Kong clothing: Waiting for China*. London: The Economist Intelligence Unit.

Steele, P. (1988). *The Caribbean clothing industry: The U.S. and Far East connections*. London: The Economist Intelligence Unit.

Steele, V. (1988). *Paris Fashion: A cultural history*. New York: Oxford University Press.

Toyne, B., Arpan, J., Barnett, A., Ricks, D., & Shimp, T. (1984). *The global textile industry*. London: George Allen & Unwin.

Walker, A. (1995). *West European textiles to 2000: Markets and trends*. London: Financial Times.

Werbeloff, A. (1987). *Textiles in Africa: A trade and investment guide*. London: Alain Charles Publishing Ltd.

Trade Associations

British Clothing Industry Association, 5 Portland Place, London W1N 3AA, U.K.

British Fashion Council, 5 Portland Place, London W1N 3AA, U.K.

Camara Nacional de la Industria del Vestido (National Chamber of the Apparel Industry), Tolsa No. 54, 06040 Mexico, D.F.

Camara Nacional de la Industria Textil (National Chamber of the Textile Industry), Plinio No. 220, Col Polanco, 11510 Mexico, D.F.

Canadian Apparel Federation, 130 Slater St., Suite 605, Ottawa, Ontario, K1P 6E2, Canada.

Canadian Apparel Federation/Design Link, 372 Richmond St. W., Suite 112, Toronto, Ontario M5V 1X6, Canada.

Fédération Française de la Couture, 100–102, Faubourg Saint-Honoré, 75008 Paris, France.

FENECON, P.O. Box 69265, 1060 CH Amsterdam, Netherlands.

Hong Kong Trade Development Council, 38th Floor, Office Tower, Convention Plaza, 1 Harbour Rd., Wanchai, Hong Kong.

Institut Francais de la Mode, 33 rue Jean Goujon, 75008 Paris, France.

Israel Export Institute (Fashion Division), 350 Fifth Ave., New York, NY 10118.

Japan Apparel Industry Council, Room 301 Aoyama Nozue Building, 2–11–10, Kita-Aoyama, Minato-Ku, Tokyo, Japan.

Taiwan Textile Federation, TTF Building, No. 22, Ai Kuo East Rd., Taipei, Taiwan, Republic of China.

Turkish Clothing Manufacturers Association, Yildizposta Caddesi 48/18, Gayrettepe-Istanbul, Turkey.

Trade Publications

Apparel International, The White House, 60 High St., Potters Bar, Herts, EN6 5AB, U.K.

A.T.A. Journal (Asian textiles and apparel), 14/F, Devon House, Taikoo Place, 979 King's Rd., Quarry Bay, Hong Kong.

Canadian Apparel Manufacturer, 1 Pacifique, Saint Anne de Bellevue, Quebec H9X 1C5, Canada.

CAMA (Children's Apparel Manufacturers Association) Parade, 8270 Mountain Sights #101, Montreal, Quebec H4P 2B7, Canada.

DNR, 7 W. 34th St., New York, NY 10001–8191.

Fashion Femme, 1 Pacifique, Saint Anne de Bellevue, Quebec H9X 1C5, Canada.

Fashion Industry News, 250A Eglinton Ave. E., Toronto, Ontario M4P 1K0, Canada.

International Textiles, 23 Bloomsbury Square, London WCIA 2PJ, U.K.

Style Magazine, Suite 301–785 Plymouth, Montreal, Quebec H4P 1B3, Canada.

Textile Asia, P.O. Box 185, California Tower, 11th Floor, 30–32, D'Aguilar Street, Hong Kong.

Women's Wear Daily, 7 W. 34th St., New York, NY 10001–8191.

World Clothing Manufacturer, 23 Bloomsbury Square, London WCIA 2PJ, U.K.

*T*he Retailers of Fashion

*E*ventually all merchandise that is designed and produced must reach the ultimate consumers, and that is the role and responsibility of **retailers**. In the course of buying and selling goods that are acceptable to their customers, retailers also serve the industry as a series of listening posts on the consumer front. At the same time, they act as a medium for disseminating information and stimulating demand for fashion products.

Retailers of fashion outnumber fashion producers by more than seven to one and are the largest source of fashion industry jobs. It is estimated that there are approximately 110,000 retailers that specialize in fashion apparel and accessories, another 38,000 that include some apparel and accessories in their merchandise assortment, and more than 24,000 jewelry stores (National Retail Institute, 1999). Some retailers are giant companies as, for example, Wal-Mart and Sears, which are among the world's largest businesses. At the other extreme are small **"mom-and-pop" stores** run by an owner with few or no assistants. Many new **retail formats** are becoming increasingly important.

The first part of this chapter discusses the differing kinds of retail operations and the period and environmental circumstances of their origin. The second part discusses the many changes that have occurred in fashion retailing today. The readings that follow the text illustrate some of the new trends and challenges having an impact on retailing today.

Fashion Retailing in the Past

In the early 1800s, there were only about 10 million people in the United States, and most were farmers or pioneers moving westward with the frontier. Except for the few cities established along the Atlantic coast, the country was rural. Transportation was by foot, on horseback, or by horse and wagon. Roads, such as they were, were little more than Indian trails through the wilderness. Retailers that functioned in this environment were small country stores and trading posts or itinerant peddlers. The last-named group traveled from farm to farm, offering for sale such small conveniences as cutlery, tools, buttons, combs, hand mirrors, needles, and thread. They were welcome visitors to frontier people, because they brought with them bits of news and a touch of civilization. The retailing of ready-to-wear was still in the future, awaiting the development of factory-produced textiles and apparel.

It was not until late in the nineteenth century that significant amounts of ready-made clothing became available for sale in stores. Before that, the fashion operations of stores in the growing cities consisted only of selling fabrics, trimmings, and made-to-order clothing. Although custom-made clothing remained important into the 1920s, it was steadily giving way to the growing and constantly improving ready-to-wear manufacturing industry. At the same time, retailers were learning to deal in ready-to-wear. By the 1920s men's, women's, and children's apparel departments were firmly established in all big-city department and specialty stores, and ready-to-wear was also available through mail-order catalogs to customers in outlying areas.

In the early days of ready-to-wear retailing, owners of the great fashion stores worked creatively with manufacturers to produce ready-to-wear designs that would meet the fashion needs of their customers. Many retailers helped manufacturers get started by bringing them Paris models to copy and providing them with substantial orders. The retailer at that time was the main source of fashion information for consumers as well as manufacturers. There were few movies, few telephones, no television, and only a few publications to keep people up to date on what should be produced or worn. Long before the fashion show, the bridal counselor, and the college shop were commonplace, several prominent stores were publishing fashion brochures that they mailed to their customers. Lord & Taylor began such a publication in 1881, John Wanamaker in 1909, and Marshall Field and Company in 1914. As fashion traveled its long, slow route from Paris to Podunk, customers looked to their oracles, their favorite stores, for advice on what to wear.

Different Kinds of Retail Operations

In the retailing of fashion, as in fashion itself, customers call the tune. Just as fashion keeps changing to reflect changes in consumer wants and needs, so does its retailing continue to change. Historically, new and different forms of retailing have come into being in response to changes in social and economic conditions, and each has initiated certain operational methods that distinguish it from previously existing types. Today, although many once widely disparate types of retailing now overlap, many of their distinctive operational characteristics still exist. This is also a time when retailing is being dramatically transformed. Brutal forces are driving out the slow and inefficient. New retail formats are developing. In essence, many retailers are "reinventing" the store. Furthermore, retailing may not even refer to a "store" as we have known it in the past.

NAICS Codes for Retailing

In previous chapters, we considered the U.S. government's North American Industry Classification System (NAICS) codes for the manufacturing segment of the fashion industry. The NAICS system defines the retailing process as "the final step in the distribution of merchandise; retailers are, therefore organized to sell merchandise in small quantities to the general public. . . . The buying of goods for resale is a characteristic of retail trade establishments that particularly distinguishes them from agriculture, manufacturing, and construction industries" (NAICS, 1998, pp. 411–412).

Just as in manufacturing, NAICS codes denote specific segments of the retailing industry. The codes for the retailing industry are under Sectors 44 and 45. Those codes significant to the fashion industry are given in Table 10–1. As for manufacturing, all government data on the industry (sales, employees, and so on) are grouped according to these categories.

Retail experts project that the retailing industry as we know it today will change dramatically in the years ahead. Our definitions of different types of retail formats are likely to be modified greatly. The NAICS codes take into account retailing in two formats and defines them as follows:

- **Store retailers** [also known as **in-store retailers**] operate fixed point-of-sale locations, located and designed to attract a high volume of walk-in customers. In general, retail stores have extensive displays of merchandise and use mass-media advertising to attract customers (NAICS, 1998, p. 411).
- **Nonstore retailers**, like store retailers, are organized to serve the general public, but their methods differ. The establishments of this subsector reach customers and market merchandise with methods such as the broadcasting of "infomercials," the

Table 10–1	Select Branches of Fashion Goods Retailing by NAICS Code Number

NAICS Code	Branch of Industry
44	
448	**Clothing and Clothing Accessories Stores**
4481	Clothing Stores
44811	Men's Clothing Stores
44812	Women's Clothing Stores
44813	Children's and Infants' Clothing Stores
44814	Family Clothing Stores
44815	Clothing Accessories Stores
44819	Other Clothing Stores
4482	Shoe Stores
44831	Jewelry Stores
45	
452	**General Merchandise Stores**
4521	Department Stores
45291	Warehouse Clubs and Superstores
45299	All other General Merchandise Stores
454	**Nonstore Retailers**
4541	Electronic Shopping and Mail-Order Houses
4543	Direct Selling Establishments
45439	Other Direct Selling Establishments

Source: From *North American Industry Classification System, United States, 1997* by Executive Office of the President, Office of Management and Budget, 1998, Washington, DC: Author, pp. 411–457.

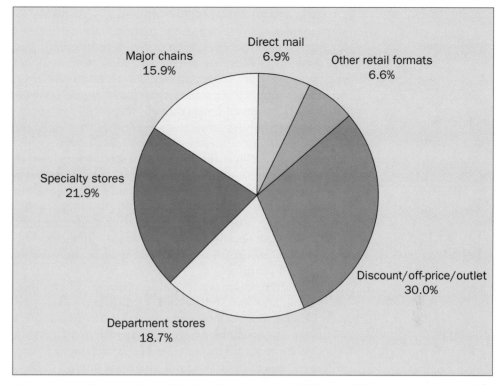

Figure 10–1

Where U.S. consumers shop for clothes (market share of apparel sales, 1999).

Source: Compiled from *Apparel Market Monitor, Annual 1999* (pp. 7–8) by American Apparel & Footwear Association, 2000, Arlington, VA: Author. Adapted by permission.

broadcasting and publishing of direct-response advertising, the publishing of paper and electronic catalogs, door-to-door solicitation, in-home demonstration, selling from portable stalls. . . ." (NAICS, 1998, p. 412).

Figure 10–1 shows where U.S. consumers buy their apparel today. In the first part of this chapter we will consider various types of in-store retailing. This will be followed by a section on nonstore retailing and its growing importance.

Department Stores

A **department store** is defined by the Bureau of Census as a retail establishment that employs 50 people or more and that carries a wide variety of merchandise lines, including (1) men's, women's, and children's apparel; (2) furniture, home furnishings, and appliances;[1] and (3) household linens and fabrics. In the trade, however, several other criteria are applied: related categories of merchandise are offered for sale in

---

[1]A number of large department stores (as they are defined by industry financial analysts) now have little or no furniture. Most do not sell large appliances, such as refrigerators or other "white goods," as they once did. Department stores have dropped a number of product areas they once carried because those departments were not profitable, required large amounts of floor space, or were not consistent with the store's image.

separate departments; each department is managed as a separate profit center; responsibilities for stocking the department are delegated to a buyer; and customers are offered many services, such as credit, return privileges, deliveries, and telephone and mail order. There are usually also such specialized services as restaurants, beauty salons, and jewelry repair, among others. In an earlier era, department stores were one-stop shopping sites for apparel and home furnishings. John Wanamaker in Philadelphia even sold airplanes at one point.

The typical department store chooses as its target group of customers people of middle to upper-middle socioeconomic status, with fairly large discretionary incomes. The fashion appeal of such a store stems from the breadth of assortment it offers in middle to upper-middle prices and in **national brand** and designer names, often augmented by its own brand name. Browsing among its broad stocks and guided by its advertising and displays, the customer can develop his or her own ideas of what to buy. When the choice has been made, the purchase can be consummated with confidence because of the store's refund policies. The offer of money back if the merchandise fails to please has been a cornerstone of department store policy for more than a century.

Department stores provide the "theater" of retailing. Their advertising and displays bring customer traffic and, because these stores cover so many categories of merchandise, they can generate more traffic than a specialized clothing store. The combination of customer traffic and appealing displays often prompts, say, a woman who has come seeking a lamp for her living room to purchase fashion items for herself, even though these were not on her shopping list. Department stores typically do more than half of their total volume in apparel and accessories for women, men, and children. In the fashion business, the department store not only represents an impressive volume of sales, but also is a medium for exposing merchandise to the customer, often with considerable drama.

Figure 10–2 shows a relatively traditional organizational structure for large department stores. Table 10–2 shows the top department and specialty department stores.

Origin of Department Stores

Most of our large, best-known department stores were founded in the middle and late nineteenth century, when mass production was developing and cities were growing. Some of their founders began as peddlers before they opened a store. Some examples are Aaron Meier, whose small general store in Portland, Oregon, opened in 1857 and later developed into Meier & Frank; Morris Rich, who peddled notions in Ohio and then moved on to Georgia to open Rich's of Atlanta in 1867; Adam Gimbel, whose descendants built the Gimbel organization on the foundation of the store he opened in Vincennes, Indiana, in 1842. Others had their beginnings as small dry goods stores such as Macy's, New York, which opened in 1858 for the sale of feathers, hosiery, and gloves and added new lines as increasing mass production made them possible (Harris, 1979).

Branches: From Suburban to National

In retailing, when a store that is well established in one location opens an additional facility in another but operates it from the original parent or flagship store, the new addition is called a **branch store**. Just as the branches of a tree depend on the trunk for nourishment and growth, so do branch stores depend on the buyers, promotion

Figure 10–2   **Organization chart of a typical large department store.**

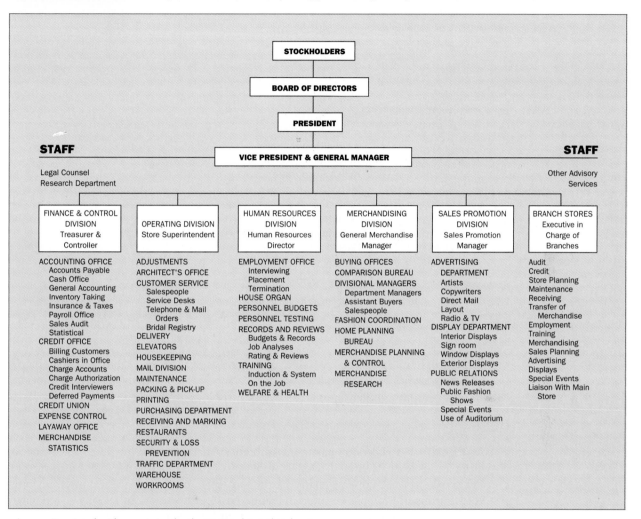

Source: Reprinted with permission by the National Retail Federation.

executives, and other members of the parent store's management team for merchandise and direction.

Where customers go, stores go. When young city families moved out to new suburbs in vast numbers in the 1950s, retailers in the central cities moved out to serve them in branches—free standing at first, but later in the shopping centers that soon developed. By the early 1970s, branches had proliferated to the point that collectively they began contributing more than half the parent firm's total value. By the late 1970s, suitable suburban areas had been exploited to the full by some stores, and these began to expand around the country, into other metropolitan areas. Thus, we find New York's Lord & Taylor with branches in Connecticut, New Jersey, Pennsylvania, Virginia, Texas, and Maryland. Dillard's of Little Rock, Arkansas, has branches in

Table 10–2	The Top Department and Specialty Department Stores	

Rank	Company	1999 $ Sales (in millions)
1	Sears, Roebuck and Co.	29,775.0
2	J.C. Penney Company, Inc.	18,964.0
3	Federated Department Stores, Inc.	18,217.0
4	May Department Stores Company	13,869.0
5	Dillard Department Stores, Inc.	8,677.0
6	Saks	6,423.8
7	Nordstrom, Inc.	5,124.2
8	Kohl's Corporation	4,557.1
9	Mervyn's	4,099.0
10	Dayton Hudson	3,074.0
11	Montgomery Ward	3,000.0
12	Neiman Marcus Stores	2,553.4
13	Belks*	2,200.0
14	Boscov's*	900.0

*Estimate
Source: Schulz, D. (2000, July). "Top 100 Retailers." Stores, S18. Reprinted by permission.

Texas, Missouri, New Mexico, Oklahoma, Florida, Kansas, and Ohio. Bloomingdale's of New York has branches in Massachusetts, New Jersey, Pennsylvania, Texas, Florida, and the Washington, D.C., area.

Competitive Changes by Department Stores

As Figure 10–3 shows, department stores lost market share in the 1990s whereas other retail formats gained. Department stores have taken bold steps to recapture lost market share, copying many of the strategies used by the discounters. Major cost-cutting efforts have resulted in leaner, more-efficient organizations. Many have consolidated divisions, streamlined buying and merchandising operations, and refined tracking and distribution systems, resulting in significant decreases in operating expenses.

Many department store groups have initiated ambitious **private-label** programs. Private-label merchandise, as used in the fashion industry, refers to goods produced exclusively for one retailer, and it carries only the name of the retailer or one of several brand names owned by the retailer. Private-label programs will be discussed later in this chapter. Although department stores will continue to carry well-known national brands, many have found advantages from well-executed private-label programs. Retailers have better profit return on private-label goods than on national brands. Department stores have more control over their own brands, permitting them to respond more quickly to changing fashion trends, to present exclusive merchandise, and to tailor their lines more precisely for their target markets. Generally, private-label merchandise accounts for about 15 to 25 percent of department stores' apparel sales.

Like their discounter cousins, some major department stores have made bold growth moves. Unlike the discounters, however, large department stores have been

Figure 10–3

Winners and losers among apparel retailers: Apparel market share trends 1989 vs. 1999.

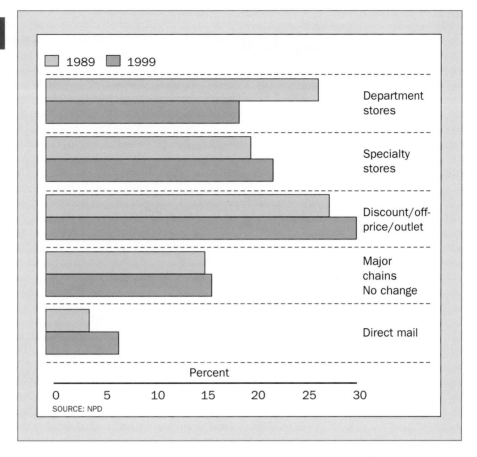

Source: Based on *Women's Wear Daily*, October 5, 1995 and *Apparel Market Monitor, Annual 1999* (pp. 7–8) by American Apparel & Footwear Association, 2000.

more inclined to buy existing store groups rather than building new ones. These mergers and acquisitions have resulted in powerful store ownership groups, better able to compete against the mammoth discounters and general merchandise chains.

Store Ownership Groups

The founding fathers to today's great department stores operated family-owned and family-run single-unit stores. Today, by means of mergers and acquisitions, nearly every such store is part of a **store ownership group**, which is a corporation that owns a number of autonomously operated retail organizations. Each store division retains its local identity and independence, has its own branches, has its own buyers and merchandise mix, operates under its own name, and presents itself to customers much as if it were still an independently owned institution.

The first and oldest of such groups was the Federated Department Stores, Inc., incorporated in 1929 by a merger of Filene's in Boston, Lazarus in Columbus, and Abraham & Straus in Brooklyn, soon joined by Bloomingdale's in New York. During the decade that followed, other corporate ownership groups were formed such as the R. H. Macy group, Allied Stores, and Associated Dry Goods. The trend continued, giving birth to such other groups as Dayton-Hudson and May Department Stores (Table 10–3).

Table 10–3	**May Department Stores: A Store Ownership Group**		
Company	**Headquarters**	**Number of Stores***	**1999 Sales**
Lord & Taylor	New York	78	$2,129 billion
Hecht's, Strawbridge's	Washington, DC	74	2,457 billion
Foley's	Houston	57	2,174 billion
Robinsons-May	Los Angeles	55	2,057 billion
Filene's	Boston	44	1,703 billion
Kaufmann's	Pittsburgh	50	1,597 billion
Famous-Barr, L.S. Ayers, The Jones Store	St. Louis	42	1,348 billion
Meier & Frank, ZCMI	Portland, Oregon	8	404 million
Total department stores		422	$13,869 billion

*Additional stores are planned for several of these companies.
Source: Based on information in *May Department Stores 2000 Fact Book.* (p. 1), 2000, St. Louis: Author.

In recent years, several of these groups were acquired by other groups or merged together, creating giant conglomerates in the department store industry. For example, Associated Dry Goods was acquired by the May Department Stores group. Federated Department Stores and Allied Stores were merged when they were acquired by Campeau Corporation. Following the eventual departure of Mr. Campeau, Federated emerged as a major department store group.

The large Federated Department Stores, Inc. absorbed Macy's in 1994, creating a retail empire with 341 stores. In 1995, Federated added the ailing 82-unit California-based Broadway Stores (formerly known as Carter Hawley Hale Stores) to its empire, and in doing so strengthened Federated's West Coast presence. In 1997, Dillard's acquired the Mercantile department store group.

The consolidation of the industry through mergers and acquisitions has transformed the department store segment of retailing from what it was 20 years ago. The industry is now so concentrated that 72 percent of all sales of the top 10 department stores are generated by just *four* companies: Federated Department Stores, Inc., May Department Stores, J.C. Penney, and Sears Roebuck & Co.[2] Because department stores have higher costs of doing business (because of the store environment and services) than specialty stores, one way to reduce those costs has been through the **economies of scale** that result from consolidations. These economies of scale permit department stores to be price competitive.

As May Department Stores, Inc. and Federated Department Stores, Inc. have acquired additional stores, they have also consolidated divisions and centralized operations to take advantage of their economies of scale. In 1986, May operated 19 department store divisions but by 1994 had streamlined these to eight large regional department store companies (divisions). This consolidation within May saved about $125 million, mostly through job cuts (May Department Stores, 1995; Sack, 1995). For example, a buyer in one of May's new consolidated companies became the buyer for all the stores in what had been two or three companies previously. Instead of buying for 10 stores, the buyer might be buying for 30 stores. Federated

---

[2]Previously, J.C. Penney and Sears Roebuck & Co. were not considered department stores. However, as both have repositioned themselves, they are now frequently considered department stores.

Department Stores participated in similar consolidations and also centralized credit operations, data processing, and accounts payable.

Few consumers realize that, for example, Lord & Taylor of New York, Foley's of Houston, and Kaufmann's of Pittsburgh are among the stores owned by the May Department Stores. Similarly, among Federated Department Stores are Bloomingdale's of New York, Burdine's of Florida, Rich's of Atlanta, and others. Indeed, few of this country's largest department stores are now independently owned. Independent and smaller department store groups have an increasingly difficult time competing against the giants; therefore, it is likely the consolidation will continue.

The consolidation of retail power has important implications for the entire fashion industry. These will be discussed further later in this chapter.

Apparel Specialty Stores: Large and Small

In contrast to the department store's wide variety of general merchandise, a **specialty store** is a retail establishment that either deals in a single category of merchandise (such as jewelry, shoes, books, furniture, apparel) or specializes in related categories of merchandise—for example, clothing and accessories for men, women, and children, or sporting equipment and active sports apparel, or televisions, radios, and VCRs. Compared to the broad appeal of department stores, specialty retailers cater to a particular type of customer and carry narrower lines of merchandise, with a large assortment within each line that is specifically geared for a well-defined targeted customer. For example, as The Gap sought to appeal to more segments of the population, the parent company launched Banana Republic and Old Navy. The highly successful Old Navy chain was created to appeal to a specific segment of the youth market.

A number of hot new specialty retailers have burst on the scene, often combined with elements of entertainment. These include Warner Brothers, Disney, Rainforest Cafe, Urban Outfitters, and Diesel. Some are associated with a sports theme, such as Nike's distinctive store on 57th Street near 6th and the National Basketball Association (NBA) store in New York City. Even the National Rifle Association (NRA) considered opening a store in the area, but political sentiment against the NRA deemed this unwise.

Specialty retailers vary widely in size. Some are single-unit "mom-and-pop" stores, some are units of chains, and some are large departmentalized stores with branches. Among consumers, the larger versions are often mislabeled department stores, because they carry wide assortments of the merchandise categories in which they specialize, offer extensive customer services, and are also organized by departments.

Large and small, specialty stores are among the biggest channels of distribution in the apparel supply chain, with a large share of the total market. The fashion impact of giants such as Saks and Neiman Marcus (some sources now consider these two in the department store group) makes a great contribution, but so also does the small, independently owned shop that offers convenience, friendliness, and an assortment carefully tuned to the wants of its clientele.

Large Departmentalized Specialty Stores

Like the department stores, many of today's large and prestigious specialty shops began in the second half of the 1800s as small, independently owned enterprises, in small towns or in the then-developing cities. Some expanded into department stores; others simply broadened their assortments in specialized merchandise categories. Filene's of Boston, for example, was founded in 1873 in Lynn, Massachusetts, by William Filene, who later bought a men's store in that city, a dry goods store in Bath, Maine, and two stores in Boston—one specializing in gloves and the other in laces. Similarly, I. Magnin of San Francisco had its beginnings in 1880, in the modest home of Isaac and Mary Ann Magnin, where wealthy San Francisco ladies came for Mrs. Magnin's exquisite, handmade, embroidered, and lace-trimmed lingerie, christening dresses, and spectacular made-to-order bridal gowns (Harris, 1979).

Like the department stores, almost every one of these great specialty stores is now part of a store ownership group. To cite but a few examples, Bullock's and I. Magnin are owned by the Federated group and Filene's by the May Company group. And also like department stores, they operate branch stores, either in local suburbs, nationally, or both.

Unlike department stores, however, they are completely dedicated to fashions in the rise and peak stages, and their assortments are both broad and deep in the upper-middle to highest-price ranges. Therein lies their competitive strength. They can more easily define their targeted customers, they develop salespeople who are fashion knowledgeable and helpful, and they provide personalized services.

Small Apparel Specialty Shops

It would be hard to find a town so small—or a city so big—that it is without independently owned, small mom-and-pop apparel or accessories shops. These are the stores owned and managed by one or two people and employing fewer than three salespeople. Each of the stores so defined generally has annual sales volume of half a million dollars or less; they neither have branch stores nor are they part of a chain. The attrition rate among them is high, but so also is the rate of replacement by new entrepreneurs. Their collective impact in the fashion business, however, is important. Bureau of the Census figures continue to show that a substantial part of fashion retailing is done in just such outlets.

From the consumers' point of view, small fashion retailers offer convenience of location and intimate knowledge of their customers' needs and tastes. Their owners know the way of dressing in the communities they serve, and more often than not, they will buy with individual customers in mind.

From the producer's point of view, according to manufacturers interviewed by the authors, the importance of these stores goes far beyond the amount of business they place. For one thing, they are loyal to the firms from which they buy. In the larger stores, the buyers may not be the same from one year to the next, and they do not have that same loyalty.

With some manufacturing firms, small specialty shops may account for a major portion of their business. With others, such as Liz Claiborne or Esprit, the minimum quantities demanded on an order will rule out the small retailer entirely. Levi Strauss & Co. created quite a stir among small retail firms when the company established a policy of selling only to companies that purchased at least $10,000 in Levi merchandise. For the industry as a whole, which is a stronghold of small manufacturing firms, the collective buying power of the small, specialized apparel retailers is very significant.

Boutiques

The term **boutique** is French for *little shop*, and for many years it referred only to those intimate shops within Paris couture houses where the customer could buy perfumes and accessories carrying the house label. In the United States the term *boutique* designates a small shop that carries highly individualized and specialized merchandise intended for a narrow, well-defined customer segment.

The proliferation of boutiques in the United States (and in London, where the trend began) was an outgrowth of the antiestablishment "do your own thing" attitudes of the 1960s. Some of today's boutiques, like their 1960s forerunners, cater to the avant garde young and others to more mature customers. Many feature merchandise at astronomical prices; others sell at more moderate levels. Some deal only in designer clothes; others deal in hand-crafted fashions. Some deal in trendy accessories; still others deal in antique clothing.

The early independently owned boutiques of the 1960s were often established by creative fashion enthusiasts to sell merchandise that expressed their individual point of view—even if they had to design or possibly produce the merchandise themselves. Generally, the merchandise was too advanced, too limited in appeal, for large stores to handle; only boutiques could do the job.

Independently owned boutiques made such an important place for themselves in the mid-1960s that large stores sought ways to appeal to boutique customers. Many stores established and still maintain groups of small, highly specialized shops on their floors in which they feature merchandise assortments keyed to a particular "total look" in apparel and accessories.

The boutique approach gained further impetus as European couture designers ventured into ready-to-wear and established their own boutiques, either freestanding or within stores selected for the franchise, or both. Among the luminaries whose ready-to-wear is offered in boutiques in freestanding stores or within larger stores are Cardin, Givenchy, Valentino, Yves Saint Laurent for his Rive Gauche collections, and such Americans as Calvin Klein, Ralph Lauren, Anne Klein, and Donna Karan. In addition, many ready-to-wear designers from other countries have entered the U.S. market by way of their own boutiques in fashionable areas—for example, the Soprani boutique on Rodeo Drive in Los Angeles and the Giorgio Armani on New York's Madison Avenue.

Today, the boutique concept is widely accepted and used by most large department and specialty stores, not only for current fashions, but also for bath accessories, gourmet food and cookware, and whatever else captures customer interest.

Chain Store Retailing

A chain is understood to be a retail organization that owns and operates a string of similar stores, all merchandised and controlled from a central headquarters office. Multiunit chains developed during the late 1800s, as transportation and communication improved. Among the early chains were the A & P (Great Atlantic & Pacific Tea Company), Woolworth's, and J.C. Penney. Each started with a single store, gradually added others, and demonstrated the feasibility of the multistore concept and the economies of centralized buying.

Chains that sell apparel are either (1) general merchandise retailers, such as Sears and J.C. Penney, whose product categories are similar to those of department stores, or (2) specialized apparel or accessory chains that focus on one or more related categories of apparel. Chains may be national, regional, or local in location. Their highly centralized, uniform store operation is quite different from what prevails among departmentalized stores that have branches or are autonomously operated retail stores that are part of the store ownership groups discussed earlier.

In the trade, the characteristics that distinguish **chain store** operations from those of typical department stores are as follows:

- There is no one big-city flagship or main parent store, as in the case of a multiunit department store with branches.
- The store units are standardized and uniform in physical appearance and in the merchandise they carry.
- The buying is done by buyers in the chain's central office (i.e., they have **centralized buying**), and each buyer is responsible for a specific category of merchandise—as contrasted with buying for an entire department.
- Merchandise is usually distributed to the units of a chain from its central or regional warehouses.
- The buying function is separate from the selling function.
- Selling is the responsibility of centralized sales managers and the managers of the individual store units.

However, as the number of branches operated by a departmentalized store increases, the parent store usually adapts several of a chain's operations, notably the separation of the selling function from the buying function. Selling becomes the responsibility of centralized store managers.

As an indication of the important role that chains play in the business of fashion, consider the following facts.

- Wal-Mart, Kmart, Sears, Target, and J.C. Penney—the five largest general merchandise chains—are considered to be the "Big Five" of retailing (Table 10–4). Their combined 1999 annual sales were $275 billion. Wal-Mart, the largest retailer in the world, clearly leads the pack, now so far ahead of the others that the sales of the next four added together do not match Wal-Mart's volume (Schulz, 2000).
- The combined sales of the eight top specialized apparel chains shown in Table 10–5 were more than $44 billion in 1999. The Gap alone had sales of more than $11.6 billion in 1999. The Limited was larger than The Gap before splitting into two entities: one from its core women's apparel group and the other from its lingerie and personal care businesses (Intimate Brands).

Table 10–4	The "Big Five" General Merchandise Chains	
Company	**1999 Sales**	**Number of Stores**
Wal-Mart*	$165,394,000,000	3,993
Sears	$ 41,070,000,000	3,011
Kmart	$ 35,925,000,000	2,172
Target	$ 33,212,000,000	1,238
J.C. Penney	$ 32,510,000,000	4,085

*Includes supercenters and Sam's Clubs
Source: Schulz, D. (2000, July). "Top 100 Retailers." *Stores*, S5. Reprinted by permission.

Company	1999 Sales	Number of Stores
Table 10–5	**Select Specialized Apparel Chains**	

Company	1999 Sales	Number of Stores
The Gap	$11,635,398,000	3,018
The Limited	$ 9,723,334,000	2,913
TJX	$ 8,795,347,000	1,357
Intimate Brands*	$ 4,510,836,000	2,110
Spiegel/Eddie Bauer	$ 3,210,225,000	560
Ross Stores	$ 2,468,638,000	378
Burlington Coat	$ 2,242,500,000	382
Talbots	$ 1,290,923,000	n.a.

*Previously part of The Limited.
n.a. = Not available
Source: Schulz, D. (2000, July). "Top 100 Retailers." *Stores*, S5–S17. Reprinted by permission.

Specialized Apparel Chains

In terms of the fashion business, the decade of the 1920s was the beginning of apparel retailing by chain stores. Before then, there were a few retail chains of "waist stores," as blouse shops were then called. Their targeted market was low-income customers seeking prices below those offered in department and specialty stores. In about 1919, as blouses went out of fashion, producers of waists began to make low-priced dresses that the waist chains added to their assortments. With department and specialty stores catering to middle- and upper-middle-income families, there was little competition for chains featuring low-priced apparel. This period saw the start of many low-priced apparel chains that catered to the new class of "working women" who had entered the workforce during the manpower shortage of World War I.

A notable example of an early waist chain is the Lerner Shops, which got its start in those years and by 1984 had 800 stores, with sales of $700 million primarily in low-priced fashions ("The Super," 1986). In 1985, this chain was acquired by The Limited stores. Other types of chains that sprang up and developed in the 1920s included millinery chains, men's hat chains, and family clothing stores. Fashion leadership was not their forte.

Chains took a different direction in the 1970s. There are now new **apparel specialty chains,** quite different from any of their predecessors. Regional or national in scope, they operate stores of relatively small individual size and feature highly selective lines of contemporary and often trendy fashions in middle price ranges. Their aim is toward mainstream American juniors, misses, and young men's sportswear customers.

Today's apparel chains derive their strength from their ability to focus on a particular segment of the consumer market and the fashion interests of that market. Unlike department stores, they are not burdened by the need to serve a broad section of the public; they concentrate strictly on the target market they have identified for themselves. As in all chain retailing, their operations are highly centralized; their store units are generally uniform in design and merchandise presentation; and they usually operate under the same name in all locations (Figure 10–4). Many have a **store ambiance** designed to appeal to the customer the store wants to attract. Typical are The Gap, The Limited, Talbots, Eddie Bauer, and Victoria's Secret.

Figure 10–4	**Composite organization chart of an apparel chain.**

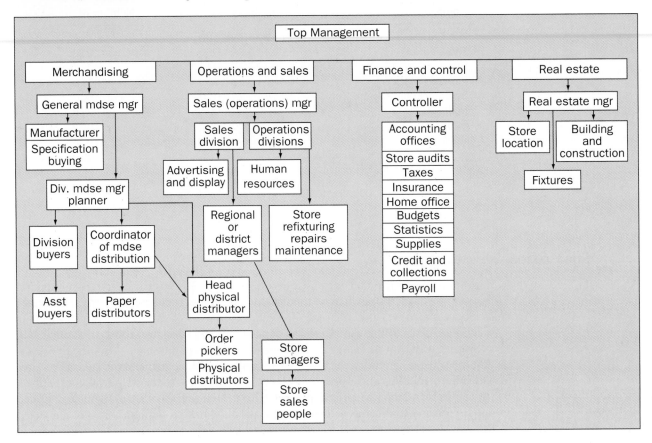

Such chains feature mainly their own private brands. Additionally, their buying power is so large that they can specify colors, patterns, styles, fabrics, designs, and whatever else they consider important.

These specialized chains became, and still are, a major source of competition to department stores because their merchandise categories and moderate price ranges are within the scope of this older form of retailing. Their competition is felt most directly in casual sportswear for juniors, misses, and young men.

Specialty stores have lost market share in recent years, as shown in Figure 10–3. Too many stores competed for the same customers in their teens through early thirties and did not change as this consumer matured. This segment of the industry is crowded, with a high degree of overlap among stores competing for the same shoppers. Even stores under the same ownership compete for the same customer. The Limited Stores, Express, and Lerner, all owned by The Limited corporation, have competed in the same markets and frequently in the same malls. Many of the apparel specialty stores established their early successes around having a few "hot" items that attracted young customers. Now that consumers are becoming more individualistic, fewer are responding to these items. Specialty retailers are finding it harder and harder to find these big fashion hits. As the stores try to avoid big mistakes in identifying these "hot" items, many resort to filling their stores with "safe" choices like denim and khaki. This has led to the "sameness" in specialty stores that have caused consumers to ask themselves, "Wasn't I just in this store?" **Differentiation** has become a new concern and industry buzzword.

Specialty retailers are finding it harder to continue to compete by using another strategy that gave them an edge over department stores. For two decades, specialty retailers made their success by being faster and more nimble than their department store colleagues. Specialty retailers were able to zero in on their customers, identify new trends, and by using the latest technology produce and replenish merchandise far more quickly than could their large, slower-moving department store cousins. For example, The Limited could identify trends and have products delivered in fast cycles that department stores could not begin to match. However, as department stores have developed partnerships with suppliers and become more proficient in producing their own private-label assortments, specialty stores no longer have this advantage.

The weak retailing climate of the 1990s caused several retail reorganizations. A number of major specialty apparel chains have filed petitions under **Chapter 11** of the U.S. Bankruptcy Code. Chapter 11 is the legal process that provides an opportunity for companies burdened by excessive debt to continue operations while plans are made to restructure the company and reschedule debt payments. This often involves selling off some divisions. All such decisions are made in negotiations with creditor and stockholder committees and are subject to approval and supervision of a federal bankruptcy judge who oversees the situation.

Among specialty store groups that filed for Chapter 11 are Edison Brothers Stores Inc., which had 2,700 units. (Store units are often referred to as **"doors"** in the industry.) In the restructuring, about 500 unprofitable doors were closed down. The company's Oaktree division was merged into its Jeans West Division. Other Edison Brothers Stores include: 5-7-9 Shops, J.Riggins, JW/Jeans West, Zeidler & Zeidler/Webster, Coda, Repp Big & Tall, Bakers/Leeds, The Wild Pairs, and Precis.

One-time top performer Merry-Go-Round stores is another specialty store chain that operated for a time under Chapter 11. Other specialty chains that ran store-closing sales during out-of-court restructuring included Charming Shoppes and Gateway Apparel. A number of these did not survive in the end. All of these once-thriving specialty chains suffered from the sluggish retail climate and the crushing competition of the 1990s.

Apparel Retailing by General Merchandise Chains

The general mass-merchandising chains have also become a factor in fashion distribution. The Penney chain had apparel and accessories from the start, but Montgomery Ward and Sears had functioned primarily as catalog houses until the 1920s. With transportation improving and the rural customer no longer completely dependent on the mail, they moved into store operations. Sears began in 1925, with a single store located in its Chicago mail-order facility. Ward's soon followed. Both companies started with stores that featured equipment and supplies primarily of interest to men. Only gradually did their stores move into apparel, and then it was for their typical customer, of modest means and modest clothing budget.

It was not until the 1960s that the big **general merchandising chains** came of age as major factors in the fashion business. In response to the increased affluence and greater fashion awareness of their targeted customers, they broadened their assortments and extended their price ranges upward. They also gave prime main floor locations to apparel and accessories.

Both J.C. Penney and Sears Roebuck have emphasized apparel more in recent years than was true in their earlier company histories. In the 1980s, J.C. Penney shifted to apparel for a greater portion of its store merchandise assortment, dropping some of its hard lines such as furniture and large appliances. In the 1990s, Sears ended years of floundering to redefine itself, settling on apparel as its primary focus. In this transformation, Sears adopted its "Softer Side of Sears" apparel campaign, which became so successful for its women's clothing that it was extended to men's and children's clothing. The retailer expanded its assortment of national and private brands, offering customers trendier and more updated merchandise. Wal-Mart has placed more emphasis on fashion in recent years—a significant move for the company, which is by far the world's largest apparel and accessories retailer—with an estimated to exceed $25 billion in sales annually.

With their enormous buying power, these great chains can have merchandise produced to their specifications and styled exclusively for them. They may not have, or even attempt to have, the fashion authority and leadership shown by department and specialty stores and by the new breed of specialized apparel chains. But what they can do, and do very well, is move a great deal of merchandise and control a substantial percentage of the fashion market. It is generally estimated in the trade that apparel and accessories represent at least 30 percent of these chains' total volume. On that basis, the combined fashion goods business of the big chains amounts to many billions of dollars, a decidedly important share of the fashion market.

Discount Retailing: Underselling Operations

Shortly after World War II, discounters added a new dimension to the world of retailing by adopting the operational techniques originated by food **supermarkets** in the 1930s. These techniques entailed offering lower food prices to depression-weary customers by using self-selection selling, low-rent locations, inexpensive decor, and cash-and-carry terms.

As generally understood in the trade, the term **discounter** applies to a retail establishment that *regularly* sells its merchandise at less-than-conventional prices, concentrating mainly on national brands. By operating with self-service and other expense-saving techniques such as no mail or telephone orders, no free deliveries, low-rent locations, and limited return privileges (in some cases), they can operate profitably on markups lower than those that prevail among other types of retailers.

The success of discounters in the 1950s stemmed from their sale of nationally advertised branded appliances at prices below the manufacturers' suggested retail prices. This was in the period just after World War II, when men returning from military service spearheaded a boom in family formation, suburban living—and babies. The two-earner household in that period was relatively rare, and incomes had to be stretched to accommodate the pent-up demand for everything young families needed, from refrigerators to ready-to-wear. As the suburban communities burgeoned, so did the discounters. They opened stores in both cities and suburbs and broadened their merchandise assortments to include low-priced, unbranded apparel.

As these households and their children prospered, many of them retained their active interest in buying at favorable prices. They were in a position to enjoy the good life—but they enjoyed it more at a bargain. This was in marked contrast with the attitude of earlier generations, among whom comfortable incomes were equated with freedom from price consciousness. Underselling retailing in various forms became more and more firmly entrenched in the 1960s, 1970s, and 1980s, without regard to business cycles, employment statistics, or consumer income figures. Value-conscious consumers of the 1990s emphasized this trend even more than had been true earlier.

Full-Line Discount Stores

Full-line discount stores, called *discounters*, have had a powerful impact on the retail industry in recent years. These stores generally sell name-brand merchandise, as well as their own store brands, at prices lower than those of the traditionally priced department or specialty stores. The major discounters are Wal-Mart, Kmart, Target (part of Dayton-Hudson), Ames, Bradlees, and Caldor.[3] These stores are economy versions of the old-fashioned store where customers could fulfill a large portion of their shopping needs in one place. Today's discounters often have more merchandise than traditional department stores.

Although the discounters are not the fashion leaders, they are the most powerful presence in the industry today. As consumers have become more value conscious **cross-shoppers**, who may shop at department stores for some items and at less-expensive stores for others, have made discounters the winners. Most notably, Wal-Mart has roared onto the scene, going from a small midwestern discount chain to the world's largest retailer. Today, Wal-Mart is also the largest apparel and accessories retailer in the world, with about 3,500 stores (not counting Sam's Club stores), and it is adding about 100 stores per year (Wal-Mart, 2000).

Discount chains, like other mass merchandisers, have massive buying power that wields a great deal of influence in the industry. Because they buy huge quantities, they can negotiate competitive prices with suppliers that permit the discounters to pass savings along to the consumer. The appetites of major discounters such as Wal-Mart are so great that some manufacturers may produce all their merchandise for only one giant chain (a strategy with many risks if that single retail customer decides to change suppliers). In fact, some of these chains are so large that few manufacturers have the production capacity to fill a major discounter's needs, even for a single product line. Consider, for example, that over 3,500 dresses are required to have only one of a single type in each Wal-Mart store. To offer a range of sizes and styles in a line quickly adds up to hundreds of thousands of items required by just this one retailer. Buyers for the discounters work in narrowly specialized apparel categories and are responsible for millions of dollars in sales annually.

Until very recently, discount chains (along with off-price and outlet stores) took market share from other retailers—at least a percentage or more of the market each year. Although a percentage or two of the market may seem slight, in the 1999 apparel market of $183.9 billion, a shift of a percentage or two is very significant when one percent represents more than $1.8 billion. Discounters, particularly Wal-Mart, have been criticized for hurting small businesses in communities where stores are opened. As Wal-Mart opens **supercenters** with 175,000 or more square feet of space, these have been estimated to equal the sales volume of 100 typical small businesses.

Discounters continue to seek well-known branded apparel to enhance sales and store image. Selling brands such as Gitano, Catalina, White Stag, Faded Glory, and Hanes continues to make discounters a growing force in apparel retailing. Wal-Mart's

---

[3]Ames and Caldor have both gone through Chapter 11 bankruptcy experiences but are still in business; Bradlees is not.

introduction of the Kathie Lee Collection, using Kathie Lee Gifford as the spokesperson, was a monumental success for the Arkansas-based discounter.

Wal-Mart may have started as a small-town operation, but the company is now legendary for many of its efficient and state-of-the-art operations that keep costs to a minimum. These efficiencies, which are translated into attractive prices for consumers, include use of technology and logistics to provide efficient warehousing, transportation, and delivery systems. The company's international growth in recent years has been phenomenal, now including about 1,000 stores in other countries.

Hypermarkets and Supercenters

Adopting a retailing format popular in Europe, several **hypermarkets** were opened in the United States. These hypermarkets are gigantic full-line discount stores and supermarkets combined, with 200,000 to 300,000 square feet of selling space and selling as many as 100,000 items. Stores sell everything, including clothing, home furnishings, tires, appliances, gardening supplies, and food and offer services such as haircuts, restaurants, banking, and free supervised play areas for children. Employees often move about these megastores on skates.

These sprawling hypermarkets began to appear in France in the 1960s and subsequently spread to a number of other European countries. Once touted as the next big boom in U.S. retailing, hypermarkets did not meet retailers' expectations in this country. U.S. consumers appeared to be overwhelmed by the size of hypermarkets. Bigger did not appear to be better in this case. This retail format has succeeded in Europe, particularly in France, apparently because other mass retailers do not compete as vigorously as in the United States. Two French retailers, Carrefour and Leedmark, opened hypermarkets in the United States but later closed them. Kmart's partnership with Bruno's supermarket to form hypermarkets in the South was not successful. To date, Wal-Mart remains the only major retailer operating hypermarkets, four of them, in the United States (D'Innocenzio, 1992).

The supercenter concept has been much more successful than hypermarkets. Both Wal-Mart and Kmart have been successful with this format, combining a very large, full-line general merchandise discount store with a supermarket. Supercenters, carrying thousands of **SKUs**, are more streamlined and user friendly than the hypermarkets. Wal-Mart appears to be placing major growth emphasis on the supercenter concept, building those rather than smaller stores in areas where population demographics show they can be successful.

Warehouse Clubs

The **warehouse clubs**, also called membership warehouses or price clubs, originated in Europe as cash-and-carry wholesalers for small businesses. In the United States, these clubs serve small businesses but also have expanded their clientele to include customers who pay a small membership fee to join. The major warehouse club groups are Sam's Club (owned by Wal-Mart Stores Inc.) and Price Club/Costco. The former Pace Membership Warehouse, owned by Kmart, was purchased by Sam's Club. Little or no advertising, stark industrial decor, low-rent locations, cash-and-carry transactions, and very fast inventory turns keep their expenses very low. The warehouse atmosphere of these clubs and their low pricing policies attract the value-conscious customer—a category that includes almost everyone who shops for commodities.

Although the warehouse clubs specialize in selling branded commodity goods in bulk, they also sell basic apparel, footwear, and home textiles. Casual wear, sportswear, and undergarments are the most frequently found apparel items, with an occasional find in designer lines. Dressing rooms are generally unavailable.

Most of the time upscale brand merchandise appears in these stores under legitimate conditions, but sometimes it gets there through **diverters**. Because many manufacturers of prestige goods do not want their status labels weakened by being sold in cut-rate stores, they refuse to sell to these retailers. However, enterprising individuals too often find ways of bending the rules, and diverters sometimes play that role in this case. In this scheme, other stores will intentionally overbuy these prestige items, with the intent of selling the merchandise to warehouse clubs or other low-cost retailers. The merchandise is "diverted" to a retailer other than the one to whom the manufacturer sold it.

Category Killers

The retail landscape has been changed dramatically in the past decade by the **"category killers"**—retailers that specialize in tremendous assortments of a single kind of merchandise. They get their name from destroying competitors who sell the same merchandise. Like discounters, these stores offer substantial savings because of high volume and low margins. Traditionally, these stores have been huge, stand-alone stores. These cavernous stores are also sometimes called **superstores** or "big box" retailers. Sometimes when Wal-Mart is included in a group with these stores, these are called the *power retailers*.

Some of the major names among the category killers are Home Depot, Toys 'R' Us, Barnes & Noble, The Sports Authority, Circuit City, Office Depot, and Bed Bath & Beyond. Although this is an exceedingly important group of retailers, industry experts generally do not identify fashion retailers in this category.

A new retail phenomenon began to occur in the mid-1990s, which some described as "demalling" or "the invasion of the category killers" (Edelson, 1995a, p. 8). As hundreds of small specialty stores close annually,[4] malls are filling their spaces with the big box stores. This move is a historical change in the classic mall concept with a few **anchor stores** surrounded by specialty stores. Traditional department store anchors then will be forced to compete against the category killers inside their own malls. This means the department stores must rethink their merchandising and consider eliminating categories the big box retailers sell. Edelson (1995a) noted that "what appears to be threatening department stores may end up benefiting them in the long run. Observers see the big box invasion as creating a hybrid retail environment that could reverse negative traffic patterns at malls across the country" (p. 8).

Off-Price Apparel Chains

Underselling stores that offer quality and fashion apparel have been on the scene for many years, but only recently have they blossomed into a major force in retailing. One of the earliest among them, Loehman's, was founded in Brooklyn in 1920 and is now a national chain of 77 stores. Others that came into the field later followed the same course, starting as individual stores and developing into national chains.

Known in the trade today as **off-price retailers**, the fashion apparel discounters came into their own in the late 1970s, growing at a much faster rate than more

---

[4]Edelson (1995b) notes that apparel retailers alone lost an estimated one million square feet of mall space in 1994.

conventional retailers. What distinguished these new fashion discounters from their predecessors was that they specialized in high-quality brand- and designer-name clothing, at deeply discounted prices—and they still do.

The target customers of these operations are the price-conscious middle class. Among them are also consumers who formerly bought top-quality merchandise without really questioning price. When apparel prices skyrocketed, some of these consumers sought the discounters—not for cheaper grades of merchandise, but for the familiar "names" and qualities at lower prices. For example, they are willing to spend $100 on a dress, sweater, or handbag, but they want one that normally sells for $150 to $200 in department and specialty stores (Figure 10–5). In these stores, the selection is limited, and returning merchandise is often more difficult than at other stores.

The two leading players in this market are TJX Companies, with 1999 annual sales of nearly $8.8 billion from 1,357 stores. The second largest is Burlington Coat Factory, with sales of more than $2.2 billion from 382 stores. Restructuring is occurring in this segment of the industry also. For many years, Marshalls was the largest apparel discounter, with 495 stores. However, TJX bought the Marshalls division from Melville in 1995.

The impact of underselling apparel retailing on conventional retailers has been more than just competition. Today one can walk into well-known department and specialty stores at the height of the selling season and find numerous off-price sales being featured. The distinction between conventional and discount retailers has become blurred, and it has become increasingly harder to determine where conventional retailing ends and off-price operations begin.

Figure 10–5

Examples of deep discounts on name-brand merchandise at off-price apparel stores.

Factory Outlets

Another important form of off-price apparel retailing has become an important force across the country—**factory outlets** owned and operated by manufacturers of top brand- and designer-name clothing. These outlets originally served as a dumping ground for out-of-season merchandise and odds and ends of factory stock, but have evolved far from that.

Today, there are about 12,000 outlet stores in all parts of the United States, compared to 3,682 in 1988. More than 500 manufacturers operate outlet stores, many with a "chain" of outlet stores. Most of these are clustered in fast-growing **outlet centers,** or outlet malls (Figure 10–6). Outlet store decor, services, merchandise assortments, and locations have been upgraded, becoming good-looking, professionally run retail stores.

Initially located on the factory grounds, these outlets began to cluster in outlet centers, which were located in outlying areas not in conflict with the shopping areas of their major retail accounts. If a major department store buys from a manufacturer, the retailer resents having the supplier establish its own store nearby and undersell the department store on the same merchandise. Outlet centers are now trying to build a more consistent base of repeat customers, and to do so, they are locating closer to traditional malls. Whereas outlet centers were 45 miles from traditional malls in 1990, they now average 28 miles. Outlet center shoppers were found to spend twice

Figure 10–6

A factory outlet center.

Source: Photo by Anthony Magnacca/Merrill/Prentice Hall.

the amount of time at outlet centers as in a traditional mall. When they invest the time to get there, it is a planned event.

Factory outlets generally do very little advertising, thus avoiding conflict with their retail accounts, but they do leave labels in the garments. In the past, outlet stores typically received manufacturers' new lines after they had been shipped to other retail customers a month or so earlier. Increasingly, however, outlet stores are featuring in-season merchandise, treating outlet centers as another distribution channel, not a place to get rid of excess inventory or seconds. In some cases, manufacturers produce merchandise specifically for their outlet stores. With the popularity of outlet stores, discounts have dwindled from more than 70 percent below the normal retail price to sometimes as low as 10 to 15 percent below. The norm now appears to be 20 to 25 percent below retail (Edelson, 1995b).

During the early years of outlet centers (the 1980s), merchandise tended to be from middle-of-the-road manufacturers that appealed to the mass market. Today, outlet developers are courting a more affluent clientele. Outlet centers have attracted fashion-forward designers including Ralph Lauren, Donna Karan, Calvin Klein, Henry Grethel, Harvé Benard, and Kenar. One center has a European store featuring merchandise from Armani and Emanuel. With the upscale orientation, the shopping environments and amenities have improved, more closely resembling traditional malls.

Retailers are even trying to get in on the successful outlet mall trend, opening outlet stores near their flagship stores. For example, Saks Fifth Avenue's clearinghouse outlet, Off-5th—Saks Fifth Avenue Outlet, opened near its Manhattan store.

Some retail experts question whether outlet centers can continue their fast-paced expansion. One writer noted, "the outlet mall boom is sowing the seeds of its own decline" (Rudnitsky, 1994, p. 46). Because of the growth of these malls, this segment of the industry, like several others, is becoming rapidly **overstored**. Total consumer spending has not increased enough to keep pace with the growing number of stores. Outlet malls are succeeding by taking market share from other retailers, but consumers may eventually lose some of their zest for outlet stores.

Franchised Retailing

Franchised operations are familiar to the public through such organizations as fast-food outlets such as McDonald's and KFC, through automobile dealerships, restaurants such as Howard Johnson's, and national networks of real estate offices like Century 21.

In a **franchise** arrangement, the **franchisor** (a parent company) provides a **franchisee** (owner-operator of a retail unit) with the exclusive use of an established name in a specific trading area, plus assistance in organizing, training, merchandising, and management, in return for a stipulated consideration. The nature of the agreement varies widely from company to company. For example, the franchising company may provide an operating program complete in every detail, or the agreement may simply specify that the franchisor will provide merchandise for the franchisee. The uniform appearance of many franchised retail outlets often gives the impression to the public that they constitute a chain, but in actuality, each store is run by an individual entrepreneur who owns the business, meets his or her obligation to the franchisor, and retains the remaining profits.

Designer-Name Franchised Boutiques

As described in the previous chapter, European ready-to-wear designers have been operating their own franchised name boutiques for the last two decades, among them the Rive Gauche franchised boutiques of Yves Saint Laurent and the Nouvelle Boutiques of Givenchy. Beginning in the 1970s, franchising arrangements began to be visible in the domestic apparel retailing field. Among the earliest and most successful were the maternity shop franchises such as Lady Madonna and Maternally Yours. Other examples are the Tennis Lady shops and the hundreds of Athlete's Foot franchised outlets.

In the 1980s, American name designers began to follow the lead of European designers, and today American designer-franchised boutiques have burgeoned in major cities throughout the United States. An outstanding example is Ralph Lauren, who has pioneered a multimillion-dollar retail business with worldwide franchises in the United States and throughout affluent areas in Europe and Asia. The growth and future role of retail stores controlled by their designer franchisors is one that bears watching.

Shopping Centers and Malls

A major retail phenomenon growing out of the migration to suburbia that followed World War II was the development and proliferation of shopping centers. A **shopping center** is a preplanned, architecturally coordinated grouping of retail stores, plus a parking area that is generally larger than the area occupied by the stores themselves. Medical facilities, banks, restaurants, and sometimes theaters and skating rinks may be part of the mix offered the shopper. These centers are usually developed by real estate interests and occasionally by the real estate divisions of very large retailers. The centers have their own managements, promotional activities, and merchants' associations to weld their stores into a cohesive group.

Since the 1960s, when shopping centers emerged as major retail sites, they have provided a prime area of expansion for department stores, chain stores, large and small specialty stores, and sometimes off-price retailers. More recently, even the category killers are locating in malls. According to the International Council of Shopping Centers, there are over 40,000 shopping centers in the United States (International Council of Shopping Centers; for updates see www.icsc.org).

The retail climate of the 1990s had an impact on the development of shopping malls. An excessive amount of retail capacity (space available)—known as overstoring—exists in the United States. Some 18–20 square feet of retail space exists for every man, woman, and child in the country, more than enough to accommodate reasonable population growth in the future. (Figure 10–7 shows the extent to which shopping center growth rates have out-paced population increases, leading to market saturation.)

Because of the glut in retail space, new shopping center construction has slowed. During the 1970s, about 25 new regional shopping centers opened in a typical year. That pace slowed to an average of around four or five new malls per year.

Numbers alone do not tell the whole story of shopping centers, however. Over the years, they have changed from open-air centers, laid out horizontally with on-site parking, into multilevel, enclosed, and climate-controlled **malls**,

| Figure 10–7 | **Shopping center growth outstrips population rise.** |

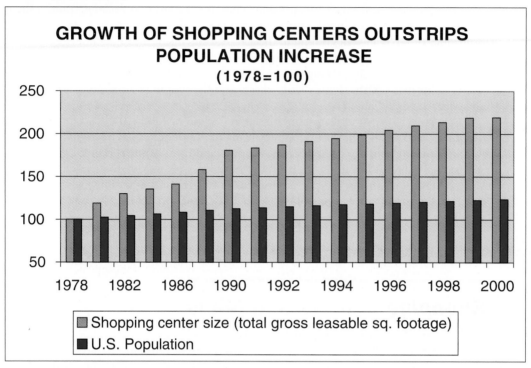

**GROWTH OF SHOPPING CENTERS OUTSTRIPS
POPULATION INCREASE**
(1978=100)

■ Shopping center size (total gross leasable sq. footage)
■ U.S. Population

Source: From *Standard & Poor's Industry Surveys: Retailing General Report*. Copyright 2001 by Standard & Poor's. Reprinted by permission.

where shoppers can spend an entire day shopping, resting, eating, even skating or seeing motion pictures. And they are no longer purely suburban phenomena; they are now in center city areas—often those associated with urban renewal enterprises. An outstanding example of an urban enterprise is Trump Tower, located on Fifth Avenue in New York. This is a 68-story building consisting of 49 floors of apartments, 13 floors of office space, and a 6-floor atrium around which are some of the most prestigious fashion stores in the world. Another example is the Water Tower in Chicago.

Another large type of shopping center has emerged on the scene in recent years. Sometimes called a **megamall**, the largest of these in the United States is the Mall of America, located in Bloomington, Minnesota, near Minneapolis/St. Paul. With 4.2 million square feet, 10 times the size of an average regional mall, the Mall of America is large enough to hold seven Yankee Stadiums. Total store front footage of 4.3 miles, distributed among more than 400 stores on several levels, makes this a shoppers' paradise. Referring to itself as "the world's premier retail and entertainment center," the mall attracted an estimated 700,000 tourists from other countries in its first year. The area near the mall is designed to accommodate visitors who come for more than a brief shopping trip; 6,500 hotel rooms are nearby. Tour groups often identify the Mall of America as their destination; over 12,000 organized tour groups and 400 Japanese groups visited in the mall's first year.

The Mall of America is the leading example of another retail phenomenon—combining shopping with entertainment. Complete with Knott's Camp Snoopy, which features seven acres of year-round theme park entertainment, the Mall of America sets the trend in creating large-scale entertainment-oriented shopping centers (Figure 10–7). As consumers have shied away from shopping and spent less and less time at malls, shopping center developers have added entertainment components to create more of a "destination." The goal is to entice the consumer to spend more time in the mall. With 45 restaurants, 9 nightclubs, 14 theater screens, and even a wedding chapel (with full wedding planning services), visitors have plenty of ways to be entertained at the Mall of America. The strategy appears to be working for at least some stores in the megamall (Figure 10–8). For example, the Nordstrom store there has surpassed all the company's other stores in the country in sales and profits.

Figure 10–8

Camp Snoopy provides various forms of entertainment to Mall of America shoppers. The Snoopy Bounce is 38 feet tall and 28 feet in diameter. Inside the giant inflated beagle, children can frolic on an air-filled cushion.

Source: Courtesy of Knott's Camp Snoopy.

Nonstore Retailing

As consumers continue to be pressed for time, many are expected to be increasingly attracted to the convenience of various types of nonstore retailing. Consumer research also indicates that this time-pressured consumer is frustrated with shopping in malls. Options that permit shopping in the convenience of one's home are becoming increasingly appealing to weary consumers. Retail consultants Kurt Salmon Associates predict that over the next few years, there will be a massive shift to nonstore retailing of all types. Figure 10–9 illustrates the shift KSA predicts from in-store retailing to nonstore retailing.

Although changes in consumers' attitudes toward shopping are critical to these predicted shifts, technology advances have created nonstore shopping options undreamed of a decade ago. Interactive technology provides access to vast amounts of information and choices, and this will increase exponentially in coming years. Consumers' computers and televisions now offer vast potential as places to shop as manufacturers and retailers discover ways to sell effectively through these media. The new wave of electronic retailers is growing fast.

Mail-Order Houses

By census definition, a **mail-order house** is a retail establishment that does the bulk of its selling to the consumer primarily through the medium of a catalog as a result of orders placed mainly by mail or phone. Perhaps the term *catalog houses* would be more accurate today, because a large portion of the merchandise is shipped to consumers by delivery services other than the U.S. Postal Service.

The concept of selling through a catalog rather than over the counter of a store was pioneered by Aaron Montgomery Ward in 1872, to be followed by Richard Sears, who issued the first Sears Roebuck & Company catalog in 1893, although he had been in business before that time.

Figure 10–9

In-store vs. Nonstore Retailing

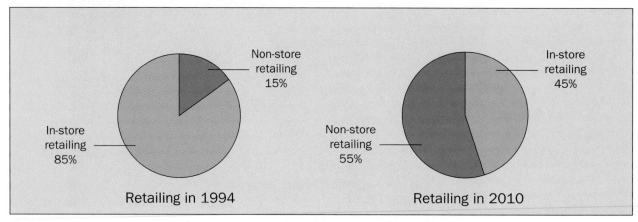

Source: Based on information in *Vision for the New Millennium . . . Evolving to Consumer Response*, p. 8, by Kurt Salmon Associates, 1995, Atlanta, GA: Author. Adapted by permission of Kurt Salmon Associates.

Among the conditions that paved the way for this nineteenth-century innovation in retailing was the then-predominantly rural nature of the country. Stocks of country stores were limited, and transportation to the developing fashionable city stores was difficult. More to the point, rural free delivery had just been introduced by the post office.

These early catalogs were the standbys of rural customers for generations. Although the fashions offered were not exciting, the prices and assortments surpassed those in rural stores, and they were a delight to the country clientele they were intended to serve (Figure 10–10). In the eyes of these customers, the catalogs indeed earned the name that came to be applied to them: "the wish book." So well, indeed, did the mail-order houses meet the needs and broadening interests of rural customers that by 1895 the Sears catalog consisted of 507 pages, and the company's annual sales exceeded $750,000 ("Merchant to," no date).

As one early mail-order company, Jones Post & Co., told its customers: "Your home, or ranch, or farm, is never so far distant that you are shut out from the great throbbing world with its mammoth commercial establishments. No longer are you forced to be satisfied with the small stock and slim assortment (of country stores) from which to make your selection at exorbitant prices" (Kidwell & Christman, 1974, p. 162).

Growth of Mail-Order (Catalog) Retailing

Beginning in the 1970s, catalog sales have been increasing rapidly and show every sign of continuing to do so. Catalog *apparel* sales account for about 7 percent of all apparel sold (AAMA, 2000).

This "buying from catalog" phenomenon results from several factors: the rise of two-earner families, in which neither spouse has much time for shopping in stores; affluent singles, whose active working and social lives leave little room for shopping; the time crunch for working mothers; crowded stores and their often inexperienced and hard-to-find salespeople; and the advent of toll-free 800 telephone numbers. The result has been an explosion not only in the number of catalog companies, but also in the variety of goods that can be bought from catalogs. Today, mail-order houses range from large, well-known retailers such as Spiegel, which sells designer-name fashions, to small specialty operations such as the Collins Street Bakery in Texas, which sells fruitcake. In fact, mail-order sellers of both apparel and other consumer products have multiplied to such a degree that there is even a publication called *Shop-at-Home-Directory* for consumers who want information about the various mail-order houses and the merchandise that each features.

Among the largest in terms of dollar sales are the general merchandise catalogs of J.C. Penney and Spiegel. Targeted at mainstream America, they sell merchandise to furnish a home, clothe a family, and equip many types of activities. For a century, Sears Roebuck & Company published its beloved "wish book." However, the company dropped the catalog in 1993 as part of a major restructuring. Following the end of Sears' "big book," many other catalog firms scrambled to secure pieces of that mail-order business. Sears has since returned to the mail-order business with specialty catalogs.

Mail-Order (Catalog) Apparel Specialists

Although apparel has been featured in mail-order catalogs since their inception, it is only in recent years that there has been an increased emphasis on upscale fashions. Many highly specialized apparel mail-order houses have proliferated, each of which focuses its effort on a clearly defined targeted group of consumers. Some, such as the

Figure 10–10   **1897 Sears Roebuck & Company catalog page.**

Source: This page from the 1897 catalog is reprinted by arrangement with Sears Roebuck & Co. and is protected under copyright. No duplication is permitted.

Horchow Collection, concentrate on high-priced, sophisticated luxury items of wearing apparel and accessories as well as home furnishings items. Other similar operations of this type are Trifles, J.A. Bank Clothiers, and the specialized fashion-forward books of Spiegel. Hartmarx's Barrie Pace catalog is directed at professional women. Another group of catalog fashion retailers specialize in classic and casual wear for men and women. Perhaps among the best known of this type are Lands' End and L.L. Bean, which mail millions of catalogs annually. Examples of others in this category include Johnny Appleseed, Eddie Bauer (owned by Spiegel), Victoria's Secret, and Talbots. There are also catalogs devoted to off-size apparel, such as King Size for men and Brylane for large-size women's apparel. Spiegel's E style is a catalog for African-American women. A number of mail-order shoe firms specialize in hard-to-find sizes.

The operations involved in buying and selling fashion goods by mail are quite different from those of stores. The preparation of a catalog is a lengthy process, and merchandise must be bought close to a year in advance of a selling season. Because apparel producers do not have their seasonal lines ready that far in advance, catalog houses must work with fabric suppliers and apparel manufacturers to develop the kinds of merchandise they want for their targeted customers. However, because most catalog retailers print and distribute millions of catalogs, their tremendous purchasing power enables them to have merchandise made expressly for them.

Catalog Operations by Department and Specialty Stores

At this point, it may be well to reread the definition of a mail-order house. Some catalog retailers may have one or more retail stores. Talbots, for example, operates more than 400 stores. However, if the bulk of a retailer's business is done through catalog sales, it is considered a mail-order house.

Originally, the primary purpose of the catalogs of conventional department and large specialty stores was to attract customers into the store. Nowadays, the same elements that led to the growth of mail-order retailing have encouraged such retail stores to increase the frequency and distribution of their catalogs and improve the efficiency with which they handle mail and telephone responses. These days, although not to be classified as mail-order houses, mail and telephone business accounts for a more and more substantial portion of the conventional stores' business. A few examples of department and specialty stores with impressive catalog sales are Saks Fifth Avenue, Neiman Marcus, Victoria's Secret, Talbots, and Nordstroms. Precise figures are not readily available, but Bloomingdale's may illustrate the point: Bloomingdale's-by-Mail is now referred to as the "second largest store" in their multiunit operation.

Catalog Showroom Retailing

A **catalog showroom retailer** is an underselling company that sells from a catalog and also maintains a showroom where samples of the merchandise can be seen and ordered. There are no deliveries, but usually the purchases can be picked up immediately at the showroom or from an adjoining warehouse. Very large, prepackaged stocks of the catalog items are on hand.

The mainstay of the merchandise assortment is usually branded housewares, appliances, TVs, stereo equipment, electronics, toys, and sporting goods at prices well below those prevailing in conventional stores. Items of apparel, cosmetics, children's sleepers, men's underwear, and jewelry are also carried, but often are not featured or listed in the catalogs. Prices reflect the low operating costs. In addition to their bare-bones operation, catalog showrooms are usually in low-rent areas. Few salespeople are needed, because customers select their items from samples and catalogs, then fill out purchase slips and pick up their packages from the warehouse.

Retail operations of this type began in the late 1960s and achieved a growth in sales ranging from 30 to 40 percent during the 1970s. The largest of these is Best Buy, with sales of over $12 billion.

The impact of such stores on the fashion business has been negligible thus far; but so was the impact of other forms of underselling stores at first. Whether or not these minimum-service retailers will make a place for themselves in fashion still remains to be seen.

Electronic Retailing

Although most goods are still being sold through stores and mail-order catalogs, various forms of electronic shopping have become increasingly important. No one can really predict the future of these forms of retailing, but nearly all industry experts agree that more and more consumers will participate in electronic shopping, viewing merchandise on either television screens or on a personal computer. In short, home shopping is going high tech.

The electronic retailing trend reflects the same social factors that explain the growth of mail-order sales—the number of working women and individuals' interest in spending spare time in more relaxed ways than shopping.

Electronic retailing occurs in basically three formats: (1) **online computer services**, (2) **home television shopping**, and (3) **CD-ROM shopping** with a compact disk run on a CD-ROM drive to show catalog collections. Each of these is discussed following.

Online Retailing ("E-Tailing")

Computer technologies permit consumers to use the Internet to shop in cyberspace. This relatively new means of doing business—e-commerce—has exploded as a sales channel for products and services. The truly revolutionary impact of the Information Revolution is being felt in this area of e-commerce. The term "**e-tailing**" is used for online retailing, a form of **business-to-consumer (B2C)** e-commerce.

Victoria's Secret showed the fashion world the potential of e-tailing when more than two million Internet users worldwide watched a Victoria's Secret fashion show in a live webcast from Cannes, France. On the day of the actual webcast, VictoriaSecret.com received roughly 15 million hits from more than 140 countries. While the general public ogled models in the latest lingerie designs, technical engineers and management used new technologies that permitted viewers to shop as they watched.

The number of consumers with home computers has mushroomed, making e-tailing a growing medium for the fashion industry. Retailers are realizing increasingly that it may be necessary to have websites as well as their conventional stores. In the new vernacular, **bricks-and-mortar** refers to retailers with traditional store sites, and **bricks-and-clicks** refer to those with both stores and online sites.

It is estimated that eventually between 20 and 40 percent of apparel sales will be online. At first, some skeptics thought that consumers would be unwilling to order apparel from online sources because shoppers would be unable to feel or try on garments. However, sales growth is encouraging. Advantages include quick comparative shopping, immediate update of products, and various features that help the consumer envision how garments would look on themselves. Innovations such as virtual dressing rooms and customized virtual models enable companies to customize the shopper's experience and the products they buy. For example, one children's wear company lets the customer order customized combinations of colors and designs to be made into a garment. Unfortunately, boo.com, an e-tailer with one of the most catchy, state-of-the-art sites and with an intended global reach, was fairly short lived in its original format. A scaled-down version later emerged.

A study that Ernst & Young conducted for the National Retail Federation queried consumers and online retailers in six countries. In general, consumer shopping online is gaining acceptance in every country surveyed. Consumers are making more online purchases, and as they do, they are spending more. Not only are more consumers shopping and spending online, they plan to make greater use of the online channel in the future. All companies interviewed said they had success online and had great expectations for the future. Some felt the online channel was more efficient than their store-based operation.

Order fulfillment is an important consideration. E-tailers must be prepared to deliver merchandise as ordered and without delay. Consumers expect shipments from online sources more quickly than from catalogs. In the Ernst & Young study, 52 percent of the retailers use their own distribution centers for warehousing and delivery. Some companies use a variety of distribution strategies. Some use three different channels depending on the product—the company's own stores may deliver, an order may be shipped direct from the supplier, or it may use third-party distribution. Entering e-tailing has required careful planning for demand and supply chain management to ensure that inventory is available when needed and that orders are accepted, picked, shipped, and monitored effectively.

Credit card use—the "plasticization of business"—is a great facilitator of e-tailing. So are the worldwide delivery services such as United Parcel, Federal Express, and DHL. With these two modern aides to business, potential global sales may be just around the corner. Technically, consumers in nearly any country can log on, order with a credit card, and have products shipped by one of the delivery services with worldwide distribution.

However, security issues have been a major concern to consumers, and many are reluctant to give their credit card numbers online. More-established e-tailers such as amazon.com appear to have now conquered this potential problem.

Another relevant issue is: Who can sell online and maintain workable business relationships? Online sellers whose primary business is retailing appear to have few conflicts of interest. However, when manufacturers attempt to sell directly to the consumer, they run the risk of alienating their retail customer. That is, the retailer feels that the supplier is competing for consumer sales and may terminate business with that supplier. For example, if Levi Strauss sells directly to the consumer, Levi is competing with many major stores that carry the Levi brand. The retail stores may decide to carry other brands rather than Levi.

Home Television Shopping

TV shopping shows have been around since the late 1970s, but most authorities date the real emergence and increasing importance of home shopping channels to the mid-1980s.[5] Home shopping channels are cable or satellite TV channels entirely devoted to selling goods and services. The two major ones are Home Shopping Network and

---

[5]Home Shopping Network was founded in the late 1970s and QVC in 1986.

QVC. Most TV shopping works like mail order; the consumer calls an 800 number after viewing the product. As cable and satellite companies upgrade to offer hundreds of channels and become interactive, home shopping has the potential of tapping into a "video mall"—offering consumers a chance to browse through channels, ask for information, order, and pay without ever leaving home.

Until the early 1990s, television shopping had featured moderate-priced merchandise directed to the masses. Major retailers had shown little interest because this medium was not being directed toward the more urban and suburban upscale customer that many merchants wanted to attract. However, a major change occurred in the TV home shopping industry when Barry Diller, who had started Fox Broadcasting Co. and made it a powerful fourth network, took the helm at QVC, the second-largest home shopping channel at the time. Diller rapidly transformed QVC into a high-profile medium attracting both manufacturers and retailers catering to a range of customers.

Under Diller's leadership, QVC became a more fashion-oriented shopping channel. Fashionable Saks Fifth Avenue made astonishing sales, confirming that upscale shoppers were attracted to this form of retailing. Other upscale stores including Bloomingdale's, Nordstrom, and Williams-Sonoma explored TV home shopping. Numerous designers have also sold merchandise on QVC, including Arnold Scaasi, Donna Karan, Calvin Klein, and Diane von Furstenberg. For many manufacturers and retailers, the sales volume per hour was phenomenal—far beyond what could have been anticipated based on previous TV shopping history. One survey found that home shoppers were younger, more educated, and more style-conscious than believed earlier; nearly half were men (Zinn, DeGeorge, Shoretz, Yang, & Forest, 1993). MTV's home shopping venture, "The Goods," featured designers such as Isaac Mizrahi, Todd Oldham, and Marc Jacobs.

Instead of thinking of TV home shopping as a competitor, for a time some retailers saw this medium as having potential to help reduce the costs associated with store retailing—namely, rent, sales help, and advertising. Even J.C. Penney, whose earlier home shopping network failed, remained open to the future of this retailing option.

During Diller's two-year stay at QVC, TV home shopping was heralded as the most important shopping format of the future. Sales were astonishing. After the initial hype, however, enthusiasm waned somewhat. Although QVC's annual sales are about $3 billion, fewer high-profile designers and retailers appear to be attracted to this medium. TV home shopping has two constraints that reduce its appeal: (1) the customer must adapt to the TV schedule, watching lengthy programs to see only a few items displayed—hardly the time-saving feature today's time-starved consumers want, and (2) TV home shopping does not permit fashion products to be presented with enough clarity and detail to make satisfactory purchase decisions. An exception to this appears to be jewelry, making TV home shopping a growing source of jewelry sales.

Shortcomings may be reduced if TV home shopping takes on more interactive features, turning the experience into an active rather than passive one. Interactive features might let the viewer point and click on products of specific interest—for example, shoes, jewelry, or undergarments—rather than having to watch what the network chooses to show. Interactive features could permit the shopper to zoom in on the product. Both TV home shopping and online computer shopping have the potential to offer these interactive features; time will tell which becomes the medium of choice.

CD-ROM Computer Shopping

This retail format involves use of a CD-ROM disk holding offerings from 25 to 45 companies. The new digital versatile disk (DVD) holds many more times the information that a CD holds. Several companies specialize in developing these disks, which are purchased by consumers. The consumer may click on icons and word commands to browse through the catalog "pages" on the screen. Shoppers may type in the names of specific items and retrieve selections from various catalogs on the disk. This format is more limited than online services because new product offerings occur only when the consumer obtains a new disk.

Flea Market Retailers

A **flea market** is a location, either indoors or out, in which a wide variety of independent sellers rent space on a temporary basis. Flea markets are growing all over the country, both in number and in size. Some are open every day, others only on the weekend. Any vendor may sell at these markets. All that is needed is merchandise and the money to rent a booth or table.

The merchandise offered for sale may be new or old, antiques and near-antiques, clothing, accessories, furniture, kitchen utensils, handcrafted and ready-made products, high-priced and penny-priced merchandise. Some flea market sellers even specialize. One may sell only used jeans, another may sell only jewelry, and so on. The variety is infinite—and this is part of the attraction for shoppers hunting for possible treasures, bargains, or unique items.

Direct Selling: Door-to-Door and Party Plans

Modern versions of the early peddlers are the **direct-selling retailers** who operate without stores. A *direct-selling* establishment is one that sells merchandise by contacting customers through either *door-to-door* approaches or some form of *in-home party plan*. Direct selling is not new in the fashion field; in the period before World War II, silk hosiery and custom-made foundation garments were successfully sold this way.

Door-to-door retailing encompasses many different types of products. Working on commission, a salesperson calls on a customer at home and attempts to make the sale. In the household goods field, such names as Electrolux and Fuller Brush are familiar; they use this method exclusively. In fashion-related fields, Avon is perhaps the best-known operation of this kind. Starting with door-to-door selling of cosmetics, it now includes jewelry as well as apparel and accessories in its merchandise mix.

The **party plan** of selling depends on the company's representative getting a local woman to organize a party of her friends and neighbors, at which the salesperson presents the company's merchandise. The hostess receives a gift, usually provided by the salesperson. This method of selling in the home is most closely associated with Tupperware, but it has also been used effectively in the fashion field by firms such as Sarah Coventry for jewelry. Doncaster is an example of fashion apparel sold by this means.

In most instances, salespeople who represent direct-selling firms use a company-produced catalog to supplement the relatively limited assortment of samples from which they sell.

The Changing Dimensions of Fashion Retailing

Very few periods in history have seen as many changes in the world of retailing as the last two decades. Although the fundamental role played by retailers in the business of fashion has not changed—the buying and selling of fashion products to the ultimate consumer—almost everything else about them has.

Until 1980, major retailers of fashion could still be easily classified as department stores, specialty stores, chains, mail-order houses, discount houses, and the like, according to their distinctive operational characteristics. Since the 1980s, however, retailers have moved in so many different directions that they can no longer be so neatly defined. *Acquisitions, verticalization, globalization, partnerships, buyouts, private labels, e-commerce, e-tailing, restructuring, consolidation,* and *superstores* have become retailing buzzwords. Today, the retail marketers of fashionable merchandise come in an almost infinite variety of shapes, sizes, corporate ownership, pricing strategies, and merchandise assortments.

The section that follows covers some of the major changes that are revolutionizing softgoods retailing.

Growth of Private Labels: Retailers into Manufacturing

In the late 1970s, as designer and manufacturers' national brand names proliferated, it seemed as if every type of retailer was featuring the same nationally advertised names—department and specialty stores, mail-order houses, chain store retailers, and hordes of off-price apparel specialists that were underselling these well-known names. In order to have merchandise that was unique to their stores and to regain their freedom from price competition, many large department and specialty stores increasingly developed and promoted their own private-label fashion products in men's, women's, and children's apparel and accessories. **Private-label** merchandise, as used in the fashion industry, refers to goods that are produced exclusively for one retailer, and it carries only the name of the retailer or one of several brand names that are owned by the retailer. Recent years have witnessed a steady expansion of private-label operations, and today the fashion business is inundated with so many different names and labels that it is hard to know whether a specific name is that of a manufacturer's national brand, a designer's name, or a retailer's private label. In a special "Infotracs" supplement on brands in *Women's Wear Daily* and *DNR*, these industry distinctions were given:

- *National/designer brand ("name brand").* A label that is distributed nationally to which consumers attach a specific meaning. Typically a national brand represents a certain image, quality level, and price-point range to consumers. Examples are Lee, Ralph Lauren, Esprit, and Hanes.
- *Private-label brand.* A label that is owned and marketed by a specific retailer for use in their stores. Examples are Stafford, Arizona, Faded Glory, Jaclyn Smith, and Kathie Lee Gifford.
- *Retail store brand.* A name of a retail chain that is, in most cases, used as the exclusive label on the items carried by that retailer. Examples are The Gap, Abercrombie & Fitch, L.L. Bean, and Victoria's Secret.

- *All other brands.* Miscellaneous labels that are not included in the preceding categories; these include licensed brands. Examples include Mickey & Co., Looney Tunes, August Silk, and Wilson.
- *Nonbrands.* A label to which consumers attach no significant identity, awareness, or meaning (Lewis, 1995, p. 3).

A survey for the "Infotracs" feature found that consumers do not make distinctions among what the industry views as different types of brands. Rather, consumers think in terms of *brands* (which include all the first four just listed) and *nonbrands.* Nearly three-fourths of the female respondents defined certain store labels as "brands," and two-thirds identified certain private labels as "brands."

In the same survey, retailers revealed that financial reasons (increasing revenues and margins and reducing costs) and differentiation were the major reasons merchants had developed private-label programs. Fulfilling a consumer need or niche was rated lower in importance (Lewis, 1995).

Today, as a result of expanding private-label operations, large retailers are deeply involved in the production process and have assumed roles that traditionally belong to manufacturers—the styling and contracting production of merchandise (Figure 10–11). Most have established special **product development** departments that create their own lines of merchandise and work with manufacturers or contractors in this country and abroad to produce their private brand merchandise according to their specifications.

Figure 10–11   **Staff in the private label division of a major retailer plan a line in the same manner as merchandisers in an apparel firm.**

Source: Photo by Elena Karpova.

The May Department Stores, for example, has a staff of more than 100 people who perform product development functions, just as a product development staff at an apparel manufacturing firm would. They develop private-label lines like the Valerie Stephens line and contract production both domestically and overseas. Many other large retail firms, including J.C. Penney, have staffs who are doing the same. Today on the classified pages of industry publications, retailers' help-wanted ads for product developers compete with those of manufacturers for the same designers and production coordinators. A large retail store product development department uses all the new computer technology for design, marker making, and so on that a modern apparel firm

Figure 10–12

The National Retail Federation has provided training for its members on how to develop and improve private label brands. Reprinted courtesy National Retail Federation.

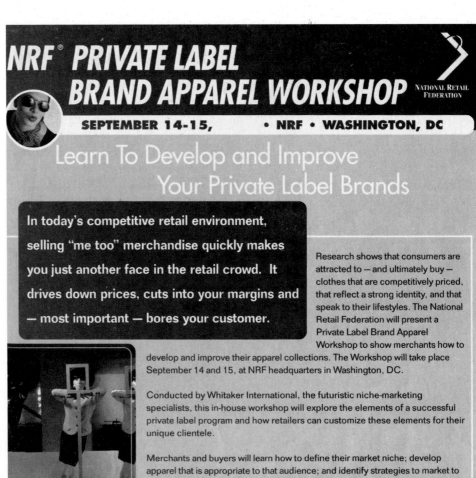

will have. Other stores work with producers that specialize in creating and producing private-label programs. Moreover, trade groups and other trade sources are available to assist retailers in producing for these programs. For example, Figure 10–12 illustrates the assistance available through the National Retail Federation.

Although it is generally estimated that 80 percent or more of private-label merchandise is produced offshore by contractors in low-wage countries, many major U.S. manufacturers with strong national brands of their own are now also producing private-label merchandise. Rather than lose business to foreign sources of supply, they are supplying retailers with exclusive merchandise to be sold under the store's own labels. While continuing to produce their own nationally branded products, they are developing private-label divisions within their own companies. More often than not, the merchandise is manufactured in the same factories by the same workers who make their national brands and is sold side by side in the same stores. Examples include the Vanity Fair division of VF Corporation (producers of its own Vanity Fair and Vassarette lines plus at times private-label merchandise for Victoria's Secret) and the Mansco division of Manhattan Industries. Even a high-priced fashion producer such as Tahari has entered the field and produces for the Privé Collection label of Saks Fifth Avenue.

Another development is the licensing and use of a designer or other well-known name as one of a store's private labels. For example, The Limited has a licensing agreement for the Moods by Krizia line. Other examples are the agreement between Kathie Lee Gifford and Wal-Mart (Figure 10–13) and between Jaclyn Smith and Kmart.

Figure 10–13

The Kathie Lee Collection was developed exclusively for Wal-Mart.

Source: Photo by Anthony Magnacca/Merrill/Prentice Hall.

Although retailers build their own brands for greater profit, more distinctive assortments, and greater control over their merchandise, most merchants continue to sell national brands alongside their private label brands. Sometimes retailers have to be concerned that their private label products do not destroy the market for name brands they have carried successfully, damaging the long-term relationships they have built with name-brand manufacturers over time. J.C. Penney's Arizona jeans is a good example of a private-label line that is compatible alongside the strong Levi brand. The Arizona label sells more than $500 million annually; however, Levi sales in Penney stores continue to grow at a healthy pace.

The proportion of private-label goods to other labels varies from store to store, but for many, the range is 15 to 20 percent of all apparel. Among chains whose store names are the same as the apparel brand, well over half the total stock, or in some cases all, may be privately branded merchandise. The Gap is a prominent example.

In the early days of private label merchandise, only a few specialty and discount chains used this strategy in securing merchandise assortments. Today, however, private-label development has proliferated into a high-volume, high-profile enterprise at major retail firms everywhere. Private-label programs have become more comprehensive, covering more categories and SKUs. The explosion of private-label programs has occurred at a time when the U.S. apparel market is already oversaturated. Growing imports have added to this excess of products in the market. The oversupply of apparel has occurred as consumers have slowed in their clothing expenditures. As these trends converge, the result is an apparel market glut in which markdowns are required just to sell the merchandise, and both manufacturers' and retailers' profits suffer.

Concentration of Retail Power

As we have discussed in earlier sections of the chapter, consolidations through buyouts and mergers have resulted in larger and more-powerful retail firms. This concentration of power and clout has many advantages as retailers respond to a bruising economic environment. Large merchants can consolidate functions such as buying, product development, and logistics to reduce costs and improve efficiency. The massive buying power of the retail giants permits them to demand very competitive prices on merchandise. These competitive prices permit the megamerchants to offer merchandise to their customers at attractive prices and to improve their own profit margins. For some retailers, even major ones, this consolidation has rescued firms that were gradually sinking into bankruptcy.

Although retail consolidations have many advantages for the industry, these changes may have limitations, also. For example, as consumers complain of too much "sameness" in stores, consolidation of buying may add to that. For example, if Federated's buyers are now making all the buying decisions for stores that were once made by Macy's buyers, this reduces prospects for variety in merchandise in the Federated/Macy's stores.

As we discussed in Chapter 6, retail consolidations may also create challenges for manufacturers who sell to the giant retailers. These large retailers make increasing demands on their suppliers because suppliers now have fewer potential retail customers who buy very large quantities of merchandise. Large, powerful retailers use this power to press suppliers to give better and better prices and to provide more services such as **preticketing** merchandise, shipping it floor-ready, and holding the extra inventory. Retailers continue to demand more chargebacks for often minor offenses. Many engage in **matrix buying**, which means those suppliers not on the matrix are unable to sell to that retailer.

Partnerships in the Softgoods Industry

As competition and a sluggish economy have created challenging business conditions for both retailers and manufacturers, both have learned there are advantages to developing closer working relationships with each other. Both are serving the same end-use consumer. Moving away from a feeling of animosity and toward one of cooperation has led to a more-integrated softgoods industry, at least for companies that choose to develop these partnerships.

As a means of serving customers more effectively and in reducing costs, retailers and manufacturers work together through **Quick Response** programs. In their book, *A Stitch In Time: Lean Retailing and the Transformation of Manufacturing*, Abernathy, Dunlop, Hammond, and Weil (1999) discuss how technological advances of the 1980s paved the way for this new concept in retailing—**lean retailing**. The fashion industry has always been vulnerable to rapidly changing styles and fickle customers, and the old way of doing business often led to stock shortages, high inventories, and costly markdowns.

Abernathy et al. note that companies like Wal-Mart have led the way in lean retailing—rethinking how products are ordered, virtually eliminating delays at the distribution center to sales floor by drawing on sales data captured electronically at the time of the purchase. The terms *Quick Response* and *lean retailing* refer to basically the same concept. The aim of each is the quick replenishment of fast-selling items to have merchandise in stock when consumers want it. The electronic linkages between suppliers and retailers rely on shared data. When the retailer sells an item, the only way the supplier knows to replenish that item is by having access to the retailer's sales data. The retailer tracks sales by style, size, and color and transmits that information to the manufacturer. The apparel firm uses the information to tailor its production to match retail sales so they can replenish stock quickly and spot trends fast.

Companies that can adapt to the lean retailing strategy can reduce inventory risk, reduce costs, and increase profitability while improving their responsiveness to ever-changing tastes of customers. Other business sectors are adapting the lean retailing concept after seeing its success in the softgoods industry.

Linkages are also set up between apparel companies and textile companies so they also can tune into retail sales. The textile firms must be prepared to respond to the fabric needs of apparel firms as they replenish retailers' inventories. The linkages are also important in retailers' development of private label lines, as shown in Figure 10–14.

Logistics and Distribution

Computers have facilitated greatly improved means for receiving merchandise from suppliers, storing minimal amounts of inventory for a store's selling needs, and distributing merchandise among a chain's multiple stores. This may be handled by the retailers' own traffic department, or may use independent ("third-party") logistics firms.

Large inventories of fashion merchandise represent major investments for retailers. **Supply chain management**, a hot industry topic, focuses on careful planning and communication between manufacturers and retailers to have merchandise on hand as needed without having costly investments in inventory. Today's efficient retailers move merchandise quickly and efficiently. Gone are the days when retailers held large inventories that languished in warehouses. Merchandise must move quickly to stores, in anticipation that sales will occur relatively fast for a rapid stock

Figure 10–14

J.C. Penney uses electronics to develop private-label lines.

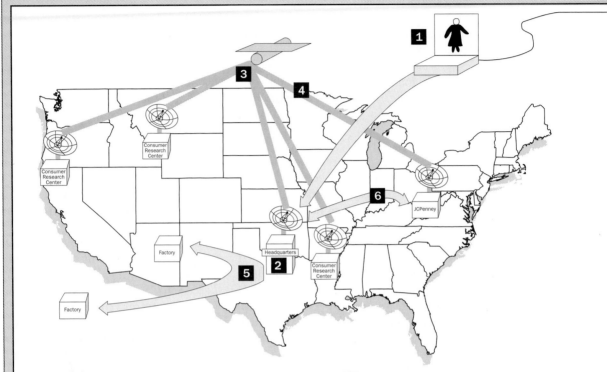

1 J.C. Penney fashion scout in Europe sees a new design, transmits a color photo via telephone lines to headquarters in Dallas.

2 At headquarters, a J.C. Penney version of the product is designed on a computer-aided design system.

3 Using satellite links, designs are shown to consumers at J.C. Penney testing centers around the U.S. The consumers "vote" on the products on personal computers. The results are tabulated at headquarters within 24 hours to help decide if the company should sell the product.

4 Using the company's direct broadcast system, merchandise is shown to buyers at 700 J.C. Penney stores nationwide. They can provide instant feedback.

5 Design and production information about the garment is transmitted electronically to factories in the U.S. and Asia. Photographs of samples may be transmitted back to headquarters for quality-control checks.

6 Sales results are tabulated daily at J.C. Penney stores and are transmitted to headquarters over phone lines. When sales of a product reach a certain level, a computer in the store may automatically reorder it. In some cases, these reorders are transmitted directly from the store to the manufacturer.

turn. Through frequent stock turns, retailers maximize their return on the inventory investment and have more profit to show in the end. The distribution system must be rapid to support that fast stock turn and to assure that plenty of new assortments are available to customers who shop the stores. For example, in The Limited's giant distribution center, most merchandise is shipped to stores within 24 hours of receiving it from suppliers.

Cross docking is an example of these efficient distribution activities. This method is used in retail distribution centers in which merchandise is received, sorted, and routed directly from receiving to shipping without spending any time in storage. Additionally, for retailers involved in QR and EDI, **advance ship notices** (electronic bills of lading) are sent electronically to the retailer when the supplier ships the merchandise. This alerts the retailer that the merchandise will soon arrive, to be distributed among multiple stores if needed.

Globalization of Retailing

Retailers have traditionally attached great significance to "thinking locally"—that is, developing relationships between merchants and consumers and tailoring merchandise assortments to each local clientele. Although retailers must continue to address the needs of local markets, many large retail firms are now thinking in much broader terms. A number of major retailers are developing global strategies.

Globalization of retailing is occurring for a number of reasons. First, many borders and barriers have vanished. The NAFTA pact has encouraged firms in North America to think increasingly in terms of one market, rather than three. Increased integration of the European Union means there are fewer borders to penetrate to sell in Europe. The fall of the Berlin Wall has opened vast markets in Central and Eastern Europe.

Second, advances in communication technology and transportation make it much easier to do business in other parts of the world. Fax machines and electronic mail permit low-cost communication with business partners worldwide. Satellite television, movies, and travel have resulted in a degree of converging tastes among consumers on all continents. Consumers almost everywhere recognize McDonald's, Mickey Mouse, Coca-Cola, Levi's, and Pizza Hut. Although cultural differences continue to exist among the peoples of the world, an amazing number of consumers everywhere want U.S. jeans and sneakers. In a report entitled *Consumer Nation: Retailing 2010, Global Retailing in a Consumer-Centric Universe* (2000), PriceWaterhouseCoopers experts assert that a "consumer nation" will be created by the Internet. Without geographic borders, this new global "nation" will be an on-line marketplace where consumers from anywhere in the world come to view the bounty of products and services available to them.

Third, changes in the economies in various regions of the world have resulted in a difference in spending potential or spending willingness. Consumers in other countries like the offerings and format that U.S. retail firms can give them. In the 1980s a number of European retailers opened stores in the United States to sell in what much of the world sees as a large, affluent market. These included Benetton, Laura Ashley, and Body Shop International Plc. However, as we have discussed previously, the U.S. fashion market changed in the 1990s. Consumers slowed their spending on apparel and other products as a result of demographic changes and shifting priorities. Therefore, the U.S. market, like that in most of the other more developed countries, has offered very little growth potential for ambitious retail chains looking for opportunities to expand. As U.S. domestic growth leveled off, a number of other regions of the world experienced high rates of both economic and population growth, particularly in Asia and some parts of Latin America. In the past, as retailers in the more developed countries wanted to expand their international markets, they added stores in *other* more developed countries. That is no longer the case. The rapidly expanding economies of countries once considered less developed are the new targets for retail expansion.

Many familiar U.S. retailers are rapidly expanding in other countries; these include Talbots, J.C. Penney, Foot Locker, Wal-Mart, Kmart, and others. L.L. Bean now issues its catalogs in more than 145 countries. Compared to European and Asian retailers, retailers in the Americas have been slow to globalize; however, many are actively pursuing expansion strategies today. Moreover, the Internet extends a retailer's offerings without the investment of building stores or mailing catalogs.

Although this worldwide retail expansion is expected to continue, individuals involved will find it necessary to recognize and respect the cultural differences in other countries. Although a "westernization" of lifestyles is occurring, marketers must realize that many tastes and preferences will differ. Just as Coca-Cola offers flavor variations in other countries and McDonald's burgers are made from a different mixture of ingredients in other nations, apparel preferences will vary also. Consumers have different views on what constitutes attractive colors and styles. Fit preferences are different; some residents in other countries may view U.S. clothing as sloppy and vulgar. Acceptable exposure of the body varies greatly among the peoples of the world. Sizes must accommodate different stature. For example, U.S. size ranges are not suitable for Asian or Hispanic markets, where individuals have a smaller build.

Global retailing offers many potential opportunities for those firms willing to take risks, study their markets carefully, work closely with local representatives who know the market, and remain committed for the long term. Global retailing will not be easy, but it may very well distinguish the winners from the losers among retailers in the decades to come.

Relationship Marketing

At the same time that retailers are expanding globally, many retailers are also striving for **relationship marketing**, that is, building a closer relationship with the domestic customer. Retailers realize that to prosper, they must strive to meet the needs of an increasingly demanding consumer. As consumers are less and less inclined to think of shopping as an enjoyable social activity, they increasingly focus on a specific destination for what they need. As consumers tire of the "sameness" in retailing, this will require a move away from *mass* merchandising.

Additionally, the Internet has empowered consumers. They are now able to shop online, comparing products and prices more quickly than ever before. Consumers are becoming more impatient, and their willingness to tolerate inattentive retailers is waning.

As retailers attempt to meet these new demands, they must attempt to know and better understand their target market. Using computers, retailers can build databases on customers to an extent unheard of until recent years, permitting **database marketing**. These computer files can amass a great deal of information on a consumer's demographic and psychographic characteristics; these files may be developed by the retail firm or purchased elsewhere. This specific information allows the retailer to develop offerings of special interest to specific customers and to build a relationship with those consumers.

New technology allows retailers to increasingly **customize** their merchandise offerings and service to more narrow niches of the domestic market. Providing products specific to consumers' needs will use **micromarketing** techniques. This requires differentiating stores, merchandise within those stores, and thinking at the lowest level of aggregation. Retailers who manage this in the domestic market may be better prepared to function successfully in global markets.

Specialty mail-order firms have used these database marketing techniques for years to reach specialized niches. Women who wear large-size apparel may find that they are deluged by catalogs from retailers specializing in large sizes, or the individual with hard-to-find shoe sizes may suddenly receive catalogs from several companies. When these strategies lead to ongoing relationships between the consumer and the retailer, the resulting information is useful to manufacturers also. That is, the whole softgoods chain is better able to serve specialized markets through various micromarketing techniques.

Readings

Retailers face many changes in how they do business today. The Internet and e-commerce have transformed the industry in ways unheard of a decade ago. At the same time, consumers expect more from retailers. These articles address some of these changes.

Retailers Are Flocking to the Web—Like It or Not

Retailers are finding that having a Web presence is necessary to complement existing business. A number have valuable success stories, and those are shared in this article.

Mackey McDonald: 2020 Vision of the Future

McDonald, who is CEO of VF Corporation, shares the company's vision of what the retail industry will be like in the future. He shares VF Corporation's plan to serve retailers and the end-use consumer through various leading-edge technology applications.

Relationships. Experiences.
Don't Hit the Market Without Them

Today's customer is tired of sameness in fashion goods and bland shopping experiences. This article asserts that customers need a visual, lifestyle experience when they shop.

Retailers Are Flocking to the Web— Like It or Not

by Vicki M. Young

New York—Damn the profitability. For retailers on the Internet, it's full speed ahead.

Regardless of costs, regardless of sales, regardless of return, or lack thereof, retailers have no choice.

Steven A. Richter, retail analyst at Tucker Anthony, concluded, "For retailers, being on the Internet is not viewed as a trade-off. It's a question of how one does it, not whether one should do it. The reality is that it's critical to have the site to be able to touch the consumer at multiple points. The consumers are demanding it. They want to do things their way."

Especially for companies heavily involved in the buying and selling of apparel, there may not be an immediate benefit to a dedicated Web site, but there is a definite penalty to the absence of one.

"An Internet presence is a requirement more than a benefit," said Joseph Teklits, analyst at Ferris, Baker Watts. "A lot of investors are less interested in a company if there is no Internet strategy. But that doesn't mean there's a premium for those that do have a Web presence."

Veronique Bardach, chief executive officer of Inshop.com, an "informediary" firm that helps retailers drive traffic to their local stores, noted that in her experience, traditional retailers who have made the jump online have done so as a response to competitive pressures.

"It is rare that a company can generate value in the short term from such a defensive action. Even if a retailer is successful online, the only value they can anticipate is goodwill from Wall Street, which is not quantifiable. Only once they're online do these retailers begin to contemplate a definitive plan that could in the long run provide shareholder value."

Jeffrey Klinefelter, retail analyst at U.S. Bancorp Piper Jaffray, pointed out, "Today's valuation in the market doesn't give companies credit for being on the Internet. It's a defense mechanism for them. If they don't do it, the valuation of their companies could come down."

Klinefelter observed that it takes longer for retailers to get credit for their migration online. "The revenue base is so large that it takes more time to grow the operation. Catalog companies, because of their fulfillment and call center infrastructure that's already in place, are given credit for their ability to migrate."

Todd Slater, retail and apparel analyst at Lazard Freres, noted, "It's critical for retailers to have an Internet presence. They will lose 10 percent of the market by avoiding it."

He added, "For manufacturers, it hasn't yet been as critical. But if vendors could do it all over again, they would go direct to the consumer and not through the retail channel. Direct to consumers has the highest return [relative] to retail, and gives firms greater ability to control their destiny."

Henry Nasella, chairman and cofounder of Online Retail Partners, which provides technological and business guidance in the e-commerce arena, observed, "More vendors are moving online as a way to maintain loyalty to the brand."

Source: From Daily News Record, *June 7, 2000, p. 16. Copyright 2000 Fairchild Publications, Inc. Reprinted by permission.*

Nasella's predicting that manufacturers will use the Web as a way to meet customers' replenishment needs for core basics, or perhaps items not available from what's sold at retail.

Erwin Ishman, managing director at Marketing Management Group, said, "The Internet may be self-defeating for the manufacturer. It's going to drive down the prices he can charge because all the information will be available to the retailer."

Analysts and consultants agreed that it's tough to get a fix on who the market share and profit winners on the Web will be.

"We can't figure out if you can ever make money selling to the consumer on the Web even though some companies say they are profitable," said Emanuel Weintraub, president of Emanuel Weintraub Associates Inc., a management consulting firm.

Walter Loeb, a retail analyst at Loeb Associates Inc., observed, "The Internet is a very difficult area to assess right now. I think the click-and-mortar companies are likely to succeed, and the plain Internet companies—where the customer doesn't have any place to return or exchange merchandise—are not likely to be as successful."

Click-and-mortars that analysts say have top-notch sites are J.C. Penney, Lands' End and The Gap.

"J.C. Penney, despite its present problems on the selling floor, has one of the most outstanding sites," said Loeb, noting it's also an easily recognizable site because of the existing customer base generated from the J.C. Penney catalog division. More importantly, Loeb said, "J.C. Penney knows how to present the merchandise on the Internet."

Jeffrey Edelman agreed. The PaineWebber retail analyst said in a research report that the company's online environment is working because "Penney is able to leverage its name, brands, 52 million customer base, 1,100 store base, and the merchandising and infrastructure of its $4 billion catalog business."

Lands' End was cited by Weintraub as having "clear, identifiable merchandise and an excellent presentation" online. "Gap is focused on just a few items, but its ability to cross-promote the brand is a major factor in its success."

The specialty retailer promotes the site at its stores, where it also provides Internet access to the site, he said. "That kind of promotion helps drive consumers to the site."

"You have to be a brand to succeed on the Internet," Loeb stated, noting that Gap and Limited have sites but that they are set up as individual branded sites and not corporate sites with links to the different brands.

Edelman also said in a research report that Federated Department Stores could be a winner in e-commerce. "Management believes its online business can be a major contender by the fourth quarter of this fiscal year, and a winner in 2001.... Management has a vision for this business, but it has to be implemented over the next quarter or so."

He wrote that Federated has significant potential, judging by its success with its WeddingChannel site. "While this area was an obvious (and perhaps the easiest) route to take online, it does validate Federated's ability to link all of its businesses together.... We believe it has been clearly documented that the combination of bricks and mortar, and an online presence, has the potential to be profitable. Size can make the difference and Federated not only has that on its side but also powerful brands, significant customer base, a high average online transaction and more than adequate fulfillment capacity to make this a profitable venture."

For Wayne Hood, retail analyst for broad lines at Prudential Securities, "The ultimate in shareholder value [for retailers] is the acquisition of new customers."

Many retailers, he said, create shareholder value through their Web presence because the sites give them a competitive advantage in reaching the consumer through another channel.

In the meantime, the players with the most likely chance of success are still the click-and-mortar retailers, Loeb said. He added, "You have to put things in perspective. J.C. Penney did a $102 million Internet business last year, and $15 million the year before. They're going to do maybe $170 million this year. But if you take into context what they do, their catalog business is $4 billion and their total retail sales are $19 billion. The Internet business is infinitesimal. Most figures on the Internet are infinitesimal right now. They may be the size of another store, but they're not the size of another company."

Mackey McDonald: 2020 Vision of the Future

by Janet Ozzard

While many people at the Fairchild CEO Summit spoke in the abstract about the Internet's impact on retail, jeanswear giant VF Corp. has a model up and running. It's called VF 2020, and it was the core of the keynote presentation given by Mackey McDonald, VF's president, chairman and CEO.

"Faced with a lot of choices and with spending hundreds of millions of dollars, we made the decision to launch this project," he said. "We've talked to futurists, to customers, and we designed a vision of what we think the retail industry will look like 20 years from now." In essence, VF's vision of its future is that of a big manufacturer that will respond to needs at the niche level, and even at the level of individual consumers on the retail front lines.

Cindy Knoebel, the company's director of investor relations and one of the contributors to the project, joined McDonald in the presentation, narrating a video simulation of how the VF 2020 model would work to transform the acts of shopping and selling in a future department store.

"We believe retailers in the future will need to create a more experience-based environment for shoppers," said Knoebel. Enter Ms. Lopez, a fictional shopper from the year 2020 who, in the video, is about to shop in a department store called Hometown Retail.

The fictional Lopez is heading for a theme boutique inside Hometown called "Hangar Up," which is merchandised to look like a 1920s aerodrome. "Here, shoppers can find the latest vintage fashion, experience the thrills and chills of single-engine flying and pick up DVDs, eat in the pilot's lounge and browse through books," said Knoebel.

Lopez's first move as she enters Hometown Retail is to swipe a card through a reader, imparting her precise body measurements as well as a history of her previous shopping visits into the store's database. When she enters Hangar Up, she's greeted by a robotic shopping aide that suggests styles she might like, based on her previous purchases.

Knoebel said this tech-supported shopping experience will fit VF because the vendor will have the flexibility to change as needed and will be equipped to help retailers pinpoint pertinent consumer information. "In coming decades, companies will compete on [the basis of] how well they know their customer base," said Knoebel. "VF is focused on new ways to gather and manage that information."

McDonald said he considered this 2020 model "an ambitious view of the future," and added such ambition is necessary for a society that is now in a state of "permanent revolution," with new technologies arriving at an increasing pace.

"At VF, we believe that knowledge will drive the apparel industry in the next 20 years, and our competitive advantage will come from the skill with which we gather and manage that knowledge."

"One thing we believe: Brands will dominate. They serve as a filter to make the shopping experience easier for consumers, who, faced with an avalanche of data on reliable and unreliable apparel choices, will stick with brands they trust."

Tech solutions are already being tried out in stores, he said, such as Internet kiosks that allow customers to look at store inventory online. Other technology to come will include kiosks that would, for example, allow a parent to see what clothes would look like on a child without having to dress and undress the child. "You can't put a price on that kind of convenience," said McDonald. "But we'll learn how."

Relationships. Experiences. Don't Hit the Market Without Them

by Tom Julian

People wonder why an advertising agency has a trend analyst. But our business isn't just about advertising: it's about creative thinking and planning for the future.

The biggest challenges concern pressures in today's marketplace. Fallon McElligott does many focus groups and surveys, but these aren't just about people talking, it's about their experiences. I've been involved in some focus groups where you have everyone from typical women shoppers to teens and business executives giving insights and reactions, and the thing that keeps coming back is they need an experience. The best way of illustrating that experience is through visuals. One woman cited Victoria's Secret as a store able to provide her with experience. But what is it about Victoria's Secret that attracts her? It's the idea that when she goes shopping, she's escaping to a place that she feels is hers—a place that doesn't pressure her, but instead speaks to her in some type of language. We know what that visual is and it is so strong it's reiterated in Victoria's Secret's catalog and commercial campaign. It's a total integrated message.

How many stores in America have the ability to tell a visionary statement to their customers every month? In terms of looking at The Gap or Banana Republic, every two weeks we see a different store statement, but we know what the brand is about. Starbucks is a great example. When we talk to shoppers, they say, "It is a destination that gives me a break from my day, with me connecting to a refreshment in a world where no one is going to intimidate me." So again, an experience factor.

How do we do that in retail today? It gets back to a company's brand, its personality. Someone asked if I had seen the Tommy Hilfiger store in California. I said, "Not only have I seen it, but I've experienced it." There is a quality factor, an information factor, a lifestyle factor. Topping the list of pressures today is this idea of creating an experience. How do you become a destination and how do you present a point of view that really correlates to a vision to your consumer? That's a tall order to fill, and it's continually filled by your mega brands, as well as your major power brokers.

In May, I had the opportunity to do the Proffitt's Broadcasting Network in Milwaukee. During that experience I heard Brad Martin speak by satellite to a group of people. About six weeks later that gentleman was the mastermind behind the Saks Fifth Avenue acquisition. Today we don't always expect who our partners could be.

I've heard a lot about international business and the catalog business. Today I look at the marketplace and, yes, there are specialty retailers. I particularly watch the Hugo Boss organization because it is running its own shops. The company is doing something unique: it's running those shops in key areas with partners who understand the marketplace and the ways to make that Hugo Boss brand come to life. How do they do that? By the experience—the visual, international and product experience. That's where the little guy benefits. That's where he's got the ability to become a player and to have this kind of partnership.

Source: From Apparel Industry Magazine, *March 1999, pp. 82, 81. Reprinted by permission.*

Department stores today are supposed to be destinations. Macy's Herald Square is pairing up with Eatzi's, a home replacement meal system out of Dallas, Texas. Why? Because it's about service today. What kind of service element can I bring to the equation that's going to make my customer solve his or her lifestyle problems better? We're going to hear more and more about it. Malls are getting into this area. The malls are acquiring a sense of community, through community rooms, literacy programs or art destinations.

Partnerships, relationships are key. How do you become a specialized partner today? We still have the ability to communicate and correspond and create our own opportunities. It's a matter of understanding what exists out there. You know your business and this marketplace. You just have to understand the common denominators that tie you into that. It's the era of integration.

How many times do you think, "Am I conveying the personality of my company at every point of contact with the consumer or my customer?" That's a challenge that requires a lot, but there are big payoffs. There are a lot of companies today that are global brands as a result. It goes back to the idea of us being a visual society today.

When we hear about this idea of shops within shops, why is that a good idea? Because no one knows your business or image better than you. Retailers today fall short in that world and that's why the Gaps, Banana Republics and Old Navys are doing such a good job at it. Whether it's at a commercial or promotional level, I am mesmerized by the way the Gaps and the Old Navys go into environments and create experiences for that community.

Another trend is the catalog business, which again reinforces consumers' need for visual experience. About a year ago I was at a financial workshop and analysts kept saying they were watching a company called Abercrombie & Fitch. When I asked why, they told me they saw the company's catalog and it was different, though they couldn't verbalize why. Well, Abercrombie's catalog is not a catalog—it's a magazine, a lifestyle statement for 18- to 25-year-olds about a way of dressing. Abercrombie & Fitch today has a major integrated statement at every retail level, from its stores and catalogs to its Internet presence and now the company is talking about getting into children's wear. If I were a children's wear manufacturer or supplier, I would very much look to partner with Abercrombie & Fitch.

As far as the really long-term future, if I had to prepare a list of things to watch and places to go, I couldn't ignore outlet shopping. Last August I made a trip to an area south of Las Vegas. It's not your stereotypical outlet operation; it's a destination experience.

And, if you've never experienced something called Jamba Juice, it exists on the West Coast and in warm-weather areas. It is a custom-made fresh fruit, vegetable drink. You've never seen a longer line of people waiting to spend $5 for one experience, and it's a quick experience. But it's the idea of "I'm getting a slice of my lifestyle in my way, customized, and it's great."

People need a visual, lifestyle experience that says something to them. In my market research, someone said to me, "I am so tired of being offered vanilla ice cream everywhere I go."

Chapter Review

Key Words and Concepts

Define, identify, or briefly explain the following:

Advance ship notices	E-commerce	Order fulfillment
Anchor stores	Economies of scale	Outlet center
Apparel specialty chain	E-tailing	Overstored
Boutique	Factory outlet	Party plan
Branch store	Flea market	"Plasticizing" of business
Bricks-and-clicks	Franchise	Preticketing
Bricks-and-mortar	Franchisee	Private label
Business to consumer (B2C)	Franchisor	Product development
Catalog showroom retailer	General merchandising chain	Quick Response
"Category killers"	Global retailing	Relationship marketing
CD-ROM shopping	Home television shopping	Retail format
Centralized buying	Hypermarket	Retailer
Chain store	In-store retailing	Shopping center
Chapter 11	Lean retailing	SKUs
Cross docking	Mail-order house	Specialty store
Cross-shoppers	Mall	Store ambience
Customization	Matrix buying	Store ownership group
Database marketing	Megamall	Store retailer
Department store	Micromarketing	Supercenter
Differentiation	Mom-and-pop store	Supermarket
Direct-selling retailer	National brand	Superstore
Discounter	Nonstore retailing	Supply chain management
Diverters	Off-price retailer	Warehouse club
"Doors"	Online shopping	

Review Questions on Chapter Highlights

1. In what types of retail establishment do you prefer to shop and why? What types do you avoid and why?
2. Why is the NAICS system relevant when studying retailing?
3. Describe the target customer of the typical department store.
4. What is a store ownership group? How does it differ from chain operations?
5. What are the competitive advantages of apparel specialty stores compared to department stores?
6. Compare the operations of a department store and its branches with chain store operations. How are they similar, and how do they differ?
7. How can off-price retailers such as TJX undersell conventionally priced retailers? What are their sources of supply?
8. How are large department and specialty stores meeting the competition of the underselling retailers?
9. Why do you think full-line discount stores are taking apparel market share from other retailers?

10. What is the difference between a hypermarket and a supercenter?
11. What do you think accounts for the success of the "category killers"? How are they a threat to conventional retailers?
12. Describe the evolution of outlet centers. What is your prediction for their future success?
13. List several kinds of nonstore retailing. Which type do you believe holds the most success for the future and why?
14. Why is mail-order retailing so important today? Name different types of retailers that are in the mail-order business.
15. What are your predictions about the future of e-tailing? On what are you basing these predictions?
16. What is the difference between private-label and national brands? How do consumers compare the two?
17. What does it mean to say "the elephants will dance only with the elephants"? In the context in which this is used, what are the problems associated with this trend?
18. Why are industry partnerships important to retailers?
19. Why is global retailing likely to increase in the future?
20. How can retailers balance the two ideas that seem very different: globalization and customization?

References

Abernathy, F., Dunlop, J., Hammond, J., & Weil, D. (1999). *A stitch in time: Lean retailing and the transformation of manufacturing.* New York: Oxford University Press.

American Apparel Manufacturers Association. (annual). *Apparel Marketing Monitor.* Arlington, VA: Author.

D'Innocenzio, A. (1992, November 24). Hypermarkets: A very big idea that never grew. *Women's Wear Daily*, pp. 1, 9.

Edelson, S. (1995a, August 9). The great mall makeover. *Women's Wear Daily*, pp. 8–9.

Edelson, S. (1995b, April 4). Once a poor relation, outlets go legit—and trouble looms. *Women's Wear Daily*, pp. 1, 8, 9.

Electronic shopping. (1994, October). *Consumer Reports*, p. 623.

Executive Office of the President, Office of Management and Budget. (1988). *North American Industry Classification System, United States, 1997.* Lanham, MD: Bernan Press.

Harris, L. (1979). *The merchant princes.* New York: Harper & Row.

Kidwell, C., & Christman, M. (1974). *Suiting everyone: The democratization of clothing in America.* Washington, DC: Smithsonian Institution Press.

Kurt Salmon Associates. (1995). *Vision for the new millennium . . . evolving to consumer response.* Atlanta, GA: Author.

Lewis, R. (Ed.). (1995, November). What's in a name? Is it a brand, a private label, or a store? "Infotracs" special supplement to *Women's Wear Daily*, pp. 1–35.

May Department Stores. (1999). *May Department Stores annual report 1999.* St. Louis: Author.

May Department Stores. (1995). *May Department Stores Annual Report 1995.* St. Louis: Author.

Merchant to the millions. (no date). Chicago: Sears Roebuck and Co.

National Retail Institute. (1999). *Retail industry indicators.* Washington, DC: Author.

PriceWaterhouseCoopers. (2000). *Consumer nation: Retailing 2010.* New York: Author.

Rudnitsky, H. (1994, August 15). Too much of a good thing. *Forbes*, pp. 46–47.

Sack, K. (annual). *Standard & Poor's industry surveys: Retailing.* New York: Standard & Poor's.

Schulz, D. (2000, July). Top 100 retailers. *Stores*, pp. S1–S19.

The super specialists. (1986, August). *Stores Magazine.*

TJX buys Marshalls. (1995, November). *Stores*, p. 9.

Wal-Mart. (2000). *Wal-Mart annual report 2000.* Bentonville, AR: Author.

Zinn, L., DeGeorge, G., Shoretz, R., Yang, D., & Forest, S. (1993, July 26). Retailing will never be the same. *Business Week*, 54–60.

Suggested Bibliography

Abernathy, F., Dunlop, J., Hammond, J., & Weil, D. (1999). *A stitch in time: Lean retailing and the transformation of manufacturing.* New York: Oxford University Press.

Abbey-Livingston, D., & Becks, D. (1997). *Maximizing store impact: A retailer's guide to profitable visual merchandising.* Toronto: The Retail Learning Initiative, Ryerson Polytechnic University.

American Express & NRF Foundation. (2000). *American retail excellence—A key to best practices in the U.S. retail industry.* New York: Authors.

Arthur Andersen & Company. (annual). *International trends in retailing.* Chicago: Author.

Baughman, L. & Mauldin, A. (2000). Retailing. *U.S. Industry and Trade Outlook 2000.* Washington, DC: U.S. Department of Commerce.

Berman, B., & Evans, J. (2000). *Retail management: A strategic approach* (8th ed.). Upper Saddle River, NJ: Prentice Hall.

Broadband possibilities promise fashion on demand. (2000, June 5). *Discount Store News*, 11.

Brough, J. (1982). *The Woolworths*. New York: McGraw-Hill.

Burnstiner, I. (1994). *How to start and run your own retail business*. New York: Carol.

Cliff, S. (1999). *50 trade secrets of great design retail spaces*. Gloucester: Rockport Publishers.

CSG Information Services. (annual). *Directory of European Retailers*. Tampa, FL: Author.

Currie, M. (1996). *Achieving customer loyalty: A retailer's guide to creating and sustaining a service strategy*. Toronto: The Retail Learning Initiative, Ryerson Polytechnic University.

DeKare-Silver, M. (1999). E-shock: The electronic shopping revolution: Strategies for retailers and manufacturers. New York: AMACOM.

Deloitte Consulting and Deloitte & Touche. (2000). *Serving the networked consumer*. New York: Author.

Drucker, P. (1999). *Management challenges for the 21st century*. New York: HarperBusiness.

Echikson, W., Matlack, C., & Vannier, D. (2000, August 7). American e-tailers take Europe by storm. *Business Week*, 54, 55.

Fairchild Publications. (periodic). *Fairchild financial manual of retail stores*. New York: Author.

First National Bank of Chicago. (annual). *The retailing industry*. Chicago: Author.

Friedman, H. (1992). *No thanks, I'm just looking: Professional retail sales techniques for turning shoppers into buyers*. Dubuque, IA: Kendall/Hunt.

Ginsburg, J., & Morris, K. (1999, December 20). Xtreme retailing: Stores fight the online onslaught. *Business Week*, 121–128.

Gold, A. (1978). *How to sell fashion* (2nd ed.). New York: Fairchild.

Harris, L. (1979). *Merchant princes*. New York: Harper & Row.

Hoge, C. (1988). *The first 100 years are the toughest: What we can learn from the century of competition between Sears and Wards*. Berkeley, CA: Ten Speed Press.

International Council of Shopping Centers. (1988). *Increasing retailer productivity*. New York: Author.

International Council of Shopping Centers. (annual). *The scope of the shopping industry in the United States*. New York: Author.

Kunz, G. (1996). *Merchandising: Theory, principles, and practice*. New York: Fairchild Publications.

Kunz, M., Bongiorno, L., Naughton, K., DeGeorge, G., & Anderson, F. (1995, November 27). Reinventing the store. *Business Week*, 84–96.

Lajoie, S. (1999, April 5). 300,000 points of light. *Forbes*, 56–57.

Lancaster, W. (2000). *The department store: A social history*. London: Leicester University Press.

Lebhar-Friedman Publications. (annual). *Chain store guide directory*. New York: Author.

Levy, M., Weitz, B., Weitz, B. (1998). *Retailing management*. Burr Ridge, IL: Richard D. Irwin.

Lewison, D. (1996). *Retailing* (6th ed.). Upper Saddle River, NJ: Prentice Hall.

Lowery, J. (1998). *Buying online for dummies*. Foster City, CA: IDG Books Worldwide.

Lynn D. Schwabe & Co. (date unknown). *The retail store*. New York: Author.

MJJTM Publications Corp. (annual). *Directory of major malls*. Spring Valley, NY: Author.

Mahoney, T., & Sloane, L. (1974). *The great merchants* (2nd ed.). New York: Harper & Row.

Marcus, S. (1974). *Minding the store*. Boston: Little, Brown.

Marcus, S. (1979). *Quest for the best*. New York: Viking Press.

National Research Bureau. (annual). *Shopping center directory* (4 vols). Chicago: Author.

National Retail Institute. (annual). *Retail industry indicators*. Washington, DC: Author.

Palmieri, J. (1999, January 20). Internet becoming bigger venue for apparel replenishment sales—NRF discussion looks at ways for retailers to make money on the web. *DNR*, p. 2.

Pardoe, P. (1999). *Planning for profit: A retailer's toolkit for financial management*. Toronto: The Retail Learning Initiative. Ryerson Polytechnic University.

Peter, G. (1992). *It's not my department!* New York: Berkeley.

Peterson, R. (Ed.). (1992). *The future of U.S. retailing: An agenda for the 21st century*. New York: Quorum Books.

Phelon, K. (Ed.). (periodic). *Sheldon's retail dictionary*. Fairview, NJ: Phelon, Sheldon & Marsar.

Plaisted, K. (2000, Feb. 7). Today's apparel consumer expects more than bargain bins. *Discount Store News*, 16.

PriceWaterhouseCoopers. (2000). *Consumer nation: Retailing 2010*. New York: Author.

Rabolt, N., & Miller, J. (1996). *Concepts and cases in retail and merchandise management*. New York: Fairchild Publications.

Rating the stores. (1994, November). *Consumer Reports*, 712–721.

Rosenberg, J. (1995). *Dictionary of retailing and merchandising*. Somerset, NJ: John Wiley & Sons.

Rossi, W. (1988). *Profitable footwear retailing*. New York: Fairchild.

Schroeder, C. (1997). *Specialty store retailing: How to run your own store*. Washington, DC: National Retail Federation.

Seckler, V. (1999, July 19). E-commerce called "Future of Fashion." *Women's Wear Daily*, p. 2.

Seelye, R., & Moody, O. (1993). *The selling starts when the customer says no: The 12 toughest sells—and how to overcome them*. Chicago: Probus.

Standard & Poor's. (annual). *Industry surveys: Retailing*. New York: Author.

Sternquist, B. (1999). *International retailing*. New York: Fairchild Publications.

Stevens, M. (1979). *Like no other store in the world: The inside story of Bloomingdale's*. New York: Thomas Y. Crowell.

Tiernan, B. (1999). *E-tailing*. Chicago: Dearborn Trade.

Traub, M. (1993). *The Bloomingdale's legend and the revolution of American marketing*. New York: Random House.

Underhill, P. (1999). *Why we buy: The science of shopping*. New York: Simon & Schuster.

Value Retail News. (periodic). *The book on value retailing*. Clearwater, FL: Author.

Vance, S., & Scott, R. (1994). *Wal-Mart*. Old Tappan, NJ: Macmillan.

Weil, G. (1977). *Sears, Roebuck, U.S.A.* New York: Stein & Day.

Williams, J., & Torella, J. (1996). *A guide to retail success*. New York: Fairchild Publications.

Worthman, E. (2000, July). How warm and fuzzy is your web site? *WEARABLESbusiness*, 99.

Trade Associations

Apparel Retailers of America, 2011 Eye St. NW, Suite 300, Washington, DC 20006.

Association of Retail Marketing Services, 3 Caro Ct., Red Bank, NJ 07701.

Confederation National Dos Directoes Loj, Rua Acre, 83 Andar, Rio de Janiero, RJ 20081, Brazil, S.A.

Direct Marketing Association, 1120 Ave. of the Americas, New York, NY 10036–6700.

Direct Selling Association, 1776 K St., NW, Suite 600, Washington, DC 20006.

FENALCO Presidencia Nacional, Carrera 4a No. 19–85 piso 7o, Bogota, D.E. 440, Colombia, S.A.

Footwear Distributors & Retailers of America, 1319 F St., NW, Suite 700, Washington, DC 20004.

General Merchandise Distributors Council, 1275 Lake Plaza Dr., Colorado Springs, CO 80906.

International Association of Department Stores, 72 Boulevard Haussman, Paris F-750–08, France.

International Council of Shopping Centers, 665 Fifth Ave., New York, NY 10022–5370.

International Franchise Association, 1350 New York Ave., NW, #900, Washington, DC 20005.

International Retail Advertising and Marketing Association, 500 N. Michigan Ave., Suite 600, Chicago, IL 60611.

Japan Retailing Center, Building 1–15–3 Minami Aoyama, Minato-Ku, Tokyo 107, Japan.

Jewelers of America, Inc., 1185 Ave. of the Americas, New York, NY 10036.

Le Consell Quebecois Du Commerce De Detail, 550 Sherbrook St., West, #1000, Montreal PQ H3A 1B9, Canada.

Mail Order Association of America, 1877 Bourne Ct., Wantagh, NY 11793.

Menswear Retailers, 2011 Eye St., NW, Washington, DC 20006.

National Association of Catalog Showroom Merchandisers, P.O. Box 725, Hauppauge, NY 11788.

National Association of Display, 468 Park Ave. S., Rm. 1707, New York, NY 10016.

National Association of Men's Sportswear Buyers, Inc., 500 Fifth Ave., New York, NY 10110.

National Retail Federation, 325 7th St. NW, Washington, DC 20004.

National Retailers Association of Mexico, Homero No. 109–11 Piso, Mexico City, D.F., 11560.

National Shoe Retailers Association, 9861 Broken Land Pkwy., Suite 255, Columbia, MD 21046.

Private Label Manufacturers Association, 369 Lexington Ave., New York, NY 10017.

Retail Council of Canada, 210 Dundas St. W. #600, Toronto, Ontario M5G 2E8, Canada.

Swedish Retail Federation, Sveriges Kopmannaforbund, S-105–61 Stockholm, Sweden.

Trade Publications

Apparel Merchandising, 425 Park Ave., New York, NY 10022.

Apparel Strategist, The, 101 E. Locust St., Fleetwood, PA 19522.

Barnard's Retail Trend Report, 17 Kenneth Rd., Upper Montclair, NJ 07043.

Catalog Age, 911 Hope St., Bldg. 6, Stamford, CT 06907.

Chain Merchandiser, Rt. 1, Box 95C, Baker City, OR 97814.

Chain Store Age Executive, 425 Park Ave., New York, NY 10022.

Current Business Reports: Annual Retail Trade, U.S. Bureau of Census, Department of Commerce, Washington, DC 20233.

Direct Marketing, Hoke Communications, 224 7th Street, Garden City, NY 11530.

The Discount Merchandiser, 233 Park Ave. S., New York, NY 10003.

Discount Store News, 425 Park Ave., New York, NY 10022.

Display & Design Ideas. 6255 Barfield Road, Suite 200, Atlanta, GA 30328.

DNR, 7 W. 34th St., New York, NY 10001–8191

Earnshaw's Infants, Girls and Boys Wear Review, 225 West 34th Street, New York, NY 10001.

Inside Retailing, 425 Park Ave., New York, NY 10022.

Loeb's Retail Report, P.O. Box 1155, New York, NY 10018.

Private Label Development, 19 W. 21st St., #403, New York, NY 10010.

MMR (Mass Market Retailers), 220 Fifth Ave., New York, NY 10001.

Retail Asia, 60 Martin Rd. #07–33, TradeMart Singapore, Singapore 239064.

Retail Business Review: The Executive, 100 W. 31st St., New York, NY 10001.

Retail Performance Monitor, 195 Smithtown Blvd., Nesconset, NY 11767.

Retail Review: Softgoods, Management Horizons, 41 S. High St., Columbus, OH 43215.

Retail Store Image. P.O. Box 41369, Nashville, TN 37204.

Retailing Today, Box 249, Lafayette, CA 94549.

Shopping Center World, 6151 Powers Ferry Rd. NW, Atlanta, GA 30339.

Shopping Centers Today, 665 Fifth Ave., New York, NY 10022–5370.

Stores, National Retail Federation, Inc., 325 7th St., NW, Washington, DC 20004.

The Retailer and Marketing News, P.O. Box 191105, Dallas, TX 75219.

Value Retail News and Off-Price News, 15950 Bay Vista Dr. #250, Clearwater, FL 34620.

VM & SD: Visual Merchandising & Store Design, 407 Gilbert Avenue, Cincinnati, OH 45202.

Women's Wear Daily, 7 W. 34th St., New York, NY 10001–8191.

Auxiliary Fashion Enterprises

*O*f vital importance in the fashion industry are the services of a variety of independently operated auxiliary enterprises that either provide services or act as advisers, sources of information, and propagators of fashion news. Some of these enterprises provide vital sources to keep the industry going. Some devote their full energies to observing and analyzing the fashion scene and assist producers and retailers in clarifying their own thinking about it.

Other enterprises aid by providing a coherent fashion message to the consuming public, thus giving impetus to trends in the making. Among these fashion business auxiliaries are fashion information and advisory services, the news media, fashion video producers, advertising and publicity specialists, and resident buying offices.

A wide array of enterprises now provide services associated with new technologies and globalization. A number of Internet companies serve the fashion industries, and other consulting firms help to install and use sophisticated computer systems in apparel firms. Other companies are available to help both manufacturers and retailers in merchandising and product development. Consultants who assist firms in importing and exporting have also become important to the industry.

This chapter discusses such enterprises, how they function, and the part they play in the fashion business. The readings that follow the text are concerned with the activities of companies that operate in this segment of the fashion business.

Fashion Information and Advisory Services

Although all fashion producers and retailers of any size have experts of their own within their firms, many use outside specialized sources of fashion information against which to check their own analyses and conclusions.

Fashion Information Services

Beginning in the late 1960s and growing in importance ever since then, a number of comprehensive **fashion information services** have developed. Their clients are located worldwide and include fiber companies; textile producers; producers of men's, women's, and children's wear; retailers; buying offices; and accessories and cosmetics companies. So all-pervading is the influence of fashion, however, that their clients also include some producers of small appliances, cars, home furnishings, and other consumer products.

In a business environment where time and timing are ever more important, these services offer specific, timely, concise, and complete worldwide information, often tailored to each client's specific needs.

The number of firms offering these services is constantly increasing, but the following are among the most important:

- Nigel French, headquartered in London. Their fabric reports cover the major fabric seasons—Spring/Summer and Fall/Winter—including the Interstoff and American fabric showings. They also issue separate color and knitwear brochures, report on New York and European designer collections, and present major season styling issues.
- Other European forecasting services include I.N.D.E.X, Global Consultants, and Bureaux.
- The Fashion Service, known as TFS, whose reports cover fashion information from all over the world. Information is also available in CD form. Examples of TFS trend information are shown in Figure 11–1.

Figure 11–1

Examples of TFS, The Fashion Service, forecasting information. TFS is an international company that specializes in color, trend, and fashion forecasting.

Source: Courtesy of TFS, The Fashion Service.

- The *International Colour Authority* (published in London) and the Color Association of the United States (with headquarters in New York) are important sources of color trend information. These are available for both women's wear and menswear (Figure 11–2).
- Here and There, whose reports cover U.S. ready-to-wear, couture collections, Japanese Prêt collections, Italian and French knitwear shows, fabric fairs (Interstoff, Ideacomo, Premier Vision, Prato), and a special feature that translates high fashion looks for mass markets.
- Promostyl, which began as a children's wear service in 1967. They now have offices or agents in 23 cities worldwide and publish 31 different handbooks annually.
- Stylists' Information Service (SIS). Their reports include "The Boutique Forecast" (twice a year), "The Children's Forecast" (twice a year), "The Eveningwear Forecast" (once a year), "The Menswear Forecast" (twice a year), "The Lingerie Forecast" (once a year), "The Women's Actualwear Forecast" (twice a year), and "The Trimming and Finishing Book" (once a year).
- Karten for Kids is published eight times a year, and Karten for Little Kids (or infants and toddlers to the age of two) is published twice a year.

| Figure 11–2 | **Examples of trend information provided by the International Colour Authority, a London-based organization.** |

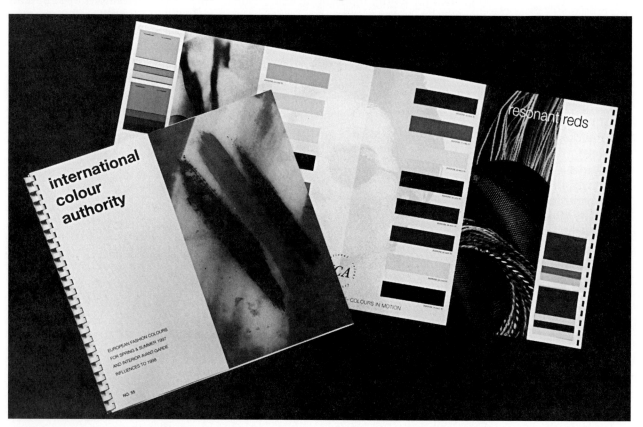

Source: Courtesy of ITBD Publications.

Fashion Consultants

A **fashion consultant** is an independent individual or firm hired by fashion producers and retailers to assist them in some phase of their fashion operation. Probably the oldest still in existence is **Tobé Associates**, founded in 1927 by Mrs. Tobé to service retailers. The firm sends to its paying clients a multipage, illustrated weekly brochure that contains information on current and coming trends, illustrated by specific style numbers with the names of the producers and the wholesale prices. As Tobé herself once described the function of her consulting firm,

> We are the reporters and interpreters of the fashion world speaking to the fashion-makers and the fashion sellers. . . . Our job is to tell the makers what the sellers are doing and vice versa. Most of all, we interpret and evaluate for each what is happening to fashion itself. . . . We make it our business to stay abreast of those economic, social, and art trends which I maintain are the great formative currents of fashion. . . . From all these we try to pick the significant trends that will change our lives, and hence our fashions. . . . We keep an eye on what those in the fashion vanguard are wearing and doing and seeing. This not only means reporting on what smart people wear. . . . It also means keeping abreast of what plays, films, and TV presentations they are seeing, which are successful, where they travel, and what books they read. . . . All of this information flows into our offices, where it is digested, sorted out, evaluated, and then disseminated through a weekly report. . . . Our clients—department stores throughout America, specialty stores in Europe, a wool manufacturer in Finland, the Export Institute in Israel—they can all shop the Fifth Avenue stores, the Paris showings, the Seventh Avenue showings, without budging from their desks. They can keep track of resort life without going to Monaco or Florida or the Caribbean. They can read about the fads, as well as the foundations of fashion, without spending much time or effort in research.
>
> So it is our business as a whole to interpret the current scene to the makers and sellers of fashion wares. (Tobé, 1957)

Another example of a retail consultant is Merchandising Motivation, Inc. (MMI), which is operated on a similar but smaller scale. There are also many other consulting firms, usually headed by former fashion practitioners, whose services are available, for a fee, to retailers or producers, or both. These firms usually deal with specific areas of the fashion industry, such as accessories, fibers, fabrics, children's wear, and menswear.

Merchandising, Buying, and Product Development Organizations

This group of organizations evolved from companies that were once known as **resident buying offices**. These began as a paid service for retailers to help them locate desirable goods in the market. They played an equally important but unpaid service for manufacturers by bringing their merchandise to the attention of retailers when it met their needs and standards.

Originally, almost every large store outside New York City was affiliated with an independent buying office, either serving that store alone or serving many non-competing retailers. Buying office functions included reporting market information, acting as a representative of its client stores, and performing related services for its retail clients. These organizations keep stores informed of fashion, price, and supply developments and act as eyes and ears for the client stores.

Eventually, the term *buying office* was only somewhat applicable to these organizations as they evolved to meet the needs of a changing retail industry. Rather than being buying offices, these groups became organizations with other kinds of services to help retail clients. The large ones assisted retailers far beyond the buying function. More recently, these organizations helped with **product development**, whereby the design staff of the buying office develops private-label merchandise specifically tailored to the needs of their client stores. Some of these organizations became broad-based business consulting organizations (i.e., **consultants**) to assist retailers with merchandising activities, sourcing, **logistics** related to importing, **management information systems (MIS)**, and a range of other areas.

The retail transformation has led to an extinction of some of the biggest players in this group, as we soon shall discuss. As retail mergers and consolidations occurred, this caused the pool of potential clients to shrink. Most retail giants now have their own internal staffs—in many cases, very large staffs—who perform these roles; thus, they do not need the services of these outside groups.

The organizations that provide the merchandising and product development services to retailers (what were formerly just buying offices), that is, **merchandising, buying, and product development organizations,** fall into two major categories: (1) those that are independently owned enterprises and receive fees from the stores they serve and (2) those that are store owned or corporate owned.

Independently Owned or Fee Organizations

Independently owned organizations, which were known as salaried or **fee offices** when they were buying offices, are run as private enterprises. Member or subscribing stores pay a yearly fee, usually based on a percentage of annual sales volume. Most such offices concentrate on serving specialty stores that carry all or most types of apparel and accessories. Others specialize in such narrow categories as large, petite, or tall sizes; bridal, maternity, or junior wear; off-price apparel; fabrics or accessories; men's and boys' wear; or home furnishings. A few concentrate on filling the needs of small department stores, representing them in all the markets of interest to these clients.

Some of the long-standing companies providing these services have closed, and others have been acquired by large firms. The Doneger Group has emerged as the largest independent apparel buying office in the country. This group, which now operates 10 specialized divisions, assists client firms with many aspects of business that go beyond the traditional buying function. Among the 10 divisions are the Doneger Buying Connection, Doneger Kids, Doneger Menswear, Doneger Tall Buying, and D^3 Doneger Design Connection. The Doneger Group assists clients in such areas as domestic and international market coverage, product development, trends in color and style changes, direct-mail programs, information on sources of store supplies, and many others.

When buying offices were first established in New York, they were vital because they offered store owners (outside the marketplace) access to new and current information, increased purchasing power because of their size, and an opportunity to share or exchange information. They were important in seeking out new and unusual resources to provide stores with distinctive merchandise. As major retailers grew bigger and their buying clout also grows bigger, buying offices tried to change their service menu. Facilitating imports and private-label programs became one of their major roles. Unfortunately, some of the large organizations were unable to change enough to survive. In effect, many of their functions had been taken over by the retail giants themselves.

Store-Owned Organizations: Cooperative Groups

Unlike the privately owned, profit-oriented fee offices, the organizations that were store owned were controlled and supported by the stores they served. Their major objectives were to provide services that the supporting stores required to assist them in operating profitably.

A **cooperative merchandising organization** (formerly a **cooperative buying office**) was one owned and maintained by a group of stores that it served exclusively. This type of office was also known as an *associated office*.

One of the major and best known of such offices was the Associated Merchandising Corporation (AMC), founded in 1918 by Filene's of Boston; F. & R. Lazarus of Columbus, Ohio; J. L. Hudson of Detroit; and Rike's of Dayton. Other major stores soon joined. Membership grew, attracting both U.S. stores and some in other countries. In the 1990s, AMC was owned mostly by Dayton-Hudson and Federated Department Stores, but it had several other major retail members. However, when large retail conglomerates bought store groups such as those who were AMC members, it reduced the client pool for services like those AMC provided. That is, the acquiring company had these services provided by its own in-house staff. Now, AMC is owned by Dayton-Hudson and is more realistically considered a corporate office.

AMC, whose headquarters were in New York, came to focus primarily on sourcing and development of exclusive products for member stores. In its prime, AMC had a staff of over 600 professionals with offices in more than 30 locations outside the United States. In these offices in other countries, staff members coordinated the production of merchandise being sourced from that region. **Overseas merchandise representatives** made major contributions to product management, in the selection and development of merchandise. The representative's knowledge of local markets was vital, and he or she often worked one-on-one with individual store merchants who travel the world in search of unique product assortments and looked to AMC's overseas staff for guidance and direction. These representatives had the client's best interests in mind as they monitored production for quality and prompt timing of deliveries. Each office was staffed with quality control personnel who tested products to see that they meet the retail client's expectations.

Formerly, the other major cooperative organization was Frederick Atkins, Inc., which also evolved from being a buying office to an entirely different type of business. The company was an international retail merchandising and marketing organization that provided market direction, exclusive merchandise programs, management information, and merchandising counseling to a group of independent and general merchandise retailers. In its heyday, Atkins boasted a roster of powerful retail member clients. Frederick Atkins, Inc. engaged in product development and distribution of exclusive private-brand merchandise as well as national brands to the member firms. The company's international division had commissionaires in 30 countries who developed and maintained resource relationships in other countries, assisted office and store personnel on overseas trips, set up meetings, and followed through on orders after the buyers had left. After 56 years of business, Atkins went out of business in 2000. A merger of AMC and Frederick Atkins, Inc. was discussed but never achieved. Now neither exists—testimonials to the dramatic changes that take place in how the fashion industry goes about its business and the need for continual change. Opportunities for exciting jobs are still there, but they exist in different forms. In this case, functions may be performed within the giant retail conglomerates rather than by hiring outside firms (Moin, 2000).

Some smaller organizations now exist to serve a few of the functions AMC and Frederick Atkins, Inc. provided. For example, Leftcoast Style is a small California-based operation that serves Dillard's and Jacobsen's.

Another, Directives West, is a retail consulting firm that provides inside information, direction, and a unique perspective on the West Coast fashion industry. Over 100 retail clients use the services of Directives West, which include: weekly bulletins on hot trends, monthly retail recaps for senior management, trend forecasting and reporting, shopping reports, in-depth fashion forums and marketing overviews, and assistance with market visits (Figure 11–3).

Corporate Offices

Another very important type of office is the **corporate merchandising/buying office**, which is owned and financed by a store ownership group and services only the stores of that group. Unlike the homogeneous mix of stores served by cooperative offices, some of the store ownership groups consist of both large and small stores. Examples

Figure 11–3

Directives West provides services such as trend forecasting and reporting to its more than 100 retail clients.

Source: Courtesy of Directives West.

are May Department Stores, T. Eaton, Belk Stores, and Batus Corp. In the case of each of these corporate offices, the combined volume of the stores it serves makes it a very important entity in the marketplace.

The large corporate merchandising/buying offices have evolved into multifaceted units, as we have discussed for the previous groups that began as buying offices. Rather than focusing exclusively on searching the markets for products for the stores in the corporation, these offices have also become heavily involved in designing, product development, and sourcing of private-label merchandise. Today's **market representatives** are frequently performing both roles.

Changes in the May Department Stores Company reflect shifts that have occurred for corporate buying offices for store ownership groups. The company's buying office, May Merchandising Company, was previously located in New York. Staff in that office searched the market for all the May companies, working with buyers from various stores in planning and securing merchandise. In the early 1990s, May Merchandising Company was moved to St. Louis to be at the corporate headquarters. May Merchandising Company identifies emerging fashion developments and merchandise trends for the department store divisions and closely collaborates with the operating companies to enhance their merchandising programs. The company's central merchants and creative group work with the design and technical center (i.e., the product development group with about 100 staff members) and May Department Stores International to develop private-label programs. May Department Stores International is the overseas buying arm of May Merchandising. It operates a network of eight offices in Asia and one in Prague and works with agents in numerous other countries. Major retailers like May now own and manage their own overseas operations, a structure that the companies feels is vital to the quick response of import programs to merchandising trends.

Computer Technology and Service Providers

Today, computer technologies undergird the entire fashion industry. These developments have rewritten the rules about how and where products are made as well as how they move through the whole channel of distribution, as shown in Figure 11–4. Examples include CAD systems, product data management systems, Quick Response/ EDI systems, POS systems, bar coding, supply chain management, logistics/ distribution systems, establishing shopping sites on the Internet, and on and on.

The Internet has spawned the e-commerce phenomenon, which is reshaping the industry at every stage. Both business-to-consumer applications and business-to-business online services have proliferated in recent years. Great numbers of "new economy" entrepreneurs have started Internet businesses that offer a potential for making the entire fashion industry more efficient in terms of time and costs. Many new Internet businesses have sprouted to support the industry.

Now, an apparel manufacturer can shop for fabrics, zippers, trims, and other components via the Internet. Rather than being limited to a small group of U.S. suppliers with whom the company did business in the past, new Internet "**dot-com**" companies provide services that enable the manufacturer to shop global markets for the best choices and prices. Other companies may help the manufacturer sell off surplus inventory. Both manufacturers and retailers may sell directly to consumers online. All in all, computer technology has given birth to a whole new industry to provide these services.

Figure 11–4

Application of information on technology throughout the fashion pipeline.

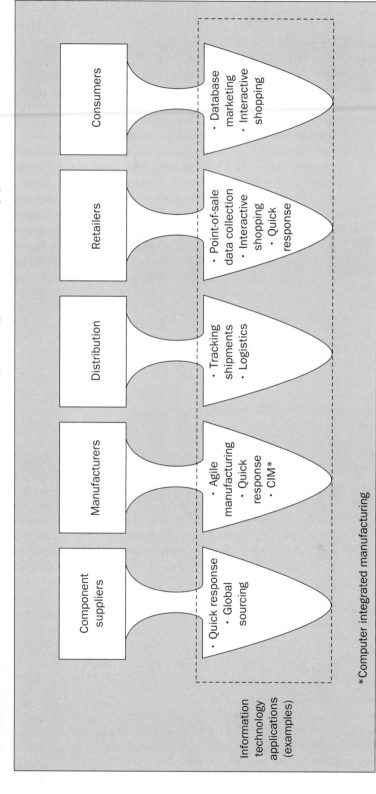

Component suppliers

Manufacturers

Distribution

Retailers

Consumers

Information technology applications (examples)

- Quick response
- Global sourcing

- Agile manufacturing
- Quick response
- CIM*

- Tracking shipments
- Logistics

- Point-of-sale data collection
- Interactive shopping
- Quick response

- Database marketing
- Interactive shopping

*Computer integrated manufacturing

Testing Laboratories and Services

A number of independent testing companies help the fashion industry by testing products and components for quality, durability, safety and so on. For example, fabrics, trims, and buttons may be tested before used in garments. Or final garments may be tested on a number of performance measures such as shrinkage, colorfastness, or flammability. Additionally, companies may need to be sure the fiber content in a garment is what they actually ordered. Regardless of the nature of the testing, these services are for hire. The client manufacturer or retailer pays the laboratory for performing the testing services (Figure 11–5).

These days when both manufacturers and retailers import large volumes of fashion goods, often from less-developed countries, these testing services have become particularly vital. Large firms may maintain their own **testing laboratories,** sometimes using their own facilities as well as the independent testing labs. Many small companies rely almost entirely on the independent testing services.

Merchandising Testing Laboratories, based in Brockton, Massachusetts, is a well-known example of these testing laboratories. The company maintains a state-of-the-art testing facility that tests fashion products as well as items ranging from household paints to Christmas lights. Today, the company has facilities throughout the world.

Figure 11–5

Staff in merchandising testing laboratories provide valuable services to the fashion industry, as well as to numerous other industries.

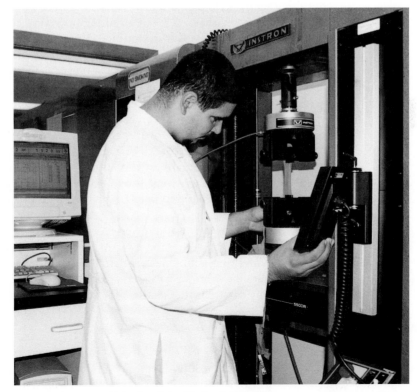

Source: Courtesy of Merchandising Testing Laboratories.

Management Consultants

In addition to the organizations we have just discussed, another type of consulting group has become increasingly important to many manufacturers and retailers. Although the groups just discussed have worked primarily with retailers and have specialized more in the past on merchandise-related areas of expertise, some others also provide various types of management and marketing assistance.

Another group consisting of **management consultants** focuses more specifically on management and market research areas, specializing in the softgoods and consumer goods distribution industries. These consulting firms tend to focus more on helping companies with management issues, such as broad strategic planning, market strategy analysis and planning, merchandising, and operations strategies, rather than on product trend analysis and selection. Examples of these include:

- *Kurt Salmon Associates, Inc. (KSA)* specializes in working with companies in the softgoods industries. Some of their divisions work more specifically with textile and apparel manufacturers, and others specialize in retailing. KSA has offices in several parts of the United States and in numerous other parts of the world. This consulting firm often conducts in-depth studies of an industry sector in a country but also works with individual firms in analyzing their operations to become more efficient and profitable.
- *PriceWaterhouseCoopers (PWC)*, the well-known accounting firm, previously had consulting services. These became a separate firm in 2001. PWC had a worldwide management and market research consulting firm with a division specializing in retailing and consumer goods distribution industries. The new company does extensive research and reporting on the retail industry in general and works with retail clients on an individual basis to improve competitiveness and profitability.
- *Deloitte & Touche*, another major accounting firm, had a division, the TRADE/ Retail and Distribution Services Group. Spun off from the parent comany, this group works specifically with the retailers, wholesalers, and apparel and textile companies. More than 400 professionals in North America and over 1,000 worldwide devote their efforts to serving clients large and small, public and private. This group serves many of the largest retailers, including 37 of *Fortune's* top 50 retailers. The Garr Consulting Group, a division of TRADE, provides engineering assistance related to logistics problems involved in retail and wholesale distribution.
- *IBM Corporation* has a Consulting Services and Distribution Industries division devoted to working with the retailing sector. Because of the nature of IBM's product areas, this consulting is obviously related to technology in some way. However, IBM's consultants consider broader areas of management and market analysis, which in many cases has implications for computer technology use.

Consultants in Technical Areas

Consultants who wish to sell their services to textile/apparel manufacturing and retailing firms offer an almost unlimited menu of expertise. Many of the organizations described in previous sections have staff qualified to provide assistance in specialized technical areas. However, some consulting firms offer services *only* in specialized areas such as the following:

- *Information technology*. Consulting firms offer a range of assistance in specialized information technology areas. Because many of the information technology systems are quite technical to put in place and adapt to a company's specific use, consultants can help firms design the systems to obtain maximum benefit from the investments.
- *Logistics*. Some consulting firms specialize in assisting businesses with the distribution processes involved in moving merchandise quickly and efficiently from the manufacturer to the customer. Some of the firms may operate only within the country, whereas others are involved in logistics related to importing and exporting. Although some fashion firms manage their own logistics, more are hiring third-party providers—that is, companies that specialize in handling shipping and other logistics activities.

Import and Export Consultants

The globalization of the fashion industry has added new dimensions to the business of producing and selling fashion goods. The complexities of sending merchandise from one country to another require specialists who stay abreast of the trade laws, documentation, and business strategies associated with importing and exporting. Although large firms may have some of these specialists on their staff, even those firms often use the services of trade specialists. Smaller firms will almost surely need to hire experts in these areas to be sure goods are delivered as expected, that trade laws are followed, and that payment occurs as intended. Because of the complexities of importing and exporting, fees paid to these consultants may actually save money and valuable time in the long run. Examples of these consultants include:

- **Import brokers** coordinate the details of importing merchandise made in other countries for buyers in the United States.
- **Trade attorneys** provide legal assistance related to importing and exporting. Trade attorneys can help companies in advance of international business activities to help firms understand the potential risks and costs involved. Some law firms may even specialize in trade laws for specific regions. For example, the Sandler & Travis firm is particularly well known for helping companies with 9802/807 production and other business related to imports from the Caribbean region.
- **Export specialists** can help firms both in marketing to make sales in other countries and then in the technical details related to shipping merchandise once it is sold.
- **Lobbyists** are law firms or consulting firms, generally located in Washington, D.C., that attempt to influence policymakers on trade policies that benefit the companies or groups who are paying them. For example, some textile firms want tough trade policies to limit imports, so lobbyists hired by this group work to try to get policies passed to restrict imports. Other lobbying firms may represent retailers, the governments of other countries that want to ship more merchandise to the United States, or even some large apparel firms that import some or all of their products; these lobbyists try to influence policymakers toward freer trade.
- **Labor auditors** are individuals or companies hired by apparel firms or retailers to monitor labor conditions in contractors' production plants. Some large firms have their own staff, but many hire outside auditors to obtain a more-objective assessment of conditions in the factories. These auditors look for situations that may involve unfair time and wage issues, unsafe working conditions, worker abuse, or other issues not deemed acceptable by human rights organizations and/or the popular press. These auditors can help assure appropriate treatment of factory workers and at the same time save the client firm many public relations nightmares.

News Media for the Fashion Industry

Fashion is news, and the news media cover it, both in editorial treatments and in paid advertising messages. This statement applies not only to newspapers and magazines but also to broadcast media and the Internet. Thus, a vital means of communication between the industry and the consumer, and between related parts of the industry, is activated in the daily newspapers, news magazines, women's and men's magazines, specialized fashion publications, and those segments of the trade press that affect the fashion business, radio, and television. The impact is enormous.

Fashion Magazines

Fashion magazines, whose major activity is to report and interpret fashion news to the consumer, together with additional features for balanced reading fare, have been functioning in this country for more than a century. *Godey's Lady's Book,* which was started in 1830, carried pictures of the latest fashions, gave advice on fabrics, contained other helpful hints, and of course, included advertising. Its distinguished editor, Sara Joseph Hale, gave early proof that a woman could have a successful career in the business world even in the days of hoop skirts and cinched waists. Its masculine counterpart, *Burton's Gentlemen's Magazine,* also had an editor whose name acquired luster: Edgar Allan Poe. His editorial career there was brief, however—from 1839 to 1840.

The present-day roster of fashion magazines is in the midst of an explosive change. The old tried and true magazines such as *Harper's Bazaar, Vogue, Glamour, Mademoiselle,* and *Seventeen* have suddenly been subjected to a barrage of competition from new and exciting magazines. The entrance of *Elle* as an important fashion publication started an avalanche that now includes *Mirabella* (started by Grace Mirabella, the longtime editor of *Vogue*), *Vanity Fair, Details, In-Style, Allure, M, Inc., Savvy, Model, Taxi, La Style, In Fashion,* and others (Figure 11–6). How many will stand the test of time is hard to say, but the competition for fashion readership is keen, and the established older books are experimenting with new formats and features to try to keep their circulation and revenue figures up. In menswear, *M, Details, GQ (Gentlemen's Quarterly),* and *Esquire* remain the major purveyors of fashion news.

Role of Fashion Magazines

The role of fashion magazines is a many-sided one. As fashion reporters, their editors shop the wholesale markets both here and abroad to select and feature styles they consider newsworthy for their individual audiences. As fashion influentials, these editors sometimes take an active part in the production of merchandise by working closely with manufacturers to create merchandise that they consider acceptable to their readers. They participate in distribution by contacting retailers and urging them to carry and promote the designs they feature and to emphasize the trends endorsed editorially. Finally, they provide their readers with information not only about the styles they recommend, but also about who produces them and who sells them at retail.

An important tool of their activities, and of other consumer magazines that cover fashions to a lesser extent, is the **editorial credit.** This is how it operates: The editors select garments and accessories that, to their minds, exemplify fashion news. They photograph and show these styles in their pages, identifying the makers and naming one or more retail stores in which the consumers can buy them, and usually

citing the approximate price. The magazine's sponsorship and the editorial mention encourage the makers to produce the garments in good supply, the retailers to stock them, and the customers to buy. Even in stores that do not have editorial credits for it, a fashion item featured in a strong magazine may be given special attention. If the magazine concerned has a good following among the store's customers, the editorial sponsorship becomes a selling point of the garment not only to consumers but also to the merchant. The style is then stocked, advertised, and displayed, and the magazine's name is usually featured in ads and displays. Hangtags on the garment and magazine blowups in the displays remind the customer that this is the style he or she saw in the publication. The magazine, of course, provides the tags and the blowups.

Dependence on Advertising Revenue

Like most publications, fashion magazines derive their principal revenue from the sale of advertising space. In 2000, a single black-and-white page in *Vogue, Mademoiselle,* or *Glamour* was more than $51,000, $42,800, and $70,590, respectively. For each of these, a four-color page ran more than $60,000, $52,500, and $87,300, respectively.

In general magazines such as *Reader's Digest*, the rates were about $170,400 a page in black and white, and $174,300 for a four-color ad. *McCall's* was $124,735 for a black-and-white page and $142,500 for color (Standard Rate and Data Service, September 2000). Naturally, a high ratio of advertising to editorial pages means a prosperous magazine. Although conditions vary from issue to issue and from year to year, advertising generally accounts for nearly half the total number of pages in a consumer fashion magazine.

Dependency on dollars from advertisers instead of dollars from subscribers is not always conducive to unbiased fashion reporting; it can result in a conflict between editorial comment and advertising interests. Editorial mentions of merchandise bring to producers highly desirable publicity and prestige, because the editorial pages tend to have more authority in the readers' eyes than do pages devoted to paid advertising. Thus, firms that buy space in a magazine and contribute toward keeping it profitable are likely to protest if they are not given adequate editorial attention. Such a clash of interests often makes objective fashion reporting difficult, if not impossible.

The money the advertiser spends for a page is, in simplest terms, spent to influence customers to buy its product. If a publication can show tangible evidence that it can move merchandise into the retail store and then out into the consumer's hands, its chances of selling advertising space improve.

Magazines confirm that to attract advertisers, nothing is more important to fashion magazines than their relation to stores. This fact accounts for the increasingly large staffs of departments almost unknown to their readers—promotion and merchandising. The merchandising editors act as the liaison between the fashion editors, the advertising staff, and the retail stores. Their job is to ensure that editorialized and advertised merchandise will be placed in retail stores where readers can buy it. They do this by telling the retailers what the magazine is featuring and why—and where to purchase it. Then they list for their readers' information the names of stores where the merchandise can be found. This service to the reader also helps impress the advertisers with the magazine's selling power among retailers.

Services to the Industry

The closer their relationship with both the producers and retailers, the easier it is for magazines to attract advertising. To cement these relationships, many free services are offered by fashion publications. Their staff members keep fabric and apparel producers informed on new trends and advise them on ways and means of selling merchandise. The fashion editors encourage them to manufacture items for which they anticipate a demand and, secure in the knowledge that the items will be featured by the editors, the producers will plunge ahead. The merchandising and promotion departments provide advertisers with "as advertised" blowups to distribute to their retail accounts. In addition, most magazines that are active in fashion prepare, well in advance of each season, fashion forecasts of their color predictions for the guidance of manufacturers and retailers alike. These forecasts show the colors, specific styles, and resources that will be featured in the magazine.

In developing a close relationship with retail stores, the fashion magazines make themselves a source of information for stores. To make their editorialized and advertised merchandise desirable to retailers and, ultimately, to the stores' customers, the merchandising departments prepare elaborate retail store kits that, along with the list of sources for featured garments, contain suggestions for advertising, fashion shows, and display. The kits also include selling aids such as hangtags, signs, and other promotional materials. If an important retailer requests the service, the magazine will send a representative to commentate a fashion show. Members of the magazine staff are also available in their offices at almost any time to show samples of merchandise to retailers who call, and thus encourage buyers to visit the producers of the featured apparel and accessories.

Most of the consumer magazines, including those primarily concerned with fashion, also maintain research departments. A function of these departments is to survey the readers of the magazine and compile information about their buying power, living patterns, and merchandise preferences. *Glamour*, for example, surveys young career women and college students periodically and compiles reports for retailers and manufacturers about what these women buy, how much they spend, and similar information. The fashion magazines, then, not only interpret the fashion for their readers but also interpret their readers for their industry. In the process, they serve as a clearinghouse for information in the fashion field.

Compared with consumer magazines of general interest, such as *Reader's Digest*, with a circulation of more than 15.2 million in 2000, or women's magazines such as *McCall's*, with a circulation of about 4.8 million, the fashion magazines have smaller circulations. *Glamour*, the largest, has a U.S. circulation of 2,066,500 and another 142,466 in Italy. *Seventeen* has 2,270,898, followed by *Vogue* with a readership of 1,246,037 in the United States and another 54,705 in Australia. *Mademoiselle* has 1,136,570, and *InStyle* has 966,908. For men's magazines *Esquire* has a U.S. circulation of 675,024 and another 112,161 in Great Britain. *GQ (Gentleman's Quarterly)* has a U.S. circulation of 700,020 (*Standard Periodical Directory*, 2000; *Ulrich's International Periodical Directory*, 2000).

The fashion magazines' influence in the fashion business, individually and collectively, is great and far out of proportion to their actual circulation. Fashion editors ignore styles and designers in whom they have little faith but give a great amount of free publicity to those they favor. Ordinarily, however, what they do is try to pick the most dramatic, the most exciting fashions—not always the most wearable, but the ones that will attract attention.

Newspapers and General Magazines

As mentioned earlier, almost all newspapers devote space to fashion. Coverage varies, of course, in both amount and depth. A paper with the resources of the *New York Times* may have its experts report on the Paris openings and express opinions that are read by consumers and trade professionals alike. A small-town paper, on the other hand, may assign its society editor to fill out the fashion pages with items about fashion, clipped from what the wire services send, what comes in by way of press releases, or what the local retailers supply. Each paper's policy and the interests of its readers determine how much space the publication devotes to fashion news.

Among magazines not in the fashion-magazine category there is also coverage of fashion, and it varies with the nature of the publication. Fashion editors of such media, looking at the fashion scene through the eyes of their average reader, will select for illustration and comment only the items of interest to the young mother, the working woman, the ageless city sophisticate, the sportsman, the young male executive, or whoever the particular audience may be.

Some of the general magazines show merchandise and give editorial credit; others, such as the *New Yorker*, show no merchandise but sometimes discuss what the shops are showing. The activities of their fashion editors, as in the case of newspapers, vary according to the importance that each publication and its readers attach to fashion information.

Trade Publications

There is a special field of journalism known as business or **trade publishing**. Some business newspapers and magazines in the fashion field concern themselves with a particular classification of merchandise, from raw material to the sale of the finished product. These publications are not addressed to the ultimate consumer but to the fashion professionals concerned with the manufacturing and distribution of that merchandise. Typical examples are *Textile World* and *Bobbin* magazine. Other business publications devote themselves to only one aspect of production or retailing and have a horizontal readership. Examples of these publications are *Stores* magazine, which goes to store management, and *Chain Store Age*, for chain store management. Fairchild's **Women's Wear Daily**, which is published five times a week, covers the fashion waterfront in the women's fashion business—raw materials, manufacturing, retailing, and how the trend setters among the consuming public dress. Founded in 1890 by E. W. Fairchild, it has headquarters in New York City and maintains offices in cities throughout the United States, Europe, and Asia. *Women's Wear Daily* reports collections, trade conventions, fashion events, new technical developments at all stages of production, personnel changes at the executive level, the formation of new fashion businesses—and the wardrobes and activities of prominent individuals. It is often called the industry's "bible," and no women's fashion enterprise is without its copy of *Women's Wear Daily*. The Fairchild counterpart for the textile and men's wear industry is the *Daily News Record*, now referred to as *DNR*.

Trade publications are not aimed at the general public and are inclined to discourage subscriptions from people not active in the fields they serve. They seldom appear on newsstands, except for the Fairchild dailies in the garment district. Their circulations are quite small compared with those of consumer magazines, and their advertising rates are correspondingly small, approximately $14,000 for a black-and-white page. *Women's Wear Daily*, with a circulation of 63,018 in 2000, is a giant in the field. *DNR* has a circulation of 19,948, with a black-and-white rate of $13,230 a page (Bacon's Magazine Directory, 1999; Standard Rate and Data Service, October 2000).

The capacity of trade papers for disseminating fashion information is out of all proportion to their size. Their readership, it should be kept in mind, is concentrated among people dealing in the merchandise they cover. They talk shop to such people. And, in terms of the amount of merchandise involved, when a manufacturer or merchant responds to information on fashion, that response moves a great deal of merchandise.

Trade paper editors are usually in their markets every day of the business year, and they cover every nook and cranny of their fields. They analyze fashion trends for their readers and show sketches or photos of actual merchandise, identified as to source and style number, to assist buyers and store owners in keeping abreast of the flow of new products. In addition, trade publications discuss business conditions and contain articles on how to manufacture, promote, or sell the industry's products. They analyze and report on the markets in other countries, cover conventions and other meetings of interest to the trade, report on legislative developments of interest, and write up merchandising and promotion operations of retail stores.

Market research is also part of a trade publication's work. These magazines and papers make estimates of the size of their markets, survey subscribers on buying responsibilities and attitudes toward current problems, publish directories of manufacturers, help retailers and manufacturers find sources of supply, and report on seminars and conventions appropriate to their fields.

It is important to keep in mind that trade publications are available in many other countries. Some have an international perspective, and some focus primarily on a specific country's or region's industry (Figure 11–7).

Figure 11–7

Trade publications with an international perspective, some multilingual, published by ITBD Publications in London.

ITBD, 23 BLOOMSBURY SQUARE, LONDON, WC1A 2PJ, ENGLAND
Tel: +44 (0) 20 7637 2211 Fax: +44 (0) 20 7637 2248
email: itbd@itbd.co.uk website: www.itbd.co.uk

Source: Reprinted courtesy of ITBD Publications.

Within their particular fields, trade paper editors and reporters are extremely well informed. Reading their articles is like listening to a group of experts indulging in shop talk.

Electronic Media

The impact of electronic media is tremendous, and the potential for new types and new uses in the fashion industry are almost without limits. All of these require a cadre of professionals who prepare and present merchandise through these media.

Television advertising is a powerful medium but expensive to use. Until recent years, one saw and heard little more of fashion advertising on the home screen than the institutional messages of fiber companies or the local promotions of retailers. In the late 1970s, a few retailers such as J.C. Penney began to use network TV advertising to tell their fashion stories. Today, however, both retailers and manufacturers are harnessing the power of network TV. New brands of jeans, notably Jordache and Calvin Klein, became familiar names through saturated use of this medium. Mass merchandisers including Wal-Mart, Kmart, and J.C. Penney use television advertising extensively. Sears' TV campaign to promote the "Softer Side of Sears" assisted in this major retailer's temporary turnaround from rapid decline to being more stabilized. Many producers use TV advertising; among them are Hanes, Fruit of the Loom, Levi, and Lee. Cotton Incorporated has advertised extensively to extoll cotton's comfort and utility; more recent ads have focused on image.

Because MTV and its superstars such as Madonna and Michael Jackson have demonstrated how quickly they can create demand for new fashions, fashion firms are aware of the impact the home screen can have on their customers. Particularly for young audiences, shows with models going down the runway are now old hat compared with the new fashion presentations, in which entertainment is the key word, and the emphasis is on imagination and excitement, not merely the particular outfits.

As noted in the previous chapter, home television shopping gained a great deal of attention in the 1990s. A number of well-known designers and retailers have at least tried selling on the leading shopping channels, Home Shopping Network and QVC. An entirely new cadre of fashion professionals has emerged as a result of the growing popularity of home television shopping. These include not only the television personalities who present the merchandise on the air, but also many representatives of firms whose products are being shown in a TV segment. Those individuals play important coordinating roles in having the appropriate merchandise on hand and in perfect condition to present on the air. This requires close communication with the manufacturers or retailers whose products are being presented. If a firm's products are shown regularly, a full-time representative of that firm is likely to work at the network's facilities (Figure 11–8). Numerous other specialists are required to handle the technical details of producing the program segments and assuring that home viewers can see close-up details of garments, jewelry, or other merchandise.

Fashion videos have been useful in a number of ways. Designers, among them Donna Karan, Ralph Lauren, Anne Klein, and Nicole Miller, have used videotape to capture the excitement and sales appeal of their fashion shows for their retail customers, who present the videos on their selling floors with the actual merchandise. Videotapes are used to support sales in larger stores as salespeople and consumers see the collection from the designer's point of view.

Videos have been used for in-store merchandising in another way by companies such as J.C. Penney. Videotapes were sent from company headquarters to individual stores where local department managers made merchandise selections for their stores. A shortcoming of this system, however, was that store personnel found it necessary to view a total videotape, even if they needed to order only select items. For a time, CD-ROM and DVD[1] technology has sometimes replaced videotapes for this purpose, but videoconferencing via the Internet is expected to be increasingly important.

As noted numerous times elsewhere in this chapter and others, the Internet is becoming an increasingly important media vehicle. Products are sold directly to consumers, and fabric suppliers are also able to reach their customers, the manufacturers,

---

[1]The CD-ROM catalogs may be replaced by the newer DVD (digital versatile disk) catalogs, used on DVD-ROM computers.

Figure 11–8

Industry professionals fill numerous roles at home shopping television networks and within the companies whose products are shown on the programming segments.

Source: Courtesy of QVC.

in this same way. Computer technologies will create media opportunities in the future that are literally unimaginable today.

Electronic **kiosks** have been used in a variety of ways in retail stores. Some of these simply run videotapes so the customer may view new products or to learn how to use certain items, such as creative ways to use scarfs. Other kiosks are interactive so customers can learn about merchandise or order specific sizes and styles. Lee Company has used interactive kiosks to help customers learn how to determine proper size and fit for jeans purchases. Some major bra manufacturers have also used this means to assist customers. Like other forms of electronic media, specialized professionals develop these units and adapt the technology to specific fashion products.

Videoconferencing is being used in the industry. Saving the time and costs associated with travel, buyers now have the option to watch new lines presented at the CaliforniaMart without having to go there. Through videoconferencing, executives at Levi Strauss & Co.'s San Francisco headquarters can visit with plant managers at Levi plants across the country, or Levi executives at remote locations may be interactive participants in key company meetings held at the headquarters.

Even the fax machine is used as a selling or solicitation device. Attendees who go to major trade shows may receive faxes from U.S. firms or those in a host of other countries who are seeking business partners. Sometimes headhunter firms seek candidates for executive positions through fax solicitations.[2]

Electronic media of various forms will play an increasingly important role in the fashion industry in the new millennium. These developments will not only change the way we do business but will also offer many new employment options for individuals seeking careers in the industry.

[2]Companies may buy a registration list or secure individuals' names as attendees register with exhibitors.

Advertising and Publicity Agencies

There are two ways in which producers and retailers use space in print media or time in broadcast media to get their message across to the trade or to the public. One way is paid **advertising**. The other is **publicity**—time or space given without charge by the medium because it considers the message newsworthy.

Advertising Agencies

An **advertising agency** is a service agency whose original function was simply to prepare and place ads in magazines or newspapers for its clients. Today its job encompasses much more: research of the client's consumer markets, advice on promotional needs, planning of promotional campaigns, preparation of print and broadcast advertising, preparation of selling manuals, and creation of selling aids, labels, signs, and packaging—anything that helps increase the sale of the client's product and makes the advertising itself more effective.

An advertising agency may consist of one talented, hardworking executive with a few small clients, or it may be an organization with a staff of hundreds and clients with hundreds of millions of dollars to spend each year. Approximately 65 percent of agencies' revenue is derived primarily from commissions. These are paid, not by the client, but by the media from which the agencies purchase advertising space or time. Custom has fixed the rate at 15 percent. The balance of their income is received directly from clients, generally in the form of fees for special services such as market research, and as part of the cost for producing a product for the client—for example, photography, typography, art, and layout.

When an advertising agency bids for a client's account, it studies the firm's operation thoughtfully and draws up a presentation that outlines the campaign the agency suggests and the varied services that the agency performs. When awarded the account, the agency may delve into package design, market research, and creation of selling aids and sales training material—plus its original function of preparing and placing advertising in publications, in broadcast media, and, in some cases, in transit and outdoor media.

In the fashion industries, it is usually only the largest producers of nationally or internationally distributed merchandise that make use of advertising agencies. These include some makers of finished apparel, accessories, and fragrances, plus the giant fiber and fabric sources. In recent years, however, fashion companies have made bolder use of ads on billboards and buses, as well as other media. Retailers whose audience is local or regional usually maintain their own complete advertising departments that handle their day-to-day newspaper advertisements.

Fashion Expertise

Some agencies, often among the smallest in the field, specialize in fashion accounts. In such agencies, and in those of the larger ones that serve fashion accounts, it is important to have personnel who are expert in the language and background of the fashion business: account executives who work with clients and coordinate what is done, art directors who visualize the fashion advertising, copywriters who are familiar with fashion appeals, and stylists or fashion coordinators who are responsible for the fashion slant of the ads.

The work of the fashion expert in an agency is not necessarily limited to fashion accounts. If a man's or woman's figure appears in an ad for automobiles, cigarettes, or soap, it is most likely that a fashion adviser has checked the model's outfit to make sure it is in tune with the current fashion picture as well as with the occasion and level of society being represented. Agency people also realize that fashion is a quick way to identify with whatever group of customers the advertiser seeks to reach: young, dashing, mature, conservative, or whatever. This is especially noticeable in television advertising, where the advertiser has only a few seconds in which to establish rapport with the particular viewers it wishes to influence. Compare the clothing of the characters in an investment firm's commercials, for example, with those of the characters in commercials for soft drinks. The one seeks to project a conservative image, the other a carefree, young, with-it attitude.

Thus, the advertising agency, whether or not it has a fashion account on its roster of clients, becomes involved, directly or indirectly, in the business of fashion.

Publicity and Public Relations Firms

Publicity, unlike advertising, cannot be controlled in relation to where, when, and how a particular message will appear—if, indeed, it appears at all. The publicity practitioner's control over the fate of the story he or she wishes to place with a medium rests primarily in the ability to convince the particular editor that the material is truly news of interest to that medium's audience.

Publicity's purpose, like that of advertising, is to enhance the client's sales appeal to potential customers. The space or time supplied by the media, in this case, is free, but the public relations firm's services are not. Working on a fee basis, with provision for expenses, the publicity agency develops news stories around the client's product or activities and makes these stories available to editors and broadcasters.

The key word in effective publicity is *news*. The publicity expert's first job is to find or "create" news value in a product, activity, or personality to be publicized. Next, he or she considers the media that might conceivably find this news of interest to their readers and writes the story (called a press release) in a form appropriate to the media that constitute the target. If they are likely to use illustrations, a suitable photograph may be included.

Typically, publicity activities include getting editorial mentions in consumer and trade publications, "plugs" on television and radio, school and college tie-ins, running fashion shows or other events (often with admission charges that go to a charity organization), feature articles in newspapers and magazines, and anything else that makes the products or the client's name better known and more readily accepted by the consumer—or by an industry, if that industry is the client's customer.

The publicity firm does more than merely use its contacts to place material for its client. It also prepares press releases, distributes photographs, writes radio and TV scripts, sometimes works out an elaborate fashion show, and hires and coaches professional actors to sing, dance, and model for the audience. If a medium, whether print or broadcast, is working on a special feature touching the client's field, the public relations people swing into action to provide the writer of the feature with facts, photos, and other help. Many fashion editors in smaller towns depend on press releases and photographs for the content of their fashion pages.

A broader term than publicity is **public relations**. A public relations firm does not limit its efforts to getting the client or the product mentioned in the media through press releases and similar efforts. It may supply expert advice on how to improve the client's public image and may develop some potent but less-obvious ways of getting publicity for the client: suggesting him or her as a speaker at conventions of appropriate groups, or having the client give scholarships and establish awards and foundations, for instance.

There are many independent publicists and public relations agencies that specialize in fashion publicity. As in the case of advertising agencies, their clients are generally fiber, fabric, or apparel producers instead of retailers, as retailers usually maintain their own internal publicity staffs. Insofar as the fashion business is concerned, the public relations and publicity fraternity performs the very useful function of feeding information about the industry to the news media and thus stimulates business by keeping fashion in the limelight.

Mall/Property Management Specialists

Behind the scenes of large shopping malls and other properties where fashions are sold are teams of individuals who manage and promote a group (or groups) of stores. These **mall/property management specialists** are responsible for the operation of the mall or other property, assuring that facilities are clean, attractive, and safe for shoppers. Most property management groups have a marketing staff responsible for efforts to attract shoppers to a mall or other facility. The marketing staff plays an important role in creating a lively atmosphere, filled with activities that encourage shoppers to think of that mall as a destination for a pleasant shopping experience. A staff, headed by a director of marketing, is responsible for staging special events to draw customers and doing whatever it takes to create a positive image in the community for that mall. These may range from sponsoring a visit from Santa Claus or the Easter bunny, to organizing a teen board, to coordinating theme weeks for the mall or fashion shows, to hot air balloon liftoffs to promote a special sale. The mall staff also has a vital role in helping property tenants feel a part of the "mall family" through newsletters and various events. The mall marketing staff often develops advertisements to represent the mall as a total entity; these ads may be for the print media, television, or radio.

Property management offices play a critical role in having attractive sites for the retailing of fashion goods. Individuals in these offices keep the mall industry functioning effectively, which makes them important players in the fashion industry. In an era when consumers are less likely to think of shopping as a pleasant experience, mall staffs have a particularly challenging role. Moreover, property management represents yet another group of career options. Numerous management positions are involved. Among them, marketing departments in these offices may offer potential for individuals who are creative, versatile, and resourceful and have a high energy level.

Trade Show Enterprises

A number of businesses exist for the purpose of organizing trade shows for various segments of the industry. Some of these are companies that exist solely for this purpose. Others, such as Bobbin, sponsor trade shows such as the annual Bobbin Show for the apparel industry (Figure 11–9) and also have other business activities, including publishing *Bobbin* magazine. Some trade shows are organized for the fashion segments of the industry, which retail buyers attend to secure lines for their stores. Others may be textile shows. Some are for retailers for purposes other than buying fashion merchandise (e.g., exhibitors may show computer systems, security systems, and other products or services related to store operations), textile manufacturing equipment, trims, and so on. Large trade shows require masterful coordination and need the competencies of individuals who specialize in this type of work. The activities of these trade show enterprises are important in providing a venue where different segments of the industry come together to transact business important to keeping the industry functioning.

Figure 11–9

(a) and (b) A number of trade show enterprises exist to organize trade shows for all segments of the industry. These may range from shows that feature apparel lines, those that are for textile machinery exhibitors, or that exhibit products and services for apparel manufacturers, such as the Bobbin Show shown here. The Bobbin Show has exhibitors and visitors from many countries.

(a)

| Figure 11–9 | *Continued* |

(b)

Source: Reprinted courtesy of *Bobbin*.

Trade Associations

Trade associations also play important roles in the fashion industry. Each trade association represents businesses and business executives with interests in common. These associations are composed of members who pay dues to support the operation of the group and to carry out the common goals of the members. Each organization is set up as a medium for such purposes as disseminating trade and technical information, doing research into markets or methods of operation, analyzing relevant legislation, doing public relations work for the industry or trade, and lobbying on legislation or other political matters.

Some of the largest trade associations associated with the fashion industry are the National Retail Federation (NRF), the American Textile Manufacturers Institute (ATMI), and the merged American Apparel and Footwear Association (AAFA). Like companies, trade associations sometimes merge to leverage strength. After months of talks, on August 14, 2000, the American Apparel Manufacturers Association (AAMA), Footwear Industries of America (FIA), and The Fashion Association (TFA) merged into one association: American Apparel and Footwear Association (AAFA)

(AAFA, 2000). The Intimate Apparel Council (IAC) was already under the AAMA (now AAFA) umbrella (Figure 11–10).

As many as 200 U.S. trade associations are related to the fashion industry. Some are large with fairly heterogeneous memberships, such as the three large ones named. However, some are quite small or may represent narrowly specialized groups such as hosiery manufacturers, yarnspinners, importers and/or exporters, intimate apparel producers, the leather industries, millinery firms, sportswear, children's wear

Figure 11–10

This advertisement ran to announce the merger of three important fashion industry trade associations into the American Apparel and Footwear Association.

Apparel and Footwear…A Fashionable Fit

Three great associations have agreed to work together under a new banner:
American Apparel and Footwear Association
the fashion association

The American Apparel Manufacturers Association (AAMA), Footwear Industries of America (FIA) and The Fashion Association (TFA) have recently joined forces to enhance their value to members, policymakers and U.S. consumers. This new organization is known as the **American Apparel and Footwear Association**, or **AAFA**.

Think of us as your "one-stop-shop" for policy questions related to U.S. companies involved in fashion, apparel and footwear. We don't care if you're a dyed-in-the-wool protectionist or a pinstriped cheerleader for free trade. If you need information on trade, labor or regulatory issues related to these industries, we're here for you. Likewise, if you're curious about the impact of fashion trends on apparel, footwear or textiles, check us out at the location noted below. We'll cover you like your favorite pair of sneakers.

What makes us so sure? Well, we've married the policy prowess of the AAMA and FIA with the fashion and media relations expertise of TFA. We're now pooling our resources to build a stronger U.S. apparel and footwear industry. And by working together, we'll make sure our high standards *never* go out of style.

AAFA
American Apparel & Footwear Association
the fashion association

In the fall of 2000, the AAFA began working out of a new headquarters at 1601 N. Kent St., Suite 1200, Arlington, VA 22209. We've also maintained The Fashion Association's divisional office at 475 Park Ave. S., 9th Floor, New York, NY 10016. For further information, please call us at 703/524-1864 or 212/683-5665; fax us at 703/522-6741or 212/545-1709; or visit our Web site at www.apparelandfootwear.org.

Source: Reprinted courtesy of American Apparel and Footwear Association.

producers, uniform manufacturers and distributors, or cotton growers. There are also associations for advertising and publicity specialists, fashion writers, individuals in shopping center management, and fashion designers, among many others.

The Fashion Group International

The Fashion Group International is a professional association of women who represent every phase of fashion manufacturing, retailing, merchandising, advertising, publishing, and education. Organized in 1931, its purpose was, and is, to serve as a national and international clearinghouse for the exchange of information about what is going on in the business of fashion. Headquartered in New York, it has 34 regional chapters in major cities throughout the United States and in other countries. Its membership exceeds 6,000. The Fashion Group International describes itself as a "global non-profit organization" whose mission is:

- To advance professionalism in fashion and its related lifestyle industries, with a particular emphasis on the role and development of women
- To provide a public forum for examination of important contemporary issues in fashion and the business of fashion
- To present timely information regarding national and global trends that have an effect on the fashion industries
- To attain greater recognition of women's achievements in business
- To encourage women to seek career opportunities in fashion and related industries
- To provide activities and programs that enhance networking skills and encourage interpersonal contacts so as to further the professional, social, and personal development of members (Fashion Group International, 1995)

Although many may question the female-only membership, perhaps the intent of this stipulation has been to provide networking opportunities that have long been available to men through many other organizations.

Other Fashion Enterprises

There are enterprises of many other types that play important behind-the-scenes roles in the business of fashion. Their activities, however, are too varied and too highly specialized to be described in detail. For example, display consultants design and construct fashion display materials for manufacturers, retailers, and fashion magazines. Consultants in the fields of sales promotion and marketing are also retained on a fee basis by manufacturers and retailers. Market research agencies do consumer surveys for retail stores, publications, and manufacturers or retail surveys for producers. Among the research agencies that do work for the fashion field are Audits and Surveys, which has made some interesting studies of the buying patterns of retail store customers, and Yankelovich, Skelly and White, which is noted for its demographic and psychographic research.

In short, there is a whole arsenal of auxiliary services that contributes to making the fashion business what it is today and that will undoubtedly contribute to its growth in the future.

Readings

Because the auxiliary fashion enterprises exist to serve the industry, it means that as the manufacturing and retailing industries have restructured, this segment of the industry has changed also. These readings give an inside view of some of these businesses that work behind the scenes to serve the fashion industry.

Styleexpo.com: New Venue for Trade Shows

This article describes an example of the new Internet businesses that have mush-roomed to assist fashion industry professionals who are sometimes unable to attend trade shows.

TextileWeb Introduces E-Commerce Solution for Fabric Sourcing

Fashion manufacturers can now shop for and purchase their fabrics online. This business-to-business e-commerce gives fabric buyers for a company many more choices in fabrics as well as more opportunities to compare costs.

TradeTextile: Source Link in Asia

This article describes a business-to-business website that enables companies to source for textiles worldwide.

All for One—and One for All: Footwear, Apparel and Fashion Associations Ink Three-Way Merger

This article reports on the merger of three important trade associations to form the American Apparel and Footwear Association. This merger provides combined strength in serving the industry and having a voice on matters that affect the fashion industry.

Styleexpo.com: New Venue for Trade Shows

by Wendy Hessen

New York—Now harried buyers and editors who can't quite make it to every booth at all those trade shows have an alternative.

Styleexpo.com, which went live late last month, is the first online accessories trade show for buyers and the press.

The idea came to Anibal Escobar after spending four days with his wife, Tracey Schuster, designer of the Princess Foufou handbag and hat lines, working at a trade show.

"He felt there had to be a less grueling way for buyers and designers to exchange information and thought the Internet could be the answer," said Coleman McCartan, vice president, sales and marketing at Styleexpo.com.

There will be three editions of the show per year, with merchandise available for viewing for two months at a time. During the exhibition period, designers can update their offerings as often as they would like, McCartan said.

Currently, 82 designers are exhibiting, covering all categories of accessories. Those who participated in the first round were not charged a fee, unless they needed the site to handle photographing their merchandise. Beginning with the fall edition, which will break in May, the fee for exhibitor participation will be $1,000 per show.

In keeping with the site's focus on an upscale market, McCartan said several more exhibitors will be added in the next show, but the maximum number is unlikely to exceed 120.

"Most of our designers have participated in trade shows like Accessorie Circuit or Première Classe in Paris," he said. "For fall, we will take on some younger designers and place them in a new designer area."

To spur buyer traffic, McCartan said Styleexpo.com sent mailers to upscale store buyers in the U.S., Europe and Japan. Buyers need to register and provide proof of their identity to view collections. Later this month, vendors will receive a report from the site detailing who has visited their page. They can then contact the store. Buyers are able to e-mail a designer from the site, as well.

"The hardest thing for us is to get buyers to give it a try, but once they spend 10 minutes or so on the site and move around a bit, they find it invaluable," said McCartan. "It can be a good editing tool, and is especially helpful for out-of-town buyers."

"I am a huge fan of Styleexpo," said Jennifer Wallis, a buyer at Indulge.com. "It gives me the opportunity to visualize how products will look online, which is such an important part of our business. Many of our current vendors are part of the site, but there have also been quite a few new vendors that I have been introduced to on the site."

Wallis said she visits Styleexpo.com at least once a week, both to see if there are any new designers in the assortment and to see if established vendors have added any new merchandise.

Stacey Lindseth, a buyer from Houston-based Tootsies said: "If you are somewhat familiar with a line, you could get an idea of what you would want to buy, and if you don't know a line well, the site can help you edit what you might want to see in person."

Source: From Women's Wear Daily, *February 7, 2000, p. 19. Reprinted by permission.*

Lisa Natt, owner of the Sola accessories showroom, said she liked the concept and believes that it will be successful in the long term, but hasn't had much response from buyers as of yet.

"I'm reserving judgment for now," she said. "Part of the thrill with fashion accessories is touching and feeling the merchandise. The photography isn't yet up to par, and it will need to be competitively priced with direct mail to be worthwhile. Some of my designers were a bit worried about the security of their lines, but there have been no problems with that at all."

McCartan said that some competitive manufacturers and retail chains like The Gap and Limited have attempted to gain passwords, but if their identities couldn't be confirmed, they were blocked from the site. Also, exhibitors are blocked from viewing other exhibitor's offerings.

Maria Turgeon, designer of the handbag and luggage firm of the same name, said it has already worked for her.

"It's a great idea. I have had calls from both stores and e-tailers," she said. "The other day, I was working in my showroom with a new store from Puerto Rico, and when they asked how they could review the line in the months ahead, I referred them to Styleexpo.com. It's a huge investment to take photos and send mailers, and this way I can update the site with new merchandise anytime I want."

TextileWeb Introduces E-Commerce Solution for Fabric Sourcing

by Marjorie Richardson

While the popularity of Internet commerce in the business-to-consumer arena is well recognized, marketing experts estimate that business-to-business e-commerce represents a market ten to twenty times greater. And growing. Officials at TextileWeb announced the introduction of E-commerce for Fabrics this week.

At the request of several leading manufacturers TextileWeb has launched an e-commerce platform for buying and selling fabric. Not just a promotional application, buyers can search an extensive database of fabrics and actually place orders on-line. The time and cost efficiencies of sourcing via the Internet are more than readily apparent. In the eminently democratizing style of Internet commerce, buyers can expand their sourcing options to suppliers that might not have been accessible to them previously. Including international sources.

Sellers can also extend their reach to a worldwide market of potential buyers, instantly. E-commerce allows manufacturers to transcend the well-entrenched distribution chain of the textile industry while increasing their margins in the process. "Internet commerce presents a dynamic new alternative to traditional systems of product distribution. What's more important are the cost and time efficiencies of e-commerce, allowing manufacturers to achieve higher margins selling product on-line. Sellers save and buyers save, so it's a win-win situation," explains Paul Risen of TextileWeb.

Getting set up to sell fabrics on-line through TextileWeb's E-Commerce for Fabrics is remarkably easy. Fabric suppliers provide sample yardage from which digital images and detailed product specifications are posted in a dedicated area of the *www.TextileWeb.com* site. TextileWeb manages every aspect of marketing, sales, billing and collections from there. Suppliers receive notification of orders and ship from their warehouse. The identity of manufacturers is not revealed, eliminating concerns about competitive analysis or disruption of existing distribution channels.

"Within three weeks of its inception, the program was created, implemented and produced its first order. We don't expect that this will be the be all and end all for textile distribution, but feedback from our customers indicates that we are headed in the right direction," added Paul Risen of TextileWeb.

"Who ever thought we'd be buying things like cars and stocks on-line? And fabrics? Well, the time has come and it's the savvy, progressive companies that we are seeing taking advantage of e-commerce," states Janet Bunce, Account Executive at TextileWeb. "We can effectively cover more territory and reach a wider audience than any other conventional sales channels."

It's deceptively easy for companies, and indeed any individual who has a computer, to set up a web site. Where web sites abound, few will have the required sophistication to stay ahead of lightning speed changes in technology and the principles and practices of e-commerce marketing that result. Many companies acknowledge that the time it takes to actually implement a web site can be lengthy and maintaining one requires a significant commitment of resources. Those who dally, however, may well find themselves quickly outpaced by a formerly insignificant competitor that has begun to sell their products on-line. The e-commerce platform on TextileWeb affords companies of all sizes the opportunity to engage in Internet marketing at very low risk and cost outlay.

"At TextileWeb we are in the business of creating solutions for e-commerce and business-to-business transactions. Our customers are in the business of manufacturing fabric. It makes sense for them to let us do what we do best so they can continue to do what they do best. In the next several months you'll see TextileWeb launching several business-to-business applications that take advantage of the Internet in the existing supply chain," states Paul Risen of TextileWeb.

Market pressures in an industry as competitive as the textile industry will soon place e-commerce in the position of strategic imperative rather than novelty venture. The revolution is upon us and will unquestionably affect every company in one way or another.

TradeTextile: Source Link in Asia

by Scott Malone

New York—To grab business from textile buyers who are interested in sourcing from Asia but don't know their way around the market, Hong Kong-based TradeTextile.com says it's got a simpler route to follow on the Internet.

The business-to-business e-commerce Web site, launched March 1, is the creation of Allan Cheung, who spent the past two years trying to figure out a way to bring Internet commerce to the textile industry and give a new spark to the family's textile trading operation, Dai Dai Development Co. Ltd.

In an interview from his Hong Kong office, Cheung explained that while the Far East is a very popular sourcing spot for textiles and apparel, the difference in time zones makes communications from opposite sides of the world difficult. He set up TradeTextile.com to support both auctions and direct sales, and buyers can shop an online directory of fibers, yarn, fabrics and garments and see what's immediately available, without waiting for faxes or voice mails to be returned.

"The textile industry is very fragmented, very inefficient, and requires a lot of manual work to make one transaction," said Cheung, who serves as chief executive officer of TradeTextile.com. "Imagine the time that buyers from the U.S. or Europe can save by checking the availability of products and prices from the Web."

Cheung built the TradeTextile.com business around his father's operation, which sold Chinese-made fabrics. By rolling that company into the new venture—of which the elder Cheung serves as chairman—the two hit the ground running, with the exclusive representation of six Chinese fiber and fabric producers.

Another 60 Chinese trading companies and manufacturers are offering their goods for sale on the site, but continuing to pursue other sales channels as well, Cheung said.

The site moved more than $2 million in merchandise in its first two weeks of operation, according to TradeTextile.com's CEO. Cheung said sales on the site are exceeding his plan.

The site is organized by category, offering varieties of raw materials, textiles, apparel and other garment-business related items, as well as quota rights. A check of the site's inventory last Thursday showed 633 lots of fabric, 523 of yarn, 155 of home textiles, 103 of fiber and 26 garments lots available for purchase.

It displays in English, Mandarin Chinese and Cantonese Chinese.

The site runs on software developed by Entrade Inc., a Northfield, Ill., technology concern, which has a 25 percent stake in TradeTextile.com, and like many heads of privately held tech ventures, Cheung is talking about making an initial public offering over the next year.

Right now, all fulfillment is handled by the companies selling or auctioning goods on the site. Later this year, Cheung said that TradeTextile.com, which currently has offices in Chicago, Shanghai and Hong Kong, plans to open a U.S. marketing headquarters. A North American fulfillment center for handling deliveries is also being considered, he said.

Cheung said he hopes the site will help North American buyers who are not familiar with Far Eastern suppliers to learn more about the market.

"So many people don't know much about Asian companies," he said.

"Now, through the Web, you can instantly see hundreds of suppliers and products."

Source: From Women's Wear Daily, *March 27, 2000, p. 44. Reprinted by permission.*

All for One—and One for All: Footwear, Apparel and Fashion Associations Ink Three-Way Merger

After months of talks, the new American Apparel and Footwear Association came into being on Aug. 14 following an overwhelming vote by the membership of the three separate organizations.

The new group represents a combination of three highly esteemed trade associations: the American Apparel Manufacturers Association (AAMA), Footwear Industries of America (FIA), and The Fashion Association (TFA).

The AAMA and FIA are both based in the Washington area and will relocate to a larger office in Arlington, VA, in mid-September. TFA is based in New York and will continue operating there as a division of the AAFA.

"This merger is the most important step any of our three individual organizations have undertaken in living memory," said Larry Martin, president of the AAFA, and formerly president of the AAMA. "What it will do is broaden the base of our programs ranging from government relations to high-tech research to marketing specialty products such as intimate apparel. Best of all, even as the merger enables us to do more for our members, it'll help us reduce overhead costs and operate more efficiently."

The new association includes over 700 member companies whose combined industries account for more than $225 billion in annual U.S. retail sales.

Members of each of the three groups approved a series of bylaw changes to finalize the merger. For example, the completion of the merger calls for the retirement of the AAMA's name and logo, which goes back to that organization's founding in 1960.

Fawn Evenson, president of the AAFA's FIA Division, said she views the merger as a breakthrough for U.S. footwear companies. "The fact that we now represent a much larger group of companies will translate into increased effectiveness on Capitol Hill and beyond," said Evenson, whose organization has roots stretching back to 1869. "Everybody's a winner with this new configuration. It's as natural as pairing clothes with shoes."

Eric Hertz, the executive director of the TFA Division, said he looked forward to giving the new association an enhanced focus on fashion marketing and media relations. Founded in 1955, TFA is known nationally for top-rank programs such as the annual American Image Awards, which recognize excellence in retail and apparel management. "The American Apparel and Footwear Association now has a New York address to complement its Washington base," Hertz said. "What TFA will bring to the table is an expanded focus on fashion and fashion news coverage. Being part of a larger, more diverse base of members will only strengthen TFA's already thriving programs. I'm absolutely delighted with this merger."

The merger agreement will allow AAFA members from any of the three groups to participate in all association activities, including voting for members of the AAFA board of directors and serving on association committees. The agreement also calls for both the FIA and TFA divisions to have representatives on the AAFA board.

Source: From AAFA News, July/August, 2000, pp. 1, 6. Adapted by permission of American Apparel and Footwear Association.

Chapter Review

Key Words and Concepts

Define, identify, or briefly explain the following:

Advertising
Advertising agency
Consultant
Cooperative merchandising
  organization (formerly
  cooperative buying office)
Corporate merchandising/buying
  office
Dot-com
DNR
Editorial credit
Export specialists
Fashion consultant
The Fashion Group International

Fashion information service
Fashion magazine
Fee offices
Import brokers
Kiosks
Labor auditors
Lobbyists
Logistics
Mall/property management
  specialists
Management consultants
Management information systems
  (MIS)
Market representative

Merchandising, buying, and
  product development
  organizations
Overseas merchandise
  representative
Product development
Public relations
Publicity
Resident buying office
Testing laboratories
Tobé Associates
Trade association
Trade attorneys
Trade publication
Women's Wear Daily

Review Questions on Chapter Highlights

1. List the different types of information provided by fashion information services. What types of firms subscribe to them? Why and how are they used?
2. Why would a Japanese company and a U.S. company subscribe to and use the *same* fashion information service?
3. Describe the evolution of what were once called buying offices. Why have these organizations experienced difficulty?
4. How do the activities of May Merchandising Company differ from those of the former AMC or Frederick Atkins?
5. Why are the services of testing laboratories in demand more today than in the past?
6. How do management consultants differ from fashion consultants if they are working for a fashion firm?
7. Why might a retail firm use the services of consultants in the areas of information technology or logistics?
8. Describe the roles of import and export consultants. Who uses these services?

9. Explain the relationship and services of a fashion magazine to each of the following: (a) apparel producers, (b) retailers, or (c) consumers.
10. What types of information are found in trade publications such as *Women's Wear Daily* and *DNR?* How does a trade publication differ from a fashion magazine?
11. Why and how are fashion firms using electronic media?
12. Identify the various ways in which advertising and publicity agencies assist the fashion industry.
13. Why are mall/property management specialists important to the fashion industry?
14. What is a trade association? List the names of trade associations that have been mentioned in previous chapters of the book and describe their activities.
15. Describe examples of dot-com businesses that have been developed to support the fashion industry. What are some ways these are going to change how business is done in the industry?

References

American Apparel and Footwear Association (July/August 2000). All for one—and one for all: Footwear, apparel, and fashion associations ink three-way merger, pp. 1, 6. Author: Arlington, VA.

Bacon's Magazine Directory. (1999) (47th ed.). Bacon's Information, Inc. Chicago: Bacon's Information, Inc.

Bertsch, D. (1995, November). Telephone conversation with author.

Braun, H. (1995, June 14). *Speaking globally: Information systems on a worldwide scale.* Unpublished paper presented to the International Apparel Federation, Washington, DC.

The Fashion Group International. (1995). Unpublished Fashion Group International press release.

Moin, D. (2000, April 5). Frederick Atkins closing. *Women's Wear Daily,* pp. 2, 23.

Palmieri, J. (1994, October 10). Retail pool keeps shrinking, but Doneger Group keeps growing. *DNR,* pp. 8, 12.

Standard Periodical Directory. (2000). New York: Oxbridge Publications.

Standard Rate and Data Service. (2000, Oct.). *Business publication advertising source, Part 1,* 77(11) 348, 353, 354. Wilmette, IL: Author.

Standard Rate and Data Service. (2000, Sept.). *Consumer magazine advertising source.* Wilmette, IL: Author.

Tobé. (1957, April 25). Address before Harvard Graduate School of Business Administration, Cambridge, MA. Reprinted with permission of the late Tobe Coller Davis in the 1965 edition of this book.

Ulrich's International Periodical Directory (2000). New Providence, NJ: R. R. Bowker.

Suggested Bibliography

Beaton, C. (1968). *The best of Boston.* New York: Macmillan.

Diamond, J., & Diamond, E. (1999). *Fashion advertising and promotion.* New York: Fairchild.

Dolber, R. (1993). *Opportunities in fashion careers.* Lincolnwood, IL: NTC Publishing Group.

Edelman, A. (1990). *Fashion resource directory.* New York: Fairchild.

Everett, J., & Swanson, K. (1995). *Guide to producing a fashion show.* New York: Fairchild.

Kelly, K. (1972). *The wonderful world of Women's Wear Daily.* New York: Saturday Review Press.

Pegler, M. (1995). *Visual merchandising and display* (3rd ed.). New York: Fairchild.

Perna, R. (1987). *Fashion forecasting.* New York: Fairchild.

Russell, J. (Ed.). (annual). *National trade and professional associations of the United States.* Washington, DC: Columbia Books.

Snow, C. (1962). *The world of Carmel Snow.* New York: McGraw-Hill.

Visual Merchandising and Store Design. (Eds.). (1994). *Great store design.* Rockport, MA: Rockport Publishers.

Visual Merchandising and Store Design. (Eds.). (1995). *Great retail displays.* Rockport, MA: Rockport Publishers.

Winters, A., & Goodman, S. (1984). *Fashion advertising and promotion.* New York: Fairchild.

Winters, A., & Milton, S. (1982). *The creative connection: Advertising copywriting and idea visualization.* New York: Fairchild.

Trade Associations

American Advertising Federation, 1225 Connecticut Ave., NW, Washington, DC 20036.

American Apparel and Footwear Association, 1601 N. Kent Street, Suite 1200, Arlington, VA 22209.

American Association of Advertising Agencies, 666 Third Ave., New York, NY 10017.

Color Association of the United States, 409 W. 44th St., New York, NY 10036.

The Fashion Group International, 597 Fifth Ave., New York, NY 10017.

International Council of Shopping Centers, 665 Fifth Ave., New York, NY 10022.

Magazine Publishers of America, 575 Lexington Ave., New York, NY 10022.

Public Relations Institute, 350 W. 57th St., New York, NY 10019.

Public Relations Society of America, 33 Irving Place, 3rd Floor, New York, NY 10003.

Trade Publications

Advertising Age, 740 North Rush St., Chicago, IL 60611.

Fashion Calendar, 185 E. 85th St., New York, NY 10028.

Fashion Forecast International, 23 Bloomsbury Square, London WC1A 2PJ, England.

International Colour Authority, 23 Bloomsbury Square, London WC1A 2PJ, England.

Public Relations Journal, 845 Third Ave., New York, NY 10022.

Standard Rate and Data Service, Inc., 5201 Old Orchard Rd., Skokie, IL 60076.

Visual Merchandising, 407 Gilbert Ave., Cincinnati, OH 45202.

*F*ashion Business Glossary

Accessories All articles ranging from hosiery to shoes, bags, gloves, belts, scarfs, jewelry, and hats, for example, worn to complete or enhance an outfit of apparel.

Accessorizing The process of adding accessory items to apparel for display, for models in fashion shows, or for customers' clothes on request.

Accounts Payable The financial obligations owed *by* a company to its suppliers.

Accounts Receivable The financial obligations owed *to* a company by its customers.

Acquisition A company purchased (acquired) by another firm.

Ad Valorem Tariff An import tax as a percentage of the price of the product.

Adaptation A design that reflects the outstanding features of another design but is not an exact copy.

Advance Ship Notices (electronic bills of lading) are sent electronically to the retailer when the supplier ships the merchandise. This alerts the retailer that the merchandise will soon arrive, to be distributed among multiple stores if needed.

Advertising A nonpersonal method of influencing sales through a paid message by an identified sponsor. Advertising appears in media such as newspapers, magazines, television, and radio.

Advertising Credit The mention of a store name (one or several) in a producer's advertisement, as a retail source for the advertised merchandise.

Agile Manufacturing Quick Response with a higher order of flexibility, or QR made-to-order (Clune, 1993).

Anchor Stores The department store (or other similar major stores) in a shopping mall.

Apparel An all-embracing term that applies to men's, women's, and children's clothing.

Apparel Jobber A firm that generally handles all the processes but the sewing, and sometimes the cutting, and that contracts out these production processes to independently owned contractors.

Apparel Manufacturer According to the Bureau of Census, a firm that buys fabrics and does the designing, patternmaking, grading, cutting, sewing, and assembling of garments in factories that it owns. Today, industry use of the term has a much broader interpretation to include any firm that develops garments, controls production, sells to retailers (or directly to end-use customers), and ships and bills for merchandise. Firms may or may not buy the fabrics to be used. Today, generally only small apparel companies conform to the census definition for apparel manufacturers.

Apparel Mart A building that houses the regional showrooms of apparel companies.

511

Avant Garde   In any art, the most daring of the experimentalists; innovation of original and unconventional designs, ideas, or techniques during a particular period.

Bar Code   A series of vertical bars that identify a merchandise category, the manufacturer, and the individual item.

Bilateral Agreements   Trade agreements between two countries.

Bilateral Treaty   A treaty between two countries.

Boarding (Hosiery)   Heat-setting process used to give hosiery a permanent shape.

Body Scanning   A futuristic concept to scan an individual's body electronically to make a custom-made pattern.

Boutique   From the French word meaning "little shop." A freestanding shop or an area within a retail store, devoted to specialized merchandise for special-interest customers.

Branch   In retailing, an extension of a parent or flagship store, operated under the same name and ownership.

Brand   A trade name or symbol that distinguishes a product as that of a particular manufacturer or distributor.

Bridge Jewelry   Jewelry that in price and materials is between costume and fine jewelry.

Buyer   An executive (retail) who is responsible for the selection and purchase of merchandise and for the financial performance of that person's assigned merchandise area.

Canton Trade Fair   A textile trade show held in Canton (now generally known as Guangzhou), China.

Caribbean Basin Initiative (CBI)   A U.S. trade policy that gives special privileges to countries in the Caribbean Basin.

Caribbean Basin Textile Access Program   Provides virtually unlimited quotas for Caribbean-made garments made of U.S. fabrics and cut in the United States.

Caribbean Parity   Having apparel trade privileges for the Caribbean countries equal to those for Mexico.

Catalog   A promotional book or booklet in which merchandise is offered for sale.

Catalog Showroom Retailer   An underselling establishment that prints and distributes a catalog and maintains a showroom where samples of the merchandise can be seen and ordered.

"Category Killers"   Retailers that specialize in extensive assortments of a single kind of merchandise at prices below those of conventional retailers.

Caution   French term for admission or entrance fee charged to trade customers by haute couture houses.

CD-ROM Shopping   Viewing products compiled from catalogs or other sources on a compact disk.

Centralized Buying   When all buying is done by merchandise staff from corporate headquarters.

Chain Stores   A retail organization that owns and operates a string of similar stores that are merchandised and controlled from a central headquarters office.

Chambre Syndicale de la Couture Parisienne   The French trade association that represents the haute couture houses of Paris.

Channel of Distribution   A network of organizations (and/or individuals) that performs a variety of interrelated functions in moving products from origination to consumption/use destinations.

Chapter 11   The legal process that provides an opportunity for companies burdened by excessive debt to continue operations while plans are made to restructure the company and reschedule debt payments.

Chargebacks   Financial penalties retailers demand of vendors for various reasons.

Chief Executive Officer (CEO)   The individual in a firm who has the final decision-making power for the company.

Chief Operating Officer (COO)   The individual in a firm who is head of all day-to-day operations for the company; this individual reports to the CEO.

Classic   A particular style that continues as an accepted fashion over an extended period of time.

Closeout   An offering of selected discontinued goods by a vendor to a retailer at reduced prices.

Collection   A manufacturer's or designer's group of styles or design creations for a specific season. The season's total number of styles of designs, accumulated for presentation to buyers, constitutes a collection.

Commissionaire   An independent retailer's service organization that is based in another country (or countries) and is used to represent importers abroad.

Competition   In its marketing context, it is a form of business activity in which two or more parties are engaged in a rivalry for consumer acceptance.

Computer Aided Design (CAD)   Uses software to assist in product development by saving time required to create a prototype garment. When CAD systems are linked to automatic marker making and cutting, a sample can be produced in a matter of hours.

Computer Integrated Manufacturing (CIM)   Links together via computers many aspects of a company's activities associated with developing and producing a line.

Concentration (or Industry Concentration)   The amount of an industry's business handled by a small number of the largest firms.

Confined   A line or label that is sold to one retailer in a trading area on an exclusive basis.

Conglomerate   A company consisting of a number of subsidiary divisions in a variety of unrelated industries.

Consumer   The ultimate user of goods or services.

Consumer Obsolescence   The rejection of something that retains utility value in favor of something new.

Consumer Orientation   A business gives primary attention to serving and pleasing the consumer.

Consumer-Ready   Customized products are sent directly from the manufacturer to the consumer.

Contract Tanners   Business firms that contract hides and skins to the specification of leather converters.

Contractor (Apparel)   A garment production operation that does the sewing and often the cutting for other apparel producers or retailers (so called because this work is done under a contractual arrangement). The contractor may, in some cases, be responsible for securing the fabrics.

Converter (Leathers)   A company that buys hides and skins, farms them out for processing to contract tanneries, and sells the finished product.

Converter (Textile)   A firm that buys or handles the greige goods (i.e., unfinished fabrics) from mills and contracts them out to finishing plants to have them finished (i.e., dyed, printed, etc.).

Cooperative Advertising   Advertising, the cost of which is shared by a firm and its customer for the benefit of both.

Cooperative Merchandising Organization (formerly a Cooperative Buying Office)   A service operation owned by a group of stores to assist those stores in developing (i.e., product development) and securing merchandise for their stores; other services may also be available.

Corporate Merchandise/Buying Office   A modern version of what was once the corporate buying office only; now assists stores in a store ownership group with a broader range of merchandising services (often including product development) as well as buying.

Corporation   An artificial legal entity.

Cost Price   The price at which goods are billed to a store, exclusive of any cash discounts that may apply to the purchase.

Costume Jewelry   Jewelry made of nonprecious materials.

Country-of-Origin Rules   The laws that determine the official country of origin for purposes of quota use.

Couturier   French word for (male) designer, usually one who has his own couture house. Couturière (female).

Craze   A fad or fashion characterized by much crowd excitement or emotion.

Cross Docking   A method used in retail distribution centers in which merchandise is received, sorted, and routed directly from receiving to shipping without spending any time in storage.

Cross-Shoppers   Consumers who may shop across all retail channels; they may, for example, buy outerwear at department stores and undergarments at discount stores.

Currency Exchange Rates   The number of units (i.e., the "price") of one currency in relation to another. For example, one British pound (£) may be worth $1.50 at a certain time, depending on fluctuating currency exchange rates.

Custom Made   Apparel made to the order of individual customers; cut and fitted to individual measurements as opposed to apparel that is mass produced in standardized sizes.

Customization   Tailoring products and services around the needs of individual customers.

Customized Products   Those produced for a consumer's specific needs.

Cut, Make, Trim (CMT)   Contracting to have garments cut, sewn, and trimmed as a "package" agreement.

Cutting-Up Trades   The segment of the fashion industries that produces apparel (i.e., apparel producers).

Database   An information system, generally computerized, in which a variety of factual data are organized and stored.

Data Mining   A new strategy that goes far simply analyzing POS data to help manufacturers and retailers analyze consumers' wants, needs, and spending patterns. Companies can identify which customers are spending money with them or which products are selling.

Database Marketing   Using computer files containing a great deal of information on consumers' demographic and psychological characteristics and lifestyle to target market efforts to a narrow group of consumers.

Demographics   The study of vital and social statistics of a population.

Department Store   According to the U.S. Census Bureau, a retail establishment that employs at least 50 people and that carries a wide variety of merchandise lines, including home furnishings, apparel for the family, and household linens and dry goods. Today, however, few department stores carry home furnishings or major appliances.

Design   An arrangement of parts, form, color, and line, for example, to create a version of a style.

Designers   Individuals responsible for the creative aspect of product development.

Developing Country   A poor country in early stages of economic development.

"Deverticalize"   This is a business decision by a vertically integrated company to focus on only one stage in the production-distribution process. In one example, Sara Lee sold the manufacturing part of its business to focus on being only an apparel marketer. In another example, it might also mean an apparel manufacturing company decides to close its retail stores.

Direct Marketing   A term that embraces direct mail, mail order, and direct response.

Direct Seller   A retailer that sells merchandise by contacting customers either through door-to-door approaches or through some form of in-home party plan.

Discounter (Off-Price)   An "underselling" retail establishment that utilizes self-service combined with many other expense-saving techniques. This term is commonly used to refer to the mass-merchandising discount chains.

Display   A visual presentation of merchandise or ideas.

Diverters   Questionable businesses that "divert" merchandise to a retailer other than the one to whom the manufacturer sold it. This strategy puts luxury or name-brand goods in off-price retail stores to whom the manufacturer will not sell.

Domestic Market   When referring to origin of goods, *domestic* means manufactured in one's own country as opposed to foreign made.

Domestics   Merchandise essentially for the home including sheets, pillows, towels, blankets, table linens, and other textile products.

"Doors"   An industry term for the number of stores. A chain might have 200 "doors," or a vendor might be selling to 100 "doors."

Duty   (also known as a tariff) A tax on imports.

E-commerce   Conducting business electronically, using modern computer technologies and the Internet.

Economies of Scale   The savings associated with manufacturing or selling on a large scale.

EDI   Electronic data interchange: the exchange of business data between two parties electronically.

EDI Mailbox   Where data are stored on a third party's computer, when a receiving computer is incompatible with a sending computer.

EDI Third Party   A company that provides EDI mailboxes.

EDI Trading Partner   A company with which one exchanges data electronically.

Editorial Credit   The mention, in a magazine or newspaper, of a store name as a retail source for merchandise that is being editorially featured by the publication.

807/9802 Production   A provision in the U.S. tariff rules that permits garments to be cut in this country and sewn elsewhere. When garments are returned to the United States, tariffs are paid on only the value added during the assembly process. Technically, this rule is now 9802, but much of the industry still refers to this as "807 production."

807A Production   Using U.S.-made fabrics that are cut into garments in the United States, assembled in the Caribbean, and returned virtually quota free to the U.S. market.

Electronic Retailing   Selling by means of an electronic device such as television or interactive computers.

Entrepreneur   A person who organizes, launches, and directs a business undertaking and assumes the financial risks and uncertainties of the undertaking.

Establishment Generally synonymous with *plant*, which refers to a single production facility. If the business is large, many establishments may be part of a *firm*.

E-tailing This refers to the retailing aspect of electronic commerce. This usually refers to selling directly to consumers.

European Union (EU) These are the major countries of Western Europe, which have formed an integrated area with common trade policies, common agricultural practices, and free movement of labor and capital among members.

Exclusivity Allowing a company sole use within a given trading area of a product.

Export orientation An attitude and business orientation that emphasizes the importance of exporting for a firm or country.

Exports Products or services that one country sells and ships to another.

Factor Financial institution that buys accounts receivable from sellers, assumes the risks and responsibilities of collection, and charges a fee for this service.

Factory A manufacturing plant.

Factory Outlet A manufacturer-owned retail outlet. In earlier decades the major purpose was to dispose of the manufacturer's excess inventory. Now, many manufacturers see this as another place to sell their merchandise.

Fad A minor or short-lived fashion.

Fashion (or Fashions) (1) The prevailing style(s) at any particular time. When a style is followed or accepted by many people, it is a fashion. (2) A continuing process of change in the styles of dress that is accepted and followed by a large segment of the public at any particular time.

Fashion Bulletin Written report on significant fashions prepared by fashion specialists.

Fashion Clinic Meeting of a group of persons interested in fashion (under the direction of a fashion specialist) for the purpose of presenting or discussing significant fashion trends. Clinics are usually held at the beginning of new fashion seasons.

Fashion Consultant A person who gives professional fashion advice or services.

Fashion Coordinator (or Director) A person charged with the responsibility for keeping abreast of fashion trends and developments and acting as a source of fashion information to others in his or her organization. Other responsibilities vary from place to place, as do job titles.

Fashion Forecasting Identifying which fashions or styles will be popular during a future period by looking at past experiences and current trends in the context of environmental issues.

(The) Fashion Group A national association of women engaged in the fashion business.

Fashion Image The impression the consumer has of a retailer's (or manufacturer's) position on fashion leadership, quality, selection, and prices.

(The) Fashion Press Reporters of fashion news for magazines, newspapers, broadcast media, and so on.

Fashion Retailing The business of buying fashion-oriented merchandise from a variety of resources and assembling it in convenient locations for resale to ultimate consumers.

Fashion Show or Showing Formal presentation of a group of styles, often in connection with showing the season's new merchandise.

Fashion Trend The direction in which fashion is moving.

Firm The overall business, or company. A firm may have many establishments (plants) or could have only one. Today, a number of apparel firms have no production facilities but are simply marketing companies that contract to have manufacturing done by others.

First Cost The price a retailer pays to the producer in another country for merchandise.

Flea Market A location in which a wide variety of independent sellers periodically rent space.

Floor-Ready Manufacturers send merchandise to retailers with packaging and ticketing that permits moving goods directly on to the selling floor.

Focus Groups Small consumer groups brought together to discuss their views and preferences regarding certain products or services.

Foreign Exchange The currency one country uses to buy from another.

Franchise A contractual agreement between a wholesaler, manufacturer, or service organization (the franchisor) and an independent retailer that buys the right to use the franchisor's product name or service for a stipulated fee. In return, the parent company provides assistance, guidelines, and established business patterns.

Franchisee The owner-operator of a retail unit for which there is a franchise arrangement with a franchisor, the parent company.

Franchisor The parent company which provides the franchisee with exclusive use of an established name in a specific trading area, plus assistance in organizing, training, merchandising, and management in return for a stipulated consideration.

Free Trade   Trade without barriers.

Free Trade Zone (FTZ)   An area within a country where goods may be imported and garments produced without being subject to taxes and customs duties.

Garment Center (SA)   The area to the East and West of Seventh Avenue in New York City, in which many of the women's ready-to-wear industry showrooms are located.

GATT   General Agreement on Tariffs and Trade. This has now been replaced by the World Trade Organization (WTO), which is located in Geneva, Switzerland.

Gemstones   A mineral found in nature that is used in jewelry because of its beauty, clarity, rarity, and other attributes.

General Merchandise Stores   Retail stores that carry a wide range of merchandise lines including apparel, hardware, furniture, home furnishings, and many other products.

Global Economy   A worldwide network of economies around the world brought together by computer technologies and other communication and transportation advances.

Global Marketing   Operations through which produced goods are exported and marketed in foreign countries.

Global Products   Those with components or production from multiple countries.

Global Retailing   The expansion of retailing operations on a global scale.

Global Sourcing   Utilization of worldwide production.

Globalization   A shift from a time when countries did business within their own borders to one in which almost all countries' economies are connected by various production and marketing networks.

Grainline   The direction of the warp and weft yarns in a fabric.

Greige Goods   Unfinished fabrics.

Haute Couture (literal French translation: "The finest dressmaking")   As used in the fashion business, this refers to a firm whose designer creates a collection of original designs that are then duplicated for individual customers on a made-to-order basis.

Hides   Animal skins that weigh more than 25 pounds when shipped to a tannery.

High Fashion   A fashion that is in the stage of limited acceptance.

Home Television Shopping   Selling goods and services via television, primarily on cable or satellite home shopping channels.

Hypermarket   A superlarge retailing establishment that brings food and general merchandise together in an immense area.

ILGWU   International Ladies' Garment Workers' Union, which became part of UNITE.

Import   Merchandise brought in from another country for resale or other purposes.

Import Broker   An agent middleman who brings buyers and sellers together to facilitate the buying and selling of goods from other countries in a domestic market.

Import Penetration   The portion of a domestic market taken by imports.

Income   The returns that come in periodically from business, property, labor, or other sources (i.e., revenue).

Industrialization   The social and economic changes associated with having products made by machinery rather than by hand.

Initial Markup (Mark On)   The difference between the cost price of merchandise and its original retail price.

Initial Public Offering (IPO)   The shares of stock offered by a company on the stock market when the company first becomes a publicly held firm.

Intercolor   Association of representatives of the worldwide fashion industry who meet in Paris twice annually to analyze color cycles and project color palettes for seasons two years in advance.

Interconnected Global Economy   The close linking of the economies of many countries.

International Colour Authority   A color trend service published by ITBD Publishers in London. This service is based on the predictions of color experts, and forecasts are available for fiber, yarn, fabric, and apparel producers. Color trend information is published separately for womenswear, menswear, and building interiors.

International Marketing   See Global Marketing.

Interstoff   An important textile trade fair held in Frankfurt, Germany.

Intranet   An "in-house" online communication system; this works somewhat like the Internet but operates only among members of one organization.

Jewelry   Articles of personal adornment made of either precious or nonprecious materials.

Job Lot   A broken, unbalanced assortment of discontinued merchandise reduced in price for quick sale. Also called odd lot.

Jobber   See Apparel Jobber.

Kips   Animal skins weighing from 15 to 25 pounds when shipped to a tannery.

Knock-Off   The copying of another manufacturer's fashion design.

Labor-Intensive   A product that involves a great deal of labor to produce.

Landed Cost   The cost of an imported product, which includes the cost of the merchandise, transportation, and duty.

Last   A form in the shape of a boot over which shoes are built.

Lead Time   Time necessary to produce merchandise from receipt of order to delivery time.

Lean Retailing   When retailers keep inventory levels low to reduce investments and risks. This occurs successfully only when manufacturers are prepared to provide rapid replenishment of items sold.

Less-Developed Countries   Another term for developing countries; this term incorporates countries that have advanced beyond the poorest levels.

Letters of Credit   Typical form of payment for merchandise produced in other countries.

Leveraged Buyout (LBO)   The purchase of a public company's stock made by a group of investors who borrow money from an investment firm using the company's assets as collateral.

Licensee   The person or organization to whom a license is granted.

Licensing   An arrangement whereby firms are given permission to produce and market merchandise that bears the name of a licensor, who receives a percentage of wholesale sales (i.e., a royalty) in return for the use of his or her name.

Licensor   The person or organization who grants a license.

Line   A collection of styles and designs shown by a producer in a given season.

Line-for-Line Copy   Exact copy of a style first developed by an original designer.

Lobby   A group that works together to put political pressure on policymakers to attempt to have the group's wishes carried out.

Logistics   The process of moving merchandise from manufacturers to retailers to consumers in the most efficient way possible, with concerns also for prompt delivery.

Mail Order   A firm that does the bulk of its sales through a catalog.

Mail-Order House   A retailing organization that generates the bulk of its business through merchandise catalogs.

Mall   See Shopping Centers.

Management Consultants   Business specialists (and companies) that assist client firms on broad strategic planning, market strategy analysis and planning, and merchandising and operations strategies (in contrast to fashion consultants, who assist with trend analysis and merchandise selection).

Management Information Systems (MIS)   A computerized system for managing data and putting it in meaningful form so that it is useful to management in making good decisions.

Manufactured Fibers   Known previously as "manmade" fibers, they are produced from chemical substances in contrast to fibers produced in nature (natural fibers).

Markdown   Reduction from an original retail price.

Market   (1) A group of potential customers. (2) The place or area in which buyers and sellers congregate.

Market Representative   (1) A market specialist in a corporate merchandising/buying office who covers a segment of the wholesale market and makes information about it available to client stores. (2) Similarly, a market specialist for a store ownership group or corporation who seeks merchandise lines for that company's stores.

Market Segmentation   The subdivision of a population (frequently ultimate consumers) whose members share similar identifiable characteristics (e.g., age, wealth, education level, marital status, or lifestyle).

Market Weeks   Scheduled periods during which producers introduce their new lines for an upcoming season.

Marketing   The total business interaction that involves the planning, pricing, promotion, and distribution of consumer-wanted goods and services for profit. A marketing orientation means that a company builds this around the consumer's needs.

Marketing Concept   Recognizing the importance of the ultimate consumer in the buying and selling process.

Marketing Environment   All the factors that affect how a company is able to meet its goals in developing and maintaining successful business relationships with its target customers.

Marketing Mix   The combination of factors related to product, price, place, and promotion that a company puts together to serve its target market.

Marketing Strategy   The approach a company uses to identify its customers' needs and the company's ability to satisfy those needs.

Markup   The difference between the cost price of merchandise and its retail price. Usually expressed as a percentage of the retail price.

Mart   A building or building complex housing both permanent and transient showrooms of producers.

Mass Market   The consumer market made up by a majority of the population.

Mass Merchandising   The retailing of goods on a very large scale.

Mass Production   Production of goods in quantity—many at a time rather than one at a time.

Matrix Buying   A strategy used by retailers in which they develop a list of preferred vendors who can supply the products, service, and pricing that retailers need to execute their respective strategies.

Megamalls   Jumbo malls several times larger than the typical regional mall.

Merchandisers   (1) In large firms, these individuals are responsible for developing new lines. Merchandisers plan the overall fashion direction for the coming season and give directions to the design staff about seasonal themes, types of items to be designed, and colors. (2) In recent years, this title is also being used for individuals who represent a manufacturer and work with retailers to assure that the apparel firm's line is being displayed and otherwise represented effectively within the store setting.

Merchandising   The activities involved in planning and development (or buying) of a merchandise line for targeted customers, providing them with what they want, when they want it, and at prices they can afford and are willing to pay.

Merchandising, Buying, and Product Development Organizations   The operations that have evolved from the "buying office" concept. Because most of these enterprises are involved in product development, sourcing, and activities that go far beyond buying, the old buying office term is too limited for most of these today.

Merger   A joint agreement of two or more companies to merge their business into one.

Microfibers (Microdenier Fibers)   Fibers of less than one denier per filament; this fineness gives yarns and fabrics greater softness and more silklike characteristics than traditional fiber filaments provided.

Micromarketing   Using a database to break the consumer market into smaller and smaller segments to provide increasingly specialized products and services for those small consumer groups.

Mode   Synonym for a fashion.

Modular Production Systems   One way in which garments may be produced in a factory. In this arrangement, a small empowered team (module) produces garments from start to finish, setting its own goals and often its own work rules to get the job done.

Mom-and-Pop Store   A small store generally operated by husband and wife with limited capital and few or no hired assistants.

More-Developed Countries   Those with relatively high incomes and standard of living.

Multifiber Arrangement (MFA)   A trade policy responsible for the textile/apparel quota system.

Multinational Company   A firm that conducts a portion of its business in two or more countries.

National Brand   Brand owned by a manufacturer, which is a trade name or symbol, that is nationally advertised.

National Retail Federation (NRF)   A trade association of the leading department, specialty, and chain stores in the United States.

Needle Trades   Synonym for apparel industry.

Newly Industrialized Country (NIC)   Countries that not long ago were developing countries but now have significant industrialization and fast-growing economies.

Nonrubber Footwear   All footwear that contains less than 50 percent rubber in the upper part of the shoe.

North American Free Trade Agreement (NAFTA)   A free trade policy between the United States, Canada, and Mexico.

North American Industry Classification System (NAICS)   The system for classifying various industry sectors. This system replaced the Standard Industrial Classification (SIC) after the passage of the North American Free Trade Agreement (NAFTA) so that industry figures in the United States, Mexico, and Canada would be comparable.

Off-Price Retailing   The selling of brand- and designer-named merchandise at lower-than-normal-retail prices.

Offshore Assembly Having cut garments assembled in another country.

Offshore Production Production of goods by a domestic manufacturer (including retailers) in another country.

Online Computer Shopping When consumers use online computer services to view and order merchandise.

Openings Fashion showings of new collections by apparel producers at the beginnings of a season.

Open-to-Buy The amount of money that a buyer may spend on merchandise to be delivered in a given period.

Outside Shop See Contractor.

Outsourcing When a company contracts to have functions of the business performed by companies that specialize in performing that function. Examples are sewing, logistics, and so on.

Outward Processing Trade (OPT) Sending garments to another country for some or all of the assembly.

Overseas Merchandise Representatives Individuals in other countries who assist their retail clients in the selection, development, and delivery of merchandise (i.e., sourcing) produced in that overseas region.

Overstoring The excess retail space available, relative to the population, in the United States.

Pelt Skin of fur-bearing animal.

Plants The same as *establishments*; that is, a single production facility that may or may not be part of a larger firm.

"Plasticization of Business" When credit cards are used extensively to conduct business. For example, a consumer from almost anywhere in the world can use a credit card to order an item of merchandise.

Policy A clearly defined course of action or method of doing business deemed necessary, expedient, or advantageous.

POS Point-of-sale. In retailing, that area of the store or department where the customer pays for the merchandise and the sale is recorded. This information is processed by computers and provides the basis for Quick Response systems.

Preproduction Operations Those between the time a style is accepted for the line and when a style is ready for the sewing floor. Glock, R., & Kunz, G. (1995). *Apparel manufacturing: Sewn product analysis* (2nd ed.). Englewood Cliffs, NJ: Prentice Hall.

Press Kit A collection of facts, figures, photographs, and other promotional materials assembled into a compact package and distributed to the press.

Press Release A written statement of news that has occurred or is about to occur, specifying the source of the information and the date after which its use is permissible.

Prêt-à-Porter (French term meaning, literally, "ready-to-carry") French ready-to-wear apparel, as distinguished from couture clothes, which are custom made.

Preticketing The vendor puts the price on merchandise before shipping it to the retailer. Many retailers are now requiring vendors to do this.

Primary Market Producers of fibers, textiles, leather, and furs.

Private Label Merchandise that is produced exclusively for one retail firm and identified by one or more "names" or brands that are owned by the retailer.

Privately Held Companies Those owned privately by individuals or groups rather than shareholders.

Privatized Industries Those previously operated by the government but now have been transferred to private ownership, such as those in the former Soviet Union.

Product Developer A person employed by a manufacturer to develop product lines or a retailer to create private-label merchandise for their exclusive use.

Product Development The part of apparel manufacturing (also used increasingly by retailers) that develops the line and monitors its production to assure that garments meet expectations.

Product Manager An executive who functions as the head of the product development team responsible for the planning and development of a particular product, product line, or brand.

Production Orientation A company's focus on producing what the company wants to produce or can produce, in contrast to a marketing orientation, which focuses on customers' needs and wants.

Production Package Contracting out the complete production of garments from cutting to finishing.

Productivity The amount of factory output per employee. This is a measure of efficiency of a manufacturing company.

Profit Total revenue and sales less all costs and expenses.

Progressive Bundle System The traditional way of producing garments in assembly-line fashion;

workers perform specialized tasks and then pass the garment on to the next operators.

Protectionism   Strategies to restrain imports from one's market.

Psychographics   The study of people's attitudes and values.

Public Corporation   A business that sells shares of its stock on the stock market to the public.

Publicity   A nonpaid message—verbal or written—in a public-information medium about a company's merchandise, activities, or services.

Publicly Owned   A corporation whose shares are available for sale to any person who chooses to purchase these shares; this means the shareholders (stockholders) collectively own the company.

Pull System   Determining the consumer's needs and wants and basing production on that information.

Push System   Force feeding a product line through the manufacturing and marketing process in hopes the consumer will like it.

QR (Quick Response)   A computerized partnership between different segments of the industry. Its purpose is to supply customers with products or services in the precise quantities required at exactly the right time. Computer technologies are important in Quick Response systems.

Quota   Quantitative restrictions placed on exporting countries on the number of units of specific product categories that may be shipped to a particular importing country over a specified period of time.

Rapid Replenishment   A Quick Response system that permits quick replacement of items sold by the retailer. When an item is sold, the manufacturer has a replacement item in the retailer's stock in a matter of days.

Ready-to-Wear   Apparel that is mass-produced in standardized sizes as opposed to apparel made to a customer's special order (custom made).

Real-Time Merchandising   The continuous analysis of fashion direction, consumer style testing results, and current retail sales that permits manufacturers and retailers to operate in "real time" (much closer to the selling season) rather than having merchandise tied up in the pipeline for months.

Relationship Marketing   Identifying the needs of a specific group of customers, customizing merchandise assortments around those customers'

needs, and maintaining an ongoing relationship with those consumers.

Reorder Number   A style number that continues to be ordered by buyers.

Resident Buying Office   Formerly, a service organization located in a major market center that reports market information, acts as market representative, and renders other related services to a group of stores who have their own buyers. Today, these organizations provide other kinds of services (e.g., product development, merchandising, and sourcing) and may do no *buying* at all.

Resource   A vendor or source of supply.

Restructuring   The changes a sector or company goes through in its efforts to remain competitive in response to changing market conditions.

Retailing   The business of buying goods from a variety of resources for resale to ultimate consumers.

Royalty   A compensation paid to the owner of a right (name, brand, etc.) for the use of that right.

Sales Operations   Carry out the firm's marketing and merchandising plans by physically selling the line to retail customers.

Sales Promotion   Any activity that is used to influence the sale of merchandise, services, or ideas.

Sample   The model or trial garment (may be original in design, a copy, or an adaptation) to be shown to the trade or perhaps made to check the design effectiveness and fit of the garment.

Season   In retailing, a selling period.

Secondary Fashion Centers   Regional market centers outside New York City; examples include Los Angeles, Dallas, and Chicago.

Secondary Market   Producers of finished consumer fashion products (dresses, coats, suits, accessories, and the like).

Sell Through   A measurement of the amount of merchandise sold of a particular merchandise category or style.

Seventh Avenue   An expression used as a synonym for New York City's women's apparel industry (actually, a street on which the showrooms of many garment manufacturers are located).

Shareholders (also referred to as *Stockholders*)   The individuals who own a publicly held company because they own stock in the firm.

Shopping Centers   A group of retail stores and related facilities planned, developed, and managed as a unit.

Showing   See Fashion Show or Showing.

Silhouette   The overall outline or contour of a costume. Also frequently referred to as *shape* or *form*.

SKU   Stock-keeping unit.

Smart   Having a fashionable appearance.

Socioeconomics   Pertaining to a combination or interaction of social and economic factors.

Softgoods Industry   This is a broad term that includes the production and distribution of products made of textile-related materials.

Sourcing   For retailers as well as manufacturers, the process of determining how and where merchandise (or components) will be obtained. In apparel manufacturing and retailing this term is often used to refer to where garments will be manufactured (assembled).

Specialty Store   A retail establishment that deals either in one category of merchandise or in related categories of merchandise.

Specification Buying   Occurs when a retailer contracts the production of private-label merchandise, providing precise specifications for the end product. In recent years, as retailers have essentially become manufacturers themselves (developing product lines and monitoring closely the production), this term understates the responsibilities now assumed by many retailers in the manufacturing process.

Square Meter Equivalent (SME)   A measure for tracking textile and apparel imports to restrict shipments according to quota levels.

Standard Industrial Classification (SIC)   Former U.S. system established by the U.S. Office of Management and Budget to classify establishments into industry groupings on the basis of their primary economic activity.

Stockouts   An industry term that refers to not having the merchandise a consumer wants in the desired size, color, etc. when the consumer wants it.

Store Ambience   The look and feeling of the retail store that a consumer experiences on entering and shopping there.

Store Ownership Group   A retailing organization consisting of a group of stores that are centrally owned and controlled in terms of broad policy making but are operated autonomously.

Style (noun)   A type of product with specific characteristics that distinguish it from another type of the same product.

Style (verb)   To give fashion features to an article or group of articles (as to style a line of coats and suits, for example).

Style Number   An identification number given to an individual design by a manufacturer. The retailer uses the number when ordering the item and for stock identification.

Style Piracy   The use of a design without the consent of the originator.

Style Testing   A strategy to determine consumer interest in new apparel or other products by introducing a few items and carefully watching the extent to which consumers buy them.

Stylist   One who advises concerning styles in clothes, furnishings, and the like.

Subcontracting   When contractors distribute the garment production even further; subcontracting often occurs in very small shops or in homes.

Subsidies   A form of government payment or support to exporters so they may compete more effectively in world markets.

Supercenters   A combination of discount store and supermarket with a total of 175,000 or more square feet of selling space.

Superstores   The "big box" stores that carry extensive product lines and undercut other retailers in price. These include the "category killers" or "power retailers."

Supply Chain Management   The planning and execution process for the transformation of raw materials to a useful product for the end user, using shared supply and demand information (definition supplied by Jim Lovejoy, Industry Director, Supply Chain Analysis, [TC]^2)

Sweatshops   Illegal garment production facilities that do not meet U.S. government standards for wages, benefits, and healthy working conditions.

Target Market   A particular segment of a total potential market selected by a company as the object of its marketing efforts.

Tariff   A tax leveled against imported products, also known as *duty*.

Telemarketing   Sales of products and services via an interactive system or two-way television or via telephone.

Texitalia   An important textile trade show held in Milan, Italy.

Textile Mill Products   That segment of the industry that converts fibers into finished fabrics; this includes spinning and texturing yarns; knitting, weaving, and tufting; and dyeing, printing, and other finishing.

Third World The poorer countries of the world. These are also sometimes known as the less-developed countries (LDCs) or the developing countries.

Trade The sale of goods or services from one country to another.

Trade Association A nonprofit voluntary association of businesses having common interests.

Trade Attorneys Specialists in trade law who assist their clients in importing and exporting activities.

Trade Balance The difference between a country's imports on one hand and exports on the other. A negative balance (deficit) means the country receives more imports than it exports; a positive balance (surplus) means the country exports more than it imports.

Trade Deficit A condition in international trade in which the value of a country's imports is in excess of the value of its imports.

Trade Publications Newspapers or magazines published specifically for professionals in a special field.

Trade Show Periodic merchandise exhibits staged in various trading areas by groups of producers.

Transshipment When a country that has used all its quota sends products to another with available quota so the shipment appears to come from the second country.

Triangle Shirtwaist Fire A fire that occurred in the Triangle Shirtwaist factory in 1911 and took 146 lives. The tragedy was the turning point in the "sweatshop" era because it awoke the public conscience to the labor conditions in the garment industry.

Trunk Show A producer's or designer's complete collection of samples brought into the store for a limited time to take orders from customers.

UNITE The Union of Needletrades, Industrial & Textile Employees. In 1995, the International Ladies' Garment Workers' Union (ILGWU) and the Amalgamated Clothing and Textile Workers Union (ACTWU) merged to form UNITE.

UPC Universal product code. A special bar-code symbol that has been adopted as a standard for the retail industry. The code consists of a one-digit merchandise category code, a five-digit UPC vendor number, a five-digit item number, and a one-digit check digit.

Upgrading When countries "trade up" to ship higher-priced products so they maximize what they can send under quote restrictions.

Vendeuse French term meaning saleswoman.

Vendor One who sells; resource from which a retailer buys goods.

Volume Amount of dollar sales done in a given period by a retail store or other mercantile establishment.

Warehouse Club A retail establishment that specializes in bulk sales of nationally branded merchandise at discount prices.

Women's Wear Daily Trade publication of the women's fashion industries. (The textile and menswear counterpart is *DNR*, previously known as *Daily News Record*.)

World Trade Organization (WTO) The international body that promotes free trade among nations and spells out reciprocal rights and obligations for member countries.

Select World Wide Web Sites

The following are a few relevant World Wide Web sites that readers will find useful in obtaining timely information on topics relevant to this book. The reader must keep in mind that these change frequently.

Sites for Online Job Hunting
(Most of these are general and serve all fields.)

Job Search Navigators/ Search Engines

AltaVista Careers
   www.careeraltavista.com/
Job Search and Employment Opportunities: Best Bets from the Net
   www.lib.umich.edu/chdocs/employment/
Career Paradise—Colossal List of Career Links
   www.service.emory.edu/CAREER/Main/
   Links.html
JobHunt: Outstanding Job Resources
   www.job-hunt.org
Yahoo!Internet Life: Employment Resources
   www3.zdnet.com/yil/content/profit/profess/
   empl1.html
Job Bank USA
   www.jobbankusa.com
Career Links
   www.careers.org
www.careershop.com
   www.careershop.com
Job and Career Site Links
   www.usbol.com/wjmackey/weblinks.html
Employment Spot
   www.employmentspot.com
www.about.com
   www.about.com

Job and Career Links
   www.gordonworks.com

Job and Career Sites

(Some have fees.)

Career Threads (Apparel Industry)
   www.careerthreads.com
FashionNet (under "Jobs")
   www.fashion.net/jobs/positionso.php
Retail Jobs
   www.retailjobnet.com
Retail Job Mart
   www.retailjobmart.com
Retail JobNet
   www.retailjobnet.com/cf/main/cfm
RetailSeek.com
   www.retailseek.com
Careers in Retailing
   www.careersinretailing.com
Direct Marketing Job Center
   www.dmworld.com/jobcenter/jobs.html
Textile Web
   www.textileweb.com
Career City
   www.careercity.com
The Riley Guide
   www.dbm.com/jobguide
The Job Center
   www.jobcenter.com
Career Mosaic
   www.careermosaic.com

Monster Board
   www.monster.com
CareerWeb
   www.careerweb.com
CAREERMagazine
   www.careermag.com
Job Web
   www.jobweb.org
www.internetsourcebook.com
   www.internetsourcebook.com
Interbiznet.com
   Interbiznet.com
CareerPath
   www.careerpath.com
JOBTRAK
   www.jobtrak.com
Career Shop
   www.careershop.com
America's Job Bank
   www.ajb.dni.us
FedWorld
   www.fedworld.gov
Bilingual Jobs
   www.bilingual-jobs.com
Careerbabe
   www.careerbabe.com
Careerbuilder
   www.careerbuilder.com
Recruiters Online Network
   www.ipa.com
Minorities Job Bank
   www.minoritiesjobbank.com
Fedworld Federal Job Announcements
   www.fedworld.gov
Global Careers
   www.globalcareers.com
Great Summer Jobs
   www.gsj.petersons.com
Help Wanted USA
   www.iccweb.com
Hoovers Online
   www.hoovers.com
International Jobs
   www.internationaljobs.org
Careertips.com
   www.careertips.com
Nationjob
   www.nationjob.com
JobDirect.com
   www.jobdirect.com
Occupational Outlook Handbook
   www.bls.gov/ocohome.htm

Resume Banks

(Some have fees.)

Yahoo Resume Bank
   www.yahoo.com
A+ Online Resumes
   ol-resume.com/
Resumes on the Web
   www.resweb.com
Shawn's Internet Resume Center
   www.inpursuit.com/sirc/

Sites Relevant to the Fashion Industry

Softgoods Industry Sites (Total Chain)

AMTEX
   http://amtex.sandia.gov
Demand Activated Manufacturing (DAMA)
   http://dama.tis.llnl.gov
Textile/Clothing Technology Corp. [TC]^2
   http://www.tc2.com
Textile Information Management Systems (TIMS)
   http://www.unicate.com
Textile Institute
   http://www.texi.org

Apparel Industry Sites

American Apparel and Footwear Assn.
   www.americanapparel.org
American Apparel Producers' Network
   www.usawear.org
Apparel Net (The Apparel Market Place)
   www.apparel.net/
Canadian Apparel Federation (CAF)
   www.apparel.org
Children's Apparel Manufacturers Association
   www.cama-apparel.org
Fashion Group International
   www.fgi.org

Fashion (General)

Fashion Net
   www.fashion.net
Fashion Icon
   fashion-icon.com
Just-Style.com
   www.just-style.com

Textile Sites

American Association of Textile Chemists and Colorists
  www.aatcc.org
American Textile Machinery Association
  www.webmasters.net/atma
American Textile Manufacturers Institute
  www.atmi.org
Cotton Incorporated
  cottoninc.com/online/index.cfm
FiberSource
  www.fibersource.com
Knitted Textiles Association
  www.kta-usa.org
National Textile Center
  ntc.tx.ncsu.edu
Textile Link
  www.textilelink.com
Textile Organization
  www.textiles.org
Textile Web
  www.textileweb.com/links/

Retailing Sites

International Council of Shopping Centers
  www.icsc.org
International Mass Retail Association
  www.imra.org
National Retail Federation (NRF)
  www.nrf.com

Accessories, Intimate Apparel, Cosmetics

Footwear Industries of America
  www.fia.org
The Cosmetic, Toiletry, and Fragrance Association
  www.ctfa.org
The Fashion Beauty Internet Association
  www.fbia.com
The Fragrance Foundation
  http://fragrance.org
The Hosiery Association
  www.nahm.com
Intimate Apparel Council
  www.apparel.net/iac

Fur and Leather

Fur Information Council of America
  www.fur.org
Leather World
  www.leatherworld.com

U.S. Government Agency Sites

American Textile (AMTEX) Partnership
  apc.pnl.gov: 2080/amtex.www/amtex.html
Bureau of Economic Analysis
  www.bea.doc.gov
Federal Trade Commission
  www.ftc.gov
Fedstats
  www.fedstats.gov
FedWorld Information Network
  www.fedworld.gov
Global Export Market Information System
  www.itaiep.doc.gov
North American Industry Classification System (NAICS)
  www.ntis.gov/naics
U.S. Census Bureau
  www.census.gov
U.S. Census Bureau Retailing Reports
  www.census.gov/econ/www.retmenu.html
U.S. Department of Labor
  www.dol.gov
U.S. Customs Service (USCS)
  www.uscs.gov
U.S. Department of Commerce
  www.doc.gov
U.S. International Trade Commission
  www.usitc.gov
Environmental Protection Agency
  www.epa.gov
Federal Trade Commission
  www.ftc.gov
U.S. Office of Textiles and Apparel
  otexa.ita.doc.gov
The World Factbook (CIA)
  www.odci.gov/cia/publications/nsolo/wfb-all.htm
U.S. Big Emerging Markets (BEMS)
  www.stat-usa.gov/itabems.html

Sourcing

The Agent
  www.halper.com/agent
APPARELmart
  www.apparelmart.com
Apparel and Textile Network
  www.at-net.com
Apparel Exchange
  www.apparelex.com
Apparel Industry Sourcing Site
  fashiondex.com

ApparelNet
>www.apparel.net

ApparelSourcingNet
>www.apparelsourcing.net

FabricLink
>www.fabriclink.com

Fabric Stock Exchange (Fabrics.com)
>www.fabrics.com

Fabric Marketing Research
>www.fabricmarketing.com

Garment Industry Sourcing Corporation
>www.gidc.org

National Sourcing Database
>www.nsdb.net

Sourcing Trade Show.com
>www.sourcingtradeshow.com

Textile Source
>www.textilesource.com

Textile Web
>www.textileweb.com

Virtual Garment Center
>www.garment.com

World Trade Exchange
>www4.wte.net

Consumer Sites

American Demographics
>www.demographics.com

Consumer.gov
>www.consumer.gov

Consumer Reports
>www.consumerreports.org

Federal Consumer Information Center
>www.pueblo.gsa.gov

Consumer Product Safety Commission
>www.cpsc.gov

Conference Board (consumer confidence)
>www.conference-board.org

Consumer Expenditure Survey
>http://stats.bls.gov

Fashion Trends

Color Marketing Group
>www.colormarketing.org

Color Association of the United States
>www.colorassociation.com

First View
>www.firstview.com

International Sites

International Business Network
>www1.usa1.com/~ibnet/

International Monetary Fund
>www.imf.org

International Labour Organization
>www.ilo.org

United Nations
>www.un.org

World Bank
>www.worldbank.org

World Trade Organization
>www.wto.org

Union/Labor

Child Labor in the Apparel Sector
>http://www.dol.gov/dol/ilab/public/media/reports/apparel/lc.htm

Sweatshop Watch
>www.sweatshopwatch.org

Union of Needletrades, Industrial, and Textile Employees (UNITE)
>www.uniteunion.org

Worldwide Responsible Apparel Production (WRAP)
>www.wrapapparel.org

Media

America's Textiles International
>www.billian.com

Apparel Industry Magazine
>www.aimagazine.com

Apparel Strategist
>www.appstrat.com

Bazaar
>viabazaar.com

Behind the Seams
>www.behind-the-seams.com

Bobbin Magazine
>www.bobbin.com

Daily News Record
>www.dailynewsrecord.com

Elle
>www.ellemag.com

Esquire
>www.esquire2b.com

Fashion-Icon
>www.fashion-icon.com

Fashion Planet
>www.fashion-planet.com

Fiber Organon
     www.fibersource.com
International Fiber Journal
     www.ifj.com
Online Textile News Weekly
     www.onlinetextilenews.com
Retailer News Online
     retailernews.com
Stores
     www.stores.org
Textile World
     www.textileworld.com
Yahoo!Finance: Textile News
     biz.yahoo.com/news/textiles.html
World Apparel Magazine
     www.world-apparel.com
World Textile Business News
     www.emergingtextiles.com

WorldStyle
     www.worldstyle.com
Women's Wear Daily
     www.wwd.com

"Virtual Malls"

Apparel Net (The Apparel Market Place)
     www.apparel.net/
Fashion Trip
     http://www.fashiontrip.com
Fashion Mall (mostly accessories)
     http://www.fashionmall.com
Girlshop (funky designers)
     http://www.girlshop.com
MCI Marketplace
     http://www.internetmci.com
Shopping 2000
     http://www.shopping2000.com

The Influential Designers

These are the people who have had the greatest design impact on the fashion industry in the past several decades. Some of them are superb craftsmen and women whose knowledge of fabric, cut, and production have enabled millions to be clothed with taste and style. Others have raised fashion design to the level of art. In all cases, they have either created lasting trends, established standards of excellence, or been a major influence on future generations.

Joseph Abboud   Well-known American designer of menswear, blending European styling and American practicality.

Adolfo   Began as milliner, added separates, custom blouses, long skirts in late '60s . . . devoted following of status dressers.

Gilbert Adrian   MGM's top designer, 1923–1939, for stars such as Crawford, Hepburn, Garbo . . . wide shoulders, tailored suits.

Azzedine Alaia   Sexy clothes that cling to every curve from this contemporary Paris ready-to-wear designer.

Walter Albini   Early Italian rtw designer.

Hardy Amies   British couturier for men and women, noted for his tailored suits, coats, cocktail and evening dresses.

Giorgio Armani   Major Italian rtw force for men and women . . . beautifully tailored clothes . . . now at peak of his powers.

Source: Includes some information drawn from WWD: 75 Years in Fashion 1910–1985 *and* WWD Profiles, *September 1999.*

Laura Ashley   Romantic Victorian looks in fabrics and fashion . . . built a London-based empire in clothes and home furnishings.

Cristobal Balenciaga   One of century's greatest . . . innovations include semifitted jacket, cocoon coat, balloon skirt, bathrobe coat, pillbox hat . . . disciples include Givenchy, Courreges, Ungaro.

Pierre Balmain   Opened own Paris house in 1945 . . . classic daytime looks, extravagant evening gowns.

Patrick De Barentzen   "Daring" member of Italian couture in the '60s . . . whimsical . . . enormous Infanta skirts.

Jean Barthet   Influential milliner of the '50s and '60s . . . customers ranged from Princess Grace to Sophia Loren.

Geoffrey Beene   Considered by many to be one of America's most creative designers, was inadvertently omitted from this article. Known for his innovative combination of textures, fabrics and unusual designs.

Bill Blass   Mr. Fashion Right . . . taste, durability and a consistent high level of talent since the late '50s.

Marc Bohan   Joined House of Dior in the early '60s and was there until 1989. Replaced by Gianfranco Ferre (couturier for Dior).

Donald Brooke   Most successful period was the '60s . . . also did much work for Broadway stage.

Stephen Burrows   Body-conscious clothes in vibrant colors . . . noted for his draped matte jerseys.

Roberto Capucci Started in Rome at age 21 . . . very hot in the '50s . . . known for drapery, imaginative cutting.

Pierre Cardin King of the licensing game . . . top innovator of the '50s and '60s, became first Paris couturier to sell his own rtw . . . now involved in everything from rock to restaurants.

Hattie Carnegie Influential in the '30s and '40s . . . began as milliner, then designed custom and rtw . . . influenced Norell, Trigère, McCardell.

Bonnie Cashin An American sportswear original—casual country and travel clothes in wool jersey, knits, tweeds, canvas, leather.

Antonio Del Castillo The Infanta silhouette . . . designed for Lanvin from 1950 to 1963, then opened his own house in Paris.

John Cavanaugh One of Britain's best in the '50s . . . headed Curzon St. . . . known for nipped-waist, full-skirt New Look.

Hussein Chalayan A leading British designer at the turn of the millennium with strong technical qualities, reflecting his interest in technology and architecture.

Coco Chanel Chanel No. 5 . . . the house on the rue Cambon . . . the Chanel suit: braid-trim, collarless jacket, patch pockets . . . feminism before it was fashionable . . . the one and only.

Aldo Cipullo Jeweler for Cartier's in the '70s . . . elegance, but with a light approach.

Liz Claiborne Contemporary sportswear . . . executive dressing . . . great commercial success.

Ossie Clark Enfant terrible of British fashion in the '60s . . . HotPants, maxi coats . . . started '40s revival in 1968.

Sybil Connolly Ireland's most prestigious designer.

Andres Courreges The Basque tailor . . . hot in the '60s, with suits and roomy coats . . . Tough Chic . . . the great white way.

Angela Cummings Designed jewelry for Tiffany's, now on her own . . . inventive and tasteful.

Lilly Dache From the '30s to '50s, U.S.'s top milliner . . . draped turbans, brimmed hats, snoods . . . fantasies for films.

David Dart Contemporary California designer of the '90s . . . winner of many design awards for his chic contemporary designs.

Donald Davies English shirtmaker who is based in Dublin and went to shirtdresses in the '60s . . . he used featherweight Irish tweed in a variety of colors.

Christian Dior Launched the New Look in 1947, becoming fashion's most famous name until his death 10 years later.

Jean Dresses Designed from 1925–1965 . . . his Jean Dresses Diffusion, a lower-price line for America, the start of mass production by a French couturier.

Perry Ellis Appeared in the '70s as one of the avant-garde young sportswear designers . . . gave classics a high-fashion twist.

Alberto Fabiani One of Italy's top couturiers of the '50s . . . "surgeon of coats and suits" . . . conservative tailoring . . . wed Simonetta Visconti.

Jacques Fath Enfant terrible, showman, ran own Paris house from 1937–1954 . . . sexy clothes, hourglass shapes, plunging necklines.

Salvatore Ferragamo Italian shoemaker who became international success . . . pioneer of wedge heel, platform sole, Lucite acrylics heel.

Gianfranco Ferre Architectural approach has turned him into one of Italy's leading rtw designers.

Anne Fogarty Spearheaded the revolution in junior sizes in the early '50s.

Fontana Sisters One of Italy's leading couture houses in the '50s, started by mother, Amabile, in 1907, continued by daughters Zoe, Micol and Giovanna.

Tom Ford Inspired young American designer hired to play a leading role at Yves Saint Laurent after Gucci acquired YSL.

Federico Forquet Big in the '60s in Rome, noted for coats and suits in blocks of bold color . . . went into interior design in 1972.

Mariano Fortuny Mushroom-pleated silk tea gowns . . . his clothes now are collectors' items.

James Galanos Born in Philadelphia, studied in New York, worked in Paris, opened own business in Los Angeles . . . one of America's most elegant fashion creators.

Irene Galitzine Palazzo pajamas of the '60s an important concept . . . now in cosmetics, furs, linens.

John Galliano Givenchy's replacement following the great master's retirement. Specialization of bias-cut evening wear.

Jean-Paul Gaultier One of Paris's trendiest and more controversial rtw designers for men and women.

Rudi Gernreich Avant-garde sportswear . . . maillots . . . topless swimsuit, 1964 . . . see-through blouses . . . the No-Bra.

Hubert de Givenchy   A major couturier since he opened own House in Paris in '52 . . . influenced by Balenciaga . . . most famous client: Audrey Hepburn.

Alix Gres   Originally a sculptress . . . couturiere since 1934 . . . known for statuesque and molded gowns "sculpted" on live model.

Aldo Gucci   Head of Florence-based family business . . . manufacturer and retailer of leathers, luggage and apparel . . . GG.

Halston   Began as milliner at Bergdorf's, did Jacqueline Kennedy's pillbox hat, 1961 . . . opened couture business in '68, rtw in '72 . . . simple classics . . . name licensed by J.C. Penney.

Norman Hartnell   London's biggest couture house in the '30s . . . coronation gowns for Queen Elizabeth.

Edith Head   Probably Hollywood's best-known designer.

Jacques Heim   Successful Paris couturier from 1923 until the early '60s . . . designer of Atome, the first bikini.

Stan Herman   Designer and owner of Mr. Mort during the '60s and '70s . . . popularized "fashion at a price" . . . revived chenille as a fashion fabric in the '80s and '90s . . . leading uniform designer of the world . . . three-time Coty Award winner . . . President of the Council of Fashion Designers of America.

Tommy Hilfiger   Masterful designer/marketer of Americana casualwear, first for men and later for women. His lines caught on early with urban youth, with great popularity among rappers.

Barbara Hulanicki   Mod look, the early '60s . . . a founder of Biba . . . the Total Look: coordinated color in clothes, cosmetics, hose.

Irene   Top designer for movie stars for many decades, also had own rtw business in the '60s.

Mark Jacobs   Influential in introducing the grunge look when he designed for Perry Ellis. Now designs for Louis Vuitton.

Charles James   The Eccentric One . . . ran own custom business in the '40s and '50s . . . innovative shapes . . . the Dali of design.

Mr. John   One of America's best-known milliners, especially in the '40s and '50s—the heyday of hats.

Betsey Johnson   Big in the '60s . . . low prices, offbeat fashions . . . designed for Paraphernalia, cofounded Betsey Bunky, Nini.

Stephen Jones   London's extraordinary milliner who designs hats for such notables as Lady Di.

Norma Kamali   Her contemporary sweatshirt clothes made high fashion affordable by a young audience.

Jacques Kaplan   Headed Georges Kaplan, New York furrier . . . innovator and promoter . . . a pioneer of "fun" furs.

Donna Karan   High-profile designer of elegant sportswear, with appeal to customers in the U.S. and many other countries. Previously Anne Klein's assistant, then her successor before launching her own company.

Rei Kawakubo   Comme des Garcons . . . one of the first of the New Wave from Japan in the '80s.

Kenzo   Left Japan for Paris in 1965 . . . light, whimsical rtw.

Emmanuelle Khanh   One of the first major rtw designers in Paris in the '60s . . . kicky, young clothes.

Charles Kleibacker   Journalism, show business, then fashion . . . opened own business in New York in 1960 . . . known for bias cuts . . . later fashion educator.

Anne Klein   A major American sportswear designer . . . associated with Junior Sophisticates, 1951–1964 . . . classic sportswear.

Calvin Klein   Pure American looks in sportswear and rtw . . . clean lines, sophistication and a wide range of prices.

Michael Kors   Stresses spare, simple designs that are wearable, liveable, timeless.

Christian Lacroix   Energized the sleeping, sedate House of Patou and the Paris couture with his dramatic "operatic."

Karl Lagerfeld   Outspoken, controversial, avant-garde . . . designed for Chloe, now for Fendi and Chanel.

Helmut Lang   Viennese designer whose designs became popular in the 1990s. His audacious techno-hip style gives minimalism a new edge.

Jeanne Lanvin   One of earliest Paris couturiers . . . peak years between two World Wars . . . her perfumes: My Sin and Arpege.

Ralph Lauren   Noted for his Americana-influenced designs . . . highly successful marketer of lifestyle fashions that speak of class and style. Began in the fashion industry as a tie designer.

Lucien Lelong   Great name in Paris couture from the '20s to '40s . . . didn't design himself, but inspired workers such as Dior, Balmain, Givenchy, and Schlumberger.

Jean Louis Not only a successful Hollywood designer, but also headed his own couture firm.

Claire McCardell Perhaps the most profound influence on American sportswear design . . . hot in the '40s and '50s.

Mary McFadden Socialite who first started designing exotic jewelry . . . her pleated evening dresses became the rage in the late '70s.

Alexander McQueen A leading British designer by the turn of the millennium, known for his aggressive, provocative style.

Mainbocher One of America's first custom designers in Paris . . . dressed Duchess of Windsor . . . specialized in quiet quality.

Germana Marucelli Avant-garde Milanese couturiere of the '50s and '60s.

Vera Maxwell Pioneer of American sportswear.

Nicole Miller Made her mark by specializing in unique prints for scarves, men's ties, and so on. Expanded into a much broader line, still using her prints.

Missoni One of the early Italian rtw families . . . known for knits in original colors and designs.

Issey Miyake Avant-garde Japanese designer, predated Japan's New Wave.

Anna Molinari Italian designer whose fashion is a mix of sensation and cultural influences, revisiting the past while divining the future for the romantic and glamorous woman. Lines include her name line, Blumarine, Blugirl, and Blumarine Vomo (the last for men).

Capt. Edward Molyneux From the '20s to '40s, his purity of line drew the rich and famous to his Paris salon. Brief revival in the '60s.

Claude Montana Contemporary French rtw . . . big shoulders . . . leathers . . . architectural shapes.

Hanae Mori Comes from Japan, shows in France . . . tasteful clothes in beautiful colors . . . innovative beading.

Digby Morton Early British couturier . . . opened house in 1933 . . . specialized in tailored suits, cableknit sweaters, Donegal tweeds.

Thierry Mugler Tongue-in-chic fashion from one of Paris's New Wave designers.

Jean Muir Started in the '60s in London . . . elegant, intricately detailed young clothes.

Norman Norell Brought American fashion to the level of Paris couture.

Todd Oldham Creator of simple shapes, often in bold colors and embellished with beading and embroidery.

Frank Olive Sophisticated and slick hats have been his forté since the '60s.

Andre Oliver Associated with Pierre Cardin since 1955 . . . created clothes for men and women.

Paquin One of the first Paris couturiers . . . house opened in 1891 and lasted until 1956.

Mollie Parnis One of the most successful women designers and manufacturers on SA.

Jean Patou A businessman and showman as well as a designer of elegant, ladylike couture clothes in the '20s and '30s.

Mme. Paulette Leading American milliner in the '50s and '60s . . . associated with Saks Fifth Avenue.

Sylvia Pedlar Put high fashion into loungewear . . . founded Irish Lingerie and designed there 40 years.

Elsa Peretti Revolutionary jewelry designer . . . diamonds by the yard . . . made small diamonds fashionable . . . innovator in silver.

Robert Piquet Ran his Paris couture house from 1933 to 1951 . . . influenced Givenchy and Dior, both of whom were employed by him.

Paul Poiret One of first French couturiers to free women from constraints of underpinnings . . . leader of early 20th century.

Thea Porter Antiestablishment London designer of the '60s and '70s . . . fantasy long clothes . . . Orientalia.

Anna Potok A key influence in fur design . . . founder of Maximilian.

Miuccia Prada Emerged from the family's luxury leather business to become one of the most influential designers of the 1990s. Responsible for bringing Conservative Chic, Thrift Chic and new length hems—stopping at or just below the knee—into prominence.

Emilio Pucci His prints on thin silk jerseys revolutionized Italian fashion in the '50s and '60s.

Lilly Pulitzer Her printed-cotton shift, the "Lilly," swept the nation in the '60s and '70s . . . floral prints . . . Palm Beach.

Mary Quant A miniskirt pioneer synonymous with the "swinging London" look of the '60s . . . Carnaby St.

Madeleine de Rauche Renowned sportswoman who created sports clothes for herself and friends . . . made functional clothes in the '30s.

Oscar de la Renta Came to U.S. to work for Elizabeth Arden in the early '60s . . . one of SA's "luxury" designers.

Zandra Rhodes A London original . . . outrageous evening looks . . . fantasy colorings for hair and makeup.

Jacqueline de Ribes A socialite-turned-designer . . . her love of couture quality is reflected in her rtw.

Nina Ricci Opened her house in Paris in 1932 . . . dressed mature, elegant women . . . pioneered showing lower-priced clothes in a boutique . . . her fragrance: L'Air du Temps.

John Rocha One of Britain's most successful designer exports of the '90s, going to Paris, but returning to London . . . known for innovative, experimental use of fabric and color, layering of textures, and simplicity of silhouette . . . designs sometimes viewed as "nonfashion" fashions.

Marcel Rochas Elegant French Couture of the '30s and '40s . . . packaged a perfume called Femme in black lace.

Carolyne Roehm Oscar de la Renta's former assistant, who married a financier and designs the kind of clothes her socialite friends love to wear.

Sonia Rykiel The genius of sweater dressing.

Yves Saint Laurent One of the century's greatest influences on fashion and taste.

Jill Sander One of Germany's fashion powerhouses, now a successful international apparel and cosmetics business. Her clothes combine quality with modernity of fabrics and shapes, minimal but on the edge of forward.

Count Fernando Sarmi Beautiful evening clothes . . . chief designer at Elizabeth Arden, 1951–1959, then head of his own business.

Jean-Louis Scherrer His soft, refined dresses popular in the '60s . . . opened own Paris house in 1962.

Elsa Schiaparelli The Great Schiap . . . one of the true avant-garde designers in Paris from the '30s to '50s.

Jean Schlumberger Legendary jeweler whose exuberant fantasies have pleased women such as Bunny Mellon and Babe Paley since the late '40s.

Mila Schoen Important Italian designer of the '60s and '70s.

Ken Scott Expatriate from Indiana who settled in Milan . . . fabric and dress designer since 1956 . . . Art Nouveau influenced.

Simonetta One of the first of the Italian couture designers . . . married Albert Fabiani.

Adele Simpson One of SA's durables . . . in her own business since 1949 . . . known for conservative good taste.

Stephen Sprouse Contemporary, controversial designs, strongly influenced by the '60s.

Gustave Tassell Started own business in Los Angeles, 1959 . . . refined, no-nonsense clothes.

Pauline Trigère A pioneer American designer . . . started own business in 1942, still going strong.

Emanuel Ungaro Once known as "the young terrorist" of fashion, built one of the most successful fashion empires, with licenses for women's lines, men's wear, accessories and perfume, and boutiques and in-store shops. The house of Ungaro was bought by Ferragamo in 1996.

Valentina Russian-born, opened own couture business in America in 1928 . . . dramatic clothes . . . dressed Garbo, whom she resembled.

Valentino The Chic . . . one of the most important European couturiers since the mid-'60s . . . taste, elegance, timelessness.

Philippe Venet Givenchy's master tailor, 1953–1962, then opened own business . . . noted for lean suits, rounder shoulders.

Gianni Versace Italian rtw . . . an innovator for men and women in leathers and other fabrics. After his untimely death in the '90s, his fashion business has been headed by sister Donatella.

Sally Victor From mid-'30s to mid-'60s, one of America's most prominent milliners.

Madeleine Vionnet The inventor of the bias cut and a major influence on fashion since early in the 1900s.

David Webb Known for his enamel-and-jeweled bracelets in the '60s.

John Weitz Women's sportswear with menswear look . . . big in the '50s and '60s . . . now only in menswear . . . once "designed" a cigar.

Vivienne Westwood Contemporary, controversial English designer . . . runs World's End, off-beat London boutique.

Charles Frederick Worth Dressmaker for Empress Eugenie and "founder" of French couture when he opened his own house.

B. H. Wragge Owner-designer of Sydney Wragge, pioneered concept of sportswear separates . . . important in the '40s and '50s.

Yohji Yamamoto Oversize, dramatic Japanese clothes.

Ben Zuckerman The master tailor . . . major influence on American coats and suits.

Career Opportunities in Fashion

Fashion is everywhere, and so are career opportunities for those who combine a knowledge of the fashion business with their own talent, ambition, and ability. Consider that a fashion career may open up anywhere along the road from raw materials to the final consumer purchase; stores, mail-order houses, other forms of retailing, manufacturing companies, advertising agencies, newspapers, magazines, commercial photography studios, and public relations firms are among the student's targets in the quest for a foothold in fashion.

Personal attributes suggest the direction a beginner should take. An outgoing personality helps in sales work at all levels, in showroom work, in public relations, and especially in jobs such as that of fashion coordinator, in which one often needs persuasive skills to sell one's ideas to other executives in the organization. The gift of a great figure (or physique, for men) or a photogenic face can make modeling a possibility and, through that work, a chance to learn from inside many other phases of the fashion business. Visually creative people do well in design, display, advertising, photography, and sketching for designers and fashion information services. Analytical minds adapt well to the multiple problems of managing retail fashion assortments or planning factory production, and thrive on market research.

The rewards of fashion careers are as varied as the jobs themselves. Some pay fabulously; others provide only a modest living. Some positions demand worldwide travel, to buy or observe, or to do both. Virtually all positions in the industry require an understanding of textiles and apparel in the global economy, even if one does not actually travel. Some jobs permit one to live at home and commute to an office, retail store, or manufacturing establishment. But all of them, and hundreds more, offer the student of fashion a chance to work, learn, and grow in the endlessly exciting, unceasingly stimulating business of fashion.

Most careers in the fashion industry today involve use of computer technologies. As the industry continues to transform itself in dramatic ways, individuals must continue to learn new skills (computer and other) and new approaches to doing business so they can adapt to changes in the business. Learning does not stop when one graduates from college! Otherwise, one will get left behind. Industry professionals must also stay abreast of worldwide and national news, reading all types of publications to be in touch with latest events and trends. These include business publications such as the *Wall Street Journal*, fashion trade materials, and any other publications that help one to stay on top of political, economic, and other news. One's work is likely to be affected by many of these current events.

The following is a guide to entry-level jobs in the fashion industry. It was originally prepared by Phyllis Madan and Marilyn Henrion of the Placement Department of the Fashion Institute of Technology, New York. For this edition of the book, these positions have been updated and modified somewhat. To be relevant for college students, entry-level positions are emphasized here. For an excellent summary of jobs in the apparel industry (including those beyond entry level), see the excellent Internet site developed by the Professional Leadership Council of the American Apparel and Footwear Association: www.careerthreads.com

Entry-Level Jobs for Fashion Design Graduates

- Assistant designer
- Cutting assistant
- Sketching assistant
- Sketcher (assistant to designer)
- Sketcher/stylist
- Junior designer

The personal qualities needed for all of the following jobs in the design room are similar. Applicants must be well organized, flexible, fast workers, and have the ability to work under pressure in often cramped working conditions. Fashionable grooming and neat appearance are essential. Most jobs require creativity and a good eye for trends in silhouette, color, and fabric. It is also important to have an understanding of the fashion industry (i.e., the "big picture") and the economic aspects of producing a line—that is, the enterprise must be *profitable* as well as creative to stay in business.

Assistant Designer

An individual in this role is responsible for executing designers' ideas by creating a first pattern from CAD computer files, slopers, or draping. Instructs and supervises the work of samplehands. Often required to keep records, order fabrics and trim, and do follow-up and clerical work. Although job is primarily technical in nature, one may be asked to shop stores for trends, sketch, and possibly consult with designer about fabric choices and designs.

Requirements: Fashion Design degree, good knowledge of garment construction (sewing), computer skills, strong technical skills (making first patterns, draping, and sketching). Beginners must have a portfolio.

Cutting Assistant

This may be a beginning assistant position in companies where there are several assistant designers. Cuts samples, alters patterns, generally assists in design room. Once ability is proven, may have opportunity to assist patternmaker or do draping.

Requirements: Fashion Design degree preferred, computer skills, good patternmaking skills, draping skills helpful, knowledge of garment construction.

Sketching Assistant

In this position an individual sketches principally for designers' records—precise technical sketches of constructed garment swatched with fabric and trim. May sketch freehand or by computer. May sketch and prepare artwork for presentations. Writes specification sheets on how garments are constructed. Usually orders fabric, handles a variety of clerical and follow-up duties. May do market research.

Requirements: Fashion Design degree and computer skills necessary. Ability to do precise technical sketches rapidly, either by computer or by hand, sometimes both. Portfolio required.

Sketcher (Assistant to Designer)

This person sketches freehand or computer illustration-quality sketches for designers' ideas, may be asked to contribute own design ideas, may deal with buyers, do promotional work. Hours are often long and irregular. Must be available to run errands and generally assist the designer.

Requirements: Fashion Design degree a must. Ability to do computer or freehand illustration-quality sketches at a fast pace. Outstanding portfolio required.

Sketcher/Stylist

An individual in this position works directly with principals of firm and product development staff. Shops stores for current trends, sketches ideas, works with patternmaker in developing these ideas, may not do technical work of draping and patternmaking. Participates in fabric selection, coordination of the line; may be involved in working with buyers in merchandising the line.

Requirements: Fashion Design degree, excellent portfolio, good eye for trends in silhouette, color, and fabric.

Junior Designer

This person sketches original designs, executes own first pattern, frequently sews sample. Does market research in fabrics and trends. Must be able to provide company with new design ideas and make accurate predictions on what will be salable in coming season. Must be able to design garments within company's price range. Job is fast-paced and a high-risk position because continuation of employment may be based on success of line.

Requirements: Fashion Design degree required. Strong creative ability as well as excellent computer and technical skills (draping, patternmaking, sewing). Good eye for trends (silhouette, color, fabric). Portfolio must show evidence of strong creative ability in designing coordinated line of apparel.

Entry-Level Jobs for Textile/Surface Design Graduates

- Textile/surface designer
- Colorist
- Assistant to stylist
- Lace and embroidery designer
- Screen print artist
- Woven fabric designer
- Painted woven designer
- Knit designer
- Assistant stylist

Jobs for Textile/Surface Design graduates are available in textile converting houses, vertical manufacturing (garment manufacturers that produce their own fabric), textile/surface design studios, department stores (private label), architectural firms (interior fabrics, wall coverings, carpeting), rug manufacturers, contract manufacturers/consultants, paper products manufacturers, china and giftware companies, color forecasting services, and computer graphics design firms.

Requirements: Degree in Textile/Surface Design. Excellent portfolio of designs exhibiting versatile skills and ability to meet professional standards. Must have strong computer skills, as much of this design work is done on computers today. Other requirements include initiative, reliability, following instructions, and meeting deadlines.

Textile/Surface Designer

Does original textile designs; may also do color combinations and repeats.

Colorist

Does various combinations for existing designs or products and may do original designs.

Assistant to Stylist

Not to be confused with assistant stylist, an upper-management position. Sets up appointments for stylist, acts as liaison with mills, works with clients and salespeople in stylist's absence, keeps clerical records.

Lace and Embroidery Designer

This position requires providing detailed technical drawings on graph paper of designs for lace and embroidery. Limited use of color.

Screen Print Artist

A person in this role executes designer's ideas through screen print process. Knowledge of color separations, layouts, repeats, and sample printing is required. An understanding of color and a knowledge of color formation is mandatory. Designers express themselves through the screen print process as a means of executing screened croquis and custom printing (limited or exclusive yardage) for both home furnishings and apparel. Again, much of this work is done on computers today.

Woven Fabric Designer

This individual does original designs and executes designer's ideas on handloom. Acts as an aide to stylist, sends out mill specs, does quality control, research, and resource work.

Painted Woven Designer

This person executes painted woven designs and colorations using ruling pen and airbrush; designs may be developed on computers.

Knit Designer

In this role, an individual executes knit swatches and designs on knit machines for apparel. Knitting skills are required. An understanding of the production process is necessary.

Assistant Stylist

This is a managerial position in a design firm or studio. Works with stylist in compiling lines, preparing storyboards, and forecasting; acts as liaison among stylists, designers, and clients.

Entry-Level Jobs for Advertising Design Graduates

- Pasteup and mechanical artist
- Layout artist
- Assistant art director

Jobs for Advertising Design graduates can be in either advertising or graphic design areas.

Advertising artists may work on trade or consumer accounts in advertising agencies, in-house advertising departments, or printing firms. They may work in print (magazines or newspaper) or television advertising.

Graphic designers develop "collateral material," which may consist of brochures, annual reports, packaging, logos and trademarks, corporate image projects, and so forth. They also may work in publishing, doing editorial layout for books and magazines. Board persons do the finished art to prepare it for the printer. They may work in either advertising or graphic design companies. Jobs require creativity, computer skills, and other graphic design skills.

Pasteup and Mechanical Artist

This artist prepares art for printer by pasting together elements of layout (type, illustration, photography), does color separations using T-square and ruling pen. May work for advertising agency, graphic design studio, service studio, printer, publication, or in-house corporate art department.

Requirements: Advertising Design degree or Illustration degree. Must have computer skills. Must have taken course in pasteups and mechanicals and have portfolio demonstrating precision and accuracy in executing mechanicals and color separations.

Layout Artist

This person designs layout for ads, usually under the supervision of the art director. Specifies typeface, does "comp" rendering to indicate what finished ad will look like when printed. May do own mechanicals.

Requirements: Advertising Design degree, portfolio demonstrating advertising layouts, thorough knowledge of typefaces, computer expertise, skill at "comp" rendering and mechanicals, neat and precise work habits.

Assistant Art Director

The individual in this role works directly with art director. May perform any or all of the following duties depending on the size and structure of the agency or firm: assist in developing concepts for advertising campaigns, rough and finished "comp" renderings, specifying type, mechanicals, pasteups, layout, and graphic design.

Requirements: Advertising Design degree, strong portfolio indicating thorough development of creative concepts through fast, crisp "comp" rendering; computer skills.

Alternate Entry Jobs for Advertising Design Graduates

Because of the highly competitive nature of most of the jobs just noted, graduates sometimes begin their careers by accepting nonart positions in the field such as Guy or Gal Friday, advertising assistant, or advertising production/traffic assistant. This is an excellent way to gain experience and contacts and get a foot in the door.

Entry-Level Jobs for Fashion Illustration Graduates

- Freelance illustrator
- Staff illustrator
- Sketcher

Freelance Illustrator

Jobs in illustration tend to be freelance rather than full-time. Freelance illustrators may do work for advertising agencies, retail stores, manufacturers, textile and fiber houses, pattern companies, display houses, and publications.

Requirements: Illustration degree required. Must have excellent portfolio indicating distinctive illustration style and creativity. Computer skills necessary today. Should be well organized and have ability to run own freelance business (negotiating contracts, setting rates, billing, keeping own records). Must work successfully from photographic references, as models are not provided in the industry.

Staff Illustrator

Staff illustrators may work for buying offices, retail stores, pattern companies, and some publications. However, most illustration work is done on a freelance basis. Increasingly, these illustrations require at least some use of computers.

Requirements: Illustration degree required. Must have excellent portfolio. Computer skills increasingly important.

Sketcher

Apparel manufacturers may hire sketchers on a free-lance or full-time basis to sketch garments for their records. These sketches are not used for reproduction and are not considered illustrative. They are tight sketches showing clear details of garment construction. Computer product data management programs fill this role increasingly.

Requirements: Illustration or Fashion Design degree, knowledge of garment construction, ability to do detailed sketches with tight hand, computer skills.

Entry-Level Positions for Fashion Buying and Merchandising (FBM) Graduates

Career possibilities for FBM graduates fall into these general categories:

- (1) Retail stores and (2) merchandising, buying, and product development organizations (formerly resident buying offices)
- Manufacturers *(1) retail stores and (2) merchandising, buying, and product development organizations*

Management Trainee

Most department stores and some specialty chains have formal executive training programs. Firms recruit trainees as potential managers and buyers. Each store has a limited number of openings for the training program, and competition is keen. For the majority of training programs, a bachelor's degree is necessary (especially with department stores). Each training program is unique and includes components of on-the-job training and formal instruction. Trainees are given exposure to merchandising as well as management areas.

Requirements: A high grade point average (especially in math) (a minimum grade point is required by some department stores [e.g., 2.8 to 3.0, depending on the company]), analytical ability, computer skills, strong communication skills, leadership ability, initiative, high degree of motivation and energy, maturity, fashionable grooming.

Long-Range Career Goal: Buyer, retail store manager, or other retailing executive positions.

Department Manager

Many stores hire candidates directly for managerial positions. Previous experience in sales and management in the store for which they are hired is desirable. A bachelor's degree may be necessary, depending on the prerequisites of the firm. Responsibilities are training and supervising sales associates, handling all department operations such as opening and closing the register(s), scheduling, merchandising and displaying goods, some direct customer contact.

Requirements: Similar to that of management trainee.

Long-Range Career Goal: Retail store manager, buyer, or other management positions.

Assistant Store Manager

These positions are available with specialty chain stores. Duties vary depending on the size and structure of the company and store, but usually involve assisting the manager in all phases of running the store. Positions *do not* usually lead to buying careers.

Requirements: Strong retail sales background. Computer familiarity. Duties are similar to those of department manager. With a small chain store or boutique, the manager must understand the needs of customers and provide buyers with feedback about sales and inventory. After a proven success record of store management with a specialty chain store, career growth into a district or regional manager position is possible. (Ultimately, the responsibility for growth and volume with a designated number of stores rests with the district manager.)

Long-Range Career Goal: Store manager, possibly district manager.

Buyer's Clerical

This is usually an entry-level position more commonly found in some of the few remaining large central buying offices (CBO). The job duties are often consistent with clerical duties of an assistant buyer trainee in a smaller firm and include keeping accurate records, scheduling appointments, follow-up work, possibly answering phones.

Requirements: A high degree of detail orientation is essential as well as strong math aptitude, computer skills, and communication skills.

Long-Range Career Goal: Assistant buyer and beyond.

Assistant Buyer Trainee (or Assistant Market Representative)

Often an entry-level position in some of the few remaining CBOs. The trainee works directly with the buyer and performs a variety of duties such as keeping unit control records, accompanying the buyer to the market, scheduling appointments, placing reorders, and following up on shipments. Usually the position is a five-day workweek, although overtime may be required during peak seasons.

Requirements: Necessary qualifications are similar to those of buyer's clerical.

Long-Range Career Goal: Market representatives (or buyers)—make trips to the market and spend a large portion of time researching trends, merchandise, and resources. Qualifications include a high degree of communication skills, solid math aptitude, ability to analyze data and make sound business judgments. A good fashion and color sense is also important.

Distribution Planner

Usually a position found in a large retail firm or CBO. Includes working with computer to determine distribution of merchandise to branches of the retail firm. Additional responsibilities include keeping records of unit-control, communicating with buyers and merchandise coordinators. Computer skills are essential.

Requirements: Strong problem-solving and analytical skills as well as computer skills are essential.

Long-Range Career Goal: Head distribution planner, buyer, or controller.

Product Development Trainee

Jobs in product development combine business, technical, and creative aspects and can be found in large retail organizations, private-label apparel manufacturers, or independent consulting firms. Entry-level jobs may include preparing specs, handling paperwork and follow-up, dealing with clients, overseas communications, and fashion research. As training progresses, additional responsibilities will include working with product development manager and buyers in coordinating garment styles or lines that meet buyers' expectations in regard to delivery, quality, and price point. Once orders are placed, duties include completing the necessary paperwork, providing breakdown information (sizes, colors, quantities), and approving samples for fit, color, and quality. Communications with overseas or domestic production facilities, approval of production samples, and development of yarn and fabric blends and resources are also included in product development. The job may eventually involve travel overseas, negotiating with factories on pricing, working out delivery schedules, and investigating new factories for possible future sourcing.

Requirements: Understanding of merchandising and fashion trends, basic knowledge of garment construction, textile science, and apparel manufacturing processes. Computer skills. Ability to do technical sketches, excellent communication and organizational skills, analytical and problem-solving ability, strong business sense, high energy level. Ability to interact effectively with staff in other countries.

Long-Range Career Goal: Head of a retail company's product development division.

Manufacturers

Positions with manufacturers involve work in the following general areas: (1) promoting or selling the product line, (2) merchandising or planning the line, and (3) overseeing the production and operations of manufacturing the line. In smaller companies, career positions may include duties in several of those areas, such as sales plus merchandising. In a larger firm, positions may fall more neatly into one particular area. Many jobs involve on-the-job training with regular workweeks (occasional overtime during peak seasons).

Entry-Level Positions

- Showroom sales trainee
- Showroom receptionist
- Clerical assistant
- Product development trainee

All of the positions just listed may be very diversified depending on the size and nature of the firm. Responsibilities include any of the following—showing and selling the line to clients, dealing with buyers in person and on the phone, reception, greeting clients, keeping sales records, faxing, follow-up on deliveries, writing up orders, possibly modeling garments, and attending meetings.

Requirements: Necessary qualifications include fashionable appearance, assertive personality, excellent oral and written communication skills, computer skills, and a high level of organization. Past sales experience is often helpful.

Long-Range Career Goals: Showroom sales and showroom manager—responsible for sales with own list of clients. If manager, supervise showroom sales force and staff; coordinate sales meetings. Road salesperson—sales outside of showroom in a particular geographic territory. Usually occurs with a large company after proven showroom sales record.

Retail Sales Coordinator

These positions are unique in that they provide an opportunity to gain exposure to manufacturing as well as retailing. One facet of the job involves duties in the showroom (usually serving as the home base) such as showroom sales, coordinating sales among retail store locations, analyzing inventory reports, and ordering and reordering goods for retail store locations. A second facet of the position includes promoting the manufacturer in a retail department store setting through customer service, displaying and merchandising the goods, and preparing sales and inventory.

Requirements: Excellent interpersonal and communication skills, high energy level, math aptitude, flexibility, sales ability. Computer skills. Past sales experience can be helpful.

Long-Range Career Goal: Potential growth as merchandiser or in sales.

Merchandising Assistant

Duties include working with the merchandiser in planning upcoming product lines; researching the market for trends and colors; keeping records; dealing with sales force, design staff, and customers.

Requirements: Ability to be highly organized and detailed is essential. Good fashion and color sense, team worker, analytical aptitude, and follow-through ability are important. Computer skills. Sketching skills may be helpful.

Long-Range Career Goal: Merchandiser, with responsibilities for planning the overall line, investigating colors and fabrics, giving direction to the design staff, estimating prices. In a smaller firm the owner or designer usually fulfills the role of merchandiser.

Assistant Piece Goods and Trim Buyer

Duties include assisting with ordering fabrics and trims, keeping track of inventory and records,

maintaining swatch file and samples, accompanying buyer on trips to fabric market to learn resources.

Requirements: Interest in textiles, detail oriented, well organized, ability to make good business judgments. Course work in textiles or garment construction may be helpful.

Long-Range Career Goal: Piece goods and trim buyer—to resource piece goods and trim market, price and cost goods, make purchases in conjunction with needs of design staff, possibly give direction to design staff for fabrics and trims.

Production Assistant

Duties involve assisting production manager in keeping records relating to production, sales, shipping, and inventory; keeping track of orders; writing up cutting tickets; costing garments; acting as liaison among factory, sales staff, and customers; heavy phone contact with factory. If production is done overseas, may assist in coordinating imports.

Requirements: Important qualifications include high degree of organization, tolerance for stress, communication skills, planning, follow-up and problem-solving ability, math aptitude, computer skills. Increasingly, second-language skills are valuable.

Long-Range Career Goal: Production manager—coordinates and supervises all aspects of producing the line. Usually works out of factory. If overseas manufacturer, makes regular visits to factory to check quality and coordinate production and importing.

Administrative Assistant

This position can be very diversified and usually involves assisting an executive of the firm (vice president, sales manager) in the following capacities: scheduling appointments, keeping records, filing, follow-up work, coordinating information, typing memos. For a college graduate, this is generally a job one takes just to get a foot in the door, with an eye toward moving to a more career-oriented position.

Requirements: The ability to organize efficiently is essential. Detail orientation, strong communication skills, computer skills, and potential for advancement are also important.

Long-Range Career Goal: Upper-level management—position in a specialized area (sales manager, operations manager) involved in policy making and overall managing of the firm.

Entry-Level Jobs for Apparel Production (or Manufacturing) Management Graduates

- Production control assistant
- Import coordinator
- Junior industrial engineer
- Costing analyst
- Quality control specialist
- Assistant plant manager

Graduates of an apparel production management program generally work for apparel manufacturing and importing firms. Increasingly, however, product development divisions in large retailing firms also seek graduates with this preparation. The work site may be based in a corporate office or at a manufacturing plant. Jobs in the office may or may not involve some travel to factory sites, domestically or overseas.

Production Control Assistant

Working in the corporate office as assistant to the production manager, this entry-level position may include any combination of the following responsibilities: serving as liaison between marketing and production, expediting orders, preparing cutting tickets, maintaining production records, piecegoods and trim inventory, ordering piecegoods and trim, following up on and coordinating shipments, receiving and allocating goods, dealing with contractors, production scheduling and follow-up, maintaining fax and e-mail communications with overseas resources, preparation of cost sheets, overseeing of sample production, quality control, entering and retrieving computer data.

Requirements: Organizational ability, quantitative aptitude, computer skills, accuracy, thoroughness, assertiveness, high stress tolerance, good communication skills, detail orientation, problem-solving ability.

Import Coordinator

A person in this role coordinates and monitors overseas production and shipments. Constant interface is required with shipping, warehousing, merchandising, and design areas. This individual makes certain production schedules are met, coordinates deliveries with sales orders, and meets completion dates. Other duties include: prepares specifications and documentation, obtains duty rates, adds quotas, figures markups, prepares data for computer entry. Maintains daily electronic communications with overseas resources and contractors. May be involved in matters pertaining to customs regulations, trade policies, and payment methods (e.g., letters of credit).

Requirements: Organizational ability, quantitative aptitude, computer skills, accuracy, thoroughness, assertiveness, high stress tolerance, good communication skills, detail orientation, problem-solving ability, appreciation for cultural differences in other countries, an understanding of textiles and apparel in the global economy. Facility with other languages a valuable asset.

Junior Industrial Engineer

A person in this role works at an apparel manufacturing plant studying operations and practices. Does time-and-motion studies, methods analyses, rate setting, plant layout, monitors efficiency of plant. Reports findings to management and makes recommendations for improvements.

Requirements: Maturity, organizational skills, strong analytical problem-solving and mathematical ability, computer skills, good at details and follow-through.

Costing Analyst

This position requires breaking down cost of manufacturing garments and taking into account such factors as piece rates, materials costs, import duties, and so forth.

Requirements: Good mathematical skills, analytical ability, computer skills, good at details.

Quality Control Specialist

An individual in this position usually works for an apparel manufacturer or importer, though jobs may also be found in large retail organizations with centralized buying. The person examines garments (may include fiber, textile, color, as well as sewing construction) to see that production specifications are met. The person must check assembly operations, identify problems, and work with production staff and management to correct problems. May develop specifications and inspect merchandise as it comes in from overseas as well as from domestic sources. Job often involves travel to factories.

Requirements: Detail oriented, good at follow-through, ability to work under pressure, high energy level, good communication skills, analytical and problem-solving ability, computer skills. Ability to work effectively with individuals from very different backgrounds from one's own. Second (or more) language skills are an asset.

Assistant Plant Manager

An individual in this job assists in running a factory—oversees work flow, maintains production schedules, distributes and keeps track of work. He or she assists in staffing plant and supervising various plant operations including cutting, sewing, pressing, warehousing, shipping.

Requirements: Must be a self-starter, have strong interpersonal skills, supervisory and organizational ability, high energy level, ability to work well under pressure, problem-solving ability, computer skills.

Entry-Level Jobs for Textile Development Graduates

- Assistant converter
- Assistant stylist (fabric or yarn)
- Product development assistant (textiles)
- Textile technologist
- Sales trainee
- Fabric librarian

Because textiles constitute a key component of the apparel industry, graduates of this major have a broad range of career options related to both business and technology. The entry-level jobs listed here represent some of the more typical ones available, but by no means cover the entire range of possibilities.

Assistant Converter

This individual assists the converter in overseeing and expediting the various processes involved in the transition of greige goods to finished fabric (dyeing, printing, finishing). Serves as liaison among mills, dyeing and finishing plants, knitters, and clients; heavy phone work. Projects greige goods needs, figures yardage and poundage, prepares dye orders, schedules printing, tracks yarn and finished goods. Processes customer orders and follows up on orders to see that deadlines are met. Figures costs, losses; maintains inventory control.

Requirements: Good at details and follow-through, problem solving, gathering and analyzing data, computer skills, oral communications, working with figures, memorizing, confronting, mediating.

Assistant Stylist (Fabric or Yarn)

In this role, a person may work for textile firm or yarn producer. He or she assists in developing seasonal lines and colorations. Duties may include any of the following, alone or in combination: surveys competitors and forecasts, researches market trends. Assists in preparing presentation boards and sales aids. Works with customers on development and refinement of patterns and colors. Places lab dips, follows up on sample yardage. Works with artists to make sure work is done on time. Obtains approval from customers. Maintains fabric library, keeps it current and organized, locates samples and data. Handles administrative and follow-up details related to line development.

Requirements: Excellent color sense, fashion awareness, organizational ability, communication skills, good at details and follow-through.

Product Development Assistant (Textiles)

This position requires one to be involved in knit or woven fabric development. The person helps develop product from technical point of view, prepares specification graph layouts to be executed at mill level and art room level. Translates clients' and salespeople's ideas into what is technically feasible, advises as to machine capabilities. Has samples made up, checks yarns, follows up on production, sees that finished goods are executed properly. May involve some travel to mills. Utilizes market research findings, maintains records, handles follow-up work, serves as liaison between design room and mill. Maintains phone contact with mills and factories to make certain piece goods shipments are met. Reviews fabric lines brought in by textile salespeople or may go out into market to assist in piece goods selection. May order piece goods, trims, and notions, and may make substitutions when goods are unavailable. Maintains electronic communications with overseas resources.

Requirements: Analytical ability, organizational skills, fashion awareness, color sense, strong communication skills, problem solving related to purchase orders and reorders. Skills in negotiating, confronting, record keeping, handling details and follow-through, gathering and analyzing data, use of computer, problem solving, juggling multiple demands, organizational ability, color sense.

Textile Technologist

In this role a person may work for a testing laboratory, retailer, or manufacturer. Responsibilities may include any of the following duties, depending on the setting: performs various lab tests on fabrics, yarns, fibers, and garments to determine color fastness, washability, shrinkage, and so forth. Textile components may be tested before and/or after being made into garments. Analyzes fabric construction, fiber content, finishing properties; compiles data; prepares reports on findings. Identifies problems, helps maintain standards. Develops and verifies care labeling.

Requirements: Systematic, good at details, well organized, able to follow instructions and work alone. Good communication skills; oral, written, and analytical ability; computer skills.

Sales Trainee

This individual may work for a textile mill, converter, or yarn producer. He or she calls on manufacturers (or textile firms) to sell the line and service accounts. Training may include visit to mill or assisting in showroom. Initially will be given list of accounts to work with; ultimately will be expected to generate new accounts. May deal with designers, merchandisers, piece goods buyers, or production people. May suggest end uses for product, explain properties. Gathers information and provides feedback to management on customer needs in terms of styling, product development. Follows up on orders and shipments, services accounts.

Requirements: Initiative, outgoing personality, excellent communication and interpersonal skills, problem-solving ability, good memory, color sense, high energy level, self-starter, competitive spirit.

Fabric Librarian

In this role, a person may work for a fiber or textile firm, trade association, or pattern company. Responsibilities may include any combination of the following duties: maintains up-to-date fabric library, prepares sample cards and seasonal presentations. Works with color file system, runs groups of colors in response to requests. Researches and compiles fabric resources list, may go out to review fabric lines at various resources and select appropriate fabrics for library. Assists users in locating, identifying, and selecting appropriate fabrics for library. May work in a setting that serves as a resource for internal design staff only, or may deal with clients representing other firms.

Requirements: Knowledge of textiles, excellent color sense, design and fashion awareness, ability to match textile products and potential end uses, organizational ability, systematic, good memory, good communication skills.

Index

Note: **Boldface** page numbers indicate definitions or descriptions of designers and companies.

AAFA (American Apparel and Footwear Association), 498–499, 507
AAMA. *See* American Apparel Manufacturers Association (AAMA)
Abboud, Joseph, **528**
Abend, J., 401
Abercrombie and Fitch Co., 11, 62
Abernathy, F., 16, 457
Accessories industry
    Accessory Web, 324
    brand names, 325–326
    business of accessories, 323–325
    designers, 346
    economic importance of, 325
    glove industry
        economic importance of, 339
        glove construction, 340
        introduced, 338–339
        marketing, 340
        nature of industry, 339
    handbag industry
        economic importance of, 337
        global activities, 338
        handbag construction, 337
        introduced, 336–337
        nature of, 337
        small leather goods, 338
    history of
        in 1900s, 357
        in 1910s, 357–358
        in 1920s, 358
        in 1930s, 358–359
        in 1940s, 359
        in 1950s, 359–360
        in 1960s, 360
        in 1970s, 360

        in 1980s, 360–361
        in 1990s, 361
    hosiery industry
        economic importance of, 333
        global activities, 335–336
        hosiery construction, 333–334
        introduced, 332–333
        marketing, 334–335
        nature of, 333
        retail channels of distribution for, 336
    introduced, 322–323
    jewelry industry
        bridge jewelry, 344
        costume jewelry, 345
        fine jewelry, 343
        introduced, 342–343
        marketing, 344, 345
        precious jewelry, 344
    men's accessories, 309
    millinery industry
        economic importance of, 341
        introduced, 340–341
        marketing, 342
        millinery construction, 341–342
        nature of industry, 341
    other accessories, 345
    shoe industry
        athletic shoes, 328
        competition from imports and, 330–332
        economic importance of, 328
        introduced, 327
        marketing, 329–330
        nature of, 327
        shoe construction, 328–329
        U.S. consumption of nonrubber footwear (1968–1998), 330

        small leather goods, 338
        trade shows, 324
        U.S. footwear market by country of origin (1998), 332
Accessory Web, 324
Accounts payable, 220
Accounts receivable, 220
ACTWU (Amalgamated Clothing and Textile Workers Union), 286
Adams, J., 201–202
Adams, W., 173
Adler, J., 130
Administrative assistant (manufacturing), **539**
Adolfo, **528**
Adrian, Gilbert, **528**
Adrover, Miguel, 58
Ad valorem tariffs, 92
Advance ship notices, **459**
Advertising
    cooperative, 239
    fashion magazine revenue, 487–488
    television, 492
    women's apparel, 239–240
Advertising agencies, **494–495**
After Six, 288
Agile manufacturing, **223**
Agins, Teri, 50, 117, 226, 322, 376, 407–410
Air jet shuttleless looms, 183
Alaia, Azzedine, **528**
Albini, Walter, **528**
Alderfer, E., 171
Amalgamated Clothing and Textile Workers Union (ACTWU), 286

Amalgamated Clothing Workers of America, 286
Ambiance of stores, **431**
American Apparel and Footwear Association (AAFA), 498–499, 507
American Apparel Manufacturers Association (AAMA), 124, 283, 341, 350, 421, 445, 498
  Apparel Market Monitor, 82
  Focus: An economic profile of the apparel industry, 349
  FOCUS: Economic Profile of the Apparel Industry, 391
American fashion, 57–63
American Fur Industry, 190
American National Standards Institute (ANSI) X 12, 182
American Textile Manufacturers Institute (ATMI), 4, 82, 83, 159, 168, 170, 187, 498
American Textile Partnership (AMTEX), 185–186
Amies, Hardy, **528**
AMTEX (American Textile Partnership), 185–186
Anchor stores, **437**
Annual reports, **12**
ANSI (American National Standards Institute) X 12, 182
Antimerger (Celler-Kefauver) Act of 1950, 144
Apparel. *See also* Accessories industry
  boys'. *See* Children's apparel industry
  girls'. *See* Children's apparel industry
  intimate. *See* Intimate apparel industry
  jobbers, 245
  market share trends (1989 versus 1999), 425
  men's. *See* Menswear apparel industry
  NAICS groupings for, 211–212
  ready-to-wear
    early, 213–214, 215
    U. S. imports (1990–2000), 400
    U. S. imports by major source (1984, 1995), 391
  women's. *See* Women's apparel industry
Apparel Exchange and Fabrics Online, 184–185
Apparel firms
  distribution, 237–238
  functional areas of, 220
  globalization and, 72–73
  line development
    designing, 224–228

final stages of, 235–237
  merchandisers and, 228
  preadoption process, 224, 227–228
  preproduction process, 230–232
  product sourcing, 232–235
organization of, 219–220
publicly owned versus privately owned, 215–217
relationships with retailers and, 241–242
size of, 246–248
top U. S. (2000), 244
Apparel industry. *See* Fashion industry
Apparel Industry Magazine, 244, 247
Apparel manufacturers, Web sites for, 268
Apparel manufacturing mills, NAICS group for, 8
Apparel marts, 258–262
  for menswear, 304
Apparel production, management opportunities, 540–541
Apparel specialty chains, **431–433**
Armani, Giorgio, **528**
Armstrong, G., 125, 128
Aron, Francoise, 409
ASEAN (Association of Southeast Asian Nations), 397–398
Ashley, Laura, **528**
Asian Tigers (countries), 392
Assistant art director, **536**
Assistant buyer trainee, **538**
Assistant converter, **541**
Assistant designer, **534**
Assistant market representative, **538**
Assistant piece goods and trim buyer, **539**
Assistant plant manager, **541**
Assistant store manager, **537**
Assistant stylist, **535**
Assistant stylist (fabric or yarn), **541**
Assistant to stylist, **535**
Associated Dry Goods, 425–426
Associated Merchandising Corporation (AMC), 78, 479–480
Associated offices, **479**
Association of Southeast Asian Nations (ASEAN), 397–398
Astrade, A., 58
Athletic shoes, 328
Atlanta Apparel Mart, 261
ATMI (American Textile Manufacturers Institute), 4, 168, 187, 498
Audemars, Swiss chemist, 161
Auxiliary enterprises, 74
Avant-garde fashion, **37**

Baby boomers, 129, 148–149
Bacon's Magazine Directory, 490
Baker, Frank, 202
Balenciaga, Cristobal, **528**
Balmain, Pierre, **528**
Bannon, L., 265
Barber, B., 13
Bar coding, 181
Bardach, Veronique, 463
Barnathan, J., 393
Barthet, Jean, **528**
Bassuk, David, 273–275
Beard, Thomas, 327
Beaton, C., 38
Beauty industry. *See* Cosmetics industry
Beene, Geoffrey, 58, 247, **528**
Behling, D., 44
Bell, Q., 47
Bensoussan-Torres, Robert, 410
Berge, Pierre, 376, 408
Bergler, E., 13
Bespoke tailor (custom tailor) shops, 293
Bibb Company, 172
Bierce, Ambrose, 34
"Big Five" of retailing, 430
Big Four Asian countries, 88
Bilateral agreements, **85**, 87–89
Bird, L., 130, 242
Black, P., 131, 247
Blackwell, Roger, 21, 149
Blass, Bill, 55, 57, 246, 251–252, **528**
Bloomingdale's, 15, 303
Blue jeans, 59–60
Bobbin, 496–497
Body Fashions/Intimate Apparel, 240
Body scanning, 24, 25, 230
Bohan, Marc, **528**
Bottom-up theory, **44–46**
Bounds, W., 242
Boutiques, **428–429**
Bow, Josephine, 411–412
Boyle, R., 71, 122
Boys' apparel. *See* Children's apparel industry
Branch stores, 422–424
Branded concept shops (in-store shops), 303
Brand names
  accessories, 325–326
  defined, **164**
  fibers, 164–167
  initiate apparel, 350–351
  menswear, 300
Brando, Marlon, 59, 62
Brannon, E., 53
Bricks-and-clicks, **448**
Bricks-and-mortar, **448**
Bridge jewelry, 344
Brigance, Tom, 215

British Apparel and Textile Confederation, 384
British Fashion Council, 384
Brooke, Donald, **528**
Brooks Brothers, 313–317
Browning, William C., 5
Brunnschweiler, D., 163
B2B (business-to-business) relationships, 29–30
B2C (business-to-consumer) e-commerce, 448
Bunce, Janet, 504
Bundle system, 234
Burlington Industries, 23, 171, 202–204
Burns, L., 38
Burrows, S., 57
Burrows, Stephen, **528**
Burton's Gentlemen's Magazine, 486
Bush, Barbara, 51
Business-to-business (B2B) relationships, 29–30
Business-to-consumer (B2C) e-commerce, 448
Butterick, Ebenezer, 213
Buyer's clerical, **537**
Buying offices, **477–478**
Byron, J., 194, 196, 338, 339
Byte Systems, Inc., 237

CAD (Computer-aided design), 8–9, 182, 228–229
CAF (Canadian Apparel Federation), 387, 388, 389
California Apparel News, 240
California International Menswear Market (CIMM), 307
CaliforniaMart, 259–261
Calvin Klein. *See* Klein, Calvin
CAM (computer-aided manufacturing), 182–183
Camera Nazionale dell' Alta Moda Italiana, 378
Cameron, D., 57
Camp Snoopy, 443
Canadian Apparel Federation (CAF), 387, 388, 389
Canadian ready-to-wear industry, 387–389
Canadian Textile Institute (CTI), 389
Canton Trade Fair, 179
Capucci, Roberto, **529**
Carats (karats), 343
Cardin, Pierre, **529**
Careers in fashion
administrative assistant (manufacturing), **539**
apparel production (or manufacturing) management opportunities, 540–541

assistant art director, **536**
assistant buyer trainee, **538**
assistant converter, **541**
assistant designer, **534**
assistant market representative, **538**
assistant piece goods and trim buyer, **539**
assistant plant manager, **541**
assistant store manager, **537**
assistant stylist, **535**
assistant stylist (fabric or yarn), **541**
assistant to stylist, **535**
buyer's clerical, **537**
colorist, **535**
costing analyst, **540**
cutting assistant, **534**
department manager, **537**
distribution planner, **538**
fabric librarian, **542**
fashion buying and merchandising, 537–538
fashion design opportunities, 533
freelance illustrator, **536**
import coordinator, **540**
introduced, 533
junior designer, **534–535**
junior industrial engineer, **540**
knit designer, **535**
lace and embroidery designer, **535**
layout artist, **536**
management trainee, **537**
merchandising assistant, **539**
painted woven designer, **535**
pasteup and mechanical artist, **536**
product development trainee, **538**
production assistant, **539**
production control assistant, **540**
production development assistant (textiles), **541**
quality control specialist, **540–541**
retail sales coordinator, **539**
sales trainee (textiles), **542**
screen print artist, **535**
sketcher, **537**
sketcher (assistant to designer), **534**
sketcher/stylist, **534**
sketching assistant, **534**
staff illustrator, **536**
textile development opportunities, 541–542
textile/surface designer, **535**
textile technologist, **542**
woven fabric designer, **535**
Care Labeling of Textile Wearing Apparel Act of 1972, 144

Caribbean Basin Initiative (CBI), 94
Caribbean Basin Textile Access Program, 94
Caribbean contractors, 399–401
Carnegie, Hattie, **529**
Cashill, A., 63, 150–151
Cashin, Bonnie, **529**
Casual Fridays, 39, 295
Casual office wear, 295–296
Catalog houses, **444**
Catalog operations. *See also* Mail-order houses
catalog showroom retailers, **447–448**
by department and specialty stores, 447
Category killers, **437**
Caution fees, 375
Cavanaugh, John, **529**
CBI (Caribbean Basin Initiative), 94
CD-ROM computer shopping, 451
Celler-Kefauver (antimerger) Act of 1950, 144
Central European countries, 398–399
Centralized buying, **430**
CEO (chief executive officer), 220
Chain stores, **430**
apparel specialty chains, 431–433
"Big Five," 430
general merchandise chains, **433**, 433–434
introduced, 429–430
Chalayan, Hussein, **529**
Chambre Syndicale de la Couture Parisienne, 370–371, 372, 373
Chambre Syndicale du Prêt-à-Porter, 371–373
Chan, Vincent, 202
Chan, Wing, 202
Chanel, Coco, 47, **529**
Channels of distribution, 6–7
menswear, 302–304
Chapter 11 of the U.S. Bankruptcy Code, 433
Chardonnet, Count Hilaire de, 161
Chargebacks, 137, 241, 242
Chemical fiber producers, 162–167
Cheung, Allan, 506
Chicago Apparel Center, 261
Chicago fashion center, 258
Chief executive officer (CEO), 220
Chief operating officer (COO), 220
Children's apparel industry
marketing, 264–265
nature of, 262–263
specialization in, 263–264
Chinese contractors, 396–397
Chirls, S., 159, 172
Christman, M., 5, 284, 285, 445

Cianciolo, Susan, 58
CIM (computer integrated manufacturing), 221, 233
CIMM (California International Menswear Market), 307
Cipullo, Aldo, **529**
CIT Group, 254, 255
Claiborne, Liz, 50, 72, 138, 226, 244, 247, 268–269, 346, 428, **529**
Clark, Ossie, **529**
Classics, defined, **36**
Clayton Act of 1914, 143
Click-and-mortars, 464
Click-Tex, 201, 202
Clinton, Hillary, 51
Closeouts, B2B relationships and, 29
Clothing Manufacturers' Association (CMA), 306
Clune, R., 223
CMA (Clothing Manufacturers' Association), 306
CMG (Color Marketing Group), 198–199
Cobrin, H., 237, 285, 300
Coca-Cola, 24
Cocooning lifestyle, 133
Cole, David, 21
Color Association of the United States (CAUS), 176–177
Color decisions, 176–177
Color forecasting, 198–200
Colorist, **535**
Color Marketing Group (CMG), 198–199
Comia, R., 105
Commissionaires, 78
Commodization of fashion, **50**
Competition, federal laws regulating, 143–144
Component suppliers, 6
Computer-aided design (CAD), 8–9, 182, 228–229
Computer-aided manufacturing (CAM), 182–183
Computer integrated manufacturing (CIM), 221, 233
Computer technologies, 481–482
  influence of, on fashion industry, 14–16
  logistics industry and, 20
Cone Mills, 71
Connolly, Sybil, **529**
Consignment, defined, 192
Consultants
  display, 500
  exports, 485
  fashion, **477**
  import, 485
  management, 484
  technical, 484–485

Consumer-ready manufacturing, 143
Consumers, 73
  changes in, 21
  cross-shoppers, 117, 362, 435
  fashion expenditures of (1974–2000), 13
  fashion industry and, 12–13, 116–117, 121–123
  globalization and, 73–74
  Hispanic, 146–147
  power of, 119–121
  predictions for, 142–143
  product labeling laws protecting, 144
  sociocultural trends affecting fashion spending of, 117–118
Contractors
  in Caribbean, 399–401
  in Central Europe, 398–399
  in China, 396–397
  in Eastern Europe, 398–399
  in far east, 411–412
  in Hong Kong, 393–395
  introduced, 245, 370
  in Latin America, 399–401
  in newly industrialized countries, 392–397
  in Singapore, 396
  in South Korea, 395
  in Taiwan, 395
  in Third World, 397–398
  in Turkey, 398–399
Converters, 175
COO (chief operating officer), 220
Cooperative advertising funds, **239**
Cooperative merchandising organizations, **479**
COP (customer order processing) software, 237–238
Corporate merchandising/buying offices, 480–481
Cosmetics industry
  introduced, 352–355
  world's top 10 companies in, 353–354
Costa, Victor, 258
Costing analyst, **540**
Cotons de France, 179
Cotton Incorporated, 160–161
Country-of-origin rules, **90–92**
Courreges, Andres, 47, **529**
Couture, **370**
Couturier, **369**
Couturière, **369**
Crafted with Pride in U.S.A. Council, 97
Credit cards, 16
Cross Colours, 62
Cross docking, **459**
Cross-shoppers, **117**, 362, 435
CTI (Canadian Textile Institute), 389

Cummings, Angela, 529
Cuneo, A., 51, 131
Currency exchange rates, exports and, 100
Customer order processing (COP) software, 237–238
Customer targeting, 125–127
Customization, increased, 23–24
Custom tailor (bespoke tailor) shops, 293
Cut, make, and trim (CMT), 81
Cut orders, 234
Cutting, 234
Cutting assistant, **534**
Cutting tickets, 234

Dache, Lilly, **529**
Daily News Record (DNR), 452, 490
Dallas fashion center, 258
Dallas International Apparel Mart, 259
DAMA (Demand Activated Manufacturing Architecture), 186
D'Andrea, M., 151, 180
Dart, David, **529**
Database marketing, 460–461
Data mining, 136–138
Davies, Donald, **529**
Dawson, C., 172
Dayhoff, Richard, 258
Dayton-Hudson, 425
DCs (distribution centers), 237
Dean, James, 59, 62
De Barentzen, Patrick, **528**
Del Castillo, Antonio, **529**
DELiA*s, 268
Deloitte & Touche, 484
Demand Activated Manufacturing Architecture (DAMA), 186
Demographics, 126
Denim, 59. *See also* Jeans
  history of, 285
  major producers of, 172
de Nime, 285
Department manager, 537
Department of Commerce. *See under* United States
Department stores
  branch stores, 422–424
  catalog operations by, 447
  competitive changes, 424–425
  defined, 421–422
  introduced, 422
  menswear apparel and, 303
  organization chart, 423
  origin of, 422
  store ownership groups, 425–427
  top U. S. stores by sales (1999), 424

Designer-name franchised boutiques, 441
Designers
 accessories, 346
 American, recognition of, 158
 hosiery and, 335
 of intimate apparel, 350–351
 licensing agreements and, 251–252
 line development role of, 224–226
 menswear, labels and licensing, 300–302
 responsibilities of, 228–230
 role of, in fashion development, 46–47
 trunk shows, 240
Designers' Collective, 307
Designs, defined, **35**
DeVaney, Lynne, 198, 199
Deverticalization, 18
Diana, Princess of Wales, 36, 44
Dickerson, K., 4, 5, 6, 71, 74, 96, 122, 140, 393, 394, 397, 398
Differentiation, 433
Dillard's, 423–424
Diller, Barry, 450
Dior, Christian, 40, 47, 157, **529**
DiPaolo, N., 302
Direct exporting, 99–100
Direct ownership, 101
Direct sales, B2B relationships and, 29
Direct selling, **451**
Discount retailers
 category killers, **437**
 factory outlets, **439–440**
 full-line discount stores, 435–436
 hypercenters, **436**
 introduced, 434–435
 off-price retailers, **437–438**
 supercenters, **436**
 warehouse clubs, 436–437
Display consultants, 500
Distribution, for women's apparel industry, 237–238
Distribution centers (DCs), 237
Distribution channels, 6–7
Distribution operations, 141–142
Distribution planner, **538**
Diverters, **437**
Dividends, **11**
Dixon, Joe, 313, 315–316
DKNY, 60
DNR (Daily News Record), 452, 490
Dodd, Annmarie, 311–312
Dominion Textile, 172
Doneger Group, 61, 478
Doors (store units), 433
Door-to-door retailing, **451**

Doran Textiles, 172
Dot-com businesses, for textile industry, 184, 201–202
Dressers (firms), 190
Dresses, Jean, **529**
Drop, **289**
Dual distribution system, **304**
Duck Head Apparel, 15
Dunkin, A., 116
Dunlop, J., 16, 457
Dunn, W., 389
DuPont, 23, 101
Duties, import, 92–95

Early fashion adopters, 44
Earnshaw's Infants-Girls-Boys Wear Review, 265
Eastern European countries, 398–399
E-commerce, 16, 463–464. *See also* "E-tailing"
 for apparel industry, 267–269
 for Asian textile sources, 506
 business-to-business, 29
 business-to-consumer, 448
 for fabric sourcing, 504–505
 order fulfillment and, 449
 security and, 449
 for textile industry, 184–186, 201–202
E-commerce tools, product development and, 273–275
Ecom-Textile.com, 201
EcoSpun polyester fiber, 187–188
Edelman, Jeffrey, 464
Edelson, S., 437, 440
Editorial credits, 486
E-3 (Encourage Environmental Excellence) award, 186–187
807/9802 Production, 94, 95, 257
807A production, 94, 97
Electronic data interchange (EDI), **14**, 181, 242
Electronic interactive retailing, 16
 CD-ROM computer shopping, 451
Electronic kiosks, **493**
Electronic media, 491–493
Electronic retailers
 home television shopping, 449–450
 introduced, 448
Electronic retailing, 448–449
Electroplating, 345
Ellis, Joe, 108
Ellis, Perry, 57, **529**
Encourage Environmental Excellence (E-3) award, 186–187
End of Fashion (Agins), 50
Engardio, P., 393

Environmental issues, 186–188
Environmental Protection Agency (EPA), 195
EPA (Environmental Protection Agency), 195
Escada, 385, 409
Escobar, Anibal, 502
Esprit, 72, 101, 428
Establishments (plants), 349
"E-tailing," 448–449
Evenson, Fawn, 507
Events and personalities, fashion and, 50–51
Everyday Wear, 295
Export consultants, 485
Exports, 68
 currency exchange rates and, 100
 direct, 99–100
 fur industry and, 193
 introduced, 188–189
 leather industry and, 195
 U.S. efforts to promote, 97–98
Export specialists, 485

Fabiani, Alberto, **529**
Fabria.com, 201
Fabric and Suppliers Linkage Council (FASLINC), 185
Fabric librarian, **542**
Factoring, 252–254
Factors Chain International (FCI), 254
Factory outlets, **439–440**
Fads, defined, 36
Fair Packaging and Labeling Act of 1966, 144
Fake fur, 193
Farah, 288
Far Eastern contractors, 411–412
Fashion
 American, 57–63
 avant-garde, 37
 changes
  application to merchandising fashions, 42
 changes in
  evolutionary nature of, 39–40
  fashion cycle, **40–42**
  introduction of, 37–38
  psychological reasons for, 38–39
  rational reasons for, 39
 classics, **36**
 commodization of, 50
 consumer acceptance and, 35–36
 defined, **35**
 development of
  designers' role in, 46–47
  introduced, 46–47
 fads, **36**
 forward, 37

Fashion *(continued)*
  high fashion, **36–37**
  history
    in 1920s, 48, 53
    in 1930s, 48, 53
    in 1940s, 49, 53
    in 1950s, 49, 53
    in 1960s, 48, 53
    in 1970s, 48, 53
    in 1980s, 49, 53
    in 1990s, 49, 53
    power of, 12–13
    prediction
      introduced, 52–53
      recognizing and evaluating
        trends for, 53–54
      sources of information for,
        54–55
    rapid transfer of, 21
    as reflections of their times,
      47–50
    research and development
      color decisions, 176–177
      fashion presentations,
        177–179
      fashion staffs, 176
      introduced, 175
      textile design, 177, 178
      textile trade shows, 179
    retro, 63
    secondary fashion centers,
      257–258
    social movements and, 51
    social values and attitudes and,
      51–52
    technological developments
      and, 52
    trends, **37**
    volume, **37**
  impact of, on hosiery, 335
  language of, 34–35
  leadership, theories of
    bottom-up theory, **44–46**
    introduced, 42–43
    marketing implications, 46
    trickle-across theory, **44**
    trickle-down theory, **43–44**
  market centers, 254–257
  mass fashion, **37**
  newsworthy events and
    personalities, 50–51
Fashion Association, The (TFA), 307
Fashion business, defined, 2
Fashion buying and merchandising
  (FBM) opportunities,
  537–538
Fashion consultants, **477**
Fashion cycle, **40–42**
Fashion Forecasting: Research,
  Analysis, and Presentation
  (Brannon), 53

Fashion-forward industries, 392, 393
Fashion Group International, 500
Fashion industry
  background of globalization of,
    74–75
  classification system for, 6–8
  computer technologies and,
    481–482
  consumers and, 12–13, 116–117,
    121–122
  defined, 2
  distribution channels, 6–7
  e-commerce for, 267–269
  economic importance of
    global importance, 3–4
  federal legislation affecting,
    143–144
  globalization. *See* Globalization of
    Fashion
  globalization and, 68–70
  jobs in. *See* Careers in fashion
  NAICS categories of, **7–8**
  national importance, 4–5
  overview of, 2
  producers, foreign. *See* Foreign
    producers
  product development and
    showings, 8–10
  profit motive and, 10–12
  scope of, 3
  socioeconomic factors and, 13–14
  trends
    changing consumers of, 21
    deverticalization, 18
    electronic-information age,
      influence of, 14–16
    globalization, 18–20
    improved industry relationships,
      23
    increased customization, 23–24
    logistics industry, 20
    mergers and acquisitions, 16–17
    rapid transfer of fashion, 21
    redefinition of business by
      companies, 23
    reduced response time, 22
    social responsibility, 24–25
    vertical operations, 17–18
    virtual companies, 20
  U.S. history of, 5–6
  Web sites related to, 523–527
Fashion information services,
  474–476
Fashion magazines, 486–489
Fashion pipeline, softgoods industry,
  7
Fashion presentations, 177–179
Fashion Service, The (TFS), 475
Fashion staffs, 176
Fashion Trip software, 15
Fashion videos, 492

FASLINC (Fabric and Suppliers
  Linkage Council), 185
Fath, Jacques, **529**
FBM (fashion buying and merchan-
  dising) opportunities,
  537–538
FCI (Factors Chain International),
  254
Federal Register, 168
Federal Trade Commission (FTC) of
  1914, 144, 171
  jewelry guides, 344
Federated Department Stores, 16,
  425–426, 464
Fédération Française du Prêt à
  Porter, 379
Fee offices, **478**
Fernandez, M., 147
Ferragamo, Salvatore, **529**
Ferre, Gianfranco, **529**
Fiber Economics Bureau, 161, 162
FiberMatch.com, 202
Fiber producers
  chemical fiber producers,
    162–167
  introduced, 158–159
  NAICS Subsector 325, 161
  natural fiber suppliers, 159–161
Fibers
  manufactured (chemical),
    162–167
  manufactured (man-made),
    157–158, 161
    brand names, 164–167
    high-performance, 163–164
    microfibers, 163
    producers, 161
    temperature-resistant, 164
    types of, 163
    U.S. consumption of
      1950–2000, 161–162
  natural, defined, **157**
  solution-dyed, **157**
  yarn-dyed, 158
Field, Marshall, 69
Filene, William, 428
Finance, B2B relationships and, 30
Fine jewelry, 343
Finished product suppliers, 6
Fink, Joseph, 138
Finnie, T., 172
First cost, 92
Fisher, Donald, 60
Fisher, G. Chrysler, 409
Five Rs in marketing concept,
  141–142
Flammable Fabrics Act of 1953, 144
Flea markets, **451**
Floor-ready merchandise, 143
Fogarty, Anne, **529**
Foley, C., 44

Fontana Sisters, **529**
Footwear. *See* Shoe industry
Footwear Industries of America, 330
Ford, Tom, 376, **529**
Forde, Roseann, 198
Forden, S., 73
Foreign-owned factory shift to U.S., 401–402
Foreign producers. *See also* Globalization of fashion industry; Offshore production; Overseas production
  foreign-owned factory shift to U.S., 401–402
  introduced, 369–370
  in lower-wage countries
    introduced, 389–390
    labor costs, 390–392
Forest, S., 135
Forquet, Federico, **529**
Forte, Gabriella, 408
Fortuny, Mariano, **529**
Foundations, 348, 351
France
  haute couture in, 370–377
  ready-to-wear industry in, 378–379
Franchised retailing, 440–441
Franchisee, **440**
Franchising agreement, **376**
Franchisor, **440**
Frank, B., 220
Frastaci, M., 265
Frederick Atkins, Inc., 78, 479–480
Free-lance illustrator, **536**
Free trade, 83
Free trade zones (FTZs), 392
French Haute couture, 370–377
Friday Wear, 39, 295
Friedman, A., 262
Friends of Animals, 190
Fruit of the Loom, 174
FTAdirect, 202
FTC (Federal Trade Commission) of 1914, 144, 171
  jewelry guides, 344
FTZs (free trade zones), 392
Fubu, 105
Fur industry. *See also* Leather industry
  flowchart, 191
  impact of fashion on, 192–193
  imports and exports, 193
  introduced, 189
  manufacturing of fur garments, 190–192
  marketing fur garments, 192
  nature of, 190
Fur Information and Fashion Council, 190

Fur Information Council of America, 190
Fur Products Labeling Act of 1951, 144, 191
Fur Retailers Information Council, 190

Galanos, James, **529**
Galitzine, Irene, **529**
Galliano, John, 409, **529**
GALS (guaranteed access levels), 94
Gap, The, 11–12, 17, 19, 60, 62, 73, 149, 244, 427, 456, 464
  sales in 1999, 430
Garment District (New York City), 255
Garvey, 315
Gates, Bill, 50
GATT (General Agreement on Tariffs and Trade), 83
Gaultier, Jean-Paul, **529**
Gellers, S., 293, 302
Gemstones, 344
General Agreement on Tariffs and Trade (GATT), 83
Generalized System of Preferences (GSP), 93–94
General merchandise chains, **433**, 433–434
Generation X, 50, 51, 130–131
Generation Y, 131–132, 312
Generation Z, 132
Generic names, **164**
Generra, 300
GERBERcutter automated cutter, 235
Germany
  IGEDO show, 385, 386
  ready-to-wear industry in, 385
Gernreich, Rudi, **529**
Gimbel, Adam, 422
Girbaud, F., 60
Girbaud, M., 60
Girls' apparel. *See* Children's apparel industry
Givenchy, Hubert de, **530**
Glacé leathers, 105
Glasgall, W., 393
Globalization of fashion industry, 18–20, 405. *See also* Foreign producers; Offshore production; Overseas production; Trade
  apparel firms and, 72–73
  cosmetics industry, 352–355
  fashion industry and, 68–70
  impact of, on softgoods industry, 72
  importance of preparing for, 103
  of intimate apparel industry, 351

overview of, 70
  protectionism versus free trade, 83–84
  retailers and, 73
  retailing and, 459–460
  textile producers and, 71
Glock, R., 220, 230
Glove industry
  economic importance of, 339
  glove construction, 340
  introduced, 338–339
  marketing, 340
  nature of industry, 339
Glynn, M., 45
Godey's Lady's Book, 486
Grading patterns, 230
Great Britain, ready-to-wear industry in, 383–385
Greenberg, A., 45
Greif & Company, 288, 300
Gres, Alix, **530**
Griege goods, **158**
Gromek, Joe, 313–317
Gronbach, K., 149
GSP (Generalized System of Preferences), 93–94
Guaranteed access levels (GALS), 94
Gucci, Aldo, **530**
Guess, 18, 60, 300
Guilford Mills, 23
Guitierrz, Daphne, 58

Haber, H., 252
Haggar, 288
Hahn, Nick, 201, 202
Hair styles, 51
Halston, 47, 57, **530**
Hamilton-Chandler, Beverly, 311–312
Hamm, Jacqueline, 27–28
Hammond, J., 16, 457
Hammonds, K., 116
Hand, Bert, 312
Handbag industry
  economic importance of, 337
  global activities, 338
  handbag construction, 337
  introduced, 336–337
  nature of, 337
  small leather goods, 338
Hand tailoring, 293
Hanes, 23, 61
Hanz, E., 105
Harris, Bill, 201
Harris, J., 343
Harris, L., 422, 428
Hartmarx, 288, 300, 304
  brand and product segmentation, 301–302

Hartnell, Norman, **530**

Hats. *See* Millinery industry

Haubegger, C., 146, 147

Haute couture

    Chambre Syndicale de la Couture Parisienne, 370–371, 372, 373

    Chambre Syndicale du Prêt-à-Porter, 371–373

    defined, **369**

    designer-name couture houses, 373

    economics of, 375–377

    French, 370–377

    introduced, 370

    Italian couture, 377–378

    loss of primacy, 407–410

    Paris directory for, 372

    semiannual collections and showings, 373–375

Hawes, Elizabeth, 215

Hayes, Chuck, 189

Hazzard, Tracy, 198

Head, Edith, **530**

Hearle, J., 163

Heaton, H., 171

Heels of shoes, 328–329

Heim, Jacques, **530**

Heller Commercial Services, 254

Henderson, George, 203

Here and There, 476

Herman, Stan, **530**

Herrera, C., 58

Hertz, Eric, 507

Hessen, J., 325

Hessen, Wendy, 502–503

Hester, Mark, 258

Hides, 193–194

High fashion, 41

    defined, **36–37**

High-performance fibers, 163–164

Hilfiger, Tommy, **530**

Hill, S., 138

Hines, J., 190

Hispanic consumers, 146–147

HKTDC (Hong Kong Trade Development Council), 395

Hoeschst, 167

Home Shopping Network, 449–450, 492

Home television shopping, 449–450, 492

Hong Kong contractors, 393–395

Hong Kong International Leather Fair, 195

Hong Kong Trade Development Council (HKTDC), 395

Hood, Wayne, 464

Hooper, C., 71, 122

Horizontal exchanges, B2B relationships and, 29–30

Hosiery industry

    economic importance of, 333

    global activities, 335–336

    hosiery construction, 333–334

    introduced, 332–333

    marketing, 334–335

    nature of, 333

    retail channels of distribution for, 336

Howe, Elias, 214, 370

Hugo Boss, 300, 385

Hulanicki, Barbara, **530**

Hypermarkets, **436**

I. Magnin, 428

IBM Corporation Consulting Services and Distribution Industries Division, 484

ICA (International Colour Authority), 177, 476

Ideacomo, 179

IGEDO show, 385, 386

Ihman, Erwin, 464

ILGWU (International Ladies' Garment Workers' Union), 217–218

Import brokers, 485

Import consultants, 485

Import coordinator, **540**

Imports, **68**

    buying methods of retailers for, 77–79

    versus domestic production, 81–83

    fur industry and, 193

    introduced, 188–189

    leather industry and, 195

    by manufacturers, 80–81

    preferential programs for, 93–95

    of private-label lines, 79–80

    reasons for, 75–77

    shoe industry and, 330–332

    tariffs/duties on, 92–95

    types of U.S fashion, 75

Independently owned organizations, **478–479**

Industrial Revolution in America, 170

Information Revolution, 16

Information technology consulting firms, 485

Initial public offerings (IPOs), **217**

Innerwear, 347

Inside shops, 234, 244

Insoles of shoes, 328

In-store shops, 243, 393

Intercolor association, 177

International Colour Authority (ICA), 177, 476

International Council of Shopping Centers, 441

International Fashion Fabric Fair, 179

International Kids Fashion Shows, 264, 265

International Ladies' Garment Workers' Union (ILGWU), 217–218

International Organization for Standardization (ISO) 9000, 186

International Wool Secretariat, 160–161

Internet, 16, 30, 481, 492–493. *See also* Web sites

Interstoff Textile Fair, 179, 385

"In the blue," 195

Intimate apparel industry

    annual production (1998), 349

    economic importance of, 349–350

    globalization and, 351

    industry segments, 348

    introduced, 346–348

    marketing, 350–351

IPOs (initial public offerings), **217**

Irene, **530**

Iron maidens, 348

ISO (International Organization for Standardization) 9000 standards, 186

Italian couture, 377–378

Italian ready-to-wear industry, 381–382

ITBD Publications (London), 491

I-Textile.com, 202

Ivins, M., 41

J. C. Penney, 14, 15, 20, 23, 78, 133, 135, 147, 426, 433–434, 464

    private label development, 456, 458

    sales in 1999, 430

Jackson, Andrew, 170

Jackson, Michael, 62

Jacobs, B., 401

Jacobs, Mark, **530**

Jacobsen, James, 404

James, Charles, **530**

Japan, ready-to-wear industry in, 385–387

Jayaraman, S., 142

Jeans, 59–60. *See also* Denim

Jewelry industry

    bridge jewelry, 344

    costume jewelry, 345

    fine jewelry, 343

    FTC guides for, 344

    introduced, 342–343

    marketing, 344

    precious jewelry, 344

Jockey, 23, 72
John, Mr., **530**
Johnson, Betsey, 58, **530**
Johnston, Denise, 27–28
John Wanamaker, 419
Joint ventures, 101
Jones, Kate, 258
Jones, Stephen, **530**
Jones Apparel Group, 247
Julian, Tom, 466–467
Junior designer, **534–535**
Junior industrial engineer, **540**

Kamali, Norma, 57, **530**
Kaplan, Jacques, **530**
Karan, Donna, 47, 57, 255, **530**
Karats (carats), 343
Karl Kani, 105
Karten for Kids, 476
Karten for Little Kids, 476
Kawakubo, Rei, **530**
Kelley, Kathryn, 267–269
Kellwood Company, 14, 247
Kennedy, Jackie, 51
Kennedy, John F., 62
Kenneth Cole, 60
Kenzo, **530**
Kerwin, K., 132
Kessler, J., 401
Khanh, Emmanuelle, **530**
Kidwell, C., 5, 284, 285, 445
Kim, Jennifer M., 61–62
King, Bill, 317
King, C. W., 44
Kiosks, electronic, **493**
Kips, 194
Klein, Anne, 57, 246, 251, **530**
Klein, Calvin, 60, 72–73
Klinefelter, Jeffrey, 463
Kmart, 78
    sales in 1999, 430
Knight, M., 59–60
Knit designer, **535**
Knitting, 157–158
Knitting Yarn Fair, 179
Knock-offs, 249–250
Knoebel, Cindy, 465
Koret of California, 27–28
Kors, Michael, 57, **530**
Kotler, D., 125, 127, 128
KSA (Kurt Salmon Associates), 142–143, 222, 273, 444, 484
Kunz, G., 219, 220, 230
Kurt Salmon Associates (KSA), 16–17, 21, 24, 142–143, 222, 273, 444, 484

Labor auditors, 485
Lace and embroidery designer, 535

Lacroix, Christian, 407, 409–410, **530**
Lagerfeld, Karl, 37, 408, 410, **530**
LaGrega, Angelo, 270–271
Landed costs, 92, 392
Lands' End, 15, 464
Lane, A., 37
Lang, Helmut, 58, **530**
Lanvin, Jeanne, **530**
Larsen, Jack Lenor, 176
Lasts of shoes, 328
Latin American contractors, 399–401
Lauren, Ralph, 47, 50, 57, 62, 72, 226, 251, 288, **530**
Layout artist, **536**
Lean retailing, 16, 457
Leather Industries of America (LIA), 195
Leather industry. *See also* Fur industry
    environmental concerns, 195–196
    hides and skins, 194
    imports and exports, 195
    introduced, 189, 193
    nature of, 193–194
    processing leather, 194–195
    small leather goods, 338
Ledes, John, 408
Lee, H. D., 59
Lee Company, 24
Lee Union-All, 59
Lelong, Lucien, **530–531**
Lerner, M., 128
Letting-out process, 191
Leveraged buyouts, 216
Levi Strauss & Co., 10, 17, 47, 59–60, 72, 128, 135, 287, 288, 300, 428
Lewis, Robin, 362–363
LIA (Leather Industries of America), 195
Licensees, 250
Licensing agreements, **98–99**, 250, **376**
Licensing Letter, The, 250, 251
Licensors, 250
Life coaches, 151
Lifestyles, 133
Limited, The, 15, 21, 73, 244, 455, 464
Lindseth, Stacey, 502
Lingerie, 348
Liz Claiborne. *See* Claiborne, Liz
L.L. Bean, 20
Lloyd, B., 261
Lobbyists, 485
Lobel, L., 13
Loeb, Walter, 464
Logistics, **478**, 485
    distribution and, 141–142

Logistics industry, 20, 70
London
    Fashion Week in, 384–385
    ready-to-wear industry in, 383–385
Long johns, 61
Loom types, 183–184
Lord & Taylor, 69, 419, 423
Los Angeles fashion center, 257
Louis, Jean, **531**
Loungewear, 348
Lowell, Francis Cabot, 170
Luthra, Vikas, 201

McCardell, Claire, 57, 215, **531**
McCartan, Coleman, 502–503
McCraig, Mary, 198–200
McDonald, Mackey, 121, 465
McElligott, Fallon, 466–467
McFadden, Mary, 58, 176, **531**
McGuire, P., 330
McQueen, Alexander, **531**
Macroenvironment, 128
Made-to-measure (tailors-to-the-trade) firms, 293–295
Magazines
    general, 489
MAGIC Trade Show, 307, 308
Magnin, Isaac and Mary Ann, 428
Mail-order houses. *See also* Catalog operations
    apparel specialists, 445–447
    defined, **444**
    growth of, 445
    introduced, 444–445
Mainbocher, **531**
Mall of America, 442–443
Mallory, M., 135
Mall/property management specialists, **496**
Malls, **441–443**
    virtual, 527
Malone, Scott, 184, 506
Management consultants, 484
Management information systems (MIS), **478**
Management trainee, 537
Manufactured fibers, NAICS group, 8
Manufactured (man-made) fibers
    brand names, 164–167
    high-performance, 163–164
    temperature-resistant, 164
Manufacturer-owned retail stores, 304
Manufacturers, women's apparel, 244
Manufacturers' retailing
    manufacturer-owned retail stores, 242–243
    manufacturers' shows within stores, 243

Manufacturing, agile, **223**
Marker making, 231, 233
Market centers, 254–257
Marketing
  accessories, 325–327
  approach to
    introduction, 124
    marketing environment, 128
    marketing mix, 127
    target customers, 125–127
  children's apparel, 264–265
  concepts, 124
    five Rs, 141–142
    manufacturing/distribution,
      141–142
  database, 460–461
  defined, 124
  designer labels and designer li-
    censing, 300–302
  fashion leadership and, 46
  fur garments, 192
  gloves, 280
  hosiery, 334–335
  intimate apparel, 350–351
  jewelry, 344
  macroeconomic factors affecting,
    128–135
  menswear
    at apparel marts, 304
    brand names and, 300
    designer labels and designer
      licensing, 300–302
    dual distribution system, 304
    manufacturer-owned stores, 304
    retail channels of distribution,
      302–304
    targeted customer approach,
      300
    by trade associations, 306–308
  micromarketing techniques, 461
  millinery/hats, 342
  process, 124
  Quick Response, as marketing
    strategy, 138–140
  relationship, **460–461**
  strategies, 124
  women's apparel
    advertising and publicity,
      239–240
    designer trunk shows, 240
    introduced, 238
    new technology, 241
    presentation of lines, 238–239
    reliance on sales force, 239
Market representatives, **481**
Market research agencies, 500
Markets
  defined, **125**
  fashion market centers, 254–257
  secondary fashion centers,
    257–258

segmentation, 126
target, 125–127
Marketspace, defined, 16
Market weeks, 259, 260, 304, 305,
  350
Marshall Field and Company, 419
Martin, Larry, 404, 507
Martin, Peggy, 258
Mart Management, Inc., 74
Marucelli, Germana, **531**
Mass fashions, **37**
Mass markets, 17
Matrix buying, 242, **456**
Matteson, R., 63, 150–151
Maurice Malone, 105
Maxwell, Vera, 215, **531**
May Company, 78
Maycumber, S. Gray, 163, 168
May Department Stores, 390,
  425–427
  changes in, 481
  offices in Asia, 390
Megamalls, **442–443**
Meier, Aaron, 422
Mellet, Jarlath, 313–314, 316
Menswear apparel industry
  accessories, 309
  brand names, 300
  causal office wear, 295–296
  economic importance of, 283
  geographic locations of, 288–289
  history and development of
    introduced, 283
    twentieth century, 285–287
  introduced, 282
  major producers in, 288
  marketing
    at apparel marts, 304
    brand names and, 300
    designer labels and designer li-
      censing, 300–302
    dual distribution system, 304
    introduced, 299–300
    manufacturer-owned stores,
      304
    retail channels of distribution,
      302–304
    targeted customer approach,
      300
  nature of, 287–289
  nineteenth century, 283–285
  sales by type of retail channel,
    304
  sizes for, 291–292, 298
  sportswear
    collection concept, 299
    development of lines, 297–298
    introduced, 296
    production, 298
    seasonal lines, 296–297
    sizes, 298

tailored clothing
  custom tailor (bespoke tailor)
    shops, 293
  development of lines, 290
  hand tailoring, 293
  introduced, 289
  made-to-measure (tailors-to-the-
    trade) firms, 293–295
  production, 290–291
  seasonal lines, 290
  sizes, 291–292
  trade associations, 306–308
Menswear weeks, 304, 305
Menzer, J., 107–108
Merchandisers, 303
  for line development, 228
  responsibilities of, 228–230
Merchandising
  defined, **124**
  fashion cycle and, 42
Merchandising assistant, **539**
Merchandising Motivation, Inc.
  (MMI), 477
Mergers and acquisitions, 16–17
Merton, R., 13
Mexico
  expansion to, by textile industry,
    189
MFA (Multifiber Arrangement),
  84–87, 93
  quota phaseout schedule, 88–89
Miami fashion center, 257–258
Michl, H., 171
Microenvironment, 128
Microfibers, 163
Middleton, W., 372–373
Miller, Nicole, 253, **531**
Milliken & Company, 10
Millinery industry
  economic importance of, 341
  introduced, 340–341
  marketing, 342
  millinery construction, 341–342
  nature of industry, 341
Millinery Institute of America,
  341
Millinery turnover, 342
Millman, J., 71
MIS (management information
  systems), **478**
Missoni, **531**
Mitchell, A., 150, 151
Miyake, Issey, **531**
Mizrahi, Isaac, 408
MMI (Merchandising Motivation,
  Inc.), 477
Modular production systems, 235
Mohair Council logo, 160
Mok, Benjamin, 202
Molinari, Anna, **531**
Molyneux, Capt. Edward, **531**

"Mom-and-pop" stores, 418, 427
Mondi, 385
Monget, K., 348, 350, 351
Monsanto, 167
Montana, Claude, **531**
Montgomery Ward, 122
Mori, Hanae, **531**
Morrissett, B., 172
Morton, Digby, **531**
Mouclier, Jacques, 408
MTV, 492
Mugler, Thierry, **531**
Muir, Jean, **531**
Multifiber Arrangement (MFA),
    84–87, 93
    quota phaseout schedule, 88–89
Munk, N., 132
Murphy, Dennis, 115, 123

NAFTA (North American Free Trade
    Agreement), 88, 93, 387,
    460
NAHM (National Association of
    Hosiery Manufacturers),
    333, 336
NAICS (North American Industry
    Classification System)
    for apparel, 211–212
    men's and boy's groupings, 287
    for retailing, 419–421
    subsector 325 (manufactured
        fiber producers), 161
    textile component producers,
        167–168
Nainsook suit, 61
NAMSB (National Association of
    Men's Sportswear Buyers),
    306
Nano-Tex LLC, 203–204
Nasella, Henry, 463–464
National Association of Hosiery
    Manufacturers (NAHM),
    333, 336
National Association of Men's
    Sportswear Buyers
    (NAMSB), 306
National brands, 422
National Retail Federation (NRF),
    454, 498
Natt, Lisa, 503
Neiman Marcus, 303
Neuborne, E., 132
Newly industrialized countries
    (NICs), 392–396
Newman, Ed, 176
Newspapers, 489
New York fashion center, 254–257,
    262, 288–289
NICs (newly industrialized
    countries), 392–396

Nigel French, 475
Nike, 20, 23, 62, 72, 135, 269
NikeTown, 18
Nonrubber footwear industry, 328
Nonstore retailing
    versus instore (1994, 2010),
        444
Norell, Norman, 249, **531**
North American Free Trade
    Agreement (NAFTA), 88, 93,
    387, 460
North American Industry
    Classification System
    (NAICS), 7–8
    for apparel, 211–212
    men's and boy's groupings, 287
    for retailing, 419–421
    subsector 325 (manufactured
        fiber producers), 161
    textile component producers,
        167–168
North Face, The, 269
Noselli, Nicole, 58
NRF (National Retail Federation),
    454, 498
NuStart industrial park (Mexico),
    189
Nylon, 161
Nystrom, Paul H., 12–13, 35

Off, Joe, 223
Office of Textiles and Apparel
    (OTEXA), 99–100, 188
Office wear, casual, 295–296
Off-price retailers, **437–438**
Offshore assembly method, 81
Offshore production, 80–81, 370.
    See also Foreign producers;
    Globalization of fashion
    industry
Oldham, Todd, **531**
Old Navy, 427
Oliver, Andre, **531**
Online shopping. *See* E-commerce
Open-line goods, 179
OPT (outward processing trade), **91**,
    393–394, 401
Order fulfillment, **449**
Ortenberg, Art, 77
Ostroff, J., 21, 389
OTEXA (Office of Textiles and
    Apparel), 188
Outlet centers, **439–440**
Outlet malls, 18
Outside shops, 234, 245
Outsourcing, 20
Outward processing trade (OPT),
    91, 393–394, 401
Overseas merchandise representa-
    tives, **479**

Overseas production, 141. *See also*
    Foreign producers;
    Globalization of fashion in-
    dustry
Oxford Industries, 288
Ozzard, Janet, 73, 465

Painted woven designer, **535**
Palmieri, J., 303
Panko, Donna, 312
Paquin, **531**
Parker, S. J., 57
Parnis, Mollie, **531**
Parola, R., 307
Partnerships, 10
Party plan retailing, **451**
Pasteup and mechanical artist, **536**
Patagonia, 187–188
Patou, Jean, **531**
Pattern grading, 230
Paulette, Mme., **531**
Pearson, Scott, 315
Pedlar, Sylvia, **531**
Pelle Pelle, 105–106
Pelts, 190
Pelz, L. R., 339
Pendleton, 288
People for the Ethical Treatment of
    Animals (PETA), 190
Peretti, Elsa, **531**
Perez, Enrique, 147
PETA (People for the Ethical
    Treatment of Animals), 190
PET (polyethylene terephthalate),
    187
PGR (Piece Goods Reservation),
    290–291
Phillips, S., 116
Phillips, Sara, 252
Phillips-Van Heusen, 304
Pickler, Jack, 271, 272
Piece Goods Reservation (PGR),
    290–291
Piece rate system, 234
Pierre Cardin, 99
Pietrafesa, Richard, 317
Pietrafesa Corp., 317
Pincus Bros. Maxwell, 288
Piquet, Robert, **531**
Place, 127
Plants (establishments), 349
Poe, Edgar Allan, 486
Point-of-sale (POS) data, 136–137
Point-of-sale (POS) systems, 15
Poiret, Paul, 40, 47, **531**
Polo, 60
Polyethylene terephthalate (PET),
    187
Polymer Group, Inc., 172
Polysindo, 172

Poon, Paola, 202
Porter, M., 387
Porter, Thea, **531**
POS (point-of-sale) data, 136–137
POS (point-of-sale) systems, 15
Potok, Anna, **531**
Potter, Clare, 215
Poulson, B., 171
Power, C., 51, 131
Power retailers, **437**
Powers, M., 34
Prada, Miuccia, **531**
Precious jewelry, 344
Precious stones, 344
Prediction of fashion
    introduced, 52–53
    recognizing and evaluating trends
        for, 53–54
    sources of information for, 54–55
Première Vision, 179
Preselling, 179
Pretanning, 194–195
Prêt-à-porter. *See* Ready-to-wear;
    Ready-to-wear industry
Preticketed merchandise, **456**
Price
    defined, 127
Price WaterhouseCoopers (PWC),
    484
Private-label merchandise, 79–80
Private labels, 334, 424, **452–456**,
    456
Privately held companies, **10**,
    286–287
Product development, with
    e-commerce tools, 273–275
Product development assistant
    (textiles), **541**
Product development assistant
    (textiles) position, 453
Product development organizations,
    478
Product development teams, 228
Product development trainee, **538**
Production
    overseas, 141
Production assistant, **539**
Production control assistant, **540**
Production package, 81
Production patterns, 230
Production systems
    bundle, 235
    modular, 235
    single operator, 234
    unit, 235
Productivity of textiles mills, 180
Products, defined, 127
Profit motive and fashion industry,
    10–12
Progressive bundle system, 234
Projectible looms, 183

Promostyle, 476
Promotion, defined, **127**
Property management specialists,
    496
Protectionism, 83
Psychographics, 16, 126
Publicity, 239–240, 495–496
Publicly held companies, **10–12**,
    286
Public relations firms, 495–496
Pucci, Emilio, **531**
Pulitzer, Lilly, **531**
Pull system, 140
Push system, 139
PWC (Price WaterhouseCoopers),
    484

QR (Quick Response). *See* Quick
    Response (QR)
Quality control specialist, **540–541**
Quant, Mary, 383, **531**
Quick, R., 351
Quick Response (QR), 22, 136,
    138–140, 457
    for apparel manufacturers, 242
    TALC/SAFLINC and, 181–182
    textile industry and, 180–181
    VICS and, 182
    for women's apparel industry,
        221–223
Quimby, H., 327
Quintero, F., 147
Quotas, 85, 87–89
    exemptions from, 93–95
    getting around, 89–90
QVC electronic retailing, 449–450,
    492, 493

Rabon, L., 339
Ralph Lauren. *See* Lauren, Ralph
Ramberg, Ken, 312
RAM Reports to Retailers, 55
Rapid replenishment strategies, 222
Rapier shuttleless looms, 183
Rauche, Madeline de, **531**
Rayon, 161
Ready-to-wear apparel, 213–214,
    215, 370
    in Canada, 387–389
    men's, 283–284
Ready-to-wear industry
    European schedule for, 380–381
    in France, 378–379
    in Germany, 385
    introduced, 370, 378
    in Italy, 381–382
    in Japan, 385–387
    in London, 383–385
Reagan, Nancy, 51

Real time merchandising (RTM),
    222, 223
Reda, S., 148–149
Reebok, 62
Regional showrooms, 258–262
Reichard, R., 160
Relationship marketing, **460–461**,
    466–467
Renta, Oscar de la, 58, 247,
    251–252, 532
Research agencies, 500
Resident buying offices, **477–478**
Retail channels of distribution,
    302–304
    for hosiery, 336
Retail distributors, 6
Retailers, 73
    apparel sales market shares in
        U.S. (1999), 421
    buying methods for imports of,
        77–79
    catalog operations
        catalog showroom retailers,
            447–448
        by department and specialty
            stores, 447
    chain stores
        apparel specialty chains, **431**,
            431–433
        "Big Five," 430
        general merchandise chains,
            433, 433–434
        introduced, 429–430
    changes in
        concentration of retail power,
            456
        globalization of retailing,
            459–460
        logistics and distribution,
            457–459
        partnerships in the softgoods
            industry, 457
        private label growth, 452–456
        relationship marketing,
            460–461
    department stores
        branch stores, 422–424
        catalog operations by, 447
        competitive changes, 424–425
        defined, 421–422
        introduced, 422
        organization chart, 423
        store ownership groups,
            425–427
        top U. S. stores by sales (1999),
            424
    direct selling, **451**
    discount retailers
        category killers, 437
        factory outlets, **439–440**
        introduced, 434–435

off-price retailers, **437–438**
warehouse clubs, 436–437
electronic interactive
home television shopping,
449–450
electronic retailers
CD-ROM computer shopping,
451
"e-tailing," 448–449
home television shopping,
449–450
introduced, 448
online services, 448–449
flea markets, 451
franchised retailing, 440–441
globalization and, 73
history of, 418–419
in-store, 420
versus nonstore (1994, 2010),
444
introduced, 418
mail-order houses
apparel specialists, 445–447
defined, **444**
growth of, 445
introduced, 444–445
malls, **441–443**
as manufacturers, 244
market share trends (1989 versus
1999), 425
megamalls, **442–443**
nonstore, 420–421
relationships with apparel manufacturers and, 241–242
shopping centers, **441–443**
specialty stores
boutiques, **428–429**
catalog operations by, 447
introduced, 427
large departmentalized specialty
stores, 427–428
small apparel specialty stores,
428
as virtual companies, 20
Retail formats, 418
Retailing
electronic interactive, 16
in London, 383
NAICS codes for, 419–421
NAICS group, 8
Retail sales coordinator, 539
Retro fashion, 63
Rhodes, Zandra, **532**
Ribes, Jacqueline de, **532**
Ricci, Nina, **532**
Rice, Susan, 409
Rich, Morris, 422
Richardson, Margorie, 504–505
Richter, Steven A., 463
Risen, Paul, 504, 505
Rissi, Gina, 258

Robinson, D. E., 13
Robinson-Patman Act of 1936, 144
Rocha, John, **532**
Rochas, Marcel, **532**
Rodriguez, Maria, 258
Rodriguez, Sam, 311
Roe, J., 44
Roehm, Carolyne, **532**
Rogers, E., 40
Romero, E., 132, 306
Ross, D., 51, 131
Ross, Vicky, 409
Royalty fees, 250
RP55, 105
R's, Five, in marketing, 141–142
RTM (real time merchandising),
222, 223
Rudnitsky, H., 440
Russell Corporation, 174
Rykiel, Sonia, **532**

SAFLINC (Sundries and Apparel
Findings Linkage Council),
182
Saint Laurent, Yves, 376, **532**
Sakany, L., 254, 255
Saks Fifth Avenue, 78
Sales, defined, **124**
Sales trainee (textiles), **542**
Sample makers, 224
Sander, Jill, **532**
Sant'Angelo, Giorgio di, 57
Sapir, E., 42
Sara Lee Corporation, 18, 23, 101,
138, 172, 247
Sarmi, Count Fernando, **532**
SA (Seventh Avenue), 255–256
Scanners, 181
Scanning, 24, 25
Scassi, A., 57
Scherer, Jean-Louis, **532**
Schiaparelli, Elsa, **532**
Schlumberger, Jean, **532**
Schoen, Mila, **532**
Schuster, Tracy, 502
Schwarzenegger, Arnold, 62
SCIP (Supply Chain Integration
Program), 186
Scotese, Pete, 201
Scott, Ken, **532**
Screen print artist, **535**
Sears, Richard, 444
Sears Roebuck & Company, 23, 78,
135, 247, 426, 433–434,
445
sales in 1999, 430
Seasonal lines, 224
tailored clothing, 290
Seckler, V., 21, 130, 217
Secondary fashion centers, 257–258

Seventh Avenue (SA), 255–256
Sewing machines, development of,
214
Shakespeare, William, 34
Shapewear, 348
Shareholders (stockholders), 10
Sharoff, Sharoff, 261
Sharp, John, 61
Shaver, Dorothy, 215
Sherman Anti-Trust Act of 1890, 143
Shirk, Alfred, 202
Shoe industry
athletic shoes, 328
competition from imports,
330–332
economic importance of, 328
introduced, 327
marketing, 329–330
nature of, 327
shoe construction, 328–329
U.S. footwear market by country
of origin (1998), 332
Shopping centers, **441–443**
Shuttleless weaving, 183–184
Silberman, C. E., 51
Silver, Jeff, 202
Silverman, D., 130, 132
Simmel, G., 44
Simonetta, **532**
Simonin, Richard, 408
Simpson, Adele, **352**
Singaporean contractors, 396
Singer, I. M., 61, 214
Single Income, No Spouse (SINS),
150–151
Single operator system, 234
SINS (Single Income, No Spouse),
150–151
SIS (Stylists' Information Service),
476
Sizing
for men's sportswear, 298
for men's tailored clothing,
291–292
Sketcher, **537**
Sketcher (assistant to designer), **534**
Sketcher/stylist, **534**
Sketching assistant, **534**
Skins, 193–194
SKUs (stock-keeping units), 436
Slater, Samuel, 170
Slater, Todd, 463
Slops, 284
Small leather goods, 338
Smart cards, 24
Smelser, Neil J., 41
SMEs (square meter equivalents), 87
Smith, W., 164
Smith, Willi, 57
Smyth, J., 172
Soane, David, 203–204

Social movements, fashion and, 51
Social responsibility, fashion industry
    and, 24–25
Social values, attitudes, and fashion,
    51–52
Softgoods industry
    defined, 6
    impact of globalization on seg-
      ments of, 72
    logistics management in, 142
Sole proprietorships, **10**
Soles of shoes, 328
Solution-dyed fibers, **158**
Sourcing, B2B relationships and, 29
Sourcing for production, 232–233
South Korean contractors, 395
Soviet block country (former) con-
    tractors, 399
Specialty stores
    boutiques, **428–429**
    catalog operations by, 447
    defined, **427**
    introduced, 427
    large departmentalized specialty
      stores, 427–428
    small apparel specialty stores, 428
Specification buying, 79
Spinning mills, 170–171
Splits (hides), 194
Sportswear
    production, 298
    sizes, 298
Spreading, 233
Sproles, G., 38
Sprouse, Stephen, **532**
Square meter equivalents (SMEs), 87
Staff illustrator, **536**
Standard Industrial Classification
    (SIC), 7. *See also* North
    American Industry
    Classification system
    (NAICS)
Standard & Poor's, 12
    Stock Reports, 11
Standard Rate and Data Service,
    488, 490
Standards
    International Organization for
      Standardization (ISO) 9000,
      186
Stark, M., 148
Steidtmann, Carl, 407
Sterling, defined, 343
Stitch in Time, A (Abernathy,
    Dunlop, Hammond, and
    Weil), 16
Stockholders (shareholders), **10**
Stock-keeping units (SKUs), 436
Stockouts, 137
Stonecutter Mills, 172
Store ambiance, **431**

Store-owned organizations, 479–481
Store ownership groups, **425–427**
Strauss, Levi, 59–60, 285
Streetware, in Europe, 105–106
Style, defined, **35**
Styleexpo.com, 502–503
Style numbers, 35
Style piracy, 249–250
Style samples, 230
Stylists' Information Service (SIS),
    476
Subcontracting, **402–403**
Subsidies, 391–392
Sui, A., 58
*Suiting Everyone: The
    Democratization of Clothing
    in America* (Kidwell and
    Christman), 5
Sundries and Apparel Findings
    Linkage Council (SAFLINC),
    182
Super, 436
Supercenters, **435**
Supermarkets, 407
Superstores, 437
Supply Chain Integration Program
    (SCIP), 186
Supply chain management, **457**
Sweatshops, **217**, 402–405
Swift Textiles, 172
Szware, Jean, 376

TAG (Tanners' Apparel and
    Garment) Show, 195
Tailored clothing
    custom tailor (bespoke tailor)
      shops, 293
    development of lines, 290
    hand tailoring, 293
    made-to-measure (tailors-to-the-
      trade) firms, 293–295
    production, 290–291
    seasonal lines, 290
    sizes, 291–292
Tailors-to-the-trade (made-to-mea-
    sure) firms, 293–295
Taiwanese contractors, 395
Taiwan Textile Federation (TTF),
    395
Talbots, 133
TALC/SAFLINC, 181–182
TALC (Textile and Apparel Linkage
    Council), 182
Tanners' Apparel and Garment
    (TAG) Show, 195
Tanning, 195
Tarde, G., 42
Target customers, 125–127
Target department stores, sales in
    1999, 430

Target markets, 125–127
Tariffs, 92–95, 257
    effects of, on fashion merchandise
      prices, 92
    exemptions from, 93–95
Tassell, Gustave, **532**
[TC]² (Textile/Clothing Technology
    Corporation), 6, 25,
    222–223
TDAdirect.com, 201
Technological developments, and
    fashion, 52
Teklits, Joseph, 463
Television home shopping, 449–450
Temperature-resistant fibers,
    163–164
Testing laboratories, 483
Texitalia, 179
TEXNET (Textile Industry Data-
    Sharing Network), 186
Textile and Apparel Linkage Council
    (TALC), 182
Textile/Clothing Technology
    Corporation [TC]², 6, 25,
    222–223
Textiledge, 201
Textile Fiber Products Identification
    Act of 1966, 144
Textile industry
    CEO priorities, 122
    comparison of wages in, 86
    e-commerce for, 184–186
    environmental issues, 186–188
    expansion to Mexico by, 189
    global importance of, 3–4
Textile Industry Data-Sharing
    Network (TEXNET), 186
Textile mill products industry
    economic importance of,
      168–169
    geographic location, 173–174
    history and growth
      acquisitions, mergers, and con-
        solidation, 171–172
      eighteenth century, 170
      industry evolution, 171
      introduced, 170
      nineteenth century, 170–171
      major U.S.-based firms by sales
        (1999), 173
    NAICS Sector, 8, 167, 313–314
    types of firms
      converters, 175
      introduced, 174
      specialized, 174–175
      vertically integrated firms, 174
Textile mills, NAICS group, 8
Textile producers, globalization and,
    71
Textiles, development opportunities,
    541–542

Textile/surface designer, **535**
Textile technologist, **542**
TextileWeb.com, 504–505
TexTrade.com, 202
TexWatch.com, 202
TFA (The Fashion Association), 307
TFS (The Fashion Service), 475
Theory of the Leisure Class (Veblen), 38
Third World nations, 397–398
Thomas F. Pierce & Son, 327
Thoreau, Henry David, 34
Tobé, Mrs., 477
Toledano, Ralph, 407–408
Tommy Hilfiger, 50, 57, 60, 72, 83, 135, 226
Tools, e-commerce, and product development, 273–275
Tracy, David, 201
Trade, 70. *See also* Globalization
   free, 83
   politics of, 96–97
Trade associations, 306–308, 498–500
Trade attorneys, 485
Trade deficits, **81**
Trade Development Act of 2000 (TDA), 94
Trade publications, 490–491
Tradeshow enterprises, 496–497
Trade shows
   French ready-to-wear, 379
   German, 385
   Italian ready-to-wear, 381–382
   menswear, 306–308
   online, 502–503
   textile, 179
TradeTextile.com, 506
Transshipment strategies, 90
Treber, J., 328
Treece, J., 116
Triangle Shirtwaist Fire (1911), 217
Trickle-across theory, **44**
Trickle-down theory, 43–44
Trigère, Pauline, 58, **532**
Trunk shows, 240
T-shirts, 61–62
TTF (Taiwan Textile Federation), 395
Tucker, J., 283
Tultex, 172
Turgeon, Maria, 503

Ullman, Brent, 105
Ulrich's International Periodical Directory, 489
Undergarments, 347–348
Underhill, Paco, 115
Ungaro, Emanuel, 409, **532**

Unglass, Derek, 313
Union of Needletrades, Industrial & Textile Employees (UNITE), 83, 218, 403, 405
Union suit, 61
United States
   annual production of intimate apparel and undergarments, 349–350
   apparel imports (1990–2000), 400
   apparel imports by major source (1984, 1995), 391
   apparel market of, 82
   apparel sales market shares (1999), 421
   casual office wear in, 295–296
   consumption of nonrubber footwear in (1968–1998), 330
   Department of Commerce, 4, 117
      Bureau of Economic Analysis, 13
      Office of Textiles and Apparel (OTEXA), 188
   exports of textile and apparel products, 98–101
   fashion expenditures (1970–2000), 13
   fashion imports to, 75–77
   fashion in, 57–58
   fashion industry history of, 5–6
   federal legislation affecting fashion industry, 143–144
   fiber consumption in, 161–162
   footwear market by country of origin (1998), 332
   foreign-owned factory shift to, 401–402
   imports of textile and apparel products, 82
   major textile firms in, 173
   population groups in, 129–135
   promotion of domestic products in, 97–98
   quotas and, 87–89
   reasons for free trade position of, 83–84
   sweatshops in, 217, 402–405
   textile and apparel trade deficit of, 81–82
   top department stores by sales (1999), 424
UNITE (Union of Needletrades, Industrial & Textile Employees), 83, 218, 403, 405
Unit production system (UPS), 233, 235
Universal Product Code (UPC), 181
Upgrading, 87

Uppers of shoes, 328
UPS (unit production systems), 233, 235
Urban Trends & Trading Co., 105

Valentina, **532**
Valentino, **532**
Value Line, 12
Vamps of shows, 328
Vanity Fair, 247
Van Zeeland, Franz, 271
Veblen, Thorstein, 38, 44, 46
Vendors, **254**
Venet, Philippe, **532**
Versace, Gianni, **532**
Vertical exchanges, B2B relationships and, 29
Vertical integration, **174**
Vertically integrated firms, 174
Vertical operations, 17–18
VF Corporation, 14, 17, 247, 269–272, 465
Vibe Style, 306
VICS (Voluntary Interindustry Communications Standards), 182
Victor, Sally, **532**
Victoria's Secret, 51, 138
Videoconferencing, 27–28, 493
Videos, fashion, 492
Vincent, C., 147
Vinkesevic, Marinko, 105–106
Vionnet, Madeleine, **532**
Virtual companies, 20
Virtual malls, 527
Volume fashion, **37**
Voluntary Interindustry Communications Standards (VICS), 182
Vryza, M., 190

Wallis, Jennifer, 402
Wall Street Journal, 12
Wal-Mart, 14, 16, 73, 78, 107–108, 122, 435, 436, 455, 457
   sales in 1999, 430
Ward, Aaron Montgomery, 444
Warehouse clubs, **436–437**
Warnaco, 247
Water jet looms, 183
Weaving, 157–158
Webb, David, **532**
Web sites
   for accessories, 324
   accessories, intimate apparel, cosmetics, 525
   apparel industry, 524
   apparel manufacturers and, 268
   Bugle Boy Industries, 268

Web sites *(continued)*
  for Canadian apparel industry, 389
  consumer, 526
  DELiA*s, 268
  fashion (general), 524
  fashion trends, 526
  fur and leather, 525
  international, 526
  job and career sites, 523
  job search navigators/search engines, 523
  Liz Claiborne, 268–269
  media, 526–527
  Nike, 269
  North Face, The, 269
  resume banks, 524
  retailing, 525
  softgoods industry, 524
  sourcing, 525–526
  textile sites, 525
  TextileWeb.com, 504–505
  TradeTextile.com, 506
  union/labor, 526
  U.S. government agencies, 525
  virtual malls, 527
Weil, D., 16, 457
Weinstein, Joan, 409
Weintraub, Emanuel, 464
Weitz, John, **532**
Wellman, Inc., 187–188
Westwood, Vivienne, **532**
White Stag, 288
Whitney, Eli, 170
Wilde, Oscar, 34
Williamson-Dickie Co., 59

Wilson, 23
Wilson, E., 190, 192
WIP (work-in-process), 233
Wolfe, D., 61, 62, 149
Women's apparel industry
  apparel marts, 258–262
  economic importance, 210–211
  factoring, 252–254
  fashion market centers, 254–257
  history and growth
    early working conditions in, 217–218
    industry restructuring, 217
    introduced, 212–213
    nineteenth century, 213–214
    twentieth century, 214–217
    unions, 217–218
  introduced, 210
  knock-offs and, 249–250
  licensing agreements, 250–252
  marketing
    advertising and publicity, 239–240
    designer trunk shows, 240
    introduced, 238
    new technology, 241
    presentation of lines, 238–239
    reliance on sales force, 239
  producers
    apparel jobbers, 245
    contractors. *See* Contractors
    manufacturers, 244
  Quick Response for, 221–223
  size of apparel firms, 246–248
  specialization by products and prices, 248–249

Women's Wear Daily, 240, 259, 265, 452, 490
Woolmark pure wool logo, 159
Wool Products Labeling Act of 1939, 144
Work-in-process (WIP), 233
World Trade Organization (WTO), 83
Worldwide Responsible Apparel Production (WRAP) Certification Program, 404, 405
Worth, Charles Frederick, 370, **532**
Woven fabric designer, **535**
Wragge, B. H., **532**
Wrangler, 59
WRAP (Worldwide Responsible Apparel Production) Certification Program, 404, 405
Wright, G., 148
WTO (World Trade Organization), 83

X to X Exchanges, 30

Yamamoto, Yohji, **532**
Yang, D., 51, 131
Yarn, **158**
Young, Vicki M., 130, 463–464

Zinn, L., 51, 131
Zuckerman, Ben, **532**

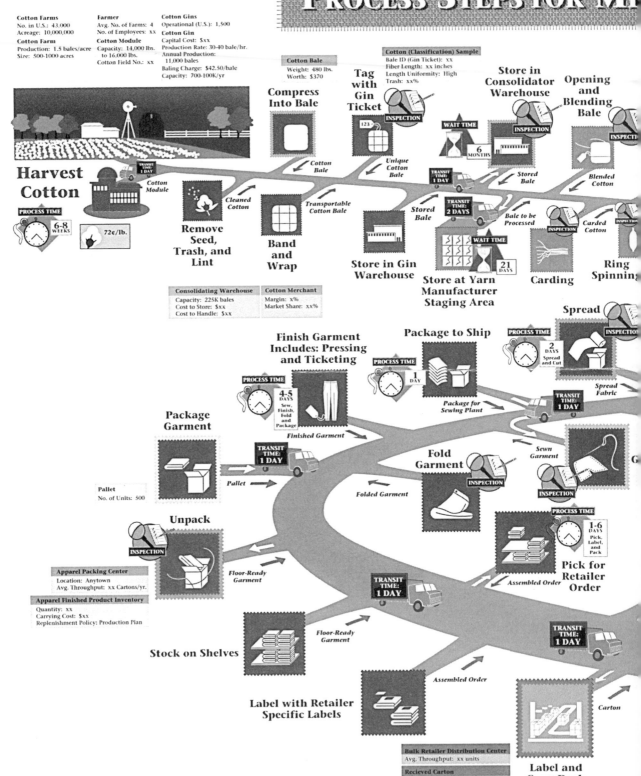